D1737779

twayne

companion to contemporary literature in english

from the editors of *the hollins critic*

first edition

twayne

companion to contemporary literature in english

from the editors of *the hollins critic*

r. h. w. dillard
amanda cockrell

editors

volume

2

macleod–williams

TWAYNE
PUBLISHERS™

New York • Detroit • San Diego • San Francisco • Cleveland • New Haven, Conn. • Waterville, Maine • London • Munich

THOMSON
GALE

Twayne Companion to Contemporary Literature in English: From the Editors of *The Hollins Critic*

R. H. W. Dillard and Amanda Cockrell

THE HOLLINS CRITIC

Assistant editor
Karen Adams Sulkin

Research assistants
Lisa Bower, Marian Crowe, Lindsey Paris,
Jodi White

Illustrations
Lewis O. Thompson

TWAYNE/GALE
Frank Menchaca, Publisher, Twayne Publishers
Stephen Wasserstein, Senior Editor

Project Editor
Matthew May

Proofreading
Melissa Dobson

Indexing
J. Naomi Linzer

Data Capture
Gwen Tucker

Imaging and Multimedia
Dan Newell, Lezlie Light, Leitha Etheridge-Sims

Product Design
Michelle DiMercurio

Composition
Evi Seoud

Manufacturing
Rhonda Williams

Permissions Hotline:
248-699-8006 or 800-877-4253, ext. 8006
Fax: 248-699-8074 or 800-762-4058

Original articles copyright © 1975–2002 by *The Hollins Critic* have been revised and updated. *The Hollins Critic* gratefully acknowledges the cooperation of the publishers and individuals who have permitted use of copyrighted material in this publication.

LIBRARY OF CONGRESS CATALOGING-IN-PUBLICATION DATA

Twayne companion to contemporary literature in English from the editors of the Hollins Critic.
    p. cm.
    Edited by R.H.W. Dillard and Amanda Cockrell.
    "Original articles copyright © 1975-2002 by The Hollins Critic have been revised and updated"—T.p. verso.
    Includes bibliographical references and index.
    ISBN 0-8057-1703-X (set) — ISBN 0-8057-1704-8 (v. 1) — ISBN 0-8057-1705-6 (v. 2)
    1. American literature—20th century—History and criticism. 2. English literature—20th century—History and criticism. I. Dillard, R. H. W. (Richard H. W.), 1937- II. Cockrell, Amanda. III. Hollins critic.
PS225 .T88 2002
                                                        810.9"0054—dc21
                                                        2002006431

Printed in the United States of America
10 9 8 7 6 5 4 3 2 1

Contents

"Such Meticulous Brightness": The Fiction of Alistair MacLeod

Alistair MacLeod (b. 1935) is a writer of fiction who is also a professor of English Literature and Creative Writing at the University of Windsor (Ontario). Much of his early life was spent in Canada's Maritime provinces, specifically Nova Scotia, to which he returns as often as possible to devote the attention to his writing that his duties as a full-time university teacher and family man often will not allow him. Many of MacLeod's stories are set in these same Maritimes; moreover, all but one of them is placed somewhere in Canada, where he has over the past few decades established a considerable reputation for himself on the basis of only two rich volumes of seven short stories apiece. However, he has also been anthologized outside of Canada, and not merely in prize-story collections; as a result, academics and students in the United States and elsewhere have begun to respect the output of this slow and careful worker (he has published about one story per year on the average) whose first American-issued collection should be in print sometime around the appearance of this survey. With fiction both old and new about to reach a much larger audience, then, it seems appropriate to devote some time to at least a rudimentary critical assessment of Alistair MacLeod's work to date.

MacLeod's two collections are entitled *The Lost Salt Gift of Blood* (1976) and *As Birds Bring Forth the Sun and Other Stories* (1986). These draw upon the worlds of MacLeod's direct personal experience—usually by means of the involvement of his own labor—coal mining, farming, fishing, teaching. Moreover, they present us with characters typical of MacLeod's own ethnic stock or that predominate in his own neglected and (these days) often economically depressed corner of the earth and the sea: Scots and Irish Celts, often still speakers of Gaelic; and Canadians of other origins, such as the descendants of the Loyalists who fled the new United States rather than renounce allegiance to the British monarchy. Perhaps it is inappropriate to talk here of influences upon MacLeod's writing, particularly foreign ones; but since it is characteristic of those of his characters who have done some reading to make comparisons between "real-life" situations and those in books, one might then fairly mention that Hemingway is one of the writers so cited. And the sense of clan and of the clan in history in his stories, one might go on to observe, cannot but remind the reader of the handling of such matters—and, in general, the use of Time—in the fiction of William Faulkner who, after all, was writing about people of much the same origins, albeit in a far-removed locale.

Perhaps it is ironic that MacLeod's fiction is to be first published in book form in the U.S. by the Ontario Review Press run by Joyce Carol Oates and her husband, Ray Smith, when one considers the disparity between the prolific Oates—often absurdly disparaged for just that trait—and the comparatively plodding MacLeod, Oates's onetime University of Windsor colleague. Likely, she simply appreciates the distinctive qualities of MacLeod's stories, which include a sense of pacing—and of having no sort of hurry whatever about the need to get things said—that in its quasi-stateliness is almost in a way like the product of a

Alistair MacLeod

Alistair MacLeod was born in 1936 in North Battleford, Saskatchewan, and lived on the Prairies until his parents returned to the family farm in Cape Breton. After obtaining his Teacher's Certificate from Nova Scotia Teacher's College, he attended St. Francis Xavier University. He did graduate work at the Universities of New Brunswick and Notre Dame. He taught at the University of Indiana (1966–69) and then at the University of Windsor. He has also been fiction editor of *The University of Windsor Review*. His short fiction has appeared in Canadian and American journals since the mid-fifties. "The Boat" (in 1969) and "The Lost Salt Gift of Blood" (in 1975) have been included in the annual collection *Best American Short Stories*. Much of his work is permeated with a sense of Cape Breton and of the sea.

MacLeod's first novel, *No Great Mischief* (1999), won several awards: the Trillium Prize, the Thomas Head Raddall Atlantic Fiction Award, and the Dartmouth Book and Writing Award for Fiction,

all in 2000; and the International IMPAC Dublin Literary Award in 2001. *Island: The Collected Short Stories of Alistair MacLeod*, appeared in 1989. ■

prior century, as well as a clarity and simplicity of expression which may, as noted above, be the result of the influence of Hemingway or, even more likely, be the Canadian-English equivalent of the way things are put in Highland Scots Gaelic. At any rate, one notes in MacLeod's work the employment of a kind of floating present tense within which past and future become merely logical accommodations, together with a relative absence of contracted forms which lends itself to the feeling of having time enough to say which was mentioned above. Beginning with the last story in the initial collection, "The Road to Rankin's Point," moreover, there is an increased use of what grammarians would term the "sentence fragment" for a deliberately induced concision of expression, something familiar in a more mannered form from the novels of J. P. Donleavy. These formal qualities make for an often-startling seeming irruption into a "timeless" text of an apparent anachronism from the present day, but the latter is usually simply the result of the hypnotic efficacy of the former. MacLeod presents us with a traditional way of life which, whatever its response to the pressures of the present age to scatter and assimilate, nevertheless maintains as a way of responding to an often harsh, brutal, and violent existence a hedge in the form of rites of passage which seem to illuminate, even as they do not quite dispel, the workings of a dour Celtic sensibility which finds patterns of fatality and doom in all.

Alistair MacLeod is also a poet, but few poems can outdo his fictions for the sheer loveliness of his presentations of a sometimes-hostile Nature, and the candid acceptance with which he takes in Nature's harder truths. The ability to combine both stark candor and sensibility to sheer beauty is often characteristic of the male characters in MacLeod's stories (which is not to say that his females lack them, either), and in this respect he is something of an anomaly among writers of fiction in North America, especially the United States. In the lead story in *The Lost Salt Gift of Blood*, "In the Fall" (which has been fairly successfully filmed in Canada), the sensitive males outnumber the pragmatic female—within the family context—by three to one. But the latter is not without sympathy, given her attempt to impose a managed order on a difficult sort of existence. In a Maritime setting, a farmer who winters as a coal miner is seen worrying about a "him" who turns out to be a horse he has rescued from mine work; "the man" and "the horse" are bound together in terms of the mutual existence they have been saved from. The horse's loyalty is recounted in a narrative about a time when the man became drunk on a winter's night, and the horse faithfully waited for him. This of course does not impress the wife, with six children to care for. She does not worry over living by selling capons for cash, the trading of animal for human life by which the family earns its existence. A neighbor boy undercuts the father's sensibility as something he "feels…because he is Scottish, and…Scotsmen are never any good at raising poultry or flowers because they think such tasks are for women and that they make a man ashamed." The neighbor is a Dutch lad, who might well mistake "poultry or flowers" as mere commodities, but he is wholly wrong about the father's affection for the ailing horse. The narration's steady present tense is briefly abdicated for a time when the father leads the trusting horse into a knacker's truck, and there is a remembering of times when the horse led the father. As the mother had wanted, the "useless" horse is driven away and the family's younger son vents his fury at this betrayal upon his mother's cash-crop capons. Against the backdrop of an oblivious Nature, the narrator sees his parents reconciled to a mutual sacrificial loss in a scene suddenly sexual in its implications:

> I stop and turn my face from the wind and look back the way I have come. My parents are there, blown together behind me. They are not moving, either, only trying to hold their place. They have turned sideways to the wind and are facing and leaning into each other with their shoulders touching, like the end-timbers of a gabled roof. My father puts his arms around my mother's waist and she does not remove them as I have always seen her do. Instead she reaches up and removes the combs of coral from the heaviness of her hair. I have never seen her hair in all its length before and it stretches out now almost parallel to the earth, its shining blackness whipped by the wind and glistening like the snow that settles and melts upon it. It surrounds and engulfs my father's head and he buries his face within its heavy darkness, and draws my mother closer toward him….

"The Vastness of the Dark" is another present-tense story told by a young man setting out from home in search of better opportunity than what his depleted mine-country community can offer. The darkness of the title extends to the carefully-described mining experience, the boy's father's drunkenness, the mother's future prospects, and even the mental state of the boy, who realizes on leaving that his freedom to leave is a dubious one at best: that he will never be wholly free of his origins. Somewhat "explained" towards the ending, the story is deftly concluded on a note of commonality. The writer's observance of local speech extends to that of the boy's grandmother, who takes the news of his departure calmly with "It is just as well. There is nothing for one to do here anyway. There was never anything for one to do here." The narrator calls this "the Gaelic inflection of her youth and…that detached third-person form which I had long ago suggested that she modernize."

But the pulls toward and against "modernization," and the notion that past and present can be smoothly reconciled through candor, are not so easily dealt with. In the collection's title story, "The Lost Salt Gift of Blood," the narrator drives into a Newfoundland harbor village, lovingly described; he falls in with one of a group of young boys out fishing, and is invited to visit the home of the boy by the young person's grandfather. Restless at night, the narrator yearns to enter another room where, we suddenly are let know, lies his "one son sleeping." The transitions from reflections on the son's room to the dead girl who used to sleep there and to the folk belief that presumably played a part in their affair are superb instances of narration by implication, and the reader is led to understand the price the narrator paid when he decided to leave his lover behind to resume his career at a distant university.

Bittersweet is the contrast between the narrator's receiving the gift of a sea-polished stone from his lost son, whom he cannot bear to dislodge from his Newfoundland milieu, and the selfish question asked by a stranger's son at an airport stop: "What did you bring me?" "The Lost Salt Gift of Blood" is a story best praised by simply urging it upon a larger readership.

"The Return" is a memory story, also first-person, of a boy journeying with his parents from the prim environment of his mother-dominated Montreal household to the rougher world his father once knew—the mining country of Cape Breton Island. Here again, it is the boy's father who proves the more sensitive parent, and the story consists of a remarkable series of introductions to the earthy ways of the local menfolk, including the witnessing of the mating of a bull and cow, as well as the grimy honorary investiture of the boy (by his grandfather) in the fellowship of the miners. "We have come from a great distance and have a long way now to go," the story concludes; and only the speaker—and the reader—know exactly how much longer that journey has become. Another rite-of-passage story is "The Golden Gift of Grey," unusual among MacLeod's fictions in being set in northern Indiana among displaced Kentuckians (MacLeod's final degree is from Notre Dame, and he taught for some time in Indiana). Essentially, however, it parallels the Canadian stories: the Kentuckians are country-mannered former miners; and the young man who is the protagonist is being drawn by education into a "higher" mode of existence. But when he is given the answer to a dilemma about what to do with the parent-rejected earnings of his secret vice (shades of *East of Eden*!)—playing pool—by another Kentuckian, a father-figure, he also receives a lesson in the sorts of compromises over absolutes his new existence will require of him: the ambiguous bequest of the title.

In "The Boat," the sheer number of references to the vessel of the title suggest that an ambiguity of meanings is again in the works; indeed, an ambiguity of the values of certain gifts is also again being adumbrated. The narrator is yet another son reminiscing about his Nova Scotia past. The boy's father had slept alone in a room he kept in a messy state, but he displayed his finer nature in his capacity for reading—fisherman by trade though he was. The mother, fine-featured, was also religious and practical, by way of contrast. There is a fine portrait of the father in his fishing boat—which requires a helper to crew—enjoying himself by giving tourists a ride and later drinking with them and singing for them Scots songs from both sides of the Atlantic, some of them ancient. When the young man decides that his place is on the boat with his father, the father makes it clear that he thinks his son should go off to school; but the son stays determined and his mother later comments that the son has added "years to his life." Yet after a season of fishing together, the father suddenly disappears overboard on the very day the season normally comes to a close. Is it an accident or a willed death? Whatever the case, it frees the young man to go off to university and change his life. In the story's final paragraph, the description of the sea-changed body of the father is an extraordinary one (and note the equivocal quality of the word *physically*):

> But neither is it easy to know that your father was found on November twenty-eighth, ten miles to the north and wedged between two boulders and the base of the rock-strewn cliffs where he had been hurled and slammed so many many

times. His hands were shredded ribbons as were his feet which had lost their boots to the suction of the sea, and his shoulders came apart in our hands when we tried to move him from the rocks. And the fish had eaten his testicles and the gulls had pecked out his eyes and the white-green stubble of his whiskers had continued to grow in death, like the grass on graves, upon the purple, bloated mass that was his face. There was not much left of my father, physically, as he lay there with the brass chains on his wrists and the seaweed in his hair.

The final story in this first collection, "The Road to Rankin's Point," finds a young man—only the reader and his grandmother find out that he is doomed to die young, presumably of leukemia—driving up a road very different from the one going in the other direction—the one which leads to the major centers of the continent—for this road leads to a rough patch of land that is his family's ancestral home, where his grandmother (the subject of her family's concern) now lives out her old age. (The grandfather had died much earlier on this same road in an accidental fall while coming home drunk.) When the family arrives en masse from the country down below, there is a general festivity at the relief caused by the news that young Calum will stay behind and live with his failing grandmother, and there is a singing of old Highland songs that the grandmother joins in by playing her violin; the narrator contrasts this music with what the grandmother's descendants are gyrating to at the Toronto end of the road. The narrator defines his grandmother's role in his family's development in terms of strength—a strength summed up in a saying of hers the first sentence of which MacLeod himself is apt to repeat more than once a day: "No one has ever said that life is to be easy. Only that it is to be lived." The story has characters speak of having prophetic gifts, and the narrator lies in his bed later wishing to take on more of the history of his clan; suddenly he hears his grandmother's dogs on the road above bewailing her death on the same day she had played the old tunes which still beset his mind so that he cannot tell whether the music is within him or without, just as the darkness outside and inside him "reach to become as one." MacLeod's first collection closes with this narrative of invigorating beauty.

A full decade later, MacLeod released his second assemblage of seven tales. But the first story to appear in it actually dates from the year of the earlier volume. "The Closing Down of Summer" is another piece derived from MacLeod's knowledge of the world of mining: its narrator is a central figure in a group of shaft miners enjoying a last bit of seaside summer sun on a Nova Scotia shore from which they must soon depart for work wherever their company sends them—South Africa, say. Another present-tense story, it is also another instance of a narrative poised on the verge of enormous change; as time ticks by and the day winds to a close, the narrator's unhurried voice lulls the reader like the August sun. And yet that voice also presents the often horrific details of life below ground, as well as its speaker's growing sense of isolation from a domestic life he seldom participates in. Death seems to wait for the narrator and his colleagues to rise up from the beach where their bodies' imprints are quickly effaced by the waves; yet the world his wife bustles about in seems an uncomprehending polar opposite: "Little about me or about my work is clean or orderly and I am always mildly amazed to find the earnings of the violence and dirt in which I make my living converted into such meticulous brightness." The process is reminiscent of MacLeod's fiction generally, if not of course in quite this sense; and if MacLeod allows his speaker's single year of university to account perhaps for his articulateness, that fact also allows for a certain irony to inhere in the narrator's compulsion "to tell…something of the way my years pass by on the route to my inevitable death"—to speak of "beauty of motion on the edge of violence, which by its very nature can never long endure." Hemingway again, perhaps; but the narrator also admires the passion he has noted in the singing and dancing of the Zulus, something missing in his own aboveground existence. His university year experience comes back to end the story as his associates pass the moonshine around and drive westward toward futures both uncertain and yet somehow certain; he recalls a medieval poem the last lines of which are "Death is to man the final way— / I wende to be clad in clay."

The two stories which follow concern Christmas. "Winter Dog" has the thoughts of its narrator, while watching his children romp with a neighbor's dog in the pre-dawn on a day before Christmas (in present time, and in a place like MacLeod's present Windsor, Ontario), move backwards to an experience that could be superficially termed a Londonesque adventure yarn— a boy's being saved from drowning off an ice floe by a big dog useless for other labor—were it not for the presence here of another meditation on death. There is a possibility of having to drive east because a family member is dying; the weather is bad. "Should we be drawn by death, we well might meet our own. Still, it is only because I am alive that I can even consider such possibilities." The irony of the story's scenario, then, is that one dog, in reminding the speaker of another in the distant past, also brings to mind the way a life has been saved in order to have it deal with death another day. The second story, "To Every Thing There Is a Season," also presents a superficial appearance—that of a newspaper Christmas story, short as it is (and indeed that is how it made its print debut); it is told as the memory of a boy who, old enough to disbelieve in Santa Claus, is made to stay up with the adults to take part in the gift-bringing of an older sailor brother. But though he is old enough to understand about Santa Claus, the boy does not at that time realize the meaning of what his father, who seems to be dying of consumption, means at the story's ending: "'Every man moves on,' says my father quietly, and I think he speaks of Santa Claus, 'but there is no need to grieve. He leaves good things behind'."

"Second Spring" presents, with a calm factualness about animal births and deaths, the reminiscence of someone who in youth had belonged to a "calf club," the purpose of which was to have each member breed and raise his own calf. The story's details of farm life's realities are closely observed and establish an atmosphere in which the young man's cow, Morag, is mounted and inseminated by a Faulknerian neighborhood bull who simply walks through fences when the breeding urge is on him. The resulting astonishment at the uncontrollable power of Nature of all concerned, reader included, is neatly conveyed by the narrator's revelation of how he deserted calf-breeding for baseball, at which "In my small area of the earth it seemed that everything was under my control." At the other end of the age spectrum is Archibald in "The Tuning of Perfection," a 78-year-old Cape Breton singer of traditional songs (his people came from the Isle of Skye) who has been "discovered" by folklorists and now has been offered a chance to appear on TV with members of his family, who join the show's producer in urging him to compromise the authenticity of his performances in order to suit the requirements of the medium. But Archibald, who usually expresses dubiety in the face of the assaults of the questionable with a noncommittal "Mmmm," stands firm, particularly after having a dream visit from his dead wife singing. The story neatly parallels Archibald's integrity with the fiercely independent ways of the eagles who nest in the vicinity, and it ends with an acknowledgement of Archibald's stature by a party of drunken singers.

The past is also crucial in a very different way to the title story of the collection, "As Birds Bring Forth the Sun." Not until well into the story do we learn that its beginnings, originally purposely vaguely indicated, are in the nineteenth century; and even then, the reader may be unsure whether the setting is Scotland or the Maritimes. This folktale quality is emphasized by the narrational texture; here, for example, is the story's opening paragraph:

> Once there was a family with a Highland name who lived beside the sea. And the man had a dog of which he was very fond. She was large and grey, a sort of staghound from another time. And if she jumped up to lick his face, which she

loved to do, her paws would jolt against his shoulders with such force that she would come close to knocking him down and he would be forced to take two or three backward steps before he could regain his balance. And he himself was not a small man, being slightly over six feet and perhaps one hundred and eighty pounds.

This self-consciously narrational stance creates both a sense of timelessness and also a suspension of reader disbelief; against both of these, subsequent scenes such as that of the breeding of the big grey dog (referred to throughout the rest of the story by the Gaelic equivalent) and the violent death of the man himself at the teeth and claws of the dog's six offspring stand out in relief all the more shocking for being couched in such ostensible gentleness. This extraordinary story, which traces the history of a family haunted by a fatalistic belief in its own doom, finds its ending in a modern hospital setting where, the narrator speculates, circumstances may once again become confused with causes—the apparent meaning of the evocative title. MacLeod, in reading "As Birds Bring Forth the Sun" in live performance, confirms the reader's impressions of this tale by delivering it in an almost incantatory, quasi-bardic manner that serves to heighten its unforgettable impact.

If "Birds" possesses a Faulknerian power of the grotesque to instill awe, the volume's final and longest item, "Vision," displays genuine Faulknerian complexity of narrational mosaic in moving the reader through a familial saga taking generations to come clear—if that is the word to use in describing a story so complicatedly exploitive of the many meanings suggested by its title. As in "The Road to Rankin's Point," second sight is referred to; and as with "The Closing Down of Summer," the narrator feels compelled to speak, having himself become his narrative—or rather, having had it become him. Like the narrator, the reader is forced to accommodate himself to inadequate information; he is introduced to the narrator's fisherman father early on, for example, but he does not learn that the father is blind until thirty pages later, though there are clues in the narrative if one knew enough to watch for them. A nautical landmark, the point of Canna, sets the father to telling his son a story within the outer story, and soon there are layers and layers of history to cope with and make something of a single account out of. The father, as a young man, and his brother set out to visit their grandparents, but by mistake they are taken to the house of a strange old woman whom they eventually realize is blind, but whom they cannot as yet "recognize" to be their actual grandmother. When they encounter their grandfather, they do not know him at first—though what they find him up to in the barn is a clue, if they could spot it, to the excess sexuality that is responsible for their existence. Like Archibald's "Mmmm," a mild "Oh" appears repeatedly in this story to indicate an insufficiency of response to a meaningful matter—casualness, uncertainty, evasiveness. MacLeod carefully arms the reader with information that will be needed later on: for instance, that in the past the poor local residents would think nothing out of the ordinary about eating lobster sandwiches does not strike one as anything but curious when first mentioned, but twenty pages later it is required knowledge at a point where explanation would prove intrusive; and the blind old lady's odd reference to her dogs as "twins" makes sense another twenty pages later when it is revealed that she had once given birth to twins, one of whom died. A question by the blind woman—in Gaelic—to her onetime lover, "Who's there?", is answered finally, "It is myself"; but not until the question returns to consciousness in a way that saves the father's life (though he loses his sight) in combat during World War II does the father, now a grown man, start to reap the fruit of understanding of the question's full implications. (And another blinding, ironically, brings an end to clan feuding.) This magnificent story is in its very structure ample proof of how "forever difficult [it is] to see and understand the tangled twisted strands of love." That is to say: the "tangled twisted strands" of narrative are turned to binding rope by the reader's acknowledgment of the power of love.

A new story, "Island," as yet unpublished, is to be included in the Ontario Review Press edition of MacLeod's work, and it has been read in manuscript form for this survey. As the absence of an article in the title implies, the theme of the narrative is that of isolation, in particular the emotional aloneness of Agnes MacPhedran, the last of a family which for years has tended a lighthouse on a coastal island which has gradually acquired their name. While she is still young, she meets and is attracted to a red-haired fisherman who understands her loneliness "as if he were reading her mind." He goes away but returns ("I told you I'd come back") and asks her to marry him; she assents and they speak of going "somewhere else" to live. Her response to all these promises of change is largely a matter of "Oh yes" that becomes simply "Oh" as they make love in a shanty away from her parents' purview, and "Oh" is all she says on hearing her father's offhand mention of the death of that red-haired young man in a lumbering accident. Of course, she is pregnant; and she leaves the daughter she bears with her aunt, on the mainland. She herself shortly becomes solely responsible for the lighthouse, and there is a striking later scene in which she gives herself to a party of mackerel fishermen she has helped take advantage of a spawning run—this at the spot where she had declared her love for the red-haired man. Passing years are telescoped into a few pages of narrative during which the woman becomes thought of as a local eccentric, and finally—after she learns that the government will no longer require that the lighthouse be manually cared for—a young red-haired fellow appears at her door, eventually identifying himself as her grandson from Toronto. He promises to return, and when he does, he is in appearance and manner of arriving and speech a duplicate of her long-dead lover. He takes her to his borrowed boat, saying it is time they went to "live somewhere else." The eerie narrative, a culmination of MacLeod's apparent fascination with folk belief in the occult, concludes with the fatal finality of a folktale:

> A dog barked once. And when the light revolved, its solitary beam found no MacPhedrans on the island or the sea.

In its length, "Island" resembles "Vision"; and the writer is apparently at work on a novella. These developments can only fuel curiosity about new developments in MacLeod's art at what might be a crucial point in his career. What is "crucial" includes not just possible changes in MacLeod's approach to fictional forms, however; it involves the point with which this survey began: MacLeod's arrival within the awareness of an even greater readership. Of course, that process has long since begun: Simone Vauthier of the Université de Strasbourg has written two entire papers on "The Road to Rankin's Point" alone—one in French, on the use of the present tense, and the other in English, on the concepts of time and space employed in the story; and Arnold E. Davidson of Michigan State University has intelligently discussed the role of "displacement, substitution, and elision" in the second collection. Nor has MacLeod been without honor in his own country. Ken MacKinnon, in a review, has cited the major theme of MacLeod's work to be "the long homeward journey from exile." Other Canadian reviewers have simply praised MacLeod's craft, so low-keyed at first encounter that its efficacy may elude the hasty reader. That craft, they have usually noted, is centered upon an emotional quotient almost unbearable in some of MacLeod's stories—were it not for the steady voice that keeps excess response at bay. But as MacLeod has said in a newspaper interview, "I think most art begins in the emotional part of man." Readers of his stories will not be surprised to find that one area of MacLeod's academic interests is the fiction of Thomas Hardy; and they may also find that MacKinnon's characterization of MacLeod's central theme acquires extra resonance when MacLeod is paralleled with Hardy. Questions of resemblances aside, however, one is left agreeing with the many Canadian reviewers who have called MacLeod one of the finest Canadian practitioners of the short story form presently writing. Though MacLeod would doubtless be pleased with such a description, his new audience—noting the universality inherent in the lit-

■ **BOOKS BY ALISTAIR MACLEOD**

A Textual Study of Thomas Hardy's "A Group of Noble Dames." Notre Dame, Ind., 1968 (Ph.D.) Thesis.

The Lost Salt Gift of Blood. Toronto: McClelland and Stewart Ltd., 1976.

As Birds Bring Forth the Sun and Other Stories. Toronto: McClelland and Stewart Ltd., 1986.

The Lost Salt Gift of Blood: New and Selected Stories. Toronto: Ontario Review Press, 1988.

Island: The Collected Short Stories of Alistair Macleod. Saskatoon: Thistledown Press, 1989.

No Great Mischief. New Providence, N.J.: BPR Publishers, 1999.

erary means by which he has exploited the emotional resources of his native region—may well question the need to include the proper adjective.

John Ditsky
February, 1988

UPDATE

Although less read in the U.S. than in his native Canada, and although his output has been modest, MacLeod is nevertheless recognized as a master of the short story. His collected stories were generally greeted with acclaim, and praised on the dust jacket by such writers as Joyce Carol Oates and Frederick Busch, although a *New Republic* review was mixed: "They are written in an earnest, almost liturgical prose of careful simplicity and frequent beauty, and with a kind of clumsiness and carelessness about cliche that suggests a stern disdain for aestheticism. . . . MacLeod is indeed a real writer, but his strengths are inseparable from his weaknesses; the sincerity that produces his sentimentality also stirs his work to a beautifully aroused plainness." The same review suggested that MacLeod's old-fashioned style of writing may partly explain his limited American following.

Now as an award-winning novelist, MacLeod has gained new fans. Steeped in the history of Canada, *No Great Mischief* is the story of a Cape Breton orthodontist who lives a privileged life far different than the hardscrabble existence of his forebears, whom he cannot stop thinking about. *Quadrant* praised it as "a meditation on love and loyalty, history and kinship. It works like a Celtic design or a Gaelic song, forever circling on itself and embroidering the same few motifs. It is true art because it transcends the grief which helps power it." It also admitted that the last scene, of nursing home residents holding hands to sing a song from their past, "is reactionary humbug of the worst kind. But others, the open or secret supporters of the exiled party of Memory, will know they must read it because it will have the heart out of their breast."

"Following a Serpentine Brick Path:" The Fiction of Bobbie Ann Mason

In her 1982, and first, collection of short fiction, *Shiloh*, Bobbie Ann Mason established herself as a brave new voice in contemporary American writing. Less than a decade before, she had published volumes that draw upon her academic training—a "guide" to Nabokov's *Ada*, and a feminist survey of series books in girls' fiction. It will fall to the eventual graduate student to make the salient connections between the Russo-American fictionist, and his antiworld named for a character whose name puns on "ardor," and the prepossessions of the headily active domain of recent feminist readings of literature. Less than a decade later, she had evidently subsumed both interests into her own reworking of the themes of structural innovations and the thematic concerns of women writing. Though merely the first of only five volumes of fiction to date, *Shiloh* quickly established Mason as a force to which attention must be given.

The sixteen stories that comprise *Shiloh* also laid Mason's claim to a heretofore largely ignored portion of, if not the traditional literary South per se, then certainly at least the western precincts of Kentucky, a region in a border state whose local notion of a city must inevitably mean Paducah. The writers who provided the blurbs for this first collection were unanimous in spotting its strengths: an "impressive" ability to convey a sense of character and place and dialogue that unsentimentally places those characters in situations without easy solutions. Moreover, these stories show Mason employing authorial devices which she would sustain in later work, though in increasingly more subtle ways.

For instance, the story "Detroit Skyline, 1949" concerns a visit to her relatives in the North by Peggy Jo, whose aunt now lives in a suburb so distant from the big city that getting to the latter briefly becomes a kind of Grail quest, and then an abandoned dream glimpsed only briefly as a skyline visible in the fuzzy image provided by a vintage TV set. With all its conspicuous later problems, Detroit retains its stunning image to the eyes of any beholders in Canada to the south; yet it is the mind's skyline that concerns Mason: something yearned for, but ultimately declined in favor of returning home again, like Moscow in Chekhov's play—but possessing an allure only apparent from afar. This unreal Oz, El Norte, or Camelot, we must remember, was the place that drew thousands from Kentucky and other parts of the South during the War, when it was heralded as the "Arsenal of Democracy." Peggy Jo's relatives, then, are the temporal descendants only a few years removed from the memorable characters in Harriette Arnow's masterwork, *The Dollmaker*; they are Kentuckians who have, by their lights, caught on and thrived.

The Brazilian composer Heitor Villa-Lobos once wrote a piano piece purportedly based on the image of the New York skyline transposed onto sheet music. Mason's Detroit provides an image neither so ostensibly specific nor ultimately impressionistic. Rather, it is a goal both physical and internal, and Mason's fictions are full of journeys that are both topographical and devel-

Bobbie Ann Mason

Bobbie Ann Mason was born in 1940 near Mayfield, Kentucky, where she was raised on her parents' dairy farm. The first person in her family to go to college, she earned a degree in journalism at the University of Kentucky in Lexington in 1962. She moved to New York and worked for Ideal Publishing Company as a writer for fan magazines like *Movie Life* and *TV Star Parade* before quitting to earn an M.A. in literature from the State University of New York at Binghamton, and a Ph.D. from the University of Connecticut. Her doctoral dissertation was an analysis of garden symbolism in the novel *Ada* by Vladimir Nabokov and was subsequently published as *Nabokov's Garden: A Guide to Ada.* The following year she wrote *The Girl Sleuth: A Feminist Guide to the Bobbsey Twins, Nancy Drew, and Their Sisters.* She taught journalism at Mansfield State College (now Mansfield University) in Pennsylvania before turning to fiction, but by 1979 she had left her teaching position to write full-time. Her first book, *Shiloh and Other Stories,* won the Hemingway Award in 1983, followed by a grant from the Pennsylvania Arts Council, and fellowships from

the National Endowment for the Arts, the National Academy and Institute of Arts and Letters, and the Guggenheim Foundation. Her first novel, *In Country,* appeared in 1985, followed by a second, *Spence + Lila,* another collection of stories, *Love Life,* and her most recent novel, *Feather Crowns,* which won the 1993 Southern Book Award. She lives in Kentucky with her husband, writer Roger Rawlings. ■

opmental—often one in the guise of the other. Blurring the spiritual component is often a panoply of specific referents—referents fixing the story in both time and place. Peggy Jo's declined migration begins with her noting the different way her assigned Detroit-suburban play-mates say and do things—pronouncing "hair," for instance, in two syllables instead of one, Peggy Jo is thus easy to label as an outsider, but in the process she finds the inner resources to claim her own identity, and to relate it to her home. It is true that there was once a song whose lyrics ran "Oh, how I wish again / I was in Michigan / Back on the farm," but it has never caught on; Bobbie Ann Mason's old Kentucky home is an address whose sentimental appeal needs to be reckoned with, even while it stays in the heart of the pilgrim—like, say, Faulkner's Mississippi.

Thus there are those details, like ads along roads that can be subliminally registered but also ignored. In the present story, a family watches Arthur Godfrey and Milton Berle. One person watches Jack Carter or Howdy Doody; someone else smokes Old Golds; and others shop at Woolworth's or hanker after Cunningham's ice cream. In the kitchen one finds a Mixmaster; on TV, Gorgeous George. Whole families fear contagion from polio in public pools, and "reds"—whatever they are—in the auto plants. It's Toni in the bathroom and Fab in the laundry; Fred Waring, "Little Orphan Annie." One could scan a Mason story for the capitalized nouns and get at least part of the point and, unlike some authors, Mason's knowledge of period trivia seems unassailable. No less a writer than John Updike, for instance, in his heavily-researched most recent novel *In the Beauty of the Lilies,* errs when he relies on memory for the names of the train stations called out on the Jack Benny radio show and calls them "Anaheim, Mazuza, and Kukamunga." The gaffe obtrudes because Updike has been dropping names so often, so long, arguably to excess; yet one can hardly imagine Mason doing such a thing. But in neither writer can such allusiveness be thought to have been intended as a substitute for genuine character development.

It would seem sensible at this point to give more extended coverage to the title story, "Shiloh," to which Mason also gave pride of place in her collection. (Moreover, "Shiloh" is frequently anthologized, so that the teaching experience is inevitably bound up with consideration of the story both in its own right and also as a piece chosen by anthologists because it presumably serves contemporary political agenda.) Yet "Shiloh" resists ready compartmentalization; its protagonist finds herself heading off in new directions on the basis of no external proselytization, but rather on having discovered more to herself than she had been told would be there. Students are apt to identify her first names, "Norma Jean," as an allusion to Marilyn Monroe—but without quite knowing what to make of the fact. (Similarly, Leroy Moffitt's name seems to suggest a downhome type with a pretentiousness implied at its start, a claim to a kingship he cannot quite manage to live up to.) When the story opens, Norma Jean is already lifting a barbell, at work on strengthening her pectorals; her disappointment that one arm's muscle is not as hard as the other's is given a fairly lame rationale by Leroy—she is right-handed, after all.

In fact, "lame" is the operative word here. Leroy has "injured his leg in a highway accident," and though on the mend, is "frightened" about the prospect of going back on the road as a trucker again. Thus the "king" is wounded grievously, while his recuperative therapy has inspired his wife to assert her own physicality. Leroy now occupies himself, as his wife builds her muscles, with hobby kits; and he wants to build Norma Jean a full-sized log cabin to be the house he has always promised her. Of course, this throwback of a residence is hardly what she wishes for. Their rented house "does not even feel like a home," he understands; and while he plays the homebody, his wife is out selling cosmetics for a living. Additionally, they have lost their only child in its infancy, and Leroy knows "that they must create a new marriage, start afresh." True enough, while Leroy watches Donahue, Norma Jean is rediscovering her youth by playing sixties songs on the electric organ Leroy has bought her.

Leroy is dismayed by the thought that his little town has changed so during his brief life; he continues (with the help of marijuana) his unreal dream of building the log house while his wife goes on with her self-development. Norma Jean's mother, Mabel, who has become a member of the United Daughters of the Confederacy, has her own sort of pilgrimage in mind: to the battlefield at Shiloh. She thinks the trip is her daughter's duty, even as she deprecates Leroy's needlepoint "Star Trek pillow cover":

"That's what a woman would do," says Mabel. "Great day in the morning!"
"All the big football players on TV do it," he says.

Despite her own willful rootedness in an obsolete past, including her sexist notions of what is a productive occupation for a man, Mabel identifies Leroy's malaise exactly: he doesn't know what to do with himself.

Norma Jean prepares a casserole, her obeisance to women's magazines no less profound than the way both spouses attend to the commercial names that are dropped in their paths daily. In a now-characteristic haze, Leroy can only repeat an old refrain of his, the motto of his fecklessness: "Well, what do you think?" It is as if he has just met Norma Jean for the first time: "They could become reacquainted." Mabel uses Leroy's log-house blueprints for a coffee rest, meanwhile hilariously displaying her obtuse refusal to listen to a correcting of her way of saying the name of that supposedly dangerous breed of dogs, "datsuns." A cloud of guilt over the death of the infant hangs over the relationship, furthered by Mabel's discovering Norma Jean smoking.

Norma Jean is now taking an English composition course, starting by writing about women's-magazine soup-can-based recipes, but soon her cooking has become more adventurous as well: "tacos, lasagna, Bombay chicken." Mabel repeats her long-standing suggestion that the couple travel to Shiloh for a "second honeymoon." Before they do, Norma Jean informs Leroy that his name means "king," but his question as to whether he is still king of his castle is deferred as Norma Jean, flexing her muscles, says that she is seeing no one else. She adds that her name was originally Marilyn Monroe's, but that also "Norma comes from the Normans. They were invaders." At which she agrees to go to Shiloh. One can only assume that Mason was aware of the famous Bellini opera *Norma*, in which a Druid priestess and her Roman lover walk into the flames together at the finale. But Mason's Norma has her own heroic path in mind, and suicide is no part of it.

At their picnic in Shiloh, Norma says to Leroy—she having given up smoking; he still toking a joint—that she intends to go off on her own: "I want to leave you." "Don't do me that way," is Leroy's feeble response. Could we start over again? he asks; and her response is that they have, and this is where they are. Norma Jean scoffs at the idea that this is a "women's lib" thing, and "starts walking away." Leroy can only try to sort through the confusion of history, American and their own, in his mind, and at least realize that the log house has been a bad idea. When he opens his eyes, he sees Norma Jean walking along a "serpentine brick path" through the cemetery. There follows a final paragraph that reminds the reader of the dust ruffle Mabel had made for them, to hide whatever had been under that bed that should not be seen:

> Leroy gets up to follow his wife, but his good leg is asleep and his bad leg still hurts him. Norma Jean is far away, walking rapidly toward the bluff by the river, and he tries to hobble toward her. Some children run past him, screaming noisily. Norma Jean has reached the bluff, and she is looking out over the Tennessee River. Now she turns toward Leroy and waves her arms. Is she beckoning to him? She seems to be doing an exercise for her chest muscles. The sky is unusually pale—the color of the dust ruffle Mabel made for their bed.

Hobbled husband, rapidly walking wife: this ending is ambiguous only in the minds of certain readers. Thus the story's endpoint provides a fine means of rereading the whole. When Norma Jean waves, what are we to make of her semaphore?

The creative-writing class signals are out all through "Shiloh," though its naming of names—particulars caught on the sly, as if by candid camera—becomes progressively less important as Mason moves towards her first full-length fiction, *In Country* (1985), her first story apparently readily adapted to screen purposes. Whereas the journey to "Shiloh" can be seen, in spite of its ultimate seriousness but because of its seemingly lighthearted depiction of border-state domestic life, as something ironically less than fraught with heavy intent, *In Country* is by no means what the story might be argued to be: a fictional take on the breakup of a marriage, the substance of such songs as Johnny Cash and June Carter's celebrated "Jackson," in which that city becomes an imagined Grail of liberation from marital chains. Rather, it is the harrowing account of the trip to the Vietnam Memorial by a young girl, Sam Hughes, and her uncle Emmett, like her father Dwayne a fighter in the abortive war—but unlike the father, a survivor.

Sam, a spunky 17, has struggled long to come to an understanding of the father who died before she was born. On her present journey, Sam and Emmett are accompanied by Sam's grandmother, Mamaw, who is merely a clone of "Shiloh's" Mabel. Sam's beloved VW beetle develops transmission trouble, stalling the story at the end of Part One in Maryland, almost if they were an army about to descend on the capital. When Emmett complains, in their comfortable motel room, that (with a Carson/Rivers rerun on TV) "Nothing's authentic anymore," Sam reflects "that everything is more real to her, now that they are on the road." Thus—and all this casually—a Mason female protagonist (this one is also a runner in her spare moments) identifies authenticity with being on the road. In this presumably existentialist sense, then, self-discovery is identified in a parallel way with linear motion, surely some sort of rightful usurpation of a traditionally male perquisite throughout American literature.

The habit of using topical referents so evident in the story collection also animates *In Country*, where they do nothing to undercut seriousness of narrative purpose, but instead, ground the story in the reality of a western Kentucky in a particular time, a place (and by extension, time) that Sam feels makes it a kind of island—cut off as it is from the rest of the state by flood-control dams and the artificial lakes they have created. Part Two, the longest part of the book, shows us Sam and Emmett and how they became the twosome on their pilgrimage, which doesn't resume until near the end of the volume; it is a long hiatus that makes the brief conclusion seem a release, a letting out of breath, an exorcism of tensions built up over the years of Sam's fatherless upbringing.

Sam's mother thinks that her brother Emmett has been "messed…up" by the Vietnam War, like so many others. Emmett's sensitivity to sudden loud noises is part of that psychological legacy, but there is a physical component as well. Sam thinks Emmett suffers from the effects of Agent Orange, but massive denial is going on among officials, and the doctor Emmett consults dismisses his facial outbreaks as adult acne. But something like rosacea would not cause such fears as Sam has for Emmett's future health, or that of any children he might have. A typical activity for Sam and Emmett to join in is the habitual watching of *M*A*S*H* reruns, empathizing as they do with the frustrated caregivers who deal through irony with the vicissitudes of their roles in that "forgotten" war in Korea. Ten years after its conclusion, the one in Vietnam has become one that elicits an embarrassed shunning.

Trying to reach back in time towards an understanding of her dead father, Sam listens to old music of his era; "Hearing it, Sam felt the energy of the sixties, like desire building and exploding. But there was something playful in the song, as if back then were a much better time to be young than now." Perhaps it was; yet one also sees Sam as applying to her father's lifetime, in the attempt to bring it back to life, just those sorts of narrational devices that Mason herself uses, such as those meant to animate Sam's own times. Sam is that sort of rare young person who understands that the lives of one's parents are essential clues as to the nature of one's own personhood.

By the same or a similar token, the reader might be tempted to see in the Bobbie Ann Mason of the jacket photographs of this time a pictorial suggestion of the personalities of her protagonists: vibrant, competent, aware. However questionable the validity of such an exercise, it is paralleled by the passage in which Sam studies the only known photo of her father that she owns, and which she keeps in her dictionary:

> In the picture, Dwayne Hughes had on a dark uniform with a cap like the one Sam had worn when she worked at the Burger Boy. His face was long and thin, and a blemish on the bridge of his nose stood out like a connecting point between his eyebrows, like a town on a map. His hair was so short she could see his scalp. His ears stuck out.
>
> The boy in the picture was nineteen. Lonnie [her boyfriend] was going on nineteen. Sam looked at her face in the mirror—fat, sassy, stubborn. Her father's face was so scrawny. She couldn't see any resemblance to him.

But what, then, had been Dwayne's legacy to Sam?

Sam gets involved with local war veterans, including one fellow, Tom, who while considerably more mature than Lonnie, of course, feels in his *gravitas* something more akin to fatherly concern for Sam. She even tries to give herself to him sexually, but Tom has been physically and/or psychologically unmanned by the experience of combat, which in his case had been particularly horrifying; they end by falling asleep together, her arms around him. The core experience of Part II concerns Dwayne's journals, which Mamaw provides for Sam to read. Sam discovers in them a hard truth: that her father had killed Vietnamese even as his fellow soldiers died around him, and even as he tried to think from time to time about "the baby" back home. Having preferred to think of him as fighting for those "in the World," Sam is sickened by the diary entries: "Her stomach churned, and she felt like throwing up." Her father's dispassionate accounts of what he endured have worked on her imagination to the point where she spends a night in a state park/swamp, not far from a safe tourist boardwalk but subjected to bites and some discomfort. Yet she knows that without the terrible noises of night combat, let alone the Doors and their apocalyptic dronings about the coming end, it is a sham. She emerges to find Emmett waiting. Carrying around a mannish version of her own name, Samantha, is no substitute for finding her own self. The journey to Washington is ready to begin as, this time, it is the man who walks ahead and disappears into the woods.

With the voyage resumed, Part III shows a Sam having gone "sort of crazy" after her rite of initiation. En route, she reflects on how her country truly does deserve to be called "America the beautiful," yet now she cannot help but see it, in "flashes," as it must look to a returned veteran. Arriving in Washington, and as they head for the Memorial, Sam is bothered by the display of federal business-as-usual that surrounds the site, which she is the first to identify: "It is massive, a black gash in a hillside, like a vein of coal exposed and then polished with polyurethane." Mamaw quietly observes, "It's black as night." When they find Sam's father's name, it is too high to reach; but a borrowed ladder enables first Mamaw, then Sam, to touch the carved inscription: "She feels funny, touching it. A scratching on a rock." Unsettled, dissatisfied, Sam rushes to consult the directory of names, hoping to find her father listed again. Instead she finds her own name, or that of a "Sam Hughes" who died a month to the day short of his eighteenth birthday, a Texas boy whose name fixes her to that wall forever as she touches it, feeling oddly, "as though all the names in America have been used to decorate this wall." The last glimpse we have is of Emmett, sitting "cross-legged in front of the wall" where he has sought out his dead buddies, and "slowly his face bursts into a smile like flames."

This beatific vision of Emmett, which closes the novel, must remind the reader—through Emmett's posture and Mason's simile—of the Zen spirit of the monks who protested the war by burning themselves to death. It is a note of final acceptance that brings closure to this family's quest—offering, if one wishes, the hope Mamaw finds in a flower growing from a cranny; but certainly, for Sam, a new understanding of who she herself is beyond that frozen moment when her father died. *In Country* does not focus on combat per se, as do the novels written by such fine writers as Tim O'Brien, but like O'Brien's most recent novel, *In the Lake of the Woods*, it does what protesters once promised to do: bring the war back home.

In Country's ending could easily have been made mawkish, or at least sentimental, but Mason has kept it uncondescendingly strong. So too with the substance of Mason's next published work, *Spence + Lila*, where the narrative of a health crisis in the lives of a small farmer and his wife speaks of love—of individuals for one another and of the soil—in a way that is reminiscent of that next major Kentucky writer just to the east, Wendell Berry. Published in 1988, *Spence + Lila* (its title suggestive of a lover's carving into a tree bark) is an even shorter novel than its predecessor at 176 pages, including some blank pages and several of illustrations; indeed, it was issued as part of the Harper Short Novel Series. It is in any event a work of daring economy.

When the work opens, Spence is driving Lila to Paducah for a biopsy on a lump that has been found in her breast; the couple are frightened but determined to brave the situation out. Their daughters and son will be helping, but Spence is set on taking care of himself in Lila's absence. Within the space of the chapter's brief length, they have entered the hospital's chilly interior; it is like a "meat locker," Spence decides. The daughters arrive while Lila is beginning to experience the first waves of memory that sweep over her, this time dating to the earliest days of her marriage. She is prepared to lose a breast—"My big jugs," she calls them—though it is an index of her marriage that Spence might feel the loss of one more than she, affectionately giving them both humorous names as he has been fond of doing.

At home on his farm, Spence is also remembering—as he feeds his little herd, each member having her own familiar name, and as he prepares his simple meal in the microwave. Again, the ample intrusion of the new into our lives is documented by Mason, but it is as if the references to specifics are less intrusive than ever. Back at the hospital before Lila's exploratory surgery, Spence finds the orderlies in their greens to be like "leprechauns." The patient's condition is aggravated by the bewildering barrage of hospital terminology they are made to endure. Hating hospitals, Spence tries to get outside for a while, but memories dog him down. Meanwhile, Lila's lump is malignant, and the more drastic surgery proceeds; Mason deftly sketches her mental state on emerging from her anesthetic.

Lila's characteristic defense is her public humor, but it is little help in her moments alone. Before her strokes dictate a second procedure, angioplasty, Lila lies in her hospital bed, the prosthetic artificial breast she had been jokingly tossing around earlier like a beanbag waiting in the drawer next to her. She remembers wondering, the week before, about missing her breast.

> …how they disposed of it: Did it all come out in one hunk, or did they hack it out? She thought about dressing a chicken, the way she cut out the extra fat and pulled out the entrails. She thought of how it was so easy to rip raw chicken breasts.

But when she is ready to leave the hospital at last, Lila becomes herself again as she regales a new roommate:

> "Oh, I've been through the wringer!" Lila cries. "I've had my tit cut off and my neck gouged out and staples put in, and I've been stuck with needles all over like a pincushion and put down in cold storage long enough to get pneumonia…"

At the same time, Spence has been throwing himself into his farming, wanting to surprise Lila with the yield of the land he feared she might never see again. He has even taken a ride in the crop-dusting plane of his neighbor, realizing that the latter has been reaping a tidy profit on marijuana with which he has seeded Spence's land.

All this time, both Spence and Lila have been reliving key moments in their marriage, seemingly realizing in the process the intricate ways in which their separate lives have become intertwined. Spence even remembers scenes from the war; Lila, her trips. In the final chapter, Lila returns home, pleased to see her cat, Abraham—just as Spence has made use of the company of his dog, Oscar. But where they come together is over the garden she has missed so much that she immediately throws herself into premature yard work. Her husband discovers her coming back with her arms full of produce, like some indomitable Ceres. On the last page of the novel, Mason brings its key images together, as Spence—whose biggest surprise is that he has stocked the pond with "oversized catfish" he can't wait to watch her catch the first of—looks at his wife anew:

> Her face is rosy, all the furrows and marks thrusting upward with her smile the way the okra on the stalk reach upward to the sun. Her face is pretty as freshly plowed ground, and the scar on her neck is like a gully washed out but filling in now.

And he imagines the marijuana growing amidst his soybeans like hummocks in the Everglades, "mounds like breasts." When he uses a vegetable image to make a randy suggestion, Lila laughs her hearty laugh, "the moment he has been waiting for." Like that stocked pond, presumably, "her face is dancing like pond water in the rain, all unsettled and stirring with aroused possibility." Literally and figuratively, *Spence + Lila* is an earthy celebration of life and love.

All during the period when Mason was preoccupied with getting her first novels, one more or less standard length and one quite short, into print, she was continuing to publish short stories in some of the nation's top fiction venues. This ability to attract the finest markets hardly detracts from the value of what Mason had been about during this period, any more than it should be in the least a remark to be taken as derogatory to note that her story quality remained consistent with what had gone before, and into her first collection. To the inquiry, Has she improved? it could readily be answered, Improved on what? In any event, the new collection, *Love Life*, appeared in 1989. On no more logic than repeated coin tosses, we might take as typical the story "Sorghum"—the only one in the collection to have been published in the prestigious *Paris Review*.

Liz's husband, Danny, arrives home late at night in a great "screeching" of tires; "I'm home!" he yells, as if he were Ozzie Nelson just a bit late from the office. "When he was drunk, he made love as though he were plowing corn," Liz reflects, "and she did not enjoy it." Liz listens to a radio psychic, whose clientele seem incredibly passive about receiving shattering news, and is told that Danny is also cheating on her. Danny, for his part, cannot understand why Liz always wants something more—like a fancy dinner out. Hasn't he just bought her a microwave? he asks. A quest after homemade sorghum, which Liz hasn't had since childhood, leads her to an old fellow who makes the stuff—and thus, to his son, Ed. Ed takes her malling and then for Cajun chicken and a margarita; Liz has not met with such romance before, and wonders about her options. Ed proposes that she run off with him for a game-dinner outing with his friends.

Before this happens, however, Eve's sorghum-molasses search has led her to Ed's father, Cletus, who remembers when "An old-timey sorghum-making had a picnic, and the whole neighborhood helped." But Liz's game-dinner escapade takes place among the folks with wealth down at that geographical anomaly Reelfoot Lake, itself created almost overnight by a seismic catastrophe. Having burned her bridges with Danny and her family, though not yet having told them, she finds herself in her "loud red dress" still feeling out of place. The expensive lakeside property includes a bathroom with a bubbling Jacuzzi, which causes Liz to fret, for "She had heard about orgies among trendy sets of people." At the dinner table, she contemplates the prospect of enduring the company of such people yet again.

Dinner consists of quail, rabbit that "used a quart of tenderizer," possum that "looked like cat paws" that her host has "just blasted" out of a tree, goose with a cream sauce, duck cooked with cherries that feels "leathery," seemingly "pickled" rabbit, and liver stuffing for the quail. Liz, feeling ill, heads for the bathroom and finds her appearance in the mirror still "young, innocent." She ends by stripping off her red dress and sinking into the welcoming tub. Recollecting the dishes served at a dinner she could not eat, she remembers "a picture she saw once" that, in its impossible assemblage of flowers, could only have been a still life, a *nature morte* and thus a display of approximate death—though Mason does not use the artist's term. The tub reminds her of the ocean, where she has long wished to visit, "just once in her life. That was the one thing she truly wanted." And so she indulges herself:

> She touched her toe in the hot water. It seemed too hot to bear, but she decided that she would bear it—like a punishment, or an acquired taste that would turn delicious when she was used to it.

Liz's liberation, archetypically represented by the act of bathing, frees her of both the catalytic figure Ed, with his retinue of new-Kentuckian types, and also Danny, whose inattentiveness is no solution to her very valid needs. In a very real sense, she follows a middle path, the one she took when she went in quest of real sorghum molasses—which no longer requires a mule walking a circular trail to make. Like many a Mason protagonist, she is on her own and learning to control her own destiny.

For what it may be worth, the jacket illustration for *Love Life* provides a neat summation of many of Mason's prepossessions. In a bare room, a television set, turned on, bears as its freight a vase of flowers, a channel selector, and five apparently familial photos—sepia, black-and-white, and tinted—that perhaps represent as many as five generations of women. The TV is turned on, however, and the "reality" it displays is a partially clad rock singer with a female backup singer behind him, both in garish color. That assemblage might well be taken as emblem of Bobbie Ann Mason's art. But many of the usual signs of that art can be said to be missing in Mason's most recent, 1993, volume, *Feather Crowns*. At 454 pages, it is a book startlingly longer than her previous four; and not only does it lack the standard Mason guideposts of timely name referents, but it also adapts its pace to that of a woman whose experiences are not simply those of a short-fiction protagonist with concentrated happenings occurring that will thrust her onto a new road of fulfillment, but rather the slowly resolving tapestry of an individual, Christianna Wheeler, "Christie," whose act of giving birth to quintuplets in 1900—the last year of the prior century—sets her on a lengthy path through a long life and into the spans of our own.

Christie's uncomfortable pregnancy is finally followed by protracted parturition, with no advance idea of what was in store for her and the husband and family that bustle about her bed during the novel's early chapters. When the book's first section comes to a close, Christie has done what nobody does, she is told; "the beatin'est thing to hit this country since President Jackson bought it from the Indians," avers one bystander, and "Since that earthquake way back yonder," returns the first speaker. Indeed, from the number of mentions of Reelfoot Lake in this narrative, one supposes that Mason sees Christie as another local phenomenon, one fit to mention on road signs to attract tourists.

A second section dips backward in time to show how Christie, and her lusty husband, James, had arrived at this point: "And it even seemed fitting that there were so many babies. She and James had gotten carried away with their secret pleasures, and finally it had caught up with them." Nor are these their only children. But it is the remarkable fivesome that people start flocking to see, once the news hits the local and area newspapers. The callous sort of freak-seekers who would most typically be found at carnival sideshows find the Wheeler house, barging in on the family—even through the window—and besieging the babies to the point of manhandling them. A relative attempts to collect admission at the door; local bigwigs promise assistance. Then one baby weakens and dies; the set is no longer complete. Finally, the other four sicken to death. Christie does not have the heart to awaken her sleeping James, who opens his eyes to find "the still baby placed under the outing flannel on the pillow beside him, like a gift…" Speechlessly they hold onto one another. Then the peculiar Little Bunch tears open the bolster, plucking one "nest woven of feathers" after another out of the down:

"Feather crowns!" cried Amanda. "I should have known."

Christie felt the blood draining from her face and the room went dim. She started across the room to see the feather crowns, but her knees gave way.

"It's all right, Christie," Amanda said soothingly. "It means the babies are in heaven."

Here the novel's plot takes a bizarre twist, as Christie takes her five dead babies, embalmed to a turn with a taxidermist's art, on the road to display at just the sort of sideshow venue mentioned above. The America of P. T. Barnum has made of a bereaved mother, her glass-encased infants, and their feather crowns, something worth paying to gape at. Watching the crowds that come to see her babies, Christie's reactions vary from anger—"Get your eyes full"—to cold objectivity—"My babies was wooled to death—pure and simple. By people just like you. But now nobody can touch 'em." At times, her mother's grief makes Christie tempted to believe, as she has been told, that the "deaths really have been a greater gift to the world than their lives might have been," but when she and James look at their "changeless features" now, the "dolls" hold "no lost meanings or fresh messages. She stoppered up her feelings the way her mother bottled grape juice with her mail-order bottle-capper."

We remember as readers the historical case of the Dionne quints, as Christie, a very different woman now thirty-seven years after the birth of her own babies, tries to visit the Canadian quints. Through a gallery glass, she watches the Dionnes at play—having noted the many similarities to her situation in 1900, but briefly angry because "Hers could have lived," too. Waiting to meet Mme. Dionne, Christie reflects:

> In her mind, Christie listened again to the children's voices that she had heard through the closed gallery windows while she watched the girls at play. It was the squealing of five small children, all equal but separate and different, the joy of small children who haven't encountered any pain yet except the pain of birth itself. There was nothing more precious on earth than that sound.

Christie decides to leave before the meeting: they don't speak the same language, and she doesn't want to bother the other mother.

Christie's long road has been both an external one measured in highway mileage as with other Mason women, and also an interior one, ditto. In the final and brief 1963 section, Christie is a widow on her ninetieth birthday, reflecting on her life for a tape interviewer's benefit. She has learned how people will "eat you alive. And families can smother you." What she realized she needed were friends, not kin—"the free and unattached generousness of a stranger meeting a stranger, where nothing familiar can cast a shadow of obligation on you, or a mirror reflection. No influences, no judgements." In a chapter where a reference to Elvis startles, Christie knows that part of what she felt when her babies were alive was that it made her "feel like somebody. It gave me something to look forward to. Women didn't get to do things back then like they can now." And with a passing mention of a President who wants to send men to the moon—and who is to die shortly—Christie is ready to go there herself. But though she has stopped mourning, she notes she and James both lost their conventional faith long ago, gazing on their dead infants.

Despite her memories, but quickened by a sprightly old age, Christie in her final words reflects on the here and now in an upbeat passage reminiscent of the ending of *Spence + Lila*:

> But I don't aim to live out my days all hunched up over my memories. I want to watch the sun come up and hear a hen cackle over a new-laid egg and feel a kitten purr. And I want to see a flock of blackbirds whirl over the field, making music. Things like that are absolutely new ever time they happen.

Christianna Wheeler's life, including its bitterest experiences, has not left her deadened; rather, she is still able to rejoice in the constant new birth of the world around her—multiple birth.

It seems safe to predict that another Mason volume will appear shortly. After all, *Feather Crowns* was published a good three years ago, and its predecessor, a collection of short stories, has

■ BOOKS BY BOBBIE ANN MASON

Nabokov's Garden: A Guide to ADA. Ann Arbor, Mich.: Ardis, 1974.

The Girl Sleuth: A Feminist Guide. Old Westbury, N.Y.: The Feminist Press, 1975, Athens: University of Georgia Press, 1995.

Shiloh and Other Stories. New York: Harper & Row, 1985, New York: HarperCollins, 1990, Athens: University of Georgia Press, 1995.

In Country. New York: Harper & Row, 1985, New York: (HarperCollins), 1986.

Spence + Lila. New York: Harper & Row, 1988, New York: (HarperCollins), 1989.

Love Life: Stories. New York: Harper & Row, 1989, New York: (HarperCollins), 1990.

Feather Crowns. New York: HarperCollins, 1993, New York: HarperCollins, 1994.

Midnight Magic: Selected Stories of Bobbie Ann Mason. Hopewell, N.J.: Ecco Press, 1998.

Clear Springs: A Memoir. New York: Random House, 1999.

Zigzagging Down a Wild Trail. New York: Random House, 2001.

been available some seven years now. Moreover, during those years new short stories have continued to appear at a fairly regular pace, and her growing readership will have been eager for more of her writing for some years now. It should be stressed, furthermore, that any new work will only be this writer's sixth—a rate that, while hardly indicating Oatesian prolificacy, surely marks an output of creative energy that seems to have been unflagging since the hiatus between her early critical work and her first fiction. Additionally, her first collection, issued when she was still only 42, produced the story first considered here, "Shiloh," and on that basis she made it almost immediately into the survey course anthologies where permanent reputations are supposed to be made (and unmade); and one does not hear the least suggestion that the recent wave of political correctness in inclusion choices had anything to do with this salient phenomenon.

There is no reason to doubt that Bobbie Ann Mason is a writer just entering her performance prime. This brief overview has been meant to point to features of her artistry that seem perfectly timed to snag the sensibilities of readers of the final decade of the present millennium. It would seem hopelessly and unjustly normative and reductive to express this artistry as it seems to have been thus far adumbrated here: as a matter of women finding themselves by exercising their abilities, by some means or another, to walk. But, like "Shiloh's" Norma Jean, it is hard not to see them as basically "walking through the cemetery, following a serpentine brick path."

John Ditsky
October, 1996

UPDATE

Bobbie Ann Mason, still a popular and celebrated writer, has since published two collections of stories, *Midnight Magic: Selected Stories of Bobbie Ann Mason* (1998) and *Zigzagging Down a Wild Trail* (2001), and *Clear Springs: A Memoir* (1999). *Booklist* called the stories in *Midnight Magic*, many first seen in *The New Yorker* or *Atlantic Monthly*, "remarkable," and those in *Zigzagging*, "exotic, strange, and mysterious, a looking-glass world." When she published her acclaimed memoir, *Publishers Weekly* called it "a loving embrace" of Mason's small Kentucky hometown and the people who raised her, "a richly textured portrait of a rapidly disappearing way of life."

Further into Darkness: The Novels of Cormac McCarthy

■ **I**

Born in 1933 in East Tennessee, Cormac McCarthy has demonstrated the abiding fictional potential of his native region—and in the process added to the stature of the American Southern literary tradition—in four remarkable novels: *The Orchard Keeper* (1965), *Outer Dark* (1968), *Child of God* (1973), and *Suttree* (1979). All of these were published in the United States by Random House, and the last of them—*Suttree*—was in fact begun before the publication of *The Orchard Keeper*, a detail worth noting when making the inevitable comparisons of style and subject a reading of all four suggests. As with *A Death in the Family* by McCarthy's co-regionist James Agee, McCarthy's novels are fitted out with interchapters which accomplish passages of time and increments of action by means of refractive prose—changes in angle of vision. But the comparisons with other Southern writers, chief among them Faulkner, that the novels of Cormac McCarthy bring to mind are beyond our fully considering here; suffice it to observe that in the case of Faulkner, that "Dixie Limited" which, in Flannery O'Connor's memorable phrase (and she having said so much that is pertinent to McCarthy's writing, without mentioning the man, in her essays), comes roaring down on the "mule and wagon" of every other writer from the South who attempts to raise his or her own unique voice, the possibility of comparison with McCarthy does not seem to have inhibited the latter in the least. Dictionally, tonally, McCarthy simply goes *beyond* Faulkner.

It is that journey beyond Faulkner—though without sustaining a continuing reference to the older writer—that I intend to survey in this paper. If the writing of William Faulkner can be called "Gothic," "grotesque," and in diction "florid" or "obscure," "arcane," then Cormac McCarthy has gone him one better. Though doubtless operating under some degree of Faulknerian influence, McCarthy writes as though Faulkner had never existed, as if there were no limits to what language might be pushed into doing in the last half of the twentieth century. The clash between near-incredible erudition and resources of diction and the actual subject matter—the characters, the actions, the settings—of his books creates in McCarthy's work an enormous and disturbing energy and power to move the reader. By means of this energy and power, he is able to carry that reader further into darkness than even Faulkner, seemingly, dared go—to that place where those reside who have rejected the covenant: those "children of the kingdom" mentioned in Matthew 8:12 whose rejection of grace has earned them "weeping and gnashing of teeth." It is this rejection, I should think, that accounts for the titles of two, or perhaps three, of McCarthy's books, and the seemingly motiveless malignancy of certain of his characters that makes their passages through this world seem so chilling—although their portraits, in their extremity, do not become the less familiar (which redoubles the chill).

This arguably Biblical presentation of character is abetted by a similarly Biblical narrative flow; in spite of the resources of diction already mentioned, McCarthy's stories are told with the

Cormac McCarthy

Cormac McCarthy was born July 20, 1933, in Providence, Rhode Island. He is the son of Charles Joseph and Gladys McGrail McCarthy, and was educated at the University of Tennessee. His awards include the Ingram-Merrill Foundation grant for creative writing, in 1960; the American Academy of Arts and Letters traveling fellowship to Europe, from 1965 to 1966; and the William Faulkner Foundation award, in 1966, for *The Orchard Keeper*. In addition, he won the Jean Stein Award from the American Academy and Institution of Arts and Letters (1991); the National Book Award for fiction (1992) and the National Book Critics Award for fiction, both for *All the Pretty Horses*; the Lyndhurst Foundation grant; and an Institute of Arts and Letters award. He has contributed to *The Yale Review* and to *The Sewanee Review*. ■

economy of folktales. Or parables. They focus in on basics, on the here-and-now, on the earth itself, in a manner which the language used for summing up, for commentary, makes seem the starker, the more extreme. Here, for instance, is (excluding from consideration the first of the interchapters alluded to earlier) the very first paragraph, entire, of McCarthy's "first" novel, *The Orchard Keeper*:

> For some time now the road had been deserted, white and scorching yet, though the sun was already reddening the western sky. He walked along slowly in the dust, stopping from time to time and bobbling on one foot like some squat ungainly bird while he examined the wad of tape coming through his shoe-sole. He turned again. Far down the blazing strip of concrete a small shapeless mass had emerged and was struggling toward him. It loomed steadily, weaving and grotesque like something seen through bad glass, gained briefly the form and solidity of a pickup truck, whipped past and receded into the same liquid shape by which it came.

This is one of McCarthy's seething monsters afoot, filled with resentments at all who cross his path, cross *him*, making his life futile and filled with bile. If Hart Crane's "The Bridge" shows us, in "The Tunnel," "love / A burnt match skating in a urinal—" (to choose one of several possible cliches among quotations), what shall we say of hate in McCarthy? To cite the resemblance of this opening paragraph to the beginning of *As I Lay Dying* simply will not serve; the bad taste it produces, the foretaste it advances, is simply too strong. One notes the loaded negative words: "deserted," "squat," "ungainly," "wad," "shapeless," "struggling," "grotesque," "bad," etc. If this is the South, it is the South perceived by Vladimir and Estragon.

Yet almost immediately, there is a characteristic switch to a more elaborate diction, descriptive passages creating the image of a Knoxville region where "Clay cracks and splits in endless microcataclysm and the limestone lies about the eroded land like schools of sunning dolphin, gray channeled backs humped at the infernal sky," and where the forest floor "has about it a primordial quality, some steamy carboniferous swamp where ancient saurians lurk in feigned sleep," and where even the shacks of mountaineers can be seen "squatting over their gullied purlieus like great brooding animals rigid with constipation." *Mosquitoes*, yes; but not even Faulkner quite so consistently made up images like these. The "poetic" excess of these passages—McCarthy does become more "restrained" in time—serves as index to this book, and to its author's canon.

Impossible, too, not to think of various Faulknerian "suspended moments" wherein action is frozen in a stasis of reader attentiveness, as when the novel's principals meet in a frieze of rigid violence:

> …Then Sylder stood, still in that somnambulant slow motion as if time itself were running down, and watched the man turn, seeming to labor not under water but in some more viscous fluid, torturous slow, and the jack itself falling down on an angle over the dying forces of gravity, leaving Sylder's own hand and bouncing slowly in the road while his leaden arm rose in a stiff arc and his fingers cocked like a cat's claws unsheathing and buried themselves in the cheesy neckflesh of the man who fled from him without apparent headway as in a nightmare.

Not until Sylder discovers that he has killed the other man, his own hand having shriveled "into a tight claw, like a killed spider," in the process, does time again resume motion. And a few pages later, as if to confirm the devilish suspension of normal reality, there is introduced an old man who carries a pole of hickory, hewn hectagonal and "graced…with hex-carvings—nosed moons, stars, fish of strange and pleistocene aspect." In McCarthy's three shorter novels, manipulation of time becomes more than a device; it is an atmosphere: of timelessness, or being out of time.

The habit of omitting quotation marks around dialogue is but one of the devices by which McCarthy intensifies reader experience of violent action—in this book, for instance, including the collapse of a tavern porch into a gully and the crash of an automobile into a creek. The interplay of present event and memory assists in this process of making experience vivid. But for the most part, McCarthy's achievement—in this novel which contains a Faulknerian hunt for reputed "treasure" and which ends in contemplation of the peace of the dead, *The Mansion*-like—depends upon his splendid choices of imagery. In mid-novel, for instance, amid a snowy landscape and "brilliant against the facade of pines beyond, a cardinal shot like a drop of blood." And this is the meditation on the dead just alluded to:

> Evening. The dead sheathed in the earth's crust and turning the slow diurnal of the earth's wheel, at peace with eclipse, asteroid, the dusty novae, their bones brindled with mold and the celled marrow going to frail stone, turning, their fingers laced with roots, at one with Tut and Agamemon, with the seed and the unborn.

It will be argued that this verbal richness is simply flamboyant overwriting, that little is gained by such a purpled and mannered cast. The answer—which cannot, of course, mollify all potential detractors—lies in the reading, in the effects achieved: in the tension mentioned earlier between materials and narrative style.

■ II

Moreover, McCarthy's later work shows evidence of increasing care in the lavishing of verbal embellishment (if that is indeed the proper term). Yet "materials," as noted above, continue to attract him; he grounds his language in matter—as any of the quotations already included will attest—like one of Steinbeck's country folk drawing with a stick in the earth while dealing with a problem. *Outer Dark* continues this attention to the material, the vengeance enacted upon its wanderers and those they chance upon augured and adumbrated in the state of nature itself, like the dream with which the novel begins. At once the dreamer, who has committed incest with his sister and fears it will be discovered, is distracted by the noise of a passing tinker and wonders "what new evil this might be." The baby born of this relationship is abandoned in the woods, and the description of its protests echoes those of Benjy Compson:

> It howled execration upon the dim camarine world of its nativity wail on wail while he lay there gibbering with palsied jawhasps, his hands putting back the night like some witless paraclete beleaguered with all limbo's clamor.

What exactly does all this *mean*? It is the poetic flow of a writer who creates a Brothers-Grimm world of uncertain date, one in which a tinker poised upon a bridge brings a troll to mind for the reader, and in which a confused sinner sits on a roadside stone "and with a dead stick drew outlandish symbols in the dust." McCarthy portrays a society reduced again to primitivism—if indeed it has ever emerged—and communicating through barbarous violence and magical runes. When the victim sister seeks out the grave of the infant she has been told is dead, she moves "with quiet and guileless rectitude to stand before a patch of black and cloven earth": good and evil confront one another in stark extremity, again as in fairy tales; evil triumphs, and only death brings peace. The brother flees, found out, and raises "his clenched hands above him threatful, supplicant, to the mute and windy heavens." Naturally there is no answer.

Indeed, the next scene is of the arrival of the three dreadful avengers, who bring horror and death wherever they go; McCarthy daringly likens them to figures in some piece of W.P.A. post-office art: "parodic figures transposed live and intact and violent out of a proletarian mural and set mobile upon the empty fields…" Later in the book, hanged men remind the reader of scenes out of some Breughel painting, the horror thus evoked being timeless, everlasting. Nor is this the limit of language's wizardry in this book where Faulknerian nobles are called "squire"; within a space of three pages, McCarthy uses these three examples of yoked opposites: "static violence," "furious immobility," and "violent constraint." Travelers on their wagon-borne chairs appear, in their "black immobility," like "stone figures quarried from the architecture of an older time." And the sister searching for her child wakens in the woods to see "toy birds with sesame eyes regarding her from their clay nests overhead." But what but fantastic language will serve to describe a world in which violent arguments break out over the making of butter, and in which hanged men are encountered casually, in the middle of a field, attended by a pair of buzzards merely? It is, needless to remark, our world precisely, rendered as dream and thus heightened in effect; hence McCarthy's diction.

One of *Outer Dark's* greater sequences involves a near-epic crossing of a river by ferry; the crossing, which goes disastrously awry, leads directly into the camp of the three avengers, and to a scene of great menace. It is almost as if these two poor souls, the brother and the sister both, had let loose all the demons in the world by the fact of their fornication. Their lives become nightmare; they are haunted by emblems of judgment:

> …She crouched in the bushes and watched it, a huge horse emerging seared and whole from the sun's eye and passing like a wrecked caravel gaunt-ribbed and black and mad with tattered saddle and dangling stirrups and hoofs clopping softly in the dust and passing enormous and emaciate and inflamed and the sound of it dying down the road to a distant echo of applause in a hall forever empty.

These events, it will be noted, occur generally in a void; they rivet attention because they are all that exists, and they take precisely the time it takes to read of them to happen.

McCarthy parallels some of Faulkner's great horse scenes with what must inevitably remind the reader of the Biblical account of the Gadarene swine; the herd of hogs being driven by in *Outer Dark* can carry men along with them, but first there is a discussion in which one character mentions Jewish dietary laws and the other replies, "What's a jew?" What then occurs acquires its power because to these people, it has not happened before: they do not know they are repeating a pattern of possession and atonement. There is some suggestion in the novel, moreover, that the three killers—or at least their leader—are operating out of some sense of the injustice of human destiny; but at once, and abruptly, the child—which moments before had dangled from a man's hands "like a dressed rabbit, a gross eldritch doll with ricketsprung legs and one eye opening and closing softly like a naked owl's"—has its throat slit. The novel ends when the brother, having found that the road he is following ends in a "spectral waste out of which reared only the naked trees in attitudes of agony and dimly hominoid like figures in a landscape of the damned," turns back, wondering why "a road should come to such a place." But on his journey back, he passes a blind man going to the place he has just returned from. He says nothing. He merely notes that "Someone should tell a blind man before setting him out that way."

■ III

Well yes; someone should. Denials of responsibility, along with unwarranted assumptions of authority, run through Cormac McCarthy's four novels. *Child of God* is as illustrative of this notion as any of the others, but here the prose has been stripped to its absolute leanest; in its starkness and simplicity of means *Child of God* comes near to being a tour-de-force. In one of those ironic characterizations that nearly give his hand away, McCarthy encapsules his central character on the novel's second page: "A child of God much like yourself perhaps." Said child of God is seen threatening an auctioneer almost immediately; more to the point of McCarthy's presentation of his ordinariness, Lester is soon seen urinating, defecating, and masturbating. The atmosphere, particularly within the abandoned house where Lester takes up residence, is one of rot and decay; man is but another particle within a material nature in this novel. Within a few pages, a fox hunt rushes right through Lester's new home (and later on he witnesses a boar hunt). Life's value is far from assured here.

Among the more horrific grotesqueries in *Child of God,* certain simple jokes nestle: the names of a dumpkeeper's daughters (taken from a medical dictionary), "Urethra, Cerebella, Hernia Sue"; pigeons that are exploded (as in Wendell Berry's *Nathan Coulter*) by means of rectally-applied firecrackers. But for the most part, the humor is of a black sort, designed to chill and repel. And often, a poetically rendered scene turns sour when Lester intrudes: a girl found sleeping outdoors in her nightgown turns into a feral self-defending beast; a young girl watching fireworks is unwittingly attracted to this dangerous stranger:

> …And you could see among the faces a young girl with candyapple on her lips and her eyes wide. Her pale hair smelled of soap, woman-child from beyond the years, rapt below the sulphur glow and pitch-light of some medieval fun fair. A lean skylong candle skewered the black pools in her eyes. Her fingers clutched. In the flood of this breaking brimstone galaxy she saw the man with the bears watching her and she edged closer to the girl by her side and brushed her hair with two fingers quickly.

The young girl's movements sum up the power of McCarthy's style: by combining elaborate diction with terrible deeds, he creates a tension of attraction-repulsion. Evil fascinates with its lurid beauty.

Quentin Compson's protests that he doesn't hate his South (at the end of *Absalom, Absalom!*) would have to be amplified at an even shriller pitch to cover what is depicted in *Child of*

God. Within a very few pages, we are shown a blacksmith's ritual of proud and careful effort being ignored by a loutish countryman, an infant chewing the legs off a captured robin, a scene of necrophilia with an element of voyeurism thrown in for good measure, the main character shopping for clothes to deck out his dead beloved, a fire that consumes this favorite corpse and sends the protagonist to a cave to live, and the killing of a fresh beloved (and the leaving of her idiot child to die in another fire). At last, Ballard has created his underground kingdom of the dead in the image of his own graceless soul:

> He followed this course…through a tunnel that brought him to his belly, the smell of the water besides him in the trough rich with minerals and past the chalken dung of he knew not what animals until he climbed up a chimney to a corridor above the stream and entered into a tall and bellshaped cavern. Here the walls with their softlooking convolutions, slavered over as they were with wet and bloodred mud, had an organic look to them like the innards of some great beast. Here in the bowels of the mountain Ballard turned his light on ledges or pallets of stone where dead people lay like saints.

It is hard not to draw in the breath at one of these chapter-ending revelations. This is the world beyond good and evil, where only the unbridled intelligence exists, playing God: "Disorder in the woods, trees down, new paths needed. Given charge Ballard would have made things more orderly in the woods and in men's souls." Ballard, who has taken to wearing the clothing of his victims, is even seen telling the snow to fall faster ("and it did"), and wondering "what stuff" the stars were made of, "or himself."

Thus McCarthy has endowed this "child of God," supposedly like overselves, with the capacity to protest his fate, to attempt to rewrite the order of things. We find him saving his corpses from a flood, the heroic effort required seeming mock-Biblical or mock-epical and leaving him "gibbering, a sound not quite crying that echoed from the walls of the grotto like the mutterings of a band of sympathetic apes." But when a deputy asks an old man if people are meaner than they used to be, the old man replies, "No…I don't. I think people are the same from the day God first made one." In Ballard's career human history is telescoped and reversed. Contemplating the fields renewing themselves in the springtime, Ballard drops his head and weeps; later, he dreams a dream of an idyll in nature, riding on muleback and resolved to go on riding, "for he could not turn back and the world that day was as lovely as any day that ever was and he was riding to his death." Fleeing his enemies later, Ballard finds an "ancient ossuary" deep in the bowels of the earth, where there are the bones of "bison, elk," and a jaguar whose eyetooth Ballard takes along. Ascending to the surface of the earth again, Ballard turns himself in to the county hospital, and dies of pneumonia before he can be charged with any crime. His body is reduced to spare parts, like Gary Gilmore's in Norman Mailer's *The Executioner's Song*:

> He was laid out on a slab and flayed, eviscerated, dissected. His head was sawed open and the brains removed. His muscles were stripped from his bones. His heart was taken out. His entrails were hauled forth and delineated and the four young students who bent over him like those haruspices of old perhaps saw monsters worse to come in their configurations. At the end of three months…Ballard was scraped from the table into a plastic bag…

But there is more—the discovery of the cave filled with corpses, which then have to be hauled forth, like this one:

> The rope drew taut and the first of the dead sat up…Gray soapy clots of matter fell from the cadaver's chin. She ascended dangling. She sloughed in the weem of the noose. A grey rheum dripped.

It is terrible stuff, deliberately so, yet it is not the mindless gore of Fifties comic books; instead, it is yet another version of Yeats' "terrible beauty."

Cormac McCarthy's concise history of mankind takes a more naturalistic turn in his first/fourth novel and most recently published work, *Suttree*. It is, in length and approach, a considerable departure from what has gone before. It is perhaps as long as the other three books put together, and it is an urban novel whereas the other three are rural. It is tied to a specific city, Knoxville, Tennessee, and to a fairly specific time, whereas the others, for all the occasional clues one might find therein, are without time and almost without place too. In a peculiar and doubtless unplanned (or not totally planned) sense, *Suttree* completes the others, makes them a square, takes them into another dimension.

Sheer length and density of presented experience prevent adequate critical consideration of *Suttree* here, but it may be possible to fit the work within McCarthy's canon generally, for certain stylistic traits are in evidence here as much as in the other three novels. For one, McCarthy's handling of dialogue is as superb here as ever—a point difficult to establish without extensive quotation, and one which nevertheless can be cited as common to several of the writers of the American South in our time. We might distinguish Suttree himself as observer and absorber from McCarthy's other protagonists, for his intelligence and articulateness mark him as having the gifts to cope, albeit painfully, with the anguishes of his time, as none of his creator's other characters seem able to do. Indeed, though the novel is set in Knoxville in the Fifties, Suttree himself is nearly a stereotype of the Sixties—a gifted and conscious dropout (as they used to be called) from a rotten society. "Blind slime. As above, so it is below," Suttree comments on the possibility that there are caves below Knoxville. Thus this vision of the world as scarcely created, or as created badly, is what the character Suttree seems to share with McCarthy the author. What persists of the writer's standard "first novel," arguably, is this projection of the self into the figure of the central character—one who, nevertheless, is better at suffering and being there than at acting.

Knoxville has had, arguably, more and better talent devoted to its fictional depiction—James Agee, David Madden, Cormac McCarthy—than any other American city, once size is considered and weighed accordingly. McCarthy's Knoxville is rather akin to Eliot's Waste Land or Unreal City; in McCarthy's case, however, Knoxville becomes the all-too-real city. A fragment of the novel's initial reverie, italics removed, reads:

> …Encampment of the damned. Precincts perhaps where dripping lepers prowl unbelled…The buildings stamped against the night are like a rampart to a farther world forsaken, old purposes forgot. Countrymen come for miles with the earth clinging to their shoes and sit all day like mutes in the marketplace. The city constructed on no known paradigm, a mongrel architecture reading back through the works of man in a brief delineation of the aberrant disordered and mad. A carnival of shapes…

Thus we are not too surprised to find that "the city is beset by a thing unknown" which simply to dwell upon is to invite in. Alas, the thing is human nature, an image of ourselves presented at the gates which we are compelled to take in and worship—and which turns, immediately, into our ruin.

When we first encounter Suttree, he is fishing; what is caught, instead of fish, is a suicide, a grappling hook wedged into his face giving him a "crazed grin. They raised him so, gambreled up by the bones of his cheek. A pale incruent wound. He seemed to protest woodenly, his head awry." The hook comes away at last, brings with it facial flesh. What of it? We have been to McCarthy's anatomy classes before; have sat still for these "delineations" and their artistic products. Suttree catches fish, and takes one to a hermit; the hermit accepts, and offers a communion Suttree refuses. This is our body, our blood. To read McCarthy is to take part in a spectral Eucharist, a not-quite-black Black Mass. We stir our spoons through our soup, wondering what next we will be asked to take for part of Chowder.

If McCarthy's dialogue can be attributed to a regional Ear, some of his other prose can seemingly only be called the product of a poet's sense of rhythm. Here is, perhaps, a particularly Celtic evocation of moment, not otherwise demanding of attention (cf. Donleavy, Beckett?):

> He crossed the cabin and stretched himself out on the cot. Closing his eyes. A faint breeze from the window stirring his hair. The shanty-boat trembled slightly in the river and one of the steel drums beneath the floor expanded in the heat with a melancholy bong. Eyes resting. This hushed and mazy Sunday. The heart beneath the breastbone pumping. The blood on its appointed rounds. Life in small places, narrow crannies. In the leaves, the toad's pulse. The delicate cellular warfare in a waterdrop. A dextrocardiac, said the smiling doctor. Your heart's in the right place. Weathershrunk and loveless. The skin drawn and split like an overripe fruit.

Or consider this meditation by the once-jailed Suttree, the survivor of a pair of twins, upon what age reveals (we combine extremities of a pair of paragraphs):

> From all old seamy throats of elders, musty books, I've salvaged not a word. In a dream I walked with my grandfather by a dark lake and the old man's talk was filled with incertitude. I saw how all things fall false from the dead.... I followed (my twin) into the world, me. A breech birth. Hind end fore in common with whales and bats, life forms meant for other mediums than the earth and having no affinity for it. And used to pray for his soul days past. Believing his ghastly circus reconvened elsewhere for alltime. He in the limbo of the Christless righteous, I in a terrestrial hell.

McCarthy's vision has come back to Tennessee again by way of France.

Again, space prevents an adequate consideration of the subject of humor in McCarthy's works, for what strikes the reader as amusing may also serve to judge that reader; long exchanges of dialogue, further demonstrations of how finely tuned McCarthy's ear is, eventually become demonstrations of attitude. As in the fiction of the South generally, laughter is generally accompanied by cruelty—to animals or persons—and pain. But one of the most hilarious passages one might have read anywhere in recent years is surely the section of *Suttree* in which the character Harrogate is introduced. A walking actualization of all our cliches about simple and naive country boys, Harrogate has a secret passion, indulged in the dark of night, that gets him sent to prison: he fornicates with watermelons. It is as if there is no end to the deviltry a clouded human imagination can invent for itself; McCarthy's novels accomplish the non-theological proof of the existence of what once would have been called Original Sin. His characters are wandering harrowers of a present "terrestrial hell"; as the ending of *Suttree* has it,

> Somewhere in the gray wood by the river is the huntsman and in the brooming corn and in the castellated press of cities. His work lies all wheres and his hounds tire not. I have seen them in a dream, slaverous and wild and their eyes crazed with ravening for souls in this world. Fly them.

Thus ending echoes Prologue; the hunter is within the gates.

By avoiding the space-wasting device of plot summary, this essay, it is hoped, may pique the curiosity of readers heretofore unfamiliar with Cormac McCarthy's fiction. By concentrating on the salient features of his style, however, and by attempting to summarize the categories of character and event encountered in that fiction, it may have left the impression that McCarthy is a compiler of horrors merely, an indiscriminate creator of cheap shock effects. Nothing, I feel, could be further from the truth. Nor by this time should it still be possible to dismiss his verbal ingenuity as mere

■ **BOOKS BY CORMAC MCCARTHY**

The Orchard Keeper. New York: Random House, 1965.

Outer Dark. New York: Random House, 1968.

Child of God. New York: Random House, 1973.

Suttree. New York: Random House, 1979.

Blood Meridian; or, the Evening Redness in the West. New York: Random House, 1985.

All the Pretty Horses. New York: Random House, 1992.

The Stonemason: A Play in Five Acts. Hopewell, N.J.: Ecco, 1994.

The Crossing. New York: Knopf, 1994.

The Gardener's Son: A Screenplay. New York: Ecco, 1996.

Cities of the Plain. New York: Random House, 1998.

The Border Trilogy (contains *All the Pretty Horses, The Crossing,* and *Cities of the Plain*). New York: Knopf, 1999.

posturing, or as some last gasp of Southern decadence extinguishing itself even as it blazes wildly. Cormac McCarthy may have certain features in common with the early Joyce Carol Oates, the early John Hawkes; yet he is still his own man entirely, indebted neither to such writers as these nor to the shade of William Faulkner, with which we began. "I never worried about the influence of *any* good writer," he has recently written me. "More the better, to my way of thinking."

"The style comes *out* of the place, material, characters, etc.," he continues in the same letter, referring to the differences between *Suttree* and the rural novels (his next book is "about Americans in northern Mexico in 1849, which will be a different style again"). "The free-floating anxiety that provides *ambiance* in some of my books is something I have found in the world and so I put it in," he concludes, understandably reluctant to discuss further "the confrontation of evil" in his works (because "then I'd be an essayist, and I aint"). One can hardly blame him: the novels speak eloquently for themselves, and ultimately the reader must go to them, or return there, and accompany this spendid prophet further into darkness.

John Ditsky
April, 1981

UPDATE

McCarthy has since written four novels: *Blood Meridian; or, The Evening Redness in the West* (1985); *All the Pretty Horses* (1992), *The Crossing* (1994), and *Cities of the Plain* (1998). The last three books make up *The Border Trilogy* (1999). He also has written *The Stonemason: A Play in Five Acts* (1994) and his script *The Gardener's Son* (first produced by the Public Broadcasting System, 1977) was published as *The Gardener's Son: A Screenplay* (1996).

The Southern-raised and -based McCarthy has been compared with such esteemed Southern writers as William Faulkner, Carson McCullers, and Flannery O'Connor. According to the *Dictionary of Literary Biography*, McCarthy shares with those writers "a rustic and sometimes dark humor, intense characters, and violent plots . . . [and] their development of universal themes within a highly particularized fictional world, their seriousness of vision, and their vigorous exploration of the English language." The *New York Times* has noted, "His characters are often outcasts—destitutes or criminals, or both. Death, which announces itself often, reaches down from the open sky, abruptly, with a slashed throat or a bullet in the face. The abyss opens up at any misstep." Indeed, the extreme violence that continues to mark his work has drawn mixed, and sometimes harsh, criticism: some critics find the violence excessive and gratuitous; many do not. Some find his punctuation-lean style difficult and even irritating. Critics do agree, however, on the lyrical beauty of his writing.

In 2000, *All the Pretty Horses* was made into a critically acclaimed film, starring Matt Damon and Penelope Cruz. Because of that, and because of the awards for his books—and despite his avoidance of publicity—McCarthy is becoming increasingly well known.

A Men's Club: The Fiction of Leonard Michaels

The term *minimalist* is no more satisfying or exact when it is used with respect to literature than when it is applied to music, but if the term has any appropriate critical relevance, it should be right to use it in connection with the stories of Leonard Michaels, who can be said to have been writing "minimalist" fiction when certain currently popular practitioners of the genre were still in grammar school. Michaels may not himself care for the term, but he writes pieces with such enormously concentrated coiled energy that they can almost be termed elliptical; the reader comes away from them feeling as if a full literary meal has been consumed, single lines somehow having contained more than single lines ought by rights to contain. In letters accompanying his statement of cooperation with the writing of this article, Michaels states: "Virtually everything I've ever written is terse." And again: "I publish very little compared to various contemporaries, and never publish anything too heavy, that is, long." Michaels's equation of length with sheer bulk is revealing, positing as it does a credo, an eschewal of turgidity, with which his output has been wholly consistent.

That output consists of four slim volumes published over little more than two decades, and by the same fine publisher. Each has been slightly shorter than its predecessor, almost as though the author had made doing so a point of honor. The first of these, *Going Places*, collects fiction first published during the late 1960's, and to read these again after twenty years or so is to recognize how well Michaels captures the tone of that most romantic era. *I Would Have Saved Them If I Could* (1975) is very much the stylistic mate of the first book, a point to be discussed later on. *The Men's Club* appeared in 1982, and was subsequently turned into a film with a Michaels screenplay. Though this vehicle did not apparently sit well with the critics, a recent home viewing convinced this writer that those critics might not have known just what they were watching; certainly the writing is sharp and crisp and recognizably Michaelsian. And last year, *Shuffle* appeared, an assemblage that the jacket blurb calls "autobiographical fiction in the form of confession, memoir, journal, essay, and short story." Other pieces have yet to be gathered together.

It is this "autobiographical fiction" aspect of Michaels's writing that has to be dealt with at the outset. Michaels apparently appears in many of his own pieces, frequently under the alias of Phillip Liebowitz. Doubtless, some future biographer will have a field day relating Michaels's life to his fictions, the writing is so full of naked candor, particularly with respect to relationships with women. (Three of the books are dedicated to females only by first names; the fourth appears to be meant for Michaels's parents.) This article, however, is intended to deal with these fictions purely as fiction, and to avoid all possible taint of literary gossip, even to the point of avoiding asking personal questions that Michaels might well have been willing to answer.

Yet as an author, in his awareness of his Jewishness and in his honest portrayal of male sexuality, and especially in his rigorous intellectuality, Michaels is reminiscent of a better-known

Leonard Michaels

Leonard Michaels, an American short story writer and novelist, was born the son of a barber on January 2, 1933, in New York City. Michaels received his B.A. from New York University and his M.A. and Ph.D. from the University of Michigan. A Guggenheim Fellowship and a National Endowment for the Humanities Fellowship are two of the awards he has received. He was also the recipient of the National Book Award Nomination for his collection of short stories, *Going Places*, and the American Book Award Nomination for his novel *The Men's Club*. Michaels has taught at Patterson State College (now William Patterson State College of New Jersey), the University of California, Davis, and has been visiting professor at such colleges as Johns Hopkins University and the University of Alabama. Michaels is currently a professor of English at the University of California, Berkeley, and the editor of the *University Publishing* review. ■

writer whose upbringing took place just across the Hudson from Michaels's New York childhood (he now teaches in California), Philip Roth. In fact, Roth and Michaels—and Alexander Portnoy!—are of an age; all were born in 1933, the year the Nazis took power. Comparisons of the work of Philip Roth and "Philip Liebowitz" are inevitable; this article intends to avoid them as much as possible. If comparisons between Michaels's characters and, say, Roth's Nathan Zuckerman result from this article, however, its author will not mind at all.

Leonard Michaels's fiction is energized by a novel sort of tension between an often academic intellectuality and an only seemingly indulgent sexuality, itself a symptom of a Romantic and arguably immature lifestyle on the parts of many of his characters. The drama of these supposed opposites is only initially jarring, and perhaps not at all, for those who swim in the rivers of academe. In Michaels, there is dramatic irony between the elevated workings of the mind and the frequently contradictory impulses of the will, as expressed through the body. Rarely connected with conventional love, sexuality is thus fairly often a spasm, a twitch, that marks the electrical wattage given off by synaptic activity. Sex becomes a language usually at odds with the "purely" verbal; or if it is a language in a more familiar sense, it is that language's means of emphasis—ejaculation, if you will, in at least a pair of meanings of the term.

Going Places is off and running with a story about a college woman who, returning from a car ride on which she has been raped, sees a dummy in a store window and finds herself relating to it; let down by her self-centered boyfriend, she ends up a suicide just before a dormmate comes by her room to meet her. "Manikin" captures a pre–*Roe v. Wade* era with a university environment that is full yet barely sketched out, but its Turkish rapist who thinks macho aggressiveness elicits love is hardly an obsolete type. "City Boy" begins, like some Italian play, breathlessly, with a couple plummeting toward sex thirty feet from the girl's parents, while the girl repeats, "Phillip, this is crazy." Discovered by her parents, Phillip runs naked out the door, rides down the elevator with the reproving doorman, tries unsuccessfully to get into the subway, returns, finds that the girl's father has had a heart attack, and at the end has the daughter again demanding sex: "The clock ticked like crickets. The Vlamincks spilled blood. We sank into the rug as if it were quicksand." All this is carried off in a bizarre mix of panic and references to Freud and Dürer, the Vlamincks and Utrillos on the walls, and garbled Sartre. Similarly, "Crossbones," in only four pages, tells in onrunning sentences the violent relationship of a New York Jew and a Minnesota Scandinavian that culminates in marriage when a promised paternal visit does *not* quite come off.

"Sticks and Stones"—most Michaels titles contain their implied ironies—concerns the relationship between two men in an intellectual atmosphere reminiscent of the vapidity—or brilliance, depending on the strength of one's nostalgia—of the films of the '50s and '60s, when that genre was touted as the indisputable one for our times:

> I yawned and scratched my cheek, though I wasn't sleepy and felt no itch. Our eyes slipped to the corners of the squalid world. Life seemed merely miserable.
>
> Afterwards, in my apartment, I had accidents. A glass slipped out of my hand one night, smashed on the floor and cut my shin. When I lifted my pants leg to see the cut, my other leg kicked it. I collapsed on the floor. My legs fought with kicks and scrapes till both lay bleeding, jerky, broken and jointless.

The mannered prose of the piece includes a recital of what seems to be the plot of Antonioni's *Eclipse,* followed by a discussion of art during which "my head fell off." By story's end the character Phillip is "a head on legs. Running"—another dreamlike fusion of the worlds of life and art.

"The Deal" concerns an encounter between a woman and a pack of street youths, and seems to center around the question of how circumstances may require one to become a commodity in the eyes of others. "Intimations" is all of a page and a half in length, and deals with a visiting Jewish mother whose ability to discern pork from chicken elicits a culture clash between her son and his shikse wife—the couple from "Crossbones"—whose name is naggingly repeated throughout until a ringing phone accomplishes a role-reversal. "Making Changes" presents that datedly hip aspect of '60s life, the artsy orgy. The protagonist, Phillip, wanders a landscape of copulating bodies in a search for one "Cecily"; in the end, a suitable Cecily is found and taken home, where "We had D.H. Lawrence, Norman Mailer, triste…. She kissed me. We had Henry Miller." Michaels unblinkingly satirizes a society in which life is lived accordingly to scenarios gleaned from literature and films.

The matter-of-factness with which certain aspects of the day's culture are treated is a major part of the deftness of Michaels's style. "Mildred" begins and ends with inanities about her appearance, and indeed, the first several pages are sheer dialogue only interrupted when drugs are produced and abortion becomes the topic of conversation. Suddenly Mildred "showed us her womb" and, told it looks edible, takes it to the stove. "I had a bite," the narrator says; then:

> She cried. I made fists and pummeled my head. She cried. I pummeled until my head slipped into my neck. She stopped crying. I smashed my mouth with my knee. She smiled a little.
>
> "Do it again."
>
> I started eating my face….

"Fingers and Toes" is a masterpiece of party talk featuring Phillip and his unfortunate friend Henry (from "Sticks and Stones"); in it, intelligent people copulate and laugh ("Nee, nee") and make Sartrean references before Phillip slips away like a hero of Romance into a night reminiscent of something out of Dylan Thomas: "I slipped into it nose first. It nosed into me. I twitched like a fish and went quivering through dingy dingles, from blackness to blackness to blackness to blackness."

The contemporaneity of much of Michaels's work is apt to obscure for the reader its grounding in a middle-European surreality, but a story like "Isaac" serves as a useful reminder of a vanished archetype, a world of Kafka and Chagall. "A Green Thought" mocks the pastoral Marvell as it returns us to the lives of Phillip and Henry, Marjorie and Cecily, where university-trained intellectuals carry on like the lower mammals. "Finn" takes us to the world of the university and of assimilationist Jews trying to adjust to a milieu whose rules they haven't made; it ends with "a little waking dream," a dream-montage of a dance, another cinematic dissolve. The title piece ends the collection: "Going Places" questions just that process, showing us a former cabbie, beaten during a mugging, who becomes an assistant to a paint contractor instead and discovers that no life is without hazard. Work this story's implications back through the whole of Leonard Michaels's first collection, and one sees a pattern of questioning certain basic American cultural assumptions that include—almost as though his characters did not recognize what their relevance might actually be—explicit or implicit allusions to the works of various artists (Chekhov, Borges, Mamet, Elkin, Magritte, etc.), some of whose work Michaels's stories in fact precede.

I Would Have Saved Them If I Could appeared in a rather different climate in America. The Nixon presidency had been shot down in flames, but not before bringing an effective end to the idealism (and hedonism) of the '60s—nor before the figure of Henry Kissinger had managed to suggest an identity between sexuality and power. The Vietnam War having ended, a more or less characterless decade resumed its dull pace towards worse things. Leonard Michaels's fictions continued to image the America of those times, but he also responded in technically innovative ways to the new dispensation. Coverage of his first book here took the approach of including piece after piece in the order in which they were published in book form, but there is no reason to confine this discussion to that single format. Indeed, an analysis of the collection's structure should say more about Michaels's evolving sense of form, as well as of historical, political, and literary concerns.

Structurally, *I Would* consists of thirteen stories. The series is bookended by two "Phillip" stories, one about Michaels's alter ego as an inquisitive youth, the other showing him as an ambitious married man on the corporate make. After "Murderers," the opening story, there appears "Eating Out," the first of three sustained mosaic fictions in the collection, each characterized by being divided into subsections all of which are given their own individual "sub"-titles. The first and second of these hark back to the "Phillip" material of the first collection, and thus spin a web between such matter and the opening and closing of the present volume (which contains other Phillip stories as well). The third, the title work, is as personal as the first two, but in a less traditional way; it is a "Phillip" piece in the sense of being a fictional survey of the making of an artistic conscience. Among these longer pieces are sandwiched the other eight ingredients of the mix.

The "bookend" stories are only superficially conventional. "The Murderers" is a little masterwork about coming of age as an American Jew that Philip Roth might have written, and also might envy. Indeed, as the other best treatment of the theme of "Jews on a Roof," it at least rivals Roth's early "The Conversion of the Jews." In the story, which it would be unfair to wholly summarize, "Phillip Liebowitz" and his pals make another visit to a precarious tenement rooftop perch in order to watch the young rabbi and his wife dance naked and then make love. What ensues has the rabbi calling the boys "Murderers," though death takes another and surprising form in this powerful juxtaposition of sex and death in a young man's unique rite of passage. At the other end is the almost-surreal "The Captain," in which a grown Phillip, eager for a job, decides that the way to earn one is to advance upon the prospective employer's wife at a party, whereupon the two have sex in an exhausting variety of ways. Meanwhile he has allowed his wife, to the same end, to flirt with the employer. In the end, having decided that he has cinched the job, Phillip finds that his wife has done the trick for him. Amidst these events, Phillip sees himself as "a young captain in a novel by Conrad. First opportunity to command.... I notice it's a moral storm. The worst kind." A moment of doubt passes, then "I was walking, and all right. I was the captain." Yet the common reader might well wonder if this captain is in charge of his own soul, or even owns one; the dispassionately clinical narration, although first-person, leaves all such judgments entirely to the reader.

"Some Laughed," which precedes "The Captain," is a satire on the world of academic publish-or-perish, and thus makes for an entertaining segue to the final story. On the other hand, after "Eating Out," the first lengthy and innovatively-structured narrative, there appears "Getting Lucky." Phillip Liebowitz finds himself being groped to the point of orgasm in a crowded subway car; neatly tucked in place thereafter by his anonymous nonacquaintance, Phillip leaves the train wondering which of the faces in his vicinity belongs to his assailant/benefactor, male or female. Beset by ambiguity over the meaning of this encounter, Phillip reaches the street, ready to run if approached:

> In the brilliant windy street, Liebowitz hailed a cab. Before it stopped he had the door open. The meter began ticking. Ticking with remorseless, giddy indifference to his personal being and yet, somehow, consonant with himself. Not his heart, not the beat of his viscera, and yet his ticking self, his time, quickly and mercifully growing shorter. "I'll be dead soon," he thought. Tick-tick-tick.

Challenged by the cabbie to give an address or leave, Phillip lights a cigarette and tells the cabbie to shut up, that he is ready to pay to go nowhere. Having gone places, having gotten lucky, Phillip listens to the sound of his life running up the meter with something like relief.

"Eating Out" and "Downers" are the first two longer stories constructed out of narrational bits separately titled, fragments but also self-contained, elements in a matrix that is itself a part, one of two or three such parts, in a larger matrix that is the present collection, and arguably also part of the evolving constellation that is Michaels's work. The Jewish mother, the troublesome friend, the disappointing sexual relationships: all return here in miniatures left to the hand of the reader to put into their places, like pieces of a puzzle. Here, for instance, is all of "Eating Out"'s "The Hand," a vignette about the inheritance of absences, by now material familiar from each day's TV talk shows:

> I smacked my little boy. My anger was powerful. Like justice. Then I discovered no feeling in the hand. I said "Listen, I want to explain the complexities to you." I spoke with seriousness and care particularly of fathers. He asked, when I finished, if I wanted him to forgive me. I said yes. He said no. Like trumps.

The strains of heredity of education, of upbringing, in Phillip have gone to producing an offspring capable of designing his own wry reaction to life—his own game version, with rules both created and learned, and capable of being "won," moment by moment, by the deft application of an ironic twist.

"I Would Have Saved Them If I Could" takes its title and applies it thereafter to the entire collection, from a letter from Lord Byron in which he describes the decapitation of three prisoners while he is in Rome on a visit. The letter itself is filled with a tension, alarming to a lay reader but familiar to the artist, between the need to observe and record and transform on the one hand, and the desire to change by means of human intervention on the other. In a larger sense, and with respect to Michaels's own times, the story questions literature's ability to deal with life's terrors by means of conceits and ironies—as with Borges and his subsequent school of "magic realists"—even as it uses its own conceits and ironies to make its point. In a central section, "The Screams of Children," Borges's character becomes part of a gathering-together of the various strands of Michaels's own story:

> THE NEW TESTAMENT is the best condemned-prisoner story. Jesus, a "suspected" Jew, sublimates at the deadly moment. In two ways, then, he is like Jaromir Hladik. Insofar as the Gestapo gives birth to the ecstatic Hladik, he and Jesus are similar in yet another way. Both are victims of parental ambivalence, which tends to give birth to death. One could savor distinctions here, but the prophetic Kafka hurries me away: humanity, he says, is the growth of death force. For reasons of discretion the trains rolled before dawn, routed through the outskirts of Prague. Nevertheless, you could hear the screams of children.

But you must read the whole story to have an inkling of what to make of this passage or, for that matter, to see how this difficult and serious piece then segues into the surreal visit to a Chinese Jew in a hospital, "Hello Jack," thence to the penultimate "Some Laughed," and finally the portrait of Phillip as a man, "The Captain."

In sum, Michaels's second collection of short fiction has been used here to draw attention to the writer's sense of structure, both in terms of the overall assemblage and within each separate piece—just as the first collection was read in thematic terms. And as establishing a judgmental stance towards his materials is largely left to Michaels's readers, so too must the intrinsic interrelationship between matter and form be seen in the act of reading Leonard Michaels. For the always "terse" Michaels is quite capable of approaching arguably bizarre content through conventional fictional means, while at other times his subjects are perceived through the tunnel vision of the dream, the nightmare, the drugged state, or—at the other end of the mind's workings—the essay, the philosophical disquisition, and the associative leaps of poetry. In 1981's *The Men's Club*, Michaels creates his "first novel" by sustaining a narrational matrix within which excerptable single stories are embedded. The characters take turns telling their stories yet the whole is greater than the simple sum of its parts. It is a classic literary structure—as if confessing as much, indeed, one of the club "members" is surnamed Canterbury.

The Men's Club is *echt*-Michaels, in the sense that it dares to deal with a topic other writers might not come near. That men have anything to say to one another as men seems, in these "politically correct" times, a form of heresy. One weekly column in *The New York Times Magazine*; and Robert Bly's followers out in the bush: these have come to seem atavistic concerns at best. The novel's narrator deals with this issue in the book's first two pages:

> …I supposed there could be virtues in a men's club, a regular social possibility. I should have said yes immediately, but something in me resisted. The prospect of leaving my house after dinner to go to a meeting. Blood is heavy then. Brain is slow. Besides, wasn't this club idea corny? Like trying to recapture high-school days. Locker-room fun. Wet naked boys snapping towels at each other's genitals. It didn't feel exactly right. To be wretchedly truthful, any social possibility unrelated to wife, kids, house, and work felt like a form of adultery. Not criminal. Not legitimate.…

"*Like a form of adultery*." It is typically Michaelsian to frame the issue in such a sexual way; if men are to socialize, their motivation must be explained away as a kind of harmless play: Boys will be boys. "Maybe men played more than women. A men's club, compared to women's groups, was play. Frivolous; virtually insulting. It excluded women. But I was thinking in circles. A men's club didn't exclude women. It also didn't exclude kangaroos. It included only men." In our time to admit to wanting to share time with one's own gender has become, for men, an embarrassment, an implied affront to one's personal sense of *pudeur*.

Before long, the club's first meeting well along—men have "clubs," women "groups"—Kramer, the host, cheerfully offers his guests the fare already prepared for the next day's meeting of his wife's group; and to sacramentalize the event he proffers "a case of zinfandel. It is good, good California. Men, I offer to you this zinfandel." Suddenly some vestigial Hemingway DNA seems to have asserted itself. The narrator reflects:

> …We were "lucky," said Kramer. Lucky maybe, to be men. Life is unfair business. Whoever said otherwise? It is a billion bad shows, low blows, and number one has more fun. The preparations for the women's group would feed our club. The idea of delicious food, taken this way, was thrilling. Had it been there for us, it would have been pleasant. But this was evil, like eating the other woman.…

"Eating," again, is equivocal at the least, and in fact suggests at least three possible meanings. What is clear enough is that the men's club deals with the food for the women's group—circle, coven??—as one invading and primitive tribe might have dealt with the trappings of another. These spoils are to be consumed and the powers of their makers taken on. When Kramer, the host, brings wine to his men, "his dark eyes glowed. His voice was all pleasure. 'This is a wonderful club. This is a wonderful club'." The pleasure obtained here has its patent element of desecration in it, a primitive form of revenge against a dominating order.

In a sense, all of Leonard Michaels's writing can be referred to as a "men's club." With the exception of such pieces as "The Deal," the imagined persona—if indeed imagined—is male; and the stories they tell, or that are told about them, can be seen as interrelated in far more than an autobiographical way. Granted, Michaels does not make use of such transparent ruses as those frequently employed by the late I. B. Singer: Three Jews decided to pass the time by telling stories. What other writer of our time has tried so determinedly to enter the male psyche, starting with the premise that there is such a thing, as Michaels? Never having met a woman who has read Michaels, this writer cannot gauge his ability to transcend the limits of gender as regards readerships, but there is to his work a certain *frisson*, a naughtiness born of complicity, that the narrator of *The Men's Club*, a professor, puts very well:

> Saint Augustine confesses to a night of vandalism with a gang of boys. They stole some pears. No big deal, but it troubled him that human company inspired evil. He hung out plenty. There was his mother, his mistress, his students, and always there were men.…

The flip side of that allusion, of course, is Augustine's formulation of the notion of Original Sin, the end product of hanging out with a gang that steals pears. Michaels's theme can be said to be just what his narrator imputes to Augustine, "that human company inspired evil."

Again, like Bly's men in the wilderness rediscovering their maleness, Michaels's characters reach a peak—before their host's wife comes home—during which they throw knives at a door and commence communal, feral howling:

> We sounded lost, but I thought we'd found ourselves. I mean nothing psychological. No psycho-logic of the soul, only the mind, and this was mindless…it seemed we were one in the rising howls, rising again and again, taking us up even as we sank toward primal dissolution, assenting to it with this music of common animality, like a churchly chorus, singing of life and death.

The boys return to their real lives, singing of their host (in trouble with his wife), "singing of Kramer, jolly good fellow we'd left in his dining room peering after us, waving goodbye. Jolly good fellow. Which nobody should deny." They *can*, mind you; but they *should not*. Let he who is without sin cast the first stone. *Honi soit qui mal y pense.*

As *The Men's Club* presages the "Me Decade" and Reaganism, his most recent collection, *Shuffle* (1990), is as ostensibly fragmented as we feel ourselves to be at that decade's end. Perhaps only a Jewish mother could be ready for such an age, dependably anticipating disaster as she would. Here is "I Would"'s "Ma"—part of "Eating Out"—in its entirety:

> I SAID, "Ma, do you know what happened?" She said, "Oh, my God."

In that same collection, on the opening page of the splendid seven pages of "Murderers," Michaels makes what might be the only other use of the word that becomes his collection's title: Uncle Moe, who dies in the story's first line, is said to have "shuffled away his life." One might otherwise have conjectured a card deal, or a movement in the general direction of Buffalo. True, *Shuffle* is an odd mix, a literary luck of the draw, but it is also about a sometimes seemingly aimless movement through life, a life increasingly difficult to dissociate from the writer's own.

Like many a contemporary poem unified anecdotally rather than by means of images or, to put things more narrowly, like many an anecdote unified primarily by narrational voice rather than by conventional means of construction, *Shuffle's* "Journal" opens on a note of sexual dysfunction among characters incapable of doing more than pay lip service to traditional mores. The personages who appear in it have managed to outrage the experienced norm, such as the writer high on cocaine who sits at his typewriter reassured that he is so good he doesn't even have to write. A certain outrageousness, in fact, is taken *as* the norm, one meant to be casually outdone. As in the prior piece in which a young son is quoted, the object seems to be to "trump." Even in death, the narrator's father surprises his widow with a

> dumb little smile on his face, as if it weren't bad being dead. He'd gone like himself, a sweet gentleman with fine nervous hands, not wanting her to feel distressed. It's a mystery how one learns to speak, the great achievement of a life. But when the soul speaks—alas—it is no longer the soul that speaks.

Taking the reader where he or she might not be capable of following, the "Journal" in *Shuffle* is both intelligent and candid, even as it is also simultaneously private and public, like the celebrated journals of the musician Ned Rorem, themselves no less enchanting for their sense of *voice*.

There follow four autobiographical sketches, all of them predictably brief. In the first, "The Father," Michaels presents a humble individual grateful to have survived his Polish origins, grateful for whatever life allows him of pleasure. At the end, the narrator remembers when he, on his way to an assignation, encountered his father on the street, and their relationship is encapsuled in a bit of atavism:

> ..."Do you need money?"
>
> "No."
>
> "Here," he said, pulling coins from his coat pocket. "For the subway. Take."
>
> He gave.
>
> I took.

This is a relationship instinctively understood on the father's passing when the rabbi, leaving the parents' apartment, notices the narrator and instructs him in Yiddish to "Sit lower," which the latter acknowledges to be right.

"To Feel These Things" concerns the narrator's mother, and the farmer's attempt to imagine his origins through her stories of life in Poland. He concludes, "Eventually, I figured it was bad for Jews the way *it* is said to be raining. I didn't know what *it* was, only that *it* was worse than Hitler, older, absolutely unreasonable, strong, able to do things like fix the plumbing and paint the walls. *It* was like animals and trees, what lives outside, more physical than a person, though *it* appeared in persons." That this primordial source of fear can be dealt with through literature is the gist of "Literary Talk," in which the narrator suddenly glimpses the connection between *The Winter's Tale* and the big eyes of a doomed ball-turret gunner remembered by his teacher. Finally, "The Abandoned House" shows the narrator in graduate school, trying to pilfer furniture from a rural Michigan house, and encountering, eerily, a palpable presence in the house that makes him flee to the predictable "universe of silence" of present time.

The final and longer piece, "Sylvia," concerns a relationship with a woman encountered in what was left of Greenwich Village in 1960; the territory is lovingly described—as can be attested to by anyone who was there then—the way the best cultural anthropologists can summon up the spirit of a vanished civilization. But the narrative is about relationships. Michaels, in one of his tightly lucid *Threepenny Review* essays, has speculated about the meaning of this word, three-quarters composed of abstractions as it is; he quotes Kafka to the effect that it seems pointless to have a city as large as Vienna when all that is needed is a single room:

> The incomprehensible city is "relationship," or what you have with everyone in the abstract and lonely vastness of our social reality. The room, all one needs, is romance, love, passionate intimacy, the unsophisticated irrational thing you have with someone; or what has long been considered a form of madness, if not the universal demonic of contemporary vision.

(Note that "relationship" is, like the "it" of "To Feel These Things," an external force exercising an absurdly rational authority over what makes the human truly human, itself.) When Sylvia cuts her wrists "superficially," on the basis of previous experience, the narrator rushes in to her with food, at which she picks "sullenly, as if conceding that there might be a reason to live." Neurotically jealous, seemingly in perpetual PMS, Sylvia is capable of complaining that her nose is "a millimeter too long." This is the "universal demonic" of the "irrational" relationship.

One returns, necessarily, to the question deliberately being ignored here, a question that nonetheless hovers in the air while reading Michaels: even if we do not raise the issue of how closely the fiction resembles the author's "life," do we need to wonder about its accuracy as reportage? No is the safest answer, and yet a feminist, for instance, might raise the issue of the presentation of female characters, not to mention their supposed models. For the moment, the question is moot, and yet the dead-on accuracy of Michaels's reminiscences of New York in the '60s only intensifies it, as when the writer confirms for us the importance of films in "his" developing consciousness: "We carried away visions of despair, exacerbated through relentless boredom toward thrilling apprehensions of this moment, in this modern world, where emptiness could be exquisite, even a way of life, not only for Monica Vitti and Alain Delon but for us, too. Why not?" Or, again echoing earlier stories, there is this reflection on the academic life at Columbia:

> …Our friends knew they were going to be fired, since it was the department's tradition to fire people, but they weren't absolutely sure when it would happen, or if, by some miracle, the department would choose to keep them. They were saved from nervous breakdowns by the hope of being among the chosen, lots of marijuana, downers, uppers, and occasionally heroin. Eventually they lay before their senior colleagues who, like ancient Mayan priests, cut out their hearts. To their credit, they tried to destroy themselves first with drugs.

■ **BOOKS BY LEONARD MICHAELS**

Going Places. New York: Farrar, Straus and Giroux, 1969.

I Would Have Saved Them If I Could. New York: Farrar, Straus and Giroux, 1975.

The State of Language. Ed. with Christopher Ricks. Berkeley: University of California Press, 1980.

The Men's Club. New York: Farrar, Straus and Giroux, 1981.

Shuffle. New York: Farrar, Straus and Giroux, 1990.

West of the West: Imagining California. Ed. et al. San Francisco: North Point Press, 1989.

Slyvia: A Fictional Memoir. San Francisco, Mercury, 1992.

To Feel These Things: Essays. San Francisco, Mercury, 1993.

A Cat. New York: Putnam, 1995, London: Souvenir, 1995.

Time Out of Mind: The Diaries of Leonard Michaels, 1961–1995. New York: Putnam, 1999.

A Girl With a Monkey: New and Selected Stories. San Francisco: Mercury, 2000.

Not only does this passage, with its ironies and only slight exaggerations, tie the world of the Michaels consciousness to the grotesqueries of drug visions and thus, in this sense, confirm the vision of some of the early stories, but it serves as a bridge from the earlier quote on films to the ending when, overdosed on Seconals, Sylvia leaves the narrator with "emptiness…nothing, nothing at all."

If the intensity of "Sylvia" makes magnificent use of Michaels' "I" voice, the piece's subthemes—referred to above—adumbrate his other strengths. He has deepened as an artist even as he has developed a sense of how to write a commercial property. A new long story, "Viva la Tropicana," set for publication in *Best American Short Stories* and based in Miami and Havana, uses Michaels's more serious concerns as subtext for what is basically a color-charged adventure yarn in exotic locales—something perhaps only someone who both wrote a tight essay on Rita Hayworth and *Gilda* and saw all those Antonioni flicks could have turned out. Leonard Michaels is clearly a writer who deserves a far greater readership than he seems to enjoy at present. It would be ironic—one of those ironies that play about in his titles like light on water—if the film medium were to help make that expansion possible. "Sylvia" pauses to mention the decade when "movies" became "films." Perhaps the pretentiousness implicit in that change has evaporated by now. "Viva la Tropicana" might make a great film. It might even make a terrific movie.

John Ditsky
December, 1991

UPDATE

Since this essay appeared, Leonard Michaels has published *Sylvia: A Fictional Memoir* (1992), *To Feel These Things: Essays* (1993), *A Cat* (1995), *Time Out of Mind: The Diaries of Leonard Michaels, 1961-1995* (1999), and *A Girl with a Monkey: New and Selected Stories* (2000).

Reviews of his work can be somewhat mixed. *Booklist* called Michaels' story collection *A Girl with a Monkey* "career-defining" and wrote: "Michaels' trenchant, direct, and lyrical style, with not one word wasted, works as a tight springboard for conveying his vast knowledge about why we love who we love." Yet a *Library Journal* labeled it "uneven": "The characters and places are powerfully presented, but often the realism is too hard-edged to engage the reader. . . . [T]his collection—one story of which was included in *Best American Short Stories* 1991—is clearly the product of an author who strives too hard for perfection."

Even so, Michaels is highly regarded by many discerning readers and critics, and has a significant "cult" following. According to a *Dictionary of Literary Biography* essay, "Two things are incontestable: the power of Michaels to tell a gripping or hilarious story, and the elegance of his narrative and descriptive prose style."

Dickinson with a Difference: The Poetry of Josephine Miles

■ **I**

In the Good Old Days, when I was in the Middle School, we used to compose themes upon such topics as "Sir Roger de Coverley in the 20th Century," just as if there could have *been* a Sir Roger in the 1930's, or a village where health and plenty cheered the laboring swain, or a spacious firmament proclaiming its great Original from pole to pole. Nevertheless, I propose to begin this essay in a similar vein, just as if Emily Dickinson could have been University Professor at Berkeley, an accomplished scholar, and a poet with ten published volumes to her living credit.

Here is Professor Miles:

Kind

When I think of my kindness which is tentative and quiet
And of yours which is intense and free,
I am in elaboration of knowledge impatient
Of even the patientest immobility.

I think of my kind, which is the human fortune
To live in the world and make war among its friends,
And of my version, which is to be moderately peaceful,
And of your version; and must make amends

By my slow word to your wish which is mobile,
Active and moving in its generous sphere.
This is the natural and the supernatural
Of humankind of which I grow aware.
    (Prefabrications)

And here, as rendered by the Middle School laureate, is ED's version:

One is a quiet person
Particular and Pale—
Too great an operation
Her neighborhood would fail.

Another like the turmoil
God fingered into flowers
Sets planets at provincial
And claims them—may be—ours.

So natural, the violet,

Josephine Miles

Josephine Miles was born June 11, 1911, in Chicago. She took her B.A. in 1932 from University of California at Los Angeles. In 1934 she took her M.A. from the University of California at Berkeley and in 1938 earned her Ph.D.

She was awarded Guggenheim, N.E.A., and U.S. Fellowship in the Arts grants. In 1956 she won the National Institute of Arts and Letters Award. She was a member of the Academy of American Poets, the Poetry Society of America, and the American Academy of Arts and Sciences.

Josephine Miles retired from the faculty of the University of California at Berkeley where, since the 1940's, she had been professor of English. She won more awards and honors before her death: the Lenore Marshall/*Nation* Poetry Prize (1983) for *Collected Poems, 1930–1983*, which was also nominated for the Pulitzer Prize in poetry (1983), and the Fred

Cody Memorial Award (1984). She died of pneumonia, May 12, 1985, in Berkeley. ■

So crucial, the sun,
Only the nicer sciences
Observe connection.

Well, yes, there is all the difference, and perhaps I am merely playing tricks. There is nothing in the movement of the Miles poem that suggests Dickinson, and yet its translatability into the Dickinson mode was at once apparent to me, and my sense of connection was further supported by the following poem:

Well Made

Familiar to our readers
In all its special vein
Is the form of the tale in the author's careful form.
The incident beginning
And then begun again
With love and care to keep the cockles warm.

The palpitant unfoldment
And dear and sudden end,
The shape of the tale in the author's burning hope
Familiar to our readers
But not the blind
Looking around of the mind for the shape.
(**Local Measures**)

I ask you to re-read it, omitting the long lines 3, 6, 9, and 12. What have you got? If I am correct, you've got the very accent of ED, the best and brightest ED, omitting the "drivelling after redbreasts and the nauseating sensibility to weeds and insects"—phrases proffered in 1807 against Wordsworth, and quoted by Miles in her essay on his subject.

I cannot explain the kinship, which may even be news to Miles. It is certainly not a question of influence, and it is the reverse of imitation (my poem is an imitation). Nor is it a matter of culture: there is more than a continent between yesterday's Amherst and today's Bay Area. Nor do I think it a matter of sex and temperament, though the madwoman-in-the-attic theorists might be able to make out a case. I think most of us who write have found ourselves at times speaking in tongues (thinking in tongues?) of fellows far removed from us, and to some of whom we should vehemently disclaim any relationship (e.g., T. S. Eliot to D. H. Lawrence). Something surfaces from the depths of the imagination and establishes connections where no explicable link exists. "Light breaks where no sun shines: / Where no sea runs, the waters of the heart / Push in their tides." We have a great deal yet to learn about the esemplastic power. We may labor to bring forth a line that turns out to be by Homer, or for that matter by Thomas Hood. The parallelism is easily dismissed by calling it unconscious assimilation, as it often is. In the more frequent case of contemporary echoing, we can chalk it up to common concern, common culture, common language. But that answer is not altogether satisfactory. We still cannot explain the familiar experience of coming into a completely strange place and "knowing" that we have been there before. There is more in heaven and earth than is dreamt of in Harold Bloom's philosophy.

To compound the mystery, Miles has other lyric voices that, to my fatally historical ear, sound closer to the Elizabethan than to the Puritan song-makers. For instance, this fourth of "Four Songs".

> In friendship feeling quiet
> I spent a time asleep,
> And when I woke the marrow
> Out of my bones ran out
> That you were the friend I dreamt for
> But not the dream I woke for.
> And so I put this down for
> Doubt. For doubt.
> **(Neighbors and Constellations)**

■ II

Anyone familiar with Miles' work will by now thoroughly doubt my eclectic choices. The poet has herself claimed that she writes "lyrics of speech and talk rather than of song." And so, for the most part, she does. Her poetry is peopled by newsboys, steam-fitters, shoe-salesmen, movie-goers, students. It includes long and often dull satires on academic and political bureaucracy. ("Government Injunction Restraining Harlem Cosmetic Company," from *Poems on Several Occasions,* is a brilliant exception.) Its landscape is urban: throughways and subdivisions, with a distant glimpse of mountain and shore, and an ever-present consciousness of times of day, the lighting of the lamps in heaven and earth. Her eye is ever open, and her ear pretends to be colloquial.

> But there is the sea, I said, off the far corner
> Through that vacant land:
> And there the pile of prefabricating panels
> And the cement blocks swiftly
> Rose in the sand.
> **(From "Summer,"** *Prefabrications***)**

The bulk of Miles' poetry clearly belongs, by intention, to the School of Whitman, as almost all contemporary American poetry does. To be sure we have a few formalists, in the traditional sense; more who fall somewhere between the formal and the "free," and some who have moved from the first to the second (never, I think, the reverse). But when Lowell moved from the Castle nearer the ocean, he paid his back bills and took all his baggage with him. His move is typical of our poetic population, and his sons and daughters may live to see the Castle razed and Sweet Auburn revitalized by the Rouse Company.

Miles presents, to my ear, an uneasy compromise that manifests itself in certain word-choices and syntactical constructions that are far from colloquial. I refer the reader back to "Well Made," with its mixture of modes, and to "Kind" with its very unspeechmanlike "I am in elaboration of knowledge impatient." She will write a fine poem like the following:

City
1.
Into our brick acropolis returns
The pascal lamb
New to this brith of his but hungry at
His horrid pen.

And keeps our health that we may nourish him
Alive and young
To spring in springtime out the leafage as
The world began.

And keeps our brick resorts as pliant as
Block upon block we yield to such a leap,
The frolic pasture in his city and
The planners' hope.
(Prefabrications)

And then in the third section of the same poem she will commit lines like

This is the given, that stem leaps from earth,
That chlorophyll hollers in the mum alley.

It is as if she were not quite at home in the culture and century she so stubbornly inhabits. Her technique betrays a dislocation that her humanistic principles deny.

I feel that Dickinson is dislocated from the inside, dislocated (again omitting the robins) to denial and death, a true Puritan child. But her style at its quirky best resolves and triumphs. Miles apparently triumphs at some personal center, but her verse which works from the outside is disturbed and injured from the outside.

She describes *To All Appearances* as "acceptance and praise of all appearances, however alien they may seem to the truths underlying them: the appearance of magnitude in the appearance of power, of confidence in doubt, of death in age, of joy in simplicities, of large ideas in small talk." I am baffled by this statement. I find the Whitmanesque in practice means small ideas in large talk, but Miles' talk is modest. I can understand not reaching after final conclusions, and remaining in the midst of doubts and difficulties. But I cannot understand praising (mere) appearance, unless Miles is saying that appearance *seems* alien to truth, but truly is not so. Or that appearance is all we've got to work with. That the casual and the trivial and the daily are to be seen as Beauty, and therefore Truth. Praising appearance would certainly account for our general inability to create form out of a perennial center, our lack of confidence before the real, even our going wholly over to the irrational.

Miles has several poems which seem to me (I am not at all sure) to be about Ultimate Questions. For example:

Riddle

You are a riddle I would not unravel,
You are the riddle my life comprehends.
And who abstracts the marvel
Abstracts the story to its sorriest ends.

But not your riddle. It is patent,
Never more than it says, and since that is
Impossible, it is the marvel
Nobody, as I am nobody, believes.
(Prefabrications)

As might be expected, this witty and imageless poem begs the question. I do not offer the remark as a criticism. I think of our largely imageless painting, our complex but tuneless (there is no other word) music, our poetry reduced so often to a near-prose diary. And I am tempted to play Philistine, and say "he paints those stripes because he can't draw." I know this to be, despite appearances, untrue. Miles is a case in point because she *can* do the formal lyric beautifully. She can never wholly let it go. But she fights it all the way. Why?

■ III

A consideration of Miles the literary historian is perhaps not properly part of a commentary on Miles the artist, and yet a brief glance at the prose casts some light, I think, on her—and our—poetry. The titles alone indicate the nature and range of her investigations: *Wordsworth and the Vocabulary of Emotion; Major Adjectives in English Poetry; Eras and Modes in English Poetry; The Continuity of Poetic Language* (comprising the primary language of poetry in the 1640's, 1740's, 1840's and 1940's). The learning is vast—how many of us know Creech and Oldham, Denham and Phillips? The patient accumulation of linguistic evidence puts to shame our student scorn of word-counters, and verifies our professorial conviction that the clue to, say, James or Faulkner is precisely in vocabulary and sentence structure. Neither in criticism nor in poetry does Miles start with the Grand Idea; indeed, as she would be first to admit, she seldom arrives at it. But her every insight is founded on scrupulous induction.

She has tabulated, for instance, proportions of adjectives to nouns to verbs in the first 1,000 lines of 130 poets (*Eras and Modes*), and the words most often used by ten poets (Wyatt to Whitman). She has considered clausal and phrasal constructions over five centuries. She has endeavored, by this close technical look at poetic practice, to discover the descriptive principle of period sequence. In the course of this labor she has drawn some very astute conclusions, of which I cite a couple of examples.

After quoting Spenser's *Amoretti,* sonnet 1 ("Happy ye leaves when as those lilly hands"), she remarks,

The poem is an exclamation, not an argument. It rests in its adjectives, *happy, trembling, starry, lamping, bleeding, blessed,* in the physical sense of bodily images which are also symbols. *Handle, look, behold,* and *please* are the few significant actions, and they are subordinate to the substance. Connections are provided by participles, and these together with descriptive adjectives are half again as many as the verbs.

This is the mode which would give us the heavens and earth of *Paradise Lost,* the cosmological reaches of Akenside, the rich detail of Thomson, the personifications of Collins, the great aesthetic and social divine wars of Blake, the figure of Keats's Autumn, the vigor of symbol and celebration in Whitman and Henley. In our own day [1951] such poets as Dylan Thomas may lead us back to it. The style of which this mode is an enduring part has been given no name by the literary historians, though the 18th century poets themselves often called it 'sublime'. It is an extreme we have not met in our language strongly for almost two centuries.

I ask you to consider how many of us could link Spenser to Whitman, and prove the link? Or Herrick to Auden:

The lines of inheritance have meaning as they suggest basic modes of thought. The Herrick, Landor, Auden line is such a one, with its sharp delivery of accepted thought...

For Auden, Herrick's stanza has loosened and at the same time become sonorously complicated, more out in the world, speaking less in its author's tones.

Miles finds that the poetic pattern of an "age," roughly a century, follows a sort of hero's way; rebellion, transition, and reconciliation (as characterized by vocabulary, syntax, verse form, reference).

The Skeltonic satiric poet of 1500 wrote an extremely clausal poetry, as did Wyatt and Surrey and their followers in mid-century; then the final thirty years were the golden Elizabethan years of a relatively balanced mode. The seventheenth century began with the clausal verse of Jonson, Donne, and Herbert, and continued with that of Cowley and Vaughan; after 1670 came again the balance of the neo-classicists. The eighteenth century began with Prior and Thomson and continued with Collins and the Wartons the opposite extreme of phrasal emphasis, countered slightly by the classicism of Pope and Johnson, until finally in 1770 the new balance began to be achieved with Goldsmith, Crabbe, Rogers, even finally Wordsworth. The nineteenth century then began with the active clausal balladry of Coleridge, Byron, Moore, Landor, proceeded with that of the Brownings and the Pre-Raphaelites, and ended again, after 1870, with the balanced modes of Swinburne, Bridges, Thompson, Phillips, Hopkins—to begin again in the twentieth century the clausal revival of the Donne tradition, in Housman, Hardy, Cummings, Frost, Auden.

This theory offers a tentative solution to some of the questions I raised in section II. If we have had rebellion (Eliot, b. 1888), and transition (Miles, b. 1911), could we be heading for an end-of-century calm? I have heard it bruited about that painting is going to return to the image, and poetry to a modified sort of song. Miles, then, might be in the position of Arnold (b. 1822), between two worlds whose conflicting claims made his poetry jagged. The three stages may, Miles suggests, be a matter of generations, or "the feeling of a beginning or an ending century." History, of course, impinges on linguistic practice: the twain converge. And how greatly may it impinge as we near the millennial mark?

■ IV

However much history may account for our speech patterns, and, no doubt, for the concerns we voice in literature, it will never provide us a satisfactory explanation for the occurrence or development of an individual artist. It cannot account for Dickinson except as a mutation, and even then it cannot explain why a poet whose particular strength is her way of saying ("Safe in their Alabaster Chambers") can so often say so badly ("Oozed so in crimson bubbles / Day's departing tide"). No more can I account for the failure of a poet like Miles to live up to demonstrated capacities. For it must be admitted, however much one comes away liking the poetic personality, that the bulk of Miles' poetry is pedestrian. The best of it is contained in *To All Appearances: Poems New and Selected,* and most of the poems quoted above, here assigned to their original volumes, can be found collected there.

One could drag in, by way of excuse, the historical cliché of our century: that we cannot have an affirmative and whole art because we live in a protesting and divided world. I subscribe to this cliché insofar as it applies to poets of potential "cosmological reach," though excellent poems have been made before not only out of chartered streets and bloody palace walls, but also out of exile, loss, philosophical stalemate, and spiritual starvation. At any rate, Miles eschews cosmology, as well as the deeper implications of our tawdry-becoming-tragic American scene. When she remarks, "I think my poems are peaceful and peaceable, but am glad they got written where the action is," she is accurate—so long as the action is limited to traffic patterns, asbestos poisoning, and student vagaries.

The new book, *Coming to Terms,* is typically erratic. It contains pleasant if insignificant poems of everyday incident like "Fund Raising," "Evening News," "At the Counter," "Why We Are Late":

> A red light is stuck
> At the corner of LeConte and Euclid.
> Numbers of people are going in and out of the 7 Palms
>   Market,
> Some sitting with beer at La Vals,
> Lots lugging bags to the Laundromat—Open—
> A couple thumbing rides up the hill, fog curling in over
>   newsracks,
> Low pressures.

It contains poems of general comment like "Center," which goes

> Did you come
> Out of the borderlands dear to the south
> Speaking a language Riveran, Nerudan, and saying
> *Aqui esta un hombre:* my first lesson?
> And come as Quixote, the man of romance
> In its new century, tilting
> At windmill giants of concrete,
> Slim lance at the ready? Woe to them
> That join house to house, that lay field to field
> Till there may be no place that they may be alone
> In the midst of the earth.

The poem reminds me of the conclusion to the big *Continuity* book:

> My interest has been in the similarities, rather than in the differences, of poetic practice, and so has run counter to much of the best work done in our time. I have asked, not what sets one poem or poet apart from another, not what distinguishes a style, not what separates poetry from prose, but rather, what in frequency and abundance most centers and joins.

An admirable and a useful interest, surely, so long as we do not forget its opposite: "It is better to study the changes in which the being of the Human Heart largely consists than to amuse ourselves with fictions about its immutability" (C. S. Lewis). I, for one, feel a good deal more centered and joined by the extraordinary Chaucer or Milton than I do by Akenside or Thomson. Though I daresay *more* people have been centered by Henley's unconquerable soul than by Hopkins' Holy Ghost.

The best of the new volume is its more overtly than usual autobiographical poems, such as this one where the child in the plaster casts is doubled by her broken doll:

We made a special trip to the doll hospital
To pick her up. But, they can't fix her after all,
    my father said,
You'll just have to tend her with her broken cheek.
I was very willing. We opened the box, and she lay
In shards mixed with tissue paper. Only her eyes
Set loose on a metal stick so they would open
And close, opened and closed, and I grew seasick.

■ V

I think, coming finally to terms, that I have been trying to force Miles into a mold of my own design: with her demonstrable lyric talent she *ought* to be writing more graceful poems. With her obvious sociological compassion, she *ought* to be making more significant statements. With her proven expertise in Eng. Lit., she *ought* to employ the resources of the Tradition. The fact that she does not fit the critic's choice is perhaps one reason for her critical neglect. It is our pretension, not hers, that would have her meet our cultural and aesthetic demands. Trying to see her in her own terms is not going to make her more than a minor poet. But at least it can free her from the imposition of standards and the achieving of goals which she does not set for herself. I myself have been put straight by Steven Helmling's essay on Stevie Smith in *Parnassus*, winter '77.

Mr. Helmling does not discuss Miles, but in a parenthesis he places her in the company where she belongs, the company of Smith, Moore, and Bishop, to which we might add that of Edith Sitwell. It is a company of eccentric, independent, and unabashedly single ladies. They are modest, they are impulsive, they are *humorous*. Not unacquainted with private pain and public anger, they do not capitulate to them. They do not distrust literature's capacity to give pleasure. It may be that their very lack of presumption allows their dull passages, or their trivial ones. In common with their rebellious successors, the practitioners of Body Language, they are bad at abstractions. One thinks of Moore and Bishop with their peculiar eyes for the odd detail, their small, slow-paced revelations. Smith and Miles are more apt to start from the casual encounter—a scrap of conversation, the headlines, a committee report, a street incident—and to pass rapidly on. Sitwell, unlike Miles, exploits her ear, but like Miles she falls flat when she tries, however feelingly, to deal with "history." I think also, in this context, of Welty, O'Connor, and Murdoch. Welty, to be sure, can handle mythic pattern, and O'Connor can take us off the face of the earth—but our taking-off place is the pig-pen.

I am aware that I am playing at centering and joining; there is a vast distance between Sitwell's imaginary gardens (with real toads) and Miles' suburban backyards (with plastic pelicans). Different as they are in background, technique, even (c. 25 years) age, these artists are linked by a certain wry wit not usually attributed to women. Women are encouraged to be playful, or to be dumb-funny, but "motherwit," in my line of work, is seen as an attribute of deans and admissions officers, and the really funny jokes are left to the men. Stevie Smith is downgraded for the same qualities that make Betjeman popular. But my good-humored group is linked in a more serious way. They seem to seek (Bishop) or find (Miles) what women, and I suppose other human beings, most desire: being at home in the world. For these *grandes*

■ BOOKS BY JOSEPHINE MILES

poetry

Trial Balances (anthology of young poets) edited by Verna Elizabeth Grubbs. New York: Macmillan, 1935, Toronto: Macmillan, 1935.

Lines at Intersection. New York: Macmillan, 1939.

Poems on Several Occasions. New York: New Directions, 1941.

Local Measures. New York: Reynal & Hitchcock, 1946, Toronto: McClelland & Stewart, Ltd., 1946.

Prefabrications. Bloomington: Indiana University Press, 1955.

Neighbors & Constellations: Poems 1930–1960. Bloomington: Indiana University Press, 1960.

Civil Poems. Berkeley, Calif.: Oyez, 1966.

Kinds of Affection. Middletown, Calif.: Wesleyan University Press, 1967.

Fields of Learning. Berkeley, Calif.: Oyez, 1968.

American Poems. Berkeley, Calif.: Cloud Marauder Press, 1970.

To All Appearances: Poems New & Selected. Urbana: University of Illinois, 1974.

Coming to Terms. Urbana: University of Illinois, 1979.

Collected Poems, 1930-1983. Urbana: University of Illinois Press, 1983.

prose

Wordsworth and the Vocabulary of Emotion. Berkeley: (*Publications in English*, v. 12, no. 1) University of California Press, 1942, New York: Octagon Books, 1965.

Pathetic Fallacy in the Nineteenth Century. Berkeley: (*Publications in English*, v. 12, no. 2) University of California Press, 1942, New York: Octagon Books, 1965.

Major Adjectives in English Poetry. Berkeley: (*Publications in English*, v. 12, no. 3) University of California Press, 1946, Norwood, Penn.: Norwood Editions, 1978.

The Vocabulary of Poetry. Berkeley: University of California Press, 1946.

The Primary Language of Poetry in the 1640's. Berkeley: (*Publications in English*, v. 19, no. 1) University of California Press, 1948.

The Primary Language of Poetry in the 1740s and 1840s. Berkeley: University of California Press, 1950.

The Primary Language of Poetry in the 1940s. Berkeley: University of California Press, 1951.

The Continuity of Poetic Language. Berkeley: (*Publications in English*, v. 19) University of California Press, 1951, Toronto: Oxford University Press, 1951, New York: Octagon Books, 1965.

Eras and Modes in English Poetry. Berkeley: University of California Press, 1957, London: Cambridge University Press, 1957.

Eras and Modes in English Poetry (2nd ed., rev. & enl.). Berkeley: University of California Press, 1964, London: Cambridge University Press, 1964.

Renaissance, Eighteenth Century, and Modern Language in English Poetry: A Tabular View. Berkeley: University of California Press, 1960, London: Cambridge University Press, 1960.

Ralph Waldo Emerson. Minneapolis: (pamphlet series) University of Minnesota, 1964.

Saving the Bay. San Francisco: Open Space, 1967.

Style and Proportion. New York: Little, Brown & Company, 1967.

Poetry and Change. Berkeley: University of California Press, 1974, Brittian: University of California Press, 1974.

Working Out Ideas: Predication and Other Uses of Language. Berkeley: University of California Press, 1979.

edited

Poem. New York: (Prentice-Hall English literature series) Prentice-Hall, 1959, London: Prentice-Hall, 1959.

Classic Essays in English. New York: Little Brown & Company, 1961.

dames, as for ED, speech is one symbol of their affection for that home, be it an English manor, a London flat, a Georgia farm, or a Berkeley classroom.

They remind me of my mentors in the Middle and Upper School, whom I once discussed with my fellow-Baltimorean Adrienne Rich. They knew their semicolons and their restrictive clauses, their Caesar and their Shakespeare, their Algebra and their frog's guts backwards and forwards. Some of them bound up birds' legs, some of them bound books, and one of them brought women's lacrosse to the U.S.A. (Bishop played ping-pong, Moore was a Dodger fan, and Sitwell dressed even more oddly than Miss Goodbody.) Many of them had graduate degrees from Bryn Mawr or Hopkins. All of them knew what cant was, and despised it. All of them welcomed (in those days) Eliot and Joyce. All of them, these days, fulminate against revision of the Prayerbook, because they know what language is and means. They are not backward-lookers, but standard-bearers: courageous, dedicated, tireless, witty, civilized: examples to us of what fortitude the soul contains. As Adrienne and I agreed, we shall not see their like again.

> Praise then
> The arts of law and science as of life
> The arts of sound and substance as of faith
> Which claim us here
> To take, as a building, as a fiction takes us,
> Into another frame of space
> Where we can ponder, celebrate, and reshape
> Not only what we are, where we are from,
> But what in the risk and moment of our day
> We may become.

Julia Randall
June, 1980

UPDATE

Before her death in 1985, Josephine Miles published two more books: *Working Out Ideas: Predication and Other Uses of Language* (1979) and *Collected Poems, 1930–1983* (1983). In addition, Miles's poems were recorded on audiocassette by the Archive of Recorded Poetry and Literature, Washington, D.C. (1981).

Miles, a distinguished teacher as well as a respected poet, was the first woman to receive tenure in the English department at the Universtiy of California, Berkeley, where she stayed for her entire academic career. She edited numerous anthologies and texts, and wrote books on language, but it is as a poet that she is chiefly known. Although criticized early on by a few reviewers who saw too much restraint, her work developed and soon earned widespread admiration. Her scholarship, rather than existing in a separate sphere, served to inform her poetry, and she wrote in an accessible style on a wide range of large topics, including the goodness of humanity as well as its failings, birth, death, civil rights in America, the Vietnam War, culture, and the pursuit of beauty. *Benet's Reader's Encyclopedia of American Literature* stated: "Her poetry is typically based on common speech, and reflecting the passing moment."

Parnassus praised her 1979 collection, *Coming to Terms*, and noted that her "landscapes . . . are naturally enough the narrowly defined foregrounds of her home in Berkeley. On the other hand her scenes are very thickly peopled." When her celebrated *Collected Poems* came out, the *San Francisco Review of Books* noted "a remarkable unity of tone," even for a span of 50 years. "Miles takes more liberties with open forms as she gets older, but the same sane voice prevails."

When Miles won the Lenore Marshall award for *Collected Poems: 1930–1983*, one of the judges, Alfred Corn, remarked in *Nation* that "Miles's American dialect is recognizable as a variant of daily speech, but it's not Williams's nor Frost's nor Bishop's," and he cited A. R. Ammons's comment that this collection is "one of the finest and solidest bodies of poetry to be found in this country."

The Fiction of W. O. Mitchell

■ **I**

It is safe to say that of all the best Canadian writers of the present day, only one of them, W. O. Mitchell, is without a substantial reputation among American readers. Margaret Atwood, Robertson Davies, Margaret Laurence, Mordecai Richler, Alice Munro, and even passing-through Canadians like Brian Moore and senior-citizen Canadians like Morley Callaghan: all have sizeable American readerships, sizeable enough to allow them all to "pass" as U.S. writers when not drawing attention to their citizenship suits their purposes—however much they may play the nationalist role at home. It isn't that W. O. Mitchell isn't known here as a Canadian. It's that he isn't really known at all.

Mitchell seems to have become this sort of anomaly because he has not made any special effort to capture his due share of the American market; or perhaps his publishers have not done so for him. He is, in fact, an energetic enough participant in the lecture-and-reading circuit in Canada, a circuit made even more remarkably active by considerable governmental subsidies. But though he is a familiar figure at writing conferences and at university creative-writing seminars (currently, he is writer-in-residence at the University of Windsor, Ontario), Mitchell seems not at all displeased at having become (till now) a purely domestic institution—unopposed as he is to still greater celebrity. He has been content to be a fine Canadian writer writing about universal human concerns as epitomized by actions happening on the stage which is Canada, especially the Canadian West. He is a regionalist in the best of senses, as was Faulkner. The present paper is an attempt to make a case for the just and natural widening of W. O. Mitchell's audience.

Born in Saskatchewan in 1914, William Ormond Mitchell held a variety of jobs during his university years—he majored in philosophy—while he was accumulating the experiences and techniques which have since become the staples of his trade as writer. But he had been writing since as early as 1933, finally placing his first story with a respected Canadian magazine in the early 1940s. A couple of pieces from what would become his first published work of fiction were accepted by *Atlantic Monthly*, where the reader was Wallace Stegner—a writer with similar origins and attitudes. The result was the inclusion of these excerpts in the 1946 Martha Foley *Best American Short Stories*, continuing magazine publication in both countries, and the 1947 appearance of Mitchell's first novel, *Who Has Seen the Wind*.

Who Has Seen the Wind is the all-time Canadian best-selling novel, and it is frequently adopted as a course text in Canadian high schools and universities. Whether or not its particularity—it is set in a small Saskatchewan prairie town during the Depression, and concerns a young boy's coming-of-age—makes it more appropriate reading for Canadian youth than *Huckleberry Finn*, as I once heard a Canadian critic claim, it seems that *Wind's* echo of prairie

W. O. Mitchell Born on

March 13, 1914, William Ormond Mitchell grew up
in Weyburn, Saskatchewan, Canada, where he lived
with his parents, Ormond S. and Margaret Letitia
Mitchell. In 1932 he enrolled in the University of
Manitoba, which he attended until 1934. He
received his B.A. from the University of Alberta in
1942, at which time he married Merna Lynne Hirtle.
They had three children and lived in Calgary, Alberta, Canada. Mitchell's career experiences ranged
from that of salesman, to teacher, to seaman, to high
school principal. From 1968 to 1987 he was the
writer-in-residence at a number of Canadian universities. His various awards and honors include: the
President's medal from the University of Western
Ontario, 1953; *Maclean's Magazine* Novel Award,
1953; and the Stephen Leacock Memorial Medal for

the best humorous book by a Canadian author, 1962
(for *Jake and the Kid*). Mitchell died of cancer in
1998. ■

childhood has touched a responsive chord in the hearts of Canadian readers of all manner of
backgrounds and regions. Its Canadianness aside, *Wind* can and must be studied as Mitchell's
first and most celebrated claim to fame—one in a series of only five volumes of fiction to date
(a sixth is in the works), a publishing record that might look slight were it not for Mitchell's
continuing involvement with theatre (a love affair that began at the University of Manitoba,
continued with a playwriting course at the University of Washington, and eventually resulted
in a considerable career in writing radio scripts and plays for the stage); a volume of his plays
has just seen print in Canada.

Like *Huckleberry Finn, Who Has Seen the Wind* is episodic in character—a format no less
appropriate to the picaresque novel than it is to fiction of experience—of "growing up"—generally. *Jake and the Kid*, another of Mitchell's fictional works, is episodic to an even greater
degree: it represents a culling of the apparently best sequences in what had originally been a
phenomenally successful radio series in Canada; and perhaps it also represents in the purest
possible form Mitchell's ability to mine the crystals of experience. With respect to both region-
alism and *Huckleberry Finn*, it can be said that Mitchell resembles the American writer of the
previous century in the way both men exploit the local in the interests of the universal—what
Mitchell calls, in a note to me, "that impossible magic" by which art relies not on the direct
conveyance of "transcending truth—therefore abstract," but rather on "the specifics (geography—sensuous fragment)."

Mitchell is as candid about the sources of the lessons he has learned as a writer as he is
quick to squelch assumptions of influence. For instance, he acknowledges that Clemens, Steinbeck, and Virginia Woolf were important in helping him "realize that illusion lives in the world
of the many rather than the one," while Thomas Mann and Henry James were negative examples of the same abiding principle: "Thematic and narrative structure must not damage the illusion." Even Wallace Stegner, whose writing in its integrity seems to singlehandedly validate

Mitchell's thesis about regional particularities, is to Mitchell never an influence, but rather a parallel evolutionary development. In another note to me, Mitchell says:

> Wallace Stegner and I were stained in our young, litmus years by the same Southern Saskatchewan geography—its isolated emptiness. In his words to me: "We are both products of the short grass culture."

Comparative articles on Mitchell and such figures as Steinbeck and Stegner, one assumes, are still some distance down the critical road—though in time they will be written, and probably prove helpful.

■ II

Who Has Seen the Wind, its title taken from a Christina Rossetti poem, concerns the childhood experiences of Brian O'Connal, who like W. O. Mitchell grows up on the Saskatchewan prairie. Again like Mitchell, Brian loses his father at an early age; so that *Wind* becomes simultaneously the necessary instance of the autobiographical novel in the career of W. O. Mitchell, and also the first substantial demonstration of the process by which memory—conscious or subconscious—is subsumed into art. Thus the hook or hitch which sometimes becomes the obstacle to development in what eventually is seen as a "single-novel" writer is turned, in Mitchell's case, into the means of further onward propulsion. If *Wind* is no *Finn*, its writing is hauntingly evocative, though occasionally self-consciously so. Here is a section ending from *Wind*, its language even in its excesses redolent of Cather at her best, or else exceeding her:

> In the summer sky there, stark blue, a lonely goshawk hung. It drifted low in lazing circles. A pause—one swoop—galvanic death to a tan burgher no more to sit amid his city's grained heaps and squeak a question to the wind.
>
> Shadows lengthen; the sunlight fades from cloud to cloud, kindling their torn edges as it dies from softness to softness down the prairie sky. A lone farmhouse window briefly blazes; the prairie bathes in mellower, yellower light, and the sinking sun becomes a low and golden glowing on the prairie's edge.
>
> Leaning slightly backward against the reins looped round his waist, a man walks homeward from the fields. The horses' heads move gently up and down; their hoofs drop tired sound; the jingle of the traces swinging at their sides is clear against the evening hush. The stubble crackles; a killdeer calls. Stooks, fences, horses, man, have clarity that was not theirs throughout the day.

In reviewing Mitchell's latest book, the critic George Woodcock charges *Wind* with "shallowness, combined with a kind of softness in the writing and imagery" which he also identifies with an unwillingness on Mitchell's part to be "penetrating in his vision of Canadian social realities." To the extent that this is valid, Woodcock has both distanced *Wind* from *Huck Finn* and also measured the Canadian critic's obsession with thematic concerns—matters of overriding imagery and nationbuilding tendentiousness. Mitchell is no less Canadian than his critics are, but refuses to subordinate his artistry to momentary and rhetorical purposes. Though the text gets structurally more fragmented at the time of Brian's father's death, *Who Has Seen the Wind* retains a praiseworthy objectivity in which death is simply a fact of life like any other:

> He heard a wagon on the road behind him, but he did not hide as he had done the day before. It was Ab. He stopped the team and sat silently, a high and waiting grasshopper upon the wagon seat. Brian's legs refused to lift him. Still holding the reins in one hand, Ab leaned forward and Brian felt the pull of him as he helped him up.

Ab did not start the horses. Upon his wry little face lay an expression as gently as a benediction. He cleared his throat.

"Yer Paw," he said. "Telegraft lady phoned us last night, kid. Yer Paw down to Rochester—he went an' died."

Wind remains Mitchell's enduring legacy to his own Saskatchewan past, and also his personal testament to the pioneer generation whose errors—even in fiction—are not to be made much of.

Jake and the Kid (1961) can be considered as an even more daring facing of the realities of a nostalgic market on Mitchell's part—one in which the temptation to simply cash in on a successful product (in this case, that memorable radio series) must have been nearly overwhelming. After the fact, *Kid's* artistry shines through—in spite of the overlapping and sometimes repetitious nature of its character introductions and incidents; in spite of the necessarily fragmented quality of a collection of popular short pieces which never quite cohere as a novel (nor need be said to be meant to). Despite what Mitchell has said about a lack of specific influences, the sentimental pairing of older hired man and the young boy to whom he acts as foster-father will seem to many to derive from Steinbeck's *The Red Pony*, though it lacks *Pony's* unifying device of overriding theme and underlying development. What *Kid* does have in quantity is a rich sense of place (it's Crocus, Saskatchewan, during a World War II that has taken away the Kid's father). But a passage like the one that follows gives ample evidence of another sort of influence:

> There was me, and I was just a fly on a platter, the way she is on the prairie when you have a real moonlit night; wherever you go there's the black rim of the prairie round you, and some real far-off stars over top, and the wind in the grass like a million mad bees going all at once and everywhere. Just a fly walking across a black, flat plate.

The boy's floor-shot point of view, his colloquial "the way she is" undercutting the surprisingly delicate observation of nature, otherwise inexplicable or arguably excessive—this is the artistry of a Mark Twain, surely, and must remind the reader of the best passages in *Huck Finn*. So too do the places in *Kid* where Jake's tall-story exaggerations provide narrative catalysts—a technique that might also bring Faulkner to mind.

■ III

This further mention of Mark Twain suggests that this might well be the place to talk about W. O. Mitchell's platform manner. Few members of Mitchell's audience would not think, in watching him at work, of Mark Twain's platform appearances—or, at least, of Hal Holbrook's impersonation of Mark Twain. It might well be accurate to describe Mitchell as the finest raconteur of his sort *since* Mark Twain. As he is in private conversation, Mitchell in public seems the careful combination of the crusty and the genial, of the erudite and the slangy and the rough. As he ages, Mitchell has perfected the role he has begun to grow into: that of artful codger. It's a manner eminently well suited to his material, which has to do with the dredging up of regional memory for purposes of transmuting it into art. He becomes Saskatchewan speaking; the mustache and the snuff are part of an amazing equation of the style and the man.

Mitchell has himself added to his personal legend the fact that his mother had for a time nursed Mark Twain; and he has let himself be quoted as wondering if he might not be Mark Twain's illegitimate son. Writers do not say this sort of thing without full cognizance of the effect they might cause; in Mitchell's case, the literal four-year hiatus of possibility between the elder American's death and the Canadian's birth does not render the suggestion wholly absurd. It doesn't take much in the way of psychological-interpretational skills to see the unfathered Mitchell as Mark Twain's "spiritual" son after all (someone who might have given balance to that household of women Mark Twain occupied!). (Mitchell himself, by the way, is both very married and also the proud parent of talented children, all by now grown.) As for the man himself, perhaps the important point is that the folksiness is part of the art, and that none of his auditors are fooled for a moment except to the degree that they are willing to be fooled. It's part of the balancing act which Mitchell views both life and art as—a notion he apparently shares with e.e. cummings. Yet at the same time Mitchell is emphatic about the difference between source and end-product: "Life Ain't Art" is one of his mottos.

The succession of odd jobs that led to a career in radio are mirrored in this life-art tension in Mitchell's work. One sees it in the disparity between the Kid's thoughts and his spoken utterances, even if one is hardly bothered by it at the time. Perhaps it is also part of the reason why Mitchell's venture into a more serious sort of fiction met with something less than enthusiasm from his audience. *The Kite* (1962) has even been described—by Wayne Grady in a recent *Books in Canada*—as "pessimistic," but the reasons for this response escape this reader, at least. The story of a reporter coming back to the Alberta foothills to do a story on the 111-year-old Daddy Sherry contains the standard Mitchell ingredients of missing fathers and male bonding, true enough, but the account of the oldster whose life span exceeds that of his country itself is, in the end, a compelling testimonial to the ability of the human spirit to survive, to stretch itself against all odds. Childhood memories of a kite-flying experience that never happened in the end become merged and redeemed, for the reporter, in the final flying of a kite by the old man and the young boy who has befriended both the reporter and the oldster. Whether or not the novel's last line—a sighed "Aaaaaaaaaaaaaaaaah........." is the expression of Daddy Sherry's pleasure or his resigned acceptance of his death at that moment, the spending of his spirit, is hardly relevant; he has had his moment of triumph, and he has passed the baton of kite-string-stick on to young Keith, with the instruction to "Keep her up there forever." Three generations, representing beginnings, fruition in the form of love, and endings, are combined in the final tableau. It is a novel which deserves more readers than it has had to date.

The Kite exists also in a stage version, and one can easily understand how readily adaptable might have been a work which so clearly reflects Mitchell's experience in radio. The generation which grew up in radio's Golden Age will easily note the way Mitchell handles flashbacks through radio techniques: what begins as spoken recollection segues into dramatization of past events, and the narration yields to direct experience. This naturally makes the work—again—episodic; and indeed one critic at the time complained of Mitchell's "emphasis on the anecdote at the expense of the overall design." But it is hard to see how being episodic is in itself a negative quality, especially when the results are a Faulknerian richness of texture enlivened by such tall-tale "stretchers" as the account of Daddy greeting the American Immigration officials who come to investigate Daddy's house—which has illegally crossed the U.S. border in a flood—with "Take me...to your cannibal chief." Daddy Sherry is meant to be outrageous; he is a larger-than-life projection of Mitchell's own values in both life and art, and the fusion or resolution of tension is nowhere better encapsuled than in the scene in which the old man ventures forth on a homemade trapeze because he has always wanted to be a trapeze artist (as in a very real sense he is), and then threatens his caretakers that unless he gets his own way "I'll break every goddam glass bone in my body." This kite survives its makers.

■ IV

The progressive modernization of W. O. Mitchell's prose style and formal approach to fiction writing continued with the 1973 publication of *The Vanishing Point*, Mitchell's most ambitious (and longest) work to date. In a valuable interview with David O'Rourke in *Essays in Canadian Writing* (Winter 1980–81), Mitchell speaks of how he created a character after his own daughter, then living "the hippie, Gypsy life" and seemingly "about to be destroyed":

> ...my daughter is Victoria Rider, the Indian girl who's lost. And Blake's thing of the little lost girl is that the good guardians come and find her in the cave with the beast, and what do you know? The beast is life, and she hasn't been destroyed after all....

Mitchell goes on to discuss his indebtedness to Blake, seemingly using the insights of the poet to clarify his own rejection of what in the United States has been expressed in the once-popular nonsense of Charles Reich's *The Greening of America*:

> ...And you see in *The Vanishing Point* it's possible to say that the answer for Indians—for man—is to go back to the primitive childhood, and back to the living whole, but the green ghetto is as horrible as the asphalt ghetto. It's a dreadfully serious novel...

Indeed it is. Its funny passages cannot blur the impression of seriousness with which *The Vanishing Point* leaves the reader, as if by this single work Mitchell had intended to lay to rest once and for all what he calls his "folksy old Foothills fart" image. It is also his longest work of fiction, one which deals effectively with the clash of white, urban culture and the Indian's traditional existence in Nature. The redemption of the Indian girl Victoria Rider from the former "ghetto" and the redemption of the teacher Carlyle (!) Sinclair from despair at failing to change the urban one—both redemptions are accomplished by the act and state of love, as if to echo not only the Scot's Yea but also Arnold's "Dover Beach." It's not a mindlessly optimistic work by any means, but it is life-affirming in a way which depends for its effect upon a splendid coming-together of plot motifs at the end. Not the least of these are the classic North American motif of the highway (and its implications for the title, which is the name of something which only appears to exist) and the classic Canadian motif of the Country Mouse, especially an Indian, caught in the toils of the City. And perhaps Mitchell's Calgary is Blake's London here as well, remembering as we should the novelist's acknowledged debt to Blake.

Rather than quote from this impressive novel, I should like to speak of the elements of that "coming-together" of plot motifs mentioned above. Aside from road and city metaphors, there is that of the title itself; and there are also the complementary images of the vehicle (one long-stalled gets going again on the final pages) and the bridge (an actual one, and the manner in which Mitchell treats human relationships) and the river (a dry stream flows again at the novel's close). There are also images from the world of bird and animal, images which are picked up in the surnames of the Stony Indian men and women. Finally, there is Mitchell's use of Indian culture itself, usage which culminates in a scene at a tribal dance when the returned Victoria calmly approaches Carlyle Sinclair to share with her former teacher the Rabbit Dance—and his bed. As I have already suggested, these separate strands come together at the novel's close in a manner reminiscent of poetry.

■ V

After *The Vanishing Point*, Mitchell occupied himself with stage and film work, and also began a novel with a university setting—he has worked at quite a few—only to set the manuscript aside to begin work on *How I Spent My Summer Holidays*, which was published to enormous critical acclaim in 1981. *Holidays*, in spite of its tongue-in-cheek title, is about the Discovery of Evil; and the shock provided, given the otherwise idyllic prairie setting, exceeds what Willa Cather gives her readers in *A Lost Lady*. Apparently the university novel, upon which Mitchell has now resumed work, also concerns corruption and its effects; and so there is ample reason to conclude that the days in which Mitchell's name was popularly associated with prairie nostalgia exclusively are just about over. At least one critic has noted, unsurprisingly, that if *Wind* is

Mitchell's *Tom Sawyer, Holidays* must be his *Huckleberry Finn*. Such a distinction, neatly repudiating one with which we began, is also a measure of how far W. O. Mitchell has come in terms of sureness of technique and stylistic control since *Wind*—and, by extension, of the strides made by Canadian literature generally into the cosmopolitan postmodern literary world. The innocence lost in *Holidays* is thus its central character's, is Mitchell's, and is Canada's.

Yet the assurance with which *Holidays* is written comes at no cost to the work's ability to evoke—just as *Wind* and *Kid* had—a sense of just that country from which Mitchell himself emerged. Hugh, the grown boy remembering his past who is the novel's central figure, is only two years older than Mitchell himself; his perceptions of his remembered world must tally closely with those of the author, and the grown Hugh's realization of what the child could not have understood at the time is the source of the novel's powerful resonances. Here, for instance, is a passage which begins a section of the opening chapter of *Holidays*; in it, Hugh remembers his boyhood indulgence in the pleasures of the swimming hole (there were two to choose from):

> AT THE MENTAL hole, or further upstream at the CPR hole, I was always the first one into and out of the water, crawling up the clay bank, clutching for purchase at willow roots or grass tufts or wild-rose bushes. Under the drip of wet boys' bodies the clay usually baked and cured to hard adobe under the prairie sun, very quickly became a greased slide, and then grey and sucking mud.

Thus far, this might have been a paragraph out of *Who Has Seen the Wind* or *Jake and the Kid*. What's different is what's fictionally adumbrated here, and what's shortly to come. The sheer physicality of Mitchell's description tallies with the perseverance of Hugh's ability to recollect—and hence with the workings of the creative process itself, according to Mitchell's "messy method" theory of retention of artistic materials. But that is not the point. The association of details, their sensuality, brings together such elements as the boys' nakedness, their experience at the swimming holes as central to the novel's plot, and the way in which their emerging sexualities express themselves—if ever so innocently—in holes in Nature, in places of wet sucking clay that becomes "a greased slide" of "grey and sucking mud."

So too with the novel's moral dimension. Within a few lines and pages Hugh has connected his alacrity ("first one into and out of the water") with his developing sense of genital insufficiency—aggravated by the chill water—and of course with his changing adolescent's consciousness of the world around him. Sexual awareness colors his perceptions: shortly thereafter Hugh takes part in a decorating of naked bodies, especially including genitalia, with alkali silt—a shocking white which makes it possible to frighten yet another group of boys at the chapter's end. This instinctive adoption of a kind of tribal initiation ritual—rite of passage into manhood—is handled with superb subtlety by Mitchell; Hugh's "art" is tied to his ability to manage and proclaim his sexual identity. This self-discovery, however, soon expands into a series of discoveries about the nature of the world around him, to which sexuality provides the key. What begins as lighthearted and humorous quickly turns troubling, then ugly and perverse; and before the process has run its course, or when it does, the life force reaches its natural endpoint in death. How to make sense of it all, to balance the forces in play in Hugh's obsessive memories of another man's career? "I hope that he has haunted me for love!", the novel concludes; the book is, once again, an open-ended one.

Thus W. O. Mitchell can be seen as a writer whose mission is to define and clarify possibilities and the choices open to us all—and not as someone who imposes answers on his readership. In *Holidays*, his art has attained a concision that finally justifies the earlier, lighter, exercises in nostalgia. One looks forward to that academic novel, now in its final stages. He has—

■ BOOKS BY W. O. MITCHELL

Who Has Seen the Wind. Toronto: Little, Brown, 1947; Toronto: Macmillan, 1960, 1961.

The Kite. Toronto: Macmillan, 1962, 1974, Toronto: Bantam Seal, 1983.

The Black Bonspiel of Wullie MacCrimmon. Calgary: Frontiers Unlimited, 1965.

The Devil's Instrument. Toronto: Simon & Pierre, 1973.

The Vanishing Point. Toronto: Macmillan, 1973 (serialized in *MacLeans Magazine,* 1953–1954, as "The Alien"; Toronto: Bantam Seal, 1983.

Jake and the Kid. Toronto: Macmillan, 1974.

How I Spent My Summer Holidays. Toronto: Macmillan, 1981; Toronto: Bantam Seal, 1983.

Dramatic W. O. Mitchell. Toronto: Macmillan, 1982.

Since Daisy Creek. Toronto: Macmillan, 1984.

Ladybuy, Ladybug. . . Toronto: McClelland & Stewart, 1988.

According to Jake and the Kid. Plattsburgh, N.Y.: McClelland & Stewart, 1989.

Roses Are Difficult Here. New York: Bantam, 1991.

For Art's Sake. Plattsburgh, N.Y.: McClelland & Stewart, 1992.

An Evening with W. O. Mitchell. Plattsburgh, N.Y.: McClelland & Stewart, 1997.

Mitchell has—also recently published *Dramatic W. O. Mitchell*, a collection of his best theatre pieces. Well into an eighth decade of undiminished artistic and personal vigor, W. O. Mitchell has finally clarified and firmed up his hold on a distinguished and permanent place in the history of Canadian writing. He deserves to extend that celebrity south of the border as well.

John Ditsky
April, 1983

John Montague: Dancer in a Rough Field

If I were, as I am, beginning a re-reading of John Montague, or if I were advising others where to begin reading him, I would go, and send those others to the heart of his collection *Tides,* which had the Poetry Book Society Recommendation in 1970. And to two works there, one of them a quite horrifying prose-poem entitled with a cold irony that is typical of Montague: "The Huntsman's Apology." As you will see, it is not likely to be used as an argument for the defense by the unspeakable who pursue the inedible, or by those genial knee-booted Kerrymen who know by the inner voice that little hunted hares really love the chase. This is it:

"You think I am brutal and without pity but at least I execute cleanly because, like any true killer, I wish to spare the victim. There are worse deaths. I have seen the wounded bird trail her wing, and attract only the scavenger. 'Help me,' he croaks as he hops near. One dart of her beak would settle him, for he is only a pale disciple of death, whom he follows at a distance. But when she needs sympathy and when he calls "I am more unhappy than you" her womanly heart revives and she takes him under her broken wing. Her eyesight is poor and her senses dulled but she feels an echo of lost happiness as he stirs against her breast. She does not realize that he is quietly settling down to his favourite meal of dying flesh, happily enveloped in the smell of incipient putrefaction. The pain grows and spreads through her entire body until she cries aloud but it is too late to shake off his implanted beak. He grinds contentedly on and, as she falls aside, his bony head shoots up, like a scaldy out of a nest. His eye is alert, his veins coursing with another's blood, and for a brief moment as he steps across the plain without looking back, his tread is as firm as a conqueror's."

The second work is brief, called "A Meeting," and is from the ninth-century Irish:

"The son of the King of the Moy
met a girl in green wood a mid-summer's day:
she gave him black fruit from thorns
and the full of his arms
of strawberries where they lay."

The startling thing is that both are poems about varieties of love, or about love at different stages, of development or decay. They come at the heart of a book that holds other fine love-poems and in which the blurb, with perhaps an echo of the poet's voice, says with a great deal of justification that the directness and passion of Montague's love-poems have been admired, and his feeling for people and landscape, and claims that in this collection, *Tides,* all these are seen as a part of a larger struggle where life and death are interwoven like the rhythms of the sea. Love in green woods at midsummer has its black fruit from thorns and a plenteousness of strawberries. Love can also be a rasping and cankerous death.

John Montague

_{John} Montague was born on February 28, 1929, in Brooklyn, New York. He was educated at Saint Patrick's College in Armagh and at University College, Dublin, where he received his B.A. and M.A. degrees. He studied at Yale University as a Fulbright Scholar and received his M.F.A. degree from the University of Iowa.

Montague worked on the State Tourist Board in Dublin from 1956 until 1961. He acted as a professor of the Poetry Workshop of the University of California at Berkeley in 1964 and 1965 and at University College, Dublin, in 1967 and 1968 and again from 1972 to 1988. He has taught at the Experimental University of Vincennes, University College, Cork, and at the State University of New York, Albany.

He received the May Morton Memorial Prize in 1960 and is a member of the Irish Academy of Letters. Montague has also won an Alice Hunt Bartlett Memorial Award (1979) and a Guggenheim fellow-

ship (1979), and he was named the first professor of poetry in Ireland in 1998.

He also served as the literary director of Chaddagh Records. ■

He has a nightmare in which he lies "strapped in dream helplessness" and some hand unseen, unknown is cutting up the body of the beloved, till the rhythm of the blade rising, descending, "seems the final meaning of life." Released from the dreadful dream, he lies in a narrow room, "low-ceilinged as a coffin," while outside the Liffey knocks against the quay walls and the gulls curve and scream over the Four Courts: Gandon's great domed building, the flower of the eighteenth century, the heart in Ireland of unalterable law. There is much agony in these love-poems, a something not allowed—for when, in one of the most celebrated passages of raving about love, Shakespeare allows Berowne to take off for seventy or so lines, and a lover's eye will gaze an eagle blind, a lover's ear will hear the lowest sound, a lover's feeling is more soft and sensible than are the tender horns of cockled snails: but Berowne had not at that moment, and as Shakespeare well knew, arrived at consummation not to speak of satiation. Montague, lean and sharp and soft and sensible, as Berowne uses the word, sees his lovers absurdly balanced on the springs of a bed, shadows swooping, quarreling like winged bats, bodies turning like fish "in obedience to the pull and tug of your great tides." A windswept holiday resort on the shore of the North sea becomes a perfect setting for the monster of unhappiness, "an old horror movie come true," to crawl out of the moving deeps and threaten love. The hiss of seed into a mawlike womb is the whimper of death being born: and lovers whirl and turn in their bubble of blood and sperm before, from limitless space, the gravities of earth claim them. Back from the business of loving, resuming workaday habits with the putting-on of clothes, the lover finds himself, comically driving through late traffic, and changing gears with the same gesture that a while ago had eased the "snowbound heart and flesh" of the beloved. It is a bitter sort of comedy.

■ II

It is scarcely then by accident that he places in the middle of all these love-poems the best rendering, from the Irish of the ninth century, of the love-dirge, or bitter memory of past loves and bitter consciousness of bodily decay, of the *Cailleach Beara*, the Hag or Old Woman of Beare: which is the southwestern peninsula between Bantry Bay and Kenmare Bay, the land of the O'Sullivans. The Cailleach, a formidable ancient, overburdened with all knowledge and weariness and sometimes, all wickedness, is a recurring figure in Celtic mythologies and shows her face, on occasions and on various bodies, in Montague's poetry.

A one-eyed hag, she—or the poet who interpreted her, as Montague does eleven centuries later—reckons that her right eye has been taken as a downpayment on her claim to heaven; a ray in the left eye has been spared to her that she may grope her way to heaven's gate. Her life has come to be a retreating sea with no tidal return. Gaunt with poverty she, who once wore fine petticoats, now hunts for rags to cover her body. The great and generous gentlemen who once made love to her have now ridden on into eternity, their places taken by skinflints, well-matched with girls who now think less of love than of money: and she looks at her arms, now bony and thin, that once caressed with skill the limbs of princes. Yet she gives thanks to God that she has lived and loved and feasted royally and misspent her days, even though now, to offer up that gratitude, she prays by candlelight in a darkened oratory and drinks not meat nor wine with Kings, but sips whey in a nest of hags: a memory. Never more can she sail youth's sea, she hears the cry of the wave, "whipped by the wintry wind," and knows that today no one will visit her, neither nobleman nor slave: and the poem rises to that recurring consideration of lift as ebb and flow, and it may be that it was that very image that attracted Montague so strongly to the ancient poem:

> *"Flood tide*
> *And the ebb dwindling on the sand!*
> *What the flood rides ashore*
> *The ebb snatches from your hand*

> *"Flood tide*
> *And the sucking ebb to follow!*
> *Both I have come to know*
> *Pouring over my body....*

> *"Man being of all*
> *Creatures the most miserable—*
> *His flooding pride always seen*
> *But never his tidal turn.*

> *"Happy the island in mid-ocean*
> *Washed by the returning flood...."*

In this collection, one of the two most striking poems is certainly "Life Class." It opens calmly, clinically, a cool detailed survey of the body there to be studied, the hinge of the ankle-bone defining the flat space of a foot, the calf's heavy curve sweeping down against the bony shin, the arm cascading from shoulder-knob to knuckle, shapes as natural, as inanimate almost, as sea-worn caves, as pools, boulders, tree-trunks. This is the artist in the neolithic cavern recording in wonderment the skeleton of the life he sees, an art that may have been as utilitarian as modern engineering. Until the awakening comes to the existence of secret areas: "hair sprouting crevices, odorous nooks and crannies of love awaiting the impress of desire." Thereafter, the frenzy of the desert father tormented by images and visions that drag man down "to hell's gaping vaginal mouth." Until the eye and the mind swing the other way and the phantom of delight (Wordsworth did not follow it neither into the desert nor to hell's mouth—as far as we know, that is) becomes an ordinary housewife earning a few shillings extra, a spirit, good or evil, yet a woman too: and the very soul of the machine blossoms, "a late flower," into a tired smile over a chilled cramped body.

The other poem, "The Wild Dog Rose," follows the woman into more terrible and more holy places. It confronts again the *cailleach,* the ancient enchanted hag who recurs in our mythologies and in Montague's poetry. The image of the *cailleach* in this poem is a figure who haunted his childhood, lived in a cottage, circled by trees and with a retinue of whinging dogs, on a hill-slope in South Tyrone. A grown man, a young poet, he walks to see her and the outside appearance is as it was when she used to terrify his boyhood: the great hooked nose, the cheeks dewlapped with dirt, staring sunken eyes, mottled claws, a moving nest of shawls and rags. But she talks to him gently and sadly about her memories of youth, her own unimportant sorrows: she is kin to the *Cailleach Beara* and in her own *coulisse* in time, and the dogrose shines in the hedge: and there is no sense of horror until she tells him of the night when a drunken oaf staggered into her cottage and attempted to rape her. She prays to the Blessed Virgin for help and after a time she breaks his grip, he sleeps and snores on the floor, then awakes in shame and lurches away across the wet bogland:

"…. The wild Rose
is the only rose without thorns,
she says, holding a wet blossom
for a second, in a hand knotted
as the knob of her stick.

"Whenever I see it, I remember
the Holy Mother of God and
all she suffered."

That image of the Cailleach reappears again when in his poem-sequence "The Rough Field" he stands squarely facing into the past and present of his own place and people, and meditates also on some of his own personal agonies. He has a regulated passion for retracing his steps, changing and rearranging.

There is much more in the collection, *Tides,* than I have here indicated: more than love and lust, and woman, young and old, and ancient mythologies. There are, for instance, wise words to and about Beckett, and about Joyce, and a moving farewell to places and parents, and a seagull's view of his own town which misses only history and religion: which Montague is not to miss when later he takes a more-than-seagull's view of Garvaghey (Garbh Achaidh), "The Rough Field," where he comes from. The collection, too, is rich, as is his earlier poetry, with the preoccupations of a man who has known, and to the bone, the ways of three countries: Ireland, France, and the USA.

■ **III**

He was born in New York in 1929 of Irish parents who had left Ireland in the confusion following the Troubles of the 1920's. From an early age, as he said to Mary Leland in an interview article in *The Irish Times,* (Nov. 23, 1976), he was aware of the confusion of the time through the unhappiness of his parents and had also an "emerging sense of bi-location" out of which he was to make a theme. As a child he was shipped back to Ireland and grew up on a farm in

South Tyrone, in Ulster, with his father's unmarried sisters, somewhat isolated from the rest of his family, a situation that has also left its mark on his work.

Something of this I myself was aware of from away back. In my final year in high school, in 1936, a young fellow called Montague, American-born, came into third year and right away became of a group who were attempting to found a school magazine. Several of us then thought that this young man was so bright in a literary way that he was destined, or doomed, to become a writer. As it happened he became a medical doctor, and it wasn't until the late 1940's that a young man, whose name I was already aware of in the magazines and elsewhere, came into my house in Clontarf, in Dublin city, with some other college people of the time and said, quietly and confidently, that he would be the writer of the Montagues and that I had, for a while, gone to school with his elder brother.

By his own words, written down two years ago for a revised edition of his first collection, "Poisoned Lands," he was not at that time as confident as he seemed. In the early 1950's he was "discovering with awe" that he might possibly "be able to write something like the kind of modern poetry" he admired. But in the "acrimony and insult" of the poetic world of Dublin at the time he found out that the atmosphere was against doing anything of the kind. To explain the subtleties, more social than literary, involved in all that would need an essay five times as long as this one. The easiest way to understanding would be to do as I have done: come to Dublin permanently, say at the age of twenty and in 1940, and live there ever since, seeing it, I hope, steadily and seeing it whole. Voltaire, you'll remember, suggested to somebody who was anxious to do something of the sort that one way to found an enduring religion would be to be crucified and to rise from the dead.

■ **IV**

In 1977 he reworked his first collection, *Poisoned Lands,* which had originally appeared in London in 1961. The nature of the revisions, additions and subtractions, from one edition to the other, has been thoroughly examined by the poet Seamus Deane, in a review in *Hibernia* for June 10, 1977. Montague himself said: "It became not so much the case of an older writer wishing to correct his younger self as of trying to release that earlier self from chains of time and place." He pleasantly recorded that in the years between, Mr. T. S. Eliot had said: "I have, indeed, found Mr. Montague's poems worthy of study." We are all allowed those little moments in the sun, eyes happily closed when, that is, we get the chance to enjoy them.

Sidney Keyes, the young English poet who went to his death in the battle of North Africa, was garrisoned for a while with the British Army in my native town of Omagh, Co. Tyrone, sixteen miles away from Montague's Rough Field—Garvaghey or Garbh Achaidh. A friend of mine (now living in Indiana but coming from that same garrison town) who knew Keyes well, says that he told her that he, an Englishman, was never happy in Ulster; he said the land brooded, waiting. A pity that the young American-Irish Montague and the doomed English soldier-poet never could have met: they could easily have walked within arm-reach of each other on Omagh street: and right in the middle of "Poisoned Lands," and for reasons that have to do with the same long history of the off-shore islands, Montague senses the brooding and waiting that had disturbed Keyes.

"At times," he writes, "on this island at the sheltered edge of Europe.... green enclosure of monks and quiet poetry.... we are afraid as the hints pile up a disaster.... Our best longings," are, "helpless, as the clouds begin banking for a more ominous day." So he considers and incantates in a time of peace: and a brutal farmer who hates country people strides across symbolically-poisoned lands with four good dogs dead in one night and "a rooster, scaly legs in air, beak in the dust." The poet remembers how, as a boy, he carried water twice a day from a spring-well, and he sets the scene and crystallizes the experience in a poem as pure and lucid as the water, and hopes to stylize that experience "like the portrait of an Egyptian water-carrier," but is halted and entranced "by slight but memoried life": a phrase of great subtlety and significance. The Cailleach, the Sean Bhean Bocht (the Poor Old Woman) of myth and of patriotic balladry, appears to him "her eyes rheumy with racial memory." She could be Mother Ireland, she could be that lovely Cathleen who followed St. Kevin to his cave in Glendalough and was, by the chaste and irate saint, thrown into the deeper of the two lakes. The poet, at home on his own hills, climbs up through red cornfields at the end of summer to see on the summit the secret spirals on the prehistoric burial stone and to wonder "what hidden queen" lies there in dust: and turning the page from that moment he comes on one of those golden phrases that happen only to the most fortunate poets: "Like dolmens around my childhood, the old people." It is one of his most important and most memorable poems and later on he is to work it into the intricate pattern of "The Rough Field." He remembers some old people Orange and Green, who lived around his early rural years. He concludes splendidly:

> "Ancient Ireland, indeed! I was reared by her bedside,
> The Rune and the chant, evil eye and averted head,
> Fomorian fierceness of family and local feud,
> Gaunt figures of fears and friendliness,
> For years they trespassed on my dreams,
> Until once, in a standing circle of stones,
> I felt their shadows pass.

"Into that dark permanence of ancient forms."

In that poem and, generally, in *Poisoned Lands,* and in the following collection, *A Chosen Light,* he has hammered his thoughts, and his places, into unity, and, also, the past and present of his own country. The shape of his mind has been made clear and his style has a sinewy sort of seeming nonchalance on which he is steadily to work and rework giving "slight but memoried life" a deep, universal significance. He casts a careful eye even on an old-style country byre and sees the milking-machine at work, and the old ways changing. He follows Murphy, an Irish worker, to the factories of Manchester, and balances his lot there against the possibilities of stagnation and madness in an Irish midland village.

He walks among mythologies on the grassy mounds of the hill of Tara, that was the residence of the High Kings of pre-Christian Ireland, and wonders was it a Gaelic acropolis or a smoky hovel, and sees wolf-hounds "lean as models," follow at the heels of heroes out of the sagas: a sardonic bringing-together of the images of two ages. In Bernini's baroque Rome he watches Irish pilgrims, "matrons, girdled in nun-like black," marching with bead and book relentlessly toward their God. The strangest variety of objects and people become symbols before his clear and wondering eye: an aging Irish priest watching bathing beauties on an Australian coast and remembering his own youth: a crazy old priest on an Irish street seeing young girls lifting their light skirts, hearing them (or imagining he hears them) cry out at a listless man in sunshine, wearing black: the pantomimic figures of the rural mummers, St. Patrick, St. George, Satan, remembered from a winter in boyhood: a tortured Catalan Christ seen in a cultural center in New Haven, Connecticut: tired travelers dwarfed by snowy mountains at a bus-stop in Nevada: thirty quids worth of silky hair, a neighbor's dog, "shameless manhood, golden fleece.... with a visage as grave as Richelieu," that he walks in the Champ de Mars in Paris...This is a rich and varied world.

In a mountain-brook, as a boy, he fingers for trout and years later, in a Paris street, he can feel on his hands the taste of the terror the hunted has for the hunter. Remembering a girl who spent herself too easily, and for whom he had a sort of distant, undefined affection, he realizes that in that countryside "even beauty cannot climb stairs." He walks with an Irish virgin in the Dublin mountains: and crosses the American continent to meet a love not so virginal: and an uncle, a folk-musician, leaves for the New World in an old disgrace, and the nephew watches the abandoned violin gather dust and decay, and remembers that uncle in a poem and knows that "succession passes through strangest hands."

By the end of his second collection, *A Chosen Light,* he has gathered together and arranged like ornaments his foreign experiences, he can cast a calm eye even if it is an eye of foreboding, on his own country: and the calmness and foreboding can burst into bawdy laughter when he walks out at a folk-music festival in Mullingar at which, to judge by reports at the time, fornication was rife:

> "At the Fleadh Cheoil in Mullingar
> There were two sounds, the breaking
> of glass, and the background pulse
> of music. Young girls roamed
> the streets with eager faces,
> Pushing for men. Bottles in
> Hand, they rowed out for a song:
> *Puritan Ireland's dead and gone*
> *A myth of O'Connor and O'Faolain.*"

■ **V**

Utter assurance comes to Montague with the composition and arrangement of *The Rough Field,* his most remarkable book and one of the most interesting statements made in this century about Ireland past and present.

From a rump parliament of old friends who spend a night discussing a crate of bottles in a mountain cabin, the poet staggers home through the sleeping countryside. He peers over a humped bridge, listening in the dark to the

> "Unseen rattle of this mountain
> Stream, whose lowland idlings
> Define my townlands shape."

He remembers the day he climbed to find the stream's source, through the lifeless, lichened thorn of MacCrystal's Glen and on and up until he came to a "pool of ebony water fenced by rocks," and groped under the rocks in the pool for the monstrous legendary trout to find only the cold source of the stream's life, the spring beating like a heart. Wondering if that was the ancient trout of wisdom he was meant to catch he goes seven-league-booting it on through the darkness, remembering an old man who raged at him to keep cows away from a well that is now "boarded-up," like the old man himself, remembering how he and the old man's son had once at that place kicked honeycombs around the grass until their boots smelled sweet for days afterwards, remembering how "every crevice held a secret sweetness" in summers gone forever. Now in the night:

> ".... all around, my
> Neighbors sleep, but I am
> in possession of their past
> (The pattern history weaves
> from one small backward place)
> Marching through memory magnified:

Each grassblade bends with
Translucent beads of moisture
And the bird of total meaning
Stirs upon its hidden branch."

There, you could perhaps say, is the core of *The Rough Field*. It is a unity, a movement and sequence of poems as strong and steady as the mountain stream descending on the lowlands to define a world, taking with it the past and present of that one small backward place, but a place over-burdened with history: for it is part of the country of the great Hugh O'Neill who warred for nine years against Elizabeth the first of England. Montague glosses his text, indeed, with fragments of ancient history, with a clipping now and then from current news, even with a bigot's letter pushed through a letter-box and ranting against the Romish wafer.

The bookmaker, Liam Miller of the Dolmen Press, a supreme artist in the making of books, has ornamented this one with woodcuts from John Derricke's: "The Image of Irelande with a Discoverie of Woodkerne, 1581." The result is a book of full meaning and exceptional beauty, and Montague's steady advance towards his mastership in verse brings him to great achievement.

The place, as I've said, is Garvaghey, a rough field, on the road between Ballygawley and Omagh as you go north: I pass it myself on the way to my own early haunts. The father who stayed in New York, when the infant son was brought back to Ireland, revisits the family, and father and son walk Garvaghey together, not smiling, "in the shared complicity of a dream," for when "weary Odysseus returns, Telemachus must leave." But the memory of his father stays with him on those hills and in New York City. Family history and his own personal agony, and the history of the place over three and a half centuries, onward from the end of the great O'Neill to the calamities of the present, are all twisted together, strands in a strong rope. Beginning this book he goes west by bus from Victoria station in Belfast and the historical gloss tells us how that Lord Mountjoy who had inherited the land from Charles Blount, the victor for Elizabeth over O'Neill at the battle of Kinsale, arrived first on the same route by coach in Omagh all that time ago. Ending almost the book, he celebrates the city of Derry through which from the transalantic liner, the poet himself came home to Garvaghey.

Nowhere in the book is the tight razor-edged discipline of his verse and his uncanny knack for gathering the ages together more on display than in the movement that deals with the present problems of Derry City, "A Second Siege." Derry (Doire) the Oak-Grove of the Celtic St. Colmcille is there, and the Londonderry of the settlement by the London merchants of the seventeenth century, and of the first renowned seige in the wars between William of Orange and James Stuart, and the shattered Derry of the bombs and the battle in the Bogside in the last nine dreadful years:

"Once again it happens
Under a barrage of stones
and flaring petrol bombs
the blunt, squat shape of
an armoured car glides
into the narrow streets
of the Catholic quarter
leading a file of
helmeted, shielded riot police;
once again it happens,
like an old Troubles film,
run for the last time.... "

An extra dimension is introduced from his experiences elsewhere and Irish troubles are seen as part of the world's experiences. He was in Berkeley, California, for the beginning of the campus tumults there, and bombs in the Bogside and napalm in Vietnam are all part of the human condition:

"Lines of protest
lines of change
a drum beating
across Berkeley
All that Spring
invoking the new
Christ avatar
of the Americas
Running voices
Streets of Berlin
Paris, Chicago
Seismic waves
Zigzagging through
a faulty world."

He means faulty as in earthquakes and he surveys a world that may, as because of the San Andreas fault, California may, fall apart any of these days. Although he can be agonized and terrified by memory it could still be that he is happiest with those old people who, like dolmens, surrounded his childhood: Jamie MacCrystal, who sang to himself a broken song without tune; Maggie Owens, who was "a well of gossip defiled"; the Nialls, who lived among blooming heather bells but were all blind; Billy Harbinson, who married a Catholic servant girl and was forsaken by both creeds, but who still aggressively wore bowler and sash when the great day came around. Dolmens may be immune to earthquakes.

He is so well aware that he was reared by the bedside of an ancient Ireland that another poet said "knew it all." He knows (as I've quoted) the rune and the chant, the head averted from the evil eye, the Fomorian fierceness of feud. Even when he wrote those words he never dreamed that they could become as bitterly true as they have become in northeast Ulster since 1969. Standing in his rough field on a Tyrone hillslope he surveys his world and finds it precarious. He travels south through the county of Cavan and sees the same changing patterns from Ulster to the Ukraine and wonders as he also does in the "Hymn to the New Omagh Road" on the balance sheet of change:

"Harsh landscape that haunts me,
Well and stone, in the bleak moors of dream
with all my circling a failure to return
to what is already going,
going....
Gone.

■ VI

Since *The Rough Field* there have been two collections, *A Slow Dance* and *The Great Cloak*. Little space have I left myself to consider them, but you will find that they richly reward reading and rereading, right through—so to speak, for the pace, arrangement, and continuity are insistent, and they amply justify Robin Skelton's strong claim that Montague is "clearly one of the most skilled and interesting poets alive, and one of the most original and disturbing." The poet, approaching fifty, has the confidence and assurance, and for very good reasons, that the young man thirty years ago pretended to have. The pared-down lines are rich in irony, humanity, the sense of transience and mortality in love, in men and women, in nations and civilizations: a keen, exact expression.

That slow dance is a dance of life and death, of calm observation alternating with strange fantasy:

"Darkness, cave
drip, earth womb

We move slowly
back to our origins

the naked salute
to the sun disc

the obeisance
to the antlered tree

the lonely dance
on the grass"

He sees a sawmill on the road to Geneva: sees life emerge, a calf licked clean by a cow, from the cave of an old limekiln in Ireland: life and death and despair in a wintry courtyard with (in a fine refrain) snow curling in on the cold wind: writes a song for the shade of John Millington Synge: studies a snail, whorled house and all, that playing children have left on the table full of books at which he works: speaks for an old bitch of a dowager in a western castle: returns home to walk with neighbors under Knockmany hill: sees strange symbols, a Celtic Moloch, a modern high-rise hotel gutted by terrorist bombs, in the Cave of the Night: "Godoi, godoi, godoi! Our city burns and so did Troy." Sees his father returning from America through the customs at Cobh, and travels with him to a moment of recognition. Sees an old French colonel in his final retreat in a Normandy chateau. Writes a lament "so total" that it mourns no one but the great globe itself.

"The Great Cloak" is an intensely personal poem-sequence about the death of love, and abandonment and betrayal, about the birth and growth of a new love:

"As my Province burns
I sing of love,
Hoping to give that fiery
wheel a shove."

The only poem I can compare it with, and it is very much a unity and no haphazard collection, is George Meredith's "Modern Love": yet if it can, at times. be tense with agony and regret, it does not end as Meredith does in a sort of half-resigned despair, but rises to hope and renewal and a new life being born. No mortal who has realized that life is not a straight line can fail to be moved by this poem: happier people should cross themselves and thank whatever gods there be for something like good fortune.

"I'll tell you a sore truth, little understood.
It's harder to leave, than to be left.… "

"A feel of warmth in this place.
In winter air, a scent of harvest.
No form of prayer is needed,
when by sudden grace attended.

■ **BOOKS BY JOHN MONTAGUE**

Forms of Exile. Dublin: Dolmen Press, 1958.

The Old People. Dublin: Dolmen Press, 1960.

Poisoned Lands and Other Poems. London: MacGibbon and Kee, 1961, Chester Springs, Penn.: Dufour, 1963, Dublin: Dolmen Press (revised edition), 1977.

Six Irish Poets (with others) edited by Robin Skelton. London: Oxford University Press, 1962.

All Legendary Obstacles. Dublin: Dolmen Press, 1966.

Patriotic Suite. Dublin: Dolmen Press, 1966.

Home Again. Belfast Festival Publications, 1967.

A Chosen Light. London: MacGibbon and Kee, 1967, Chicago: Swallow Press, 1969.

A New Siege. Dublin: Dolmen Press, 1969.

The Rough Field. Dublin: Dolmen Press, 1972, London: Oxford University Press, 1972.

Hymn to the New Omagh Road. Dublin: Dolmen Press, 1968.

The Bread God: A Lecture, with Illustrations in Verse. Dublin: Dolmen Press, 1969.

The Planter and the Gael with John Hewitt. Belfast: Arts Council of Northern Ireland, 1970.

Tides. Dublin: Dolmen Press, 1970, London: Oxford University Press, 1970, Chicago: Swallow Press, 1971.

Small Secrets. London: Poem-of-the-Month Club, 1972.

A Fair House (translations from Irish). Dublin: Cuala Press, 1973.

The Cave of Night. Cork: Golden Stone, 1974.

O'iada's Farewell. Cork: Golden Stone, 1974.

A Slow Dance. Dublin: Dolmen Press, 1975, London: Oxford University Press, 1975. Winston-Salem: Wake Forest University Press, 1975.

The Great Cloak. London: Oxford University Press, 1978, Winston-Salem: Wake Forest University Press, 1978.

The Leap. Dublin: Gallery Press, 1979, Deerfield, Mass.: Deerfield Press, 1979.

Selected Poems. Winston-Salem: Wake Forest University Press, 1982, Toronto: Exile Editions, 1982, Dublin: Dolmen, 1982, London: Oxford University Press, 1982.

Deities. New York: At-Swim Press, 1982.

The Dead Kingdom. Dublin: Dolmen, 1983, London: Oxford University Press, 1983.

Lost Notebook. Cork, Ireland: Mercier Press, 1987, Chester Springs, Penn.: Dufour Editions, 1987.

Mount Eagle. Oldcastle, Ireland: Gallery Press, 1988.

The Figure in the Cave and Other Essays. Syracuse, N.Y.: Syracuse University Press, 1989.

New Selected Poems. Oldcastle, Ireland: Gallery Press, 1990.

Born in Brooklyn: John Montague's America. Fredonia, N.Y.: White Pine Press, 1991.

An Occasion of Sin. Fredonia, N.Y.: White Pine Press, 1992.

Time in Armagh. Oldcastle, Ireland: Gallery Press, 1993.

About Love. Riverdale-on-Hudson, N.Y.: Sheep Meadow Press, 1993.

Collected Poems. Winston-Salem: Wake Forest University Press, 1995.

Chain Letter. Poetry Ireland, 1997.

Smashing the Piano. Oldcastle, Ireland: Gallery Press, 1999.

Love Present and Other Stories. Dublin: Wolfhound Press, 1999.

Company. New Providence, N.J.: BPR Publishers, 2001.

short stories

Death of a Chieftain and Other Stories. London: MacGibbon and Kee, 1964, Chester Springs, Penn.: Dufour, 1967.

edited

The Dolmen Miscellany of Irish Writing. Dublin: Dolmen, 1962.

A Tribute to Austin Clarke on His Seventieth Birthday (with L. Miller). Dublin: Dolmen, 1966, Chester Springs, Penn.: Dufour, 1966.

The Faber Book of Irish Verse. London: Faber, 1974, New York: MacMillan, 1977.

Naturally, we fall from grace.
Mere humans, we forget what light
led us, lonely, to this place."

As I end this essay I see in *The Irish Times* a new Montague poem: writing, as Spenser and others did about Mutabilitie but with, you might say, a touch of return divilmecarum:

"Sing a song for
things that are gone,

minute and great,
renowned or unknown.

"The library of Alexandria,
the swaying Howth tram,
the Royal city of Hue,
the pub of Phil Ryan.

"Now, nearing fifty, I
have seen substantial things
hustled into oblivion.... "

John Montague has since published more than a dozen books of poetry, two books of essays, and a memoir, and he has edited two books of Irish literature. "John Montague is one of the few indispensable voices coming out of Ireland today," states the *Dictionary of Literary Biography*. "A poet of great sensitivity and intelligence, he has spent the last three decades trying to awaken from the nightmare of Irish history even as he has been drawn by the thin, insistent music—sound of fiddle, sound of drum—which serves as a ground bass to everything he writes." Although he was born in Brooklyn, and later educated in the United States, he was raised in Ulster, Ireland, and has an Irish sensibility. Influenced by such Anglo-Irish figures as Oliver Goldsmith, William Carleton, Samuel Beckett, Austin Clarke, Patrick Kavanagh, and, especially, William Butler Yeats, "Montague has listened attentively to the language of his place."

He is best known in Ireland but is gaining readers in the United States, especially since the publication of his *Collected Poems*. "[T]he ingenious peregrinations in Montague's writing, from loss to revival across public and private parishes, qualify his work as a great achievement," wrote R. T. Smith in a *Southern Review* critique of the *Collected Poems*, adding that "no age is wholly dark when dedicated artists offer their labors to illumine the path, and no pain or anger falls beyond the range of penance and subsequent joy."

Smashing the Piano (1999), his most recent poetry collection, drew similar admiration. "Like his great predecessor [Yeats, whom he writes about], Montague has reached a position as a respected senior poet, from which he can survey the past from a serene and even playful perspective," stated a *Publishers Weekly* review. "These poems show mastery not only of form and technique, but also of the conflicting emotions of a life in poetry."

Although Montague has written fewer short stories than poems, his stories do have an appreciative readership. *Publishers Weekly* wrote of his collection *Death of a Chieftain and Other Stories*: "Clairvoyant in its descriptive force . . . Montague's collection penetrates the obscure corners of man's social and psychological experience. . . . [T]hese technically proficient stories [are] musical, oddly arresting and morally complex."

Benedict Kiely

To Be in the Presence of a Mountain Gorilla for Even One Hour Simply Rips Your Soul Open with Awe: The Work of Sy Montgomery

In her first book, *Walking with the Great Apes*, Sy Montgomery gave a powerful portrait of Dian Fossey, the martyred gorilla researcher and defender. Montgomery describes Fossey speaking about her work among the gorillas: "'I can't tell you how rewarding it is to be with them…their trust, the cohesiveness, the tranquility….' Words failed her, and her hoarse, breathy voice broke. 'It's really something.'"

It's a moving glimpse. There is a kind of eloquence in that failure of speech. Fossey was attempting to say something that she couldn't express, and that she probably was reluctant to express. In a different context, "It's really something" would be a non-statement, but here it is poignant, pregnant with the depth of feeling behind it.

What Fossey was unable to articulate in that moment, Montgomery expresses, sketches in, beautifully constructs. Few writers are more gifted in the "It's really something" response— both in having it and in giving it voice. She has other gifts as well, but one of the central things is her ability to articulate awe.

Walking with the Great Apes is a study not only of Fossey but of Jane Goodall and Biruté Galdikas as well—the triumvirate of primate researchers Louis Leakey sent into the wild, with historic results. Not only did they succeed in providing much new insight into the lives of humanity's closest non-human relatives, they also pioneered a style of observation that challenged both the methods and the assumptions of conventional science. They discovered individuality in the study species, and they did not disallow emotion, on either side of the species divide.

In the chapter I've referred to, Montgomery describes several specific encounters that Fossey had with the gorilla she named Digit, the individual with whom she developed the strongest bond. It was a strong bond indeed. Montgomery says that it was as powerful and rewarding as any in Fossey's life, non-human or human, and it's unlikely that Fossey would have said otherwise. One memorable encounter with Digit took place when Fossey was sick, as she often was. She had been asthmatic as a child, she smoked throughout her adult life, and the air in the mountains where she lived was thin and often cold. The phrase "gorillas in the mist," made famous by the Sigourney Weaver film based on Fossey's story, conjures a beautiful image, and it's easy to forget that the mist was chill and raw. Often Fossey nursed broken bones. On this occasion, she hobbled out on a broken ankle to be with the gorillas. Soon Digit came over and sat beside her. Montgomery writes:

> He chose to remain beside her throughout the afternoon, like a quiet visitor to a shut-
> in, old friends with no need to talk. He turned his great domed head to her, looking
> at her solemnly with a brown, cognizant gaze. Normally a prolonged stare from a
> gorilla is a threat. But Digit's gaze bore no aggression. He seemed to say: I know. Dian

Sy Montgomery

Sy Montgomery, the daughter of a U.S. Army general, was born in Frankfurt, Germany, on February 7, 1958. She attended Syracuse University, earning dual B.A.'s in French/psychology and magazine journalism in 1979. She married Howard Mansfield, also a writer, in 1987. She has lectured on conservation topics at the Smithsonian Institution, American Museum of Natural History, California Academy of Sciences, and other schools, universities, and conservation organizations. Research for her books has taken Montgomery to places all over the world: "To research my books and articles, I have been chased by an angry silverback gorilla in Zaire and bitten by a vampire bat in Costa Rica. I have spent a week working in a pit with 18,000 snakes in Manitoba. I have been deftly undressed by an orangutan in Borneo, hunted by a tiger in India, and…swum with piranhas, eels, and dolphins in the Amazon."

Walking with the Great Apes: Jane Goodall, Dian Fossey, Biruté Galdikas earned the Best New Nonfiction award from the New England Writers and Publishers Project. She has contributed to such journals as *International Wildlife, Geo, Nature, Animals Magazine, Orion, Boston Globe Sunday Magazine*, and *Ranger Rick's Nature Magazine*, and *Encyclopedia Britannica*. She is the author of a monthly column for the *Boston Globe* and of radio commentaries on nature for National Public Radio's *Living on Earth*

program. Her script for *Mother Bear Man* won the Chris Award for Best Science Documentary at the 1998 Columbus Film Festival.

Montgomery has said of her work: "I write for both adults and children in order to help us remember our duty to the earth. Children are a particularly important audience for they have an intuitive connection with plants and animals I hope to help honor and foster in my work. If our kind is to avert the poisonings and extinctions now in progress, today's children will do it." ■

would later write that she believed Digit understood she was sick. And she returned to camp that afternoon, still limping, still sick, still troubled, but whole.

Another time Fossey was on the opposite side of a ravine from the gorillas. It had taken considerable time and enormous patience to reach the point where the gorillas became habituated to her presence, but eventually Fossey went well beyond merely being tolerated. In this instance, the gorilla group came across the ravine to her. Last in line was Digit, who, Fossey wrote, "came right to me and gently touched my hair.… I wish I could have given them all something in return." What she gave them was complete devotion, and ultimately her life. Montgomery adds, "At times like these, Dian wept with joy. Hers was the triumph of one who has been chosen: wild gorillas would come to her."

Many people are suspicious of such encounters. To some, the topic of relationship across species boundaries (unless the other species is their dog, cat, or horse) is either sentimental or unsettling. When "the other" is a species that bears such resemblance to us as chimpanzees, gorillas, or orangutans do, the question of relationship becomes even more provocative. To certain religious persuasions, of course, breaching the human divide is a form of blasphemy—and I don't think it is only the rabid anti-evolutionists who are upset by it. Many feel threatened when humanity's presumed central, distinct, and favored place in the scheme of life is in any way challenged. For centuries we denied that animals have feelings (some still do), and that was part of the related denial that they have souls—whatever souls may be. Enterprises such as Fossey's, Goodall's, and Galdikas's are problematical for some scientists as well. All three faced criticism for methods that some thought violated objectivity, and therefore science, such as giving names to study subjects, thereby introducing the risk of humanizing the animals, though the intention was only to individualize creatures that the three women knew, increasingly well, were very much individuals.

Dian Fossey was an extreme case, with an extreme personality. She was volatile, and could be fierce. She underwent great suffering, both physical and emotional. Her life contained drama and tragedy. (Hers is the only life of the three that has attracted the attention of non-documentary filmmakers.) But while she inhabited an exotic place in more ways than one, hers may well have been one of the central lives of the twentieth century. I would say the same of Goodall and Galdikas, but Fossey's story has a special intensity. Because she attached herself to mountain gorillas, she was on the front lines of an apocalypse: species extinction, the human presence overwhelming the wild on a scale and with a finality that it never had before. Because she was fierce, even violent, in their defense, her story throws into sharp contrast the question of whether and how animals and their habitats can be protected. Going head to head with local government and local people, she provided an heroic example of what would not work—though in saying that one must also say that without her, the mountain gorillas of Rwanda might have been exterminated before more subtle plans for their preservation could evolve. Because she loved the gorillas so much, she gave an example of the human connection to something other than the human, to the larger web of life; she gave not just an abstract argument, but a visceral, spiritual example.

Montgomery is a writer well-suited for understanding and communicating the intensity of Dian Fossey's link with the gorillas. She is like Fossey in her capacity to feel the exhilaration and comfort of animal presence. Though she has a keen eye and ability to describe, she goes beyond being an observer. The sentence that I've used for the title of this essay is hers. Does it sound like a wild claim? It isn't, really. The tone of the sentence is that of a straightforward report. (The word "simply" is perfect there.) Montgomery is one who has had her soul ripped by awe and yet stayed whole. If such soul-ripping is beyond us, she will make it real. At the very least, she will point the way through the spells of her language. Like Fossey in her best moments among the gorillas, she is an animal ecstatic.

■ ■ ■

But don't let me scare you off. Reading Montgomery, one does feel the electricity of her excitement, and the openness of her awe. Her language is strong, brightly colored, sometimes lush as jungle orchids, dramatic as tiger stripes. But at the same time her intelligence is also extremely tough and flexible. She has a gift for assimilating and structuring not just far-ranging information, but different worlds. *Walking with the Great Apes* is as admirable for its structure as it is for its compelling engagement with its subject. "Organization" is a mundane sounding word, but let me talk a little about organization.

Her task called for three portraits, but at the same time she had the three companion species to take into account as well: Goodall and chimpanzees, Fossey and gorillas, Galdikas and orangutans. And then there was Louis Leakey, the famed anthropologist whose intuition it was that female researchers, and ones with qualifications quite different from those of trained scientists, might be especially suited for the job of long-term field study. Montgomery's solution to organizing her several-faceted subject was to write three essays on each of the women, and to present them in a sort of rotation in three sections, each section viewing them from a particular angle. Part One is called "Nurturers," and here we meet each woman in relation to an individual ape who had special importance to her. Part Two is "Scientists." Here Montgomery places her chapter on Leakey, and then gives three more portraits of the women in their unconventional routes to, and sometimes uneasy relationships with, the world of science. Part Three is called "Warriors," in which their differing conservation strategies are examined: Goodall, "the crusader"; Fossey, "the sorceress"; Galdikas, "the diplomat." Then there is something left over, a theme implicit throughout the preceding chapters, which is the question of boundary between human and non-human, and the possibility of crossing it. Montgomery deals with this in an epilogue titled "Shamans"—a risky chapter which rounds out the book with a haunting and quiet power. The book is as firmly and smoothly structured as a snail's shell.

■ ■ ■

What might it mean to cross over to the animal? In traditional cultures, shamans are believed to travel from realm to realm, from the world of daylight human consciousness in the community to the worlds of animals and spirits. The travelers can see what was unseen, possibly exert influence, bring back information. In "Shamans," Montgomery surveys a number of variations of the crossing: the vision quest of the Oglala; anthropologist Colin Turnbull's account of the leopard-men of Africa; a story from ethnobotanist Mark Plotkin of an encounter with a shaman of the Panomamo Indians of Peru; biologist E. O. Wilson, who keeps a colony of ants in his office and says, "The ants give me everything, and to them I will always return, like a shaman reconsecrating the tribal totem." These and other examples form a backdrop for discussing the crossings of the three "ape women."

The chapter isn't long, but it makes a persuasive case that for each of them, the research project grew into a kind of sacred journey among the animals. What did these three bring back? Much data; many insights. But as they immersed themselves in the lives of other species, they absorbed something more than recordable data. They each learned something about ape manners, language, and body language, and it wasn't merely an intellectual kind of learning. They were impressed, sometimes troubled; they were *affected*. Montgomery gives moving details of how close they drew to the apes, but she also notes the limits of such relationships: Goodall backing away from the word "friendship" as a description of what she had with the chimps; Galdikas describing her enormous fascination with orangutans, verging on a desire to merge, but also saying, "Maybe you can be a chimpanzee; maybe you can be a gorilla. But you can't be an orangutan. If you step back you realize you're fooling yourself. But that's what gives them their majesty, their nobility—they don't need anybody."

Only Fossey seems to have crossed over to an extent that renders ordinary human understanding inadequate. In a way that Goodall and Galdikas did not, she made gorillas, as one colleague put it, "her surrogate race." Galdikas said that when she last met with Fossey, she realized that "Dian's soul was already tinged and had already merged with gorillas." Ian Redmond, a scientific colleague of Fossey's in the field, reported that when she was killed, three gorilla groups that had been at some distance from her camp moved steadily and inexplicably toward it. Fossey was already dead when *Walking with the Great Apes* was written, so, being unable to interview her subject, Montgomery decided to consult a friend who is a medium. The medium reported that in the other world, Fossey had become a gorilla.

This last research technique is not calculated to win over skeptics or positivists, but Montgomery includes the medium's report among the other views and testimonies. This is characteristic of her. Deeply respectful of science, she isn't limited to science's version of the truth. Though she has a strong beam of reason, she is not cowed by rationality, nor by what rationality cannot explain. A phrase of Walt Whitman's applies well to her: "aplomb in the midst of irrational things." She has a remarkable openness; a radiant, hungry sort of intelligence. She is an adventurous writer, and not just because her writing takes her to jungles.

There is a passage from Henry Beston's classic *The Outermost House* that is justly famous:

> The animal shall not be measured by man. In a world older and more complete than ours, they move finished and complete, gifted with extensions of the senses we have lost or never attained, living by voices we shall never hear. They are not brethren; they are not underlings; they are other nations, caught with ourselves in the net of life, fellow prisoners of the splendor and travail of the earth.

It's a statement hard to match for balance, precision, and eloquent respect for the other. In a more ecologically advanced society, we might learn it as we learn the Pledge of Allegiance or The Star-Spangled Banner; people might say it in church, temple, or mosque to fill out what their religions and prayers usually omit. Montgomery quotes this passage in the "Shamans" chapter, and then she returns to it in the book's final paragraph, where she proposes that scientific consciousness and methods might not be incompatible with traveling "within their nations, to allow oneself to become transformed, to see what ordinary people cannot normally see." It is a large ambition, but one that animates all her writing.

■ ■ ■

Introducing the Beston quotation, Montgomery wrote: "The line separating man from the apes may well be defined less by human measurement than by the limits of Western imagination. It may be less like a boundary between land and water, and more like the lines we draw on maps separating the domains of nations." Having said that near the end of her first book, near the beginning of her second, *Spell of the Tiger*, a study of the man-eaters of the Sundarbans region of India and Bangladesh, she wrote:

> The very name of Sundarbans is a dreamlike blur of meanings: sundar, the Bengali word for beautiful; sundari, a beautiful, silvery mangrove, once the dominant tree; samudraban, forests of ocean. Indeed, here the forest and ocean are often indistinguishable, one bleeding into the other like tints in a watercolor: blue-grays, olive greens, muddy browns. In the morning mists, the water joins the sky; in the water the tides dissolve the earth—as the Self, Hindu mystics say, dissolves into the mind of God.

And then in her third book, *Journey of the Pink Dolphins*, set in the Amazon, she began with this paragraph:

> The days are full of water. The wet season has drowned the village soccer fields and banana groves and manioc gardens, even flooded some of the less carefully placed stilt houses along the river. Young saplings are submerged completely, and fish fly like birds through their branches. Huge muscular trees stand like people up to their torsos in water; epiphytic orchids and the tree-hollow nests of parrots and bamboo rats are at eye level when you stand in your canoe. On the wide branches, tank bromeliads, plants related to pineapples with spiked, succulent leaves, are

themselves tiny lakes. The leaves mesh to form an overflowing bowl. Some five hundred different species—centipedes, scorpions, tree frogs, ants, spiders, mosquitoes, salamanders, lizards—have been recorded living in a bromeliad's bowl, a miniworld of rainwater.

Montgomery is drawn to the places where boundaries are fluid and shifting, where it is clear that scale and separation are not absolutes. It isn't just lines drawn on maps that are somewhat arbitrary. At the same time, Sundarbans and the Amazon are places where the wild fecundity of the earth envelops most powerfully. Here, always present along with the beautiful and the amazing, whether in the foreground or the background, above the surface or below, is the huge, implacable power of nature, which gives birth, and sustains, and takes back all things. In *Spell of the Tiger* an Indian man puts it concisely: "Here you know you are at the mercy of something else." In *Journey of the Pink Dolphins*, Montgomery says, "…the river, the mother of this place, could swallow one of us whole." In all kinds of ways, in these books neat definitions and safe boundaries are washed away.

Both books evoke similar, very complex visions. We can visualize the worlds Montgomery describes on a double axis, like the four directions. Picture it laid across the mangrove forests of Sundarbans, or the Amazon. At one pole is scientific knowledge. Opposite that is mythology. In Sundarbans the mythology is drawn primarily from Hinduism, but it has roots even older than that and has power for Muslims as well. In the Amazon, the mythological realm is the Encante, a world believed to exist in the river, under the surface of the water—a line which dolphins literally breach in breathing, and which in legend they sometimes cross in a more radical way. If science is north and mythology south, in the east is a particular species, a creature which has qualities that make it a totemic animal of the place and the presiding presence of the book. Finally, at the pole opposite the tiger or the dolphin are human beings, the people who live in the place and those who come for science or other reasons. Montgomery's journeys are not only to Sundarbans or the Amazon; they are also along these axes, and she honors all four directions. The books are about ecology and culture. Ecology, as the dictionary says, is "the relationship between organisms and their environment." But the ecology of these places, Montgomery argues without really arguing, but rather by describing, by weaving scores of stories, hundreds of details, cannot be understood without including "the other world."

There are two especially remarkable things about the tigers of Sundarbans. First, they are the only tigers in the world that regularly prey on humans. Second, the tiger is regarded by the local people as the next thing to a god. Those of us in the Judeo-Christian-Islamic traditions are quite used to thinking of monotheism as an advance, but in another sense, given the shimmering, billion-faceted, infinite nature of the universe, full of complements and contradictions, polytheism has its advantages as a way of describing the world. In Sundarbans there is a tiger god, Daskin Ray, and a forest goddess, Bonobibi, whose shrines and stories are the intermediaries between the human and the non-human. But even the tiger, the animal itself, is god-like. In its strength, its stealth, its ability to appear and disappear with astounding suddenness, its ability to carry a person from one world to another in an instant in its jaws, it has impressive credentials. These tigers defy what seems normal or natural, drinking saltwater, swimming so well that they are sometimes seen at sea. They are also the protectors of the forest, and the forest is the basis of life for the people—though sometimes those who go there do not return. Montgomery evokes this majesty and power. And then there is the fact that the tigers take more human lives here than anywhere else. "Yet," Montgomery writes, "there is no eradication campaign directed against the tigers of Sundarbans. Here the tiger is feared but not hated; here it is worshipped but not loved." This ecological situation fascinates her, and with equal respect for the tigers and the people who live near them, she brings it vividly to life.

Tigers, of course, are among the most dramatic and storied of all animals. They are also among the most endangered. It isn't a coincidence that Montgomery followed her book on the great apes, all endangered, with one on tigers. She is both a celebrant of animals and their passionate defender. In the Introduction to *Spell of the Tiger*, she asks the basic question: "What if tigers vanish from the earth? Do we need tigers in our world?" The entire book is an answer. In the Epilogue, she answers in a few words: "If we eradicate the tiger, we murder a god." Throughout the book she has explained how the tiger is a god. Knowing that there will be resistance to the divinity of the tiger or any other animal, she answers in another way: "If, in the height of our hubris, we exterminate the tiger, we risk losing sight of the deepest truth our kind has ever known: that we are not God."

A polytheism that allows for a tiger-god and god-like tigers is perhaps less far-fetched, and is certainly less arrogant and nearsighted, than a monotheism that holds that human beings, apart from all the others, are the ones made in the image of God.

■ ■ ■

In *Spell of the Tiger*, we contemplate an animal that verges on being a god. In *Journey of the Pink Dolphins*, the focus is on an animal which inhabits a mystical place, Encante, but which is also on the verge of becoming human. Not only do their pink faces have a certain aquatic humanoid appearance, but the local stories about dolphins place much emphasis on their power to take on human form, to become humans of irresistible handsomeness and beauty, and in fact to come ashore and take human lovers back with them. This is of course craziness, right? But when Montgomery asks Don Jorge, an elderly man who has lived his whole life along the Amazon, he says, "It is certain bufeos [dolphins] transform into people. This isn't a story. I saw this myself. It really happened."

This exchange is recorded in a chapter called "Time Travel." In the chapter along with Don Jorge is Gary Galbreath, an evolutionary biologist; in fact, Galbreath goes with Montgomery when she visits Don Jorge. This is the kind of company Montgomery likes; she's equally interested in what the scientist and the storyteller have to say, and in their respective knowledge and powers.

Before the interview with the old man, Montgomery and Galbreath spend the day on the river, and she discovers that the scientist is a time-traveler:

> Gary, I found, often travels back in time. He can go there without blinking. As we journeyed through the rain forest…sometimes the normally loquacious professor would become suddenly quiet; he would get a dreamy look in his eyes, and one could see that he was gone. Gary sees nothing mystical about his ability, and in fact would be horrified at the suggestion that he possesses anything similar to shamanic powers. He is a scientist, first and foremost, and doesn't believe in trances or gods or powers outside those of the laws of physics.
>
> And yet, sometimes he would say to me, "Let's go back to the middle Jurassic," or propose, "Suppose we go back into the Cretaceous," the way other people might suggest a trip to the mall.

The chapter is a wonderful demonstration of synthesis. Montgomery lets both the scientist and the traditional storyteller state their cases, their vastly different versions of reality, with their equal clarity and confidence. She also points out the underlying common ground. Reports of dolphins turning into humans, expressed in haunting stories, and evolutionary accounts of land mammals going back to the water, based in the hard rock of fossil evidence, are held next to each other and turned in such a way that we can begin to see their connection. Montgomery describes the imagination of a scientist so that we can see, hear from his own lips, how science too is a form of myth—myth, of course, not meaning something that is false, but something that expresses a large truth. One must not be too damn literal-minded in trying to understand the world, nor in reading Montgomery. She is, as I said before, a master of assimilation, and reading her is an excellent remedy for one-dimensional thinking.

Personally, I do not believe that dolphins transform into humans, attend human parties, and beguile people with their beautiful bodies and their dancing. Of course, I don't live on the Amazon, haven't even been there—but it sounds unlikely. Don Jorge says they do these things, for sure. And what does Montgomery believe? She doesn't quite say. But clearly she believes that we'll get a subtler, fuller version of the truth if we reject neither science nor myth—if we let them flow side by side, like the place in the Amazon where two rivers join and flow as one—two streams, two colors, one river. In her head and her heart, the different ways of knowing flow together, work together, and in a way become one.

■ ■ ■

Walking with the Great Apes opens with a scene of Biruté Galdikas and a doctor removing maggots from an orangutan's infected vagina. "Maggots," "orangutan," and "vagina" are not words that commonly appear together in the same sentence. When they do, they make a startling combination, and also a kind of poetry.

In *Spell of the Tiger* we learn what ghosts and snakes have in common besides the ability to come and go silently. In Sundarbans the people believe that ghosts and reptiles are both restless in the rainy season. We hear about the kalash, only "moderately poisonous," which likes to slip into bed with people in order to get warm and dry.

In the Amazon, Montgomery and her photographer companion Dianne Taylor-Snow were sunburned while on the river looking for dolphins: "One night, I slept all night on top of a big wooden clothespin and never realized it, because my senses were flooded with pain from my sunburn. The itching that followed was even more annoying, especially once I located its source: hundreds of tiny brown ants discovered the bounty of my shedding skin and weeping blisters, and would flood into my bed each night to drink the fluid and collect the skin to carry it away. ('I hate it when insects eat my flesh,' I had commented to Dianne. 'Yeah,' she agreed, 'especially when you're still alive. It's OK when you're dead, though.')"

That was bad, but not as bad as the nausea she experienced after taking the drug Ayahuasca in a ceremony, hoping to experience a visionary glimpse of the dolphin realm—an example of her commitment to her research. She did not receive the vision hoped for. There were visions, and one especially surprising one at the end, but the sickness was more memorable than the visions:

> The ceremony went on and on, and so did the nausea. I began to think that of all ailments I had suffered, this was the worst. This was worse than the time I got sea-sick shark-tagging with a biologist: Just as I was turning green from the chop, he had decided this was the time to lure the sharks, and poured overboard a bucket of fish blood. This was worse than all the diarrhea I'd suffered in four trips to India. This was worse than the time I got dengue fever. I'd been with Dianne at a Dayak tewa in Borneo, drinking rice wine flavored with the corpse of a fetal deer out of a human skull—but at least with dengue, I had gone unconscious for three days, and missed the discomfort. Dianne had watched over me then, and before I passed out, I gave her instructions that if my body began to stink she should call my husband to tell him I'd died.

I call this a kind of poetry because of its vividness—unsettling, visceral, and high-spirited all at once. Montgomery has a gift not just for awe but also for the awfulness of nature. And yet, this form of poetry has its complement in lyrical passages that evoke the beauty of the natural world with the same precision touch with which she describes the grotesque. For example, part of dolphin research is following them in a boat with electronic tracking devices. But this can give way to something else:

> …We were supposed to be working with the telemetry, in pursuit of a single electronic answer to a simple question: "Where are you?" "I am here." Nonetheless, I put down the telemetry and unplugged the earphones, seduced by the pleasure of their game. I lost myself in their play, and let their motion flood my senses: wet skin gliding against wet skin, the kiss of air, wind and sun on arched backs, the embrace of the cool water. Over and over, they surfaced and plunged, sliding, timeless and weightless, between water and air. No wonder botos enter human story as lovers; they glide through the elements the way lovers slide through one another's bodies, a tension of tenderness and hunger, poised on the threshold of joy. As the sunlight poured over us, heavy as honey, sweat drenched my hair, my bra, my shirt, my socks, my shoes. Sweat ran into my eyes and mouth and ears. But I never noticed until they left us, and then my mouth would water as if hungry, and I would feel tears stinging my eyes.

Montgomery has a terrific, you might say preternatural, ability to describe the otherworldliness of the world, which exists everywhere but at especially heightened levels in certain primitive places:

> In this spirit-drenched tiger forest, the gods are as close as breath, as alien as dreams; what seems at first obscenely obvious may, the next moment, sink from sight and transform itself to its opposite. Looking into these forests is like glancing absently at your own hand and finding in its place a claw.

Usually it is the details of the natural, physical, mortal world that create the rich texture of her books, but there are moments when the timeless and transcendent rises and breaks the surface: "…once, out near the Bay of Bengal, I glimpsed an olive ridley sea turtle as it surfaced for a breath of air. My looking at that spot at that moment seemed as improbable and as blessed as chancing to witness the opening eye of the slumbering Vishnu, the Supreme Hindu Being who, while universes bubble from his pores, sleeps upon a fathomless ocean." Elsewhere she writes: "Listen to the voice of the Absolute: 'This am I,' sighs the moon-driven surge of the sea; 'This am I,' promises the white egret in flight; 'This is I,' says the sun's gold mirrored on the water."

Three pages after this last passage, we come to a little story about returning home from a day in the Sundarbans forest. Montgomery's guide and friend Girindra buys a couple of crabs from two boatmen they meet along the river:

> From the shallow aluminum pot in the dark hold of the little country boat, the older of the two men, his head wrapped in a gamcha, his feet wrinkled and callused like an elephant's, selected two fat, greenish crabs from the mass of windmilling pincers. He set them on the deck…. "Lady and gentleman crab," Girindra announced; he knew because he had once worked as a crab fisherman.
>
> Immediately the male grabbed the female by the eyestalk and pulled off her eye. With his other claw he crushed through the shell of her head. At the same moment, with pincers like pliers, she ripped his right claw from its socket, her eyestalk still clutched in his chitinous grip. Then gentle Girindra, seeing our afternoon snack about to self-destruct, grabbed the crabs, snapped off all their claws and legs, and dumped them, still living, into the water bucket.

And then, right at this moment of battling crabs and the casual, brutal intervention by the gentle Girindra, without other comment, Montgomery returns to the refrain: "Listen to the voice of the Absolute: This am I."

The cumulative effect of this poetry is to allow us to begin to sense how the earth is really beyond our categories of "beautiful" or "grotesque."

■ ■ ■

Montgomery's books are alive with curiosity, broad strokes of compassion, flecks of sex, flashes of insight, sparks of humor. In *Walking with the Great Apes*, her stance was more reportorial; she stood outside her subject, mostly not visible herself. In the subsequent books, she is a participant, a character in the narrative, and her personality is clearly in evidence. She's tough, funny, passionate, sometimes reckless, but in the large ways, very sane. She does not shy from truths that most prefer not to think about: "Thanks to the tiger, the people of Sundarbans still understand what the rest of us pretend to ignore: that all who share the sacred breath of life—chital and boar, frog and fish, idiot and genius—are made of meat." She has an excellent ear for the wisdom of what other people say. She asks a herpetologist about the thought processes of reptiles:

> "You can't speculate what goes on in their brains too much," he had said to me as he released a five-inch wood turtle back into the alder thicket where he'd found it. Humans, we agreed, are unduly impressed with the fact that we think; but animals know. "But they have such a history, and they're united to it in a way we are not. Whatever he knows," David had said of the turtle, "goes back to two hundred million years ago, to the first turtle. A lot of his messages are from that reserve, and beyond."

She asks an official of the Forest Department in Sundarbans why his men must set off firecrackers to keep tigers from coming to worship the tiger god along with the people:

> …wouldn't the people be safe if the tigers were occupied by religious duties? Mr. Mondal smiled. "The problem is, there is no assurance that all the tigers who would come are true believers. They might only be hungry tigers."

If there seems to be a lot of God/god talk, I don't mean to give the impression that Montgomery is a pious writer. She's anything but pious, just as she's anything but stuffy. Montgomery's liveliness extends to the Acknowledgments page, where she says: "Finally, I thank my husband, the writer Howard Mansfield, who discovered after my third trip to India that I had no life insurance. Sorry about that."

■ ■ ■

"Charismatic megafauna," people sometimes say, with a little condescension, when speaking about the appeal of the likes of gorillas, tigers, and dolphins to the human imagination and emotions. They like to point out that while rhinos or blue whales are impressive, and pandas lovable-looking, insect or amphibian species are, in the big picture, perhaps more important to ecosystems. The loss of orangutans would perhaps not be as serious as that of a certain species of carrion-eating beetle. While Montgomery and many others make strong cases for the importance of the big ones, and for their simple right of existence in the face of human self-centeredness and proliferation, and while the books I've been discussing focus on charismatic megafauna, it is probably apparent by now that her interest and regard are not limited to "glamorous species." They are all glamorous—worthy, fascinating, beautiful in their own ways—to her. Her view of life is large, her sympathies and admirations seemingly boundless. Her praise extends to not-often-praised creatures. For example, the caiman, the South American crocodilian that looks like a leaner, meaner version of an alligator. In a lake at night the canoe that Montgomery is riding in is surrounded by caimans staring up in the darkness, their eyes reflecting red in the spotlights, "glowing balls of blood." Not everyone would take this occasion to compliment reptiles, but she does: "They seemed immobile, waiting with an elegance no mammal knows."

I haven't yet mentioned Montgomery's essays, most of which were written for her column "Nature Journal" in *The Boston Globe*, and which have been collected so far in two books, *Nature's Everyday Mysteries* (a title chosen by the publisher, and which the author says she detests) and *Seasons of the Wild*. They are crisp, compact essays on a multitude of wild subjects, generally closer to her New Hampshire home than her book-length studies. They usually have two-part titles, often wonderful ones that sound like titles of term papers by a student who has broken through to wonder: "The Croak of the Wild: Frogs' Mating Rituals," "A Porcupine's Private Life: How the Prickly Rodents Mate and Mingle," "In Praise of Flies: Rethinking a Bothersome Insect."

Recently Montgomery has started writing children's books. Her first was *The Snake Scientist*, in Houghton Mifflin's Scientists in the Field series, on herpetologist Bob Mason and the garter snakes of the Narcisse Snake Dens in Manitoba, where thousands of snakes pour out of the ground in a slithering river. Mason and Montgomery are a good team to guide children into this phenomenon, both of them free of the snake-repulsion reflex that afflicts most humans. Montgomery tells her young readers, "Many people are afraid of snakes. But don't be afraid! You'll miss out on some amazing and mysterious animals. Some people claim snakes are more interesting than dinosaurs…and they aren't extinct." At the end of *The Snake Scientist* she writes, "Snakes are fascinating, but unless you are working with a scientist like Bob, you should never disturb them in the wild. Although most snakes are shy, many will bite in self-defense if they feel threatened, and some are poisonous. It is always best to observe wild animals from a respectful distance. They are happiest being left alone." These comments are good advice to children, and for all their simplicity, they also suggest very nicely some of the major themes that run through Montgomery's work.

■■■

But does Montgomery follow her own advice about leaving them alone? There is no doubt about respect, but what about distance? There are passages in *Journey of the Pink Dolphins*, for example, where her longing to be among the dolphins takes her right up to an edge. There is the desire to go physically among them, to swim with them and see them close up. "Simply being with the botos was worth a great price." When she realizes that her menstrual period is beginning, she sees it as an opportunity to test whether the stories that say that menstrual blood attracts dolphins are true, and she takes six aspirin to increase the flow—even though it is not entirely certain that there aren't piranhas in that part of the river. When she swims with them, she goes far out. Called back, she returns to shore, and her friend says, "Jesus, I thought they were taking you away." Montgomery writes: "How willingly I would have gone with them. I had surrendered to their Encante. In the water, I was a creature transformed: no longer terrestrial, no longer bipedal, I shed the world of earth and air: I left behind the way I breathe, the way I move, the very weight of my body…. I swam in the womb of Mystery." This is a powerful, sacred, but also dangerous longing. How often in reading do we feel a protective concern for the author?

But I am not talking just of physical danger here. I want to return to the question I raised earlier: What is the significance of this desire to approach, gaze over, even venture across the boundary between the human and the animal?

I'd like to think a little about this desire, and suggest some possible ways of understanding it. In doing so, I'll draw from two primatologists, both, as it happens, women. The first is Biruté Galdikas. In her book *Reflections of Eden*, Galdikas discusses Dian Fossey. Informed by personal relationship and the kinship of their pioneering field work, she speaks of her colleague with great feeling and insight. At one point she says, "…I've been quoted as saying that Dian 'became a gorilla.' I meant this metaphorically." She may have been referring to *Walking with the Great Apes*. Then Galdikas goes on to say, "Dian never thought that she was a gorilla. But to some degree she did learn to think like a gorilla, and she sometimes behaved like a gorilla." And she goes on to say, "Her empathy with her subjects went beyond expertise. In time, she became accepted almost as a family member in gorilla groups." And she goes on to say, "Even her harshest critics admitted that nobody understood gorillas like Dian." And she goes on to say, "Certainly, Dian's relationship with Digit was unique."

Maybe it is not possible for a human being to become a gorilla. And yet, as Galdikas's comments suggest, it is possible to make the approach. One can describe that approach and all it entails by saying, metaphorically, "she became a gorilla." Metaphor. Sy Montgomery's mind, too, is richly metaphorical. And the person most gifted in metaphor is sometimes the person who thinks about metaphor the least.

■ ■ ■

If one looks at a gorilla and sees kinship, is one thinking metaphorically?

■ ■ ■

Elsewhere in her book Galdikas says:

> When I look at orangutans I am reminded that we are only human. Our appearance on the earth was relatively recent; orangutans are far older, as a species, than we are. I wonder, when Homo erectus strode into Asia: were orangutans watching from the trees? It is a humbling thought.

So that is another part of it: to be humbled. To see ourselves in our newness, a part of the greater continuum of life. Galdikas continues:

> Looking into the calm, unblinking eyes of an orangutan we see, as through a series of mirrors, not only the image of our own creation but also a reflection of our own souls and an Eden that once was ours. And on occasion, fleetingly, just for a nanosecond, but with an intensity that is shocking in its profoundness, we recognize that there is no separation between ourselves and nature. We are allowed to see the eyes of God.

An orangutan's eyes are the eyes of God because they are the eyes of creation, inconceivably older and larger than ourselves (though not so inconceivably when seen in those eyes). To realize one's connection with this, to feel how there is "no separation between ourselves and nature," is one source of awe.

When we as humans see likeness in the non-human world, what we are seeing is where we came from; we are seeing our connection to all of nature, our evolution; we are seeing how inseparable we are from all of creation. I believe this sense of connection and kinship is part of what Montgomery feels and is moved by in her contemplation of animals. But it is only part, and maybe the lesser part. And here I'll quote the second primatologist, Alison Jolly, of Princeton University. In her book *Lucy's Legacy: Sex and Intelligence in Human Evolution*, Jolly discusses the role of women in primatological studies, and in animal studies in general. She considers various possible reasons why women have played such a great role in this field. She notes that there are actually about the same number of men as women in primatological societies, commenting, "Perhaps the perception that women dominate just means that we have finally achieved equality!" After discussing various factors that may have contributed to women's suc-

■ **BOOKS BY SY MONTGOMERY**

Walking with the Great Apes: Jane Goodall, Dian Fossey, Biruté Galdikas. Boston: Houghton Mifflin, 1991; Boston: Houghton Mifflin, 1998.

Nature's Everyday Mysteries: A Field Guide to the World in Your Backyard. Boston: Houghton Mifflin, 1993.

Seasons of the Wild: A Year of Nature's Magic and Mysteries. Boston: Houghton Mifflin, 1995.

Spell of the Tiger: The Man-Eaters of the Sundarbans. Boston: Houghton Mifflin, 1995; Boston: Houghton Mifflin, 1996.

The Curious Naturalist: Nature's Everyday Mysteries. Camden, Maine: Down East Books, 2000.

Journey of the Pink Dolphins: An Amazon Quest. New York: Simon & Schuster, 2000; New York: Simon & Schuster, 2001.

for children

The Snake Scientist. Boston: Houghton Mifflin, 1999; Boston: Houghton Mifflin, 2001.

The Man-Eating Tigers of Sundarbans. Boston: Houghton Mifflin, 2001.

Encantado. New York: Houghton Mifflin, 2002.

---

cess in the field, she focuses on feeling, specifically "the love of wild animals that grows out of respect and awe at their difference from ourselves." She says, "The best description I have read of our actual feelings is Sy Montgomery's introduction to her triple biography of Jane Goodall, Dian Fossey, and Biruté Galdikas." In that introduction, Montgomery described an experience she had when, before she had written any books, she was involved in field work in Australia. She had several close encounters with a group of three emus. My comment earlier about her being an animal ecstatic owes something to this passage. She says of seeing the birds, "I was stricken. I thought them the most alarming, most painfully beautiful beings I had ever seen." Fully aware of their dangerous strength and extreme otherness, she says, "My trust was simply this: being with them was worth a great price." Her encounters with the emus extended over several days, and of leaving them for the last time she writes:

> "You have eased in me a fear more gripping than that you feel when you are separated from the others. You have given me a comfort more soothing than the feel of your feathers passing through your beaks under the warm sun. I can never repay you, but I want you to feel my thanks."
>
> This speech was one of those expressions like laying flowers upon the graves of the unknowing dead. The recipient doesn't know or care. But the human species is like this: we have to utter our prayers, even if they go unheard....

Jolly says:

> Montgomery testifies to the love of wild animals that grows out of respect and awe at their difference from ourselves. It is a love that does not expect anything in return but their tolerance of our presence and our curiosity. Far from treating them as babies (which they are not) or as sentimental projections of an ideal of nature (field biologists see nature raw) or as grist for one's own career, wild animals are wondrous to us precisely because they are wild. For those who are endlessly fascinated by them, our love is for the Other. This is not a trait of women or men; it is a trait of naturalists.

And of certain writers.

■ ■ ■

In 1952 Rachel Carson wrote that "there has never been a greater need...for the reporter and interpreter of the natural world." In the half-century since then, nature writing has flourished, there has been some advance in ecological awareness; yet humankind and the earth's other creatures are in greater jeopardy than ever, and the need is not any less.

Sy Montgomery is among our best nature writers. Her reporting is strong, and her interpretative powers are brilliant. She is wilder than most, irresistibly drawn to animal mysteries and other mysteries. She is writing to save the world, to protect endangered species, to expand human consciousness—and in the process she writes lively, fascinating, immensely readable books. A very human writer, she sometimes seems a little other or more than human—more adventurous, earthy, passionate, and inspired. At times, it's as if some transformation might take place.

Howard Nelson
October, 2001

New Myths and Ancient Properties: The Fiction of Toni Morrison

In a 1978 interview Toni Morrison commented on the purpose behind storytelling: "People love to hear a story.... That's the way they learn things. That's the way human beings organize their human knowledge—fairy tales, myths. And that's why the novel is so important." Toni Morrison's careful craft and her consistent interest in technique are only half her story. Morrison is a builder of myths. Like Alice Walker, Morrison believes in the "everyday use" of literature in its essential relationship to a kind of knowing.

As Joseph Campbell asserts, the "literally read symbolic forms" of a culture actually support the civilizations, their morals, "their cohesion, vitality, and creative powers." Loss of these "life-supporting illusions" can cause the disintegration of a culture. For the Black American culture whose symbols are always under assault, Morrison may be viewed as a shaper, a rediscoverer, a revitalizer of these symbols for use in living and belief. In Morrison at her best the ancient myths of Africa may be rediscovered, and where a myth to live by is lacking, she, like her characters Sula and Nel, "[sets] about creating something else to be."

Morrison's novels must be called mythic not because they contain "literally read symbolic forms" but because she is concerned with the question "whence?" rather than "why?"—a distinction Kerenyi made about myth in an early essay written with Jung. Many of the characters and their ritualistic actions participate in a sacred time, a primordial experience. Morrison reveals ancient, communal forms in a baby's rescue, in the return of a spirit, in a plague of robins, in a blind vision, even in the way a door is opened or the way food is left in a front yard. Her work does not explain the issues of the Afro-American culture so much as it reconnects the culture to its origins, recalling and re-creating the deep presence of ancient ritual and wisdom in contemporary life.

Perhaps Morrison is most notably associated with the womanist or black feminist concerns of Alice Walker, Paule Marshall, Gayl Jones, or Gloria Naylor. Such a category is functional but misleading, for the novels of these women are diverse and rich with their individual interests. The five novels of Toni Morrison—*The Bluest Eye* (1970), *Sula* (1973), *Song of Solomon* (1977), *Tar Baby* (1981), and *Beloved* (1987)—are as distinctive from one another as the names indicate. Each novel partakes of a new concern: Morrison herself has designated the themes of the first three novels as self-image and cruelty in *The Bluest Eye,* a community's response to good and evil in *Sula,* and male perceptions of love and dominance in *Song of Solomon.* The two novels of the 1980's examine the losses which can accompany a falsely valued beauty in *Tar Baby* and the killing nature of mother love in a world without choices in *Beloved.* Morrison is an astute explorer of psychology, literature, history, and folk tradition. She is distinguished in her range, her acuity in perceiving human nature, and her ability to offer mythic models and spiritual solutions to a group of characters separated from their sources. And with her art emerges a

Toni Morrison Born Chloe

Anthony Wofferd, February 18, 1931, Toni Morrison
was educated at Howard University (B.A. 1953) and
Cornell University (M.A. 1955). She is known for
her unique and sensitive portrayals of black American families, as well as for her stylistic freshness
and authentic dialogue. Both a novelist and editor,
she has also taught at several universities Her writings include *The Bluest Eye*, *Sula* (nominated for
National Book Award in 1975), *Song of Solomon* and
Tar Baby. Morrison was also a National Book Award
and National Book Critics Circle Award and won the
Pulitzer Prize for fiction, Robert F. Kennedy Award,
and American Book Award (Before Columbus Foundation) (1988), all for *Beloved*. She won the Elizabeth Cady Stanton Award from the National Organization of Women, the Nobel Prize in Literature
(1993), and the National Book Foundation Medal
for Distinguished Contribution to American Letters
(1996). Her novel *Beloved* was adapted for a 1998

film of the same title, starring Oprah Winfrey and
Danny Glover. ■

distinctive reworking of the personal relationships among men and women in the Afro-American culture. Within the multiple, contradictory traditions to which she is heir, Morrison
emerges as a social critic, a *griot,* and a healer.

In the course of Morrison's five novels one sees a shifting, perhaps a progression, of concerns about constructive ways of living against an unchanging picture of the political terrain
of the United States. Whether the novel is set in the 1870's or 1970's, the mental landscape
upon which the African in the West must travel does not seem to change significantly. This
constant feature of the novels sets the stage for the dramatic variations in the portrayal of
male and female relationships. What begins in social criticism is countered by the absence of
customary social prescription. Certainly in the first and fourth novels there is a didacticism
about the contemporary social ills in the United States; however, the central focus of the
novels rests in choices, alternatives, questions—in imperfect experiments, as Morrison
explains it, with "love and how to survive...*whole*." The constant landscape of a world
turned upside down by the values of slavery, racism, capitalism, and colonialism constitutes
the problem of each novel; however, whites, as a group, are peripheral to the novels, though
less so in *Tar Baby* and *Beloved,* and enter in only as their culture creates a conflict in values
for the principal characters. The primary mode of the novels is to allow personal drama to
illuminate communal conflict and to show a need for the artist as both historian and maker
of these essential stories. Thus, a picture of Morrison's work includes a survey of the political
landscape, the love relationships, and the mythic characters who draw others closer to
African sources.

■ ■ ■

The unchanging background to Toni Morrison's picture of the world is an intrusive, alien value system which calls mercilessness, mercy; vice, virtue; work, child's play; beauty, ugliness; down, up; or loss, progress. This relentless function of the dominant society is not so much explained as assumed. *Tar Baby,* named for a character who is almost white, contains the most straightforward description of the wrongs of this capitalist system which seduces its victims. The heroic Son meditates on these values as he watches his white host:

> Valerian [was] chewing a piece of ham…[and] approving even of the flavor in his mouth although he had been able to dismiss with a flutter of the fingers the people whose sugar and cocoa had allowed him to grow old in regal comfort; although he had taken the sugar and cocoa and paid for it as though it had no value, as though the cutting of cane and picking of beans was child's play and had no value; but he turned it into candy, the invention of which really was child's play, and sold it to other children and made a fortune in order to…build a palace with more of their labor and then hire them to do more of the work he was not capable of and pay them again according to some scale of value that would outrage Satan himself.…

This theme of exploitation and inverted values is constant in Morrison's work and emerges in both imagery and characterization. The candy in the passage above functions similarly in *The Bluest Eye* when Pecola purchases sweets called Mary Janes and her mother Pauline loses a front tooth eating candy in the movie theater. Through such examples the reader can observe the ironic way in which the victim is an accomplice to her pain.

The hunger for sweets may also indicate a deprivation of appropriate nourishment, as it does in the last novel. Beloved, the wraith of Sethe's murdered child, has an insatiable appetite for sweets. Her hunger is, to state the obvious, unnatural, as was the social situation which caused her loving mother to choose between the child's death and enslavement. Beloved has lost the natural nourishment of her mother's milk, first through her mother's delayed escape and next, through the child's untimely death. The candy, the sweets, and the refined sugar which Susan Willis argues, forms one base of capitalist profit, are treacherous substitues for more natural nourishment and nurture.

A corollary to the candy motif in the novels is the waste that accompanies the industrialist of *Tar Baby*; waste is the result of a separation from the land, a need to control rather than live with nature. Son, one of "that great underclass of undocumented men," expresses his view of the problem in his unspoken diatribe against Valerian's attitudes: "That was the sole lesson of their world: how to make waste, how to make machines that made more waste…and how to despise the culture that lived in cloth houses and shit on the ground far away from where they ate." Valerian's purchase of the island, his house, his changing of the landscape all constitute a violation of nature on *Isle des Chevaliers*. Nature, and the people who live in harmony with it, are despised or trivialized by this American culture. In Son's mind, the preoccupation with "bathing bathing washing away the stench of the cesspools" is the reaction of a culture "new at the business of defecation." But the waste does not only mean the creation of a festering swamp in *Tar Baby,* it also means the assault on the humanity of a dissimilar culture. Obsessions with cleanliness, whiteness, straightness, blondness in both the white and black cultures all are a part of the sickness of a value system which tries to insulate itself from the vagaries and laws of nature. Such an evasion is signified by Valerian's air-conditioned greenhouse with the piped music on an island luxurious with growth. For Morrison such behavior indicates a sort of blindness, a conditioned inability to shape what she calls a "full recognition of the legitimacy of forces other than good ones." For her, insulation from plagues, weather, natural disasters, even meanness of spirit, indicates a far more tragic separation from nature and humanity altogether.

Morrison dramatizes the damage inflicted by the worship of a commercialized blue-eyed beauty. "Physical beauty," the author comments in *The Bluest Eye,* is one of "the most destructive ideas in the history of human thought." The repeated invocations of Shirley Temple, Greta Garbo, Ginger Rogers, Jean Harlow, and Claudette Colbert form a litany and then a dirge for Pecola Breedlove and her "Alice-and-Jerry Storybook eyes." The irrational yoking of goodness with this idea of beauty and the obsessive desire for the touted purity of whiteness contribute to the multiple catastrophes of this work. Pecola, however, pays the greatest price. Claudia, the youthful narrator of several sections, comments:

> All our waste which we dumped on her and which she absorbed. And all of our beauty, which was hers first and which she gave to us. All of us—all who knew her—felt so wholesome after we cleaned ourselves on her. We were so beautiful when we stood astride her ugliness.

The terrible psychology of self-hatred that leads to Pecola's final ostracism and madness is tapped later in *Song of Solomon* when Hagar, dismissed by Milkman and mad with her unrequited love, tries to recover her beauty through a desperate journey to department stores and beauty shops: "The cosmetics department enfolded her in perfume and she read hungrily the labels and the promise. 'Myurgia [sic] for primeval woman who creates for him a world of tender privacy where the only occupant is you....'" Hagar's fatal attempt to be loved for "penny-colored hair" and "lemon-colored skin" cost Reba and Pilate every bit of money they had; it was necessary to take up a collection for Hagar's funeral.

In two characters from *Tar Baby* we see this obsessive response to the dominant culture's endowment of beauty with qualities like truth and goodness. Margaret Street, a white woman who is dubbed "The Principal Beauty of Maine," attained her status as the wife of wealthy Valerian Street because she looked "like the candy that had his name." Her functionless life as object leads her to express her resentment through a secret abuse of her son. Her role as beauty creates an artificial, almost edible character who is both pathetic and cruel.

More complexly rendered is the coveted model and conscientious student of art, Jadine. For Morrison, Jadine is an ironic image of the tar baby, a light-skinned black character who seems orphaned by her own culture and sold on the civilized accoutrements of the West: a graduate of the Sorbonne, a specialist in cloisonne, a model who travels "in what the Americans call the fast lane." Jadine is accepted by other women who act as objects, who want to "make it" in New York, but she is found wanting by the women who value the "ancient properties" of respect for elders, love of community, mothering. The crisis of the novel occurs because of Jadine's fear of two acts: accepting her own womanhood, as defined by those women who haunt her, and relinquishing the status she has achieved in the white culture. Jadine's beauty and her continual separation from her family have created a girl who is not a daughter. The aunt explains,

> "Jadine, a girl has got to be a daughter first. She have to learn that. And if she never learns how to be a daughter, she can't never learn how to be a woman. I mean a real woman: a woman good enough for a child; good enough for a man—good enough even for the respect of other women.... All you need is to feel a certain way, a certain careful way about people older than you are."

For Morrison the cold, packaged, marketed beauty of the West is a snare, a sticking place, a diminution of what it means to be human.

In all the novels the names used by the dominant society have subverted or disguised the meanings of the people and places. The Bottom, a black neighborhood first established by a slave who was to be given fertile valley land, is "up in the hills." The trickster in this episode is "a good white farmer." When the slave, having done Herculean tasks to attain his freedom and his land, questions its location, the master argues, "It's the bottom of heaven—the best land there is."

Song of Solomon, a novel whose title is undecipherable until the end, contains the best developed commentary on the loss of accurate names. In a novel that begins with an explanation of the naming of Not Doctor Street and No Mercy Hospital, a novel which takes for its female hero a generous and loving character named Pilate, meaning must be carefully sought, uncovered. Milkman discovers the care that must be given a name:

> He read the road signs with interest now, wondering what lay beneath the names. The Algonquins had named the territory he lived in Great Water, *michi gami.* How many dead lives and fading memories were buried in and beneath the names of the places in this country. Under the recorded names were other names, just as "Macon Dead," recorded for all time in some dusty file, hid from view the real names of people, places, and things. Names that had meaning. No wonder Pilate put hers in her ear. When you know your name, you should hang on to it, for unless it is noted down and remembered, it will die when you do.

Milkman's liberating discovery of his ancestors' names and the final revelation of the story of the flying Africans allows him to learn his own name and value his heritage.

In *Beloved* names given in love are continually contrasted with names furnished for chattel, "bill-of-sale" names. The misnaming reveals the perversity of a culture that would deprive a race of its identity, history, and continuity. Morrison's hard irony about white perceptions shows Garner naming three brothers Paul A., Paul D., and Paul F. Called Jenny by the Garners for years, Baby Suggs finally discovers and rejects her bill-of-sale name, preferring the one given her by the "'husband' she chose." The pre–Civil War Kentucky farm is a misnamed property; in fact, her memories of Sweet Home made Sethe "wonder if hell was a pretty place too." But not only are many people and places misnamed, some words and sources are altogether destroyed. Sethe recalls being told that she alone of her mother's children was given "the name of a black man" and preserved when other babies, half-white, were thrown away without names. Even this fearful history for Sethe had to be recovered with a struggle as "she was picking meaning out of a code she no longer understood." Though Sethe recovers these experiences, the distinctive medium of the speech itself had been lost: "What Nan told her she had forgotten, along with the language she told it in. The same language her ma'am spoke, and which would never come back." Only Sethe's name is preserved.

Morrison shows us that for the slave as for the contemporary black in the United States, the loss of names is a distortion of values and a deprivation of ancestral strength. At the outset of each novel the reader is faced with a dominant culture which has killed the spirit, buried the past, and subverted the concept of virtue in the black community.

■ ■ ■

Morrison does not deliver any gratuitous optimism about change in the racial politics of the United States; she does dramatize the possibility for her characters to combine community and creativity in new and richer ways. Her great characters all wrestle with these poles of experience which, when they exist together, allow health and wholeness.

There are essentially three conditions in which the reader finds Morrison's characters: Some, like Pauline Breedlove or Ruth Dead or Jadine, have been dispossessed of the values of their own heritage and espouse the soul-killing standards of the white society. Others, for instance Cholly, Sula, or Sethe, disconnected by the abuses suffered in their personal lives from any community, experience a sort of dangerous freedom which can turn creativity into the destruction. In both these types the potential of the intellect and spirit to enrich a community is lost. The third type of character is one in whom the untamed qualities of creativity find a grounding in a genuine community which is informed by the African ancestors. Pilate in *Song of Solomon,* Son in *Tar Baby,* and Baby Suggs, before the killing of Beloved, have the generosity of spirit associated with these ancestral connections.

It is important to note here that no character is a model of perfection, and every character holds within his or her make-up the potential of this loving spirit. Sula, for instance, portrays the most highly developed creative nature, but she tragically loses her grounding in the community. Morrison makes clear that being human involves corruption. She faults the dominant society for its effort to cleanse the world of the wildness of nature and reality of evil—an effort which kills the very soul.

In *Sula* Morrison discusses the black neighborhood's understanding of the nature of things:

> What was taken by outsiders to be slackness, slovenliness or even generosity was in fact a full recognition of the legitimacy of forces other than good ones. They did not believe doctors could heal—for them, none ever had done so. They did not believe death was accidental—life might be, but death was deliberate. They did not believe Nature was ever askew—only inconvenient.... The purpose of evil was to survive it.... They knew anger well but not despair, and they didn't stone sinners for the same reason they didn't commit suicide—it was beneath them.

Morrison presents an acceptance of nature, an acceptance of events truly beyond human control, and a sturdy ongoingness of the human spirit.

This assertion is juxtaposed to what Morrison sees as a Western notion that one must overcome or eschew evil rather than survive it. Morrison contends that the human being cannot live divorced from corruption and the effort to do so is the heart of human destructiveness, intolerance, compulsion, spiritual death. Speaking about Valerian Street's "crime of innocence," his evasion of the truth about his abused son, Morrison acknowledges that "knowing more was inconvenient and frightening." Central to Morrison's concept of good and evil is the idea that "An innocent man is a sin before God. Inhuman and therefore unworthy. No man should live without absorbing the sins of his kind...." The third type of character in Morrison, a figure of health or wholeness, is also always corrupt, specifically corrupt because of grounding in and acceptance of a specific human community.

With these understandings about imperfection, creativity, and separation, we can watch Morrison explore her primary concern with the nature of the relationships between men and women in the black community. Morrison's treatment of male figures in the early novels has been criticized as gratuitously negative and stereotypical, especially because she portrays female characters who inspire awe or sympathy. Morrison's novels express understanding of, if not sympathy with, all characters, male and female, who inflict pain. However, one can observe a shift in the later novels toward greater willingness to create complex male characters—increasingly idealized.

The five novels must first be seen as experiments with what it means to do more than survive as a black woman in the United States, with the essential fact that black women must "[create] something else to be." The first two novels focus on a definition of the black woman's traditional exploitation and negative self-image and clear the way for alternatives. The men in these novels, if important, are lost in their cruelty or madness. Other male characters of less importance have a vague, temporary quality; they can be identified with the image of the wanderer which emphasizes a limited mode of autonomy for men in the myths of many cultures, particularly the Afro-American. The women of the first two novels receive a primary focus and shape the complexity of the story; Morrison's movement from Claudia-Pecola to Sula-Nel rings changes in the identities of the women, showing the potential for wholeness. The next two novels balance their attention to men and women; they show both sexes experimenting with new roles, especially pairing magical female guides with young men who will be initiated into their community. Morrison, having established her case about the black woman's predicament, experiments with the changes that are inevitable if the women are to cease to be victims. *Beloved* returns to the single focus on a female household, exploring the grace and curse of making motherhood define the self.

The treatment of these relationships pivots upon two points: an active distrust of romantic love and a regard for ancient myths and "ancient properties." Morrison's most exceptional characters embody a response to these issues—revealing the value Morrison places on the freedom of intellectual curiosity, inquiry, independence, as well as a conviction that to be constructive one must belong to a community and its sources.

In *The Bluest Eye,* when Morrison attacks the preoccupation with physical beauty, she adds "the idea of romantic love" as "the most destructive ideas in the history of human thought. Both originated in envy, thrived in insecurity, and ended in disillusion." Pauline Breedlove acquired these two ideas through "her education in the movies." The separation from her own family and community, the destructive freedom of Cholly Breedlove from any human responsiveness, and this miseducation combine to ruin Pauline Breedlove and to maim her child. As Morrison points out about Pauline's regard for "romance as a goal of the spirit,"

> It would be a well-spring from which she would draw the most destructive emotions, deceiving the lover and seeking to imprison the beloved, curtailing freedom in every way.

This sort of love as the way to establish identity leads inevitably to hatred in Morrison's novels. "Possessive mating," a central action of the novel, is a form of destruction for both Pauline and Cholly Breedlove. It does not acknowledge "lust and simple caring for." It obviates freedom altogether, negating and sealing the spirit.

Each of the first four novels examines the entanglement and destruction predicated by romantic love. Nel, in *Sula,* imprisons her imagination and perception when she chooses a relationship with Jude: "She didn't even know she had a neck until Jude remarked on it, or that her smile was anything but a spreading of her lips until he saw it as a miracle." The primacy of romantic love conceals Nel's true feelings about "missing" Sula until the end of the novel. Even Sula, who is freer than any other character in the novels and more capable of respecting that freedom in others, once succumbs to "possessive mating" in her relationship with Ajax. Shortly after the conjurer's son leaves, Sula learns that she "didn't even know his name." Thus romantic love undermines perception.

In a secondary theme of *Song of Solomon,* the tragic Hagar reveals the destructive power of a romantic obsession. In Hagar's sort of love, Morrison asserts, is all one needs to know of hate. For Hagar, when she is rejected by Milkman, must kill what she loves as the only way to insure possession. She cannot listen to Guitar:

"You can't own a human being. You can't lose what you don't own. Suppose you did own him. Could you really love somebody who was absolutely nobody without you? You really want somebody like that? Somebody who falls apart when you walk out the door…? You're turning over your whole life to him. Your whole life, girl. And if it means so little to you that you can just give it away, hand it to him, then why should it mean any more to him? He can't value you more than you value yourself."

Guitar understands love as something which does not possess nor encumber; he sees that a possessive love destroys the value and the freedom of an individual. Hagar's inability to separate herself from this poisonous conception predicates her own death: "It's a bad word, 'belong.'"

The character Son in *Tar Baby* accomplished in a rage what Hagar failed to do: He killed his faithless wife and lived with the regret. Son, like the women in preceding novels, addresses the horror of a possessive love. His passionate love affair with Jadine shows a set of conflicts reversed from those in *The Bluest Eye*. The Breedloves' confirmed belief in their own ugliness is replaced by the overwhelming beauty of *Tar Baby*'s main characters. Pecola's generosity of spirit also stands in contrast to Jadine's meanness, her absorption with things and "making it," the absence of "simple caring for." With Son and Jadine the reader witnesses a profound fascination not without its beauties, but such a consuming passion cannot live in a community or sustain a family. Jadine flies from Son, to escape the images and restrictions of a community and to maintain her agenda for "making it." The male-female patterns are reversed here: Jadine becomes the transient; Son tries to come home to Jadine and to the mythical blind horsemen of the island. The victim in Morrison's conception of romantic love is not always a woman; here a man loves unwisely, his good judgment distorted by his obsession.

Passionate love without possession seems most possible in *Beloved*, since the two men whom Sethe loved are sensitive and giving, almost fantastically so. The jealous sexual love of other novels is absent here; Sethe and Paul D. feel shyness, sorrow, then a disinterested interest after lovemaking. As Paul D. acknowledges in the end, echoing Six-O's axiom, "It's good, you know when you got a woman who is a friend of your mind." In *Beloved*, the possession, both miraculous and deadly, is love between mother and child. For mother love, Sethe held onto life when she left Sweet Home and Halle, and again for mother love, Sethe committed a crime, the news of which drove Paul D. away. Morrison gives two portraits of viable sexual relationships, but Sethe's love for her child is "too thick" and the world is too dangerous for such love to last. Both men have an admirable sensibility and gentleness; however, both are lost or diminished by the demonstrated power of another bond. Male and female sex roles are varied in Morrison's novels, but nowhere does an intense romantic passion last.

The liberation from sexual roles in Morrison accompanies another sort of liberation: Her increasing interest in the magical challenges the limits of Western empiricism. Wraiths, Conjurers, shamans, and healers most distinguish the characters of Toni Morrison from those of other novelists. Sula, Pilate, Milkman, Son, and Sethe make the indelible impressions of epic figures, primary types. Such characters seem larger than life, highly individuated, and capable of wondrous deeds—though Morrison insisted in a recent television interview that her characters are not larger than life, that people are "that big."

Several characters in the early novels have the features of a shaman, a medicine man who can interpret the signs, cure a disease, or set a spell in motion. More specifically, Joseph Campbell explains that a shaman is "a person who in early adolescence underwent a severe psychological crisis, such as today would be called a psychosis." This magical one, often a guide to the initiation of others, becomes a master of knowledge beyond the personal—beyond the circumference of conscious perception. Both Pecola and Shadrack fit such a pattern; each internalizes the outward madness of the world. This experience leads to an expanded perception of, and sensitivity to, the world in which they live. Like shamans, Shadrack and Pecola live perilously, feared and sometimes blamed for things that go wrong. Ironically, neither of these figures is able to articulate insight; however, their actions somehow cleanse the community of an evil inadequately perceived. They are precursors to the magical characters to come.

The triads of manless women in four of the five novels also draw from ways of knowing which are obscure, powerful, ultimately magical. The three whores or "merry harridans" of *The Bluest Eye* hate men "without shame, apology, or discrimination," yet they, alone among the adult community, do not despise Pecola. They have the clear eyes, full smiles, and rich laughter lacking in the black community of Lorain, Ohio. Far more magical in its way of knowing is the Peace matriarchy of *Sula*. These women, who have learned to deal with the perverse social institutions of their time, read dreams and know signs. Both Eva and Sula have knowledge of what they have not seen. Their household has both a charming and a dangerous freedom and funkiness. Sula is especially feared as a witch who does indeed cast a spell on her neighbors when she returns to the Bottom with a plague of robins.

The sinister quality of these first two groups changes radically in the *Song of Solomon* with Pilate, Reba, and Hagar. These women, who live independently of men, do not despise them. For the alienated Macon Dead they reveal a hauntingly appealing community, as he observes them, unobserved himself:

> He crossed a yard and followed a fence that led into Darling Street where Pilate lived in a narrow single-story house whose basement seemed to be rising from rather than settling into the ground. She had no electricity because she would not pay for the service. Nor for gas. At night she and her daughter lit the house with candles and kerosene lamps; they warmed themselves and cooked with wood and coal…and lived pretty much as though progress was a word that meant walking a little farther on down the road.

The song these women weave draws the cold-hearted Macon Dead into their warmth. Though Pilate is far more essential to the novel than her daughter or granddaughter, the three women constitute a household unlike others, a house of eccentricity and acceptance, of passion and compassion, of attunement to the deeper rhythms of human experience. Pilate's spells bring the hero Milkman into being.

In *Beloved* Morrison presents a shifting triad of women who have learned mostly to live apart from their men, and apart from the black community at their front gate. For years Baby Suggs, Sethe, and Denver live at the house called 124 with the lively presence of a murdered daughter's ghost. Sethe's two sons run from this haunting as soon as they reach puberty. After the death of Baby Suggs, Sethe and Denver live together with the ghost. Paul D.'s appearance at Sethe's front door, his routing of the ghost, and his effort to rejoin the women with the community are ineffectual. For the wraith of the exorcised ghost, the smooth and shining Beloved, returns to dominate the household. Though he already has, in effect, been run out of the house by Beloved, Paul D. chooses to leave 124 when he learns from Stamp Paid about Sethe's murder of her daughter. The male dissociation from Sethe's crime stands in stark contrast to the female ability to live with the history and even with the potentiality of such violence. As Paul D. says to Sethe, "Your love is too thick." The haunting spirit of the house—strong enough to drive away two boys, a man, and Here Boy, the dog—is understood by the women "as well as they knew the source of light." In fact, the supernatural events of 124 have a sort of normalcy to Halle's mother, wife, and surviving daughter: "Not a house in the country ain't packed to its rafters with some dead negro's grief. We lucky this ghost is a baby." The women of *Beloved* are isolated, not because they are mad, but because their perceptions embrace those things beyond the visible, parts of the past which can ensnare the rememberers.

These matriarchies offer not only social alternatives to the traditional male-female relationships and patriarchal structures, but also a set of values not determined by maleness or whiteness. These funky, disorderly, sometimes sinister households tap the resources of the magical; for them, ghosts, dreams, aberrations, names, and symbols are alive with meaning.

In *Song of Solomon* and *Tar Baby*, there is a strong juxtaposition of a citified black culture which demonstrates many of the modes of the dominant culture and a more ancient, animated world that lives in harmony with its mythology. These novels are journeys during which the heroes become heroes because they are able to cross from the first world to the second. The stories are not *nostoi*, or epics of return, so much as they are discoveries of a land and a history lost, a land only the ancestors have walked. The guides are women who have not abandoned the gifts of these ancestors.

Tar Baby, a novel of extreme temperatures, addresses the distance between these two worlds. Son, who belongs to the magical community of *Isle de Chevaliers*, like Ulysses, passes through maelstroms, transforms himself from a bum to a prince, learns the terrain and the people, and defends the exploited. Yet he passionately pursues Jadine, a stepchild of Western materialism, one who loves dead seals' skin and *objets d'art* more than the living. Son is divided between his passion and his knowledge. Finally, at the end of the novel, he joins the ancestral blind horsemen, through the agency of Therese, his Teiresias, whose "eye of the mind" guides him back to the island. This homecoming is abrupt and indefinite.

Only in *Song of Solomon* does the Western child, Milkman, fully accept the African sources to which he belongs. Because his aunt, Pilate, has instinctively carried her name and her sources with her, Milkman can recover his own. Beginning in pride, like a Gilgamesh, Milkman uncovers his ancestral past, and in doing so, recovers harmony with the land and generosity of spirit. This transformation is demonstrated in the last scene in which both Milkman and Pilate face a death which is not a death. Pilate, shot by Guitar, says, "I wish I'd a knowed more people. I would of loved'em all. If I'd a knowed more, I would a loved more." Like her father, Pilate asks for a song, and like Pilate, Milkman sings, "Sugargirl, don't leave me here…" (340). When Milkman says there must be "at least one more woman" like Pilate he does not realize that he is the one, as he freely offers his life to Guitar. The crossing from the West to Africa is complete, it is made by both man and woman, and it defies the traditional limits of death: "If you surrendered to the air, you could *ride* it."

Through such characters the ancient myths of the flying Africans and the blind horsemen are recovered, as are the ancient values for the ancestors and the land. But the mythic heroes emerge in new forms, in forms which give access to the contemporary black community. These characters are Morrison's crafted versions of archetypes; they tap the deeper instincts and living signs which have been subverted. They allow her novels to live in two worlds, to be themselves a crossing.

Beloved, too, is a crossing. In this historical novel the characters do not move from a contemporary black community to African traditions. This novel ponders the difficulties of a movement from conditions of slavery to what one might call self-possession. Once across the Ohio, Sethe observes, "Freeing yourself was one thing; claiming ownership of that freed self was another." This final novel examines a woman whose identity is not undermined by a romantic love but by her role as mother. Sethe, at the center of the novel, is exhausted with the struggle to see herself, not Beloved, as her "best thing." But Denver finally emerges whole from

■ BOOKS BY TONI MORRISON

The Bluest Eye. New York: Washington Square Press, 1972.

Tar Baby. New York: Knopf, 1981.

Sula. New York: Knopf, 1974, New York: NAL Penguin Inc., 1982.

Song of Solomon. New York: Knopf, 1977, New York: NAL Penguin Inc., 1987.

Beloved. New York: Knopf, 1987.

Jazz. New York: Knopf, 1992.

Playing in the Dark: Whiteness and the Literary Imagination. Cambridge, Mass.: Harvard University Press, 1992.

Collected Novels of Toni Morrison. New York: Knopf, 1994.

Conversations with Toni Morrison (with Danielle Taylor-Guthrie). Jackson: University of Mississippi Press, 1994.

The Dancing Mind. New York: Knopf, 1997.

Paradise. New York: Knopf, 1998.

Baby Suggs' holiness, from Sethe's tenacity and intellectual honesty, from the unhealthy hunger of Beloved. This last daughter's delivery by Amy Denver, a garrulous white girl with "fugitive eyes" and a "tender-hearted mouth," was as remarkable as her crossing the Ohio to freedom. But even more miraculous was Denver's deliverance from the isolation of her childhood. She becomes a woman for whom a white man at the front gate will never mean murder or something worse. She emerges from the haunted 124 as her mother's nurturer and a member of the community. The insatiable demands on mother love are exorcised.

In *Beloved*, as in *The Bluest Eye*, Toni Morrison is "saving her real affection for the unpicked children," just as Lady Jones did. For the murderer Sethe, "which was not beloved," is vindicated. Toni Morrison, a storyteller, a *griot* or historian of her race, has taken the most irredeemable crime—the murder of a child by her mother—and revealed its grace. Her story shows that under the conditions of slavery, "Unless carefree, motherlove was a killer." Morrison has taken up an act of apparent depravity and shown its origins in a great love and endurance which coexisted with the unthinkably perverse slave culture. And Morrison has let Sethe exorcise her own guilt. As Mr. Bodwin arrives at 124 for Denver, Sethe does not assault the child, but the image of the villain she could not fight eighteen years before.

Beloved is a gift of history. In the place of a murderer, Morrison gives back to us the loving, complex, unflinchingly honest mind of a Sethe who saved her children from something worse than death. The outraged ghost is satisfied, and in the third generation of this matriarchy, one woman emerges "whole."

And it shall be that in the place where it was said to them, 'You are not My people,'
There they shall be called children of the living God.
Romans 9:26

Anne Warner
June, 1988

UPDATE

Toni Morrison, the eighth female and first black winner of the Nobel Prize for literature, has since published two more novels: *Jazz* (1992) and *Paradise* (1998).

The Dictionary of Literary Biography described Morrison as "an anomaly in two respects": "she is a black writer who has achieved national prominence and popularity, and she is a popular writer who is taken seriously."

Paradise, Morrison's latest novel and the third in a trilogy that began with *Beloved* (thought by many critics to be her masterpiece) and *Jazz*, is the story of a black community whose members seek to isolate themselves from the whites and light-skinned blacks who persecuted their enslaved ancestors, but who, in their zeal, are tyrannized by themselves. It was considered controversial even before it was in bookstores, and early reviews were mixed. The *New York Times* called it "a clunky, leaden novel" and *The New Yorker* dubbed it "the strangest and most original book that Morrison has written." A *Time* magazine article was more embracing: "Everyone who cares about contemporary fiction will doubtless be talking about *Paradise*, and not only because of the renown of its author. To read the novel is to be pulled into a passionate, contentious and sometimes violent world and to confront questions as old as human civilization itself." Likewise *The Antioch Review*: "Morrison is at her best in this mythic realm where fantasy, fear, and retribution rule." And, although the reviewer also found Morrison's writing to be somewhat uneven, "Her vision is balanced by darkness and virtue, despair and hope."

Morrison's works continue to be extremely popular. Her novel *Sula* was chosen by Oprah Winfrey as her last book club selection, a guarantee of booming sales. It is the fourth time a book by Toni Morrison was chosen by Winfrey; the others were *Song of Solomon* in 1996, *Paradise* in 1998, and *The Bluest Eye* in 2000.

Paul Muldoon: Time-Switch Taped to the Trough

If, as the philosopher Richard Rorty argues, the "subject" achieves a sense of reality only through language, the poet with a supreme power of language is a king of the real. Language being, as Saussure would have it, a "concrete entity," it has it all over the subject, that almost fictional creation that only language can harness. Granted Rorty is right—only for this literary moment, of course, for tomorrow that may be another subject or, like the author, now "dead," no subject at all—then the supreme subject is the poet himself, he who wields that instrument that alone engages with the real. Still, even that self, that subject, wobbles along with his unconscious wherever that leads him. When he holds the less fictional power, that concrete power that language itself controls, he is at least less dubious than the anonymous, less skilled, the inept user of language, the tool without which humans stagger and fall. Those without the power of language become not only inarticulate in an unfathomable universe but cannot communicate their own anomalous place within it.

Among all the poets of his generation today (born 1951), even among his own contemporary Irish poets, Paul Muldoon is the supreme user of language—consequently, an astute decipherer of the real. What a gift to be born in Ireland where language and wit huddle together as if they were mated in those Gaelic bogs. That Joyce and Yeats inhabited that land doesn't hurt either. And with due respect to the Irish, Muldoon's own, it hasn't hurt that the poet has come to America where he now teaches at Princeton University. Consider, for example, how the Irish poet right here in America can hear the echoes of the American language of John Ashbery, who, like Muldoon, can refer in a single stanza to the streets, to the library, to global war and commerce, to folk or rock or punk or Mahler even as he turns to "these lacustrine cities." To both postmodernists, allusion and appropriation (parodic, witty, ironic) are all. Neither are purists, ever. While Ashbery, however, who lived in Paris for a decade, may throw in lines of French here and there Muldoon has the advantage of the more mysterious Irish. Since most American readers, like this writer, know no Irish, the exotic look on the page of the italicized Irish words somehow is marvelously amusing. You know that Muldoon is being naughty or bold or plain funny.

One mustn't labor too seriously, of course, a Muldoon-Ashbery connection (though even Baudelairean voyages take place in both poets' work, as in Ashbery's "The Skaters" and in Muldoon's "Yarrow"). Certainly the older poet is sympathetic to a very different, we mustn't say meaning, but a very different over-all worldly perplexity, a Heisenberg inderterminacy, a writer of Cagean aporia. Though Ashbery is often as funny as Muldoon, he is less the innocent. Muldoon likes to remember his boyhood on the farm and his adolescence. Unlike Ashbery he is not obsessed with the theme of absence: he does not brood over his loss of childhood. Would he ever write as Ashbery does, "Nevertheless these are fundamental absences, struggling to get up and be off themselves." Muldoon delights in his own childhood, in sexual discovery and boyish pranks and adventures—and always in the midst of all these remembrances, as if they were

Paul Muldoon

Paul Muldoon, an Irish poet, was born June 20, 1951, in County Armagh, Northern Ireland. In addition to his own work, he has also edited several books, including *Scrake of Dawn: Poems by Young People From Northern Ireland* (Blackstaff, 1979) and *The Faber Book of Contemporary Irish Poetry* (Faber & Faber, 1986). Muldoon was also responsible for the selections in *The Essential Byron* (of the essential poets collection). Muldoon is the director of the creative writing program at Princeton University and has taught poetry at Oxford University since 1999. Recipient of a Guggenheim fellowship in 1990, he has also won the T. S. Eliot Prize (1994) and the Award in Literature from the American Academy of Arts and Letters (1996). ■

absolutely a part of them, he unselfconsciously alludes to books and characters, mythic and historic, as if they were still alive. As they are in his verse, as in the following stanza of "Yarrow":

> I'd be surprised if this were some kind of time-switch
> taped to the trough, that the click of a zoom
> such nausea (from *navis*, a ship) as I'd not felt since
> the *Pequod*.

"Time-switch" is a clue to the works of Muldoon. The reader is never in one time. He/she reading the poet is as restless to be on the move as Muldoon. The poet is always on a journey, but the journey is not really in time; it is in a simultaneous, concurrent time or no time. There is perhaps in a metonymical sense no time at all for this poet. Sylvia Plath, the Trojan War, the American bomber, the modern artists Schwitters and Arp, Ovid, *Guernica* at MoMa are in the same habitat, the same time span. It is as if there is no stable Paul Muldoon, no definable Ulysses, no stable Joyce, no veritable boyhood friends of the poet. The young woman friend, a cocaine addict, who has to be detoxed, is as much Maud Gonne as herself. The Trojan War, the boxer poet Arthur Cravan who disappeared in 1918 in Mexico after his marriage to Mina Loy, spitfires, Mao, Pearse, Barthes. *The Bell Jar*, they all exist together, for

> As we hunkered there in the projection-booth
> the projector had gone, like totally out of whack:
> the freeze-frame of Maud Gonne from *Mise Eire*
>
> had S —— strike up her all-too-familiar refrain
> 'The women that I picked spoke sweet and low
> and yet they all gave tongue, gave tongue right royally.'

Are all events, all peoples of all times in one time because they have been plugged from a projection booth? Is it all the result of TV, the computer, the Internet, E-mail? (It is not hypertext!) Is this simultaneity, the historical potpourri, the result of an acceptance of Chaos theory where little events are not mere flicks in large events but their very sources? Or is this all a memory jam?

> For I'd not be surprised if this were a video
> camera giving me a nod and a wink
> from the blue corner, if it were hooked up not to an
> > alarm
>
> but the TV that I myself am laid out on a da-
> venport in this 'supremely Joycean object, a nautilus
> of memory jammed next to memory', that I'll shortly reel
>
> with Schwitters and Arp....

Or is it not that we have all fallen together—all of us from history and myth, from the arts, from the poems—into one heap of timelessness, not transcendence but the be-all of existence that is just a poet's dream (or some improbable God's). Or is it just "misrememberings," for

> I should, I guess, help Mina rake
> over these misrememberings for some sign of Ambrose
> > Bierce,
> maybe, if not her own Quetzalcoatliac.

If it is all a "misremembering" it has philosophical or perhaps more accurately magical overtones like Baudelaire's "Le Voyage," or even a confirmation of what Ashbery wrote in *Three Poems*, "the magic world really does exist." It is a world often of hilarious metamorphosis and gives the poet the opportunity of being punster and parodist of sex, art, history, myth, and philosophy.

Are the people in the poet's immediate family and his loved ones the only persons actually fixed in time? "Yarrow," the poem from which I've been especially quoting that appears in *The Annals of Chile* (for which the poet received the T. S. Eliot Prize), introduces, as many of Muldoon's earlier poems do, his mother and father. We begin to know "da" (a farmer of mushrooms) and "ma." It is "ma" whose presence is frequent in the poem "Yarrow." So many of the short poems within the longer poem are elegies to her. I quote the introductory poem of the long sequence of "Yarrow" in which the poet introduces the elegiac tone:

> Little by little it dawned on us that the row
> of kale would shortly be overwhelmed, that even if my da
> were to lose an arm
> or a leg to the fly-wheel
>
> of a combine and be laid out on a tarp
> in a pool of blood and oil
> and my ma were to make one of her increasingly rare
>
> appeals to some higher power, some *Deo*
> this or that, all would be swept away by the stream
> that fanned across the land.

Less foreboding in the same poem is his loving remembrance: "Mother o'mine. Mother o mine. That silver-haired mother / o mine."

In this same volume although there is a lovely short poem about the birth of the poet's daughter, there is another elegy, a remarkable poem called "Incantata," about the death of a young woman artist friend, Mary Earl Powers. Though the world of death runs through this last book, the sonnet to his daughter evokes beginnings, but hard beginnings because "though she's been in training all spring and summer / and swathed herself in fat / Saran- / Wrap like an old-time Channel swimmer / she's now got cold feet / and turned in on herself, the phantom 'a' in Cesarian."

There's a lot of intimacy here of all kinds. Even a timeless construct doesn't annihilate love for Muldoon. It's like reading about kin when Muldoon informs us

> That was the year my ma gave me a copy of Eleanor Knott's
> *Irish Classical Poetry* and I first got my tongue
> around *An Craoibbin Aoibbhiin* (Douglas Hyde).

The autobiographical elements exist side by side with the whole world of history, its art and literature. In the same poem with its haunting echo of "Mother o mine. Mother o'mine" the poet recalls a Keatsian and Shakespearean lament. Again scrambling even literary time, he writes: "…Dost thou know Dover? / the foul fiend haunts poor Tom in the voice of a nightingale."

In Muldoon's jumble of time, there is something of Gertrude Stein's irksomely teasing, quite wonderful essay *Composition as Explanation* that she delivered as a lecture at Cambridge and Oxford. In that essay she explains what she means by a "continuous present" which, in a way, antedates Muldoon's historical stew. She wrote:

> Everything is the same except composition and as the
> composition is different and always going to be
> different everything is not the same. So then I as
> a contemporary creating the composition in the beginning
> was groping toward a continuous present, a using
> everything a beginning again and again and then
> everything being alike then everthing very simply
> everything was naturally simply different and so I
> as a contemporary was creating everything being alike
> was creating everything naturally being naturally simply
> different, everything being alike.

But perhaps this analysis of a "continuous present" is much too rational for a much more hallucinatory Muldoon! But clearly Muldoon has Stein in mind. At one point he has fun with a very likely imagined anecdote involving Stein and Alice B. Toklas in his poem "The More a Man Has the More a Man Wants" in his book *Quoof*:

> Her *grand'mere* was once asked to tea
> by Gertrude Stein,
> and her *grand'mere* and Gertrude
> And Alice B., *chère* Alice B.
> with her hook-nose,
> the three of them sat in the nude
> round the petits fours
> and repeated *Eros is Eros is Eros*
> If he had to do it all over again
> he would still be taken in
> by her Alice B. Toklas
> Nameless Cookies
> and those new words she had him learn:
> hash, hashish, *lo perfido assassin*.

Muldoon, as a postmodern, frequently invokes narrative. It's as if he plots his poems like a novelist, yet he leaves out more than he puts in. There is a certain abruptness, a fragmentary, even Frostian element in his storytelling—something elliptical in the stories he tells. In his 1980 book *Why Brownlee Left*, for example, the title poem is tantalizingly like a medallion. Brownlee's departure remains forever in limbo, and his horses evoke everything in his life and nothing. Muldoon writes:

> By noon Brownlee was famous;
> They had found all abandoned, with
> The last rig unbroken, his pair of black
> Horses, like man and wife,
> Shifting their weight from foot to
> Foot, and gazing into the future.

The volume contains the long poem *Immram*, of intricately patterned 10-line stanzas, that is a story as much derived from ancient ancestral legend as of a contemporary West Coast world of dealers and drug pushers. The slang, the puns, the parodies, and the invention of the strange wanderings of Muldoon's father, who the poet is told in "Foster's pool-hall," "Your old man was an ass-hole. / That makes an ass-hole out of you." As for the mother, who "had just been fed by force, / A pint of lukewarm water through a rubber hose," the poet casually explains

> I hadn't seen her in six months or a year,
> Not since my father had disappeared.
> Now she'd taken an overdose
> Of alcohol and barbiturates.
> And this I learned was her third.
> I was told then by a male nurse
> That if I came back at the end of the week
> She might be able to bring herself to speak.

Even in this poem of mules and drugs we meet Caulfield, Mr. and Mrs. Alfred Tennyson, a Sears Roebuck catalogue, Salami on rye along with (naturally for the punster) Salome, F. Scott Fitzgerald, Baskin-Robbins (in particular their banana-nut ice cream!), and the reminder that "how over every Caliban / There's Ariel, and behind him, Prospero." Oh well, the whole world for this surreal, sophisticated, realistic, hermetic, magical poet is more than an oyster. It may be rather for "any other pilgrim" on Main Street "Foster's pool-room."

"Any other pilgrim" on Main Street certainly was Gallogly in the poem mentioned above, "The More a Man Has the More a Man Wants." Gallogly, a kind of American free floater (who is also known as English, and who allows Muldoon an opportunity for a satire on the Troubles), who steals, etc., crosses the country, is on the road, who uses either street language or makes references to the street or to ordinary American life—even of course at the same time, since it is Muldoon who is telling the story, makes literary and historical allusions—is suddenly in Ireland among the Irish working class, orating

> "I'll warrant them's the very pair
> o'boys I seen abroad
> in McFarland's bottom, though where
> in under God —
> *for thou art so possessed with murd'rous hate —*
> where they come from God only knows.
> 'They were mad for a bite o'mate
> I s'pose.'

Muldoon in this poem ignores no Americana, even our today's still violent frontier society (and our notorious use of Valium):

She was standing at the picture window
with a glass of water
and a Valium
when she caught your man
in the reflection of her face.
He came
shaping past the milking parlour
as if he owned the place.
Such is the integrity
of their quarrel
that she immediately took down
the legally held shotgun
and let him have both barrels.
She had wanted only to clear the air.

Are these lines by an Irishman or an American? Of course at the moment both, but it is astonishing how the essentially Irish poet understands the lure of violence for Americans. The art critic Adam Gopnik of *The New Yorker* in a May 8, 1995, issue of the magazine argued that the Oklahoma City bombing was not an American anomaly but the result of a long tradition of "killing" as "a kind of symbolic speech, a form of show business, engaged in for its publicity value." Gopnik also gave a lecture at the New York Public Library called in Poe's famous phrase, "The Imp of the Perverse," in which he showed how the "romantic rhetoric" of violence is intrinsic to the American "heartland," to the extent that it has been widely portrayed in its art—as much by Edgar Allan Poe as by the painter Benjamin West. And here is Muldoon with a parodic succinctness in verse saying very much the same thing.

Madoc: a Mystery (1991) is also concerned with violence, though with a violence that is more overtly political. It plays with the actual plan in 1794 of the poets Robert Southey and Samuel Taylor Coleridge for an emigration to America to establish a utopian community on the banks of the Susquehanna. This pantisocracy was never established, but Muldoon assumes that the poets had actually crossed the Atlantic and had set up their ideal society in the woods of northern Pennsylvania. It is the poem *Madoc* that tells us through a very unreliable narrator, whose knowledge of Western thought is very murky indeed, what would have happened had the Romantic poets' plan actually worked out.

The narrator's view of the world is awry. Everything is juxtaposed in a manner that surprises him. To him the world is lovely. It is rather a cocky and mad world, but as Muldoon's syllables as he relates this world dance together, the madness is all joy, a cacophonous lilting joy. As in the later poem *Annals of Chile* so in the poem "Cauliflowers," for example, in this volume, past, present, Belfast, Oregon, Magritte, his father, his uncle Patrick Regan are happily together—even if they are "all gone out of the world of light." Life and death are all one, all very natural. To remember is to be in the present—therefore, the faculty of "misremembering" is the human faculty that makes out of memory not a reservoir of tragedy but a resource for a collagist's deft, frequently comic manipulations. As the poet plays with the word "pipe"—even with the famous "Ce n'est pas un pipe" of Magritte (which he does not quote but implies as if the world of his uncle Patrick is as familiar with the Magritte painting as a sophisticated Dubliner) he is with equanimity remembering the slightly ridiculous vegetables that "in an unmarked pit...were harvested by their own light."

In *Madoc* as elsewhere Muldoon's lyricism is a rare pleasure, but there is always a kind of tension in the lines that may be related in *Madoc* to the tension he is suggesting between idealism and violence. The poet's wit here has a kind of gayety as if, perhaps to use an inappropriate metaphor, the sun has lightened each word that has been struggling to darken its neighbor. This interfering sun, however, leaping with syllabic rays turns all to light, but a light that like the sun doesn't last long. Whatever is happening with the syllables, however, is the result of Muldoon's carefully disciplined word witchery. That is his other world of magic, a metrical and verbal one. It is really as if the very words create myth and ritual. In the volume *Quoof*, for example (*Quoof*, by the way, the poet said recently at a reading, he himself was surprised to learn from his family meant nothing at all, a word he himself had made up!), there is a poem called "Yggdrasill." The title refers to a Scandinavian myth, and within the poem words not necessarily Irish, such as "cairn" and "tonsure" occur, and suddenly the poet writes: "someone opened a can of apricots." So closely does the ordinary, the can of apricots, exist side by side with the mythical that the mythical simply becomes the ordinary. The Muldoon juxtapositions make the mythic completely quotidian.

In one of his earliest poems in *New Weather* (published in 1973 when the poet was 21), titled "Wind and Tree," nature itself, magical as it is, becomes ordinary because that is how the world is since we are its very center: "In the way that most of the wind / Happens where there are trees, / Most of the world is centered / about ourselves." But despite its optimistic title, *New Weather*, the poet, as usual—and more so in these early poems—is cynical: "Yet by my broken bones," he writes, "I tell new weather." But the verbal play is so quirky anyway, so surreal, that because nothing can astonish the poet or us reading him we are never in a Larkinesque gloom.

In this same early volume in the poem "The Waking Father," death itself is so ordinary, so much part of a world where all things exist at once, like words, strange or not, the poet writes of "my father (who had) stood out in the shallows,"

...I wonder now if he is dead or sleeping.
For if he is dead I would have his grave
Secret and safe;
I would turn the river out of its course
Lay him in its bed, bring it round again.

No one would question
That he had treasures or his being a king,
Telling now of the real fish farther down.

Ah, the "real fish farther down"—nature cohabits with the imagined.

Muldoon is the author of ten collections of poetry. Among those not yet mentioned are *Mules*, *Meeting the British*, and *Selected Poems (1968–1986)*. Interestingly enough, his residence in the United States led him to write a libretto for an opera of the very American Frank Lloyd Wright called *Shining Brow*. But the Irish are always, fortunately, Irish—Muldoon has edited the *Faber Book of Contemporary Irish Poetry* and still publishes in Ireland.

Though some critics have said that Irish politics are not Muldoon's concern, that he is apolitical, I find that a misreading of his poems. Muldoon lives very much in this world, and it is a broad world, despite his being the director of the creative writing program at Princeton University. He is hardly "academic," not at all elitist, immersing himself, as I have indicated, not only in "high" but "low" art as well. Mark Ford, the English critic, puts it very well when he writes that Muldoon's poetry

has always reflected political events in the most
delicate of styles, avoiding overt judgments,
sentimental ideals, commitments or solutions,
instead teasing out angles of irony and embodying

states of impasse—'that eternal interim', as he
calls it in 'Lull'—with a sophistication that must
be its own reward.

All Muldoon's poems are steeped in the real contemporary Western world. His feeling for Ireland comes through from his first published poems. His inventions, his use of Irish myth, Irish
heroes, its farms (that lovely poem in *Quoof* called "Gathering Mushrooms"—"we have taken our
pitchforks to the wind"), its people whose language is never ignored reveal political histories in
themselves. The poems are spare and evocative, never dogmatic, never parading any special ideology but always humane and caring, always demonstrating a subtle historical awareness, and
that awareness includes, as I have indicated, an understanding of how violence and idealism are
frequently joint partners. Is the title of the last volume *The Annals of Chile* supposed to suggest
some kind of parallel between Ireland (there is an allusion to an O'Higgins in the poem) and the
political horrors Chile endured with the murder (or possible suicide) of Allende when the army
coup overthrew his socialist regime in 1973? There is a hint of that event. The poet writes:

'For every Neruda,' mused the bloody-nosed Countess Irina,
'must have his, like, Allende':
with that she handed back to Prince Peter the scarab

for which he'd paid a thousand guilders
and went back to cutting the line of coke with the line
of dalk, from the Anglo-Saxon *dalc* or *dolc*, a brooch
or torc.

The poet Neruda, whose death in 1973 followed soon after, seems to be evoked as a symbol for
the necessary though dangerous, precarious consequences of political involvement. It is the
drug addict young woman—S—with a muse's ability to prophesize, who warns:

'Take Neruda...a poet who dirtied his hands
like a *bona fide* minstrel boy
gone to the wars in Tacna-Arica:

if he's not to refine
himself out of existence, if he's not to end up on
methadone,
the poet who wants to last

must immerse himself in Tacna-Arica and Talca';
the larva, meanwhile of *Pieris*
brassicae was working through kale and cauliflower *et*
al.

The political upheavals in Latin America are thus introduced almost matter-of-factly in an
atmosphere of drugs and drug-dealing. But the poem "Brazil," from which the volume's title is
taken, is romantic, even nostalgically, boyishly fanciful. In this elegy for a mother who had died
of cancer, the poet writes in the opening lines remembering the mother:

When my mother snapped open her flimsy parasol
it was Brazil: if not Brazil,

then Uruguay.
One nipple darkening her smock.

My shame-faced *Tantum Ergo*

■ **BOOKS BY PAUL MULDOON**

Knowing My Place. Ulsterman, 1971.

New Weather. London: Faber & Faber, 1973.

Spirit of Dawn. Ulsterman, 1975.

Mules. London: Faber & Faber, 1977.

Names and Addresses. Ulsterman, 1978.

Why Brownlee Left. London & Boston: Faber & Faber, 1980.

Immram (illustrations by Robert Ballagh). Dublin: Gallery Press, 1980.

Out of Siberia. Deerfield, MA: Deerfield Press, 1982.

Quoof. London: Faber & Faber, 1983. Chapel Hill: University of North Carolina Press, 1984.

The Wishbone. Dublin: Gallery Press, 1984.

Mules, and Early Poems. Winston-Salem, NC: Wake Forest University Press, 1985.

Selected Poems, 1968–1986. London & Boston: Faber & Faber, 1986.

Meeting the British. London & Boston: Faber & Faber, 1987.

Madoc: A Mystery. London & Boston: Faber & Faber, 1990.

The Prince of the Quotidian. Loughcrew, Ireland: Gallery Press, 1994.

The Annals of Chile. London: Faber & Faber, 1994.

Six Honest Serving Men. Oldcastle, Ireland: Gallery Press, 1995. Chester Springs, PA: Dufour Editions, 1995.

The Last Thesaurus. London: Faber & Faber, 1996.

New Selected Poems, 1968–1994. London & Boston: Faber & Faber, 1996.

Hay. New York: Farrar, Straus & Giroux, 1998.

Bandanna. New York: Faber & Faber, 1999.

The Birds. Loughcrew, Newcastle: Gallery Press, 1999.

Poems 1968–1998. New York: HarperCollins, 2000.

---

struggling through thurified smoke.

Perhaps there is a connection here with the earlier poem "Immram" in which the poet imagines his father settling in Brazil. There is so much in the poetry of Muldoon that displaces the real with a fantasy world, and yet whether an actual or made-up world the details are so vivid that a reader accepts each world—makes a leap or stays put.

It's hard to know where the poet will go as his residence in the States lengthens. It hardly seems likely that his poems will lose their manic, marvelously wild quality. Surely there still will be verbal pyrotechnics, impossible to understand passages, but perhaps there will be as in the long poem "Yarrow" in the last volume a more open (though still mysterious, and difficult) structure. There's no doubt that a reader now frequently gets lost as episode piles upon episode without apparent meaningful linkage. Puzzles abound and are not solved. And that is of course part of the delight. Maybe, however, in new volumes there will be less frustration, less bafflement over Irish words (who has an Irish dictionary anyway?) but it's hardly likely there'll be less pleasure. What will the mood of the poet be, he who is so attuned to a historical moment, even as he delights in a tumultuous historical and mythical potpourri? What will the continuing violence in America and in the world do to a poet whose personal losses and awareness of an impossible idealism already have made him turn memory into the only fixity and the world's history and art mere playthings of the mind? Even memory, however, "slips,"

> there's something about the quail's 'Wet-my-foot',
> and the sink full of hart's-tongue, borage and common
> > kedlock

> that I've either forgotten or disavowed;
> it has to do with a trireme, laden with ravensara,
> that was lost with all hands between Ireland and
> > Montevideo.

"Montevideo?" Oh, Montevideo. "Little did I know…. "

Harriet Zinnes
February, 1996

UPDATE

Since this essay appeared, Muldoon has published three per books, p.107books of poetry, *New Selected Poems: 1968–1994* (1996), *Hay* (1998), and *Poems 1968-1998* (2000). In that time, he also has written lyrics for a song cycle, a libretto, and poetic text for a book of photographs; edited two other books; and won an Award in Literature from the American Academy of Arts and Letters.

A leading Irish poet, Muldoon is considered an original. His "short lyrics, modified sonnets and ballads, and dramatic monologues touch on themes of love, maturation, and self-discovery, as well as Irish culture and history," according to *Contemporary Authors*. In a review of *Hay*, *The New Republic* stated, "at a time when poetry has all but forgotten the possibilities of adventurous form . . ., Muldoon's ability to construct his poems is rare, and admirable."

The Figure in the Linoleum: The Fictions of Alice Munro

Of the Canadian writers of the present day who have established reputations for themselves beyond the borders of Canada as well as within it, Alice Munro is practically alone in having done so almost entirely on the basis of the short stories she has published, rather than—as is more customary in suiting the tastes of the time—by means of the conventional novel. Indeed, her vision of the novel form as such seems to lean towards the sequence of separately-titled and interrelated chapters rather than the lengthy and more ambitious pursuit of some larger and more recognizably "novelistic" objective. Though it won the Governor General's Award when it was first issued in Canada, *Dance of the Happy Shades* (1968), her first collection, did not appear in the United States until her first American publisher, McGraw-Hill, had a volume to go with it that could be designated as a "novel"—*Lives of Girls and Women* (1971). A later volume, *The Beggar Maid,* was published in Canada in 1978 under the title *Who Do You Think You Are?*, but issued a year later in the U.S. as *The Beggar Maid,* apparently because the publisher (Alfred A. Knopf this time, and thereafter) did not think the American audience would understand the colloquialism on which the Canadian title was based. Knopf was wrong, of course, but though its own choice of title implies a dimension not necessarily present in the collection as a whole, the important point to remember is that Munro characteristically revises her work even after it has seen magazine publication, and often only then begins to shape each element of the eventual mosaic into a new and larger conception.

This contemporary mistress of the short-story form was born in 1931 in Wingham, Ontario, and attended the University of Western Ontario in London, to the south. Some fourteen years of magazine publication went into the writing of *Dance of the Happy Shades,* but Munro had been writing stories long before that; and many of her stories are set in one or another fictional counterpart of Wingham, often a town called Jubilee. Indeed, her celebrated *Lives of Girls and Women* begins with a disclaimer—"My family, neighbors and friends did not serve as models"—that has unusual pertinence in the case of Munro's fiction, so accurately does she capture the speech and the patterns of living of her native region and town. Not all her former fellow townspeople approve of the picture of Wingham that emerges from this talented daughter of a family which was hardly one of Wingham's "best."

Yet the economic hardship of Alice Munro's childhood was hardly unusual in Wingham, which is a town in the northern part of southwestern Ontario, the portion of the province which becomes a kind of peninsula pointing, however tentatively, at the State of Michigan. Wingham is largely a farming community set in the rolling hills out of which the Maitland River emerges and broadens on its way to Lake Huron. Wingham and all of Huron County, moreover, are part of an area which in winter is subject to the locally notorious "snow line" that results from winds blowing eastward off the lake and can, with its sudden and unpredictable "whiteouts" and drifting, quite isolate a community like Wingham from the more populous

Alice Munro
Alice Munro was born on July 10, 1931, in Wingham, Ontario, Canada. She attended the University of Western Ontario from 1949 to 1951. Among her honors and awards, she has received the Governor General's Literary Award in 1969, 1978, 1979, and 1987. She also received the Canadian Bookseller's Award in 1972 for *Lives of Girls and Women*. She has also won the Marian Engel Award (1986); her second Canada-Australia Literary Prize (1994); the Lannan Literary Award, W. H. Smith Award, and Canadian Booksellers' Award (all 1995); a finalist designation for the *Los Angeles Times Book Review* Award (1995); a National Book Critics Circle Award for Fiction (1998) for *The Love of a Good Woman*; and a nomination in the fiction category (2001) for *Hateship, Friendship, Courtship, Loveship, Marriage: Stories*. In 2001 she was given the Rea Award for lifetime achievement, for her significant contributions to the short-story genre.

She has three children by her first marriage and is married to Gerald Fremlin. She currently resides in Clinton, Ontario. ■

parts of the province to the south and east. Isolation, and the attempt to surmount it by breaking through to another human being, is not surprisingly a major theme of Alice Munro's fiction.

Moreover, the relative hardness of much of the life in Munro's remembered Wingham is aggravated in its effects upon the individual personality by that sort of narrowness which may be typical of small towns everywhere, but which in that part of Ontario may seem especially puritanical—almost as if the true heritage of the Calvinist rigors of old New England were to be found there, in Ontario, as much as in the American South. Small wonder, then, that Munro, in listing her formative reading for Geoff Hancock for an interview in *Canadian Fiction Magazine*, named four American women writers from the South—Katherine Anne Porter, Eudora Welty, Flannery O'Connor, and Carson McCullers—before naming any men, and then named three more southerners!—William Faulkner, Peter Taylor, and Reynolds Price. (Elsewhere, she speaks as well of the influence of James Agee, yet another southerner.) This recasting of the American South in the form of a parallel, but snowbound, South of Canada is a process which must be understood if Munro's fiction is to be seen in its broader and more international context, just as it probably partially explains how readily her large American readership has taken to her carefully expanded list of works—many of them first appearing with some regularity in the pages of *The New Yorker*.

None of the above is meant to diminish Munro's stature as something of a Canadian original, any more than it is intended to portray her as merely a modern representative of the local-color tradition, a strain of writing holding on rather more tenaciously in Canada than it has in the U.S., since allusion to distinctly local names and myths has been until quite lately, if not still, a guaranteed means of affirming and participating in the buttressing of a distinctly Canadian identity. Munro's Canadianness requires no artificial emphasis, no chauvinistic italicizing; her sense and knowledge of her native region is so authentic and undeniable that it becomes, like Faulkner's famous "little postage-stamp of native soil," the key to her international recognition—accompanying the writer, as it were, even in her fictional forays to such very different locales as Victoria, B.C., and Toronto.

To narrow the focus of this assertion to matters strictly literary, it can be said that even in her very first collection Alice Munro is for the most part recognizably her own person as a writer. Though some of the pieces in *Dance of the Happy Shades* now seem to her to be closer in quality to some of her earliest attempts at fiction, she only occasionally displays in these the sort of dictional bravado which, in traditional local-color writing, so often serves to demonstrate the superiority of the writer to his or her materials. Though it would only be natural for someone of Munro's background to want to show how her education has distanced her from her origins, words draw attention to themselves as words in the earlier Monro not simply out of the author's intoxication with language for its own sake so much as to fix with great precision the nuances of her own observations. "The Shining Houses," a story about the changeover from an older style of living to that of a modern subdivision, is for Munro perhaps overexplained; and yet it yields such a lovely remark as, "There is nothing you can do at present but put your hands in your pockets and keep a disaffected heart." Flannery O'Connor's influence is especially strong in "A Trip to the Coast," in which a traveling salesman literally hypnotizes a grandmother to death, and "Thanks for the Ride," in which two boys pick up a couple of girls in a small town for an evening's fun and one of them gets rather more than he bargained for (here, a widow's casual telling of her husband's decapitation at the mill and the presence of a demented grandmother remind us not merely of O'Connor but of Faulkner's grotesques—as well as the hard-edged dialogue of a book like *Sanctuary*). But these are exceptions, and even here the stories glitter with little jewels of observed detail and insight.

Munro struggles with the matter of achieving a balance of included detail, she says; it is too easy to let a story ride on the strength of its surface verisimilitude. Too much detail and nothing stands out. "Sunday Afternoon" is a solid telling of a day in the life of a maid who works for a family so removed from reality by wealth that one daughter can ask the maid, "Do you think I ought to start to neck this summer?", while when the maid yields to a family cousin's interest in her and looks forward to further contacts with this relative of her employers, she comes to anticipate "a tender spot, a new and still mysterious humiliation." In such a story, Munro reveals the abiding importance of social class—and what as a result is "done"—in small-town Canada. "The Peace of Utrecht" insightfully examines the struggles of two generations of sisters to escape the strictures of life in their small community. "I had forgotten certain restrictions of life in Jubilee," the narrator muses, "…and also what strong, respectable, never overtly sexual friendships can flourish within these restrictions and be fed by them, so that in the end such relationships may consume half a life." This finely realized piece is also a testimony to Alice Munro's sense of artistic balance.

Munro is a feminist writer perhaps only, or primarily, in the sense that she is a writer who happens to be a woman. Her observations about the way in which women are put upon in the world she writes about, or the world she inhabits, are not really different in nature from the ones she makes about the lot of the poor, or of the lower classes generally. Rigidified expectations are just as likely to involve money as gender, and her story "Boys and Girls" (also from the first collection) is perhaps as close as Munro comes to raising a general complaint about women's lot. The story is about a fox farm where horses are killed for food. When the girl who later, as a grown woman, tells the story sets free one horse in a futile attempt to save its life, her father answers a complaint against her with this remark:

"Never mind," my father said. He spoke with resignation, even good humour, the words which absolved and dismissed me for good. "She's only a girl," he said.

The narrator reflects, as the story ends, "I didn't protest that, even in my heart. Maybe it was true." Of this story Munro has written elsewhere that the "denial of action" as a real possibility to the female "gives her a kind of freedom the young male in most societies must give up...It is permissible to have fine feelings, impractical sympathies, if you are a girl, because what you do or say does not finally count..." Yet this business of roles constricts the males as well; so that what emerges from any examination of Munro's vision is not only, once again, the recognition of her sense of *balance*, but also the degree to which that balance is implicit within her narratives, so that further authorial commentary after the fact—however lucid—is not truly necessary.

That balance is achieved as a result of considerable effort, however. Munro's temptation to go on revising her materials even after publication has its origins in her approach to fiction itself. She starts with character, or a glimpse of a personage not yet fully realized as "character"; and since she disbelieves in the importance of "event" *per se,* the development of her story line is liable to consist less of a succession of happenings than an extenuating of character as colored by the prism of mood. As she told Geoff Hancock, the thing that makes a story interesting for her is "The thing that I don't know and that I will discover as I go along." Rather than beginning with a clear idea of where she is going, Munro enters a "limbo," a "kind of shady area" where she will "look for the story" rather than "think very clearly about it." If her creative state is not precisely a "total fog," nevertheless "I'm just always on a search that is touch and go." "I like looking at people's lives over a number of years, without continuity. Like catching them in snap-shots. And I like the way people relate, or don't relate, to the people they were earlier," she continues. "This is the sense of life that interests me a lot." This disconnectedness, or the awareness of it, is echoed by the narrator of another of the stories from her first collection, "An Ounce of Cure," when she reflects on "the development of events on that Saturday night" when she got drunk for the first time and decides that she "had had a glimpse of the shameless, marvellous, shattering absurdity with which the plots of life, though not of fiction, are improvised. I could not take my eyes off it." Of course, it is *other* people's fictions that Munro's narrator refers to here; to her readers, the remarkable thing to note in these instances is the ways in which Munro's conceptions of life—as the writer who is duty-bound to record or invent it—are congruent with her notions of the difficulties of the task of the writer herself wrestling "at secondhand" with those selfsame materials.

In *Lives of Girls and Women* (1971), the narrating woman recalls the childhood experience of finding a dead cow and wondering about it: "Why should the white spots be shaped just the way they were, and never again, not on any cow or creature, shaped in exactly the same way?" It is yet another metaphor for the character-as-artist in Munro's work, paying attention to shapes "as if the shape itself were a revelation beyond words, and I would be able to make sense of it, if I tried hard enough, and had time." *Lives of Girls and Women* is itself something of a puzzling shape, for although—as already mentioned—its publisher apparently felt obligated to market it as a "novel," the reader of Munro's other fictions will have no difficulty thinking of these separately titled chapters (seven, plus an "Epilogue") as bound together primarily by their sharing of the same female narrator, who recollects seven key events in her maturation from childhood to adulthood. In the end, we see the narrator poised to leave the town of Jubilee, those narratives now constituting a freight of authorial responsibility she will have to become a writer to rid herself of: to see at last the shapes implied by the patterns of color on the hide of that cow. Deprive the whole book of that consistent speaking voice, however, and *Lives of Girls and Women* can be seen to break into its relatively independent constituent elements, a "novel" in the sense that *Winesburg, Ohio* can be called a novel.

Novel or not, *Lives* displays its small share of literary influences—among them surely James Agee, whose dreamlike childhood Knoxville seems echoed in Del Jordan's memories of falling asleep upstairs as her parents played cards below to while away a winter's evening:

> …And upstairs seemed miles above them, dark and full of the noise of the wind. Up there you discovered what you never remembered down in the kitchen—that we were in a house as small and shut up as any boat is on the sea, in the middle of a tide of howling weather. They seemed to be talking, playing cards, a long way away in a tiny spot of light, irrelevantly; yet this thought of them, prosaic as a hiccup, familiar as breath, was what held me, what winked at me from the bottom of the well as I fell asleep.

Or are we in the mind of a sensitive Faulkner character—a Darl Bundren, say? Faulknerian, too, is the story of Uncle Benny, who marries and then loses a woman he knows nothing of, and then gives up the search for her because he cannot fathom the traffic around Toronto; Uncle Benny's world is described as "a troubling distorted reflection" of the narrator's world, and "luck and wickedness were gigantic and unpredictable" there. In the Epilogue, Del Jordan talks about the novel she has been writing about her home town, and about such characters she has created as the retarded younger brother she has inserted into a real family she knew, a young man "happy once a year, when he was allowed to ride round and round on the merry-go-round at the Kinsman's Fair, beatifically smiling." The young man is to have a sister, a free spirit "wayward and light as a leaf" who "bestowed her gifts capriciously on men"; with her *"bittersweet flesh, the color of peeled almonds"* (here the fledgling writer indulges experimentally in a sensual bit of purple prose-writing) she also survives all the men who make use of her ("burned men down quickly and left a taste of death"). "I got this of course from Frankie Hall, that grown idiot who used to live out on the Flats Road," the narrator discloses in a parenthesis; but it is not wholly true, for she—and Munro—got this brother and sister from Faulkner's Compsons, with a little of Temple Drake for seasoning.

And there is, again, Flannery O'Connor. "Age of Faith" is an extremely well-told story of a phase in Del's young life in which she investigates other churches in order to find some certitude about God which she cannot get in her own United Church services, nor from her agnostic mother, an encyclopedia salesperson. In a typically O'Connor-ish ending, Del loses her faith in anything but a God—excluding her italics of epiphany —"real, and really in the world, and alien and unacceptable as death…God amazing, indifferent, beyond faith," only to find that she has managed to pass her previous form of religiosity on to her brother Owen, who as he sinks to his knees in prayer leaves Del wondering, "Do missionaries ever have these times, of astonishment and shame?" Yet Del, at an earlier stage, can sound awfully much like Huckleberry Finn:

> I realized that I did not care a great deal, myself, about Christ dying for our sins. I only wanted God. But if Christ dying for our sins was the avenue to God, I would work on it.

Or in "Baptizing," the final full-length story, which superficially sounds like yet another first-time-drunk narrative: here Munro truly resembles O'Connor in telling of the passsionate romance between a girl of superior intellect and a born-again Baptist boy from the Jericho Valley. Here the refusal of a simulated baptism brings a relationship to an end; yet even here Munro is her own woman, as when she nicely observes of her hometown mentality, "We could not get away from the Jubilee belief that there are great, supernatural dangers attached to boasting, or having high hopes of yourself."

Yet here also Munro is returning to her theme of the stultifying effect local convention has upon concepts of what is acceptable, especially when gender is involved. In "Heirs of the Living Body," two sisters tend to women's work while a reputedly intellectual brother hacks away at a boring account of regional history. (Pretensions to intellectuality are some of the temptations which Del has to deal with—by rejecting scholarship for its own dry sake in favor of a healthy discovery of her own sensuality; mention is even made of a local woman who says "things like 'he told her and I' instead of 'her and me'—a common mistake of people who thought they were being genteel." Indeed, Munro has here zeroed in on a grammatical fault—along with the reason for it—so widespread in Ontario that students report being taught it in their schools.) In the book's title story, the young woman becomes the passive victim of a bachelor's moment of sexual assertiveness just before the man leaves his local sweetheart in the lurch; Del's mother reflects, as if to emphasize the title within the title, "There is a change coming in the lives of girls and women. Yes. But it is up to us to make it come…" But Del considers her mother's advice and decides that it is just more propaganda defining females as "damageable" while men were supposed to encounter experience without fear of shame. Del has decided not to wait for change, but to make it arrive by living the way men do. Most powerful, perhaps, is the story "Changes and Ceremonies," which tells of the abortive romance between a high school teacher, female, who winds up drowned in the Wawanash river, and a certain Mr. Boyce, who steadily refuses the woman teacher's gambits—in the background of the fuss caused by the local production of a school operetta—and is reported at the end to have moved to the city of London, Ontario, "where there were some people like himself." Munro's—or Del's—brief line is a fairly breathtaking ramming-together of the two separate levels of the story, adolescent and adult, in a moment of insight which, once achieved, is simply too late to act upon. In a summation found in Del's "The Photographer" Epilogue, the narrator reflects upon the difficulty of interpreting even those materials close at hand: "People's lives, in Jubilee as elsewhere, were dull, simple, amazing, and unfathomable—deep caves paved with kitchen linoleum." Linoleum, the tapestry of the poor, has been thrown at Munro as a favorite image; yet the image of a young girl bent over and staring, uncomprehendingly, at the pattern on the floor of her experience can hardly be considered irrelevant to the fiction of Alice Munro.

But if Del Jordan is shrewd enough to realize that she cannot escape Jubilee and what it stands for by making a local marriage, like her onetime girlfriend Naomi, she also comes to see that she cannot simply follow her mother's advice by sacrificing part of herself to the goal of an academic career: she knows the need for passion in her life; and she understands that a sterile academic career would be just another way of taking Jubilee with her. Munro's next collection, *Something I've Been Meaning to Tell You* (1974), consists of thirteen stories possessing little if any overall unity; and yet even though these pieces—written during the time Munro was living in Victoria, British Columbia—are set in a variety of places, the themes and approaches are by now familiar ones, however much their literary quality displays Munro's ability as having hit full stride. If the influences of such writers as O'Connor and, perhaps, Welty persist in this collection, they have also long since been subsumed into something wholly Munro's own.

Slickly Weltian, for example, is "How I Met My Husband," wherein the narrator—a maid—waits in vain for a letter from a barnstorming pilot she has fallen for only to decide at last that there were "women just waiting and waiting by mailboxes for one letter or another" and "women busy and not waiting," and so she contrives to marry the mailman. But the new sort of setting is to be found in "Material," in which a woman once involved with a man who has turned out to be a famous literary figure realizes, to her shock, "that what was all scraps and oddments, useless baggage, for me, was ripe and usable, a paying investment, for him." Nicely observed is the special status accorded writers, for "Outrageous writers may bounce from one blessing to another nowadays, bewildered, as permissively reared children are said to be, by excess of approval"; and when these writers appear on the lecture platform, "Girls, and women too, fall in love with such men, they imagine there is power in them." The volume's title story, moreover, itself neatly encapsules whole lifetimes of frustrated desires.

But *Something I've Been Meaning to Tell You* is also about indulgence in desire: about the discovery of secret yearnings in the act of doing something about them. It might be glib to suggest that a more hedonistic West Coast "scene" is responsible for the presence of this strain in Munro's new fiction, but the volume certainly reflects the trendy permissiveness of the 1960s and '70s; the hippie presence is felt here, along with all the jargon of that vanished era. And though Munro is not as singularly attentive to younger or older characters (leaving the middle ground to others) as she seems to think, she does connect both youngsters and oldsters with the erotic in a pair of stories. "Marrakesh" ends with a grandmother's discovery of her own voyeuristic tendencies as, "trembling, her knees weak," she watches her granddaughter and an acquaintance take off their clothes and prepare to make love, "Flaunting themselves in the light as if nothing mattered, guzzling and grabbing now, relishing and plundering each other." In "The Found Boat," a young girl becomes an adult in the instant in which she, skinnydipping on a dare, finds herself facing a naked boy boldly—"quivering from the cold of the water, but also with pride, shame, boldness, and exhilaration":

> Clayton shook his head violently, as if he wanted to bang something out of it, then bent over and took a mouthful of river water. He stood up with his cheeks full and made a tight hole of his mouth and shot the water at her as if it was coming out of a hose, hitting her exactly, first one breast and then the other. Water from his mouth ran down her body…

Within seconds, Eva has learned what a power her own emerging sexuality has given her; and moments later, she learns to subordinate other concerns to this one as she formulates, casually, a defensive lie.

But Munro is Munro here yet, as when she ends "The Spanish Lady" by having its narrator react with puzzlement to the death of a total stranger—"As if we were all wound up a long time ago and were spinning out of control, whirring, making noises, but at a touch could stop, and see each other for the first time, harmless and still." This undeliverable "message" tallies with the bewilderment of the teller of "Winter Wind," who once has "tricked…out and altered…and shaped" such stories as that of her grandmother, but now, "being as careful as I can," decides that "People carried their stories around with them" so that "we get messages another way, that we have connections that cannot be investigated, but have to be relied on." "The Ottawa Valley" ends with the narrator throwing up her hands at the possibility of "making a proper story" out of real events so as to exorcise them, only to admit that she "could go on, and on, applying what skills I have, using what tricks I know, and it would always be the same." Suspecting the validity of meanings read into experience, Munro instead emphasizes the sort of accurate observation of felt life that places the reader in the position of her characters: would-be artists trying to reduce experience to orderly patterns.

That accuracy of observation, as Canadian poet Leonore Langs has reminded us, extends to Munro's faithful reproduction of life in Wingham and elsewhere; not only events such as the bingo games, the Orangemen's Day Parade, the afternoons spent at the cemetery, the falling asleep under bedroom ceilings of pressed tin; but also the local expressions—many of them indicators of social class—which seem derived in great part from Irish usage. This is especially true of *Who Do You Think You Are?* (1978), published in the U.S. as *The Beggar Maid: Stories of Flo and Rose*, in which Munro's artistry seems absolute. As John Gardner confessed, this book may be either a collection of short stories or "a new kind of novel"—like Munro's second volume— but the distinction does not seem finally to be of importance at all. These ten stories do amount to a kind of lengthier fiction, and one of the two key characters, Rose, does go on to become the book's final focus even as Flo recedes from view, and yet the single pieces which constitute *Who Do You Think You Are?* all had initial and separate magazine publication or else seem to have a separate integrity of their own. But by switching from a first-person voice to an omniscient third-, Munro surprisingly increases not only the objectivity but also the immediacy of her work. Just as Munro came back from British Columbia to Clinton, just down the road from Wingham, so too does her fiction move from "Jubilee" to "Hanratty" as well, her character Rose ventures out into the world from Hanratty as Munro did (characters in Munro's work can be fairly accurately assessed in terms of the cities they move to: Windsor, London, Toronto), leaves Toronto for B.C., and then returns to check on the condition of her roots. The book combines the themes of the earlier volumes in a concentrated and more concise fashion (this is far more the "novel" than *Lives of Girls and Women*), in the process exploring social mores and the politics of crumbling relationships much as John Updike was doing in the literature of the United States.

The Beggar Maid—the American edition's title comes from an identification of Rose with the subject of a Burne-Jones painting made by a young man she would shortly marry—is so densely textured that it defies excerpting; and indeed, the reader deserves to be teased into investigating its superb qualities for him/herself. But here, for instance, is a section in which Rose encounters what we would now refer to as the "lifestyle" of the family of the man she is to marry. It's Vancouver Island; the American referent would be the film *Five Easy Pieces*:

> …Size was noticeable everywhere and particularly thickness. Thickness of towels and rugs and handles of knives and forks, and silences. There was a terrible amount of luxury and unease. After a day or so there Rose became so discouraged that her wrists and ankles felt weak. Picking up her knife and fork was a chore; cutting and chewing the perfect roast was almost beyond her; she got short of breath climbing the stairs. She had never known before how some places could choke you off, choke off your very life…

This sort of Oatesian study of enervation has seldom, if ever, been handled better; and in general it can be observed that in its quickening of reader nerve-ends *The Beggar Maid* is something of an Alice Munro unqualified triumph.

In 1983 Munro published her most recent collection of stories, *The Moons of Jupiter*, and on the evidence of it her virtuosity continues unabated. That virtuosity can express itself fairly traditionally and straightforwardly, as in "The Turkey Season," wherein Munro connects the gutsy speech and lifestyles of the women who work as turkey-gutters at a turkey farm with the work they do for a living. This Steinbeckian performance follows on one that seems to echo Agee, "Connection," in which a woman's growing impatience with her husband's condescending attitude towards the habits and diction of her native region finally results in her throwing a plate at him; the piece ends gently with a reverie of recollection ("I lie in bed beside my little sister, listening to the singing in the yard. Life is transformed, by these voices, by these presences, by their high spirits and grand esteem, for themselves and each other.") As the round "Row, Row, Row Your Boat" comes to an end, voice after voice drops away until but two are left:

> Then the one voice alone, one of them singing on, gamely, to the finish. One voice in which there is an unexpected note of entreaty, of warning, as it hangs the five separate words on the air. *Life is*. Wait. *But a*. Now, wait. *Dream*.

It's terribly lovely stuff; but there are also instances in this collection of a growing complexity of structure in Munro's work, the result of the taking on of the challenge of dealing with the way a character's mind will slip back and forth in time, seeking clues to those associations which are the result of, yet do not clearly explain, our uniqueness as human beings.

In "Dulse," for instance, Munro describes the visit of a writer, Lydia, to an island off the New Brunswick coast. Lydia is sorting through the ruins of the relationships of her life, and trying to make sense of them. She meets an elderly gentleman, Mr. Stanley, who is a devoted fan of Willa Cather's life and work (yet another American woman fictionist, by the way; and one especially drawn to things Canadian) and who looks at life as he thinks this admired artist would have. Lydia's attentions focus on the men who work on the island, while Mr. Stanley pursues a local woman to whom Cather is reputed to have given advice at a critical moment in her life. The story comes to final focus on a bag of dulse, the dried seaweed which Maritimers ingest as a kind of candy, which one of the men leaves for Lydia. Lydia offers some to Mr. Stanley, jokingly wondering if Willa Cather had ever eaten dulse:

> "Dulse," said Mr. Stanley thoughtfully. He reached into the bag and pulled out some leaves and looked at them. Lydia knew he was seeing what Willa Cather might have seen. "She would most certainly have known about it. She would have known."
>
> But was she lucky or was she not, and was it all right with that woman? How did she live? That was what Lydia wanted to say. Would Mr. Stanley have known what she was talking about? If she had asked how did Willa Cather live, would he not have replied that she did not have to find a way to live, as other people did, that she was Willa Cather?

Lydia's impatience with the equanimity with which Mr. Stanley assumes that the world can be reduced to an artistic construct as if invented by, and therefore thoroughly understood by, an artist is nothing else but Munro's own and parallel impatience. Doubtless, she would agree with that other Canadian writer W. O. Mitchell when he insists, "Life ain't Art." The narrator of this collection's title story puts it another way when she attends a planetarium show and finds comforting the assurances scientists make about remote worlds they have never visited: "Why did they give out such confident information, only to announce later that it was quite wrong?" For Munro, it is the function of the artist to search for meanings, not to act as though the knowledge of them was implicit in the artist's role.

Alice Munro's heightened degree of surface verisimilitude has distracted some of her readers from the presence of this doubt, this quest, within her work. Content has been considered rather than style and structure, as critic Louis K. MacKendrick has pointed out in his recent and valuable collection of new Munro criticism, *Probable Fictions*—a title itself meant to emphasize the fact that in her stories, it is "fictionality" that delights; "their realities are constructs of rare skill and masterful invention." Such a Nabokovian view of Munro necessarily startles the casual reader who seemingly recognizes this or that "real" element in a Munro story. Yet as Alice Munro herself told Geoff Hancock, "I never write from an idea, a myth or a pattern." The pattern begins to emerge from the process of staring hard at what MacKendrick calls a "facsimile" of life, rather than existing beforehand.

It would have been tempting to end this essay where it began, as if by drawing attention to the ways in which Munro's native region seems to animate her work one could then refer to her as the spokesperson for Canada's South—even if a fifth or more of Canada's population live south of Wingham. That might distract us from Munro's quest for what Henry James liked to call "the figure in the carpet." Of course, in the world from which Munro and her characters spring, it's likelier to be linoleum—and worn linoleum at that—that covers the floor as it draws and perplexes the eye. It is the figure in the linoleum that makes the fictions of Alice Munro as excitingly important as they are.

John Ditsky
June, 1985

■ **BOOKS BY ALICE MUNRO**

Dance of the Happy Shades. Toronto: Macmillan, New York: McGraw-Hill, 1973.

Lives of Girls and Women. Toronto and New York: McGraw-Hill Ryerson, 1971.

Something I've Been Meaning to Tell You. Toronto and New York: McGraw-Hill, 1974, Scarborough, Ontario: New American Library, 1985.

Who Do You Think You Are? Toronto: Macmillan, 1978. Published in the U.S. as *The Beggar Maid: Stories of Flo & Rose.* New York: Knopf, 1979, Markham, Ontario: Penguin Fiction Series, 1982.

The Moons of Jupiter. Toronto: Macmillan, 1983.

The Progress of Love. New York: Knopf, 1986.

Friend of My Youth: Stories. New York: Knopf, 1990.

Open Secrets: Stories. New York: Knopf, 1994.

Selected Stories. New York: Knopf, 1996.

The Love of a Good Woman: Stories. New York: Knopf, 1998.

Queenie: a Story. London: Profile Books in Association with London Review of Books, 1999.

Hateship, Friendship, Courtship, Loveship, Marriage: Stories. New York: Knopf, 2001.

UPDATE

Short-story writer Alice Munro has since published seven books of stories: *The Progress of Love* (1986), *Friend of My Youth: Stories* (1991), *Open Secrets: Stories* (1994), *Selected Stories* (1996), *The Love of a Good Woman: Stories* (1998), *Queenie: a Story* (1999), and *Hateship, Friendship, Courtship, Loveship, Marriage: Stories* (2001). She also has contributed to *Night Light: Stories of Aging* (1986) and *Best American Short Stories* (1989). She also is a frequent contributor to periodicals, such as the *Atlantic, Canadian Forum, Chatelaine, Grand Street, Queen's Quarterly*, and *New Yorker*. Her story "Connection" was filmed by Atlantis Films in association with the CBC in 1986.

Her work is hailed by critics and readers alike, both in her native Canada, where her stories are usually set, and the United States. Her characters often are the farmers and townspeople of southwestern Ontario, and she writes about their "ordinary experiences so that they appear extraordinary, invested with a kind of magic," according to the *Dictionary of Literary Biography*, and she often explores the shadows cast by men over the lives of women. "Few people writing today can bring a character, a mood or a scene to life with such economy," wrote *Publishers Weekly*. "And [Munro] has an exhilarating ability to make the readers see the familiar with fresh insight and compassion." In the *Ontario Review*, Joyce Carol Oates once wrote of the feelings behind Munro's stories, of "the evocation of emotions, ranging from bitter hatred to love, from bewilderment and resentment to awe. . . . In all her work, there is an effortless, almost conversational tone, and we know we are in the presence of an art that works to conceal itself, in order to celebrate its subject."

In a review of her most recent story collection, *Hateship, Friendship, Courtship, Loveship, Marriage: Stories*, the *New York Times Book Review* wrote: "Things may be very bad for the people in Munro's stories, but they do not always get worse. Instead, the stories may see what can be said in favor of life in dire circumstances, not by comforting or defiant formulations but by attending for whatever may come up in the way of a favorable sign."

Against Consolation: Some Novels of Iris Murdoch

■ **I**

I picked up my first Iris Murdoch in a bookshop in South Wales, summer '74, for 30p. It was called *Under the Net*. Next morning I left it under the Gideon along with Gerald Durrell on elephants. Congenial company, thought I, since the Murdoch seemed to be about this German shepherd named Mars, a retired film-idol. Both books were supposed to be veryvery funny. The *Net's* epiphany was certainly funny: the hero (whose name immediately escaped me) was as rapt as Gregor Mendel in the garden when somebody's tabby gave birth to two tabbies and two Siamese. At Aberystwyth I bought up all the minor Hardy.

A twelvemonth later, Towsonbooks special-ordered *Under the Net* for me ($4.01 paper). I have begged, borrowed, and stolen the other fifteen or sixteen novels and read them straight through in a six-week marathon, without knowing any more about the author than the blurbs provide. My knowledge is subsequently extended by Murdoch's book on Sartre, her Leslie Stephen lecture, *The Sovereignty of Good over Other Concepts*, several more of her articles and interviews, and the by now considerable critical literature, including full-length studies to date by A. S. Byatt (1965) and Peter Wolfe (1966). It is difficult for me as a devotee of Wordsworth, Rilke, Stevens, Dickens, James, and both Eliots, to account for my attraction. Murdoch's true Penelope may be Gilbert and Sullivan. Or she may be Mozart. But there's a semblance of a theme here: the solidity and significance of the world external to the self (Wordsworth); the angels Eros and Thanatos (Rilke); living in the world without subscribing to any concept of it (Stevens); contingency, comedy, and horrors (Dickens); moral truth and consequences (James); compassion (Eliot, G.); conscience and culture (Eliot, T.); English Institutions (Gilbert and Sullivan); versatility, wit, and High Seriousness (Mozart).

These are high compeers for a writer who commits every stylistic cliché we learned to avoid in workshop, e.g. omniscience, switching viewpoints in mid-scene, planting obvious props (if there's a swimming pool, somebody's going to drown in it), and sometimes growing symbols *in*organically. She introduces black masses in the bowels of government buildings, imprisoned princesses, Irish patriots, bog suck-ins, airport shoot-outs, and as many varieties of murder, sex, accident, and suicide as the *Daily Mail*. She has been called Gothic, Metaphysical, Naturalistic, and lately by Daiches (*Critical Inquiry*, June '75) "not modern." But none of these portmanteaux contains her. Sometimes outrageous, always sceptical, always observant, hypersensitive to the hide-and-seek of human relationship, cultivated, funny, tolerant, uncommitted to systems, committed to Truth and Virtue insofar as we can know them, and to Freedom as vision rather than choice, Iris Murdoch is an accurate and undespairing projector of our age. She is able to envision a meaningful life without myth, and to retain a kind of free-form belief in values that are "existential" without being, as they are in Sartre, selfish or arbitrary. Suffering is real, the more so because it is not purgatorial ("Who minds suffering if there's no death and

Iris Murdoch

Born on July 15, 1919, in Dublin, Jean Iris Murdoch was educated at Somerville College, Oxford, and received a degree in 1942. She also attended Newman College, Cambridge, and held the Sarah Smithson studentship in philosophy from 1947 to 1948.

From 1942 to 1944 Murdoch served as Assistant Principal with the British Treasury. She then worked with the United Nations Relief and Rehabilitation Administration until 1966. Murdoch was named a fellow of St. Anne's College, Oxford, in 1948 and was also made a university lecturer in philosophy. She was a member of the Formentor Prize Committee.

Murdoch contributed to the *Listener*, the *Yale Review*, the *Chicago Review*, and other magazines. In addition, she won several more important awards and honors: she was named Commander of the Order of the British Empire (1976) and later Dame Commander (1986); she won the Booker Prize (1978) for *The Sea, the Sea*; she was granted an honorary doctorate by Oxford University (1987) and, posthumously, another honorary doctorate by Cam-

bridge University (1993). She was awarded the medal of honor for literature from the National Arts Club (1990). Murdoch died from Alzheimer's disease in 1999. ■

the past can be altered?"). Life is the recognition of the reality and impenetrability of others—primarily people, but also animals, vegetables, and the elements. The universe is not susceptible to reason; we cannot solve it, but we have much to learn from it. The consolations of form—religious, philosophical, social, aesthetic—are many and great. Murdoch is sympathetic to them. She puts sharp words into the mouths of dull clerics. She is acquainted with the perfect release that can come to us in contemplation of the masterworks of art (especially visual art) and nature. But she is against consolation, and on this count Mr. Daiches is wrong about her modernity, although he is correct that she is no less concerned than Jane Austen with class, money, and marriage. Her "form," as I shall presently demonstrate, is most often that of romantic comedy. Nothing new here. No tergiversations of time, space, language, or consciousness. But I can think of nothing more needed in modern art or modern thought than to be fully cognizant of our doubts and difficulties, to rest in them, and still to give pleasure.

■ II

It is clearly impracticable to consider individually the works of so prolific a novelist. Besides, Murdoch is not, so far as I can tell, a developer. Some novels are more complex than others, some are bigger, some are better, but there does not seem to be any major change in technique or preoccupation between *Under the Net* (1954) and *A Word Child* (1975)—indeed both deal with the relation of words to actions. *The Net, The Unicorn, The Bell, The Flight from the Enchanter, A Fairly Honorable Defeat, A Severed Head* have received the most critical attention, possibly because they verge on the moral fable and thus tempt the interpreter. He may have helpful things to say, but he always fails to convince me that Murdoch is in need of his services (or mine). Common readability, as I have already implied, is one of her delights. We hardly need to be told that the medieval bell dredged from the bottom of the lake, with its scenes from the life of Christ—"eyes stared at them out of square faces"—and its motto *Vox ego sum Amoris, Gabriel vocor*, represents the Old Culture; that the plunge of Gabriel back into his watery grave, à la Excalibur, means the impossibility of that particular rebirth or resurrection. The true and the quasi-religious communities of the novel are not derided. The anti-Sartrean Abbess remarks that our duty "is not necessarily to seek the highest regardless of the realities of our spiritual life as in fact it is, but to seek that place, that task, those people, which will make our spiritual life grow and flourish; and in this search we must make use of divine cunning." Divine cunning, for the Abbesss, includes Red Cross life-saving. But the focus of *The Bell* is relationship, not religion; Gabriel is more important as plot-device than as symbol. *The Unicorn* is better approached through fairy tale than it is through Plato or Paul, and it is best approached through Henry James, e.g. this sentence about the somewhat Stretherian hero: "Effingham was of course, as he had hundreds of times since told himself, stripped, prepared, keyed up, attuned, conditioned." If anything, Murdoch disarms philosophy. "The novel," she writes, "is properly an art of image rather than of analysis, and its analysis is, to borrow Gabriel Marcel's terminology, of a mystery rather than of a problem."

My own favorites are what I might call "middle Murdoch," though not in a chronological sense. They are "pure" domestic comedies, perhaps somewhat less striking than the above group. They include *The Nice and the Good, An Unoffical Rose, The Sandcastle*, and my exemplum, *An Accidental Man*.

Ludwig Leferrier, twenty-two, is the budding intellectual son of French-German Protestants who have emigrated to Vermont in disapproval of Hitler. He is in London about to take up a fellowship in Ancient History at Oxford, having torn up his U.S. draft card. As the novel opens, he has just become engaged to Gracie Tisbourne, whom he has met through Austin Gibson Grey, father of his Harvard friend, Garth. Gracie is reluctantly present at the death of her grandmother, long cared for by her maiden aunt, Charlotte. In a surprise and spiteful will, Grandmother leaves Gracie her Chelsea house and fortune.

Austin Gibson Grey, the accidental man, has just lost his job ("recession"). In childhood he has lost the flexibility of his right hand through a fall caused in his imagination (perhaps really, we never know) by his elder brother Matthew, now Sir Matthew, a successful diplomat operating in the Mysterious East. Austin G. G. has also lost his first wife, Garth's mother, in an accidental drowning which he likes to present as a suicide due to her imagined involvement with Matthew. His second wife, Dorina (the spiritual ingenue to Gracie's sexual ingenue), has gone for safe-keeping to her sister and self-constituted guardian, Mavis, described as a Bloomsbury Catholic with a failed life. Gracie's Aunt Charlotte and Mavis Argyll have both in earlier days loved Matthew.

Matthew returns from the Orient, baffled in his desire to join a Buddhist monastery (if only to sweep azalea leaves, or perhaps sweep away the doom visions that becloud the Western mind) by lingering guilt about his brother. He finds Austin G. G. refuged with Mitzi Ricardo, a seedy six-foot blonde whose athletic career has been ruined ten years past by a tennis accident. Mitzi keeps a sort of rooming-house where Ludwig also resides. Matthew picks up with Mavis. He rents Gracie's grandmother's house; Aunt Charlotte rents Austin's apartment. Garth G. G. returns. He has thrown up Harvard philosophy for East End social work. En route he has lost the mss. of a novel, à la Miss Prism. Gracie has separated him from Ludwig; he takes up being kind to the dispossessed Charlotte and the incarcerated Dorina.

A broken engagement, a blackmailing, two attempted suicides (Charlotte and Mitzi), two accidental deaths (a child run over by Austin and Dorina electrocuted in a bathtub), three cocktail parties, four epistolary interludes, and some four hundred pages later, Garth (published) is married to Gracie (pregnant), Charlotte is living in the country with Mitzi and Pyrrhus (a dog), Mavis is rehabilitating Austin, and Ludwig has returned to America and prison accompanied by Matthew.

Minor characters omitted in above précis: Gracie's parents and their circle; Ludwig's parents; Gracie's homosexual brother Patrick; Ludwig's homosexual and/or bibulous Oxford colleagues-to-be; Mavis's char, Mrs. Carberry, and her retarded child; Mr. and Mrs. Monkley, mother and stepfather to the child run over by Austin; a Physician; a Parson; an Owl; a Sung bowl; an automobile named Kierkegaard; a yacht named Annapurna Atom; Chorus. A catalogue worthy of Nanki-Poo.

Such a superficial summary is sufficient to establish the comic pattern, knots dramatically unknotted; true identities revealed; society celebrated in a marriage-feast. Ourselves revealed as ridiculous, relovable, re-employable, reconciled with the past and present—in sum, maneuvering onward very much as before.

Except for the batches of letters (the senior Leferriers and Patrick Tisbourne appear exclusively by post) and the New Yorkerish repartee of the cocktail parties, the story moves along rather like a subway train: we think of the stations (dramatized scenes) and not of the dull connecting stretches like these:

> I'm boring, her, he thought. They were having lunch at the Café Royal. Matthew had no servants at the villa yet. He had thought that food and drink would help. Now they had both eaten and drunk too much in desperation.
>
> Gracie was a pale miniature-looking girl with a small well-formed head and a small eager face. She had glowing powdery flesh, very light blue eyes, and wispy half-long silvery-golden hair.

The writing, in short, is often flat and sometimes inexact (what is "glowing powdery flesh"?). Even so, there are verbal surprises, as when Mitzi pleads, with Charlotte in the same words Charlotte has used to Matthew: "Thank God I've got the dignity of real love to support me, I haven't got anything else." Matthew rejects Charlotte, who weeps because "a certain occupation of dreaming was gone forever." But Charlotte, recognizing her own late dream in Mitzi's plea, finally responds without illusion. Pyrrhus (the Retriever Retrieved for the nth time from the Battersea Dogs' Home) wags at this triumph of Amor.

Dorina, longing for relief just before her lonely death in a hotel room, asks

> Is there any prayer or place of gaze still left which is not mere enchantment? There should be such, even now, even without God, some gesture which would bring automatic world-changing wisdom and peace. *Pliez les genoux, pliez les genoux, c'est impossible de trop pliez les genoux.* Who had said those beautiful words to her and what did they mean? Then suddenly she remembered. It had been her skiing instructor at Davos.

A "fine" writer Murdoch is not, but such devices have at the very least the style of ironic intelligence.

An Accidental Man lacks a big climactic scene such as the collapse of the bridge in *The Bell*. The turning-point is Dorina's death. Ludwig, en route to the Reading Room, has just recognized the runaway in the street and passed her by. Her accident precipitates his decision to return to America; her name has often come up in his arguments with self-centered Gracie, who forbids him to get involved in Austin G. G.'s troubles. Love's desire to isolate (possess, protect, or in some cases punish) is one of the themes of the novels. Dorina is the innocent victim of others' neuroses and conventions, akin to Hannah Crean-Smith (*The Unicorn*) and Catherine Fawley, the failed religious aspirant (*The Bell*). Besides activating Ludwig's conscience, her death releases Austin from his dream-wife and sends him flying to Mavis, released of her dream-child. Matthew, released of Austin, flies to Ludwig; Charlotte, released of Matthew, flies to Mitzi; Gracie, released of Ludwig...etc.

If Dorina, who "attracts poltergeists," is a half-spiritual (Murdoch's world is full of such marginal people, half-intellectuals, half-contemplatives, half-artists), her Prufrockian husband, the titular hero, is spiritually impotent. Asthmatic, hysterical, maimed, he cringes in a psychic prison of which Matthew is the unwilling jailer. Matthew is the power-figure (psychopomp, magus, confessor), the agent of change, in company with Mischa Fox (*The Flight from the Enchanter*), Julius King (*A Fairly Honorable Defeat*), Honor Klein (*A Severed Head*), and Monty Small (*The Sacred and Profane Love Machine*). These figures have suggestive names, foreign origins or connections, sinister secrets, and they burst *ex machina* into the story. Loved and feared like the gods they mimic, they engender the complications which, when finally resolved, leave everyone who is still alive in somewhat closer touch with "reality." Matthew has come home to free Austin from his compulsions, a freeing symbolically accomplished when Humpty-Dumpty Austin smashes Brother's beloved collection of Oriental pots. But his real mission is to Ludwig, the newcomer to the circle. He brings no directives, but he listens to Ludwig's scruples as Gracie will not. When the hero departs, the god goes with him, much to everyone's relief.

Ludwig is a fairly dull boy. But he has a good first-generation Puritan conscience that will allow him neither to fight in (presumably) Vietnam, nor to get on with Aristophanes. The reason that his decision is moving (he is genuinely in love with both Gracie and his work) is that it is really "for nothing"—except what he feels to be honor, and what is honor? etc. There is no Authority to define "the Good," or virtue, or truth, or courage—and yet somehow they will not go away. Garth's novel, *The Lifeblood of the Night*, is inspired by his witnessing a murder on the streets of New York—witnessing and passing by. One is reminded of Camus' Clamence, haunted by the cry to which he did not respond. A recurrent memory of Matthew's is a scene in Red Square in which an innocent stranger greets a group of protesters and is hauled off with them by the police. Ludwig has passed the desperate Dorina by in the street. Now he will go home to *bear* witness, to please his pro-American parents, and probably to wreck his career. Nobody waves the Stars and Stripes. We are free to think Ludwig a cad or a fool, since we have not the consolation of good faith.

Here and elsewhere (in *The Red and the Green*, in the Lusiewicz brothers and Nina the refugee dressmaker of *Flight*) the larger course of history impinges, as in Virginia Woolf, on the tiny events of particular destinies. The everyday world is also solidly present. Murdoch's people work, eat, dream, take the 88 bus, know the white-faced coots in the park, grow roses, get rained on, catch colds. They are acquainted with Plato, Tintoretto, grief, adultery, the welfare state, and the occult. They try, with uneven success, to be good parents and faithful friends. They are less interested in money than in love; more often than not they make both quite well. Peter Wolfe, speaking of the novelistic continuum linking Austen, Eliot, and Murdoch, says accurately that all three sympathize with their characters without condescension or sentimentality. But he adds, "each, in spite of a compassionate awareness of humanity, is perhaps less successful in the creation of male characters than in other areas of fictional art." As I find Murdoch *especially* good at men, I can only account for this difference of opinion by supposing that male readers are not even yet used to viewing themselves from the female perspective. Men of all shapes and sizes contribute to *my* sense, at least, of the authenticity of Murdoch's world.

No less authentic to our experience is her introduction of horrid surprises. Illusory gods descend; one's child is run over in the street; one is fired, arrested, deserted, betrayed; the economy collapses again, God is dead, and the Wallace Collection loses its charm. Even so, Ludwig's decision—unlike Austin's reclamation, which like everything else in his life is accidental—is the decision of a free moral agent. Matthew quixotically concludes:

> From the good good actions spring with a spontaneity which must remain to the mediocre forever mysterious. Matthew knew with a sigh that he would never be a hero. Nor would he ever achieve the true enlightenment. He would be until the end of his life a man looking forward to his next drink. He looked at his watch and drifted down to the bar.

■ III

Murdoch's 1974 novel, *The Sacred and Profane Love Machine*, is labored and, in my opinion, unsatisfying. The author's voice is obtrusive:

> Each person doubtless has a sort of form or structure or schema (only that would not have been Harriet's word) into which his consciousness lazily stretches itself out when unconcerned, and which is, however unglittering and inglorious, his happiness. Emily did deeply love her son, however, only she could not help constantly using him as a weapon against her lover.

Blaise Gavender is "a man of two truths," these being his mistress Emily and their illegitimate son Luca, and his wife Harriet and their son David. Monty Small, the Gavenders' neighbor, is a retired magus; his secret sorrow has long since amputated him from responsible involvement with others. Blaise (a lay analyst, ha) must unify his life. The two women meet, but nothing is resolved until Harriet is conveniently shot by sheer happenstance in an airport fracas. The only real casualties are Luca, with whom Harriet has established a bond and who as a result of the events has to be institutionalized, and Harriet's dogs, who are promptly put out. There are a few dreams (Freudian), murders, and seductions around the edges of this stodgy piece. Murdoch has written her way out of adultery far more successfully.

In *The Sandcastle*, schoolteacher Mor returns to his conventional wife after his fling with the Visiting Artist. In *An Unoffical Rose*, nurseryman Randall Peronnet elopes with his mistress (on the proceeds of the sale of the paternal Tintoretto), leaving domestic Ann to keel the family pot. Both of these solutions are fictionally successful. We have known ever since Homer that human ends simply do not harmonize, and that the vision of a rational order, or the dream of justice (even for children and dogs) are only the most expensive of our consolations. We do not really care whether fictional people are good (Ann Peronnet) or bad (Randall Peronnet), but we hate them to be moral eunuchs like Gavender, who bounces with all the élan of a dead tennis ball between his nagging Queen of the Night and his self-righteous wife. His Titian has dressed both sacred and profane ladies in matching motley, and it is only an arbitrary act of violence that decides between them.

Christian freedom rested on the assumption that, although every love kindled within us arises of necessity, the power to arrest it is within us, and that we are judged according as we use this power to garner and winnow good and evil loves (*Purgatorio* XVIII). I think that a great deal of modern literature has been designed to test this theory, and that by and large it has not been found wanting. But what if desire is a machine, and the power to arrest the machine is *not* within us? What if love (physical love at any rate) is simply the destroyer, a destroyer that theology has no power to circumvent, psychology no power to appease? Such seems to be the sceptical suggestion of this novel.

Throughout her work, Murdoch blurs her versions of freedom, virtue, knowledge, and the good, until they all seem to come to the same thing, best epitomized by Effingham Cooper's vision in *The Unicorn's* bog:

> Since he was mortal he was nothing, and since he was nothing all that was not himself was filled to the brim with being, and it was from this that the light streamed. This then was love, to look and look until one exists no more, *this* was love which was the same as death. He looked and knew, with a clarity which was one with the increasing light, that with the death of the self the world becomes quite automatically the object of a perfect love.

Well, the self cannot die until the heart ceases to beat, or so we used to think. And in real life, the world, because it includes the self, can never become the object of a perfect love. But in art the Hero is the one who has the vision of the thousand-faced Other, the Not-Self, and this vision is his knowledge is his freedom is his virtue is his good. The Old World would have called it his salvation. Consolation is a very different matter. Consolation says Somebody (something) loves me, or in a pinch it says I love somebody (something)—"and at least I have the dignity of real love to support me."

The supreme artists (Sophocles…but I leave the reader to name his own game) have never dealt in consolation at all. The next greatest have admitted consolation corrected by vision, and have thereby provided the hope of the world. A novel in which vision (Monty) is unloving, loving (Blaise) is blind, and the Not-Self manifests its power in a slaughter of innocents, leaves this critic, for one, disconsolate.

■ IV

Hilary Burde, the word child, protagonist of Murdoch's latest novel, is, until the final episodes, an example of "form" without vision. Murdoch perhaps intends to show up those who are students rather than practitioners of language. "Nothing humbles human pride more than the inability to understand a language…. God wanted us to see that goodness is a foreign language."

Hilary has raised himself from an orphanage background to a fellowship at Oxford because he is "good" at words. He is master of half-a-dozen foreign tongues; his friends say he reads poetry for the grammar. But there is little poetry in this prosy volume, except for a few tucked-in tags from Webster, Shelley, Yeats, Eliot, and the Hymnal. The metaphor of the subway train is more than applicable. When Hilary is not making love to another man's wife, or performing his low-level job in Whitehall, our underground man is riding the Inner Circle, with leisurely stops at the station bar in Liverpool Street or Sloane Square.

The "word act" (human communication?) comes a cropper on the sex act (the machine?). Oxford Hilary is having an affair with the wife of his senior colleague, Gunnar Jopling. When she announces that she is pregnant by her husband and wishes to stick by him, Burde drives his car at 100 m.p.h. across the motorway. Anne Jopling is killed; Hilary's career is ruined. We meet him twenty years later, living in a sloppy flatlet in Bayswater, attending to his small job, and otherwise riding the tube to his weekly dinner appointments with the familiar elegant homosexual, his spiritual adviser (Monday); a young man carbuncular, his only inferior at the office (Tuesday); the usual middle-aged social couple (Thursday); his ex-mistress Tommy (Friday); his sister Crystal (Saturday). Crystal is the imprisoned innocent of this novel, an uneducated bespectacled sometime seamstress, kept lonely, televisionless and dog-less by Hilary so that she may share his *burde-ns*. "I loved Crystal…as if I knew that she was my only hope. My younger sister had to be my mother, and I had to be her father."

■ BOOKS BY IRIS MURDOCH

Sartre: Romantic Rationalist. New Haven: Yale University Press, 1953; Cambridge: Bowes & Bowes, 1953; New York: Hillary, 1963; London: Bowes & Bowes, 1965; London: Fontana, 1967.

Under the Net. New York: Viking Press, 1954; London: Chatto & Windus, 1954; New York: Compass Books, Viking Press, 1964; London: Longmans, 1966; New York: Bard Books, Avon; London: Penguin.

The Flight from the Enchanter. London: Chatto & Windus, 1955; New York: Viking Press, 1956; London: Penguin, 1964; New York: Compass Books, Viking Press, 1965.

The Sandcastle. New York: Viking Press, 1957; London: Chatto & Windus, 1957; London: Penguin.

The Nature of Metaphysics (contributor). London: Macmillan, 1957.

The Bell. New York: Viking Press, 1958; London: Chatto & Windus, 1958; New York: Bard Books, Avon; London: Penguin.

A Severed Head. New York: Viking Press, 1961; London: Chatto & Windus, 1961; New York: Compass Books, Viking Press, 1963; New York: Bard Books, Avon, 1970; London: Penguin.

An Unofficial Rose. New York: Viking Press, 1962; London: Chatto & Windus, 1962; London: Penguin, 1964.

The Unicorn. New York: Viking Press, 1963; London: Chatto & Windus, 1963; London: Penguin, 1966; New York: Bard Books, Avon, 1970.

The Italian Girl. New York: Viking Press, 1964; London: Chatto & Windus, 1964; London: Penguin, 1967; New York: Bard Books, Avon.

The Red and the Green. New York: Viking Press, 1965; London: Chatto & Windus, 1965; London: Penguin, 1967; New York: Bard Books, Avon.

The Time of the Angels. New York: Viking Press, 1966; London: Chatto & Windus, 1966; London: Penguin, 1968; New York: Bard Books. Avon.

The Nice and the Good. New York: Viking Press, 1968; London: Chatto & Windus, 1968; New York: Signet Books (NAL), 1969.

Bruno's Dream. New York: Viking Press, 1969; London: Chatto & Windus, 1969; Toronto: Clarke, Irwin, 1969; New York: Dell Books, 1970.

A Fairly Honourable Defeat. New York: Viking Press, 1970.

The Sovereignty of Good. New York: Schocken Press, 1971.

Gunnar Jopling, now an important bureaucrat, reappears, remarried to Lady Kitty, and the machine grinds. Burde falls in love with her, under cover of freeing both Gunnar and himself from the nightmare of Anne's death. He is incapable of resisting a clandestine correspondence and clandestine meetings in the park, preferably under the statue of Peter Pan (another word child?). However, despite the fact that Kitty proposes that Burde give her the child Gunnar can no longer engender, he finds too late the power to resist, to arrest. "We must resist the irresistible and we can," he is in process of telling her when Gunnar appears, and in the ensuing struggle Kitty falls into the river.

But from this small good of intended resistance, other goods spring. Hilary conceals his part in Kitty's death from Crystal; he thereby becomes "not her"; she becomes a not-self, and the Oedipal bond is loosed. Crystal (who wants a real child) marries the young man carbuncular. Hilary presumably marries Tommy (who wants a real child). In the marriage ceremony the word act and the sex act become one.

■ V

Nobody will ever forget the story of *Robinson Crusoe*, the setting of *Wuthering Heights*, the character of Emma Bovary, the method of Henry James, or "happy families are all alike." The trouble is, everything about Iris Murdoch is eminently forgettable. Even her fans can be caught asking "What's the one where the boy gets trapped in the sea-cave?" I would argue—to use the traditional terms and not to enter into any debate about the hierarchy of literary forms—that comedy is less memorable (or perhaps more readily suppressible) than epic or tragedy. I think of Orestes before I think of Aeschylus, of Hamlet before I think of Shakespeare, but I think of Molière or Trollope before I can call up a player or a scene. In the same way I think of "Mur-

An Accidental Man. New York: Viking Press, 1971.

The Black Prince. New York: Viking Press, 1973.

The Sacred and Profane Love Machine New York: Viking Press, 1974.

The Three Arrows and the Servants in the Snow (two plays). New York: Viking Press, 1974.

A Word Child. New York: Viking Press, 1975.

Henry and Cato. New York: Viking Penguin, 1977.

The Fire and the Sun. New York: Oxford University Press, 1978.

The Sea, the Sea. New York: Viking Penguin, 1978.

A Year of Birds: Poems by Iris Murdoch. Tisbury, U.K.: Compton, 1978.

The Servant: An Opera in Three Acts, music by William Mathias. London: Oxford University Press, 1980.

Nuns and Soldiers. New York: Viking Penguin, 1980.

Reynolds Stone. London: Warren Editions, 1981.

The Philosopher's Pupil. New York: Viking Penguin, 1983.

The Good Apprentice. New York: Viking Penguin, 1986.

The Book and the Brotherhood. New York: Viking Penguin, 1988.

Acastos. New York: Viking Penguin, 1988.

The Message to the Planet. New York: Viking Press, 1990.

Metaphysics as a Guide to Morals. New York: Viking Penguin, 1992.

Joanna Joanna: A Play in Two Acts. London: Colophon with Old Town Books, 1994.

The Green Knight. New York: Viking Penguin, 1994.

The One Alone. London: Colophon with Old Town Books, 1995.

Jackson's Dilemma. New York: Viking Penguin, 1996.

Existentialists and Mystics. New York: Viking Penguin, 1998.

Something Special. New York: Norton, 2000..

doch." With a little further effort I call up M. Jourdain's prose, the Signora Vesey Neroni's couch, and the Veneerings' dinner party (but which novel was *that* in?). From Murdoch I call up Honor Klein surprised in bed with her brother, and from Flannery O'Connor the removal of Hulga's artificial leg by the Bible salesman. The grotesque subsides to the ordinary, and I remember Randall taking farewell of his roses, and Mor getting his son off the roof. I suppose the fact is that we like to recognize ourselves in The Heroic Temperament, whether it is St. Theresa or, more digestibly, Dorothea Brooke. Of course Dorothea is no more St. Theresa than Mr. Casaubon is Northrop Frye. But she is given with a depth that stirs our own; *there,* we say, and with the grace of God, go I. But hardly anybody wants to be grotesque, few of us like being laughed at, and nobody outside the prayerbook wants to be ordinary. Murdoch's people are grotesque, funny, and ordinary. O'Connor's good country neighbors never recognized themselves in her stories. Such people, they cried, do not exist, or certainly not in Georgia.

I think the sword-swinging Honor Klein, the pigeon-killing Radeechy, the jokester Julius King, and the enchanter Mischa Fox probably do not exist. They are Grendels, in Gardner's or any other rendition, straight out of the psychic cave. In good Anglo-Saxon tradition, Murdoch simply introduces dragons onto the scene. They become a dimension of daylight life, a daylight garishly colored by our hopes and fears. Sir Matthew Gibson Grey is a good example, fangless as he is except when it comes to the chocolate mousse. It is the *idea* of him—as Cain, Buddha, Lover—that promotes the action; he is powerless *except* in the imagination of others. For Murdoch, as Byatt notes, imagination is something which invents objects of desire in order to avoid the pressure of reality. This Austin G. G. invents the Dorina who is to rescue his life from accident by giving it form and clarity. But the real Dorina is too fragile to bear the Beatrice-burden, and the vision fades upon the fall of an electric heater into the bathtub. In an analogous way

Hannah Crean-Smith, the unicorn, invites others to project their pain and guilt upon her, and properly enough she vanishes into the sea. Murdoch employs what Frye would call apocalyptic and demonic imagery, the park and the pit. I think she would disagree that the world of "nightmare and the scapegoat, of bondage, pain, and confusion" represents the world as it is "before the human imagination begins to work on it." For her the slimy snakes and the happy living things are co-eval figments, and as far as I can see there is nothing in mythology to indicate that they are not. Caliban and Ariel inhabit the same isle, but Naples is across the bay. Imagination is not reality, because reality is not a construct of the mind. "The only way to regenerate the imagining spirit is to join it to the world of action."

Such a regeneration seems to be Murdoch's concern. It is dangerous to deal in may-be's but I suspect that she may be a greater artist than she appears to be from a contemporary perspective. The prose of *The Unicorn* and the delicate characterization of *The Bell* bear me out. But she abjures such magics. "The pattern which he had seen in his life existed only in his own romantic imagination. At the human level there was no pattern" (Michael Meade in *The Bell*). In a world deprived of general truths, we must forgo an absolute aspiration, both in art and in life. We must live on the human level. Neither the way up nor the way down is for us. We will be to the end of our lives readers looking forward to our next novel. We have at least, that consolation.

Julia Randall
February, 1976

UPDATE

The prolific Dame Iris Murdoch maintained a steady output of work after this essay appeared, and went on to write nine more novels before her death from Alzheimer's disease in 1999: *Henry and Cato*, *The Sea, the Sea*, *Nuns and Soldiers*, *The Philosopher's Pupil*, *The Good Apprentice*, *The Book and the Brotherhood*, *The Message to the Planet*, *The Green Knight*, and *Jackson's Dilemma*. Although interest in Murdoch's work has never really waned, there was a surge when her husband, John Bayley, published his 1999 memoir, *Elegy for Iris*, and, especially, when the Academy Award–winning film *Iris* came out in 2001, starring Dame Judi Dench and Jim Broadbent.

Long known as a champion of reason and intellectual freedom, Murdoch has been revered for her ability to create engaging, highly original "novels of ideas" that encompass all manner of human relations, situations, and philosophies. Upon her death, Malcolm Bradbury wrote in *Time* that she was "one of postwar Britain's greatest novelists," and that her books were "every one distinctive and different, all displaying that exotic, fantastic imagination that can only be called Murdochian."

Her body of work created wide ripples, and influenced not only twentieth-century literature but philosophy as well. The *Concise Dictionary of British Literary Biography* noted that "[s]he draws eclectically on the English tradition" of Dickens, Austen, and Thackeray "and at the same time extends it in important ways." And the *New Criterion* wrote, "The qualities that made Iris Murdoch a great novelist" include "her technical skill, richness of imagination, philosophical ideas, and moral vision."

Murdoch's final novel, *Jackson's Dilemma*, was greeted with enthusiasm, and her readers did not realize it would be her last. *Booklist* called her "brilliant and charming" novel with the playwright's touch an "homage to that master of convoluted comedy, Shakespeare." A *Contemporary Review* critique called it extraordinary: "Intricately plotted, there is space for moments of haunting reflection on human nature. The language is assured and rich in discourse poetic and philosophic. Here, of course, is a novelist of stature, working at the height of her powers. . . . . Arguably, *Jackson's Dilemma* is the summation of her talent, the gathering of all the strands. . . ." The review added that Murdoch never pokes fun at her characters, despite their often complicated moral predicaments. "Iris Murdoch's intelligence is matched by her sympathy."

The Ornamentation of Old Ideas: Gloria Naylor's First Three Novels

In 1982, when Gloria Naylor exploded onto the scene with her award-winning novel *The Women of Brewster Place*, it was only the beginning of a career in which the artist would continue to draw substantially from other writers' works to enhance her own presentation of novelistic ideas. Henry Louis Gates has characterized this strategic style as "signification," that is the utilization of others' characters and themes to provide a foundation from which to springboard off into one's own variations. Slave narrators did it with their reinforcement of certain themes such as an oppressive South, the value of education, and flight to northern freedom. The brilliant Ralph Ellison, with his *Invisible Man* (1952), did it as he drew upon Richard Wright's *Native Son* (1940) to create his own version of the black American male. In more recent years we have seen Alice Walker relying on Zora Neale Hurston's *Their Eyes Were Watching God* (1937) to provide, in *The Color Purple* (1982), her own rendition of the quest for self-actualization.

The literary process of borrowing ideas has been going on for quite some time, but Naylor is one who has perfected the technique. One need only have read Ann Petry's *The Street* (1946) to be struck by the similarity between it and *Brewster Place*. First of all, both novels ended with a terrible death that contributed to a most profound meaning. In Petry's novel the death involved protagonist Lutie Johnson killing lecherous Boots Smith, a black nightclub entertainer who promised himself to do all that he could to get Lutie's body. He had promised her a singing job, and at one point pulled his car to the side of a deserted road and held her "so tightly and his mouth was so insistent, so brutal, that she twisted out of his arms, not caring what he thought, intent only on escaping from his ruthless hands and mouth." So desperate was he to achieve his goal that when physical force failed he concluded that "if he couldn't get her any other way, he'd marry her," not due to anything even faintly resembling love, but as yet another means whereby he might attain the object of his lewd desires. He was no different from the white business proprietor, Old Man Junto, who warned, "Leave her alone. I want her myself." No different from the janitor, William Jones, who planned to rape her. No different from Mr. Crosse, of the Crosse School for Singers, who stipulated, "If you and me can get together a coupla nights a week in Harlem, those lessons won't cost you a cent." Lutie picked up an inkwell and hurled it at that propositioner's face, "the ink paused for a moment at the obstruction of his eyebrows, then dripped down over the fat jowls, over the wrinkled collar, the grease-stained vest." She dared to strike back, but her reaction, at that time, was against only one of the despicable male characters. When a half crazed Boots finally resorted to extreme violence, declaring, "Maybe after I beat the hell out of you a coupla times, you'll begin to like the idea of sleeping with me," Lutie picked up an iron candlestick and:

> kept striking him, not thinking about him, not even seeing him. First she was venting her rage against the dirty, crowded street. She saw the rows of dilapidated old houses; the small dark rooms; the long steep flights of stairs; the narrow dingy hall-

Gloria Naylor

Gloria Naylor was born on January 25, 1950, in New York City, to a transit worker and a telephone operator. She received her B.A. from Brooklyn College of the City University of New York and her M.A. from at Yale University. Naylor worked as a Jehovah's Witness missionary from 1968 to 1975 and as a telephone operator in New York City until 1981. Naylor is best known for her book *The Women of Brewster Place*, a novel about the situation of black women in America. Naylor won the Lillian Smith Book Award from the Southern Regional Council (1989) for *Mama Day* and the American Book Award from the New Columbus Foundation (1998) for *The Men of Brewster Place*. She has been writer in residence or visiting professor at numerous institutions. ■

ways…the smashed homes where the women did drudgery because their men had deserted them. She saw all of these things and struck at them.

Bludgeoning Boots in this way, she imagined she was destroying all the dreadful obstacles that had prevented her and other black women in like situations from attaining respectability.

In *Brewster Place* the killer resides in a housing project and is a lesbian who has just been raped by C. C. Baker and his cohorts. C. C. and the other gang members escape but Lorraine kills Ben, a janitor who years earlier had been a cause for his own daughter's turn to prostitution. That daughter had come to Ben and told him about the sexual improprieties she had been forced into under the auspices of doing maid work for a white landowner. Ben resolved "that if he sat up drinking all night Friday, he could stand on the porch Saturday morning and smile at the man who whistled as he dropped his lame daughter home." Notwithstanding the social inequities in force between black and white men, it is evident that Ben could have done more before his daughter fled, leaving a note that stated, "If she had to earn her keep that way, she might as well go to Memphis where the money was better." In a literal sense Ben's death is accidental, but from another perspective, his death is symbolic of an end to the same phenomenon Petry's Boots represented, the lack of proper action when proper action was so desperately needed.

Kathryn Palumbo is pessimistic in her article "The Uses of Female Imagery in Naylor's *The Women of Brewster Place*," where she maintains that Naylor "offers her characters no hope and no power beyond daily survival." But in actuality the final section of the novel serves notice that a new way of life may be on the horizon. At first conceived as a means of raising money to pay for a tenants' association lawyer, a well-planned block party takes on even greater significance as:

Women flung themselves against the wall, chipping away at it with knives, plastic forks, spiked shoe heels, and even bare hands…. The bricks piled up behind them and were snatched and relayed out of Brewster Place past overturned tables, scat-

tered coins, and crushed wads of dollar bills. They came back with chairs and barbecue grills and smashed them into the wall.

That wall was the place where C. C. had led five others in rape. It was where a dazed Lorraine
had killed Ben. This was the wall that separated all project residents from the rest of society,
and now in the drenching rain while "all of the men and children…stood huddled in the door-
ways," the women dismantled this wall of seclusion and opened the way for possibility.

Petry had a somewhat similar depiction of black sisterhood. In fact, the Georgia-born out-
cast, Mrs. Hedges, saved Lutie from rape. Interestingly enough, it was the janitor (building
superintendent) who forced her down toward the basement until:

> A pair of powerful hands gripped her by the shoulders, wrenched her violently out
> of the Super's arms, flung her back against the wall. She stood there shuddering,
> her mouth still open, still screaming, unable to stop the sounds that were coming
> from her throat. The same powerful hands shot out and thrust the Super hard
> against the cellar door.

Yet in spite of that aid, Mrs. Hedges is less than satisfactory in terms of supplying a solution for
young women out on the street. Her answer was for them to become prostitutes.

Mrs. Hedges does not offer the optimum solution, but upon considering how Lutie had
been abandoned by virtually all of the men in her life, we wonder what exactly Petry had in
mind for black women's progress. Lutie's husband became mired in an adulterous affair. Her
father chose alcohol and loose women over contributing to a suitable environment for his young
grandson. And then there was that child himself who, while albeit not at an age to be fully
responsible, had already become susceptible to "gangs of young boys who were always on the
lookout for small fry Bub's age, because they found young kids useful in getting in through narrow fire-escape windows, in distracting a storekeeper's attention while the gang light-heartedly
helped itself to his stock." After Bub was caught and taken into police custody, Lutie could only
contemplate how "the little Henry Chandlers," such as those she had cared for in the plush Connecticut suburbs, "go to YalePrincetonHarvard" while "the Bub Johnsons graduate from reform
school into DannemoraSingSing." The cycle of disappointments seemed bound to continue.

As Petry had done thirty-six years earlier in her novel, Naylor likewise has three generations of males fail Mattie Michael who, first of all, has gotten pregnant by a man who won't
marry her. When she refuses to tell her father who the baby's father is, Mr. Michael "held her by
the hair so she took the force of the two blows with her neck muscles, and her eyes went dim
as the blood dripped down her chin from her split lip." Mattie continues her refusal and the
father keeps on with his punishment, beating her with a broom until it "had broken, and he
was now kneeling over Mattie and beating her with a jagged section of it that he had in his fist."
Shortly thereafter, she leaves home and gives birth to a son she names Basil. Time passes quickly as he becomes a young man and Mattie realizes she had:

> never met any of Basil's girlfriends, and he rarely mentioned them…and it sud-
> denly came to her that she hadn't met many of his male friends, either. Where was
> he going? She truly didn't know, and it had come to be understood that she was
> not to ask.

Just as the hardworking Lutie had lost her son, Bub, to the street with all of its illegal distractions, Mattie loses Basil to a barroom brawl. After he is arrested, Mattie seeks legal help. "Thank
God for ignorance of the law and frantic mothers," her lawyer says to himself. Lutie's attorney
had been just as calculating, thinking, "Now why in hell doesn't she know she doesn't need a
lawyer?" as he gave her three days to get two hundred dollars.

One is tempted to reconsider if indeed Mrs. Hedges would not be a better alternative to such devastating results. But Petry made her too much a flawed character. On the other hand, Naylor has Mattie develop into a great source of strength without losing her morality. Forced now to live at Brewster Place, she nevertheless does not exploit in the manner of Mrs. Hedges. Naylor has her strongest woman character giving an abundance of love, the sort of love that makes her wait up late for Etta Mae out on a date with the opportunist, Reverend Woods, who is attracted to Etta, strictly in the physical sense. Mattie had tried to stop Etta from going but she also understood:

> Sometimes being a friend means mastering the art of timing. There is a time for silence. A time to let go and allow people to hurl themselves into their own destiny. And a time to prepare to pick up the pieces when it's all over.

When Lucielia Louise loses both of her children and subsequently wishes to die herself, it is Mattie who gently rocks her back toward a healthy consciousness.

> She took the soap, and, using only her hands, she washed Ciel's hair and the back of her neck. She raised her arms and cleaned the armpits, soaping well the downy brown hair there. She let the soap slip between the girl's breasts, and she washed each one separately, cupping it in her hands. She took each leg and even cleaned under the toenails. Making Ciel rise and kneel in the tub, she cleaned the crack in her behind, soaped her pubic hair, and gently washed the creases in her vagina— slowly, reverently, as if handling a newborn.

It is the notion of the fulfillment of sisterly love that separates Naylor from Petry. In *The Street* Lutie finally fled New York City, and there is utter sadness as we think of her loss. The women of Brewster Place also have suffered immensely, but they "still wake up with their dreams misted on the edge of a yawn…. They ebb and flow, ebb and flow, but never disappear." We have seen the tragedy of these women's lives but anticipate prospects for a better future.

■ ■ ■

Many in our society have come to regard the massive movement to suburban-type environments as the key to progress. So it is apropos that Naylor's next novel should examine an exclusive black neighborhood where residents have gained economic success. Naylor narrates:

> Practically every black in Wayne County wanted to be a part of Linden Hills…somehow making it into Linden Hills meant "making it"…only "certain" people got to live in Linden Hills, and the blacks in Wayne County…kept sending in applications to the Tupelo Realty Corporation—and hoping.

However, on the very first page of *Linden Hills* (1985), we are given reason to suspect that not everything is as it should be. Linden Hills "wasn't a set of hills, or even a whole hill," but the northern face of a plateau that led down into the town cemetery. The main proprietor of the Tupelo Realty Corporation is one Luther Nedeed, an old, rather spooky dark man who has assumed the ownership of his father's undertaking business, an establishment which that father had inherited in turn from two previous generations of Luther Nedeeds.

One might assume in this case that an analogy can be made between moving up in terms of socio-economic prosperity and a geographic moving up within the context of Linden Hills. But on the contrary, movement downward is what these residents seek, although once reaching the bottom they mysteriously disappear. Still, "none of the applicants ever questioned the fact that there was always space in Linden Hills." Residents at the very bottom are disposed of in some way by Nedeed, whose inverted name, "de eden," means false paradise.

Naylor would have done well enough just to have depicted the superficiality of those lost in the quest for material possessions. However, she chose to innovate and use Dante's *Inferno,* written in the fourteenth century, as the framework for her twentieth-century tale. Dante's version of Hell is best conceptualized by imagining ten descending layers of circles. At the top are virtuous but unbaptized pagans. The second circle consists of inhabitants who have been lustful. Those who have been gluttonous compose the third circle. Followed, in the fourth, by both those who have been avaricious and those who have been prodigal. Then come the wrathful, the heretical, the violent, the fraudulent, and the traitorous who are trapped in circles five through nine respectively. The Devil himself, frozen from the waist down in a lake of ice, makes up circle number ten, the most frightening of all Dante's levels.

Drawing on that model, Naylor has eight concentric circles composing Linden Hills. Lester Tilson lives with his mother and sister on First Crescent Drive in "the smallest house on a street of brick ranch houses." They live on the fringe but are nevertheless part of the Linden Hills community. As Catherine Ward has asserted, "Here, like the neutrals in the vestibule outside Circle One of the *Inferno,* live those who are neither good nor evil, the uncommitted who chase after banners." The full import of that statement is realized as we view the Tilson home where:

> Its two-story wooden frame had been covered with light green aluminum siding, and three brick steps led up to a dark green door.... Willow-green print furniture sat on jade carpeting and there were green-and-white Japanese porcelain vases arranged on the tables in the living room. The curtains in the hallway and living room had avocado stripes and fern prints, and with the light coming through them, they gave a whisper-green tint to the white walls.

The color green dominates, emphasizing the degree to which money itself becomes a god. Even house walls appear green when the sun shines through avocado-striped, fern-printed curtains. Inside, the carpeting is jade; outside, the wooden frame is covered with green aluminum siding, a clue to how artificiality has covered what was once natural.

Further down on Third Crescent Drive lives Maxwell Smyth, assistant to the executive director of General Motors, whose "elaborate series of humidifiers and thermostats enabled him to determine the exact conditions under which he would eat, sleep, or sit." His life is so calculated that "the only thing his bathroom lacked was toilet paper, which he kept in the closet and brought out for rare guests since he never needed it." As Naylor says, "His entire life became a race against the natural—and he was winning." The decision whether even to smile at his secretary was one that he considered with great gravity.

On the sixth level down we come across Mrs. Laurel Dumont, who is likewise losing touch with her most valuable possession, her own inimitable soul. As an eight-year-old child she had loved the water although "she didn't swim a lick." Grandmother Roberta saw to it that young Laurel learned; in time, the youth came to be quite proficient, as comfortable in a country swimming hole as when her head was "resting in Roberta's lap, the crickets and bullfrogs competing as hard to give the light." But as Laurel grows older she finds herself first in college and then married to Howard Dumont. "And when she finally took a good look around, she found herself imprisoned within a chain of photographs and a life that had no point." The last time we see her alive she is consciously diving from a thirty-foot board into the twenty-foot end of an empty swimming pool.

In characterizing Laurel, Naylor builds on the feminist statement that was so much a part of her first novel, *Brewster Place.* Laurel was indeed trapped in a life dictated by her husband's social position and standards perpetuated by Linden Hills. But it is as we continue on with our downward movement that we get to the most disturbing portrayal of sexist oppression as we are told about the four Nedeed wives. Luwana Parkerville Nedeed bore a dark-skinned son for her husband and then faded into an obscure life of privately composing letters just to herself. A generation later, Evelyn Creton Nedeed bore the traditional dark-skinned son, thereby becoming expendable, and then starved to death. Priscilla McGuire Nedeed had the requisite son and then watched as that son cast a deeper and deeper shadow across her face, first as she observed it in family photographs and then in reality. As Ward puts it, "Without a fight, she watches as the shadows of her husband and son blot out her soul."

The latest in the line of Mrs. Nedeeds is Willa Prescott Nedeed, who wore:

> Saddle oxfords in grade school, maroon loafers in high school, platform heels in college…. She imported the white satin pumps that took Willa Prescott down the aisle six years ago and brought her back up as Willa Prescott Nedeed. Her marriage to Luther Nedeed was her choice, and she took his name by choice. She knew…that there were no laws anywhere in this country that forced her to assume that name; she took it because she wanted to. That was important. She must be clear about that before she went on to anything else: she wanted to be a Nedeed.

Her desperation to be married had been so great that she did not consider the exact nature of her compromise. Nedeed had gone to his tenth college reunion to choose from among "those who had lost that hopeful, arrogant strut," someone "more than willing to join the life and rhythms of almost any man." Willa Prescott had been just such a woman. She wanted to be a Nedeed and "walk around and feel that she had a perfect right to respond to a phone call, a letter, an invitation—any verbal or written request directed toward that singular identity." Her fate will be linked to the other Mrs. Nedeeds who preceded her, but she is the most tragic of all, for upon giving birth to a son who turned out to be light-skinned, her husband locked both her and that son in the basement where, during a six-year period, the son slowly died and the mother slowly lost her mind.

Naylor has cleverly altered the Dantean concept of Hell to include what can be experienced in this mortal life. Willa Nedeed suffered through it, as did the other three Nedeed wives. Linden Hills is Hell, and in place of morality lies the single-minded thirst for financial success. As was true in the *Inferno,* the price paid is in human souls.

The Roman poet Virgil led Dante through an afterlife Hell, and Lester leads Willie Mason through Linden Hills. It is, of course, significant that Lester is a poet who occasionally earns five dollars for getting a poem published in a local newspaper. However, Willie does not write his poems. He serves the same function as an African *griot,* perpetuating a culture through phenomenal memory. Willie had:

> already memorized 665 poems and this last one just wasn't working out. Would he have to start writing them down? He couldn't imagine that. Poetry wrote itself for him. If he had to pick up a pen and paper, he just knew there would be nothing to say…His poems only made sense in his ears and mouth. His fingers, eyes, and nose. Something about Linden Hills was blocking that.

Willie is unable to memorize more than 665 poems, which bodes well for him, considering 666 is a sign of the Devil. The young poet had wanted to continue with his craft but is appropriately wary in approaching Linden Hills. Lester is thus essential as a guide though dangerously relaxed in this evil territory.

In Canto XXI of the *Inferno* we had also seen recklessness on the part of Virgil, so sure that demons who once threatened would now let them pass. A demon chief even offered them escorts. Virgil handled all of this in matter-of-fact fashion while Dante asked the vital questions:

"O Master, what is this?" In fear I spoke,
"Alone, if thou the way know, let us start.
Such escort's aid I care not to invoke.
If thou beest wary, as wontedly thou wert,
Dost thou not see them, how they grind their teeth
And with bent brows threaten us to our hurt?"

Virgil ignored Dante's apprehensiveness on that as well as on several other occasions.

In spite of such difficulties, however, they made it through the Inferno and on to Purgatorio for a rendezvous with the illustrious Beatrice, a woman the author Dante himself first saw when he was nine years old and she was eight. Although they were never involved in any kind of physical romance, Dante did envision her as his ideal. Stewart Farnell offers insight:

> Virgil is Dante's immediate guide, but it is Beatrice who has sent Virgil to Dante. Just as Virgil is even himself, the Roman poet, and also, symbolically, much more, so Beatrice is herself, the real Beatrice whom Dante loved and who was for him a revelation of the divine glory, and she is also a symbol. Beatrice symbolizes revelation, spiritual illumination, grace, theology, salvation, and even Christ.

This would explain Virgil's flaws. Though ordained to lead Dante, he was not on a par with Jesus Christ or Beatrice, who might have been designed to symbolize either Christ or goodness in pure form.

Naylor's version of Beatrice is Ruth Anderson, previously a resident of Linden Hills but now living on Wayne Avenue and married to Norman Anderson, who comes down with "the pinks" once every year and nine months. When that psychological fit occurs it leaves him desperate to scrape off imaginary slime. "He resorted to his teeth and bare nails only after everything else had failed—jagged sections of plates and glasses, wire hangers, curtain rods, splinters of wood once part of a dresser, coffee table, or her grandmother's antique music box." Nevertheless, Ruth stays with him in their sparse apartment "with its bare wood floors, dusted and polished, and with the three pieces of furniture that sat in three large rooms: one sofa in the living room, one kitchenette set with plastic-bottomed chairs on uncertain chrome legs, one bed." Like Beatrice, she is reminiscent of Christ, who lived only with the barest essentials and with those most despised, like the lepers.

Just as Beatrice had sent Virgil to Dante, so too does Ruth suggest that Lester guide Willie through Linden Hills, in this case to look for odd jobs. When they run into difficulty with a policeman, she somehow knows of their dilemma and sends Norman with a story the policeman will accept. "Norm, you must have been sent from the gods," Willie says, to which Norman replies, "Ruth had a feeling that you two might get yourselves into a mess, walking around down here." Virgil led Dante through the levels of Hell, but Christ was the source of love and wisdom. So too with Ruth. While Luther Nedeed has held his wife in captivity six years for the most insignificant of reasons, Ruth celebrates six years of being with someone she had every reason to leave. "I rule in —," Norman starts to say before Ruth catches him as they drink from their Styrofoam cups. "Love rules in this house," he corrects himself with Christian words.

■ ■ ■

The prospect of pure love is also at the heart of Naylor's most recent novel, *Mama Day* (1988). The novel's basic structure consists of briefly rendered sections in which a formerly widowed woman and her dead first husband narrate alternatively. Ophelia recalls, "Six months of looking for a job had made me an expert at picking out the people who, like me, were hurrying up to wait—in somebody's outer anything for a chance to make it through their inner doors to prove that you could type two words a minute, or not drool on your blouse while answering difficult questions about your middle initial and date of birth." She is cynical about her move from Willow Springs (off the coasts of South Carolina and Georgia) to New York City, and it is most evident as she seeks gainful employment after two years of business school in Atlanta and seven years with an insurance company that folded because of its "greedy president who didn't have the sense to avoid insuring half of the buildings in the south Bronx—even at triple premiums for fire and water damage." She now sits alone in a restaurant, pondering her tenuous situation.

Seated at another table is George Andrews, who in his first dialogue from beyond the grave confides, "Our guardians at the Wallace P. Andrews Shelter for Boys were adamant about the fact that we learned to invest in ourselves alone." In accordance with that institutional standard, George matriculated at Columbia University and, upon graduation, went on to become a partner in his own engineering firm, Andrews & Stein. Still, he suffers from an identity crisis caused by parental circumstance. His mother had been a prostitute; his father had been one of her customers.

There is a vague resemblance, even this early on in the novel, to Shakespeare's Prince Hamlet, whose mother Gertrude committed adultery with his Uncle Claudius and then married him less than one month after that uncle killed King Hamlet in pursuit of the throne. Prince Hamlet was devastated and railed in a soliloquy:

Frailty, thy name is woman! —
A little month, or ere those shoes were old
With which she followed my poor father's body,
O God, a beast that wants discourse of reason
Would have mourn'd longer.

It is possible that Hamlet's grievance against his mother became transferred to women in general, making it difficult for him to conduct any kind of relationship with members of the opposite sex.

Naylor's George, who is indeed quite fond of Shakespeare, has been seeing one woman for five straight years, but their relationship has become stagnant. And then when Ophelia arrives on the scene, seeking employment at Andrews & Stein, George is attracted but still recommends that she try another company where, unbeknownst to her, a lecherous boss lurks in waiting. She nonetheless avoids sexual harassment by contriving a story and "a couple of coffee breaks with the office gossip and then everyone knew about my breaking up with a man who I found out had been committed twice for homicidal rages and who now took to slinking around my apartment building." This keeps the lecher out of her personal life so she can accomplish that for which she is being paid.

Some readers might wish that Shakespeare's Ophelia could have had only half so much cunning and strength so that when Hamlet demanded, "Get thee to a nunn'ry," she might have withstood it better. For was it proper to blame her, the pawn of Hamlet's testers? On the other hand, can we really blame Hamlet for retaliating against someone he saw as a spy?

Bernard Grebanier, in a rather provocative study entitled *The Heart of Hamlet* (1967), noted the wide variety of ways in which scholars have viewed Hamlet's supposed rejection of Ophelia. Many have thought that Hamlet rejected her because of his mother's inappropriate remarriage that distorted his own perspective on women. Others conclude Hamlet just was not in love. Then there is the view that Hamlet was a man of such limited energies that he could not have engaged in courtship and planned vengeance too. Some say that in earlier versions of the Hamlet story Ophelia was a prostitute. Finally, there is the opinion that Hamlet was a man so consumed with himself that he was incapable of loving anyone else.

Having presented those possible explanations, Grebanier then does something of an about-face in proposing how it was most likely Ophelia who did the rejecting. "Fear it, Ophelia, fear it, my dear sister," Laertes had advised with regard to her relationship. "Do not believe his vows, for they are brokers," added Polonius. And Ophelia apparently gave in to those entreaties, rejecting Hamlet and then reporting how she "did repel his letters, and denied his access to me." By the time she fell into the "weeping brook," we were not even sure whether she had committed suicide or accidentally fallen in. But we did know she was victimized by an ongoing state of affairs that made love a quite tangled prospect.

■ ■ ■

Writing for the *Richmond Times-Dispatch,* Robert Merritt criticizes *Mama Day* and assesses, "the clarity the story demands has faltered in what seems to be a misguided effort to make the story more structured for accessibility." *Brewster Place* was recently made into a television drama, and the movie rights to *Mama Day* have already been bought. So Merritt might be correct in insinuating that Naylor now writes with an eye toward greater remuneration than mere book sales will allow.

Still, we must consider that clarity in itself was not Naylor's goal as she wrote *Mama Day.* As it is, the woman after whom the book is named is in possession of certain powers that defy explanation. At eighty-five years of age, Mama Day "can still stand so quiet, she becomes part of a tree." The local doctor has to admit that her herbal cures are just as good as what he himself can accomplish with years of medical training. All of Willow Springs knows that she has a gift, but they do not know the gift's source.

Mama Day's great-niece, Ophelia, is another most ambiguous character. As has been mentioned, the novel's basic structure is that of a lengthy conversation between two lovers, one dead, the other alive. The novel's very last lines are, "What really happened to us, George? You see, that's what I mean—there are just too many sides to the whole story." After three hundred and eleven pages we still cannot be sure about the veracity of the events which surround their relationship. Can too many New England Patriot football games, a white ex-girlfriend, and a move to Willow Springs be the source of so much conflict? Or is it in the natural order of things that what goes on between a man and woman, presumably in love, is indeed a complex tangled web?

It is this latter point, in particular, that Naylor has drawn from *Hamlet.* Like Hamlet, George is concerned about his place in the world of "movers and shakers." But unlike Hamlet, George marries Ophelia anyway, and we get rapid hints of ensuing difficulty. "It was a pity you didn't like being called Ophelia," says George at one point. Then there is something crucial that Ophelia's grandmother and Mama Day have not told her. Those two elderly women talk, with Mama Day beginning:

> "And we ain't even told Baby Girl about…. And we should, you know, Abigail. It ain't nothing to be ashamed of, it's her family and her history. And she'll have children one day."
>
> "There's time before you saddle her with all that mess. Let the child live her life without having to think on them things. Baby Girl —"
>
> "That's just it, Abigail—she ain't a baby. She's a grown woman and her *real* name is Ophelia. We don't like to think on it, but that's her name. Not Baby Girl, not Cocoa—Ophelia."
>
> "I regret the day she got it."
>
> "No, Sister, please. Don't ever say that. She fought to stay here—remember, Abigail?"

"I could forget to breathe, easier than I could forget those months. Sitting up
with her night after night, trembling every time she choked."

In a literal sense Abigail and Mama Day are referring to the day when Ophelia was born premature, weighing less than five pounds. Born in 1953, when medical technology was not as
advanced as it is today, she indeed had to fight to survive, her success being a minor miracle.

However, there is much more to this matter than the gasps of a premature child. Naylor
wants us to ponder on the challenge undertaken at the very point when we began living, a
challenge that involves reconciling ourselves with the past. Early in the novel we are told about
Sapphira, an African-born slave sold to Bascombe Wade in 1819. Legend has it that the slave
"married Bascombe Wade, bore him seven sons in just a thousand days, to put a dagger
through his kidney and escape the hangman's noose…persuaded Bascombe Wade in a thousand days to deed all his slaves every inch of land in Willow Springs, poisoned him for his
trouble." Obviously, that narration hinges on something phenomenal, to say the least. We are
reminded of the ending in *Hamlet* where four people meet death as a consequence of the duel
between Hamlet and Laertes, Claudius dying by both sword and poison.

It is, moreover, intriguing that Bascombe's last name is Wade, perhaps alluding to another
version of his death, that he walked out into the Atlantic Ocean after Sapphira "got away from
him and headed…toward the east bluff on her way back to Africa." We think back to Shakespeare's Ophelia who "fell in the weeping brook" and met her demise. Perhaps Ophelia *did* commit suicide, and Hamlet might have done the same had he not had the task of staying for revenge.

Naylor's emphasis is nonetheless on the woman. Being a black woman herself, she is especially sensitive to this tragic history. Slavery allowed Bascombe to do a terrible injustice to Sapphira, who in other circumstances might have been able to give him as strong and pure a love
as was humanly possible. Later, as Mama Day observes, "We ain't had much luck with the girls
in this family," it is as though the females are all cursed. Mama Day thinks about how

> Most all of the boys had thrived: her own daddy being the youngest of seven boys,
> and his daddy the youngest of seven. But coming on down to them, it was just her,
> Abigail, and Peace. And out of them just another three girls, and out of them, two.
> Three generations of nothing but girls, and only one left alive in this last generation
> to keep the Days going—the child of Grace.

Who were the wives of those first two succeeding generations, totaling fourteen boys? Did they
even all get married? We are not fully told, but we do get the impression that they were not
much better off than the four wives of the Luther Nedeed generations. The names are of less
significance than the probable fates they suffered as a consequence of the era and circumstances into which they were born.

One whom we get more information about than all the others was the woman who would
be the mother of Mama Day. This mother was also named Ophelia and in addition to having
Abigail and Mama Day, she gave birth to Peace, who while still a baby, fell into a well. That first
Ophelia was so distraught that she actually tried to jump into the well after her dead daughter.
She was restrained then but would later go into a trance and wander into the Sound, a relatively narrow but deep body of water between Willow Springs and the eastern United States mainland. She died, in Mama Day's words, "trying to find peace." Naylor's ingenious use of the name
"Ophelia" and the action of death by drowning draw on Shakespeare and thereby add a certain
power to the message of repeated loss.

Of Ophelia's three children only Abigail and Mama Day are still left. Mama Day has no
children; Abigail has had three: Grace, Hope, and yet another Peace. The symbolic import of

those names becomes clear as we learn that all three of these daughters are dead. Abigail's Peace died even younger than the first Ophelia's. Abigail's Hope was the mother of Willa Prescott Nedeed; Hope died shortly after Willa married Luther.

So what we are left with is the child of Grace, yet another Ophelia who "came into the world kicking and screaming," an omen of things yet to come. After coming of age, she journeys first to Atlanta and then New York and seems bound to survive rather nicely until upon a return visit to Willow Springs, she is propositioned by Junior Lee and then cursed by his disturbed wife. There is little that Abigail and Mama Day can do as Ophelia gazes into the mirror and sees "flesh from both cheeks was now hanging in strings under my ears, and moving my head caused them to wiggle like hooked worms." Ophelia feels her face and it is normal, but later, as the curse progresses, she conveys:

> it was no illusion that they had begun to crawl within my body. I didn't need a mirror to feel the slight itching as they curled and stretched themselves, multiplying as they burrowed deeper into my flesh…they were actually feeding on me, the putrid odor of decaying matter that I could taste on my tongue and smell with every breath I took.

As it turns out, the only thing that can save Ophelia is George's love. It is as though Hamlet has been given just one more chance. Mama Day carts her rooster off to a distant cabin and then summons George to bring her hen from the chicken coop. His instructions are to "search good in the back of her nest, and come straight back" with whatever is found. The hen wages a vicious battle, dealing George several death blows, and he has found nothing but his own "gouged and bleeding hands." What he learns, however, is that with those very hands he can hold on tight to Ophelia, and, metaphorically speaking, never have to let go.

In *Brewster Place* we had been presented with a world in which relationships between males and females were devoid of the required mutuality. *Linden Hills* presented one such reciprocal relationship, rendered through the marriage of Ruth and Norman Anderson. But by casting Ruth in the mold of a Christ-like figure, we wonder what the prospects would have been for average people. Finally, in *Mama Day,* we see how love between a mortal man and a mortal woman can be strong enough to conquer anything.

James Robert Saunders
April, 1990

UPDATE

Since this essay appeared, Gloria Naylor has published two novels, *Bailey's Café* (1992) and *The Men of Brewster Place* (1998). She also edited *Children of the Night: The Best Short Stories by Black Writers, 1967 to the Present* (1995), and cowrote, with Bill Shore, the nonfiction *Revolution of the Heart: A New Strategy for Creating Wealth* (1996). *The Women of Brewster Place* was adapted as a miniseries, produced by Oprah Winfrey and Carole Isenberg, and broadcast by ABC-TV in 1989; it became a weekly ABC series in 1990, produced by Winfrey, Earl Hamner, and Donald Sipes.

Naylor, who is unquestionably in the literary mainstream, once told *Publishers Weekly* that she was dissatisfied with the "historical tendency to look upon the output of black writers as not really American literature," and added that she aims to "articulate experiences that want articulating, for those readers who reflect the subject matter, black readers, and for those who don't—basically white middle class readers."

This praise from the *Washington Post* was typical when *The Women of Brewster Place* was published: "With prose as rich as poetry, a passage will suddenly take off and sing like a spiritu-

■ **BOOKS BY GLORIA NAYLOR**

The Women of Brewster Place. New York: Viking Press, 1982, Reprinted, New York: Penguin Books, 1989.

Linden Hills. New York: Ticknor and Fields, 1985, Reprinted, New York: Penguin Books, 1986.

Mama Day. New York: Ticknor and Fields, 1988, Reprinted, New York: Penguin Books, 1989.

Bailey's Café. New York: Harcourt, 1992.

The Men of Brewster Place. New York: Hyperion, 1998.

al. . . . Vibrating with undisguised emotion, *The Women of Brewster Place* springs from the same roots that produced the blues. Like them, her book sings of sorrows proudly borne by black women in America."

When *The Men of Brewster Place* came out in 1998, it was naturally compared to its best-selling predecessor—and many critics found it weak. "The tremendous psychological insights that made the women of Brewster Place so real is sadly lacking in the majority of Naylor's male protagonists," wrote *Booklist*. "These characters remain flat, and their stories are cautionary tales, intriguing in terms of the issues they raise yet a touch too facile and melodramatic. But there are flashes of genuine insight, tragedy, and great warmth" nonetheless. It was awarded the American Book Award from the New Columbus Foundation.

Love and Pain and Parting: The Novels of Kate O'Brien

Forty or so years ago I wrote something about the novels of Kate O'Brien and, about the same time, was privileged to meet and, as an immediate consequence, to admire that remarkable woman: as everybody who is interested in such things must admire her novels. Now I try to see her as she was then: a handsome, well-built woman with a mannish hairstyle and a direct, if courteous, way of speaking; and she put you on your toes and kept you there because you knew she was listening attentively to everything you said. You also knew that as well as being in the presence of a great novelist you were in the presence of a great lady, with something else added. It was not until I heard her talk of Teresa of Avila, about whom she wrote a book, and about Spain, about which she wrote several books, that I realized what that something else was. It was a touch of the Reverend Mother, but the Reverend Mother in Extraordinary: a Reverend Mother, who, like Teresa herself, was capable of great impulses: the poet Crashaw had written of the young Teresa that she was for the East and martyrdom; and a Reverend Mother capable also not only of expressing the profoundest thoughts on life and death, love and pain and parting, and on the nature of God and man.

Then in her book *Farewell Spain,* which appeared in 1937, I came across this remarkable passage. As one among a crowd of tourists, although she had never been a tourist anywhere, she is leaving the caves of Altamira and their neolithic drawings, and returning to the moving present and the lighted world. That simple act acquires for her an eschatological significance. She writes: "But the sentimentalist—I speak for myself—always comes out of that cave in a condition of broody inertness, a condition bordering on pain of some kind. Feeling unsociable like a homeless, evicted troglodyte. Pondering the accidents and blisses of initiative and genius, and the arrogant irresponsibility of the processes of life and time."

We must remember that she called one of her novels *Pray for the Wanderer.* It was a novel of protest, an exact and forceful one, against the then prevailing Irish puritanism. The title, as we all know, came from a hymn much heard in Irish Catholic churches in her and my childhood, and, naturally enough, written by an Englishman: and by the same Englishman, Father Faber of the Oratory, who also wrote, "Faith of Our Fathers," thunderously sung or rendered, not only in Irish churches but on the Gaelic playing-pitch at Croke Park. But the use of the title *Pray for the Wanderer,* may have implied more than just a wandering from a Catholic childhood and upbringing: the most worldwide of all wanderers is man, the evicted troglodyte whose name could easily be Adam.

Turning now to a partial rereading of Kate O'Brien I open first *The Ante-Room,* simply because it was the novel that she seemed at times to prefer to her other novels, insofar as any novelist is ever quite certain of such things. Her first novel was the highly successful *Without My Cloak,* published in 1931, a chronicle of the prosperous Considine family in the solid

Kate O'Brien

Kate O'Brien, a
novelist and playwright, was born in 1898 in Limerick, Ireland, and died August 13, 1974, in Faver-
sham, England. After attending University College
in Dublin, she began her career as a journalist in
London. O'Brien later changed her focus to drama
and her first play, *Distinguished Villa*, was performed in London in 1926. O'Brien is best known,
however, as a novelist. As a writer, she concentrated
mainly on the Irish middle class and the effects of
conservative Catholicism. Her first novel, *Without
My Cloak*, was published in 1931 and received the
James Tait Black Memorial Prize and the Hawthornden Prize that same year. O'Brien also lived in Spain
and wrote several novels that involved Spanish history and culture, including *For One Sweet Grape*,
which was made into a motion picture in 1955.
Other works by O'Brien include two travel books,
My Ireland and *Farewell, Spain*; a history and criticism, *English Diaries and Journals*; a biography, *Teresa of* Avila; and the nonfiction *Presentation Parlour*.

provincial town of Mellick: and few novelists have understood as well as Kate O'Brien did the
meaning of a prosperous house, a solid middle-class family, of a town not tumultuous enough
to be a city yet escaping small-town stagnancy. That was one theme in her work yet it was related so closely, if subordinated to other themes, death, departure, and the slow comprehending
of the soul, that her town of Mellick, for which we may read Limerick, and the Considine
household are of the first importance.

She delighted in finding her material in such houses and families: not the Big Houses of
the Irish novel from Edgeworth to Somerville and Ross, not the cabins as from Carleton to one
aspect of Liam O'Flaherty, but the solemn homes that years of trading enabled a provincial
mercantile class to build, or even the better-type convent-school to which the prosperous merchants would send their children. The Considine fortunes that provide the background for the
novel *Without My Cloak,* start in a sidestreet in Mellick with a canny forage merchant, a trade
built directly on the land. From those roots the family tree grows to produce in the end Caro-
line, who has in her a touch of Emma Bovary, or Denis, who has an artist's soul, or his uncle,
who, in London, lives the life of a gay bachelor.

When the novel opens the father of Denis has just built for himself outside the town and
away from the dusty pallor that two or three flourmills give to some of the streets, the house of
his heart's desire: a visible symbol of the transition inevitable in such families where the members, still conscious of the hard gnarled roots of their being, are also shortly to become aware of
the unaccustomed and exotic. The meaning may be that it takes several generations of hard
men of business to produce in the end one son capable of being a poet.

But when three years later *The Ante-Room* was published, Kate O'Brien had moved on to matters much deeper than even the most faithful observation of social matters. The anteroom of the title is not a place where the bourgeoise suffer for a time before becoming poets but the dread hall of silence and pain where body and soul embrace for the last time before the final parting: and death and departure, suffering and sin, exile, love satisfied and yet never satisfied have been predominant themes in Kate O'Brien's novels. Balanced, though, by humor and a great human tolerance: she was a humorous and tolerant woman, and although she had a great feeling for the saint who had longed for the East and martyrdom, she also knew that it was the same saint who could remark wryly that haste was the enemy of devotion. There was no morbidity about Kate O'Brien.

The entire action of the novel *The Ante-Room* happens in and around a great house of the Mellick middle-class. This is how it is introduced to us:

> "By eight o'clock the last day of October was as well-lighted as it would be. Tenuous sunshine, swathed in river mist, outlined the blocks and spires of Mellick, but broke into no highlights on the landscape or in the sky. It was to be a muted day.
>
> "Roseholm, the white house where the Mulqueens lived, stood amid trees and lawns on the west side of the river. Viewed from the town in fine weather, it could often seem to blaze like a small sun but it lay this morning as blurred as its surroundings. It neither received nor wanted noise or light, for its preoccupation now was to keep these two subdued. And this morning that was easy; there was no wind about to rattle doors or tear through dying leaves, but only an air that moved elegiacally and carried a shroud of mist.
>
> "Agnes Mulqueen slept with her curtains open, so that at eight o'clock, though still almost asleep, she was aware of movement and light. She turned in her bed and the weak sun fell upon her face though her eyelids still resisted it.
>
> "One by one the Mass bells ceased to ring in Mellick, and as their last note dropped away the clock in the hall at Roseholm, always slow, boomed out its cautious strokes. Agnes stirred and sighed. Once, when every whisper in the house had seemed to aggravate her mother's suffering, Agnes had suggested silencing that clock. But Teresa, her mother, would not have it. 'When I can't hear it any more,' she said, 'I'll know I'm at the Judgement Seat'."

Teresa Mulqueen is dying of cancer. Grouped around her last agony, which happens over the Eve and Feast of All Saints and the Feast of All Souls, are that daughter, Agnes, in her middle-twenties; her sister, Marie-Rose, two years older; the husband of Marie-Rose, Vincent, in his late twenties; an aged and pious nursing nun and a pretty young nurse who is by no means a nun; Teresa's son, Reggie, broken and uglified by ten years of syphilis and mercury treatment; an efficient young doctor called William Curran who is in love with Agnes; the husband of Teresa, a decent, worried man: and others. Put in such summary, everything seems banal but the intricacy of the relations between these people, the intensity of their moral problems, the muted yet explosive atmosphere of that house of death submit to no summary. Agnes, hopelessly in love with her beloved sister's husband, and he tragically with her, sits at the dinner-table and reflects:

> "She, seated opposite her father at one end of the dining-table, with Vincent at her right side and William Curran at her left, with Marie-Rose glittering and curvetting on the young doctor's other side, and Reggie, next to Vincent, brooding happily, almost dreamily, above his burgundy glass, contemplating detachedly this softly-

lighted group, had felt a cold amazement stir in her that a house ostensibly surrendered to one sorrow should all at once give roof to so many unmentionable, intense and contradictory emotions. Her mother lay upstairs, waiting for God to reprieve a sentence which He would not reprieve—and because of her and her approaching death, this scene—so exciting, so reviving, so passionately alive—was set. Teresa, dying, was the reason, too, of Dr. William Curran. And she would die, but the maze they were treading tonight in her honour, one might say, and because she had forbidden them to celebrate the Eve of All Saints—when would they who were caught in it have learnt and forgotten, forsaken its intricacies."

The dance of life goes on around the central, final verity of death. Dr. Curran feels a cold sense of the futility of that life, its brevity and sadness, and thinks:

"We are helpless, ignorant and helpless. And it isn't the final impassivity of heaven that matters, though that's like a caul enclosing the world. That's unavoidable. But our worst helplessness has only to do with the affairs of this immediate life—and we'll never correct it, because we'll never find a way to learn the workings of each other. This uniqueness, this isolation—oh God, it makes the simplest day unbearable."

Discovering that the chaste and religious woman he loves is in love with her sister's husband, he walks away from the house in darkness and agony, and knows that nothing is too silly or wasteful to be a fact, nothing too destructive to be true. Even the beautiful but not too brainy Marie-Rose realizes; how shocking a thing transience was which sounded gradual and gentle. She and her husband in the early days of a marriage that has now turned sour, existed in such a marvelous sea of passion that for a while it surrounded and disguised their chill islands of self-assertion. The time of the novel is 1880: and without the strict Catholic and social morality that binds them all, the struggles of their souls and bodies would be, if not meaningless, at least otherwise and less agonizing. To release them from such social and religious clamps would be false, in art and in history.

In her novel *Mary Lavelle,* as later in Maura Laverty's novel *No More Than Human,* a young Irish girl goes out as a governess to Spain. Both novelists in their time had done exactly that. It was one way of seeing the world and learning languages. It was also another Irish way of going into exile: the word in those days, before the Atlantic could be crossed in four or five hours, still retained something of its ancient, poignant meaning: as valid a way of going into exile, say, as that of Frankie Hannafey in Seán Ó Faoláin's novel *Come Back to Erin,* when he fled for refuge to New York; or that of Patrick MacGill when he went picking potatoes or shovelling red-hot cinders with the migratory laborers in Scotland.

But Mary Lavelle, and Kate O'Brien, who wrote her story, did not lose Ireland in order to find Spain, and all through Kate O'Brien's work it was clear that her adoption of Spain had not in any way weakened the grip of the roots that held her to her own country. There is nothing of the exile's traditional nostalgia in the way in which Mary Lavelle, after six weeks in Spain, can compare Irish faces and Spanish faces, finding that the faces of Irishmen are expressive and mobile, that the faces of Spanish men are, with their arresting and reserved gravity of eye, perpetually wearing masks. But Kate O'Brien adopted only one country and not the whole world, and was preserved from becoming merely a cosmopolitan writer by that deep sense of the mystical meaning of arrival and departure, of death which is the final departure and the prelude to the last arrival. Spain influenced her so powerfully not only because she happened to go there when she was young, but because the cast of her mind had something naturally akin to the land of Teresa and John of the Cross, and even of that odd man, Philip the great king. To this I will return later.

But it occurs to me now that there is here an interesting parallel, or contrast, between the novel *Mary Lavelle,* and a later novel *The Last of Summer,* published in 1943. *Mary Lavelle* was the first of her novels to get her into trouble with the ludicrous Irish censorship of the period: for Mary, alas, had herself seduced in Spain, romantically and beautifully seduced but still seduced: and that didn't happen to Irish girls in Spain or anywhere else and even if it did other Irish girls were by no means supposed to say so. Nor Irish boys!

In passing it may be worth commenting on how apt Kate O'Brien could be at picking splendid quotation titles: *Without My Cloak, The Land of Spices, The Last of Summer, Pray For the Wanderer, As Music and Splendour.* Oratory was not lost in the world she lived in.

To return: the novel *Mary Lavelle* sent a young Irish girl to Europe. But in *The Last of Summer,* a young woman, daughter of an Irish father and a French mother, comes back to the County Clare, uninvited and as a consequence unexpected, to search for the house and the places of which she had heard her father speak so often. He had become estranged from his people for marrying not only a foreign woman but a minor actress. He is dead and so is his wife: but some homing instinct or some *pietas* draws his daughter back to the places of his boyhood. As she is unexpected, she leaves her bag at the station on the fringe of the small town and sets off walking toward some of her father's people, his home, her home. She meets some children on the way and smiles at them ingratiatingly: and one big, bright-eyed girl looks at her with unexpected animosity and says with a sneer: "What happened to your lips?" Now this was in the days when lipstick and the marks of it were as uncommon in rural Ireland as women in tight trousers:

> The other children looked alarmed but they giggled. Angele hurried past them along the empty road. She was shaking, dared not speak or look back. She felt tears of fury in her eyes. What a fool she was. Surely she knew yokeldom by now, in many countries, and was accustomed to being a stranger in places where strangers are targets.

> But in this shaft sped by a rude little girl—no novelty—she felt without reason a greater force than could have been intended; she felt an accidental expression of something which had vaguely oppressed and surprised her, these ten days, in the Irish air—an arrogance of austerity, contempt for personal feeling, coldness and, perhaps, fear of idiosyncrasy. In this most voluptuously beautiful and unusual land. She could not help the tears in her eyes. She hated the rudeness, and she heard the insult to her reddened mouth symbolically—so self-conscious was she. She heard it as an ignoble warning from the people of her father. If I could only stop being so idiotically self-conscious! If I could give up responding to every dotty little nothingness that blows my way:

> The tears did not fall. She laughed outright. At herself and at the rude little girl. What happened to your lips? Well, of all the nerve! I've a jolly good mind to go back and give her the thrashing of her life.

> She laughed delightedly and leaned on the low mossy wall of a bridge. Divine Olympian river. Of an entirely other character than the sweet English streams or the winding waters of France. And how familiar it was to her from father's description. If it *was* your river you would know it always across years of absence.

Pray for the wanderer: and the wanderer, or at any rate the wanderer's daughter, returns to encounter that semi-comic insult and censure. There is in that passage a sharp and true analysis of our Irish character. Of course in 1992 no little rural Irish colleen is likely to pass remark on a lady wearing lipstick, or anything or nothing else. In fact the little rural Irish *cáilín* is herself liable to be wearing the oddest garments.

It seems a long time since the old parish priest in a Kerry seaside resort said from the pulpit, and in the height of the holiday season, that he saw a lot of strange women going around in trousers: and it would be much more pleasing to God if they went around without them. And in the 1940s there was a character in Myles na Gopaleen who said gloomily that there was nothing but trousers in Russia.

Howandever: as a symbol of our Irish censorious instinct, the balefulness behind the laughing Irish eyes, the devil, not little and not dancing, that sneering little child will do very well. She learned the art from her elders.

The Last of Summer, is one of the easiest of Kate O'Brien's novels, yet it is filled with wonders, among them a splendid description of the Cliffs of Moher:

> "It was a hot clear day with, even here, only a gentle breeze.... the cliffs, declining, exposed an open sea, quiet and luminous, yet hardly bluer than the blue sky. The land shelved downward to the east in a composed, stripped pattern of green turf, grey walls and little houses, painted white, or pink or blue. There were no trees in sight. A few sheep grazed, and gulls and curlews cried; an empty road twisted between the field like a slack white ribbon.
>
> "Angele considered all of this with wondering pleasure. Sharply outlined clear, immaculate, and seeming on this day to overflow with light, the scene, dramatically balancing austerity with passion, surprised her very much and made her unwilling to cry out in hasty praise. Yet though so individual, so unlike other recollected scenes of beauty, it struck at her heart nostalgically, she felt. Something it held of innocence, of positive goodness, familiarised at the first encounter to emotional memory.
>
> "The water lay cold and still, very far below, profoundly shadowed by the great uneven wall of rock which stretched to left and right. There was no sound now, either of bird or wave; little frills of foam came and went on the quiet tide, a lonely, black canoe, seeming absurdly small and with three tiny shapes of men in it, moved outward, escaping from the shadow of the cliffs into blue water."

Moher has never been so well described, but the importance of the passage is not even in the fine landscape or seascape painting but in the suggestion that such a vision may also be part of ancestral memory. Yet Kate O'Brien, a rational woman, was not as far as I know (and, perhaps, in spite of her own words, quoted earlier) much given to any sentimental nostalgia: or, if she was at all affected by it, it would be for the study-hall in a convent school, for candles burning for benediction on a flower-laden altar, for gentle voices singing slightly sentimental hymns. The only pain of parting that Kate O'Brien seems to have seen as merely a human affair was the pain in a schoolgirl's heart when schooldays are over and familiar and loved places must be abandoned forever.

Yet in what is possibly her greatest novel, *The Land of Spices,* even that simple emotion is raised to a different level, or seen from a different angle, when the reverend mother who is the central character in that novel leaves the Irish convent to return to the continent to take over control of the entire Order: "Her heart was sad. Sad that a return often dreamt of would be at last to graves and empty places; sad that a departure which once she had most bitterly desired should seem at its coming so inconsistently a sacrifice. And indeed twisting about in her soul against her undisciplined pain, she marvelled how emotionalists endured their lives at all, since she who hardly tolerated feeling found its touch intolerable."

Kate O'Brien found her title for that novel in the sonnet in which George Herbert with a magnificent recurrence, names and renames the hope and miracle of prayer. It may have been one of her favorite poems: I do remember her pleasure one day when, with considerable effort, for it is an intricate poem, I managed to quote it word-perfect up to the last two splendid lines:

Church-bells beyond the stars heard; the soul's blood,
The land of spices, something understood.

The mood of the novel borrowed something from the mood of the great sonnet. But, alas, when the novel was published in 1941 it fell foul of the deplorable censors: who may not have read George Herbert. All this may now seem to people, say under fifty-five, a long time ago: but the case was so ludicrous or scandalous, or both, that it may still be worth reflecting on. Perhaps the censors thought that spices had something to do with spicy, and it would obviously be wrong to write a spicy novel about a convent. To me, it may be the best of the three great somber, meditative novels she has written: the other two are *The Ante-Room,* and *That Lady:* because in *The Land of Spices,* she is dealing, as it were, at source, with the values she applied in other novels dealing with life outside the convent walls; with the strength and weakness of human love, with life as a series of departures leading to that final and inevitable departure. But because in one brief passage the sexual nature of her father, whom the reverend mother remembers with love, yet whose fault, as she saw it, drove her away from human love, is mentioned, the book was banned, under the terms of the Act, as being in general tendency indecent or obscene. In so far as I ever heard or could make out, this was the relevant passage:

Her father's study was at the back of the house, above the kitchen. It had a long wide balcony of wrought iron which ran full across the wall and ended in an iron staircase to the garden. This balcony made a pleasant deep shade over the flagged space by the kitchen door, where Marie-Jeanne, the servant, often sat to prepare vegetables or to have a sleep. Traffic was free up and down those stairs and (her father) was not formal about access to his study, even when he was working, even when he was having a silent and solitary mood.

Helen…ran up the iron stairs, along the balcony to the open window of her father's study.

"She looked into the room.

"Two people were there. But neither saw her; neither felt her shadow as it froze across the sun.

"She turned and descended the stairs. She left the garden and went on down the curve of Rue Saint Isidore. She had no objective and no knowledge of what she was doing. She did not see external things. She saw Etienne and her father in the embrace of love."

As we have seen, Kate O'Brien began her novel-writing with that long chronicle of the Considine family, going back a century to find the origins of the people she wrote about and tracing their growth almost up to the present. But her most deliberate use of history as a framework to support her telling of death and departure and families, and sin, was made possible not by Irish but by Spanish history. In the foreword to *That Lady,* she was careful to point out that she was not writing an historical novel but an invention arising from reflection on the curious external story of Ana de Mendoza and Philip II, of Spain:

"Historians cannot explain the episode, and the attempt is not made in a work of fiction. All the personages in this book lived and I have retained the historical outline of events in which they played a part; but everything which they say and write in my pages is invented and—naturally—also are their thoughts and emotions. And in order to retain unity of invention I have refrained from grafting into my fiction any part of their recorded letters or observations."

It is a most interesting approach. For since she has clearly disavowed any intention of writing a straight historical novel (from which, as a general rule, the Lord preserve us), and since she has called the book an invention, any discussion on its truth to the period can be dispensed with, and the novel seen for what it is: a protracted case of conscience discussing with insight the problems of a good woman who has sinned, of a libertine, Antonio Perez, who has fallen in love, of a scrupulous king resenting the ability of the less scrupulous to commit the sin he shrinks from: in the exact sense of the phrase, a classical situation.

As her three great novels bear witness, Kate O'Brien was as fond of a case of conscience as any zealous Jesuit could be. Ana de Mendoza is the widow of a man who has been counselor and close friend of Philip the king. Vulgar rumor has it that she has also been Philip's mistress. Actually she is, in friendship, very close to the king and he, valuing her friendship, does probably in some obscure corner of his death-possessed soul pride himself in possessing in vulgar rumor, something that for complex moral reasons, at least, he does not possess. Ana, in her widowhood, her wealth, her family pride, her close friendship with the king becomes the mistress of Antonio Perez, a married libertine who is also a counselor of the king. A grand affair begins, is discovered and horribly punished by a king who, like most righteous people doing horrible things, is probably not at all clear about his actual motives. Nevertheless, the novelist makes it quite clear that Philip is not the villain of the story as she writes it. The quotation from George Meredith's *Modern Love* seems here inevitable:

The wrong is mixed. In tragic life, God wot,
No villain need be! Passions spin the plot;
We are betrayed by what is false within.

But there is in *That Lady,* as in *The Ante-Room,* and *The Land of Spices,* the power of feeling bursting like a shell among a group of devoted people, devoted, once again, in the exact classical sense of the word. Mary Lavelle in Spain loses her heart and her virginity, returns to Ireland with tears in her eyes and the first seeds of experience sown in her soul. The young man in *The Ante-Room* loves his wife's sister with a hopeless love and ends it, romantically and sentimentally, by looking down the barrel of a gun and thinking of his childhood: "He remembered leaning on a gun in the garden at home on a sunny day, leaning like this and talking to his mother. It was summer and she was sewing. She had said: 'Don't lean on it, Vin. It will mark your face.' Darling mother. She smiled. He could see every detail of her smile. Darling mother. He pulled the trigger, his thoughts far off in boyhood."

In *The Land of Spices,* the memory of the fearful moment when her father's secret, left-handed love had been revealed to her could not black out in the nun's mind the many memories of an endearing, civilized man who loved the poetry of Traherne, and Herbert, and Crashaw.

But in *That Lady,* Kate O'Brien deliberately sacrificed every human consolation and saw her people and their plight, or sin, against the background of a greater reality, or God. An illicit love-affair in the upper reaches of society offers to the romantic and the sentimentalist, or the merely curious, the opportunity for a lot of fun. To the rigid moralist it opens the gate for thundering judgments about scandal and the inevitability of punishment. Kate O'Brien followed her own path, saw the beauty and the pity of the doomed passion, the doubt of the sinner, the complexities of repentance, the instability of the ground on which the king stands when he, playing a sour God, contrives judgment and punishment. Ana, with her lover in her arms and fearful scruples in her mind, thinks: "Is my poor scruple greater than what I

■ **BOOKS BY KATE O'BRIEN**

Without My Cloak. Garden City, New York: Doubleday, Doran and Company, 1931, Reprinted. New
York: Viking Penguin, 1987.

The Ante-Room. Garden City: Doubleday, Doran and
Company, 1934, Reprinted. New York: Viking
Penguin, 1990.

Mary Lavelle. Garden City: Doubleday, Doran and
Company, 1936, Reprinted. New York: Viking
Penguin, 1985, as *Talk of Angels,* New York:
Hyperion Press, 1997.

Farewell, Spain. Garden City: Doubleday, Doran and
Company, 1937, Reprinted. Boston: Beacon
Press, 1985.

Pray for the Wanderer. New York: Doubleday, Doran
and Company, 1938.

The Land of Spices. Garden City: Doubleday, Doran
and Company, 1941, Reprinted. New York:
Viking Penguin, 1990.

The Last of Summer. Garden City: Doubleday, Doran
and Company, 1943.

English Diaries and Journals. London: W. Collins,
1947, (c1943).

For One Sweet Grape. Garden City: Doubleday, Doran
and Company, 1946, Reprinted. London: W.
Heinemann Ltd., 1947. Retitled: *That Lady.*

Teresa of Avila. London: M. Parrish, 1951.

The Flower of May. New York: Harper, 1953.

As Music and Splendour. New York: Harper, 1958.

My Ireland. New York: Hastings House, 1962.

Presentation Parlour. London: Heinemann, 1963.

give this man and take from him? Am I to set my little private sense of sin above his claim on me and his unhappiness? Am I cheating because I want him and have grown tired of the unimportant fuss of my immortal soul? Am I pretending to be generous simply to escape again into his power?"

Those questions leave little room for romantic illusions but they open the door to pity: not the destructive pity that obsesses Graham Greene, but a tired, welcoming pity that could be a shadow of God's mercy. Towards the end of the novel Ana talks to her friend the Cardinal Quiroga about her problems, and the novelist removes the last illusion by seeming to say that even mercy can be presumed on. Ana accepts her guilt:

> "I have repented long ago in that clear-cut sense and returned to the usual religious
> practices. And I accept these years and all that empty loneliness and forsakenness
> as a part perhaps of my purgatory. But as this purgatory was forced on me, I cannot
> seek to derive merit from it in heaven—and, in general, I can't with any honesty
> turn to God, as holy people say. Because, while accepting His ruling, I shall always
> be glad of Antonio."

The heart, and the novelist, have reasons that slip between the rigid lines of the theologian's textbook. But, and this is where Kate O'Brien shows that in an earlier century she might have been not a novelist but one of those valiant women learned in the science of God, the cardinal says: "God doesn't ask the impossible of you, you conceited woman."

The nun in *The Land of Spices* saw the truth after much experience and much lonely suffering:

> Free in her meditations on God's will and His hopes for humanity she admitted that
> human love must almost always offend the heavenly lover by its fatuous egotism.
> To stand still and eventually understand was, she saw, an elementary duty of love.
> To run away, to take cover, to hate in blindness, and luxuriously to seek vengeance
> in an unexplained cutting-off, in a seizure upon high and proud antithesis—that
> was stupidity masquerading offensively before the good God.

She meditates on the future of the girl, another Anna, reared in this upper-class convent, as indeed Kate herself was, her parents having died when she was young:

And now all was done that age may do for childhood. Anna's schooldays were closed and there was no appeal against the advance of life and the flight of innocence. She had been taught to be good and to understand the law of God. Also, she had been set free to be herself. Her wings were grown and she was for the world. In poverty, in struggle, in indecisiveness—but for some these were good beginnings. Good for Anna, Reverend Mother thought, and was glad to know that it was forward to them she was going. Prayer would follow her, prayer always could. It would have been happy to have been at hand, a little longer, to have heard something of the first flights and first returns. But such a wish was nothing. All that could be done was done. Anna was for life now, to make what she could of it. Prayer could go with her, making no weight—and whether or not she remembered the days of the poems an ageing nun would remember them. How sweet is the shepherd's sweet lot, from the morn to the evening he strays. Reverend Mother passed by the bright opening of the elm-trees and looked over the lawns to the blue lake.

Benedict Kiely
April, 1992

Imagining the Real: The Fiction of Tim O'Brien

Drafted in 1968, Tim O'Brien served in Vietnam in 1969, and in the fall of 1970 he enrolled in Harvard University's doctoral program in government. During his first year of graduate school O'Brien began writing *If I Die in a Combat Zone*, a memoir of his Vietnam experiences. Taking a year off from Harvard in 1973–74 to work as a general assignment reporter for the *Washington Post*, O'Brien also found time to write *Northern Lights*, his first novel. Realizing that the *form* of *If I Die* did not allow him to get at important psychological truths or to fully explore the meaning of his Vietnam experiences, and convinced that the life of the imagination is half of war—indeed, half of *any* kind of experience—O'Brien gave his fertile imagination free rein in *Going After Cacciato*, a highly inventive and skillfully crafted novel which won the National Book Award in 1978 over John Irving's celebrated *The World According to Garp*. Returning to the apocalyptic themes of *Northern Lights*, O'Brien's most recent work, *The Nuclear Age*, is a warning that our species will not survive if we continue to conceive of the Bomb and nuclear war as mere *metaphors*. We must, O'Brien's protagonist continually exhorts us, *imagine the real*.

A painstaking and meticulous craftsman in his own writing, O'Brien nonetheless insists that style is not the most important element of good literature. "Stylistic problems," O'Brien asserted in an interview,

> can be solved: by writing better, by recognizing your own faults and getting rid of them. What *can't* be learned, however, is passion for ideas—substance. Out of every forty books of contemporary fiction, I'm lucky to find one which gives the sense of an author who really gives a shit about a set of philosophical issues. I'm not saying that fiction should *be* philosophy, but I am saying that a fiction writer must demonstrate in his work a concern for rightness and wrongness. What I see instead is concern for style and craft and structure. I see concern for well-drawn characters, concern for plot, concern for a whole constellation of things which, however, seem peripheral to the true core of fiction: the exploration of substantive, important human values.

Dissatisfied, then, with the "contemporary tendency to examine purely personal daily concerns—the minutiae of life," O'Brien conceives of all of his work as somewhat "political" in that it is directed at big issues. Among his chief concerns: What are the meanings of courage and justice, and how can they be achieved? How does one do right in an evil situation? How and why do people become politicized and depoliticized? How do one's imagination and one's memory interpenetrate, interlock?

▪ II

Although O'Brien has written two Vietnam books, and the Indochina conflict is clearly of more than tangential concern in his other two novels, he considers himself neither a Vietnam writer

Tim O'Brien

William Timothy O'Brien was born October 1, 1946, in Austin, Minnesota. Although educated at Macalester College and Harvard University, Tim O'Brien discovered his vocation as a writer in Vietnam. He worked briefly as a national affairs reporter for the *Washington Post* before entering the army and serving a tour of duty in Vietnam, where he became a sergeant. He won the National Book Award in 1979 for *Going After Cacciato*. He also has won the Vietnam Veterans of America award (1987), the Heartland Prize from the *Chicago Tribune* (1990) for *The Things They Carried*, and the James Fenimore Cooper Prize for Historical Fiction (1994) for *In the Lake of the Woods*. He has received awards from the National Endowment for the Arts, the Massachusetts Arts and Humanities Foundation, and the Guggenheim Foundation. His works have been translated into several foreign languages. He lives in Boxford, Massachusetts. ■

nor a war writer. What Vietnam provided O'Brien was the impetus and spark for *becoming* a writer. In fact, while in Vietnam O'Brien wrote a number of short vignettes or anecdotes, including the first version of the "Step Lightly" chapter that appears in *If I Die*. At that time, however, O'Brien believed that he was merely writing in the sense that everyone does—in letters and postcards—and he did not yet think of himself as a writer. And once back in the United States, O'Brien's fundamental concern was getting through his doctoral program; writing was a kind of sidelight. At night, when he was tired of studying, O'Brien stitched together a number of his vignettes in roughly chronological order, sent his book off, and forgot about it.

Acknowledging that he did not yet "know what literature was," O'Brien feels fortunate that he got *If I Die* out of his system, or *Cacciato* might have ended up as merely another autobiography cast as fiction, and "wouldn't have been nearly so good." Intended to be straight autobiography or war memoir, *If I Die* is frequently called a novel (the spine of my Dell paperback says, "FIC"), and the book *is* written not unlike a novel: O'Brien draws scenes as a novelist would draw them, and the book's language is different from the language of nonfiction. If there is little in *If I Die* to presage the extraordinary inventiveness and originality of *Cacciato*, it is a well-written book and it introduces a number of central concerns that inform all of O'Brien's novels.

During the summer of 1968, with an induction notice tucked into a corner of his wallet, O'Brien engaged in many serious discussions about the Vietnam War. Driving around and around the lake of his Minnesota prairie town, O'Brien and his friends would move very carefully from one argument to the next. Trying to make it a dialogue and not a debate, they "covered all the big questions: justice, tryanny, self-determination, conscience and the state, God and war and love." Most of his college friends found little difficulty avoiding the war—all to their credit—and O'Brien himself concluded that the war was wrongly conceived and poorly justified. But perhaps he was mistaken, and who really knew, anyway?

Since people were dying as a result of the war, it was evil. But there was also "the town, my family, my teachers, a whole history of the prairie. Like magnets, these things pulled in one direction or the other, almost physical forces weighting the problem, so that, in the end, it was less reason and more gravity that was the final influence." A confirmed liberal, but not a pacifist, O'Brien submitted:

> I did not want to be a soldier, not even an observer to war. But neither did I want to upset a peculiar balance between the order I knew, and my own private world. It was not just that I valued that order. I also feared its opposite—inevitable chaos, censure, embarrassment, the end of everything that had happened in my life, the end of it all.

Reciting a portion of Pound's "Hugh Selwyn Mauberly," O'Brien's friend Erik concedes that they are in basic training "not because of conviction, not for ideology; rather it's from fear of society's censure, just as Pound claims. Fear of weakness. Fear that to avoid war is to avoid manhood. We come to Fort Lewis afraid to admit we are not Achilles, that we are not brave, not heroes."

At Fort Lewis O'Brien remains no less divided, no less tormented, than before he arrived. Eight weeks before he is to board a plane for Vietnam, O'Brien locates the *Reader's Guide* in the Tacoma library and looks up "AWOL and Desertion." He finds the reading interesting—he is concerned with the psychology of desertion and with what compelled the deserters to pack up and leave—but he needs something more concrete: the laws of various countries, which nations will take deserters, and under what conditions. O'Brien's research persuades him that desertion is truly possible. There is no doubt it could be done. He does not *belong* at Fort Lewis. It is some ghastly mistake. His escape plans folded up in his billfold, he spends an hour or two a day working out the details, taking notes on Swedish history, culture, and politics. He begins to learn the language. He writes letters to his family, a teacher, and some friends, trying to explain his position, his problems of conscience in participating in the war. "Mostly, though, I tried to say how difficult it is to embarrass people you love."

In a cheap hotel O'Brien thinks the whole thing through for one final night. He vomits. His AWOL bag is ready to go, but he is not. He burns the letters to his family, and the other letters he has written. "It was over. I simply couldn't bring myself to flee. Family, the home town, friends, history, tradition, fear, confusion, exile: I could not run. I went into the hallway and bought a Coke. When I finished it I felt better, clearer-headed, and burned the plans. I was a coward. I was sick."

Returning from Vietnam, O'Brien is left with only a few "simple, unprofound scraps of truth. Men die. Fear hurts and humiliates. It is hard to be brave. It is hard to know what bravery *is*." O'Brien elucidates the difficulty of arriving at a satisfactory definition of courage in a chapter of *If I Die* called "Wise Endurance." Courage is more than the charge, and it is more than dying or suffering the loss of a love or being gallant. Hemingway's "grace under pressure" is also insufficient.

O'Brien recalls his favorite prewar heroes: Alan Ladd of *Shane*, Captain Vere, Humphrey Bogart as the proprietor of *Café d'Americain*, and, especially, Frederic Henry. None of them are *obsessed* by courage. As Frederic Henry realizes, courage is only one part of virtue; love and justice are other parts. For O'Brien, proper courage is wise courage, acting wisely when fear would have you act otherwise. Moreover, courage is indissolubly linked to thoughtfulness. Growing up in a town populated by "not very spirited people, not very thoughtful people," O'Brien must also endure thoughtlessness in Vietnam. He learns "that no one in Alpha Company gave a damn about the causes or purposes of their war: It is about 'dinks' and 'slopes,' and the idea is simply to kill them or avoid them." And when he tries to pry Captain Johansen (a model of valor for O'Brien) into conversation about the war, he will only talk tactics or history; when asked to share his views about the conflict's politics or morality, he is "ready with a joke or a shrug, sending the conversations into limbo or to more certain ground." If questions of the war's morality must remain elusive and problematical, O'Brien feels compelled to engage such questions, and he is convinced that they can be engaged most effectively when imagination becomes memory's ally.

■ III

O'Brien's approach to the novel is to try to make chapters into independent, self-contained stories, and many sections of *Cacciato* originally appeared as short stories, winning four prizes. O'Brien has welded together his stories into a seamless, smoothly polished and highly original novel which can be read as the reverse, or flip side, of *If I Die*. Believing that the most compelling aspect of human nature is its imaginative aspect—what we are capable of imagining, the modes in which we imagine, and imagination's impact on our daily behavior—O'Brien unleashes his imagination to investigate whether he could have lived with the consequences of running from the war.

Cacciato opens with Paul Berlin, the novel's central consciousness, lamenting the men his squad has lost:

> It was a bad time. Billy Boy Watkins was dead, and so was Frenchie Tucker. Billy Boy had died of fright, scared to death on the field of battle, and Frenchie Tucker had been shot through the nose. Bernie Lynn and Lieutenant Sidney Martin had died in tunnels. Pederson was dead and Rudy Chassler was dead. Buff was dead. Ready Mix was dead. They were all among the dead.

When there is not death there is boredom. In ten short chapters (all entitled "The Observation Post") Berlin stands guard from about midnight until sunrise in Quang Ngai near the South China Sea. In another series of chapters episodes from his tour in Vietnam return to haunt him, interspersed with occasional recollections of his youth. The war is horrible and absurd, and Berlin prefers not to think about it. Pretending is his favorite trick to forget the war, and his imagination explores "possibilities." Berlin becomes an artist, and his hero is the dumb, crazy Cacciato, who simply leaves the war and begins walking to Paris, 8,000 miles away. Third Squad chases the AWOL Cacciato for six months, and the chapters which recount this picaresque journey give the novel its narrative thrust and power.

"I hope he keeps moving," Berlin whispers to Doc Peret early in the novel. "He does that, we'll never catch him." Cacciato leads Third Squad west, and Paul Berlin urges him on, finding the impossible escape "a splendid idea." As the elusive Cacciato lures Third Squad to Paris, they begin to walk a very thin line between duty and desertion. The chase is by no means always idyllic—at one point they fall into a tunnel system and become prisoners of war, and later, arrested by the Savak in Iran, they witness a beheading—but for most of the squad the hunt is clearly preferable to the war.

Paul Berlin's flights of imagination when he becomes an artist are his only meaningful moments in a war in which he has no stake beyond simple survival. His only goal is "to live long enough to establish goals worth living for still longer." Unlike the alienated anti-heroes so common in contemporary literature, Berlin yearns for normalcy:

Peace and quiet. It was all he'd ever wanted. Just to live a normal life, to live to an old age. To see Paris, and then to return home to live in a normal house in a normal town in a time of normalcy. Nothing grand, nothing spectacular. A modest niche. Maybe follow his father into the building business, or go back to school, or meet a pretty girl and get married and have children. Years later he could look back and tell them about the war. Wasn't that normal?

But normalcy can be only a distant dream, and Berlin needs dreaming—and pretending—to get through a terrible war. Berlin pretends that he is not in the war, that he has not watched Billy Boy Watkins die of fright. He pretends Vietnam is the Wisconsin woods: "It was the same as Wisconsin. Paul Berlin closed his eyes. It was the same. Pines, campfire smoke, walleyes frying, his father's after-shave lotion. Big Bear and Little Bear, pals forever. Lake country was always so sweet." For Berlin pretending is not dreaming, nor is it craziness. It is simply "a way of passing time, which seemed never to pass."

In his first report from "The Observation Post," Berlin wonders "about the immense powers of his own imagination. A truly awesome notion. Not a dream, an idea. An idea to develop, to tinker with and build and sustain, to draw out as an artist draws out his visions." The vision that Berlin will draw out, develop, and limn with rich, imaginative fullness, of course, is the possibility of Cacciato's impossible escape. The fact that the whole idea is crazy, Berlin muses, does not make it impossible. Even if there is only one chance in a million it might be possible. Later Berlin imagines a million possibilities. With luck and daring and courage and endurance it might be done. "It could be done. Wasn't that the critical point? It could truly be done."

Shortly after Cacciato's departure Berlin and Doc Peret discuss the deserter's chances. "I dig adventure, too, but you can't get to Paris from here. Just can't," Peret insists. "None of the roads leads to Paris." Berlin, however, is not yet entirely willing to capitulate to Peret's pessimism. In fact, "He might have even tried it himself. With courage, he thought, he might even have joined in, and that was the one sorry thing about it, the sad thing: He might have."

If it is a failure of courage, it is also a failure of imagination. At the end of *Cacciato* Berlin views "the immense stillness of the paddies, the serenity of things, the moon climbing beyond the mountains. Sometimes it was hard to believe it was a war." It is not the first time in Vietnam that Berlin has had this feeling. And the war seemed much less real before he went to Vietnam. Four credits shy of a degree from Centerville Junior College, Berlin once again feels a "vague restlessness" and drops out. "Don't you know there's a war on?" the school counselor asks.

And the truth was that he didn't. He knew, but not in any personal sense. He'd seen the fighting on TV, read about it, but never thought of it as real...And when he was drafted it came as no great shock. Even then the war wasn't real. He let himself be herded through basic training, then AIT, and all the while there was no sense of reality: another daydream, a weird pretending....

But as Doc Peret knows, "the realities always catch up with you." As Third Squad hunts Cacciato they move "with the dull plodding motions of men who move because they must." Paul Berlin himself marches "towards the mountains without stop or the ability to stop." Berlin's sense of duty and obligation is no less compelling. Sitting at a large circular table in a conference room of the Majestic Hotel in Paris is Berlin's alter ego, Sarkin Aung Wan, a Vietnamese refugee. Wan, who has become Berlin's companion during the chase, urges him not to be deceived by false obligation:

You are obliged, by all that is just and good, to pursue only the felicity that you yourself have imagined. Do not let fear stop you. Do not be frightened by ridicule or censure or embarrassment, do not fear name-calling, do not fear the scorn of others. For what is true obligation? Is it not the obligation to pursue a life at peace with itself?

The spotlight shifts to Paul Berlin. He states that he feels an obligation to see his mission to its end. He points out that his obligation "is to people, not to principle or politics or justice." But more than any positive sense of obligation, he confesses,

> what dominates is the fear of abandoning all that I hold dear. I am afraid of running away. I am afraid of exile. I fear what might be thought of me by those I love. I fear the loss of their respect. I fear the loss of my own reputation. Reputation, as read in the eyes of my father and mother, the people in my hometown, my friends. I fear being an outcast. I fear being thought of as a coward. I fear that even more than cowardice itself.

Moreover, peace of mind cannot be reduced to pursuing one's own pleasure; it is inextricably bound up with the attitudes of others, to what they want, and to what they expect. The crux of the matter is "how to find felicity within limits...Imagination, like reality, has its limits."

The meeting concludes. "There is no true negotiation. There is only the statement of positions." Or, as Berlin had concluded earlier, "Either you understood responsibility or you didn't, and she didn't." Berlin rejects Sarkin Aung Wan's alternative, yet finds his own less than satisfactory: "Guilty if you fulfilled old obligations, guilty if you abandoned them." Unable to jettison his own position, Berlin cannot imagine another one that he can live with.

At times it seems to Paul Berlin that he has wasted his whole life imagining things. As a kid he would spend long summer afternoons imagining everything he would have to do to become a professional baseball player: "Sometimes even writing down elaborate plans, working up a strategy, using his imagination as a kind of tool to shape the future. Not exactly daydreams, not exactly fantasies. Just a way of working out the possibilities. Controlling things, directing things. And always the endings were happy." Vietnam, however, affords Berlin no happy endings. The immense powers of his own imagination, celebrated in his earlier stint at The Observation Post, ultimately defer to cold-war America's definitions of duty and responsibility. If Berlin can imagine Cacciato's withdrawal from the war, he cannot *sanction* it. Like the rest of Third Squad, when Berlin confronts Cacciato in Paris it is not to accept his offer of liberation, but to bring him to "justice." Recoiling from the horrors of a war he cannot fathom, Berlin retreats into his own consciousness, but there too his range of possibilities is sharply limited.

About three quarters into the novel, in an important chapter entitled "The Things They Didn't Know," we are told that Berlin and soldiers like him did not know the Vietnamese language, or the people, or what the people loved and respected or feared or hated or hoped. They did not know religions or philosophies or theories of justice. They did not know whom to trust, or who were their friends or enemies. They did not know if it was a popular war, or a war of self-determination or self-destruction, outright aggression or national liberation.

Paul Berlin considers the possibility of returning to Quang Ngai some day to explain why he had allowed himself to go to war:

> Not because of strong conviction, but because he didn't know. He didn't know who was right, or what was right...he didn't know which speeches to believe, which books, which politicians; he didn't know who really started the war, or why, or when, or with what motives; he didn't know if it mattered; he saw sense in both sides of the debate, but he did not know where the truth lay...

He wishes he could explain to the Vietnamese people that he has "no villainy in his heart, no motive but kindness." Did not these utterly inscrutable people know that his nation's intentions were also honorable? "Even in Vietnam—wasn't the intent to restrain forces of incivility? The *intent*. Wasn't it to impede tyranny, repression, aggression? To promote some vision of goodness? Oh, something had gone terribly wrong. But the aims, the purposes, the ends—weren't they right?" In *The Quiet American* (perhaps still the best novel on Vietnam), Graham Greene quotes Byron in an epigraph: "This is the patent age of new inventions / For killing bodies and saving souls / All propagated with the best intentions." In the novel itself, Fowler lectures his American antagonist: "I hope to God you know what you are doing there. Oh, I know your motives are good, they always are…I wish sometimes you had a few bad motives, you might understand a little more about human beings. And that applies to your country, too, Pyle."

Paul Berlin had read the newspapers and magazines. He was not stupid. He was not uninformed. And because he did not know if the war was right or wrong, he saw no reason not to trust those with more experience. He loved his country. But even more than that, he *trusted* it. Berlin could hardly imagine—as the publication of *The Pentagon Papers* would help to reveal—that five American presidents from Truman to Nixon lied to the American people about what their nation was doing in Indochina.

In *If I Die*, O'Brien writes that as a high school student he became interested in politics and "tried going to Democratic party meetings. I'd read it was the liberal party. But it was futile. I could not make out the difference between the people there and the people down the street boosting Nixon and Cabot Lodge." But in *Cacciato* Paul Berlin, seeing "sense in both sides of the debate," seems unable to perceive how much alike the two sides really are. Does Berlin remember that when the momentous Tonkin Gulf Resolution passed by a vote of 416-0 in the House and 88-2 in the Senate, a *Washington Post* editorial reviled the "querulous and reckless dissent" of Senator Wayne Morse? Does Berlin recall what his high school history text said about his country's foreign policy? In an exhaustive study of high school history books Frances FitzGerald could find only *one* narrative text that explained the Vietnam War in a way that would be plausible to anyone who did not support it.

When American foreign policy congealed into a rigid anti-communist consensus shortly after World War II, dissent was equated with disloyalty, and the most crucial issues of U.S. policy, when debated at all, degenerated into discussions of *tactics* merely; fundamental assumptions were not questioned. U.S. involvement in the Indochina conflict, rather than an aberration, flowed quite ineluctably from the widespread acceptance of the Truman Doctrine and its indiscriminate containment policy.

Accentuating that his obligations are not to principles or politics, but to *people*, Paul Berlin seems unable to imagine what his nation's involvement in the war is doing to the *Vietnamese* people. Berlin can imagine—and evoke with stunning artistry—Cacciato's incredible flight to Paris. But what he cannot imagine is debating the moral and political questions that continue to haunt him except within the very narrow parameters of the cold-war consensus. In allowing U.S. policymakers to define the nature of the debate, and in uncritically accepting their assumptions, perspectives, and language, Berlin is an unwitting victim of the anti-communist consensus that continues to dominate American political life. He cannot ultimately liberate Cacciato because he cannot liberate his own imagination. In his inability to imagine alternatives or possibilities not sanctioned in cold-war America, Paul Berlin becomes complicitous in a criminal war. Asked by Lieutenant Corson what's wrong with Cacciato, Doc Peret responds, "Just dumb. He's just awful dumb, that's all." Is he?

■ **IV**

Acknowledging that *Northern Lights* is perhaps eighty pages too long—"there is so much crap surrounding the good stuff"—O'Brien intends at some point to go over his manuscript and cut it considerably before it is reissued. If *Northern Lights* as first published does indeed lack the concision of *Cacciato*, it also surely has enough "good stuff" to merit a return to print in a carefully pruned revision. As in his Vietnam books, the concept of courage is once again central, and the apocalyptic mood, images and themes of *Northern Lights* anticipate their more extended and pronounced treatment in *The Nuclear Age*.

When *Northern Lights* opens it is 1970 and, as always, there is nothing much to do in Sawmill Landing, a dying town in northern Minnesota. Paul Milton Perry, restless and afraid, awaits the return of his brother Harvey from Vietnam. No one in Sawmill Landing knows a damn thing about the war—outside of the town's orbit, it is not talked about in the drug store—"then gangbusters, bang, old Harvey gets drafted." Perry stays out of it (the war isn't real anyway), and it is only natural that Harvey the rascal, the football player, "the brave balled bullock," should be the one to go off to war.

Saying little about the war or losing an eye, Harvey does not seem bitter, and sometimes even appears to treat it all as a great adventure that, if possible, he would not mind repeating. But something is missing. "Where's my parade?" Harvey asks at regular intervals, and when he finally does participate in a Memorial Day parade, he grumbles, "Miserable parade. No class at all…I still haven't got a decent parade out of all this." Craving adventure no less than a decent parade, Harvey insists that Perry accompany him on a cross-country skiing trip into the untamed Minnesota woods. "We've got to get out and really see these woods," Harvey had declared shortly after his return from Vietnam. Lamenting that there is not enough forest any more but convinced that their woods are the best that remain, Harvey successfully persuades Perry to join him.

Overruling his wife Grace's misgivings—"it's another of Harvey's ideas and it's worse than most of them, so it must be pretty awful"—Perry emphasizes that his brother has everything arranged, including maps and "about a billion dollars worth of gear, the best stuff," and maybe this is what Harvey needs. But Perry also senses that they may be rushing too blindly into the woods, too quickly and without forewarning or proper preparation. Nevertheless, "the momentum of departure was taking hold, an inertia that seemed to have started years before, slowly growing until it was a locomotive that wailed down an incline uncontrolled, and Perry held on, following Harvey's lead."

Perry chases Harvey, but the snow soon turns into a blizzard, and Perry realizes that they are lost. Perry also realizes with perfect clarity that he is afraid. Maintaining that "it's under control," yet unable to fathom how they have become lost, Harvey declares: "We've got ourselves a challenge…Not even a bloody challenge really." Told to forget the challenges, Harvey rejoins, "No problem. Trust the old soldier." And Harvey contends that being lost is not the worst thing in the world: "What if the goddamn world ends? What if the world collapses and the fucking Russians shoot off their bombs?"

Early on their trip, listening to the fire and Harvey's snoring, Perry reflects: "A bull, all right. He knew what he was doing…they were different. Harvey knew what he was doing. Calm, building that fire, unafraid, a full-fledged undaunted hero, absolutely no question." But soon his brother becomes very ill, and Perry no longer chases Harvey, but now *leads* him. And he saves his life. Perry is forced to build his own fire from scratch (without any help or smug advice from Harvey), and he is proud of it.

Harvey, who had once saved Perry from a near drowning, rarely misses an opportunity to ridicule his brother's lack of courage. "No spine. You don't really have spine, do you?" Harvey sneers. When they stop at the town dump and Perry evinces insufficient enthusiasm for killing a rat paralyzed by their car's headlights, Harvey taunts, "Are you afraid to kill it? I'll do it if you're afraid." Closing his eyes tightly, Perry clubs the rat, but it escapes. Later, however, when they are lost in the woods, Perry kills a woodchuck for food. Harvey demeans his achievement, but Perry no longer cares. He is "exhilarated, proud, content and warm." And he even begins to think of *himself* now as an adventurer who will have some fine story to tell the townspeople, and the son Grace wanted. He can tell them that he had become "absolutely and undeniably unafraid, fearless, simply acting, thinking of the things he would tell them."

Harvey, who had once observed that a man could survive for years in the woods if he knew what was what, does not talk of their long days of being lost. But as always he continues to talk of adventure, of leaving Minnesota and going to Africa, or Paris, or Italy, or to the swamps of New Guinea, where he had earlier dreamed of beginning a new life with Addie, his Lady Brett. They would plant new seeds that Harvey had "prudently set aside for just such catastrophes." When Addie leaves Sawmill Landing for Minneapolis, Harvey vows to go to Mexico City and have a terrific time without her: "And who needs Addie? Who needs a squaw, anyway? We don't need any of that. No women, just us." For Harvey the idea is to just go and go and not come back. In a continuous flight from a confrontation with himself, Harvey has learned nothing from his experiences. His infrequent insights are always evanescent.

When Perry finally emerges from the woods, he is depressed: "There ought to have been crowds. The highway should have been jammed with well-wishers." But that he too will receive no parade is only a temporary setback. Given new life by an immersion in Pliney's Pond, Perry overcomes his habitual restless torpor; he will give Grace the child that she wants, and he decides to sell the family house and find a new job. As Harvey concedes, Perry has now "taken the old bull by the horns and who's to argue?"

Harvey suggests that selling their house might help to end his malaise, but he is reluctant to abandon its bomb shelter: "Solid as rock. It'll take anything. Hate like the devil to leave it, you know. Bad news getting caught in a nuclear war without your trusty bomb shelter." When from his bed his imperious, moribund father ordered a bomb shelter built, Harvey quit high school football to dig it. The shelter—without Perry's help—was finished just in time for the Cuban missile crisis, and there were no more jokes about the old man being crazy.

Calling to announce that their house has been sold, Bishop Markham asks, "You know what really sold 'em? The darned bomb shelter! Can you believe that? It's true, I swear…Maglione says he's gonna make it into a studio. Can't get more abstract than a bomb shelter, right?"

■ V

More than a few readers may have missed the irony of Markham's comments. That some reviewers did as well—viewing the bombshelter as "a pretty crude metaphor"—upset O'Brien, who did not intend it to be a metaphor at all: "it was just a damned bombshelter. A *real* one!" Readers (and reviewers) of O'Brien's latest work will not make a similar oversight. "Think about those silos deep in fields of winter wheat," exhorts narrator William Cowling on the second page of *The Nuclear Age*. "No metaphor. The bombs are real." A few pages later Cowling accentuates his point: "I've been around. I've seen the global picture and it's no fantasy—it's real. Ask the microorganisms in Nevada. Ask the rattlesnakes and butterflies on that dusty plateau at Los Alamos. Ask the wall shadows at Hiroshima…Take a trip to Bikini."

Cowling lives in a large expensive house in Montana's Sweetheart Mountains. There is not a neighbor for miles, but to be safe, he has purchased the surrounding land and fenced it in. He has installed a burglar alarm and dead-bolt locks on all doors. According to his wife, Bobbi, it was a lovely sort of life, but Cowling "could sometimes feel an ominous density in the world":

Beirut is a madhouse, and both superpowers continue to manufacture MIRVs. It is 1995, and Cowling's ethic is to minimize his risks, to take no chances. The hour has come to seize control, and Cowling is building a bomb shelter. His act is neither madness nor a lapse of common sense, but merely prudence.

A different diagnosis has been made by Bobbi and their skeptical and perspicacious twelve-year-old daughter, Melinda, both of whom Cowling has imprisoned in an upstairs bedroom. Fearing that her father may be trying to kill her, Melinda tells him that she could use a new father, "a *good* one this time. Get me one that's not so goddamn screwy." Bobbi has not spoken to Cowling for two months; when necessary she communicates by way of the written word, especially with poems like "Relativity," which begins: "Relations are strained / in the nuclear family." Lifting a chunk of granite, Cowling reflects:

> Relativity, for Christ sake. Metaphor. Poets should dig. Fire and ice—such sugar-coated bullshit, so refined and elegant. So stupid. Nuclear war, nuclear war, no big deal, just a metaphor. Fission, fusion, critical mass…The world, I realize, is drugged on metaphor, the opiate of our age. Nobody's scared. Nobody's digging. They dress up reality in rhymes and paint on the cosmetics and call it by fancy names. Why aren't they out here digging? Nuclear war. It's no symbol…I want to scream it: Nuclear war!

The bomb has been much more than a symbol for William Cowling for a long time; in 1958, when he was about Melinda's age, he converted his ping-pong table into a fallout shelter. Even as a kid—perhaps because he was a kid—he "understood that there was nothing make-believe about doomsday." It is terribly real, and the world is not safe. Why isn't anyone afraid? When his father finds him in the shelter, William, still half asleep, hears his name called out "in a voice so distant, so muffled and hollow, that it might've come from another planet." While his father does not openly mock him, he is too psychically numbed to have any empathy for his son, and as William takes his bath he hears his parents making jokes and hooting it up. William fails to see the humor in it.

Because his parents cannot understand the real issue—nuclear war and sirens and red alerts—William is forced to concoct "flashes" as a kind of handle on things, something they can latch on to. But William's metaphor fails, he is taken to a therapist, and all he wants to do is get back to normal. Lectured by his father that it is not healthy to dwell on all of the world's problems and dangers, and told that "we all have to keep the faith," William embraces his parents' psychic numbing and denial of the nuclear threat as the only possible solution, and, throughout seventh and eighth grades, carves out a comfortable slot for himself "at the dead center of the Bell-Shaped Curve."

Normalcy, though, is only a temporary solution. At Peverson State College, a mere forty miles from SAC's northern missile fields, William concludes that "in a time of emergency, the question will not be begged: What does one do?" Purchasing some poster paper, William writes, in simple block letters, THE BOMBS ARE REAL, and every Monday he stations himself in front of the school cafeteria. Ollie Winkler joins him a week later with a homemade model bomb, and William (no radical, not by a long shot) soon becomes involved with Ollie and three others in an underground radical movement. From 1969 to 1971 he logs perhaps 200,000 miles as the network's passenger pigeon, but it is "just a ride, and there were no convictions beyond sadness."

Having gone underground to escape the Vietnam War, William reflects on the "thick tangle of factors" that lead to political commitment. Linebacker Ned Rafferty is involved in the network only because the beautiful cheerleader Sarah Strouch is, and William acknowledges that his own motives are also not strictly political. William too is Strouch's lover, but she tires of "jumpstarting his conscience," and despises his "jellyfish attitude." For Sarah commitment is destiny, but for William it is difficult: "Two different value systems. She was out to change the world, I was out to survive it. I couldn't summon the same moral resources."

A quarter century later, able to summon even fewer moral resources, Cowling digs. It is time to retrench, and there is no reason to feel guilt, which went out with culottes. There are no more crusades; it is an era of disengagement. If you are sane you are scared, and if you are scared you dig. Or you dig if you *despair*. William once explained to Rafferty how it feels when you stop believing: "It feels fucking crazy...That's what craziness *is*. When you can't believe. Not in anything, not in anyone. Just can't fucking *believe*." He reiterates his point later, excoriating *Sarah's* lack of commitment: "You're selfish. You're fickle. You don't attach to things. You don't believe in causes *or* people, and what else is there?...You can't hold on. You can't endure...You're shallow and cowardly and vain and disgusting—you're probably mad—that's what madness *is*—can't stick, always sliding.... " If there is considerable truth in Cowling's denunciation, he undoubtedly suspects that he is also speaking about himself.

"Imagination," William's therapist once remarked, "that's your special gift, but you have to *use* it. Take charge." William himself had earlier asserted that imagination was his chief asset, but it is finally his imagination that fails him: "If we can imagine a peaceful, durable world, a civilized world, then we might some day achieve it. If not, we will not." Unable to imagine such a world, Cowling digs. His hole, he confesses, "is where faith should be. The hole is what we have when imagination fails...the hole, it seems, is in my heart."

Working on his bomb shelter two weeks earlier, Cowling was fortunate to be topside when a large boulder sheared off the north wall. It taught him a lesson: "You can die saving yourself. Even safety entails risk." Or, as Bobbi's poem "Backflash" concludes: "We destroyed this house / to save it."

■ VI

"A person is defined," Cowling believes, "by the quality of obsession." Making our most pressing issue *his* obsession, O'Brien has labored for seven years on *The Nuclear Age*. Like his novel's protagonist, O'Brien has undoubtedly often wondered, "What's wrong with me? Why am I alone? Why is there no panic? Why aren't governments being toppled? Why aren't we in the streets? Why do we tolerate our own extinction? Why do our politicians put warnings on cigarette packs and not on their own foreheads? Why don't we scream it? Nuclear war!"

Screaming, unfortunately, will accomplish very little. What *is* needed is much greater insight into what Eisenhower called "the military-industrial complex" and the other powerful forces in our culture that drive the arms race: nukespeak and the mystique of secrecy, interventionist foreign policies, the deification of science and technology, and "nuclearism," the deification of the bomb itself and our pathological dependence on weapons of mass destruction for security. And we especially need a thorough rethinking of "the Soviet threat," which is regularly distorted and exaggerated to generate support for new weapons systems and ever higher military budgets.

As *The Nuclear Age* weaves the threads from 1995 to 1958 to the turbulent sixties, it fails to connect individual madness to these larger political pathologies that have militarized the planet. O'Brien, who spares little effort in deriding the excesses and recklessness of the "peace movement," has given scant attention to the less easily discerned—but much more dangerous—madness in high places. In their ability to go beyond numbing abstractions and statistics to focus on the plight of individual human beings living under the nuclear shadow, literary works have the special capacity to assist those who might not otherwise engage the nuclear peril to begin the essential first step of "imagining the real." In this sense *The Nuclear Age* ren-

■ BOOKS BY TIM O'BRIEN

If I Die in a Combat Zone, Box Me Up and Ship Me Home. New York: Delacorte, 1973.

Northern Lights. New York: Delacorte, 1974.

Going After Cacciato. New York: Delacorte, 1978, New York: Dell, 1979.

The Nuclear Age. New York: Knopf, 1985.

The Things They Carried. Boston: Houghton Mifflin, 1990.

In the Lake of the Woods. Boston: Houghton Mifflin, 1994.

Twinkle, Twinkle. Illustrated by Emilie Kong, Racine, Wis.: Western, 1994.

Tomcat in Love. New York: Broadway Books, 1998.

ders an important service. But in failing to suggest possible alternatives to our present disastrous course, and in holding out so little hope that viable solutions to our nuclear predicament can be found, *The Nuclear Age* risks exacerbating the pervasive cynicism and sense of powerlessness that are at the heart of the problem the novel decries.

Daniel L. Zins
June, 1986

UPDATE

Tim O'Brien has since published four more works of fiction: *The Things They Carried* (1990), *In the Lake of the Woods* (1994), *Twinkle, Twinkle* (1994), and *Tomcat in Love* (1998). O'Brien's most frequent subject is the Vietnam War and its repercussions, social and psychological. He has said that his experience in that war made him a writer. In a *Publishers Weekly* interview, O'Brien explained that to write "good" stories "requires a sense of passion, and my passion as a human being and as a writer intersect in Vietnam, not in the physical stuff but in the issues of Vietnam—of courage, rectitude, enlightenment, holiness, trying to do the right thing in the world." *Contemporary Authors* called him "the author of some of the most striking narratives of warfare, both real and imagined, in the entire corpus of American literature." O'Brien once said, "War stories aren't about war—they are about the human heart at war."

His 1978 Vietnam novel *Going After Cacciato* won the National Book Award the next year and propelled him into the rank of best-selling writer. He still draws scores of readers, but critics have had mixed responses to his newest work, which branches in new directions.

"*In the Lake of the Woods* is a significant addition to [O'Brien's] body of work on Vietnam as well as a thoughtful meditation . . . on the nature of truth, narration, and mystery," wrote *The Southern Review.* The story of a young politician whose career may be hurt by a revelation about his involvement in a Vietnam massacre, it turns into mystery when his wife disappears from their northwoods cabin. When the story strays from Vietnam and the examination of the human spirit, it falters, the review continued. But when it dares "to bear witness to the mystery of evil," it succeeds. "Few writers resist easy answers as adamantly as Tim O'Brien, and few demand of themselves and of their readers a more unflinching introspection. As the narrator puts it, 'We find truth inside, or not at all.'"

O'Brien's most recent novel, *Tomcat in Love,* differs from his previous work. A lukewarm *Library Journal* review called it "a quirky character study" and predicted a small audience for the story of an "arrogant, Don Juanish character" and his search for true love. But some reviewers found it "complex and enthralling": "The tone of the novel may jar with admirers of his previous fiction," wrote the *New Statesman.* "Yet the change of direction has brought many rewards, not least the spectacle of a supremely accomplished writer thriving on, and mastering, fresh challenges."

Limning: or Why Tillie Writes

■ I

Tillie Olsen was born in Nebraska 65 years ago. In 1960, when she was 50 years old, she published her first book, a slim volume of short stories called *Tell Me a Riddle*. In 1974 she finally published a novel—*Yonnondio*—she had begun in 1932 and abandoned in 1937. To women in "the movement" she is a major literary figure, not so much despite as because of the paucity of her publications.

Since 1971, when Delta reissued *Tell Me a Riddle* in paperback, Olsen has been stumping the country, speaking about women who have been prevented by their sex from utilizing their creative talents. These are her words:

> In the twenty years I bore and reared my children, usually had to work on the job as well, the simplest circumstances for creation did not exist. When the youngest of our four was in school, the beginnings struggled toward endings.... Bliss of movement. A full extended family life; the world of my job; and the writing, which I was somehow able to carry around with me through work, through home. Time on the bus, even when I had to stand, was enough; the stolen moments at work, enough; the deep night hours for as long as I could stay awake, after the kids were in bed, after the household tasks were done, sometimes during. It is no accident that the first work I considered publishable began: "I stand here ironing." In such snatches of time I wrote what I did in those years, but there came a time when this triple life was no longer possible. The fifteen hours of daily realities became too much distraction for the writing.

> As for myself, who did not publish a book until I was 50, who raised children without household help or the help of the 'technological sublime'...who worked outside the house on everyday jobs as well.... The years when I should have been writing, my hands and being were at other (inescapable) tasks.... The habits of a lifetime when everything else had to come before writing are not easily broken, even when circumstances now often make it possible for the writing to be first; habits of years: response to others, distractibility, responsibility for daily matters, stay with you, mark you, become you. I speak of myself to bring here the sense of those others to whom this is in the process of happening (unnecessarily happening, for it need not, must not continue to be) and to remind us of those (I so nearly was one) who never come to writing at all. We cannot speak of women writers in our century without speaking also of the invisible; the also capable; the born to the wrong circumstances, the diminished, the excluded, the lost, the silenced. We who write are survivors, 'onlys.' One—out of twelve.

Tillie Olsen

Tillie Olsen was born January 14, 1912 (some sources say 1913), in Omaha, Nebraska, and had no formal education past high school. She worked as a typist-transcriber and raised her children. She is a member of the Authors Guild whose awards include a Stanford University creative writing fellowship, a Ford Foundation grant, the O. Henry award for the best American short story, a fellowship with the Radcliffe Institute for Independent Study, a Guggenheim fellowship, and an award from The American Academy and National Institute of Arts and Letters .

She has been a visiting professor and writer in residence at institutions from Amherst College to the University of California at Los Angeles. ■

I heard Olsen speak these words to a class at Dartmouth College last year, and I observed their galvanic effect on the students—mostly women—who heard them. My first exposure to Tillie Olsen was to Olsen the feminist. It was with this preparation that I first read *Tell Me a Riddle* and *Yonnondio*. I was thus unprepared for their impact on me.

■ II

For in her books, Olsen is no politician, but an artist. Her fictions evoke, move, haunt. They did not seem, when I read them, to belong to any movement, to support any cause.

And so I returned to Olsen's words about the situation of the woman writer to see if there was something I had missed, something the women's movement had missed.

In "Silences: When Writers Don't Write," originally delivered as a talk to the Radcliffe Institute for Independent Study in 1963, Olsen asks, "What are creation's needs for full functioning?" The answer *women* have heard is an echo of Virginia Woolf's "£500 a year and a room of one's own"—independence, freedom, escape from the restriction of traditional feminine roles. This is the answer Olsen herself gives on the lecture circuit. But in this early Radcliffe speech, her question seems not so much political as aesthetic.

Wondering what keeps writers from writing, Olsen turns to what writers—*men* writers—have themselves said about their unnatural silences, not periods of gestation and renewal, but of drought, "unnatural thwarting of what struggles to come into being, but cannot." She points to Hardy's sense of lost "vision," to Hopkins' "poet's eye," curbed by a priestly vow to refrain from writing, to Rimbaud, who, after long silence, finally on his deathbed "spoke again like a poet-visionary." She then turns to writers who wrote continuously, in an effort to understand what preserved them from the unnatural silences that foreshortened the creativity of Hardy, Hopkins, Rimbaud, Melville, and Kafka. She cites James's assertion that creation demands "a depth and continuity of attention," and notes that Rilke cut himself off from his family to live in attentive isolation so that there would be "no limit to vision." Over and over in these opening paragraphs of "Silences," Olsen identifies the act of creation with an act of the eye.

In order to create, the artist must see. Margaret Howth, in Rebecca Harding Davis's novel of that name, is the type of the artist for Olsen, "her eyes quicker to see than ours." And one of the special handicaps of the woman writer, confined traditionally to her proper sphere in the drawing room or the kitchen, is that she is restricted to what Olsen calls "trespass vision" of the world beyond that sphere. But although she echoes Charlotte Bronte's lament that women are denied "facilities for observation…a knowledge of the world," Olsen does not equate the reportorial with the creative eye. Vision is not photography. Olsen quotes, approvingly, Sarah Orne Jewett's advice to the young Willa Cather: "If you don't keep and mature your force…. what might be insight is only observation. You will write about life, but never life itself."

In Rebecca Harding Davis's *Life in the Iron Mills,* to which Olsen has added an appreciative biographical afterword, the distinction between vision and mere seeing is dramatized in the reactions of two viewers to the statue Hugh Wolfe has sculpted out of slag. The mill owner's son has brought a party of gentlemen to see the mill. On their way back to the carriage, they stumble on Hugh's statue, the crouching figure of a nude woman, with outstretched arms. Moved by its crude power, the gentlemen ask Hugh, "But what did you mean by it?" "She be hungry," he answers. The Doctor condescendingly instructs the unschooled sculptor: "Oh-h! But what a mistake you have made, my fine fellow! You have given no sign of starvation to the body. It is strong,—terribly strong." To the realist, a portrait of starvation must count every rib. But Mitchell, who is portrayed as the dilettante and aesthete, a stranger to the mill town and of a different cut than the doctor, foreman, and newspaperman who round out the party, "flash[es] a look of disgust" at the doctor: "'May,' he broke out impatiently, 'are you blind? Look at that woman's face! It asks questions of God, and says, "I have a right to know." Good God, how hungry it is!'"

So Olsen's vision is, in a sense, trespass vision. It is "insight, not observation," the eye's invasion of outward detail to the meaning and shape within. It is this creative trespassing that Rebecca Davis commends in Margaret Howth, whose eyes are "quicker to see than ours, delicate or grand lines in the homeliest things." And it is precisely that quality in Rebecca Davis herself that makes her so significant to Tillie Olsen, who says of her that "the noting of reality was transformed into comprehension, Vision."

Tillie Olsen's edition of *Life In the Iron Mills,* published by the Feminist Press, is central to an understanding of what she means by the creative act. It may or may not be one of the lost masterpieces of American fiction. Olsen herself admits that it is "botched." But it fascinates her because it is a parable of creation, a portrait of the artist. And significantly, that artist is a sculptor.

One of the unsilent writers Olsen quotes in "Silences" is the articulate Thomas Mann, who spoke of the act of creation as "the will, the self-control to shape a sentence or follow out a hard train of thought. From the first rhythmical urge of the inward creative force towards the material, towards casting in shape and form, from that to the thought, the image, the word, the line." Vision is perceptive seeing, which sees beneath and within the outward details the essential shape of the meaning of the thing perceived. Doctor May saw only the anatomy of Hugh's statue; Mitchell saw through to the woman's soul.

Sculpting is cutting away the exterior surface to come to the shape within the block of marble. Hugh spends months "hewing and hacking with his blunt knife," compelled by "a fierce thirst for beauty,—to know it, to create it." His struggle is first to see the beauty within and then to give it form, Mann's urge towards the material and then casting it in shape and form.

Olsen writes of Davis's art in similarly sculptural words: "It may have taken her years to embody her vision. 'Hewing and hacking'" like Hugh. The first pages of *Life in the Iron Mills* are the narrator's injunction to the reader to "look deeper" into the sordid lives of the mill workers, to ask whether there is "nothing beneath" the squalor. This preamble concludes with the artless confession that "I can paint nothing of this" inner reality, "only give you the outside outlines." But the strength of the tale is in Davis's ability to sculpt that inner reality, to dissolve the outside outlines and uncover the moral shape of her simple tale. For Olsen it is "a stunning insight…as transcendent as any written in her century."

Vision is not photography. Sculpting is not cameo carving. Rebecca Harding Davis excoriated the Brahmins she met on her trip north from her native Wheeling, West Virginia. Emerson and Bronson Alcott, she wrote in her journal, "thought they were guiding the real world, [but] they stood quite outside of it, and never would see it as it was.… their views gave you the same sense of unreality, of having been taken, as Hawthorne said, at too long a range." In other words, they imposed their vision of the world on the world of fact, pasted their carvings on the surface of things. Davis criticized them for ignoring the "back-bone of fact." To see the inner shape, you have at least to acknowledge the contour of the surface.

In her own tale of the downtrodden, *Yonnondio,* Olsen addresses the Brahmins of our day:

> And could you not make a cameo of this and pin it onto your aesthetic hearts? So sharp it is, so clear, so classic. The shattered dusk, the mountain of culm, the tipple; clean lines, bare beauty—and carved against them dwarfed by the vastness of night and the towering tipple, these black figures with bowed heads, waiting, waiting.

The aesthetic eye sees "at too long a range." It abstracts from surface detail a pleasing pattern. But the creative eye, the visionary eye, apprehends the surface in order to comprehend the inner shape which gives it meaning.

Thus by accreted detail, Olsen's definition of the creative act comes into focus. The artist stands, always, in relation to a world of fact. He can record it or he can transform it. In the one case, the standard by which he measures his achievement is fidelity to fact. In the other, his standards are formal. Between these extremes, Tillie Olsen places the creative act. Fidelity to fact, but essential fact. Form and pattern, but exposed, not imposed.

It is not surprising that, of all the literary people she met on her northern trip, Rebecca Davis should have been drawn to Hawthorne. This aesthetic stance in relation to reality that I have discerned in Olsen and Davis is also, as I understand it, the method of Hawthorne's romances. Coming to Hawthorne's tales early in her life, Davis was "verified" in her feeling that "the commonplace folk and things which I saw every day had mystery and charm…belong to the magic world [of books] as much as knights and pilgrims." *Ethan Brand,* that tale of another furnace tender, sees under the surface of fact a fable of the unpardonable sin; *Life in the Iron Mills,* as Olsen points out, is about "another kind of unpardonable sin," but its method of uncovering that sin is akin to Hawthorne's. It is not an abstraction from reality—that is the method of the cameo cutter, the formalist—but a reduction of facticity to its primary form.

■ III

When I began this study of Tillie Olsen, I was motivated by my sense that beneath the polemic about the predicament of the woman writer lay something like this more comprehensive aesthetic. What gave me this sense, or suspicion, was Olsen's fiction, which transcends her oratory. But before I turn to an appreciation of that fiction, I want to examine briefly the source of the disparity between Olsen's real aesthetic and her current feminist articulation of it.

Throughout her non-fiction writing, as we have seen, Olsen uses the metaphor of sculpture to define the creative act. To be a writer, one must "be able to come to, cleave to, find the form for one's own life comprehensions." But in an article published in *College English* in 1972, "Women Who Are Writers in Our Century: One Out of Twelve," Olsen uses this sculptural imagery to describe, not the artist, but the situation of women, who are "estranged from their own experience and unable to perceive its shape and authenticity," prevented by social and sexual circumscription from the essential act of self-definition and affirmation. The paradox of female reality, as Olsen understands it, is that immersion in life means loss of perspective, or vision.

The artist-visionary can supply that perspective, can "find the form" which constitutes the "shape and authenticity" of what Olsen calls "common female realities."

Thus in "One Out of Twelve" and on the lecture circuit, Tillie Olsen exhorts women artists to take women's lives as their subject matter, finding a therapeutic link between the situation of women in our society and the peculiar kind of discovery implicit in the aesthetic creation. Accordingly she feels "it is no accident that the first work I considered publishable began: 'I stand here ironing'."

It is possible to read the first of the four stories that comprise *Tell Me a Riddle* as an exemplum of Olsen's feminist aesthetic. The mother-narrator of "I Stand Here Ironing" looks back over a life where there has been no "time to remember, to sift, to weigh, to estimate, to total." Caught in the mesh of paid work, unpaid work, typing, darning, ironing, she has suffered, but never had time and leisure to perceive and shape, to understand, the passionate arc of motherhood. Helplessly she looks back over her memories of her daughter's childhood and concludes, "I will never total it all."

What Olsen does, in "I Stand Here Ironing," is to perceive and give form to the meaning of her narrator's motherhood, that "total" which the mother has no time to sum. As every female reader I have spoken to attests, this story movingly succeeds in articulating what Olsen calls "common female realities."

It is also possible to fit the title story of the collection into the Procrustean feminist aesthetic Olsen propounds in "One Out of Twelve." "Tell me a riddle, Grammy. I know no riddles, child." But the grandfather "knew how to tickle, chuck, lift, toss, do tricks, tell secrets, make jokes, match riddle for riddle." Why? Clearly because during all the years when she "had had to manage," to contend with poverty, to raise five children, to preserve domestic order, he "never scraped a carrot or knew a dish towel sops." The man is free, the woman bound. Women cannot "riddle" or form the experience they are utterly immersed in.

But "Tell Me a Riddle" is far more than a feminist document. In it, Olsen riddles the inscrutable by perceiving the meaning beneath and within the old woman's life and death. But this service is not rendered solely to the grandmother, but to all the characters in the story, and to the reader as well. Lennie, her son, suffered "not alone for her who was dying, but for that in her which never lived (for that which in him might never live)." And keeping his vigil by the dying woman's bedside, the grandfather achieves an epiphany, which the reader shares:

> The cards fell from his fingers. Without warning, the bereavement and betrayal he had sheltered—compounded through the years—hidden even from himself— revealed itself,
>
> uncoiled,
> released,
> *sprung*

and with it the monstrous shapes of what had actually happened in the century.

"Tell Me a Riddle" is a story about "common female realities," but it is also a story about "common *human* realities." We are all bound slaves, all immured in immanence, pawns of economic and political forces we cannot comprehend. Stepping from moment to moment, we do not see that we are pacing out the steps of a "dance, while the flutes so joyous and vibrant tremble in the air."

Olsen has made the mistake, in her recent oratory, of confusing the general human situation and the particular plight of women in our society. What she empathically knows because she is an artist she thinks she knows because she is a woman, that our greatest need is to "be able to come to, cleave to, find the form for [our] own life comprehensions." In her fiction, if not in her rhetoric, Olsen does not reserve that need to the female half of the race.

Like the mother in "I Stand Here Ironing," the protagonist of "Hey Sailor, What Ship?", the second of the *Tell Me a Riddle* stories, has spent his life day by day, immersed in "the watery shifting" from one port to another, the animal rhythm of work / pay check / binge / hangover. Yet Olsen rescues this inchoate history into meaning, by showing how Whitey fits in to a larger pattern, of which he himself is unaware. To his old friends in San Francisco, to whom he continually returns no matter how wide the arc of his dereliction, he is "a chunk of our lives." When Jeannie, the ruthless teenager, says, "he's just a Howard Street wino, that's all," her mother insists, "You've got to understand."

> Understand. Once they had been young together. To Lennie he remained a tie to adventure and a world in which men had not eaten each other; and the pleasure, when the mind was clear, of chewing over with that tough mind the happenings of the times or the queernesses of people, or laughing over the mimicry. To Helen he was the compound of much help given, much support; the ear to hear, the hand that understands how much a scrubbed floor, or a washed dish, or a child taken care of for a while, can mean.

With understanding, Whitey's sordid life is illuminated and valued. For us, who view it by way of Olsen's trespass vision, his life has meaning.

■ IV

If Olsen, like Rebecca Harding Davis, owes her aesthetic to Hawthorne, it is with another American writer that she shares her sympathies. In a revealing remark to a class of Dartmouth students, Tillie Olsen said that when she began writing her tale "From the Thirties" in 1932, she knew she would call it *Yonnondio*. Furthermore she has another unfinished novel she also calls *Yonnondio*. Like Walt Whitman's, from whom she borrowed the name, her fiction is one continuous poem, dedicated to the common man.

Yonnondio, as the subtitle reminds us, is a tale "From the Thirties." It records several years in the life of the Holbrook family, as they move from a mining town in Wyoming to a tenant farm in South Dakota to the slaughterhouses of Denver. But although the settings and their squalor have equivalents in other writing "from the thirties," Olsen is neither Upton Sinclair nor John Steinbeck. *Yonnondio* is not a protest, but a perception.

Olsen told the Dartmouth students she was "fortunate" to have been brought up "working class, socialist." She thus credited her strength as an artist, not to her sex, but to her roots, her heritage, her sense of belonging to a living culture. It is her sympathetic love for the common people she identifies with that leads her to perceive in their lives the luminous beauty she limns, to articulate the inarticulate, to give voice to what might otherwise be a note as fleeting as JimJim's song in *Yonnondio*:

■ BOOKS BY TILLIE OLSEN

Tell Me a Riddle. Pennsylvania: Lippincott, 1961, Pennsylvania: Lippincott, 1961, Pennsylvania: Lippincott, 1964, Pennsylvania: Lippincott, 1964, New York: Dell, 1971, New York: Dell, 1971.

Yonnondio: From the Thirties. New York: Delacorte Press, 1974

Silences (essays). New York: Delacorte, 1978.

Mothers and Daughters: That Special Quality: An Exploration in Photography. New York: Aperture Foundation, 1987.

a fifth voice, pure, ethereal, veiled over the rest. Mazie saw it was Jimmie, crouched at the pedals of the piano. "Ma," she said after the song was done, "it's Jimmie, Jim Jim was singin too." Incredulous, they made him sing it over with them and over and over. His words were a blur, a shadow of the real words, but the melody came true and clear.

Olsen's ears are quick to catch that ethereal melody, and her pen is incomparable at notating it.

Olsen's fiction is full of privileged moments, instants prised from the flux of time and illumined by a vision of their essential meaning. For the characters, the moments are fleeting. At the end of a day of gathering greens and weaving dandelion chains, a day wrested from the stink and squalor of Slaughterhouse City, Mazie sees her mother's face transfigured, senses in her "remote" eyes "happiness and farness and selfness." Anna's peace suffuses the place where she sits with the children, so that "up from the grasses, from the earth, from the broad tree trunk at their back, latent life streamed and seeded. The air and self shone boundless." But the sun sinks, Ben gets hungry for supper, and "the mother look" returns to Anna's face. "Never again, but once, did Mazie see that look—the other look—on her mother's face."

For Mazie, the privileged moments are so evanescent that she sometimes wonders if they ever occurred: "Where was the belted man Caldwell had told her of, lifting his shield against a horn of stars? Where was the bright one she had run after into the sunset? A strange face, the sky grieved above her, gone suddenly strange like her mother's." Snatched from the grinding, degrading poverty of her life's daily texture, such moments of beauty as Mazie had with the old man Caldwell, who directed her naïve eyes to Orion and his luminous companions, are so rare that they might never have existed, might be dreams, or promises, like the books the dying Caldwell wills her and her father sells "for half a dollar."

More often, the privileged moments do not "come to writing" for Olsen characters. "Come to writing," a favorite phrase of Tillie Olsen's, expresses her vitalistic conception of the creative process. It means the inarticulate finding words, the dumbly sensed becoming sensible, the incipient meaning finding form. For the writer, it is breaking silence. For the actor in an Olsen fiction, it is a moment of perceiving, of knowing that there is shape and direction in the ceaseless flow of what must be. Mazie comes to writing occasionally; so does her mother, Anna, who "stagger[s]" in the sunlight and moves beyond the helpless "My head is balloony, balloony" to sing her love for her eldest child and her joy in motherhood: "O Shenandoah, I love thy daughter, / I'll bring her safe through stormy water."

But more often, when Mazie is immersed in a potentially luminous moment, she perceives it as "stammering light" and when "she turns her hand to hold" it, "she grasps shadows." Anna moves through the daily drudgery "not knowing an every-hued radiance floats on her hair." As for Jim, her husband, "the things in his mind so vast and formless, so terrible and bitter, cannot be spoken, will never be spoken—till the day that hands will find a way to speak this: hands."

The hands are Olsen's hands, grasping her pen to copy a fragment of Walt Whitman's poem as the epigraph to her novel "From the Thirties":

No picture, poem, statement, passing them to the future:
Yonnondio! Yonnondio!—unlimn'd they disappear;
To-day gives place, and fades—the cities, farms, factories fade;
A muffled sonorous sound, a wailing word is borne through the air for a moment,
Then blank and gone and still, and utterly lost.

Yonnondio! That evocative word is the emblem of Tillie Olsen's aesthetic. It is her plea, and her pledge: that the unobserved should be perceived, that the fleeting should be fixed, that the inarticulate should come to writing.

Ellen Cronan Rose
April, 1976

Michael Ondaatje: Cat
Burglar in the House
of Fiction

■ **1**

Like the thieves, outlaws, and renegades who populate his books, Michael Ondaatje, the Canadian poet and novelist, operates by way of calculated subversion. If there is a House of Fiction, then he is its cat burglar, circling in shadows, playing in the fringes, lurking, always lurking. Not one to ring the door and stand waiting, he enters by alternate means: jimmying the locks, springing the trap door, picking his way through a side window. He's anything but ingratiating.

Violence informs, one might say controls and even orders, his work. The titles alone suggest a willful, almost gleeful indecorousness: images of knives (*There's a Trick with a Knife I'm Learning to Do, The Cinnamon Peeler, In the Skin of a Lion*), of genocide (*The Collected Works of Billy the Kid, Coming Through Slaughter*), of sickness (*Running in the Family, The English Patient*), of cartoon barbarism (*Dainty Monsters, Rat Jelly*). Nothing is dealt with head-on. Nothing is come at conventionally. Ondaatje explodes convention. A book-length poem is sent forth as a novel, a novel asks to be read as an epic poem, nonfiction is intimately bound up with fiction, photographs and documents rub elbows with the written word. Narrative lines are shattered. Readers' expectations are continually held hostage.

And yet there is also a reason, there is an order, to his madness. If on the surface Ondaatje's narratives seem chaotic or haphazard, the product of random, discontinuous bursts of imagination, they are anything but. Who after all understands form and structure as well as a cat burglar, conversant as he is with all the crevices and blind corners of a building? If Ondaatje wants to tear the whole house down, it's only to gather up the shards, discarding, reassembling, and rearranging to make it all new.

How best explain this apparent paradox? Perhaps the answer to this question, as to many of the important questions raised by his work, lies in Ondaatje's complicated past. By "past" I do not mean to suggest the buried hostilities and divided loyalties the Freudians would have us believe are inherent in all of us—although in Ondaatje's case, especially with regard to the troubled life of his father, there is a fair amount a Freudian could have sport with. What ought to matter most is that Ondaatje was born, in Ceylon, in 1943, that he grew up and into British colonial society, and that, at age 19, as his father continued his descent into alcoholism, the son emigrated to Canada to continue his schooling, and to write poetry. That set of circumstances alone would seem to mark him an outsider extraordinaire: born to one colonial culture, an outsider, later moving to another where, exotic caramel-skinned exile, he became a poet and novelist.

To dismiss the importance of these circumstances on the evolving writer is to potentially misread the meanings of Ondaatje's work (which, at this early stage in his career, it must be said, may not be nearly so important as his many implications). In other words, those who would see Ondaatje, with all his broken surfaces and fragmentation and shifting voices and

Michael Ondaatje Born in

Ceylon (now known as Sri Lanka) in 1943, Michael
Ondaatje moved across three continents before set-
tling in Canada in 1962. He studied at Bishop's Uni-
versity before transferring to the University of
Toronto, where he graduated in 1965. He earned an
M.A. from Queen's University in 1967.

Michael Ondaatje has since become an active
member of the literary community in Toronto and
has emerged as an internationally acclaimed poet
novelist, and film director. The winner of many
prestigious awards throughout his career, in 2000 he
won his fourth Governor General's Literary Award
from the Canadian Council for the Arts for his best-
selling novel *Anil's Ghost*. He won the Booker Prize in
1992 for *The English Patient*.■

multimedia experimentation, as primarily an exemplar of post-Modernism are missing what's
ultimately compelling about his writing.

Not that that aspect should be denied. It shouldn't—Ondaatje is, in the end, an extremely
self-reflexive writer. Simply that, though it is difficult to get a handle on any writer—especially
one who seems determined to evade all categorization—it is in the light of the outsider extraordinaire, the post-Colonial outlaw, that Ondaatje's work acquires its particular interest. The
grinding edges of his writing are those of so many expatriated writers who, though bred in the
ways of the English, continually find themselves butting up against the realities of their everyday outsider existence. Like Wallace Stevens, one of his earliest and most abiding influences,
Ondaatje, too, has a rage for order; it's his British cultural inheritance; not coincidentally, that
phrase ignites one of *Running in the Family*'s most dramatically-pitched moments. But there is
also an order for rage—the post-Colonialist's birthright.

■ II

Ondaatje's earliest poems, beginning with 1967's *Dainty Monsters*, reflect this duality. Typically,
images of birds and animals abound. In "Heron Rex," Ondaatje posits the birds as a noble race
of kings whose "blood lines" have been "introverted, strained pure / so the blood runs in the
wrong direction":

> they are proud of their heritage of suicides
> — not just the ones who went mad
> balancing on that goddamn leg, but those
>
> whose eyes turned off
> the sun and imagined it

those who looked north, those who
forced their feathers to grow in
those who couldn't find the muscles in their arms
who drilled their beaks into the skin
those who could speak
and lost themselves in the foul connections
who crashed against black bars in a dream of escape
those who moved round the dials of imaginary clocks
those who fell asleep and never woke
who never slept and so dropped dead
those who attacked the casual eyes of children and were led
away
and those who faced corners forever
those who pretended broken limbs, epilepsy,
who managed to electrocute themselves on wire
those who felt their skin was on fire and screamed
                                    and were led away

That tone—seething irony, savage understatement—is typical, as is the obvious autobiographical link-up, suggested by the first line. As *Running in the Family* relates, Ondaatje's own father, born into Ceylonese high-society, was himself a suicide, having turned to alcoholism and gone mad trying to free himself from the strictures of the British. The word "heritage," in the context of colonialism, with its double implications, is particularly damning. Prosodically, the line seems to catch the false pride of the birds, moving as it does in anapestic perfection until finally arriving at "suicide," which effectively trips, and thereby cancels, the rhythm.

In "Elizabeth," another early poem, it is the meaning of inherited ways that Ondaatje again examines. Historically based, as are many of the poems written around this time, "Elizabeth" explores myth only to explode it. Early on, images of death predominate, insinuate, as the poem traces the maturation of Elizabeth I from child to ruler. The pivot of the poem occurs in the person of a man named Tom, ostensibly Tom Seymour, a reputed early lover of the young queen. The two of them one day carry on quite heatedly. She remembers his "soft laughing," his leaving his "quick urgent love in my palm." But more vividly, and with much greater relish, does Ondaatje have her remembering his beheading, an event so vivid it merits its own stanza. There is a kind of ghoulish fascination for her, a marveling at her mastery of control, of sudden power, which Ondaatje would have us believe is to become, as leader, her character note.

■ **III**

Though not strictly a poem, *The Collected Works of Billy the Kid* "began as a poem," as a 1993 interview with Hendrik Hertzberg for PBS' *Literati* revealed. "I needed a larger arena," Ondaatje confessed, "to go for a ride on a horse." While it may be his first extended prose work, *CWBK* is not strictly a novel, either. With Ondaatje perhaps the first thing to bear in mind is that the tendency toward labeling must be immediately dispensed with. As he himself told the interviewer Catherine Bush, "I'm a great believer in the mongrel." Labels are to literature as hegemonies are to nations; they stifle, they inhibit. For Ondaatje, what's primary is to let the narrative create its own contexts as it goes along. Which does not always make for accessibility. *CWBK* is consciously, determinedly undefinable; it revels in its inability to be pigeonholed.

How then are we to properly approach it, to understand its intentions, if we don't even know what to call it? Answer: we don't. Better answer: we're not supposed to. Here as elsewhere, Ondaatje takes defamiliarization to its logical extreme. To call it a long-form poem is inaccurate; to call it a novel as prose poem is similarly missing the mark. These definitions, arbitrary as are most definitions, especially with regard to Ondaatje's work, are, in the end, as helpful as fanned fingers in holding sand.

Annie Dillard has called *CWBK* a "narrative collage"—a definition that, initially, would seem to offer a way into understanding the contents of the work. In collage, various modes of expression compete, work together. Here, too. Prose, poetry and nonprint media all have their say. The prose comes across in clipped, imagistic chunks. The poems, if they can be called that (for they make no claims for themselves as standing outside the prose), stand toe to toe with the chunks. There are the photographs—of Sally Chisum, of Billy—and the court documents, the interviews, and the newspaper clippings, all rightfully claiming our attention, not a single one slighted in context. Finally, there are the gaps, the white spaces. Ondaatje makes more of negative space than any writer I know of. Here, what's not said, what's not printed, is every bit as important as what is. Even as we read on, hoping to penetrate the mystery of Billy's world, his life and times, Ondaatje is implicating us, reminding us through these narrative blanks that all final knowledge is impossible, that gaps will always exist, and perhaps more important, that those gaps may constitute a knowledge all their own. What those gaps lead out into is possibility.

CWBK, it should be noted, is an extremely visual work—Ondaatje has remarked that what he'd done in writing it was to make the kind of spaghetti western he'd been able to afford. Taken on this level, Dillard's definition is useful. But ultimately it offers a misleading view. It suggests a randomness, a suddenness, as if Ondaatje wanted to see what a merry haphazard throwing together might yield, what discoveries might be gained. If at first glance the work would seem to have bodied forth in a single burst, on second and third glance that is clearly not the case. *CWBK*, like all of Ondaatje's work, is carefully assembled. The apparent chaos is deliberately calculated.

For want of a definition, I'd prefer cozying up to calling it a work of *bricolage*. The term derives from Levi-Strauss, whose *La Pensée sauvage* distinguishes between two types of workers: the engineer and the *bricoleur*. The latter, notes Werner Berthoff in *Fictions and Events*, "is not comparably direct in his treatment of [a project] but positively devious and refractory. He uses not a limited set of instruments appropriate to that one job but everything he has at hand; a set of instruments, that is, which bears no precise relationship to the current project, or indeed to any particular project, but is the contingent result of all the occasions there have been to renew or enrich the stock or to maintain it with the remains of previous constructions of deconstructions." In *bricolage*, it is the artful arrangement that matters most—and the arranger who stands front and center, variously undermining, elevating and implicating himself all along the way.

Like much of Ondaatje's long-form writing, *CWBK* achieves its effects by means of reciprocation, of structural tensions. Pieces are not simply laid down. In fact, the work itself is virtually seamless. Midway through, a voice—dislocated, mischievous and sneering remorselessly at our need for final knowledge—asks: "A motive? some reasoning we can give to explain all this violence? Was there a source for all this? yup —" And here Ondaatje brings in (not for the first time) one of his many documents: Walter Noble Burns's 1926 best-seller *The Saga of Billy the Kid*. Having undermined the seriousness of the historical appraisal in introducing it, Ondaatje further subverts the official, single-window, authorial viewpoint by immediately showing us Billy running amok in the old West, shooting up joints, killing for the hell of it. This careful narrative orchestration is at odds with the ostensible surface chaos he has contrived.

Burns' document is one of many Ondaatje works with, and ultimately against. Many other texts, interpretations, find their way into the text, in effect creating a text of multiple texts—of collected works. Multiple texts, multiple voices. All the major players in Billy's drama, and those who would interpret him, are given their say, with the result that all these many views and interpretations lead toward nothing in particular. Ondaatje's interest is centrifugal, not centripetal as is the historian's. Final knowledge is impossible. The single lens of history is false.

What are we left with? A shifting, multi-layered, destabilized text, thoroughly post-Colonial in its intentions, at the same time thoroughly post-Modern in its effects. Which is to say, what we are left with is artifice. Douglas Barbour has written that the work aims to free Billy, already "dead" at the start of the narrative, from the constraints. This it does, though it leaves us, paradoxically, with another myth in its place, and, ultimately, another hero—Ondaatje himself. The artist, shooting down all received notions of time, history, myth.

■ IV

Art and violence are, for Ondaatje, inextricably bound up with one another, linked acts. Indeed, it would be more accurate to say that for Ondaatje art equals violence. Or is this too only half-right? For always there is a sense that as surely as art needs—demands—violence, violence needs and demands art. It is as much Ondaatje's rage for order as his order for rage that marks him as a writer.

Three poems written at this time, "King Kong Meets Wallace Stevens," "Spider Blues" and "Burning Hills," take for their subject this very idea. In the former, the two figures never actually meet (what occasions the poem are two separate photographs), and as such, King Kong Meets Wallace Stevens is as good as any a definition of Ondaatje's style, his working method. There is Kong, uncontrolled, operating only at a single speed, "staggering / lost in New York streets again / a spawn of annoyed cars at his toes. / The mind is nowhere." And then there is Stevens who "is thinking chaos is thinking fences," Stevens who knows the need for order along with rage. "Spider Blues" posits the spider as a "kind of writer I suppose." That "I suppose" gives a clue as to the reading of the line; on one level, "kind of" and "I suppose" seem of a piece, ways of signaling a wavering in tone. Careful as he is, Ondaatje surely does not want us to accept that line as a flat-out hedge. Rather, by "kind of writer" he means to suggest a particular, a specific, writer—a writer of deadly intent. Ondaatje himself? This spider "comes to fly, says / Love me I can kill you," and thrills to the sight of his "victims in his spit / making them the art he cannot be." His control is, Ondaatje notes, "classic."

So why is the spider "blue"? The answer has to do with his awareness of the degree to which he is dependent upon the fly. Without it he cannot kill. Killing in Ondaatje's schematic is on a par with creating. The spider is dependent upon his subject. Without it he has no art. If, in "King Kong Meets Wallace Stevens," there is the artist's ambivalent self-admonishment of the need for control, in "Spider Blues" there is the artist's burning resentment of his need for subject.

In "Burning Hills," the artist, having retreated to a distant cabin, "in the burnt hill region / north of Kingston," "came to write again." Words do not come easily. There is blockage: movement in fits and starts. He comes across a handful of old photographs of long-ago summers that "were layers of civilisation in his memory." If he is to break through he must ransack the past, plundering "civilisation" for the meanings behind these pictures. This mental activity is equated with fire. There is one picture that "fuses" the five summers, and in restlessly searching their meanings, in "burning" his own hills, the artist has his breakthrough. The lantern, which hangs "on a hook in the centre of the room," takes effect: "A wasp is crawling on the floor / tumbling over, its motor fanatic." The artist, we are told, has "smoked five cigarettes," one for each of the five summers he remembers. The act of remembering, Ondaatje knows, is no passive act, no dreamy, fog-filled indulgence. Anything processed by memory, said Wright Morris, is fiction. And if the artist is not to be duped or deluded, he must learn to burn through to what's real, pillage the past for its hard truths.

In a 1984 interview with Sam Solecki, Ondaatje, speaking of the uses of tradition, said, "Consciously or unconsciously we burn the previous devices which have got us here but which now are only rhetoric."

That a verb as anarchic as "burn" should have been on Ondaatje's lips is significant in itself. That he literally should be taken at his word as to his exact intentions is without doubt.

■ V

One of the keys to unlocking *Coming Through Slaughter* is its epigraph. Ondaatje presents two illustrations, the first the only known photograph of Buddy Bolden and his band, the second a series of sonographs of dolphin sounds. The former's purpose, while not straightforward, seems the more clear-cut of the two. It demonstrates that Bolden really did exist. The latter poses more of a challenge. As Ondaatje's note explains, dolphins can make "two kinds of signals simultaneously." One of these signals is a "squawk." It is the squawk that identifies one dolphin to another. The other sound is more regular, more measured, as the evenly spaced arcs indicate; it denotes location.

Involute though it may be, the sonograph performs typically double duty. Like the dolphin, Bolden is at once bound up with the history of a place and wholly apart from it, a man who maintains, whatever his endeavor, whatever the circumstance, a consciously-hewn exclusivity; his music is at once regular, ordered and carefully structured and given to moments of manic, dizzying improvisation. The same might also be said of Ondaatje himself. "Two kinds of signals simultaneously" is as good a phrase as any to explain the tensions, the sustaining paradoxes, the mongrel strains of his particular art: poetry/prose, non-fiction/fiction, myth/fact, order/chaos. In leaving us to linger over these oppositions, Ondaatje means to tell us he will exploit them—indeed, will flaunt them.

As with *CWBK*, Ondaatje here takes as his subject a known figure, albeit a largely obscure one—Buddy Bolden, the turn-of-the-century cornetist credited with threading the seemingly disparate elements of march music and funeral music and gospel hollers into the first jazz. Having gone insane during a parade in the early teens, he never found his way onto record; Louis Armstrong came along, the phonograph was invented, the new music developed and grew into popularity, and Bolden, holed up in an insane asylum, was all but forgotten. Today, his place in jazz is secure, though largely as a creature of myth, a curious if once legendary figure in the margins of history. He is the quintessential Ondaatje hero if only because his story is full of gaps.

What's known of Bolden's life—that he worked at a barbershop, that he edited *The Cricket*, that he attacked Tom Pickett—is, as Donald M. Marquis's *In Search of Buddy Bolden: First Man of Jazz*, published two years after *Coming Through Slaughter*, argues, at best apocryphal; at worst, outright rumor. Ondaatje having done a fair amount of first-hand research himself concluded as much. So why is his Bolden, a shadowy, hard-to-pin-down character in the first place, nevertheless constructed from those few defining details? For that matter, why is the photographer Bellocq, a real-life figure of whom several important facts may at least be corroborated—none of them, it should be noted, having anything to do with Bolden—brought into the narrative? Why is Nora Bass, Bolden's wife, turned into a prostitute when all evidence suggests she was a church-going woman from a good family? Similarly, why aren't those few surviving documents that Ondaatje has compiled—for instance, his in-person interview, in 1976, with Frank Amacker, one of the few surviving members of the New Orleans jazz scene at the turn of the century—given greater say in the narrative?

These are all important questions. Obviously, Ondaatje is playing fast and loose with the facts—so much so, and to such a shocking degree, that it should become apparent he is neither sloppy nor indiscriminate, but rather consciously playing against narrative type.

To say that facts are accurate, but fiction is more truthful is to get it only partly right. A better answer can be found in "Burning Hills." What Ondaatje means to do is to burn those devices which have got us here, but which have now become rhetoric. That rhetoric says that the historical novel is constructed on facts, documents, empirical data, and that all the assembled materials must operate in concert to drive the narrative, centripetally, toward its inevitable center, toward a kind of final knowledge. Ondaatje knows there is no such thing as final knowledge, that there is no single, official window on the past, and so what he does is to create a fictional world of possibility, of multiplicity, where no single method of telling will do, where many voices compete for our attention, and where prose must admit poetry though neither may be so profound as their opposite, those telling negative spaces.

Thus, Ondaatje may use the rough, sketchy outline of Bolden's life, but in no way is he beholden to it; rather, his approach is akin to that of the jazzman: taking the facts, the details as notes, he improvises variations as he goes. Seen this way, whether the facts can be corroborated at all is beside the point, such intensity, such imagination has Ondaatje brought to bear upon them. The novel thus moves centrifugally, exploding into many different directions, each of them important, each significant. In one of what can only be called "gestures" through which the novel proceeds, and through which characters reveal themselves, we watch Bolden, obsessive, maniacal, in his private reverie in his steam-filled barbershop. The writing is compacted, imagistic, lyrical:

> "Cut hair. Above me revolving slowly is the tin-bladed fan, turning, like a giant knife all day above my head. So you can never relax and stretch up. The cut hair falls to the floor and is swept by this thick almost liquid wind, which tosses it to the outskirts of the room.
>
> "I blow my nose every hour and get the hair-flecks out of it. I cough them up first thing in the morning. I spit out the black fragments onto the pavement as I walk home with Nora from work. I find pieces all over my clothes even in my underwear. I go through the evenings with the smell of shaving soap up to my elbows. It is there in my fingers as I play. The layers of soap all day long have made another skin over me. The cleanest in town. I can look at a face and tell how long ago it was shaved. I work with the vanity of others.
>
> "I see them watch their own faces for the twenty minutes they sit below me. Men hate to see themselves change. They laugh nervously. This is the power I live in. I manipulate their looks. They trust me with the cold razor at the vein under their ears. They trust me with liquid soap cupped in my palms as I pass by their eyes and massage it into their hair. Dreams of the neck. Gushing onto the floor and my white apron. The men stumbling with no more sight to the door and feeling even through their pain the waves of heat as they go through the door into the real climate of Liberty and First, leaving this ice, wallpaper and sweet smell and gracious conversation, mirrors, my slavery here."

Later, in this same chair, under this same swirling fan, Bolden brandishing his razor slices Tom Pickett's nipple, triggering their strange skirmish. Ondaatje, alternating between Pickett's and Bolden's point of view, supplies nothing of the context necessary to understand this scene, perhaps because as the critic Douglas Barbour has pointed out, Bolden himself, edging toward madness, cannot understand his own actions. This is consonant with a text that itself "resists any form of explanation." Images are meant to suggest character development, gestures are intended as stand-ins for scenes, fragments of lyrics and song titles (shades of Sterne) are left to conjure whole "chapters." Little, if anything, is integrated, or continuous with, anything else. Meaning is continually deferred.

And yet, for all this, *Coming Through Slaughter* is carefully constructed. Chaos exists, but it is only a surface chaos. For all its "squawk," the narrative is structurally sound—to the extent that, if you were to rearrange its three parts or subsections, or remove from their immediate context any of these "gestures," you would be left with little more than an incomprehensible piece of writing.

■ VI

In each of his long-form works, Ondaatje has contrived to create his own form: a consciously mongrel narrative that seems to make up its own rules as it goes along, but that is, in reality, highly ordered, carefully structured.

Running in the Family realizes these intentions more nearly perfectly than anything he has done before, or since. It is ironic, and not coincidental, that it is at once his most autobiographical work and also his least self-reflexive. It is perhaps not ironic that it is at once his most obviously post-Colonial work and also his most personal. *Running in the Family* represents his attempt, as his older brother remarks within, to "get it right": not only the tragedy of his family, but that of Ceylon as well—for the two, as Ondaatje comes to discover, are irrevocably linked.

The personal and the social, fact and myth, fiction and nonfiction, order and rage: these are the tensions, the sustaining paradoxes, of his work, and they are here addressed as never before. Indeed, they are addressed explicitly. John Russell has pointed out that the six subdivisions reveal Ondaatje's plan for the book—a binary plan. "Ondaatje means us to see the main sections," he writes, "as working in pairs." The first, third and fifth sections are counterbalanced, or perhaps more accurately, "checked" by sections two, four and six. In the former, Ondaatje revels in the stories of his family, of their colorful variousness, of myths, of legend. There is, as Russell notes, a "stability" to these sections. The first section, for example, presents a nearly self-contained, ordered world, that of his ancestors, the "flaming youth," the wild-drinking Ceylon society of the twenties, where "Love affairs rainbowed over marriages and lasted forever—so it often seemed that marriage was the greater infidelity. From the twenties until the war nobody really had to grow up. They remained wild and spoiled." It is an impossibly sensual world, a world of continual surprise and infinite possibility, as lazy and gay and beautiful as anything out of *Gatsby*:

> "And so, while monsoon and heat moved into deserted Colombo homes, it was to Nuwara Eliya that my grandparents and their circle of friends would go. They danced in large living rooms to the music of a Bijou-Moutrie piano while the log fires crackled in every room, or on quiet evenings read books on the moonlit porch, slicing open the pages as they progressed through a novel.

> "The gardens were full of cypress, rhododendrons, fox-gloves, arum-lilies and sweet pea; and people like the van Langenbergs, the Vernon Dickmans, the Henry de Mels and the Philip Ondaatjes were there. There were casual tragedies. Lucas Cantley's wife Jessica almost died after being shot by an unknown assailant while playing croquet with my grandfather. They found 113 pellets in her.... "

In these sections, Ondaatje is playful, almost whimsical. As is the case elsewhere, photographs are more than illustration, they are narrative constituents, and as Russell notes, Ondaatje's use of photographs to introduce sections betrays his careful, architectural design.

Consider, for example, the photographs heralding the first, third and fifth sections: double portraits of his mother and father, handsome and hopeful; a group portrait of his extended family in their sarongs and robes in languorous splendor beneath a passel of palm trees, faces ironic and mirthful; and a portrait of his mother and father, under the self-penned inscription, "What we think of married life," their faces comically contorted, half ape, "half idiot." These photographs are perfectly in keeping with what follows, as Ondaatje relates the story of his parents' courtship, the world they inhabited, and his early growing up. Their separation, and Mervyn's descent into madness, is only hinted at, or revealed piecemeal through conversations with friends and relatives, neither of whom can lay claim to full, intimate knowledge of his story. If there is tragedy, it is only hinted at. Ondaatje in these sections operates by way of deferral and indirection.

The high-spiritedness, generally, of these sections owes much to the ruling presence of Lalla, Ondaatje's maternal grandmother, a "lyrical socialist," a giver, a doer, whose generosity, "exceeded the physically possible for she had donated her body to six hospitals." Ondaatje's description of her death by drowning, with its strong echoes of Joe Christmas' flight and even of Bolden's march into madness during a parade, is so fanciful and wondrous that it is difficult to regard what is typically a somber event as anything but what it is—a "magic ride." It is as if all the natural world had turned out to escort one of their own:

> "Lalla took one step off the front porch and was immediately hauled away by an arm of water, her handbag bursting open. 208 cards moved ahead of her like a disturbed nest as she was thrown downhill still comfortable and drunk, snagged for a few moments on the railings of the Good Shepherd Convent and then lifted away towards the town of Nuwara Eliya.

> "It was her last perfect journey. The new river in the street moved her right across the race course and park towards the bus station. As the light came up slowly she was being swirled fast, 'floating' (as ever confident of surviving this too) alongside branches and leaves, the dawn starting to hit flamboyant trees as she slipped past them like a dark log, shoes lost, false breast lost. She was free as a fish, travelling faster than she had in years, fast as Vere's motorcycle, only now there was this *roar* around her. She overtook Jesus lizards that swam and ran in bursts over the water, she was surrounded by tired half-drowned fly-catchers screaming *tack tack tack tack*, frogmouths, nightjars forced to keep awake, brain-fever birds and their irritating ascending scales, snake eagles, scimitar-babblers, they rode the air around Lalla wishing to perch on her unable to alight on anything except what was moving.

> "What was moving was rushing flood. In the park she floated over the intricate fir tree hedges of the maze—which would always continue to terrify her grandchildren—its secret spread out naked as a skeleton for her. The symmetrical flower beds also began to receive the day's light and Lalla gazed down at them with wonder, moving as lazily as that long dark scarf which trailed off her neck brushing the branches and never catching…"

In sections two, four and six, by contrast, Ondaatje is concerned with the "darker side" of "paradise," with the consequences wrought by colonialism. If the odd-numbered sections revel in legends, myths, sensual detail, high-spiritedness, gossip, if they present a bright, blooming order, the even-numbered sections as much as they are about anything, are about rage. Ondaatje's plan is not so schematized as to divide itself equally (or evenly) between the personal and the political. On the contrary, the two are intimately bound up with one another. But the emphasis here is clearly on the political, as evidenced by his section headings: "Don't Talk to Me About Matisse" (the title is taken from a bitter, ironical poem by Lakdasa Wikkramasinha, about the glory of art and culture that is spread in the name of savagery), "The Prodigal," and "The Ceylon Cactus and Succulent Society." Again, photographs play an important role. As Russell has observed, the photographs in these even-numbered sections all admit the possibility of "danger"; in the photograph introducing "The Prodigal," for instance, a train inches perilously over the side of a mountain.

Danger is evoked in other ways. If in the odd-numbered sections Ondaatje's narrative is lush with flora, in these even-numbered sections wild animals assert their presence: we are told of kabaragoyas and thalagoyas, either of which "can whip you to death with its tail"; of "disturbed peacocks"; of a "filthy black wild boar"; and perhaps most ominously (and symbolically) of the grey cobra and other snakes that would come into the house after his father's death. In this Ceylon that is quite literally a garden, danger, Ondaatje hints, lurks everywhere; it may at one time have been an Eden, but no more.

Similarly, the narrative in these sections is willfully discontinuous, even fractured. It is here Ondaatje's "Monsoon Notebook" entries appear, once in each; and it is here, in the second section, the prose gives way, memorably, to poetry.

Form, say the laws of art, follows function; with Ondaatje, form *is* function. Of all his narratives, perhaps nowhere else is form so crucial, so central to an understanding of the work generally, as in *Running in the Family*. No mere rhetorical device, Ondaatje's carefully ordered oppositions go beyond structure; they approach meaning itself. For even as its creator indulges happily in the wild profusion of myths and legends, these alternate sections undercut the brightness of that blooming world, insisting always that what lay behind it, vast and invidious, was colonial rule. Like the young revolutionaries whose insurgency he recounts in "Don't Talk to Me About Matisse," Ondaatje in these alternate sections mounts a rebellion of his own—against his own narrative. What is being assailed is the stability of first impressions. There is a darker side, he asserts: behind the order, rage.

As Lalla animates the odd-numbered sections, it is Mervyn who haunts the even-numbered sections. If Lalla embodies the myth of the Ondaatje family, and of Ceylonese society generally, Mervyn represents the flip side. Like the "old portraits" of Ceylon that hang on Ondaatje's brother's wall in Toronto, that grow "from mythic shapes into eventual accuracy," the book turns, symbolically, from Lalla to Mervyn. Introspective, given to brooding, and worse, as his drinking worsens, to paranoia, Mervyn is physically incapable of transfiguring his dread. He knows no gaiety. He fears for his family and himself, internalizes. As he grows older, he grows to resent, and resist, the proscribed order of things. His "last train ride," which provides the book's thematic climax, in counterpoint to Lalla's final ride is neither wondrous nor magical.

A major in the Ceylon Light Infantry, Mervyn had become "obsessed with a possible invasion" of the Japanese. The year is 1943, and he is in charge of Transport, stationed in Trincomalee. His dipsomania and paranoia get the best of him, but Mervyn, protector that he is, really does believe he is "saving" his country.

"Somehow my father smuggled bottles of gin onto the train and even before they left Trinco he was raging. The train sped through tunnels, scrubland, careened around sharp bends, and my father's fury imitated it, its speed and shake and loudness, he blew in and out of carriages, heaving bottles out of the windows as he finished them, getting John Kotewala's gun"—"Sir John Kotewala," Ondaatje notes, "for he was eventually to become Prime Minister."

Mervyn's rampage continues. Having "managed to get the driver of the train drunk," he was "finishing a bottle of gin every hour walking up and down the carriages almost naked," a pistol in his hand. The scene is a masterpiece of black comedy, bending now toward the ludicrous, now toward the terrible. Mervyn's fellow officers, wanting to contain him but unwilling to trigger a violent outburst, lest they rile the high-ranking British officers nestled within one of the carriages, have no recourse but to follow him as he creeps along the tops of the moving train. So it was that the British

> "slept on serenely with their rage for order in the tropics, while the train shunted and reversed into the night and there was chaos and hilarity in the parentheses around them."

The scene explodes, literally, that Mervyn has stumbled upon are collected and put into jeeps. In fact, they are not bombs at all but rather pots of curd that passengers had been carrying. No matter: there is Mervyn, at the Kelani-Colombo bridge, dropping "all twenty-five pots into the river below, witnessing huge explosions as they smashed into the water."

■ VII

Ondaatje's interest in filmmaking is more than dilettante's dabbling. In 1990 he was a fellow at Norman Jewison's filmmaking institute; in the years prior he made a number of short, whimsical documentaries; in this context, his remark about *CWBK* being a word-rendered spaghetti western is not as offhand as it would seem.

Like the documentary filmmaker, for whom arrangement is all, Ondaatje is interested in moments, gestures: stills. And what are stills but individual photographs? In Ondaatje's longer prose works, photos are not simply pictures but narrative constituents, as integral to the overall design as any block of text—and proof, if any was needed, of the remarkable degree to which he has constructed a destabilized, decentered, thoroughly democratized narrative.

This is worth remembering when considering *In the Skin of a Lion*, although it is Ondaatje's first long-form work that uses no photographs. It is also Ondaatje's first work to call itself a novel. At first glance, this seems a misnomer, because its rhythms, which are Ondaatje's rhythms generally, are not those of the novel. Moreover, the trademarks of the novel—character development, narrative drive, dramatic tension—are conspicuously absent. Neither is there a complex web of relationships, with its attendant rhythms of rise and fall, upon which the author will exercise a rigorous scrutiny.

Ondaatje can't be faulted for not having tried. Clearly, his intentions are otherwise. Indeed, Ondaatje had originally wanted to write about the strange, real-life adventures of one Ambrose Small, a millionaire in turn-of-the-century Toronto, until a little less than halfway through the writing of the book, when in his continuing research he lost all interest in him. It would have been surprising only if Ondaatje had built his narrative around him. In none of his narratives is any one character fully developed, fully fleshed out, in the manner of Austen or Hardy or Eliot. They remain elusive, shadowy, if not altogether intangible figures. Patrick, on whom Ondaatje eventually settled to sift the events of the story through, is himself a less than commanding presence. Some have argued that Ondaatje set out to write about him and got carried away, typically caught up in research (the history of bridge building and waterworks in Toronto, which, far more than backdrop for the novel, is its grid), and was in the end unable to braid these seemingly incompatible narrative strands. This is a fair argument, of a piece with Ondaatje's own pronouncements about his writing process. "Plot," as he remarked in a 1992 interview with David Streitfeld of *The Washington Post*, "is sort of discovered as I go along, in the writing."

But as all of Ondaatje's works are not about character so much as they are about place, or more accurately the places his characters inhabit—landscapes mental as well as physical—I don't think Patrick was ever the focus, either. In fact, more to the point, is "focus" a word that may be used with regard to Ondaatje?

If Patrick is a bit player in his own narrative, nowhere near as alive nor rounded a character as either Clara or Alice, his lovers, or Caravaggio, the thief, neither are those characters' histories as exhaustively detailed, as encyclopedically knowledgeable as those of, say, Dorothea or Jude. The point is not to force an unfair comparison, but merely to underscore that Ondaatje's aims are different. His is a shifting, decentered, destabilized text, which, forsaking the steady accretion of detail to explore its character's lives, instead catches the chance, the odd moments, freezing them, illuminating their interiors.

Perhaps I should have written "friezing." For what Ondaatje has done is to subject his characters to a larger, panoramic design, of which they make up only a part. Why has he done this? The answer, I think, has a lot to do with his choosing to call the work a "novel."

Certainly its rhythms are not those of the novel. In its compactness, its elusiveness, its openness, the work is much closer to poetry, and offers many of the same moment-by-moment sensations. But its lines are cast as prose, and its length is considerable. As Ondaatje's epigraphs provide keys to unlocking the texts that follow, it is significant that *In the Skin of a Lion* not only begins with a quotation from "The Epic of Gilgamesh," but takes its title from that enduring communal poem. Perhaps Ondaatje wants to reclaim the term "novel"? At the very least he wants to reawaken us to the imperatives of storytelling, embodied in the earliest epic poetry: to encompass history, to confront politics, and to move swiftly, seldom lingering, deriving meaning less from any exhaustive detailing of individual histories than from its structural repetitions and narrative multiplications.

■ VIII

Neither *In the Skin of a Lion* nor *The English Patient*, published six years later, are given to broken surfaces. Neither makes use of photographs, white spaces, or poetry. They would appear to be Ondaatje's least unconventional works. But it would be misleading to suggest that Ondaatje has simplified himself with age. On the contrary, his means have only become more subtle, devious; his end remains the same. Indeed, what each of these books reveals is Ondaatje's growing distrust of the novel, its assumptions, its implications, its prejudices.

Hemingway wrote that writers are either putter-inners or taker-outers. He was himself a taker-outer, having found the effects he wanted could best be achieved by paring his prose to its essences, that after all a work was like an iceberg, its meanings submerged below water, and that what was really important was the white spaces, the things not said. The mark of Ondaatje's writing is not that he is a taker-outer, but that he is so radically unlike other taker-outers.

Whereas a minimalist's work often reads as if individual paragraphs and chapters had been excised, *The English Patient* (joint-winner of the Booker Prize for 1992) reads as if an entire narrative had been sacrificed, and what remains is a ghostly spirit. That *ur*-narrative—the linear, straightforward account of four lives bound by circumstance in a ravaged Italian villa at the end of World War II—has been told many times over, by novelists both great and small, and Ondaatje seems intensely aware of that fact. What he has instead given us is a book comprised of those parts that invariably would have wound up in the trash basket of any other novelist. It is a novel of side angles.

Consciousness, the strange recesses of the mind—these are not typically the concerns of the novelist writing about war and its devastations. It is telling that Ondaatje offers as one of his four characters not a bombardier, but a bomb diffusion specialist. Nothing is come at conventionally. Nothing is dealt with head-on. A British lieutenant remarks, "If you are in a room with a problem, don't talk to it."

What Ondaatje does is to take that *ur*-narrative and play on its fringes, letting arcane bits of research, abstract conversations, and snatches from a host of sources—from Herodotus to James

■ **BOOKS BY MICHAEL ONDAATJE**

The Dainty Monsters. Toronto: Coach House Press, 1967.

The Man with Seven Toes. Toronto: Coach House Press, 1969.

Leonard Cohen. Toronto: McClelland & Stewart, 1970.

The Collected Works of Billy the Kid: Left Handed Poems. New York: Norton, 1970.

Rat Jelly. Toronto: Coach House Press, 1973.

Coming Through Slaughter. Toronto: Anansi, 1976. New York: Norton, 1976.

Elimination Dance. Toronto: Nairn, 1978.

There's a Trick with a Knife I'm Learning to Do. New York: Norton, 1979. Toronto: McClelland & Stewart, 1979.

Claude Glass. Toronto: Coach House Press, 1979.

Running in the Family. New York: Norton, 1982. Toronto: McClelland & Stewart, 1982.

Tin Roof. Lantzville, British Columbia: Island Writing Series, 1982.

Secular Love. Toronto: Coach House Press, 1984.

All Along the Mazinaw: Two Poems. Wisconsin: Woodland Pattern, 1986.

In the Skin of a Lion. New York: Knopf, 1987. Toronto: McCelland & Stewart, 1987. London: Secker & Warburg, 1987.

The Cinnamon Peeler: Selected Poems. Toronto: McClelland & Stewart, 1989.

The English Patient. New York: Knopf, 1992.

Handwriting. New York: Random House, 1999.

Anil's Ghost. New York: Knopf, 2000.

Fenimore Cooper to Kipling—fill out the story. If the narrative tends toward abstraction; if its many layers and textures, for want of a kind of controlling, ordering force, seem like so much marginalia; if its side-angle sensibility permits a certain slippage of focus, that is perhaps by design. This is not a novel about a quartet of characters and their war-torn lives. It is about the novel itself—the linear, conventional novel, which Ondaatje, having shot to hell, in piecing together the many shards left in the ruin, is trying to make sense of, to make whole, and new again.

Todd Kliman
December, 1994

UPDATE

Canadian poet, novelist, and playwright Michael Ondaatje continues to be widely read, and has since written a novel, *Anil's Ghost* (2000) and *Handwriting: Poems* (1999), and edited a nonfiction book, *Lost Classics* (2001).

In a review of *Anil's Ghost*, *Publishers Weekly* wrote: "More effective than a documentary, Ondaatje's novel satisfies one of the most exalted purposes of fiction: to illuminate the human condition through pity and terror. It may well be the capstone of his career." His poetry fares just as well. "*Handwriting*—spare, imagistic, lyrical—is a deep spell woven of history, imagination, and the chiaroscuro of fairy tale," declared a *Prairie Schooner* review.

In 1996 *The English Patient* was made into a critically acclaimed film, starring Ralph Fiennes and Kristin Scott Thomas; it won an Academy Award for best picture.

To Know the Truth: The Novels of Robert Deane Pharr

■ I

Robert Deane Pharr has been writing for a decade now, with no striking public success. His first novel, *The Book of Numbers* (1969), received modest critical praise and was eventually made into a violent "blaxploitation" motion picture. His second novel, *S.R.O.* (1971), was less successful than *The Book of Numbers,* and his third *The Soul Murder Case* (1975), was met with almost total indifference by readers and critics alike. In the ledger of modern letters, Pharr is recorded as a minor writer.

There are a number of reasons for this. In his two latest books, he has taken for his material deeply unsettling and unpleasant subjects—alcoholism, drug addiction, madness, rape, and violent crime—and he writes about them in graphic and sometimes horrifying detail. In addition, he is an uneven literary technician. His narration—particularly in the two latest books—sometimes comes to a standstill, his prose is occasionally graceless, and his fictional purpose is not always clear.

But, that said, it should be added that the literary career of Robert Deane Pharr is a remarkable story, and the uneven work he has produced forms a strikingly unified whole. The former has much to teach us about the courage—moral, intellectual, and physical—which life may demand of those who choose to write serious fiction; the latter offers startling and painful insights into the frightening, equivocal power of truth in a deceitful universe.

Pharr is a 60-year-old American black man who for much of his life earned his living as a traveling waiter, a nomad following the racing season from town to town in pursuit of the high rollers and the big tips; later he worked as a waiter at Lundy's in Brooklyn—an enormous restaurant which sometimes employed as many as 150 waiters on a given Sunday lunch shift. Much of Pharr's life has been a struggle against alcoholism, illness, and poverty. He wrote *The Book of Numbers* while living on welfare in one of Harlem's "single room occupancy" hotels—jumbled warrens which have since gained notoriety as "welfare hotels." This first completed manuscript was destroyed by a madwoman. Pharr had no copy; after a brief nervous breakdown, he sat down and rewrote the book from memory.

Lacking literary connections and credentials, Pharr got his entry into publishing while working as a waiter at the Columbia University Faculty Club. While serving lunch to Professor Lewis Leary (then chairman of the Columbia English department), Pharr asked him to read the manuscript. Leary was impressed and passed it along to a friend at Doubleday. After three years' delay, *The Book of Numbers* was published, and since then Pharr has stuck determinedly to his new career. He has recently completed a fourth novel and begun work on a fifth.

Pharr's writing is intense and sometimes painfully vivid. His characters are driven by deep feelings they can often neither understand nor control. Like prisoners hammering at the bars of their ceils, they are brave, angry, frightened, determined, and confused.

Robert Deane Pharr

Born in 1916 in Richmond, Virginia, and raised in New Haven, Connecticut, Robert Dean Pharr returned south in 1933. He graduated from Virginia Union University and did graduate work at Fisk University. After an early career as a waiter in exclusive resorts and private clubs, he won attention for his writing. He received a Rockefeller Foundation Grant in 1969, a Chapman Foundation Grant in 1971, and was named a Distinguished Alumnus of Virginia Union University in 1975.

Robert Deane Pharr died during surgery for an aneurysm, April 1, 1992, in Syracuse, New York. ■

The prison is, of course, the raw reality of black life in a white nation—racism, poverty, drug addiction, crime, indifference, and alienation. But there is a larger context as well. His characters often sense that their agony is not exclusively or even primarily of racial origin, but rather ontological—the pain and terror of any self-aware being striving to know the truth in a universe which seems inexplicably, inexorably hostile.

Pharr's characters are constantly learning new and more frightening truths about human life; his novels proceed less by means of plot or incident than through a series of painful revelations, as life flays them of their cherished illusions, one by one. There is no victory for Pharr characters. At best, they achieve a determined but precarious equilibrium which enables them to move forward in life without succumbing to loneliness and fear. Those who cannot learn this uneasy balance are doomed.

But though Pharr's chief concern is apparently for truth and the hurtful liberation it brings, his work is also valuable because he is an accomplished social novelist. He has a keen eye for the quirks of people in groups and the descriptive skill to render them convincingly on the page. *The Book of Numbers* and *S.R.O.* are skillfully written novels of black manners. They explore small subsocieties which most readers, black or white, will never enter.

The Book of Numbers is an intricate, tightly constructed work which holds the reader's attention throughout; *S.R.O.* is overlong, jumbled, and compulsively fascinating; *The Soul Murder Case* is raunchy, confused, violent, and ultimately a failure. Yet each book relates organically to the other two, and taken together they show us a writer wrestling with enormous themes and bravely making art out of his private demons.

■ II

No nigger knows the hour of his emasculation. The moment and

the place is chosen with abandon. Anywhere and everywhere it may
come. The knife has descended in crowded courtrooms, in churches,
at work, riding the public bus, or in the nigger's own castle of a cabin
while he watches his woman moan in terror and shame.

    There is no truth or nobility in the moment.

The Book of Numbers

The Book of Numbers is the story of two strong, resourceful black characters who are crushed by a malign reality—the rigid social system of the Jim Crow South of the 1930s. Dave Greene and Blueboy Harris are traveling waiters who are determined to build something which will belong only to them and, by extension, to black people. They are unwilling to accept the meager leavings that Southern society considered proper for black men—minister, schoolteacher, bank messenger, etc. They do not choose crime; it is simply the only alternative open to them.

They settle upon the durable form of illicit gambling known as "the numbers" or "policy," in which a bettor selects a three-digit number and wagers any sum from a penny up. The daily "number" is determined in some relatively public, tamper-proof fashion, such as the last three digits of the total number of shares sold on the New York Stock Exchange or the results of key races at a nearby track. The odds against winning are 999 to 1, but a winner is paid only 600 to 1. Thus, as crime goes, numbers is relatively safe and highly profitable—so profitable, in fact, that most large towns had numbers banks owned by white mobsters and protected by white policemen and judges.

But in their travels, Dave and Blueboy have found one city without a bank in being. Although never identified in the book, the city is recognizably Richmond, Virginia. Even if the book were a failure on other levels, it would still be invaluable for its portrayal of black society in the Depression-era urban South. Pharr takes an unsparing, detailed look at every level of the city's black community: the hypocritical ministers, the pathetically snobbish "socialites," the fearful, verbose college professors (at the black university, students are locked into their dormitories at curfew because death by fire is less to be feared than premarital sex).

Most memorable is the picture of the Ward, the city's black "sporting district," with its nip joints, speakeasies, kiffs, and gambling hells. At its center is Booker's Hotel, a small black hostelry which is the nerve center for a community of surprisingly gentle hustlers, gamblers, and barflies.

But *The Book of Numbers* is not just a social novel: in the rise and fall of the black numbers bank is a story of a quest for spiritual, as well as racial, justice. Dave and Blueboy wish to live as free men: but they are pitted against a universe which does not reward strength or courage. They fail because they are unable to look squarely at this malign reality; each fights against illusion, gives in to it, and fails.

Illusion and reality form a powerful theme in *The Book of Numbers*, as in all of Pharr's work. Denied any hope of meaningful achievement in the white man's world, the book's characters live in a world of myth and legend. Dave, the younger of the two protagonists, at first tries to liberate the Ward's black people from their illusions, but discovers that it is neither possible nor wise. Early in the book he approaches a group of young men in an attempt to recruit runners for the embryonic numbers bank. Trembling with excitement, the youths say they have heard that he and Blueboy are not really traveling waiters at all, but "international gamblers." Dave will not play the game; he tries to stick to facts. By their shattered reactions he realizes that they do not want the facts, and will not follow him if he forces them to face the truth. And he further realizes that it is he, not they, who is in the wrong:

Childlike, these men had handed Dave a worthless bauble, and requested him to weave a fable around it. They were like a crippled child who, knowing he cannot go on the Sunday school hike, asks to be told a fairy tale about a trip to the moon. Does that make the child stupid?

Under the tutelage of the more experienced Blueboy, Dave learns to play expertly on the illusions of his constituency. It is the book's unstated irony that, of all the black characters, only Dave and Blueboy, social outcasts and nominal criminals, are able to build anything of value to the black community. The bank flourishes, and the profits are put to work building "legitimate" business enterprises which bring money and jobs to the Ward. More important than the economic benefit, however, is the pride which all the people of the Ward take in the success of their numbers bank:

…Flick brought the Ford to a stop in front of the flower shop. Inside, Makepeace met a thrilling sight. It was not only Blueboy issuing orders, but all the young men he had around him, busy, active, using their intelligence. His legs, so much like tree trunks, quivered with the pride of anticipation. Never had he witnessed such orderly yet hectic industry by Negroes.

Yet this hectic industry, in the end, proves a very equivocal benefit. Many of the Ward's blacks are seduced by the prospects of easy riches into bankruptcy, embezzlement, alcoholism, and violence. Because it is built only on black money, the bank destroys even as it creates. And in the end it seduces even Dave, who changes from a spinner of myths into their victim. He comes to believe in the pride the bank creates, and forgets the malign reality around him.

Dave's hour comes when the corrupt white police raid the bank, hoping to take control of the profitable operation from the blacks. Obsessed by his newfound pride, Dave hopes to fight openly for control of his business. But without consulting him, the more pragmatic Blueboy arranges to combat the threat in a more time-honored black fashion. On the day of the trial, with Dave watching from the audience, the intelligent, brave, resourceful blacks of the numbers bank reappear in sinister new guise, dressed in gaudy rags, weeping in feigned terror and repentance, crying piteously to Jesus for mercy.

They play the classic white stereotype of trifling, childish blacks so well that the judge indulgently frees them; but there is an unexpected side effect. Dave's pride, his own illusion, is stripped from him; his fantasy of freedom and dignity is destroyed. Stunned and humilated, he withdraws from life, until by the book's end he is a pathetic, passive shadow.

Dave's crisis is the book's climax. For the remaining third of the novel, the characters' fortunes steadily decline. There is no material or logical reason for this: in fact, the numbers bank continues to flourish, free and independent. But Pharr makes it clear that the trouble is spiritual. Dave and Blueboy have tried too hard, have opened themselves too much to the harsh truth of human life. There is no escape for them. Blueboy, so adept at playing the white-black role, becomes weary of it and forgets his place. He refuses to accommodate a gang of larcenous white policemen; they beat him to death. Decay and dissolution afflict the raffish social order of the Ward: characters for whom we have come to care are jailed, murdered, or forced to flee. In the end, only Dave's last lover, Delilah Mazique, retains her vitality and her ability to hope; it is she who must run the bank and care for Dave.

Delilah seems to be Pharr's ideal of the type of person who can survive the pain and terror of this life. Faced with an unjust social order, she neither rebels nor submits, but somehow keeps herself and her hopes inviolate, retaining her strength while others surrender to despair. But in the final passage of the novel, Pharr tells us that even Delilah's hopes are vain, and we are left with the ambiguous knowledge that "most things do not last always, and only the things of black granite—like Delilah's own spirit, like the Numbers, and like the Niggers—are forever."

■ III

> *"Why the hell is everything a junky does unprintable?" I sputtered.*
> *"No, I'll change that: A Black Junky whore. If five white bitches were*
> *laying up on a white guy like this I bet he'd be able to write a*
> *charming little tale that Esquire or Playboy would grab in a minute."*
> **S.R.O.**

The Book of Numbers is a tightly-constructed work of the imagination; *S.R.O.* is autobiographical, discursive, and rambling. But its nearly 600 pages tell a powerful story of one man's descent into hell, and of his eventual rebirth.

The hell of *S.R.O.* is the Logan, a decaying Harlem apartment house which has been converted into a "single room occupancy," or welfare, hotel. The time is the mid-sixties, and to the Logan comes Sid Bailey, "a middle-aged black, obviously at the tail-end of a monstrous drunk." Bailey has been thrown out by his wife, Alise, and he seeks anonymous refuge in the Logan for $13.95 a week while he works at Lundy's in Brooklyn.

But there is little solitude, and no peace, in the Logan. Once again Pharr demonstrates his gifts as a social novelist, giving life and order to the Logan's universe of drifters, junkies, pushers, whores, pimps, thieves, and thugs. As in *The Book of Numbers,* where the "criminals" are the heroes, Pharr turns our expectations inside out, drawing these social outcasts as credible human beings. All are flawed; some are admirable, some brutal, but all are believable and sympathetic.

Pharr is also brilliant in his delineation of the social interaction of the Logan's tenants—the intricate rituals which have evolved to allow people to live together in a dangerous crowded warren. One memorable scene presents a seminar of drug sellers (the Logan has one per floor) seriously discussing the fine points of pusher ethics:

> These people were dedicated merchants, just as purposeful and serious about their trade and image as any member of the Junior Chamber of Commerce. Why, these people really were conducting a seminar in Leah's room. They discussed ethical questions like whether to let a sick junky have a bag for less than five dollars. Butch and Joan insisted that even a sick junky should be made to go back in the street and hustle up the full price of a fix. On the other hand, Bill and Reba believed that a sick junky is a menace to all junkies, and especially to the pushers. A sick junky should be fixed up before he does something that will arouse the community and/or the police.

The people of the Logan, even more than those of *The Book of Numbers,* are adrift in a world of illusion. Living next door to Sid Bailey are Joey and Jinny, a black-white lesbian couple; Joey, a white woman, tries gamely to pass as a black man, and the Logan's inhabitants in time accept her as one. On the floor above is College Joe, a semi literate dropout who claims to be studying psychology at Columbia. Each night he sits down to "study"; the other tenants, immensely proud of knowing a college man, tiptoe up and down the hall while Joe solemnly scans his "textbooks"—mildewed junior-high school readers he has bought in second hand stores.

Of all the Logan's people, only Sid Bailey even has the ambition of facing life as it is, and he finds the attempt painful and dangerous. The other inmates do not want to give up their illusions, and Sid soon finds it terrifying to part with his own:

> Life in an S.R.O. is ugly and it will make you just as ugly if you let it. Every S.R.O. inmate I knew had long ago learned to evade life with a skill I had not even tried to master. Even the Sinman and Blind Charlie were never so foolish as to face life head on. With his brute strength Blind Charlie knocked life out of the way, never once

attempting to deal intelligently with this something that was never intelligent. Maybe I was the only damned fool in or around Harlem who tried to reason with fate.

Because Sid does try to reason with fate, he is defenseless against the ugliness around him; one character says he is "so damn naked" that he is scary to be with. Much of *S.R.O.* concerns the loss of Sid's illusions; in many ways the book resembles a middle-aged man's *bildungsroman.* Sid's mentor is the Sinman, a white Columbia dropout turned heroin pusher, who shows him how to defend himself in the jungle of the Logan—and, by extension, of life.

The Sinman (so-called because he fancies himself a "student of sin" living among "the Devil's own") introduces Sid to two women who provide the novel with a series of notable sex scenes: Gloria, a robust black prostitute, and Sharlee, a hauntingly beautiful addict of mixed black and Eurasian descent. Though Sid comes to love both, neither can save him from the pain of trying to reason with fate. Gloria is jailed, leaving him alone, and Sharlee proves unable to shed the role of beautiful waif and confront him as an adult woman.

Sid's decline continues. He drinks more heavily, loses his job, and goes on welfare. Unable to exercise his will, he becomes a wino and finds himself unable to resist the parasites living around him. The low point of Sid's pilgrimage comes when five prostitutes systematically move in on him, sleeping and shooting up in his room and attempting to manipulate him into feeding and caring for them.

But somehow Sid's descent brings him a curious redemption. The prostitutes do not master him; he learns to dominate them, and eventually throws them out. At the Sinman's command, he begins writing to fill the time: the result is the beginning of a novel (as *S.R.O.* is almost completely autobiographical, it isn't surprising that the manuscript seems to resemble *The Book of Numbers*). Gloria is released from jail, and (like Pharr's other strong woman characters) helps redeem her man from despair by sharing her body and her strength.

They vow to escape the Logan. But before they can effect their escape, a madwoman, convinced that she is in love with Sid, destroys the manuscript (this incident, again, is based on reality; Pharr remains bitter at the New York police, who had earlier refused to arrest the woman for invading his room naked and armed with a butcher knife. The officers who came to the door and saw the woman trying to stab Pharr shrugged and suggested he go to court for an eviction order).

The loss of "my old gal," as he has come to call the novel, brings on an emotional collapse, and he enters a mental hospital. After his release, he rewrites the book, proving that whatever he has learned will be lasting; then he leaves the Logan forever, for a reunion with Gloria, who has become an ardent black nationalist. But the resolution is carefully ambiguous; as he walks out of the book, Sid tells himself only, "Now you walking, boy. Keep on, boy. Keep right on."

Despite its narrative flaws and seemingly depressing subject matter, *S.R.O.* is a powerful book, and in many ways more hopeful than *The Book of Numbers*. Its value does not lie only in its sharp picture of a small subculture which most of us will never know firsthand, but in its moving portrait of a man trying to integrate his life, against stunning odds, by his devotion to the craft of writing.

■ IV

Life is real and life is honest. And a real smart man forever wants
none of it.
The Soul Murder Case

The Soul Murder Case puzzled reviewers and readers alike. Most dismissed it as a wild, raunchy potboiler—a purposeless blend of sex, violence, and rage. Those it has in abundance, and reviewers focused on them and missed the actual, very serious, point of this curious, badly flawed novel.

The book had its genesis in the mid-fifties when Pharr was hospitalized in Freedmen's Hospital of Howard University, suffering from acute alcoholism. While undergoing treatment, he found himself sharing a ward with a number of heroin addicts being weaned from their dependence on drugs. To his surprise, their withdrawal from addiction did not seem to be the agonizing, brutal process of popular mythology, but a relatively rapid, painless procedure.

Doctors explained to him that Freedmen's had developed a withdrawal method that was radically different from those in use elsewhere. Although full details were published in 1951* the method is apparently still used only at Howard.

As the drug problem exploded in the sixties and seventies, Pharr was outraged. A simple treatment method, developed by black doctors, seemed to promise a solution to the nation's drug problem; white America had ignored it for almost a quarter-century. *The Soul Murder Case* was written to tell the world about the program; understood in this light, much of the book's apparently random madness becomes more understandable.

Bobbie Dee, a former top black singer, has lost his career as a result of heroin. He is cured at Freedmen's Hospital through the ministrations of Dr. E. Y. Williams (who is not a character at all but the psychiatrist who developed and supervised the withdrawal program).

Like Pharr, Bobbie Dee reveres Williams as "next to Gawd," and he accepts his theory that drug addiction and alcoholism are both linked directly to sexual frustration.

Discharged from the hospital, Bobbie finds his voice destroyed, and he tries to carve out a career as a literary agent serving the growing market for black-oriented screenplays. As an agent, he discovers a blues singer named Candace Brown, who is also, secretly, a poet of staggering talent.

But Candace is on the verge of suicide, for reasons which Bobbie cannot decipher. Feeling himself, with the cataclysmic suddenness which marks the emotions of Pharr's characters, desperately in love with Candace, he tries to unravel her mystery. The answer, when it comes, is one of those scarifying visions which come to all of Pharr's characters from time to time: Candace is secretly married to a white man who raped and beat her years before. The knowledge that this beautiful black poet has given herself to the white oppressor sends Bobbie running to heroin; but another black woman, Viena, saves him by luring him into bed and assuaging his pain with her body.

Bobbie then meets Candace's daughter Marion, and is drawn to her with a wild incestuous paternal love. Marion has become a drug addict, and out of pride she refuses Bobbie's offer to finance her through the Freedmen's cure, preferring to taste real life by kicking "cold turkey." A wild scene follows: Bobbie is forced to subdue Marion's self-destructive urges with physical violence, alcohol, and finally sex. When she has put drugs behind her, she devotes herself to helping Bobbie realize his love for her mother. Candace remains with her white husband out of sexual frustration, they conclude; Bobbie must seduce her and teach her the real meaning of sex.

This he does; but they are discovered by the husband, and in the ensuing fight Bobbie is knocked unconscious and Candace—freed at last from her dependence on the white oppressor—murders the husband with a switchblade. She is arrested and confined to a mental hospital; as the book ends, Bobbie is preparing to enter the same hospital to be near her.

---

* E. Y. Williams, M.D., "The Treatment of Drug Addiction: A Preliminary Report," *The Psychiatric Quarterly*, State Hospital Press, Utica, N.Y., October 1951.

■ **BOOKS BY ROBERT DEANE PHARR**

The Book of Numbers. Garden City, N.Y.: Doubleday, 1969.

S.R.O. Garden City, N.Y.: Doubleday, 1971.

The Welfare Bitch. Garden City, N.Y.: Doubleday 1973.

The Soul Murder Case. New York: Avon, 1975.

Giveadamn Brown. Garden City, N.Y.: Doubleday, 1978.

Viewed as an attempt to tell the world about the Freedmen's Hospital withdrawal program, this initially incomprehensible plot begins to make more sense. The detailed description of Bobbie Dee's stay at Freedmen's Hospital—which must have puzzled reviewers—is the core of the book; set against it, as a demonstration of the horrors of unassisted withdrawal from heroin, is the violent passage in which Marion kicks her habit. The vivid sex scenes, as well, support Williams's theories (as interpreted by Pharr) that drug addiction, alcoholism, and most other problems are caused by sexual repression.

But, that said, it must be added that in fictional terms *The Soul Murder Case* is a clear failure. The book covers much of the same emotional and social ground as did *S.R.O.* But where in *S.R.O.* the shadow-world of drugs, prostitution, and crime is rendered with cool graphic realism, in *The Soul Murder Case* Pharr has allowed the material to get out of control, spinning itself into a mad fever-dream—repetitive, confusing, and largely senseless.

However, Pharr strikes one clear theme in *The Soul Murder Case* which offers much insight into his past and present work. He believes deeply in the redemptive power of art in its capacity to transform and salvage our individual and collective lives. This note was first sounded in *S.R.O.,* where Sid Bailey rises out of alcoholism and despair by writing a novel. In *The Soul Murder Case* Pharr extends the notion. Candace Brown's poetry (which Pharr wisely does not include) is not just *good* poetry: it has a shattering, electrifying effect on all who read it, it is a revolutionary force. So powerful is art that Pharr tells us that one of Candace's songs, violently anti-American, was forcibly suppressed by the C.I.A. because it threatened national security.

Perhaps it is this theme that best gives a key to the curious, admirable integrity of Robert Deane Pharr's writing. As a man who has redeemed his own life by writing, he is willing to ask more of art than it can possibly deliver. His books are violently alive: they crackle with an energy that seems to be trying to escape the page. Pharr desperately wants us to see the truth about heroin addiction, about race relations, about the nature of reality itself.

After the failure of *The Soul Murder Case,* Pharr told an interviewer, "I'm not going to write any more serious books." But the title of his most recent unpublished novel is *Giveadam Brown*—an apt expression for the desperate caring that fills all of Pharr's writing to date. Pharr cares deeply for truth; he is willing to pay almost any price to know and to tell it. This is no mean accolade for any writer, major or minor, famous or unknown.

The work of novelist and social critic Robert Deane Pharr, who died in 1992, never attracted the kind of attention enjoyed by his contemporaries. After this essay appeared, he published two more novels, *The Welfare Bitch* (1973) and *Giveadamn Brown* (1978). When his first novel, *The Book of Numbers* was published in 1969, critics predicted a promising future for the 53-year-old author who wrote with such honesty about the black experience in white America. The *Dictionary of Literary Biography* states that the novel "confronts one of the most painful questions surrounding the Afro-American experience: How can ambitious, intelligent, energetic blacks . . . achieve the capitalist American Dream when the conventional roads to power and financial security are unjustly closed to them?"

The four novels that followed, however, were largely dismissed or ignored altogether, mostly due to the subject matter: the rough side of life, and the junkies, drunks, and prostitutes who inhabit it. A *New York Times* book review stated that Pharr's description of this world "is so vivid that one is almost forced to look away from the page to avoid the smell of . . . putrid breath and the bite of . . . terror." After his last book appeared, he apparently gave up writing. Although his work attracts few readers today, it is still of interest to scholars and critics.

Garrett Epps
December, 1976

Proving Irony by Compassion: The Poetry of Robert Pinsky

■ ■ ■

■ I

If a critic today calls a poet "traditional" he or she almost always continues by saying, "Of course I mean traditional in the energetic sense, the forward sense, in the sense of not settling for safe pieties." And so flow the disclaimers. But the damage has already been done. "Traditional" seems a burdensome stamp, a coat of single, opaque color. Even used in an avant-garde context, as Harold Rosenberg used it in his resonant phrase "the tradition of the new," it still tends to stigmatize, and that phrase hasn't had nearly the staying power you might expect. Not that people don't appreciate a paradoxical turn of phrase. But if we persist, as unfortunately we do, in dividing writers into two camps, the experimental and the traditional, it is still the latter that has all the explaining to do. And he who explains the most convinces the least.

Robert Pinsky is a traditional poet. What follows is an essay that will, I hope, serve as a disclaimer to eliminate the negative connotations of that label. Rather than begin by pointing to Pinsky's wide-ranging cultural sensibility, or his mastery of literary-historical knowledge, all of which will surface eventually, I should say at the start that this poet, in two books of criticism and three of poetry, stands out by virtue of his emotional tightness. Now such an attribute may be more stigmatizing in a cynical age than being called traditional. I mean by emotional rightness that balance of feeling and intelligence that is often hard-won but never agonized in its display. We live in an age, to put it mildly, that doesn't care much for tact. Emotional rightness is nearly a synonym for tact, but it adds to tact a sense of urgency, a willingness to break rules and transgress boundaries when necessary. It's a virtue difficult to discuss, having an ethical shape analogous to what Michael Polyani calls "tacit knowledge," that ingrained, "in-bodied" complex of awareness and standards that can't be quantified or easily transmitted. Pinsky has increasingly become a moral poet, that rarest of modern types, not by being a scourge or a satirist, but by returning to questions and matters of right and wrong, truth and error, and seeking to prove—more in the sense of test than vindication—his feelings about such matters. This is not to say (here comes a disclaimer) that his work has none of our contemporary concerns, such as fascination with popular culture, an obsessive interest in certain mythic topics, and a penchant for psychoanalytic assumptions about human behavior. Pinsky draws on such concerns and more, but he manages to be personal without being confessional, sophisticated without being glib, and knowledgeable without being world-weary or cutely playful.

Reading Pinsky offers positive delights as well as negative ones, however. His poetic language has many of the best features of good prose, as its connections and complexities flow from a straight forward approach to his subjects. His subjects, especially in his latest book, *History of My Heart,* are chosen with an eye to both scale and variety. He can write about a visit to a concentration camp, his New Jersey childhood, Fats Waller, or an apocalyptic vision, all with deft control. As for his critical skills, his book on Walter Savage Landor might be taken as a model of

Robert Pinsky

Robert Pinsky was born in Long Branch, New Jersey, in October of 1940. He received his education at Rutgers University in New Brunswick, New Jersey, and earned his B.A. in 1962. He attended Stanford University in California as a Woodrow Wilson, Stegner, and Fulbright fellow, and received his M.A. and Ph.D. (1966). He has taught as assistant professor of humanities at the University of Chicago, Wellesley College in Massachusetts, University of California in Berkeley, and at Boston University. Since 1978 Pinsky has been poetry editor for the *New Republic* in Washington, D.C. He was the recipient of the Massachusetts Council on the Arts grant in 1974. He also was awarded the Oscar Blumenthal Prize in 1978. Among Pinsky's many other honors are an American Academy of Arts and Letters Award, a Guggenheim fellowship, the William Carlos Williams Prize, a *Los Angeles Times Book Review* award and the Howard Morton Landon Prize for translation both in 1995 for *The Inferno of Dante: A*

New Verse Translation. In 1997 Pinsky was named U.S. poet laureate. ■

how to approach a neglected, less-than-major figure and show his accomplishments and pertinence to a new generation of readers. His book on contemporary poetry was the first to offer intelligent scruples about those dominant verse conventions that had become rigidified by the middle of the nineteen-seventies. The book had a positive partisan core, as such books usually do, and lately Pinsky has been closely linked with some of his contemporaries, such as Robert Hags, James McMichael, and Frank Bidart. This group works on elective affinities, however, and their work has not been advanced by any manifesto or explicit program of shared styles or subjects. All in all, a decent claim could be made for Pinsky being the most accomplished poet-critic in America under the age of fifty. But in what follows I want especially to argue that Pinsky's strength derives from his use of both irony and compassion in a way that these two attitudes, normally seen as opposites, are called into a test of one another. It is through this test that Pinsky gets at the emotional rightness that is his main focus and creates the artistic complexity that is his achievement. Taking the long view, we can say that such a test and a poet's willingness to submit to it are not the result exclusively of either an experimental or traditional cast of mind or temperament. But it is Pinsky's traditionalism, especially his use of multiple cultural and historical dimensions, that I think best accounts for the special quality of his work.

■ II

Pinsky's first book of poetry, *Sadness and Happiness,* often anchored its title subjects in an abiding sense of weather and atmospherics. The atmosphere remains one of the more traditional ways to image forth the congruence of inner and outer sensations. Weather is a trope where the pathetic fallacy is likely to overwhelm the poet, however, and "angry clouds" and "peaceful dawns" can soon do his thinking and his feeling for him. Yeats's "Lake Isle of Innisfree" with its peace that comes "dropping slow," like the morning dew from the eaves of some cottage, displayed just the sort of "emotional slither" that Pound wanted Imagism to discredit. Pinsky, ever aware of how the rhetorical can become merely formulaic, works both with and against the weather as a way of representing the emotional truth:

> Therefore when you marry or build
> Pray to be untrue to the plain
> Dominance of your own weather, how it keeps
>
> Going even in the woods when not
> A soul is there, and how it implies
> Always that separate, cold
> Splendidness, uncouth and unkind —
> **("Ceremony for Any Beginning")**

Here the language possesses a sort of decorous, Augustan control, reminiscent of Richard Wilbur and other "academic" poets of the postwar period. But the poem argues *against* decorum, at least in the sense that it warns the impersonal addressee to mistrust any compliant, automatic equation between self and world. (The poem also uses a moral tone mixed with a certain aestheticized sensibility that we will look at more closely later.) Relying on metaphors of atmosphere and weather threatens to reduce experience to a deterministic sense of the natural order. For Pinsky, the human will can be too coldly accepting of its place in the world, acting as just another force, "uncouth and unkind," among the myriad forces that sustain the physical universe. "One's life is one's enemy," the poet announces, invoking an almost Yeatsian, defiant note of self-dramatization and self-definition through antithetical struggle. If it's true, as one poem claims, that "the unseasonable soul holds forth," it is also true that "what happens / Takes over, and what you were goes away." The dialectic of self and world, of identity and experience, is an ongoing one in which neither term can be counted on to define total victory or our highest value. As another poem in the book says, speaking of the "hours which one / Had better use," the passing moments come bearing "Their burden of a promise but a promise / Limited." Here we have another turn of irony's screw that late modernism makes possible: knowing how freedom and necessity intersect, how promises and burdens make each other felt, we can learn to live with the "ordinary unhappiness" that might be our only true destiny.

Obviously a world in which promise can be burdensome is an ironic world, and potentially a bitter one as well. But if the promises are limited then so is the burden. Pinsky's "Poem About People" confronts the "hideous, sudden stare of self," and tries to adjust to a Sartrean awareness of the hell of the other's need, "unlovable" and lizard-like in its reptilian urgency. This poem ends with an image of "the dark wind crossing / The wide spaces between us," and the neurosis and bigotry and urban anomie, all the psychopathologies of everyday life, engulf us and yet link us with their windy, unenlightened chill. We are close to a gloom that matches that of the Tory satirists (Dr. Johnson's notion that there is more on earth to endure than to enjoy). But if we see this gloom as essentially that of post-Romantic irony—the Keatsian cry that "but to think is to be full of sorrow" stripped of its promise of Keatsian sensual bliss—then not only will we be more historically accurate, we will see Pinsky's way out as well.

The "ordinary unhappiness" of which Freud spoke emerges in Pinsky's work as the centering goal and condition of the poet's struggle to balance irony and compassion. This struggle comes to a peak in the "Essay on Psychiatrists." Rife with wit and social observation, the poem

features a persona whose bemusement borders on the naive and yet whose analytic sophistication almost outstrips his subject.

> In a certain sense, they are not serious.
> That is, they are serious—useful, deeply helpful,
> Concerned—only in the way that the pilots of huge
>
> Planes, radiologists, and master mechanics can,
> At their best, be serious. But however profound
> The psychiatrists may be, they are not serious the way
>
> A painter may be serious beyond pictures, or a businessman
> May be serious beyond property and cash—or even
> The way scholars and surgeons are serious, each rapt
>
> In his work's final cause, contingent upon nothing:
> Beyond work; persons; recoveries. And this is fitting:
> Who would want to fly with a pilot who was *serious*
>
> About getting to the destination safely? Terrifying idea —
> That a pilot could over-extend, perhaps try to fly
> Too well, or suffer from Pilot's Block; of course,
>
> It may be that (just as they must not drink liquor
> Before a flight) they undergo regular, required check-ups
> With a psychiatrist, to prevent such things from happening.

What is remarkable and rewarding about such a passage is the way several people—us, the
psychiatrists, their patients, other "professionals"—not only are accurately characterized but
have their concerns taken, well, seriously, though not without a saving grace made possible by
touches of comic incongruity ("Pilot's Block") and common sense that sees past the common
observation ("A painter may be serious beyond pictures"). The tone of a phrase such as "Terrifying idea" mixes mordant humor and genuine concern into an ironic texture that both relies
on and yet corrects the tendency of colloquial language to contain and conceal our habitual
anxieties. The emotional knowingness of such a passage, its sense that sadness and happiness
are inextricably joined in a way that almost cancels the purity of either, comes close to an
unspoken and banal acknowledgement that wisdom and ecstasy are forbidden if not impossible in a world of "regular, required check-ups." The voices of Pinsky's early personae often
appear to have come to terms with a late-modernist despair, a despair that purchases and
approves its own special brand of sanity. But though sane adjustment to such threats as enthusiasm, demonic concern, or even lyric rapture (now excused in post-Freudian awareness as
neurotic displacements of the self's unlovable need), is hard won, this adjustment is only part
of Pinsky's view of our emotional life.

The "Essay on Psychiatrists" reaches an apogee of wit and thoughtful balance when it uses
Euripides' *Bacchae* as a gloss on the psychiatric profession. In Pinsky's subtle reading of the
classical drama we can see both Pentheus and Dionysus as the model of psychiatric concern
and method. This double vision illustrates how Pinsky balances his irony and his compassion.
Pentheus stands as the man of affections, the compassionate but mistrusting doctor who "raises
his voice in the name of dignity." Dionysus, on the other hand, is the ironist, one who turns to
grim humor, "With his soft ways picking along lightly / With a calm smile." Obviously Pinsky
imagines that healing, especially healing our own natures, requires both perspectives, and furthermore he realizes Pentheus' compassion is threatened by his panic in the face of disorder,

while Dionysus' irony can quickly become "bland arrogance." We might take this reading of Pentheus and Dionysus as a show of Pinsky's Augustan perspectival balance and decorum, or as a wry commentary on psychiatry's frequent desire to have it both ways when explaining character and motivation. And we are also cautioned about psychiatrists near the end of the poem that "we must not / Complain both that they are inhuman and too human." Finally we realize that Pinsky's view of psychiatrists is nearly completely congruent with his view of all people, and what we have been reading is less a sociological dissertation than an updated "Essay on Man."

Pinsky's ability to use a classical text and his own gloss on it as the center of an extended poetic argument sets him apart from the great majority of his peers. (In *An Explanation of America* he uses Shakespeare's "The Winter's Tale" in much the same Augustan manner, and also uses an equally complex persona.) Such ability itself determines the special nature of Pinsky's enviable artistic achievement, as he faces language with a richly layered awareness of our inescapably linguistic condition. Language is for Pinsky both the sign and the scene of our sadness and happiness, our burden and our promise, a wealth of "terms of all kind mellow with time, growing / Arbitrary and rich." Again, our souls' weathers must be resisted or we can blindly accept as natural that which is arbitrary—in other words we must be prepared to be ironic about our own desires. But we also have to accept the rich wisdom of common sense, so often embodied in tag-lines, *loci classici*, axioms, or "old sayings," for often compassion recognizes in such ordinary language the extraordinary pressures of being human. In an epoch when experimentalism and unsubstantiated metaphoric license, often justifying itself as surrealism, form a large part of contemporary poetry's idiom, Pinsky may appear unduly conservative in his verbal invention. But I think Pinsky's poetic gifts are devoted to a just separation of the truly public and rhetorical from the glibly easy and formulaic uses of words. Put bluntly, I think Pinsky sees language as he sees people, both ironically and compassionately. This dual attitude to language involves Pinsky in a related struggle, namely the vexed question of whether any logical or verbal act can preserve the truth of our everydayness. Broadly speaking this is the mediaeval argument over nominalism, that once and future doubt that all we say (and write) is somehow discontinuous with what we think and feel, that language is doomed to betray much more than it can ever preserve out of the "blooming, buzzing confusion of the world," as William James called it.

■ III

One of the forms the argument over language has taken in the modern era is the argument between imagistic poetry and discursive poetry. In his critical study *The Situation of Poetry*, Pinsky joins this argument largely on the side of discursive poetry. By explicating Keats's "Ode To A Nightingale" as a poem struggling both against and for the desire to capture the immediacy of sensation and experience, Pinsky reaffirms the essentially abstract, conventional, and discursive nature of language itself. Poetry, especially the post-Romantic poetry dominated by the contemporary styles of imagistically dense presentation, proceeds vainly when it seeks to escape completely the discursive qualities inherent in language. Rather than recapitulate all of Pinsky's argument, it helps to focus the issue by looking briefly at one of its counter-responses, an essay by Jonathan Holden, from *Field* magazine, called "The Attack on the Image." Holden defends imagistic poetry enthusiastically and, though he grudgingly grants that Pinsky is in part persuasive, he finally says that arguments for discursiveness are arbitrary, limited, and limiting to the sensibility needed to appreciate a kind of poetry that can be "tremendously sophisticated and successful." Such polemical arguments—and this one has been a lightning rod for polemic in contemporary poetry for twenty years or so—can easily be dismissed as elaborate justifications of personal taste or shunned as extreme versions of simple truths that should be seen pluralistically or kept in balanced harmony.

In fact, such arguments often conceal fundamentally divergent assumptions, and it's to Pinsky's credit that he makes his assumptions about language as clear as possible. But obviously these assumptions in turn involve a complex set of beliefs and ideas about experience, the self, emotional structures, and even moral attitudes. Holden states his position most extremely when he argues that images are "a kind of language." He supports this position by appealing to a description of "ordinary" experience which offers points of repetition, referentiality, recall, and so forth. Such structuring moments or patterns are preverbal in Holden's account, and language is employed "in a *rather* natural way, to clarify the flux and mess of experience." (My emphasis) Precisely. But this fails to illumine how far apart are the admittedly systematic possibilities of language and that "flux and mess" that has an apparent disposition to be clarified. For Pinsky admits the "flux and mess," but insists that what is "*rather* natural" to some is strained and even duplicitous and misleading to others. And so what started as an argument about language might well end up as an argument about nature. Or one could argue the other way, working toward more precise and narrow scales of meaning and agreement, and say that even if imagery is "a *kind* of language" (my emphasis) it's still not verbal language and is equally susceptible to mis-translation, as it were, as is any other non-verbal experience.

Where I side with Pinsky, however, is not solely on grounds of logical consistency or general agreement, but on the grounds of inclusiveness. The imagistic poetry defended by Holden has to my mind grown very formulaic and stereotyped in execution, and now seems historically impoverished beyond necessity. While imagism performed a crucial function in shattering the late-Victorian doldrums of poeticized language, it eventually became the *lingua franca* of our poetic idiom and now needs to be severely challenged. Already many poetic styles can be understood in part as taking up this challenge—the madcap profusion of prose rhythms in Ashbery, or the severe experimentalism of the Language Poets, for example—and discursiveness has many relatives. While Ashbery and the Language Poets might challenge imagistic conventions by being aggressively more *non*-discursive, other poets have returned to various forms of discursive writing, such as the meditative mode, versions of natural history, narrative, and even system-building structures. What we often find in these discursive forms is a continuing interest in imagery, but imagery put to a use, to clarify thought or test emotional validity or discover experiential coherence, and not simply imagery for its own sake. Bluntly put, discursive poetry can include the virtues of imagistic writing. (On the other hand, imagistic writing is often read by being translated back into some discursive frame. Holden himself does this in his essay when he explicates a poem by Galway Kinnell to illustrate his position. However, I think he mis-reads the poem, "Getting the Mail," by missing a pun on the word "declining." Kinnell's poem is about language and its struggles with the "flux and mess" and plays with the abstract structuring of language as much as with the constellation of its images.) To insist on some sort of higher truth value for a poem that relies solely on images is to deny not only the fullness of language but also that of experience.

Perhaps a poem from Pinsky's first book will illustrate this ability to include some of imagism's virtues in the service of other ends. It is called "Waiting":

When the trains go by
The frozen ground shivers
Inwardly like an anvil.

The sky reaches down
Stiffly into the spaces
Among houses and trees.

A wisp of harsh air snakes
Upward between glove
And cuff, quickening

The sense of the life
Elsewhere of things, the things
You touched, maybe, numb

Handle of a rake; stone
Of a peach; soiled
Band-Aid; book, pants

Or shirt that you touched
Once in a store…less
The significant fond junk

Of someone's garage, and less
The cinder out of your eye —
Still extant and floating

In Sweden or a bird's crop —
Than the things that you noticed
Or not, watching from a train:

The cold wide river of things,
Going by like the cold
Children who stood by the tracks

Holding for no reason sticks
Or other things, waiting
For no reason for the trains.

Obviously this poem has a hunger for a materialistic foundation to experience. But where the poem goes beyond "the life / Elsewhere of things," that forbidding sense of otherness, both ineffable and ineluctable, is where it pivots on the "less this…than that" construction in the sixth to eighth stanzas. Pinsky turns from the things he's "touched" (invoked by that image of the air touching his wrist, suggesting the pulse and leading on to the "quickening" in stanza 3) to the things he's only seen in passing, at a distance. But these latter things, the "cold wide river," are somehow more humanized by being compared to those children standing there with their gesture of incomplete and purposeless desire.

Surely this poem has a nominalist dimension, evidenced by the Band-Aid and the cinder in Sweden, but it goes beyond the nominalist dimension to propose a somewhat incongruous but corrective dual view of thing-hood. At the same time that it avoids any sense of "deep images" or mythical totemism, it also declines to invoke any Platonic essences or elaborate any schematic system. Its approach to abstract meaning, its epistemological trust, is tentative, even existential. Philosophically speaking the poem's views are closer to Merleau-Ponty or John Dewey than to Hegel or Kant. Pinsky apparently understands the recalcitrance of the mundane, the "flux and mess of experience," but he doesn't assume that things can speak for themselves. They may, metaphorically and importantly, speak *to* and *of* the humans who made, used, and discarded them, but it is we who must put their meaning (and their meaninglessness) into words. The experience of waiting—that inner atmosphere—can be *got at*, though never exhausted or fully contained, by a representation of certain instances of people looking out for some arrival. But the abstract experience of waiting is of course never fully abstract to the one who waits, and likewise it is never exclusively specific either, since we know it only by its resemblance to other such instances, our own and even those of strangers. Poetry has for centuries in the Western tradition been the mediation of such abstract experiences and their specific instances, more philosophical than history, more spelled out than philosophy, as Aristotle argues. "Getting at" that junction of abstract and specific can be accomplished in a wide variety of ways. Pinsky's way is to combine the distance of irony and the embrace of compassion, to prove them against one another, to feel the "cold wide river" and to see the waiting children.

Pinsky's poetry does not involve a total rejection of the imagistic poetry heralded by Pound and Williams, nor does it require a return to Augustan decorum. What it does instead is use the past, both the near and distant past, as a way of making the present resound. This requires not using the past to judge or censure the present, or vice versa, but to use both cultural dimensions as a commentary on each other. As he put it in *Landor's Poetry,* his study of that poet who was both classical and romantic:

> Landor's procedure is to revitalize, through profound energies of understanding and a cleanly exactitude of style, an already established situation or observation. Stylistic perfection…demonstrates the degree to which the chosen commonplace has been comprehended, and the skill of thought so demonstrated is personal and original.

■ IV

One of the most persistent biases of modernism is the stricture against commentary and explanation. So not only in his criticism, but in the very title of his second book of poems, *An Explanation of America,* Pinsky sets himself against the grain of certain received ideas. Yet this second book invites comparison with other modernist long poems, such as Williams's *Paterson* and Olson's *Maximus Poems,* in its use of both everyday and historical materials in the matrix of a quasi-epic scale. But if Williams and Olson are the imagist and objectivist models we see distantly behind Pinsky's *Explanation* there is also the discursive, philosophical accent of Stevens, especially the *Notes Towards A Supreme Fiction.* These, however, are distant models, echoed in the subject matter of the poem and in the titles of its divisions ("Its Many Fragments," "Its Great Emptiness," etc.). Close to the poem's surface and texture (and closer to its moral vision) is the model of Horace's familiar epistles (one of which, Book I, xvi, the poem translates, glosses, and incorporates in a daringly inventive perspective by incongruity). The poetry is basically that of the middle style, in blank verse, subtle enough to incorporate diverse areas of experience, from rioting urban black youths to Jefferson's epitaph, yet integrated enough by a consistent tone of what we might call patient but genuine puzzlement, so that a rational attitude is neither despaired of nor insisted upon.

Two other structural principles animate and control the poem's explorations. Pinsky addresses the poem to his daughter, or rather his "idea" of his daughter. This enables the poem to modulate its familiar approach with more weighty attitudes. He speaks both through and to the daughter, weaving explanation with apology, instruction, conjecture, even a confessional excursus from time to time. Rather than weight the poem with sodden self-consciousness, this weaving of stances matches the diversity of material and also creates a sense of authority based not on absolute certainty but rather on an earned and skeptical reverence. He labors to get it right, to make sense, and the effort is seldom strained or postured. The other structuring device is to use and yet question certain standard topics about America, such as its love of speed and space, its conscience haunted by the recurrent moral obtuseness and civic inefficiency of electoral democracy, and so forth. This gives the poem a thematic variety that again answers to the wealth of the subject, and allows the poet to incorporate various kinds of knowledge, mythic, historical, philosophical, anthropological, commonsensical, into his "explanation."

It is not special pleading to say that all of this makes the poem difficult to quote, since it is largely through the juxtaposition of incidents and passages in the three sections that the full strength of Pinsky's invention is most apparent. But if one had to single out one overriding theme in the poem, it is the difficulty of imagining America and yet the felt need to do so that drives the poem and sustains and underlies all its many facets. The book is about imagination as a way of mediating between the abstract and the specific, the mythic or ideological "givens" and the actual historical data, the lived-with and tacit knowledge and the public, presumably plausible explanation of what one takes for granted. Such imagination is also driven to consider "if the place itself / Should seem a blank, as in a country huge / And open and potential." Such blankness involves Pinsky in a further imaginative struggle, to represent the country as it undergoes the "perils in living always in vision." Further than this, the imagination must be driven on to some conception, some picture, some phantasm of death, as the poet tries to imagine the worst possibility, an end to all imaginative and imaginable space. Such an end comes in part as an image of the American plains, but also as an inner landscape, a need to go beyond oneself to some obliterating force, "the contagious blankness of a quiet plain." (Earlier Pinsky had explored Malcolm X's remark that America was a prison; the book is loaded with images and arguments about space.)

Let me quote at some length from a passage in the second section of the poem, "The Great Emptiness." This passage is preceded by one in which the poet asks his daughter to imagine how a child could be "happy to be a thing" (the nominalist question again!), participating in the "pure potential of the clear blank spaces" of the American prairie. But then the request to imagine shifts its object to a group of Swedes or Germans, immigrants hard at work harvesting in the heat, "shoveling amid the clatter of the thresher, / The chaff in prickly clouds and the naked sun / Burning as if it could set the chaff on fire." Instead of Tolstoy's happy peasantry in bucolic harmony, we feel the hint of some infernal suffering, a lasting, deep alienation as the people try to reach some "meager shade." Then Pinsky picks out a single figure to represent the next imaginativ step:

> A man,
> A tramp, comes laboring across the stubble
> Like a mirage against that blank horizon,
> Laboring in his torn shoes toward the tall
> Mirage-like images of the tilted threshers
> Clattering in the heat. Because the Swedes
> Or Germans have no beer, or else because
> They cannot speak his language properly,
> Or for some reason one cannot imagine,
> The man climbs up on a thresher and cuts bands
> A minute or two, then waves to one of the people,
> A young girl or a child, and jumps head-first
> Into the sucking mouth of the machine,
> Where he is wedged and beat and cut to pieces —
> While the people shout and run in the clouds of chaff,
> Like lost mirages on the pelt of prairie.
>
> The obliterating strangeness and the spaces
> Are as hard to imagine as the love of death...
> Which is the love of an entire strangeness,
> The contagious blankness of a quiet plain.
> Imagine that a man, who had seen a prairie,

> Should write a poem about a Dark or Shadow
> That seemed to be both his, and the prairie's—as if
> The shadow proved that he was not a man,
> But something that lived in quiet, like the grass.
> Imagine that the man who writes that poem,
> Stunned by the loneliness of that wide pelt,
> Should prove to himself that he was like a shadow
> Or like an animal living in the dark.

To answer a blankness with a blankness, to become the shadow one feels covered by, this is a modernist theme we recognize from Conrad to Mailer. But here the flat, almost affectless presentation of the essentially melodramatic material strikes with ironic force. And as the incident is then aestheticized, by the introduction of the poet figure, as if Pinsky was retreating from his own imagination of horror, we know we are looking at the incident through the lens of modernist psychological realism (there is even the fearsome machine, with its "clattering" and its "sucking mouth"). But the treatment is almost quaint, relaxed, slightly reminiscent of Frost, especially if we remember the hidden darker side of that poet. Then follows immediately the conclusion of the passage, with an echo of Keats and an explanation of the imagined scene, somewhat in the manner of Wordsworth in the *Prelude*.

> In the dark proof he finds in his poem, the man
> Might come to think of himself as the very prairie,
> The sod itself, not lonely, and immune to death.
>
> None of this happens precisely as I try
> To imagine that it does, in the empty plains,
> And yet it happens in the imagination
> Of part of the country: not in any place
> More than another, on the map, but rather
> Like a place, where you and I have never been
> And need to try to imagine—place like a prairie
> Where immigrants, in the obliterating strangeness,
> Thirst for the wide contagion of the shadow
> Or prairie—where you and I, with our other ways,
> More like the cities or the hills or trees,
> Less like the clear blank spaces with their potential,
> Are like strangers in a place we must imagine.

If he and his daughter are "like strangers in a place [they] must imagine," they are like the tramp and the immigrants, like all Americans. The caring father sees that his aloneness in America is what makes him part of it; he sees the alienation that binds. The incident and its explanation work to fuse a strangeness and a familiarity, just as the horror of the scene is fused with its calm, deliberate description. This passage includes and cross-fertilizes several cultural contexts: the historical reality of agricultural, midwestern America, the Romantic cult of death, modern theories of imagination as the key faculty in mediating anxiety, and the fairy-tale motif of the outsider-scapegoat. The inclusiveness of the passage provides us with the imaginative space to respond, not merely with quick agreement or facile recognition, nor, one hopes, with the dismissal reserved for the manufactured or trumped-up effects of derivative art. Pinsky's long poem is as ambitious in its scope as it is modest in its presentation. The speaker's irony about his own means and his compassionate care for his daughter's education combine to make this testament into what is, finally, an intelligently patriotic poem.

■ **V**

In his third and latest book of poetry, *History of My Heart*, Pinsky leaves the epistolary style and epic subject of *An Explanation of America* to return to the scale of the intimate lyric. In doing so he gives vent to an attitude that is in part confessional, but he never relinquishes the moral and public tones of the previous book. This mix of private and public stands apart from the work of most contemporary poets, and does so in part by reversing certain obvious and hidden features of American poetry. First, Pinsky willingly makes clear his wanting to connect the large patterns of fate with his homebound destinies. There are several poems here ("The Street," "Song of Reasons," "The Figured Wheel," chief among them) that juxtapose large historical or even cosmic figurations against Pinsky's personal feelings and memories. Many poets, of course, invoke or hint at larger patterns of significance, but do so glancingly or only with protective irony. On the other hand, what Pinsky conceals or at least underplays is the tendency of the lyric to fondle its own metaphoric energies, to become intoxicated with its own tropes. (This is especially true in American surrealist poetry.) Pinsky does sometimes make his trope quite obvious, as in "The Figured Wheel," but just as often his comparisons, analogies, inversions, and closures exhibit an understatedness that can make some of the lyrics seem offhand, almost apologetic.

To illustrate this latter point, let me quote the second two-thirds of "The Questions," a poem about the people the poet met, or rather half-met, in his father's office, where hearing-aids and glasses were dispensed and where the tissue and mystery of everyday social reality were first clumsily deciphered by the son. After recalling some of the customers in a detail that occasionally reads as if it came from prose fiction ("The tall overloud old man with a tilted, ironic smirk"), he suddenly realizes a depth of feeling for them, and his compassion is soon tested by a self-correcting irony. Notice, too, how the issue of abstract charity, in the form of the nun, settles in against the particular identities of a child's first roster of adults:

Why do I want them to be treated tenderly by the world, now
Long after they must have slipped from it one way or another,

While I was dawdling through school at that moment—or driving,
Reading, talking to Ellen. Why this new superfluous caring?

I want for them not to have died in awful pain, friendless.
Though many of the living are starving, I still pray for these,

Dead, mostly anonymous (but Mr. Monk, Mrs. Rose Vogel)
And barely remembered: that they had a little extra, something

For pleasure, a good meal, a book or a decent television set.
Of whom do I pray this rubbery, low-class charity? I saw

An expert today, a nun—wearing a regular skirt and blouse,
But the hood or headdress navy and white around her plain

Probably Irish face, older than me by five or ten years.
The Post Office clerk told her he couldn't break a twenty

So she got change next door and came back to send her package.
As I came out she was driving off—with an air, it seemed to me,

Of annoying, demure good cheer, as if the reasonableness
Of change, mail, cars, clothes was a pleasure in itself: veiled

And dumb like the girls I thought enjoyed the rules too much
In grade school. She might have been a grade school teacher;

But she reminded me of being there, aside from that—as a name
And person there, a Mary or John who learns that the janitor

Is Mr. Woodhouse; the principal is Mr. Ringleven; the secretary
In the office is Mrs. Apostolacos; the bus driver is Ray.

The "Mary or John" comes with the echo of the surname "Doe," so in a sense this is anyone's remembrance of those first names, the ones that originate our sense of social interaction and, in their later recall, summon the sources of affection and puzzlement, as we realize both how we cared for such people and how little of their adult identities were ever, in fact, revealed to us. I find this a very moving poem—more than a "touching" one—and for me the quiet casualness of the last five words has a surreptitious eloquence about it.

As for the other point, the connection of large patterns and personal feelings, this is well displayed in "The Street," which begins with a description, half mythical, half historical, of the street through which the funeral procession of the Emperor's child is conducted. From this we move to Pinsky's childhood street, "Rockwell Avenue," where he watched as his neighbors all rode "the vegetable wave of the street / From the John Flock Mortuary Home / Down to the river." Here there's one incident singled out, as a betrayed husband throws his shoe at the adulterer's car being driven away with the wife inside. Somebody returns the shoe to the man:

But the man had too much dignity
To put it back on,

So he held it and stood crying in the street:
"He's breaking up my home," he said,
"The son of a bitch

Bastard is breaking up my home." The street
Rose undulant in pavement-breaking coils
And the man rode it

Still holding his shoe and stiffly upright
Like a trick rider in the circus parade
That came down the street

Each August.

Here the simile leads us into an ironic bathos drawn from popular culture. But we recall the pomp of the Emperor burying his dead child, and so we see the husband between two perspectives, one ironic, one compassionate. Of course there is irony in the pomp of the Emperor which we are likely to see as misplaced and melodramatically excessive ("Slaves throw petals on the roadway"), but Pinsky gives the husband his own dignity, however tattered and helpless, as he is caught in a public display not of his own making. But the poet makes the most of it. The personal scale of grief is measured, proven by, the juxtaposition with the public, "state" ceremony, and there is dignity and fatuity in both. The metaphor in the poem works on the surface by equating the two streets, but of course it is also the grief of the two men and the mechanics of emotional display that are truly the poem's metaphoric center. In a sense, this metaphoric transformation is hidden (or perhaps completely transparent), so the poem reads in part like a fairy tale, in part like a story by, say, Ann Beattie. But it combines the richness of each into a blend of its own, a blend that welcomes the comparison of large, abstract notions of grief with specific instances of it. Coincidentally, the poem reminds me of Randall Jarrell's "Nestus Gurley," where the everyday and the world-historical are brought into a juxtaposition at once ironic and compassionate.

I don't mean to suggest that all of Pinsky's poems are judiciously measured through a grid of perfectly balanced irony and compassion. Indeed, at least two of the poems in *History* that are most memorable, "Song of Reasons," and "The Unseen," face considerable challenges of tonal balance. The first of these uses a structure similar to "The Street": it begins with two perspectives that look at first to be totally abstruse, a change of key in the song "Come Back to Sorrento" and the right of a certain French noble family, the Levis-Mirepoix, to ride their horses in Notre Dame. The theme of the poem is how any "history or purpose arcane" that is used to explain odd facts or relations in the world manages to be both "businesslike as a dog / That trots down the street" and as phantasmagoric as "the animal shapes that sing at the gates of sleep" in our childhood. The song of reasons is just that: a lyric finesse of the rational, a way of charming and disarming the ineradicable inexplicable facticity of events and the way they express human nature. The Levis-Mirepoix have their extraordinary privilege because they "killed heretics in Languedoc seven centuries ago," and yet "they are somehow Jewish" and claim "collateral descent" from the Virgin Mary. It is a reason, and it isn't a reason. The girl in the poem (apparently Pinsky's daughter) loves the part of the daily newspaper called "The Question Man," that column of man-in-the-street responses to such inane questions as "Your Worst Vacation?" or "Your Favorite Ethnic Group?" Again, people have reasons for such heartfelt responses, and the reasons even have a history—every heart has a history as well as reasons it knows and knows not of—but the "Song of Reasons" can not offer any reason why all this should be so. Pinsky's irony appreciates the bizarre humor of claiming descent from the Virgin Mary, and his compassion appreciates the way the child's favorite newspaper feature steadies her world: "The exact forms of the ordinary...show / An indomitable charm to her." But the aesthetic charm of the poem, its ability or luck in finding a fact such as that of the Levis-Mirepoix on which to build its wry playfulness, means it cannot give or challenge any final explanation. In one sense this is only fair, as the lyric mode is not charged with providing philosophical certainty or rigorous logic. Finally, I think, the affection of the speaker for the child saves the poem, for it is here that the lyric impulse is truest. The poem is like a nursery rhyme we sing a child to sleep by, covering up the narrative or logical holes with false totality and sweet song ("and down will come baby, cradle and all"). This, too, in an oblique way is a poem about nominalism, about the refusal of certain facts to yield to classification or clarification, to offer their "indomitable charm" on any but their own terms.

But there is another poem in the book whose rhetorical authority is even more challenged: "The Unseen." The obvious point must be made at the start that no poem about concentration camps can be without flaw. Just to attempt the subject, especially in a short lyric of over fifty lines, shows moral courage or artistic aplomb beyond the ordinary. Luckily for us, Pinsky has both. So when I question the poem I do so only on the highest level. Briefly my point is this: the stance at the end of the poem is accusatory, not toward the Nazis only and obviously, but toward the Godhead, the "Lord of Hosts." But can such an accusation stand? Ordinarily such accusatory rhetoric is the privilege (if that's the right word) of mystics and rationalists. The "regular believer" cannot claim the depth of experience or the alternative ontological grounds by which to challenge the deity. (That Pinsky speaks as a Jew to a deity imaged in Christian terms alters this argument only slightly, I think.) If I'm right in this, then Pinsky's speaker (to use that old-fashioned literary convention) must base his rhetorical authority on being a rationalist (he clearly is no mystic in the poem), and not a regular believer. But the compassion of the closing lines is not a rationalist's compassion; it's that of a believer. Thus Pinsky must somehow combine the ironic scepticism of a rationalist and the compassionate acceptance of a believer. To my mind he doesn't fully succeed, though that he nearly does so is enough to make the poem gripping and memorable.

It begins almost casually, with a feeling of modernist *sang-froid* masking deep uncertainty:

In Krakow it rained, the stone arcades and cobbles
And the smoky air all soaked one penetrating color
While in an Art-Nouveau cafe, on harp-shaped chairs,

We sat making up our minds to tour the death camp.

The ironic details here—the harp-shaped chairs, the Art-Nouveau—soon give way to a grim facticity as the speaker confronts the "whole unswallowable / Menu of immensities." During the tour of the camp everything takes on a "formal, dwindled feeling." (A sure instance of emotional rightness.) The speaker remembers a childhood game where he dreamed of killing the Nazi butchers, and his reverie is broken when he arrives at "the preserved gallows where / The Allies hung the commandant, in 1947." In a sense the human vengeance ends at this point in the poem, a little past half-way. The remaining five tercets deal with the speaker's realizing that he doesn't feel "changed—or even informed" (he's obviously come to terms with it in some way before the tour), but also realizing he must accept his own attempt to "swallow" the fact of this unbelievable crime. He fights his own despair, and the poem directly addresses the "discredited Lord of Hosts" with these words:

but still

We try to take in what won't be turned from in despair:
As if, just as we turned toward the fumbled drama
Of the religious art shop window to accuse you

Yet again, you were to slit open your red heart
To show us at last the secret of your day and also,
Because it also is yours, of your night.

That is a ponderous "as if" and it saves the poem from being ruined by declamatory excess, but it still doesn't remove the language from the realm of the prophetic. By looking into the heart of God, Pinsky invokes a context that can only be that of a prophet. Especially in the five words that begin the last line, the poet doesn't flinch from an almost stately, judgmental eloquence. Here we must accept that God's love is dark, perhaps even evil. The human judges the divine at great peril, whether within or without the suppositions of religious faith. If said by a believer, these lines are truly awesome. If said by a rationalist sceptic, they are misdirected, since the real fury of the poem should then fall on the human criminals and not the divine shadow they did or did not evoke to cover their bestiality. We realize this poem was written by a post-Holocaust Jew and so if we detect in it an "unsteady" mix of rationalist scepticism and fervent compassion, we can hardly be surprised. Beyond this, I'll say no more on the subject.

■ VI

The title poem of *History of My Heart* is over seven pages long, and its scale is even longer in a way. Superficially the poem is autobiographical and might be compared to those works by Henry Adams or Stendhal that speak of education as it applies to sensibility and awareness. The education of Robert Pinsky is an education into and through desire. The record of the education has several traditional motifs: the loving mother, the bestowing of the name, the first scene of arousal, the typology of gifts, and the finding of a vocation (in this case playing the saxophone) that allows the young artist to achieve maturity. It's a song of reasons in that it tells us how and why Robert Pinsky came to feel the way he does, and it resembles "The Street" in that it relates the topography of his childhood to larger patterns of destiny. It also has the obsessive probing of *An Explanation of America*, and the turns and quick shifts in perspective of "Essay on Psychiatrists." In many ways, it's the definitive Pinsky poem.

Perhaps the best way to get at the central drama of the poem, and by extension the entire volume, is to reflect on two master terms, history and nature. (What follows draws erratically on Adorno's essay, "The Idea of Natural History," in a recent issue of *Telos*, and Susan Buck-Morss's explication of it in *The Origins of the Negative Dialectic*.) The standard meanings of the two terms allot to "nature" an unchanging, quasi-divine, eternal fixity, and to "history" a sense of change, flux, and even chaos. But in our personal lives, in the histories of our hearts, we can see where the two terms begin to overlap and even change into one another. What seems "natural" to us is often "second nature," the result of a long history of emotional patterning and appetitive habit. And the flow of our dailiness, our constant change and growth, can be felt as the bedrock of our identity—we are (only) as we come to be. Newman has an instance in *The Grammar of Assent*: someone tells you your father has just been captured robbing a bank. You instantly realize (with absolutely no empirical evidence) that it's a mistake, for you know as fully as you know anything your father couldn't be a bank robber. How do you know this? Through all the numberless acts of kindness and moral probity you've witnessed him perform over the years. Your knowledge is "second nature" to you, past any possibility of refutation or claim of statistical probability or empirical variation. We can also invoke Frost's definition of love: "Love is what we've been through together." What might seem instinctual and part of the natural law, the "way things are," is often the result of a long history of otherwise unremarkable events.

The history of one's heart, then, is the story of how we developed our "second nature," taking as given and natural that which is accidental and contingent. Such a naturalizing of what would otherwise be a shapeless congeries of events must determine our sense of emotional rightness. Now, somewhat surprisingly, Pinsky's poem begins with an incident that occurred before he was born, a visit by Fats Waller to Macy's department store on Thirty-Fourth Street one Christmas. Pinsky's mother worked in the Toys section of the store and so was able to see (and obviously begin the process of naturalizing) Waller's immensely entertaining show ("as he improvised on an expensive, tinkly / Piano the size of a lady's jewel box or a wedding cake.") This incident became for Pinsky the emblem and type of desire. For him desire needs a setting, a sense of "amazing good-luck," and reciprocity, the "mutual arousal of suddenly feeling / Desired." The poem is loaded with other incidents that explore these requisites of desire, rendering them both strange and familiar, giving us a history in the form of nature, and a nature shaped by history.

Central to desire for Pinsky is the gift. It contains and releases our feelings, and like desire it has its requisites, such as surprise and what Keats called "a fine excess." Here's the main passage about the structure of giving:

> Gifts from the heart:
> Her giving me her breast milk or my name, Waller
>
> Showing off in a store, for free, giving them
> A thrill as someone might give someone an erection,
> For the thrill of it—or you come back salty from a swim:
>
> Eighteen shucked fresh oysters and the cold bottle
> Sweating in its ribbon, surprise, happy birthday!
> So what if the giver also takes, is after something?
>
> So what if with guile she strove to color
> Everything she gave with herself, the lady's favor
> A scarf or bit of sleeve of her favorite color
>
> Fluttering on the horseman's bloodflecked armor

Just over the heart—how presume to forgive the breast
Or sudden jazz for becoming what we want? I want

Presents I can't picture until they come,
The generator flashlight Italo gave me one Christmas:
One squeeze and the gears visibly churning in the amber

Pistol-shaped handle hummed for half a minute
In my palm, the spare bulb in its chamber under my thumb,
Secret; or, the knife and basswood Ellen gave me to whittle.

This passage is immediately followed by one comparing the yet-unsatisfied heart to a "titular / Insane king who stares emptily at his counselors" until suddenly his desire is objectified and he "scowls, alert, and points / Without a word to one pass in the cold, grape-colored peaks." We are back with the grieving emperor and the child's funeral procession in "The Street," where a fairy-tale perspective is used both ironically and compassionately. Note, too, how the gift from Italo of the generator flashlight has just that tincture of nominalist indigestibility, yet captures the motif of secrecy and closeness so often found in accounts of desire.

The poem ends with a complex and suggestive passage that echoes some of the spirit of Whitman's "Out of the Cradle" and Wordsworth's *Prelude*. By this I mean it deals with the mystery of individuation, especially in terms of that rich awareness of connection-and-separation that marks the growth of ourselves as individual egos. The passage weaves around certain fairy-tale motifs of the foundling (and the changeling) as well as a kind of pantheistic yearning. Here are the first seven tercets or so:

On moonless
Nights, water and sand are one shade of black,
And the creamy foam rising with moaning voices

Charges like a spectral army in a poem toward the bluffs
Before it subsides dreamily to gather again.
I thought of going down there to watch it a while,

Feeling as though it could turn me into fog,
Or that the wind would start to speak a language
And change me—as if I knocked where I saw a light

Burning in some certain misted window I passed,
A house or store or tap-room where the strangers inside
Would recognize me, locus of a new life like a woods

Or orchard that waxed and vanished into cloud
Like the moon, under a spell. Shrill flutes,
Oboes and cymbals of doom. My poor mother fell,

And after the accident loud noises and bright lights
Hurt her. And heights. She went down stairs backwards,
Sometimes with one arm on my small brother's shoulder.

Over the years, she got better. But I was lost in music;
The cold brazen bow of the saxophone, its weight
At thumb, neck and lip, came to a bloodwarm life

Like Italo's flashlight in the hand.

The saxophone playing becomes a mediation of irony and compassion, as the young man truly gives himself over to the playing and at the same time sees himself as a performer, as someone asking for attention and affection. This joining of display and submission, ego-centeredness and altruism, feels like second nature to us, but it is in fact the working out of several life-historical patterns of expectation, need, and assertion. In the grimness of "The Unseen" Pinsky remembered a Biblical phrase: "I am poured out like water," and there the phrase had connotations of loss and waste and unrecoverability. But in "History" the image of pouring out takes on a different tonal cast, for here we sense the gesture of emptying is a gesture of both self-less love and personal fulfillment. These are the final lines of the poem:

> Sometimes, playing in a bar or at a high school dance, I felt
> My heart following after a capacious form,
> Sexual and abstract, in the thunk, thrum,
>
> Thrum, come-wallow and then a little screen
> Of quicker notes goosing to a fifth higher, winging
> To clang-whomp of a major seventh: listen to *me*
>
> Listen to *me*, the heart says in reprise until sometimes
> In the course of giving itself it flows out of itself
> All the way across the air, in a music piercing
>
> As the kids at the beach calling from the water *Look*,
> *Look at me*, to their mothers, but out of itself, into
> The listener the way feeling pretty or full of erotic revery
>
> Makes the one who feels seem beautiful to the beholder
> Witnessing the idea of the giving of desire—nothing more wanted
> Than the little singing notes of wanting—the heart
>
> Yearning further into giving itself into the air, breath
> Strained into song emptying the golden bell it comes from,
> The pure source poured altogether out and away.

"The giving of desire" is a phrase that stands as a capstone to Pinsky's work so far, for it catches up the paradoxical network of irony and compassion that takes place when a "beholder" witnesses a moment of completely passionate ecstacy, when there is "Nothing more wanted." Also, without pushing things too far, I think we can see here the sense of possessing nature—"the pure source" in all its ongoing fullness—now joined with a particular unfolding of events—that description of the musical passage, with its "thunk, thrum, / Thrum, come-wallow" capturing the essence of sequentiality.

We can read *Sadness and Happiness* as a book of emotional meteorology, and *An Explanation of America* as a book of imaginative geography. This leaves us, then, to read *History of My Heart* as a book of psychological economy. The economics of desire, what is given or taken, what is lost, what gets stored and what spent, is Pinsky's thematic center in all his books—this is why he is such a profound traditionalist; he keeps track of how and what is passed on—but especially in his latest volume such questions of economy dominate. Pinsky has laid bare his heart, often complete with a "fumbling drama," and shown us that it has stored in it the light of day and the dark of night. But the great strength of his poetry is that he also shows us how the night turns into day, and how the light was set in its firmament.

Charles Molesworth

■ BOOKS BY ROBERT PINSKY

Landor's Poetry. Chicago: University of Chicago Press, 1968.

Sadness and Happiness. Princeton, N.J.: Princeton University Press, 1975.

The Situation of Poetry: Contemporary Poetry and Its Traditions. Princeton, N.J.: Princeton University Press, 1976.

An Explanation of America. Princeton, N.J.: Princeton University Press, and Manchester: Carcanet Press, 1979.

Five American Poets, with others. Manchester: Carcanet Press, 1979.

History of My Heart. New York; Ecco Press, 1984.

Poetry and the World. New York: Ecco Press, 1988.

The Want Bone. New York: HarperCollins, 1990.

The Figured Wheel: New and Collected Poems, 1966–1996 New York: Farrar, Straus, & Giroux, 1996.

The Sounds of Poetry. New York: Farrar, Straus, & Giroux, 1998.

The Rhyme of Reb Nachman. Edmonton: Vixen Press, 1998.

Jersey Rain. New York: Farrar, Straus, & Giroux, 2000.

December, 1984

UPDATE

Robert Pinsky has published four volumes of poetry: *The Want Bone* (1990), *The Figured Wheel: New and Collected Poems, 1966-1996* (1996), *The Rhyme of Reb Nachman* (1998), and *Jersey Rain* (2000). He also coedited *Americans' Favorite Poems: The Favorite Poem Project Anthology (2000)*, and has translated and edited several other books since this essay was written.

Poet laureate Robert Pinsky "is a poet and critic whose work in both areas reflects his concern for a contemporary poetic diction which nonetheless speaks of a wider experience," according to *Contemporary Authors*. As Pinsky once said: "I would like to write a poetry which could contain every kind of thing, while keeping all the excitement of poetry."

Pinsky is perhaps best known these days as the "genius" behind the Favorite Poem Project. It was his idea to record 1,000 Americans from across the country reading or reciting the poems they love best for an audio and video archive. In an interview with *The Writer*, he discussed the project: "One thing I hope is that the Project will have some effect on the teaching of poetry. Too much of our teaching of poetry has proceeded as though the reason for a poem to exist is to have smart things said about it. . . . A poem is something that sounds terrific when it is read aloud. That's the nature of the art."

The poems also were collected in book form. *Booklist* praised the collection, which defies stereotypes, and attests "to the vital role that poetry plays in more lives than seems possible in a country that appears to pay scant attention to this quiet art form." Each poem is preceded by an introduction about the reader who chose it. "Teenagers and octogenarians, a social worker, a farmer, a nurse, a truck driver, a commodities trader, a librarian, a judge, and an alcoholic who memorizes poetry to test her sobriety selected poems by Lucille Clifton, Emily Dickinson, John Keats, Haki R. Madhubuti, W. S. Merwin, Sylvia Plath, and Dylan Thomas," *Booklist* continued. "No one person, however well read, could have created this resounding collection."

Pinsky's most recent volume of his own poetry, however, *Jersey Rain*, a collection that looks at the technology age, met with mixed reviews. *World Literature Today* wrote: "I doubt that technology is poetically as important as Pinsky thinks it is, because I think that its emotional value is limited: you will not find Catullus apostrophizing an aqueduct." *Publishers Weekly* did praise the "sheer muscle of these constructions" but was less enamored of the work as a whole: "[M]ost of the poems' occasions and insights don't quite measure up to the rhetorical firepower turned upon them. . . . [The] lighter pieces will delight fans, but the poems with more profound aspirations lack a penetrating introspection."

Dwelling in Possibility: The Fiction of Richard Powers

■ ■ ■

I dwell in Possibility
A fairer House than Prose—
More numerous of Windows—
Superior—for Doors
Emily Dickinson, Poem 657

Any reader of postmodern novels can wind up like a career coroner who, overwhelmed finally by such oppressive evidence, surrounded too long by the dead, begins to feel that living itself is a dark act of irony. Like coroners, readers must determine with joyless efficiency what has so thoroughly crushed character after character, autopsies that point to the sheer weight of this century that has produced a most familiar postmodern character: insulated, paralyzed by scale, jolted by chaotic forces that deny the merest gesture significance, dropped gracelessly into a chilling era where our relentless inquisition of the natural world has finally argued us out of the necessity of a deity that took nearly three millennia to construct. Within novels oddly suspicious of plot, wary of closure, characters must shape identity against a wearying sense of drift, like dunes rifted by winds.

Given such characters, readers begin to feel understandably lost. Further terrorized by images of brutalities that saturate a media machine that pours into every private sphere, we lock ourselves in. The century's defining events—Verdun, Auschwitz, Hiroshima, Dallas, My Lai, Bosnia—have left us to the vulnerability of the physical plane; each generation's literary voice—Hemingway, Mailer, Vonnegut, Pynchon—appropriated the metaphors of ballistics or thermodynamics to offer a descendant sense of closed possibilities. Our most stunning technological achievements Frankensteined us—the automobile, the computer, the television either interred us within our own narrow rooms or trivialized us into inconsequential bits adrift in a world too much of our making, perhaps efficient and clean but lacking only purpose and reassuring control. Taught the common sense of suspicion by the hard logic of mutual destruction promoted by the Cold War at its virulent height, we have looked to our moats, fearful of connection. Despite computers that snare us within worldwide nets, despite satellite signals that shrink the world into a pocket of chips, the more we access each other, the more we network, the more alone we are, each at our terminals.

Richard Powers, among the most promising voices to emerge in the post-Pynchon generation, senses this vast loneliness in the soul of the computer age, the heartbreaking irony of networking. Only in his mid-thirties, Powers has produced five intricate novels that have compelled enormous critical respect and enthusiastic response among readers overtired of playing coroner. Read as a cooperative whole, Powers' novels argue that we have lived too long under the hard parabola hammered over our heads by Pynchon's generation. By grappling with the

Richard Powers

Richard Powers, born in 1957, graduated (B.A., M.A.) from the University of Illinois at Urbana-Champaign, initially majoring in physics. After spending several years in southern Holland and working for a time as a computer programmer, he began publishing fiction in 1985. His first novel, *Three Farmers*, was a National Book Critics Award finalist; *The Gold Bug Variations* was listed as *Time* magazine's book of the year and was as well a National Book Critics Circle Award finalist; and *Operation Wandering Soul* was nominated for the National Book Award. For his work, Powers was named one of the youngest recipients ever of a MacArthur Foundation "genius" fellowship. He returned to Urbana in 1993 for a two-year appointment as writer-in-residence. ■

identical forces that shaped that generation's descendant sense of closed possibilities—namely, brutally efficient warfare, the proliferation of the machine, the insinuation of computer technologies, the apparent effacement of the arts, the deification of the theoretical scientist—Powers recovers an unsuspected counter-argument that resists those elements of this century that have become dark cliché: its ruthless efficiency, its banalizing of creation, its dehumanizing of the individual through the relentless application of technologies. Powers does not blink away such forces but finds within them—particularly in the metaphors of connection offered both by the computer and by the mid-century revolution in genetics—an unsuspected foundation for an ascendant vision of this century even as it wambles off to its close. Powers ministers to the dead—to his characters and to his grateful readers—by offering simple commodities that only in the harsh terrain of this century's literature have somehow become desperately ironic—hope, feeling, trust, the capacity for wonder, and supremely, connection, not only to the natural world, which these very scientific revolutions tell us explodes in unsuspected miracle just outside our locked doors, but more profoundly each to the other.

Well within the mainstream of American literature, from Hester Prynne to Holden Caulfield, from Ishmael to Sethe, Powers' fictions begin in a vast, emptying loneliness. The valiant search for connection ties Powers to the gently devastated vision of Emily Dickinson, whose dark lucidity is fundamental to any approach to Powers. He acknowledges her poetics often. Like Dickinson, Powers' characters struggle unevenly along the tortuous pilgrimage away from the moat to the horizon. His characters attempt to break free of the self through avenues familiar to American literature since Hawthorne: the head, the heart, and ultimately, the imagination. Indeed, what is critical in Powers is not innovative solutions to the persistent American dilemma of loneliness but rather the recovery of respect for each faculty in a high-tech era that has diminished each. His is fiction written very much against his own era. The mind is too quickly enervated by the trivia piled up by the age of information; the heart is too easily cheapened after the excesses of the sexual revolutions of midcentury; and the imagination is too easily ignored amid our technological theaters of accessible special effects.

The head, the heart, and the imagination provide, then, a handy rubric to the fiction of Richard Powers. Those characters who engage the world through the cerebral faculties are, perhaps, most obvious. Like Dickinson in those powerful moments when her Brain encompasses the very sky, Powers confers profound respect on those who attempt to command the contemporary world through the exercise of the taxed intelligence, that hard self-reliance of the insulated scholar holding steady in the age of information. Powers favors professions that wrestle with information: librarians, medical students, teachers, perpetual graduate students, research technicians, career scientists, computer programmers. Indeed, Powers' fiction is often cited for its erudition: not only its facile wordplay and love of the terraced, superstructured sentence but for its irresistible urge to display information about an eclectic range of topics in passages that layer the unfolding narrative. Yet, as we shall see, those who attempt to relieve the ache of loneliness through the exercise of the mind are finally limited—they connect, certainly, but to the world, to an "it," and then only through the cold energy of curiosity that leaves them stunned by revelation and solution but nevertheless quite alone. When such intelligence tries awkwardly to step into the world of fuller engagement, to exercise the heart, such brave attempts to connect the fragile, feeling "I" to some available, significant Other crash and burn, exposing the self to insuperable vulnerabilities and leaving it to fashion presence from absence in the non-time of memory.

Given a world too large to know and too brutish to permit the simple grace of the heart, we edge ourselves toward too-familiar postmodern endgames, characters with overbusy minds and carapaced hearts. Yet Powers' most resilient characters find a most satisfying resolution within the faculty overlooked in our high-tech age: the imagination, that most natural of resources that assuaged and empowered Dickinson more than a century ago. It is oddly denied in an era of films with grand mechanical special effects, too-accessible cable surfing, and the oppressive assault of domestic video imagery, from video games to VCRs to video cameras. We leave the unassisted imagination behind in the childhood world of Bert and Ernie—for grownups that world is a narcotic, a dodge, nonproductive daydreaming.

Powers reclaims its energy. He understands what American characters have understood since Hawthorne's Custom-House Surveyor: that the imagination alone reassures us that we are more part than particle. For Powers, characters, moved by the aesthetic connection, find in the imagination a most expansive, soaring energy. Unlike the head that joylessly ties "I" to the "it," unlike the heart that must find cold sustenance in absence, the imagination is a summary connecting force that is both intensely private and yet splendidly communal, tying Powers' most successful characters not only to the satisfying experience of artifacts (musical works, paintings, photographs, narratives, films) but ultimately permitting a transcendent connection to others, a place within a larger interpretative community of responsive I's/eyes, working together each and all. The imagination acts much like the fairy-tale Jack (who figures prominently in Powers' first novel), the lucky child who plants without much hope a handful of ordinary seeds only to find to his amazement the stunning intervention of possibility, magic, and wonder, an act that ultimately conflates the immediate and the fanciful. Like Dickinson's starved child who finds in the arching freedom of the stirred imagination release into a world of deep response, Powers, whose name offers a happy bit of irony that would be appreciated by his characters who seldom resist a pun, empowers the reader by recovering in the imagination the neglected stuff of survival itself.

■ **I**

The Brain is just the weight of God—
For—Heft them—Pound for Pound—

And they will differ—if they do—
As Syllable for Sound.
Emily Dickinson, Poem 633

Surely, the memory pool fashioned by our vast computer networks has made information our newest last frontier. Powers is clearly fascinated by the cool cerebral workings of those willing to head to this new frontier, by their abilities to grapple with this vast complexity using only invention and curiosity. Writing against an era that has cultivated the diminished attention span, a cult of anti-intellectualism that finds dumb stubbornly cool, Powers' fiction centers on the complicated discipline of acquiring information. His characters *need* to exercise the intelligence, info-addicts who maneuver with unnerving agility about the most intimidating terrains of the Information Age—sprawling libraries catwalked by floors of organized information; great university research complexes; vast computer systems that compile gigabytes of information in fractions of seconds. As children, these characters ingest encyclopedias or request as bedtime reading *The World Almanac*.

As adults, they aggressively, joyfully pursue information, explore the immediate world too often ignored by those so anesthetized by the assault of media technology that they settle for diminished cerebral exercise. Powers' earliest central character—a stockbroker who finds himself haunted by a World War I photograph he chances to see in a Detroit art museum during a train stopover (*Three Farmers*)—tracks down with investigative resilience the story of the photograph, along the way teaching himself much about the early history of this century. Eddie Hobson, the history teacher shaken by his wartime experience at the Alamogordo test site (*Prisoner's Dilemma*), bonds to his children by turning dinners into impromptu games of trivia and riddles. In *The Gold Bug Variations*, Jan O'Deigh resigns as a reference librarian in Manhattan to live off her accumulated savings to teach herself the science of genetics, the study of life itself, pouring over tables of rarefied textbooks without expectation of any tangible results save the lonely thrill of insight in the productive isolation of investigation.

In that same novel, Stuart Ressler, already a promising researcher in the hot field of genetics, masters not only the mysteries of cellular replication but plunges as well into a lifelong study of contrapuntal music, spurred only by an irresistible response to an esoteric Bach keyboard work. And Richard Powers, the burned-out writer who serves as narrator in *Galatea 2.2*, returns at mid-life to the womb-security of the university to repair his heart and to reignite a dangerously waning imagination and, there, must teach himself about neural networks in order to participate in a complex experiment to coax an advanced computer network to respond to selected works of literature. These characters are casebook nerds, fascinated by an irresistible urge to ask why, to forsake more normative human connections to assault their immediate worlds with cerebral vigor. Much like Poe's ratiocination that Stuart Ressler is given to read and that lends itself to part of the title of that novel, Powers' fictions celebrate the mind's ability to apprehend and process.

But there are risks. Much like Dickinson, Powers cannot unqualifiably affirm the mind's embrace of the world. Richard Kraft, the surgeon-in-residence who inhabits the dark center of Powers' fourth and most disturbing novel *Operation Wandering Soul*, reveals most painfully the problematic nature of Powers' commitment to the cerebral life, how ruthlessly the available information can short-circuit the mind's ability to sort and accept. Weary of round-the-clock hospital duty that threatens to make routine the maimings of urban brutalities, Kraft stares blankly into banks of televisions in a discount store, feeling his own interior crumble as he surrenders to the sheer scale of the world that we attempt to comprehend—its violence, its brutality, its rapacity—how irrational is the world we rational creatures have fashioned.

But the mind need not collapse to be a problem. Indeed, its larger threat may be its successful functioning, a risk as familiar as the stereotypes of the schoolyard nerd. Powers' most cerebral characters are often socially retarded, monastics who grow too comfortable behind their bunkers of information and find the complication of human company often unendurable. In dilemmas that recall Hawthorne's scientists, they can become mere applesorters, cataloguing and compiling information in the frictionless sterility of withdrawal. Geneticist Stuart Ressler is burned so completely by his need for a married colleague that he walks away from his promising scientific career to immure himself as a computer programmer; Jan O'Deigh, devastated by her need for the careless and unfaithful art student Franklin Todd, hides behind her polished desk at the library; Eddie Hobson, despite his family's fierce loyalty, cannot bring himself to bond with them save through riddles and quizzes—his brother's accidental death during World War II has taught him the problematic nature of connection.

Such characters believe that to know is somehow to protect the self from the rough injury of personal contact. But by dealing only with those questions that come with answers, they lose the magic of the fuller risk of engagement by treating others as theories or as problems that come with answers. In postures that recall Dickinson's paradoxical sense of the Brain's capacity, these characters are often left lonely, cerebrally expanded but emotionally diminished—like Helen, the neural network that Richard Powers instructs in the art of reading literature in *Galatea 2.2*, who comes to understand in "her" own way that the cerebral response without engagement creates only a Caliban, a deformity capable of poetry but shunned, a freak ultimately disempowered; or like Dr. Kraft, his mental collapse complete, alone on the roof of the hospital reeling from the grim work of repairing schoolchildren shot randomly, efficiently in yet another urban sniper incident. Despite Powers' clear fondness for data, the mind cannot suffice.

■ II

The Heart asks Pleasure—first—
And then—Excuse from Pain—
And then—those little Anodynes
That deaden suffering—

And then—to go to sleep—
And—if it should be
The will of its Inquisitor
The privilege to die.
Emily Dickinson, Poem 536

Much like Emily Dickinson, Powers explores the lonely heart's hunger for connection—for the intimate rocking of human desire, or the larger dramas of family and friendship, or even the braver campaigns to put such compassion into operation in political and social crusades. Again, Powers finds himself at odds with his own era. Much as the thrill of human curiosity is at risk in the dumbing of American culture, the complicated resonances of the heart's bonding are suspect as well in a culture turning toward the logic of the moat, bored by the heart's overexposure in the invasive forces of popular culture; now, prudently suspicious of the heart's incendiary compulsions, we are left with the unappealing options of indifference, insulation, or narcissism. It appears we cannot afford to care.

Powers, however, cannot leave us alone. In *Prisoner's Dilemma*, Powers offers his soaring counterargument in the solution to Eddie Hobson's logic problem that provides the novel its title. Two prisoners, each knowing enough to destroy the other, must learn only in the oppressive immediacy of shared captivity the value of mutual trust—self-interest, which evolution seems to favor in the brutish metaphors distilled from Darwin, is ultimately not in the interest of the self at all; rather, we must do the illogical: cooperate, trust, find the generosity to risk the smallest gestures of inclusion. Powers, himself a former computer programmer, allows an automated bank machine at the close of *Gold Bug* to articulate what is surely one of his great themes. Jan O'Deigh is moving hesitatingly toward a reunion with Franklin Todd. Although burned badly during their earlier affair, her heart cannot relinquish him. Inserting her bank card, Jan is advised by the screen, "Please, enter your transaction." And yet, as with Dickinson, this luminous transaction must involve dropping the guard, an inescapable wounding that leads irreversibly to living off memories, the cold-sweet sustenance of absence. For Powers, as with Dickinson, love is finally both necessary and impossible. It is worth noting that when Jan O'Deigh receives that message from the bank machine, she is attempting a withdrawal.

At the heart's most intimate expression, Powers' cerebral characters suffer the invasive agency of love, the bug that crashes the system. Powers understands only the tectonic rocking of intimacy. Attraction is never tepid, never pedestrian. Like Dickinson, Powers never approaches love save as the hyperbolic excess of obsession, the consuming need against logic. Characters fall in deep, immediate love with those they shouldn't—with strangers barely glimpsed or most lightly introduced; or with those damaged beyond the ability to return love. They are all mismatched affairs, poor risks. As in Dickinson, we love despite—and we pay dearly. Peter Mays and Alison Stark, Jan O'Deigh and Franklin Todd, Stuart Ressler and Jeanette Koss, Richard Kraft and Linda Espera, Richard Powers and C.—the blind, necessary pursuit of bonding gives the hungry heart its bruised identity. The paramedic ministering of the physical (the sweaty aerobics that head grandly toward the warming rush of the shared orgasm) yields slowly to the reluctant exchange of cautious, imperfect hearts. But, in each case, couples stumble toward detonation, separation, internal collapse or find only the thinnest promise—as Franklin Todd cautions Jan at their reunion that closes *Gold Bug*, "Who said anything about lasting?" (638). To love here is to risk vulnerability, treachery or, far more problematic, a thinning of emotion that Richard Powers in *Galatea 2.2* begins to feel about the edges of his great love for C., the inexplicable exhaustion of connection. Much as it was for Dickinson, the heart here is unforgettable in impact and undeniable in washing force, but unbearable in its weight.

But the heart is moved by more than the electric attraction of a single powerful other. The heart can express itself in larger acts of compassion and concern. But Powers, who came of age after the sunshine decade of the 1960s with its innocent idealism and happy child naiveté, finds in activism even darker frustrations. From Henry Ford, whose Peace Ship project to end World War I centers *Three Farmers*, to Lily Hobson's frustrated attempts to close her generation's war by campus protesting (*Prisoner's Dilemma*), to Richard Kraft, who as a student overseas in Thailand conceives of Operation Santa Claus, an ambitious project to build a school for an impoverished jungle village and who later will forsake a music career to pursue medicine and conducts twenty weeks of his residency in the pediatrics ward of a public hospital in the very heart of the East Los Angeles darkness—Powers' characters attempt to minister to the Us. Yet such gestures deconstruct—the world is too vast, too brutal to permit its own repair. The Peace Ship becomes an international joke; Lily sours, retires to unnatural seclusion in her family's house; Kraft's Operation Santa Claus ends as a cynical propaganda piece for the media machine that feeds off the misery in Southeast Asia, and ultimately the young Kraft watches helpless as a mysterious young Thai girl he follows into the jungle is blown apart by a mine she inadvertently triggers. Powers understands that such quixotic nobility, what he calls the Moses Complex, must fail, ironically, of its own assumption that the world can sustain such gestures.

But if such campaigns collapse, Powers cannot bear the sour taste of cynicism nor permit the logic of withdrawal. Against the erotic paranoia of the Nuclear Age with its relentless gospel of suspicion and self-interest, Powers offers in *Gold Bug* the metaphors of the midcentury revolution in genetics that suggest that the individual is an illusion, a counterfeit commodity that we foolishly hoard. The process of replication, the industrial production of millions of amino acids and proteins from the twin helixical sequencing of four bases, animates *all* living matter. Whether or not we accept the invitation, we are one—a reassurance proffered not as some New Age McSlogan but rather as a stunning affirmation of the collective that finds irrefutable confirmation in any high school genetics textbook. It is in our best interest to heed the simple maxim that Henry Ford inscribes on the pennies he himself mints and passes out—Help the Other Fellow. Powers leaves us the unsettling job of explicating why in this century such simple logic has become tainted with irony.

But, in keeping with Powers' resilient sense of the ascendant moment, the heart does manage to complete its work of engagement. If intimacy leaves it bandaged, if altruism leaves it frustrated, the heart reaches its potential in the smaller gestures of family and friendship. To borrow a football metaphor used in *Prisoner's Dilemma*, we complete the pass, a necessarily small act that requires nevertheless coordination and cooperation with an often distant other. Powers admires the cooperative drama of the family—the hopelessly loving unit of the Hobsons (*Prisoner's Dilemma*); the Blakes, colleagues who admit Stuart Ressler into their close family by inviting him to impromptu dinners despite his protective isolation and even provide the comforts of furniture to his austere apartment (*Gold Bug*); and the tight bond Richard Powers senses between his fellow researcher Diana Hartrick (whose name suggests she has managed to turn the trick of the heart) and her children, one with Downs syndrome, after a husband had long ago abandoned such a complicated responsibility (*Galatea 2.2*).

Apart from family, however, Powers' fictions offer stunning moments when, despite the easier strategy of looking to your moat, strangers intrude into the hermetic sphere of others in acts that do not carry the heavy excesses of eroticism nor reward the doer with anything more tangible than the most traditional satisfaction of helping. Richard Powers, as first-year graduate student in *Galatea 2.2*, opens up, awkwardly, after learning of his father's death, to C. when she is then only a student in his composition class. Indeed, despite the mesmerizing pull of twin love stories in *Gold Bug*, the more significant emotional investment comes from Stuart Ressler, a hermit past mid-life, thawing into friendship with Jan and Franklin, seeing in their tentative love a chance to redress what went so completely wrong with his own heart nearly a generation earlier. Lacking ulterior motive, he leaps away from the self, goes on-line, intervenes in their lives, permits himself to care.

That deliberate act of invasive friendship is far from the only such example of unexpected thawing. The elderly gentleman who pesters Alison Stark as she waits tables in a fashionable restaurant leaves her at the close of the novel a substantial amount in his will (*Three Farmers*). Franklin and Jan set aside their own emotional turmoil (Jan has just caught Franklin in bed with another woman) to help Stuart Ressler reprogram the vast computer network they command to reinstate the insurance coverage dropped by mistake for a congenial colleague who has suffered a massive stroke. Indeed, Jimmy Steadman is dropped initially because Stuart and Franklin attempt to program into his paycheck an unexpected bonus after Jimmy covers for them during a programming crisis. In *Operation Wandering Soul*, Nico, the brash outgoing progeric dwarf who takes over the children's ward with his nervy bravura, goes out of his way to bond with Joy, a shy girl, a refugee from Asian relocation camps, who is dying quietly behind protective stacks of schoolbooks she studies against the thin hope she might someday return to her beloved classroom. In that same novel, nurse Linda Espera comes to Kraft's pediatrics ward to supervise their emotional recuperation—she touches them, a ward of strangers, in small gestures she tenders against her own childhood trauma of molestation. And at the close of *Galatea*

2.2, Richard Powers after his massive infatuation with the artificial intelligence of Helen—including irrational panics when first a bomb scare is called into the research labs that house the machine and later when a colleague proposes slicing into "her" network to probe her amazing ability to respond to texts—notices as he departs the university that a colleague who had been largely part of the background now appears pale, thinner—Richard finds himself caring that his colleague faces an uncertain medical prognosis.

It is that turning discovery of caring that is the highest expression of the heart in Powers's fiction. It is, sadly, that gesture's very delicacy that denies the heart position as solution in the fiction of Richard Powers. The greatest love here is obsession that sours into sterile withdrawal; the noblest campaigns for humanity's improvement collapse into sad circus; and the finest gestures we are left with are the smallest units of cooperation, family and friends, minor gestures of connection, passes caught, too often overwhelmed by the brutish world that serves as their necessary backdrop. But in an oxymoron familiar to Dickinson, they are monumental in their very fragility—the merest touch that goes deep.

■ III

I never saw a Moor—
I never saw the Sea—
Yet know I how the Heather looks
And what a Billow be.
Emily Dickinson, Poem 1052

If the fullest exercise of the mind leads, ultimately, to monastic withdrawal and the noblest acts of the heart lead, ironically, to the iron weight of absence, Powers offers as solution what has provided the American literary tradition the sole satisfying counterforce to the persistence of loneliness—the imagination, inviolable, imperial, and empowering. Characters find their way to the emptying, reviving act of aesthetic connection, the inexplicable, intuitive capacity of the imagination first to respond, re-enchanting the immediate world so pressed into the quotidian by our media machines, and ultimately to create. The open imagination taps an unsuspected, vibrant dimension to a tired reality we take for granted, much as in *Three Farmers* the narrator tells of August Sander who, perfecting the techniques of photography at the turn of the century, discovers as he develops one plate a most curious double image—over an otherwise pedestrian shot of a countryside village there is the unmistakable image of a shadowy castle up in the sky. Sander assumes it is a double exposure, an error, but he is told that he has actually photographed a mirage.

More than illuminating interiors by reveling in just such unsuspected "double exposures," the imagination provides, much as it did for Dickinson, a way out of the self—although it affords perfect autonomy, it requires engagement and forges profound connections; although exercised at a distance, it creates intimacy. In responding to an offered object, in stirring to life inanimate artifacts, it enters into a larger community of other isolated sensitives responding to the same artifact. The subject of any artifact, Powers reminds us, is not "I" but rather "We." Ultimately in a most erotic connection of complicity and conspiracy, it bonds those most intimate strangers, writer and reader.

At its most immediate level, the imagination first responds—a capacity easily dismissed in an inflated age when we are visually oppressed by confected images. But Powers reinvests that most primary level of engagement with unsuspected wonder—he reminds us that the engaged imagination starts with the rare capacity to respond: not only to the unfolding miracles of the natural world but to images, to artifacts, to words, and thus to participate in the fullest realization of a culture's accumulated expressions. We can be moved and even changed by the aesthetic apprehension of a thing and, in turn, can preserve that momentary charge for a lifetime.

Despite careers devoted to the inglorious work of the technical sciences, Powers's characters are hypersensitive to the unexpected intervention of the private ecstasy of aesthetic devastation. We violate the object, we change it and it returns the favor. Characters respond deeply, inexplicably—to a black and white photograph, hanging in an exhibition, of three young Germans on the way to a dance (*Three Farmers*); to obscure Renaissance landscapes in the back galleries of a city museum or to a recording of Bach offered as a birthday present from a colleague (*Gold Bug Variations*); to the magic of children's books or to the plaintive sound of a French horn (*Operation Wandering Soul*); to the weary lines of overanthologized poetry (*Galatea 2.2*); to classic Hollywood films (*Prisoner's Dilemma*). Although apparently parasitic, such bold participation in the aesthetic response never exhausts the artifact; rather each take enriches it. Given Powers' benevolent sense of the machine (indeed, Powers' first novel opens with a review of a Diego Rivera mural in Detroit that celebrates the sensual tie between humanity and its machines), he sees the unsuspected gift of technologies is to make such artifacts—movies, art prints, recordings, narratives—accessible opportunities, unlike centuries past when such art was the protected property of a pampered aristocracy.

And so we respond—or more precisely a few of us do, attuned isolatoes finding in the imagination a way to a most fine and private luster. But such a precious appreciation marginalizes the imagination. The imagination we find in Powers' fiction not only illuminates, but it sustains, makes bearable thin lives otherwise dry and still or battered lives eye-deep in this century's horrors. The ancient cleaning lady, whose ties with the actual three farmers in the photograph remain ambiguous, recounts to the intrigued narrator her lifetime spent inventing a connection to one of the farmers in the photo, an intervention into an artifact that has sustained her for eighty years by connecting her to a dead lover who merely resembles one of the men in the photograph. For all the crosswinds of passion that shape the contrapuntal plotting of *Gold Bug*, the most persistent, the most profound, the most satisfying connection links young Stuart Ressler, a music neophyte, with a piece of Baroque keyboard music. In *Operation Wandering Soul*, Joy, losing her mobility to the uncontrollable appetite of a ruinous disease that will ultimately claim her tender life, responds with a sustaining joy to stacks of children's books she has neglected in the more serious pursuit of her American education. In such capacity, the imagination does what it has done in American literature since Hester Prynne mounted the public scaffold in Salem—it makes bearable a larger world that is terrifying in its absurdity and its brutality. After all, Joy is most deeply impressed by the diary of Anne Frank, who conceives of her invented pen pal "Kitty" as a vehicle for sustaining an irrational hope, a fragile, vital sense of possibility and dignity amid steadily encroaching atrocities—"Because paper is more patient than people" (328).

Like Dickinson, however, Powers fears that the imaginative life—those sensitive enough to respond, those creative enough to fashion—necessarily sentences its most splendid practitioners to lives apart. Powers understands particularly that the life dedicated to the productions of the imaginative energy must be spent apart—in *Galatea 2.2*, obviously autobiographical and painfully reflective, Powers confesses at one point a gently voyeuristic fascination with Diana Hartrick's simple household, a routine life of marriage, normative employment, children, ordinary potato love that he sees, at mid-life, is not coming for him. When Stuart Ressler walks away from the hurricane of the heart's engagement to commit twenty-five years to computer routing, he turns his considerable creative energies into the production of musical scores that no one hears, a sort of non-life of private constructions. When Eddie Hobson, moved as a boy by the aesthetic connection he forges for the New York World's Fair, turns as an adult to the creation of his own private world, called Hobstown, he structures his exquisite private system by dictating particulars about the town into a tape recorder. But to do so compels Eddie to stand apart from a loving family who cannot understand his obsession, there behind closed doors with only the tape recorder, a benevolent dictator forging a world of (im)possibility.

But if the imagination beaches us in luminous isolation, if it cannot connect us to others (that, after all, is the hit-and-miss mess of the heart) it can *invade* others, imaginatively possess inaccessible others in acts that are both custodial and colonial. Lily Hobson, for instance, is fascinated by an old woman who lives alone across the street. She writes a lengthy letter to her (a letter, of course, never sent) in which she imaginatively enters the woman's life, takes possession of her private sphere, touches her despite never offering her the simplest greeting. And, although at pivotal moments the Hobson children each admit to feeling frustratingly distant from their troubled father, we realize as we close the book that we have been listening to tapes made by the oldest son Artie, who has found only in such an aesthetic medium the therapeutic opportunity to delve deeply into his enigmatic father.

There is Richard Powers' massive attack of imaginative eroticism in *Galatea 2.2* when he catches sight of the attractive graduate student A. and, finding his ability to strike up a simple conversation inexplicably retarded, turns to creating her within the fuller realm of his imagination, an unassisted fantasy. Or Peter Mays' obsessive exploration into history (*Three Farmers*) that is ignited when he catches sight eight floors up of a striking redhead marching in a Veterans Day Parade in downtown Boston—a fascination that grows oddly cold as he comes finally to meet the actual woman. In each case, the imagination provides cool intimacy much as it did for Dickinson—deep connection, intimate access to others, that leaves intact the imperial self. In short, the imagination empowers loneliness. Powers cannot mock what so sustains his characters, although readers more tuned to the prosaic world surely find such imaginative invasions of others, as A. argues to Richard Powers, cold, convenient self-indulgences.

It is to risk cliché to suggest that Powers goes to such lengths merely to argue that the imagination is a most splendidly isolated and isolating experience. It is the imagination's unsuspected opportunities to provide connection that most intrigue Powers and move his fictions ultimately toward their ascendant sensibility. The imagination, it turns out, works best as a cooperative. When Lily and Rachel Hobson play a game of joint composition at a typewriter, one typing a line that goes seamlessly into the second line typed by the other sister, it suggests the larger narrative structure itself—chapters that shift narrative center among each of the Hobson family members, thus shaping a braided cooperative narrative, voices that do not talk to each other but nevertheless cooperate. We are reminded that amid the breathless possibility of reignited romance that closes *Gold Bug* as Franklin Todd and Jan O'Deigh reunite, they commit themselves to a joint act of creation: they agree to produce not a child—Jan had her tubes long ago surgically burned shut—but rather the massive narrative that we have been reading, splicing together her journal of the year spent studying genetics and examining her stubborn passion for Franklin and his dissertation on an obscure Renaissance landscape painter, now refashioned into a spiritual biography of their friend Stuart Ressler. The narrative itself then is an experiment in two lonely voices braiding into a harmony that is not so much vertical as it is horizontal, much like the intricate musical structure of Bach's contrapuntal round reveals its beauty to Stuart Ressler as he comes to understand Bach's *Goldberg Variations*.

Such connections among characters, however, are too finely text-involved for Powers, who sees more practical connections possible through the Internet of the responsive imagination. The aesthetic experience binds us—the reader, the viewer, the listener—to unnamed, indeed unnameable others who also independently approach the same artifact. As the narrator discovers in *Three Farmers*, each of us adds to, participates in the extending of any aesthetic object; we exercise actively and jointly in the fullest definition of any aesthetic sign: we extend the round, whether it is a symbol in narrative, the story itself, a painting, a poem, a film, a piece of music. By apprehending any aesthetic artifact, we collaborate in the realization of that object in secret, open conspiracy with others. "I" and "I" fuse into a "We"—like trees (to borrow Powers' metaphor) suddenly becoming an orchard. The "plot" of *Three Farmers* is really the fascination shared by a disconnected few for a photograph—the plot hangs together because the artifact connects, much as Bach's intriguing keyboard work touches each of the characters in *Gold Bug*. The architecture of contrapuntal music centers Powers' fictions: in piling up separate melodies (stories), we recover harmony (plot).

Not surprisingly, Powers celebrates most profoundly the deep union made possible by the power of words, our ability (alarmingly rarer in this odd interregnum that marks the hissing away of the age of reading) to be moved unqualifiably by the act of reading. Characters, whatever their profession, confess to salving solitude by the expansive act of reading. True, Powers acknowledges traditional frustrations over language, how experience always exceeds language's ability to encode it. In *Galatea 2.2*, the computer Helen comes to the concept of "ball" through an avalanche of data on its dimensions rather than by simply holding one. Despite the agony over language, how we fall into it only when experience fails us, Powers understands the truer wonder, indeed our singularity as an organism, is our crying need to translate our most private experiences into a code, into letters, into words that in turn spell out the endless variations of experience, much as geneticists determined that the entire range of life comes from permutations of four letters or bases. In ways that readers hard on the era of minimalism's stripped prose find unabashed, Powers' prose thrills, revels in language. His characters do not mutter in the dreary monosyllabic discourse of a past generation's K-mart realism. Characters, even in the throes of emotional implosion, are expressive, articulate, even clever, turning puns with ease. Powers' sentences are artful constructions, his diction exotic and musical—language itself, not the narrative line, can easily become the most immediate experience. It is perhaps experience at secondhand, but in Powers' hands language is a gorgeous, splendid translation, a hand-me-down gown that still lights up a room. It repairs, graces the often graceless, bruising experience it relates.

And the power of narrative revives and resuscitates. Even in Powers' starkest fiction, *Operation Wandering Soul*, even as Dr. Richard Kraft succumbs to the plane of the immediate, Powers cannot bear to close the novel on such interior devastation. Rather in a closing frame, he hands the entire narrative over to a storyteller, a father telling his children stories before bedtime as they beg him for another one, a spooky one—the horrors we have endured in Kraft's apocalyptic world have been, like any scary bedtime story, more about the ability of language to move us, to terrify us, to haunt us, tales told to those who must prepare to be set loose into their own nightworld. And as we close that narrative, we touch just this raw power of narrative—the man's daughter comes downstairs long after bedtime, her eyes "burning, wet, incredulous, on fire…'I finished it,' she blurts out, 'That book you gave me. Your old favorite. I just finished it'" (352). She is irreversibly moved by the invasive power of reading, a feverish response that ties her to a much wider network of similarly devastated, exhilarated readers—alone and yet not apart. The imagination thus binds us each to our moats and yet splits us open to the horizon.

For Powers, then, the most critical character is the participatory reader, thus celebrating a relationship that has so often been stressful in postmodern narratives that have frustrated even the most resilient readers with narrative dead-ends, multiple plotlines, deliberate obfuscations. Like Dickinson, so sensitive to the reader's critical role in filling the absences that drove her to write, Powers understands that the most satisfying connection is ultimately with the reader. It is the reader who is ultimately empowered—using open endings that confound and delight,

Powers invites us to add to the round. Who exactly are those three farmers caught in that black and white photograph and what was their fate? What has happened to Eddie Hobson in his journey back to Alamogordo, who is that specter his family senses at their backdoor long after he has vanished into the desert Southwest? What will happen as Jan O'Deigh and Franklin Todd resolve to try, *da capo e fine*, their difficult and yet somehow necessary love? Will Dr. Kraft, his interior collapsing like a house of old playing cards, find his way back to the saving touch of Linda?

Coaxing a next page for these characters is not our work but our joy. Unlike postmodern narratives that taunt the reader by reminding us ad-nauseum that storytelling is necessarily defeated by closure, here Powers invites us to keep the story alive. Reading is finally a contact sport, the exhilarating terror of committing your private resources to the work of creating. The connection to the reader becomes an erotic conspiracy of mutual respect. The writer engages us from the loneliness of the creative act; and we touch characters—moved really by ink pressed into paper—and then compel the narrative beyond its closing pages. If Powers' binge-ing on information instructs us, if his sure sense of the anatomy of contemporary love moves us, his closings ultimately free us to create, usher us (perhaps hesitating) into our own luminous worlds of possibility. These splendid novels are ours to continue.

■ IV

And I, for glee,
Took Rainbows, as the common way,
And empty Skies
The Eccentricity—
Emily Dickinson, Poem 257

It is surely the worst of times and the worst of times for the imagination. In academic worlds, it has long served as private preserve of a generation of passionate narrative experimenters who found in its rich creativity a chance to exercise control against a world that had lost all sense of boundary, elevating (or reducing) fictions to dense, self-reflexive exercises—all to celebrate, in theory, the sheer fun of invention but acting rather to alienate virtually an entire generation of readers outside the academy. And in the larger cultural community, the imagination has been diminished first by the oppressive fairy dust-storms of Disney (who emerges in a wonderful satiric subplot in *Prisoner's Dilemma* as Powers' archmetaphor for the absorbing self-interest of the imagination as pure escapism) and then by the gee-whiz bang of Lucas and Spielberg, whose brand of mechanical magic demands not only that we trade sense for sensation but that we *not* exercise the imagination but rather that it play along as our reality becomes more and more virtual.

It is Powers' importance in such an age to remind us that such atrophied energy can provide us what it provided Dickinson—the generous benediction of a wounded, imperfect life. To borrow a definition Richard Powers offers in *Galatea 2.2*, the imagination bends to kiss the birthmark. It throws fine, but sturdy filaments between and about strangers who become, nevertheless, intimates. It eases a loneliness that we cannot seem to diminish otherwise. Our literature, then, need not inter us among its dead. Matter, as it turns out, matters—because overlaying this superfluous animal is the wondrous circuitry of the imagination. We need not flounder alone in the Internet. The world can be commanded, illuminated, finally (and finely) linked by the assertion of an energy most of us too willingly leave behind in childhood, embarrassed by its riches. Nothing deserves our wonder, Powers reminds us, so much as our capacity to feel it.

Surely there lurks in Powers' fiction Dickinson's fearful sense of approaching such a feast, a terror of disappointment, a trembling sense that the world's too-sudden encroachment will

■ **BOOKS BY RICHARD POWERS**

Three Farmers on Their Way to a Dance. New York: William Morrow, 1985.

Prisoner's Dilemma. New York: William Morrow, 1988.

The Gold Bug Variations. New York: William Morrow, 1991.

Operation Wandering Soul. New York: William Morrow, 1993.

Galatea 2.2. New York: Farrar, Straus & Giroux, 1995.

Gain. New York: Farrar, Straus & Giroux, 1998.

Plowing the Dark. New York: Farrar, Straus & Giroux, 2000.

shatter our finer moments of illumination and connection. Exhilaration is never far from stillness. What most intrigues in Powers is that balance of the naive wonder of the stirred child with the dark disappointment that so mar(k)s maturity—in this Powers, at such a tender age, resembles one of his more unforgettable creations, Nico, the brash boy in Dr. Kraft's pediatrics ward suffering from Hutchinson-Gilford's disease, a nine-year-old dying of old age. Much as Dickinson teaches, we are, although damaged and bruised into loneliness, finally more than we suspect. In *Operation Wandering Soul*, the ward children take a field trip to a local Women's Club for an amateur dance night. During the fun, they dance with sudden seriousness to the old Mills Brothers' classic "You're Nobody 'til Somebody Loves You." It is left to Richard Powers to remind us, much as Emily Dickinson did from behind her closed bedroom door, how imperial, how commanding, how enduring, how connected that nobody finally is.

Joseph Dewey
April, 1996

UPDATE

The much-awarded Richard Powers has since published two novels, *Gain* (1998) and *Plowing the Dark* (2000). He continues to be heralded by critics and readers alike, mostly for his range of topics, which often embrace the scientific, and interwoven story lines.

Gain is essentially a novel about environmental pollution and one woman exposed to it, as well as a sweeping look at American history. "The result is impressive and imaginative, albeit a little puzzling," wrote *Publishers Weekly*, which also noted "clunky dialogue, flat characters, portentous commonplaces." Even so, "Powers has given us the historical novel as survey course—a curiosity that we never knew we needed but that we can't keep from admiring."

The *New York Times Book Review* called his most recent novel, *Plowing the Dark*, "audacious" and "spectacular." And *The New Republic*, mildly criticized Powers, "one of our brainier novelists," for letting his science sometimes "tyrannize" his writing. Still, the review continued, his scope is stunning: "We can find riffs on architectural history, global economics, higher mathematics, and meteorology, and also on the caves of Lascaux, musical fugues, and the Gulf War. Here is a mind so dense no idea can go unmentioned. . . . In a world in which facts become obsolete by the hour, this is the information we most urgently need."

The Arts and Sciences of Thomas Pynchon

Influential critics have ardently commended Thomas Pynchon's most recent novel, *Gravity's Rainbow,* but relatively few readers have persevered tenaciously enough to complete it. Even fewer have understood it fully and thus received its infinite riches. Understanding his two earlier novels also requires strenuous effort. As a prologue to analysis of his work an unorthodox comparison may clarify and dramatize Pynchon's accomplishments. *V.,* his first novel, resembles a Hogarth print. Some of the characters frolic drunkenly, but others reveal in their furtive expressions an awareness of doom's imminence. Both artists have a sardonic wit and pay meticulous attention to detail. *The Crying of Lot 49,* Pynchon's second novel, resembles one of Escher's works. Look for a while at the ducks flying in one direction and they suddenly seem to be flying in the opposite direction. One ultimately cannot know for sure what is happening. *Gravity's Rainbow,* like many of Bosch's paintings, teems with life, its characters tortured by hideous but unidentifiable enemies in front of a lurid backdrop. The enormous amount of detail makes it as difficult for one to comprehend the work as it would be for a person in such a scene to comprehend his situation.

The frolickers in *V.* are The Whole Sick Crew and their ilk: denizens of contemporary Gin Lanes. Their Bacchanalias alternate with the attempts of the—probably deluded—Stencils to solve the frightful mysteries of V. Pynchon never clearly reveals whether or not V. exists, much less its nature. As *The Crying of Lot 49* opens, Oedipa Maas, a housewife alienated by Southern California, learns that Pierce Inverarity, a wealthy acquaintance, has recently died and made her his estate's co-executor. Her inquiry into his estate reveals an intricate web of his enterprises and several hints that the Tristero (an alternative postal system) and the outcasts it serves may exist. And they may not. If they do, Inverarity may have created them. Then again, her paranoia may encourage her to believe those who claim that the Tristero exists. There may or may not be an alternative. The ducks, in short, may be flying either way. This book ends without definitively solving the puzzle that drives forward its plot. Approximately three hundred characters fill the canvas of *Gravity's Rainbow,* some participating in two chases. Tyrone Slothrop, the main character, searches during the last phase of World War II and the immediate post-war period for a part from the Germans' ultimate rocket, and others try to understand this weapon. The characters in the other chase pursue, spy on and experiment on Slothrop to determine why his erections predict German rockets' detonations. This action indeed has a lurid backdrop. By the time this novel begins, the war has filled Europe with wreckage, both material and human. As if this were not enough wreckage, Pynchon ranges back in time to depict more, and at this novel's conclusion, by portraying the pseudonymous Richard M. Zhlubb, he glances forward to Nixon's America. *Gravity's Rainbow* ends as a rocket descends on a movie theater to initiate the Apocalypse. The revelations in that section and elsewhere in the book are, however, enigmatic, their obscurity compounded rather than alleviated by a library-full of information.

Thomas Pynchon

Thomas Pynchon, born in Glen Cove, Long Island, New York, on May 8, 1937, received his B.A. at Cornell University in 1958. His college career was interrupted by two years' service in the U.S. Navy. After graduating from Cornell, he lived in Greenwich Village for one year and worked for Boeing Aircraft in Seattle, Washington. The winner of such honors as the National Book Award, the William Faulkner Novel Award, the Howells Medal from the National Institute and American Academy of Arts and Letters, and a MacArthur Foundation fellowship, Pynchon is one of the most acclaimed writers working today, and likely the most enigmatic.

Pynchon finished his first novel, *V.*, in Mexico in 1963; it won the William Faulkner Novel Award. *The Crying of Lot 49* won the Rosenthal Foundation Award given by the National Institute of Arts and Letters in 1967. Pynchon was co-winner of the National Book Award in 1974 for *Gravity's Rainbow*. That novel was nominated for a Pulitzer Prize, but the fiction jury's unanimous vote was overruled by the Pulitzer advisory board. In 1976 the author declined an award from the National Institute of Arts and Letters.

Being shy of publicity, Pynchon has not allowed his photograph to be printed in any publication. He is currently living in California. ■

Thus, a reader of Pynchon faces proliferating complexities. All the details in his books seem related to all the others, so a reader has difficulty deciding where to grab hold. A reader would do well to begin by analyzing Pynchon's use of science. By beginning thus a reader can discern order in these books, and with persistence and a bit of research he can understand them. More specifically, a reader has the key that most quickly unlocks Pynchon's treasure house if he recognizes that with increasing subtlety this writer has found literary uses for a few modern scientific concepts. He has explored the inter-relations among these concepts and confronted them with non-scientific concepts. He has constantly gained skill in using them until in *Gravity's Rainbow* he not only includes a vast amount of information but also integrates this material into his novel rather than strewing it around on its surface.

A reader will almost certainly consider well rewarded his efforts to proceed in this way. Despite his difficulties Pynchon is enjoyable. He displays, for example, many kinds of wit. While puzzling over Pynchon's meanings a reader will be sustained by chuckles caused by academic humor, belly laughs caused by slapstick and groans caused by puns, some very clever and some pleasantly awful. At other times a reader can observe Pynchon, a sorcerer's apprentice, demonstrate his inventiveness. Suddenly one seems to be watching life in Southwest Africa, Malta or Central Asia. One also marvels at the learning that makes possible Pynchon's inventiveness, his allusiveness and his ability to analyze intellectual issues. Moreover, nearly all the stops on his plot's mazy way are interesting, and many of his characters remain in a reader's memory.

As to science in his work, in *V.* Pynchon uses the concept of entropy and the principles of cybernetics. The former refers to Clausius' Second Law of Thermodynamics, according to which closed systems, by producing heat, inevitably lose energy. Cybernetics, or information science, developed along with the computer during and after World War II, and, explaining phenomena in the context of information dispersal, it tries to inter-relate various disciplines. The identity of the equations for thermodynamic energy loss and for information loss links entropy and cybernetics and encourages cyberneticists to use "Fentropy" also to denote increasing chaos and disorder. Pynchon's fictional world is chaotic and loses energy: the characters and the society deteriorate. In it information gathering and cybernetic concepts help explain the characters' responses to this deterioration.

Entropy appears in *V.* in four important themes. First, some action occurs among the wastes of technology and the human body. For example, Benny Profane tracks alligators through New York's sewers, where a bizarre priest had tried to evangelize the rats. Second, Pynchon reports in stomach-churning detail the disassembly of two characters: some Maltese childrens' picking apart of the Bad Priest and the plastic surgery performed on a character's nose. Third, inanimateness threatens the characters. Because of plastic surgery necessitated by war wounds, for example, Godolphin is both living tissue and dead metal and thus partly inanimate. Finally, the gallery of pseudo-intellectuals, artists manqué and fraudulent sophisticates who make *V.* sometimes seem like an updating of Moliére's plays, illustrate decadence: the social equivalent of the entropic processes working in nature.

The entropy threatening them causes some characters in *V.* to seek fast understanding, before they become part of a compost heap. Pynchon describes in cybernetic terms this search for information. For example, McClintic Sphere propounds the most frequently quoted statement in this novel— "keep cool, but care"—by thinking about a flip-flop circuit, the kind used in computers, which are based on the binary (two-term) system of numbers. He wants others to avoid a dichotomy whose two parts are in themselves insufficient. In fact, *V.* interweaves many dichotomies, from Sphere's advice up to this novel's basic structure: the interplay between The Whole Sick Crew's antics and the search for V. Also, two unusual details allude to cybernetic concepts: Esther watching oscillating objects in a plastic surgeon's office and the back-and-forth subway trips, called yo-yoing by the characters who take them. These are examples of yawing: uncontrolled oscillation caused by too much negative feedback. That is, some characters, well aware of the discrepancy between their accomplishments and their goals—this discrepancy being negative feedback—have experiences that symbolize their difficulties.

The characters in *V.* who pursue information often discover something that causes paranoia, which Pynchon explores at great length in his three novels. A few characters occasionally show symptoms of it, and Herbert Stencil's monomaniacal faith in V.'s existence often appears to be an elaborate paranoid system. Paranoia, too, makes good sense in the scientific context Pynchon creates. Boltzmann, who formulated the equations for thermodynamic entropy, described by statistical methods the behavior of gases, using Maxwell's insight that average behavior should be examined because gases do not behave uniformly in either time or space. Gibbs later applied statistical analysis to solids and liquids. Planck's demonstration that substances emit energy not continuously but in units and Heisenberg's Principle of Indeterminacy further attacked science's older epistemological bases. Many scientists, therefore, abandoned the deterministic idea that because of its continuous causes and effects they could measure nature. That is, some contemporary scientists, because they doubt that they can discern chains of causes and effects and because they fear that the very act of observation alters its object, search anguishedly for certitude, as do those of Pynchon's characters who cannot be sure what, if anything, causes their troubles and do not know whether to trust their knowledge or dismiss it as merely their own paranoia's creation. In other words, the winds from the epistemological Pandora's box that contemporary scientists opened blow over the decaying landscape of V.

As to his literary skill in V., aside from his dualistic structure Pynchon simply and loosely incorporates science as a source of references. Despite its inventiveness, V. is also a typical first novel because of its realism, especially in its plot, less so in its stereotyped (for good reason) characters. Even in this novel, however, Pynchon shows signs of his future innovations. In it he presents organizations of data, explanations, fictions. The narrators and the characters again and again compose small fictions in order to explain the world around them. Pynchon warns about this project's dangers by showing that some fictions, being paranoid, distort rather than clarify. Also, he suggests that making fictions distances one from life. The Whole Sick Crew, in contrast, experiences rather than broods. In V. Pynchon begins to wonder about the fictive nature of science, of other non-literary disciplines and of his own form of discourse.

In *The Crying of Lot 49* Pynchon does not merely refer to scientific concepts but also uses them as the dynamo that drives the plot. That is, by frequently referring to cybernetic ideas and to other scientific ideas related to information he places in a scientific context Oedipa's efforts to understand the Tristero. In order to establish this context Pynchon inserts these references at important junctures in the plot. Early in this novel, for example, driving down into San Narcisco, Inverarity's home town, Oedipa sees that it resembles a circuit diagram for a transistor radio: a means of communication. A little later she watches a production of *The Courier's Tragedy,* a play that obscurely refers to the Tristero—apparently. Postal systems such as the Tristero of course also distribute information. Because she wants to explicate these references, to understand Inverarity and to determine whether or not the Tristero relates to him, Oedipa attends a stockholders' meeting at Yoyodyne, one of his businesses. There she meets an employee who explains Maxwell's Demon to her in thermodynamic terms and refers her to John Nefastis. To build a perpetual motion machine and to refute the Second Law of Thermodynamics Maxwell proposed building a sorter, a demon, to direct low-energy gas molecules into one compartment of a box and high-energy molecules into the other. He incorrectly thought that this could be done without expending energy and that the resulting difference in potential energy between the two compartments could produce work. Nefastis explains to her that the Demon supposedly would work because it has data about the energy of gas molecules. It thus relates to information science as well as to thermodynamics and it appears to resist entropy in both the thermodynamic and cybernetic senses.

After all these clues, near the novel's end Oedipa understands her quandary. She realizes that she must choose between two alternatives. Either Southern California, which Pynchon satirizes throughout, constitutes the world—surface reality is the only reality and all hope of an alternative such as the Tristero merely demonstrates her paranoia—or an obscure and more attractive reality exists, the Tristero being its communication system. Earlier Pynchon had described this pair of alternatives mainly by using mirror imagery, suggesting that the alternative reality, if it exists, is a mirror-world. By the novel's end, however, Oedipa understands in cybernetic terms her difficulty: "the waiting above all; if not for another set of possibilities to replace those that had conditioned the land to accept any San Narciso among its most tender flesh...; waiting for a symmetry of choices to break down.... It was now like walking among matrices of a great digital computer, the zeroes and ones twinned above." Then Pynchon alludes again to this novel's first important scientific image, the circuit diagram: "behind the hieroglyphic streets there would either be a transcendent meaning, or only the earth."

Although information science furnishes the terms in which Oedipa finally articulates her problem, it does not help her to solve that problem.

Other disciplines to which Pynchon refers also clarify issues but do not solve them. Psychology, for example, partially explains the many characters who have paranoid symptoms. Dr. Hilarius—ironically, a psychiatrist—has the most serious case, and he finally locks himself in his office and prepares to resist with a rifle his "enemies." Because Hilarius worked for the Nazis, Pynchon discusses very briefly twentieth-century Germany's mass psychology, a major subject in *Gravity's Rainbow*. Many of the minor characters in *The Crying of Lot 49* have paranoid tendencies. More importantly, when Oedipa amplifies her dualism into the computer imagery near this novel's conclusion she faces the possibility of her own paranoia. In general, Pynchon considers paranoia to be a way to organize information. This book's paranoids, in other words, are frightened by connections they see among bits of data that appear discrete to other people.

Whereas in *V.* Pynchon refers to political and intellectual history, in *The Crying of Lot 49* he concentrates on the history of communications, specifically the well-documented history of the Thurn and Taxis postal system and of other official systems that succeeded it and the—probably imaginary—history of rival systems. The Thurn and Taxis began in 1305, consolidated impressive power and influence and finally expired soon after the Congress of Vienna. By emphasizing the history of communications Pynchon implicitly acknowledges a main tenet of cybernetics; one can best understand societies by examining the ways they gather and disseminate information. Norbert Wiener bases on this tenet several books that apply cybernetic ideas to many other disciplines. That is, the description of postal systems and the historical information that Pynchon adds about them relate to information science. This relation of other fields to the central one of information science, as well as many other techniques, makes *The Crying of Lot 49,* unlike his two apparently sprawling novels, obviously unified.

In *The Crying of Lot 49* Pynchon also examines artistic fictions, for example, *The Courier's Tragedy*. Although a textual problem with its key lines thwarts Oedipa's analysis of this play, analyzing a literary text can certainly explain non-literary issues for her and, by implication, for this novel's readers. Pynchon also incorporates this play into a complex system of Chinese boxes. The play and a movie that Metzger (the estate's other co-executor) and Oedipa watch on television comically resemble each other. The long plot summary of this play and occasional passages from it in turn brilliantly parody Jacobean revenge tragedy. Pynchon climaxes this tour de force with one of the great comic lines in contemporary American fiction, a line that will probably affect a reader's attitude toward revenge tragedy forever after. This play is, he writes, "like a Road Runner cartoon in blank verse." Another Chinese box system contains a painting inside this novel. It in turn depicts a tower inside which captive women embroider a tapestry, and "the tapestry [is] the world." As Oedipa realizes, by creating the tapestry the prisoners endure their plight. She also thinks that the tower symbolizes all the forces that oppress her. This complicated interplay of artistic creations shows that they partially explain each other and sometimes partially explain the world. A supreme artistic creation, such as the tapestry, can even in a sense become the world.

In *The Crying of Lot 49* Pynchon analyzes literary and non-literary fictions much more incisively than he does in *V.* In his first novel the narrators and the characters make fictions. In his second novel, however, the narrator does not; he does not interrupt the story's flow to make brief explanatory comments based on organizations of data. By thus limiting the help that the narrator gives, Pynchon places readers of *The Crying of Lot 49* in a predicament like Oedipa's. They, too, must sort this novel's often confusing data and they must evaluate the reactions to it of Oedipa and others. She considers her task imperative, as her feverish tracking of clues demonstrates. Pynchon's vitriolic portrait of Southern California justifies her intensity. Without fictions to mediate between herself and her experience she would confront that experience directly, and it might be more reality than she could bear. Thus, Pynchon's social commentary and his analysis of fictions inter-relate, and he implies that contemporary persons need the best fictions they can construct.

While he gives examples of fictions, Pynchon makes *The Crying of Lot 49* itself an intricate fiction that assimilates bits of information into a narrative and gives them an aesthetically pleasing form. In important ways this fiction resembles the contemporary physical scientists' conception of nature. For example, because the Tristero's existence remains in doubt, Oedipa's perception of her experience is crucial. Rather than having an objective heroine confront indubitable reality, Pynchon has the confused Oedipa interact with and subtly change the enigmatic reality she experiences. She thus acts as Heisenberg claims observation apparatus acts. Second, modern physicists do not conceive of experience as neatly circumscribed spatially and temporally, divided conveniently into linked causes and effects. Rather, they often think of inherently limitless fields varying in unpredictable ways that require statistical methods of description. This novel's ending is similarly open-ended. An auction (Crying) of Inverarity's stamps, some of which (lot 49) the Tristero perhaps issued, may solve Oedipa's riddle. Pynchon, however, ends the book without giving the solution. Its final words are "the auctioneer cleared his throat. Oedipa settled back, to await the crying of lot 49."

Pynchon produced his gigantic *Gravity's Rainbow* not merely by doing at greater length the things he had done in his first two novels but also by probing more deeply, connecting more subtly, generalizing more impressively. *Gravity's Rainbow*, like *V.,* makes many references to information, both scientific and non-scientific. Like *The Crying of Lot 49,* it has a plot based on science; it chronicles attempts to find the secrets of rocket 00000 and to explain Slothrop's uncanny ability to predict rocket strikes. In his most recent novel, however, Pynchon describes more voluminously the ways science and other disciplines organize information and relate to each other. As to the first new emphasis, he again refers to the Second Law of Thermodynamics, which, like other scientific laws, describes regularities in nature and is thus very general. In *Gravity's Rainbow* he refers also to science's most powerful means of generalizing—mathematics—and to the generalizing methods of psychology (building psychological systems), of the film (film theory, especially concerning film's ability to portray reality and its relation to literature) and of history (historiography). As to the second new emphasis, he connects science, the main thread in this novel's intricate tapestry, with many subsidiary topics to create a tight, carefully textured work of art.

The rocket of course lies at the center of *Gravity's Rainbow*. Appropriately, it furnishes this novel's cryptic title. It traces a parabola, like a rainbow, as it tries to defeat the force of gravity, which pulls it back toward earth. The German rocket scientists in fact hoped eventually to make a rocket that could burst gravity's bonds and reach the moon. On the one hand, then, the rocket symbolizes human efforts to escape restrictive forces. For this reason Pynchon often and ingeniously connects the rocket with sex, which he also describes as a means of liberation. He claims that the plastic from which a part is made is sexually stimulating, and he includes a long series of bawdy limericks about the rocket. On the other hand, the Germans built rockets to kill. A character recognizes that "before the Rocket we went on believing, because we wanted to. But the Rocket can penetrate, from the sky, at any given point. Nowhere is safe." Its introduction into the war thus constitutes a quantum leap in mankind's destructiveness and, conversely, in mankind's fright. Because the rocket also has many other meanings, the black Africans who seek it in order to avenge European colonialism wisely consider it a secret text.

Mathematics, the foundation of the "hard sciences," also plays a prominent role in *Gravity's Rainbow*. Sometimes Pynchon merely points out interesting analogies, such as the similarity of the shapes of the double integral sign (which appears in the equations for the rocket's flight), tunnels at a German rocket installation, the SS insignia and even lovers curled up asleep. At other times he mentions that perhaps a graph or equation can represent history. Various theories of history's flow can indeed be represented geometrically; for example, a circle depicts history's movement according to the cyclical theory. Pynchon also works into this novel statistics, which modern scientists' skepticism about determinism has made more important. Some of his characters, such as Pointsman, cling to the older deterministic conception of nature, whereas others, such as Roger Mexico, a statistician, accept the newer theory that nature is random. In one of his more interesting and fruitful analogies, Pynchon compares these scientific positions to a psychological malady that has interested him since his earliest work and to another that he invents. A paranoid believes in determinism, that everything is connected, and specifically that these connections will harm him. Conversely, belief in randomness, in the total absence of connections and in the necessity for statistical analysis has, according to Pynchon, the psychological analogue of anti-paranoia: the belief that no connections exist.

Pynchon, who has an engineering degree from Cornell, also makes good use of technological data. For example, in a séance early in this novel, Walther Rathenau, the German administrative genius, alludes to synthesis and control: two themes that recur. The discovery of plastics showed the possibilities of synthesis and it is thus, this novel suggests, one of the most important events in history. That is, by making plastic, scientists broke nature's bonds, just as the rocket scientists attempted to break gravity's bonds. Earlier scientists of course synthesized compounds, but plastics engineers learned to do so almost at will to create substances with precisely the properties that they wanted. They thus made a large contribution to mankind's battle against the limitations that nature imposes on it. By describing Slothrop's efforts to understand a plastic part of the rocket, Pynchon neatly includes in this novel these and other bits of information about plastics and synthesis.

Similarly, the rocket's centrality in the plot allows him to develop naturally the theme of control. He begins with some information about the methods of controlling its flight, and then he describes many situations in the context of control, suggesting that the rocket has made this a common way to understand phenomena. Some of the most poignant scenes, as well as some of the most distasteful and baffling, make sense in this context. Social control stifles the black Hereros (an African tribe that also appears in *V.*) and lovers and other sensitive characters on both sides of the war. Many characters develop minority tastes in sex, which Pynchon describes in the scenes that helped convince the Pulitzer Prize Committee to ignore its advisory board's unanimous opinion and not give its award to Pynchon. The strange eating scenes, such as the one about bananas early in this novel and the one later about exotic kinds of candy, also develop this theme of resistance to control. Some characters have minority tastes in music, such as a preference for Rossini rather than Beethoven and fondness for kazoo concertos.

Many characters also succumb to economic and political controls, partly because they cannot understand them. Pynchon sometimes hints that everything is in fact connected, mainly by multi-national companies and cartels that gain control by mustering their technological capabilities. He does not make it clear, however, whether these hints are words to the wise or portents for paranoids. For example, Slothrop thinks that Laszlo Jamf, a scientist aligned with massive industrial firms in Germany and other countries, gave him his predicting ability while experimenting on him. Pynchon also delineates the political pressure that military industries exerted on the German government, Shell's apparent operation on both sides of the war and the social changes that new technology created by businesses and governments during the war will cause (he also implies that this is the war's most important meaning and that military and political events merely hide it). In a world running down because of entropic forces, this interlocking source of control, The System, Pynchon suggests, tries to obtain the largest possible share of the world's dwindling energy, thus increasing the outsiders' misery.

Aided by Freudian and neo-Freudian psychology, Pynchon shapes his plot and characters so that an attentive reader will see a cluster of phenomena. Paranoia, Freud argues, results from sexual repression, and it often causes aggression. Erik Erikson in *Young Man Luther* points out the apparent connection between his subject's obsessive scatological interests and a trait in him that Erikson labels paranoid. To this cluster Pynchon adds technology and capitalism, echoing ideas Norman O. Brown expresses, particularly in his essay on Swift. Brown also argues that technological progress strengthens the death instinct. If so, it is this cluster's most important component. The rocket, like other products of advanced technology, may cause many psychological difficulties and the economic and political oppression that result from them. These themes weave in and out of *Gravity's Rainbow,* and occasionally the narrator or a character comments tentatively on them, but one can best understand Pynchon's point by recognizing this cluster's sources in psychological theory.

Pynchon also makes other references to non-scientific disciplines. As to psychology, he examines types of love and alludes to Köhler (especially the cornerstone of Gestalt psychology: the human tendency to organize data into patterns), Jung (especially his theory of the collective unconscious) and Pavlov (especially conditioning and opposites). The narrator and the characters often speculate on history, such as the causes of historical change, history's movement, crucial years (1904 is vital to this novel, as 1922 is to *V.*) and the related issue of time's properties. A few references to *Faust* indicate another way to conceive of technological man, but Rilke is the most important literary figure in *Gravity's Rainbow*. Allusions to and quotations from his work, particularly *The Sonnets to Orpheus* and *The Duino Elegies,* begin with the screaming in the first sentence and recur often. Pynchon seems to consider him to be both a representative of the culture that Hitler destroyed and a prophet of Germany's future. The novel also makes many allusions to German films of the inter-war period, particularly those of Fritz Lang. Moreover, one character, von Göll, is a composite film director of that era. More subtly, the settings often resemble the Expressionistic sets used in many films after *The Cabinet of Dr. Caligari*. One can better understand the references to film by reading Kracauer's *From Caligari to Hitler*. It helps explain the scenes that purport to be films of the action rather than narrative. These scenes examine the relative effectiveness of literature and film as portrayers of reality. Finally, the occult appears in *Gravity's Rainbow* in passing references, a séance, a Tarot reading, and most importantly as a means of defying The System: "those like Slothrop, with the greatest interest in discovering the truth, were thrown back on dreams, psychic flashes, omens, cryptographies, drug-epistemologies, all dancing on a ground of terror, contradiction, absurdity."

Even the form of *Gravity's Rainbow* accords with contemporary science's insights, and with this achievement Pynchon in another way advances beyond his first two novels. Recent scientists have discovered hundreds of differences between nature and commonsense notions about it. Similarly, readers have difficulty with *Gravity's Rainbow* largely because it assaults their common sense and violates the realistic novel's canons. It will frustrate and confuse anyone who demands three-dimensional characters, logical plots, credible actions, recognizable settings and traditional narrative methods. Like the world now described by physical science, *Gravity's Rainbow* is also in some ways random. Slothrop, for example, hunting hidden drugs, finds them in the middle of the Potsdam Conference site, looks up and sees Mickey Rooney on a balcony. This kind of incongruity creates much of the humor. The randomness, dwindling energy, increasing chaos and The System also create the humor of threat followed by release when the threat appears to be avoidable. This randomness, however, is far from total; Pynchon differs from the fashionable contemporary writers whose self-indulgent cute musings pass for novels. His ideas, even more than the elements of fiction (plot, characters, etc.), order *Gravity's Rainbow*. Moreover, patterns abound in it. An early scene, for example, describes the burning of the rocket and of a cigarette. Then appears a poem about a flame, one of Rilke's characteristic images. This echoing connects Pynchon's poem with his many allusions to Rilke.

To balance all these subtle ideas, great erudition, and advanced literary techniques Pynchon has a strong humanistic strain. As his career has progressed, this strain has intensified and he has expressed it with increasing effectiveness. Although not pervasive, his humanism seems to be sincere. In *V.* it appears mainly in McClintic Sphere's admonition to keep cool but care: unconvincing advice because it intrudes into the novel and comes from a character who has dubious credentials as a moral philosopher. A scene with a pathetic drunk in *The Crying of Lot 49* fits naturally into the plot and shows Oedipa's—and, indirectly, Pynchon's—concern for suffering. However, the passage about metaphors that follows slightly blunts this scene's effectiveness. Many such recognitions of suffering appear in his most recent book, and he integrates them into it and does not undercut them. Most notably, Pökler places his wedding ring on a half-dead woman's finger because "if she lived, the ring would be good for a few meals, or a blanket, or a night indoors, or a ride home." This scene resembles the passage about Liverpool's slums in *Redburn* where Melville for the first time in print responds compassionately to human misery and thus signals his imminent blooming as a great writer. Later in *Gravity's Rainbow* Pynchon implies that literature must have a humanistic dimension. He writes sardonically about Marcel, a "mechanical chessplayer," who is Pynchon's caricature of Proust and "who has no fakery inside to give him any touch of humanity at all."

Gravity's Rainbow is in many ways unique, but it has precursors and it probably will have imitators. It belongs to a rich but largely unrecognized tradition in American prose. Many great American books—such as *Walden, Moby-Dick* and *The Confidence-Man*—are packed with information, experimental in form and intent on examining literature's nature, on reflecting on themselves as they proceed. Reviving this great tradition is one of Pynchon's accomplishments. As to imitators, the conception of literature implicit in *Gravity's Rainbow* offers a way to escape contemporary American fiction's impasse. Many recent American novels have either nothing or everything to do with nonliterature. That is, they are, on the one hand, aimless fantasy or endless examinations of literature itself or, on the other hand, virtually journalism. Some recent fine traditional novels avoid this impasse but not as skillfully as could novels based on Pynchon's demonstration that literature is, like other disciplines, a kind of fiction, but also, because it can incorporate other disciplines, the supreme kind of fiction.

John Stark
October, 1975

UPDATE

Thomas Pynchon has since published two novels, *Vineland* (1990) and *Mason and Dixon* (1997), and a short-story collection, *Slow Learner* (1984).

Part of his mystery is that he is so reclusive. "Pynchon is so reticent about himself and so wary of publicity that it is unclear even what he looks like," stated *Contemporary Authors*. "Pynchon keeps even his whereabouts a secret from everyone but his closest and most loyal friends." It has been suggested that paranoia, which informs his fiction, is the reason, "but other evidence suggests that in his personal life this daring and iconoclastic writer is merely intensely private and intensely shy."

■ BOOKS BY THOMAS PYNCHON

V. Philadelphia: J. B. Lippincott, 1963; Toronto: McClelland, 1963; London: Jonathan Cape, 1963; Harmondsworth: Penguin, 1966; New York: Modern Library, 1966.New York: Bantam, 1968.

Crying of Lot 49. Philadelphia: J. B. Lippincott, 1966; Toronto: McClelland, 1966; New York: Bantam, 1973.

Gravity's Rainbow. New York: Viking Press, 1973; 1973; New York: Bantam, 1974.

Mortality and Mercy in Vienna. London: Aloes, 1976.

Low-Lands. London: Aloes, 1978.

The Secret Integration. London: Aloes, 1982.

A Journey into the Mind of Watts. London: Mouldwarp, 1983.

Slow Learner. Boston: Little, Brown: 1985.

Vineland. Boston: Little, Brown, 1990.

Mason and Dixon. New York: Henry Holt, 1997.

For all its praise, Pynchon's work, including his reputation-making *Gravity's Rainbow*, has also often been called intensely difficult. "Pynchon's plots resist summarization, just as his narrators resist reduction to a single identifiable voice and his range of reference seems virtually endless," according to *Contemporary Authors*. As noted above, the Pulitzer Prize editorial board denied Pynchon the award for fiction for *Gravity's Rainbow,* even though the jurors had unanimously recommended him. At the same time, *Gravity's Rainbow* was being compared to James Joyce's *Ulysses* and Thomas Mann's *The Magic Mountain*, and the *Yale Review* wrote, "Pynchon is, quite simply, the best living novelist in English."

A new work by Pynchon is eagerly anticipated by his readers, of whom there are many. His novel *Vineland*, however, was found by some critics to be a lesser book than *Gravity's Rainbow*. "*Vineland* won't inspire the same sort of fanatic loyalty and enthusiasm that *Gravity's Rainbow* did," wrote a review in *Fame*. "Call it Pynchon Lite." *Time* stated: "It is, admittedly, disquieting to find a major author drawing cultural sustenance from 'The Brady Bunch' and 'I Love Lucy' instead of *The Odyssey* and the Bible. But to condemn Pynchon for this strategy is to confuse the author with his characters. He is a gifted man with anti-elitist sympathies. Like some fairly big names in innovative fiction, including Flaubert, Joyce and Faulkner, Pynchon writes about people who would not be able to read the books in which they appear. As a contemporary bonus, Pynchon's folks would not even be interested in trying. That is part of the sadness and the hilarity of this exhilarating novel."

Mason and Dixon, the story about the two men after whom the famous American dividing line is named, with everything else thrown in, was better received than its predecessor. T. Coraghessan Boyle, writing in the *New York Times Book Review*, praised Pynchon's "sublime" method: "It allows for the surveyors' story to become an investigation into the order of the universe, clockwork deity and all, and yet at the same time to reflect the inadequacy of reason alone to explain the mystery that surrounds us," he wrote. "The haunted world, the suprareal, the ghostly and the impossible have the same valence as the facts of history as we receive them." The *Nation* noted that "from the depths of a jaunty disenchantment, [Pynchon] calls into brilliant question the very ways we measure, map and misconstrue history, landscape, time, space, stars and self."

The Double Dream of Julia Randall

■ **I**

After contemplating the poems of Julia Randall for some time preparatory to writing this essay, I must at its outset confess that I have not shaken the impression of her work with which I began. The passage of time, repeated reading, and a not always summonable familiarity with her ways, merely confirm in me a kind of superstitious awe at a poet who is totally *other*. She hears things (diction, melody, experience) I cannot hear. A brief case in point. She is more thoroughly attuned than anyone I have read to the sound of her heartbeat, nor is this merely a result of her medical training. In one poem she speaks of "the whirling dead / that knock like speech in the blood"; an early poem begins "Between the fever and the stone, / the nerve's kick and the clay's condition"; and in a third poem, although "morning's artery beats up" vigorously at dawn, at night we are apt to grow faint of heart:

> I believe in the blood
> turning small, as it must, in the evening hour,
> turning down with the sparrow,
> convicted by the vein in the cut hay.*

The way she manipulates language is unique: "turning" and "small" shift momentously their denotative scope; "cut" is postponed until it flashes out, even before the wrong word, "hay"; and "convicted" tightens the moral passion of what started as mere mood- and ego-play. Not only is she different from any poet now writing, Randall reminds me only fitfully of writers from the past—this, despite the fact that (as T. S. Eliot was audible in the three passages above) her mimicry of other poets is pervasive.

The contradictory nature of this poet can be phrased another way. I have attested to my impression that she is stubbornly strange, different; yet I must also admit that I find her, in her poems, recognizable, recurrent, even monotonous. Her stylistic decisions frequently involve her in pleonasm; she seldom refrains from, and more often than not dramatically yields the poem to, overtexturing, over-wording. A concomitant of this lush too-much-ness of many of the poems is their structural stasis; many are content not to develop ideas either associatively or syntactically, although the very syntactic ambiguity may imitate a sort of movement, whether intellectual, as in this powerful sentence fragment:

> Aquin, thy servant in the tongue
> to sip the honey, justice, tell
> proportion, recommend the strong

---

* The poetry volumes will be abbreviated as follows: *ST* (*The Solstice Tree*, Contemporary Poets, 1952); *MA* (*Mimic August*, Contemporary Poets, 1960); *PC* (*The Puritan Carpenter*, Univ. North Carolina Press, 1965); *AD* (*Adam's Dream*, Knopf, 1969); and *FW* (*The Farewells*, Elpenor Books, 1981). The three sources above are *AD* 69, *ST* 8, and *AD* 103.

Julia Randall

Julia Randall was born in Baltimore in 1923. She graduated from Bennington College, and, after a year of medical school, from the Writing Seminars at Johns Hopkins. For most of her life she has taught English, most happily at Hollins College in Virginia (1962–1973). She has been the recipient of two N.E.A. grants, of an award from the National Institute of Arts and Letters, and of the Shelley Award from the Poetry Society of America (1980). She lives in North Bennington, Vermont. ■

to a strong course, perfection's—thus
ranging, in time, perfection's match:
union, indwelling, ecstasy
in every love, as mirrors each of each.
("**Question: Of the Effects of Love,**" *ST* 16)

or whether the poem makes a lyrical statement in syntactic "gestures" whose connections are illusory (I've used italics to pinpoint the syntactic sleight-of-hand):

Over the cut stars
the weeds' heal washes.
In the old dark of the gods
their light *voices*
tender a ghost to breathe
down the long *streams* of love—
sun, serpent, maiden, dove—
for his drowned *faces*.
("**Field Mowing,**" *AD* 78)

The "plot" or order of a typical poem by Julia Randall may begin with the statement of a theme (frequently as it inheres in a quality); then follows euphonious thematic elaboration; thematic restatement from an altered perspective, perhaps by sounding a profane, impatient, worldly note; then further elaboration in the mode of this second, secular movement, or chastened return to the original rhetoric. Her method is that of accretion and digression. As befits a poet longer on ornament than argument, the favored syntax will be the laden fragment, as in the gorgeous conclusion to "Hardwood Country":

So, sourwood, a skint and vital thread.

So, tupelo, great thigh and golden head.
So, wasted Ilion, that burned for Greece,
Hekabe helled, and winter in the house
of all but poetry, whose haut amens
skitter to sleep beside the evergreens.
(*FW*, 23)

Furthermore, Julia Randall is often tempted to resolve her poems with similarly thorough rhetorical closure, seeking effects too automatically beautiful, too majestically final. These resolutions sometimes begin halfway through the work; that is, they reach so far *back* toward the origins or germ of the poem as to burn it with too much nourishment.

A third tendency accompanying those of pleonasm in the style and stasis in the structure is the profoundly serious mimicry Randall has carried out, beginning with *The Solstice Tree* in 1952 (whose 24 poems were practically swamped by their cargo of Wallace Stevens—the *Harmonium* Stevens rather than he of "It Must Be Abstract"). She has also indulged in a gentler and more exacting mimicry of that half-lit, happily anonymous world of songs and airs and ballads and hymns, as in the lovely poem that opens *Mimic August* (1960):

Who tells a color?
Fennel and rose
That sprang in winter
From the crippled ice.
Who tells my true love?
For the heart's cold
That sought a stranger's son
Low to the world.
("A Carolling," *MA* 9)

When such simplicity of voice is subjected to the high pressure of great idiosyncrasy, it yields the gnomic rhetoric of a William Blake, Emily Dickinson, or W. B. Yeats (of *Words for Music Perhaps*)—three poets who also hover over and echo through Julia Randall's work, along with the writers of the Pentateuch, the Psalms, and the Protestant Episcopal Hymnal. And these are but a handful of the spokesmen-of-the-Tradition she invokes. To them should be added the voices of G. M. Hopkins, T. S. Eliot, George Herbert, John Milton, the Romantic trio of Shelley, Keats, and Wordsworth, as well as the minor bards of her childhood, Campbell, Scott, Macaulay, Byron, Arnold, Longfellow, Moore, Kingsley, Henley, Housman, Stevenson, and Hemans. The list bespeaks a generosity of poetical effects at once wearisome and splendid.

One danger of ventriloquism on such a scale is, of course, that it may stall the poem. Where a work is most successful as echo-chamber, it may be most tentative or fragile as a habitation of one's own; and where most adept at the externals, the poem of homage and indebtedness may be least inwardly motivated, least independently flexed:

And Yeats may dine at journey's end
With Landor and with Donne
And all irascible scribbling men
Who put such passion on
For Helen's honey-banded brow
And the iron-browed God of heaven
Their hearts grew thick upon the pain
And toughened, until now
They pump a more than mortal balm

Upon our sores, and sing us calm.
      ("The Company," *PC* 15)

"The Company" is clearly more Yeatsian even than the wryly subdued Yeats who wrote the admonition "To a Young Beauty," which ends with the reference to dining in the afterlife with the two eccentric minor luminaries, W. S. Landor and John Donne. The echo from this one Yeats poem opens the sluices for all the "major" Yeatsian effects Randall brings down: the "all" intensive; the seeding of the if/then causal construction in the less assuming "such" adverb; Yeats's homely yet agile practice of double epithets; his favored phrases of disguise ("put on") and the preposition of proof or vow, "upon"—not to mention the introduction of heaven and Helen. To this lavish convocation of Yeatsian effects, Randall adds only the impudent-sounding verb "pump" and the unsavory "sores." The mimicry here is not enabling, rather programmatic.

But on the other side of the mimetic ledger are her songs, uncanny, half-literary, half-ditty, borne effortlessly forward along a crooning undermelody, in which the grotesque subjects familiar in Yeats, Dickinson, and in the more limited songs of Blake and Roethke have been alchemized by Randall into her own unique artifacts that, although transparent on the surface, are metaphorically turbid. *The Puritan Carpenter* (1965) is the watershed volume for such "metaphysical ballads," including the title sequence, the unholy "Advent Poems, 1963," the sinister "Boundbrook," the sprightly and bemused "Ballad of Eve," a child's poem called "A Windy Kerchief," a love poem, "There Was a Bird," the unassuming "Figure," the mysterious and grim "Journey," and the cryptic "Maid's Song," complete in two stanzas:

Maid's Song

I wept on cypress knees,
I made a coat of moss,
I took the glowing worm
And hid him from the grass.

The river moved but once,
I could not plant my foot,
I'd mouths about my arm.
At last my love went out.
      (*PC* 24)

This is a Daphne driven from *within* to seek the intervention of vegetative matter. No Apollo is at hand to force her; in fact the maid willingly hides the glowing worm in her very foliage. But worse than this indulgence is the failure of sexual love to withstand the torture of change by which we will our own helplessness into being: "I could not plant my foot," that is, I was as bad a tree as I was wavering and unreliable a girl. "At last my love went out," that is, not even the sacrifice of my chastity was sufficient curative for my lover's yearning for me. I am uncertain whether the mouths about her arm are the mouths of birds or fishes—has she fallen into the water? "The river moved but once." The single movement of the river carries both local setting and orgasmic suggestion: she has not been growing very long, in either "country," before being uprooted by what is more powerful than she.

Like a certain category of *written* song that does not seem to need the addition of music for its poignant force (Louise Bogan's "Masked Woman's Song" is another example), Randall's airs and quatrains are peculiarly refractory to headwork and argument. Their beauty is a function of their purity and irreducibility. Although the sheer number of these in *The Puritan Carpenter* may be daunting, the metaphysical ballads in *Adam's Dream* (1969), fewer in number, are yet more dependent on their rhetoric of airless suffering. Of particular interest are the songs that re-envision incarnation and metamorphosis in tropes borrowed from biochemistry, "Earth Science," "Singing Christmas," and the brutal "Sleep Songs":

> Put on your tradesman's gown:
> > *the ribbon in the cell:*
> the shrew is creeping all alone
> under the drowsing owl.
>
> Put off your peace:
> > *the duct, the sluice,*
> > *the tooth, the telling lip:*
> stand up.

At last, in *The Farewells* (1981), Randall brings the metaphysical ballad to fruition in poems that are both less anxious and more flexible (for example, the culminating sequence of monologues on entering heaven; or poems like "Jill upon Love & Language"); but, as I will argue shortly, the principles of the metaphysical ballad are finely embedded in her last volume in new modes and occasions, where the intensity of song is tempered by other forms of speech.

We could entertain various reductive explanations for these qualities of composite strangeness and of inclusive otherness in the work of Julia Randall. She is southern, rural, "gentry," thoroughly educated, schooled as well in matters liturgical and, willingly or no, marked out by her twisted approaches to religious faith. At the elegiac close of her wandering she expects to encounter the paradox: "in the silence, singing on the track / to the home of my fathers, no gods, / but they'd welcome me back" (*FW* 70). In addition, Randall is an initiate of the Word from the perspective of the *Dozent,* having lectured for upwards of 20 years at colleges and universities, more than 10 of those years at Hollins College, where she wrote part of *The Puritan Carpenter* and all of *Adam's Dream,* these being her first two substantial books. For a decade she was a yeoman lecturer on Dickens and George Eliot, James and Conrad, Lawrence and Woolf, as well as the major poets of the British tradition: she was not a teacher of creative writing. She has thus performed the basic task of a humanist and an educator, to simplify, generalize, categorize, and propound ideals as they are to be educed through the great books.

At the same time, unlike W. H. Auden, Louise Bogan, T. S. Eliot, and Howard Nemerov, to name only four poets who have written much good and influential prose, Randall has published very little prose, done almost no reviewing, and generally held aloof from the bourse of current aesthetic debate as well as the bright kiosks of reputation. Although one may suspect that such relative obscurity as continues to attend her may suit her temperament, this retirement from prose has had the unfortunate effect of keeping her books of poems out of the public eye, even out of print. Still, she is wise about the pitfalls of opinion, given the weaknesses of human character. She says to William Wordsworth from Virginia, "I think, old bone, the world's not with us much. / I think it is too difficult to see, / But easy to discuss" (*PC* 6). She recognizes the profound gap between discussing the world in a flawed and endlessly mediate way and seeing it in a pure and passionately immediate way—between talking (which is what most contemporary writers know too well how to do, even in verse) and singing (which is what she reflexively turns to, even when her subject is prosaic).

One of the strongest signs of Julia Randall's work is the conflict between these two modes—between a poetry whose emblems are archetypal and hermetic ("I pulled the knife out of my side, / And ashes greased the floor like blood," PC 45), and a conversation on "idle" whose constant purr tells us that the Valley Cleaners have lost her winter coat, or that she puts newspapers on the kitchen floor ("against dog tracks, / boot tracks, sink splashes, and spilled beer," AD 73). Randall has tenaciously tried to introduce the broader appetite and more leisurely discursiveness into the milieu of dense feeling. Many of her poems in the discursive mode flag, but even these may contain one or more of those passages, familiar to all readers of Randall, in which her personality asserts itself as a touchstone, her local history becomes a measure of our common humanity, and her own Eastern-basin landscapes unearth the shell and seed of the indigenous imagination: "place, too, is our ancestor." Gently, mildly, the land of the heart turns to us its human profile:

> Somewhere, Sir Thomas Browne,
> In a friend's face, dying, saw a ghost a bone
> Rise, and the family feature
> Clear off the curves of earned, familiar nature:
> Lusts, comforts, every lineament of school,
> Or private light of industry or travel.
> Pure Peter vanished, and the patient lay
> Pure Willoughby, pure Cameron, family clay
> Startled to reclamation. Then if place,
> Too, is our ancestor (that is
> The forever England concept), this low east,
> Like love, rides in the gesture of my flesh.
> ("**Maryland,**" *PC* 22)

But despite several such powerfully reticent verse paragraphs, "Maryland," which is 82 lines long, is full of strange and funny lists ("Pigeons, watermelon, Edgar Allan / Poe, the Star Spangled / Banner"), arch, aimless chatter, and a patent discomfort with the obligations of form, social and prosodic, and at the same time an eagerness to believe in, suffer for, and earn them a place. But her brisk, rational, pedagogical side with its fund of ideas and closets full of points (including points about her own poems from the outsider's vantage—"I suspect," she says in a letter, "we should all be better poets if we were less well educated") is chain-mailed to do battle against her lyrical or dream side, the deep habitual responses, the hot, straightened, and tortuous expression that sounds like pure, rippling melody, or like pure sobbing.

Adam's Dream is the volume where the two attitudes seem to lie at the greatest distance from each other. The discursive poems tend to be flat, unnecessarily detailed, dilatory; the lyrics cruel, obscure, and, as I said earlier, "airless." The dream of the title, being two-fold, may help to explain the polarity. In the excerpt from *Paradise Lost* that opens the book, Adam recalls to the emissary Raphael what it was like when he first tried to speak (he found that he knew the names of everything around him); then he called on the natural creation, by name, to tell him how he got there and who made him (VIII, 267–282). It is after this request that Adam falls asleep and is visited by a dream in which a shape divine leads him to paradise, where each fruit stirred in him a sudden appetite to pluck and eat. At this, he woke "and found / Before mine Eyes all real, as the dream / Had lively shadow'd" (VIII, 309–311). His Creator in person then shows him his new world, warns him against the Tree whose operation brings knowledge of good and ill, and encourages Adam to name the beasts. (Both before and after the first dream-of-the-earth, Adam is gifted with an automatic faculty of naming.) Then they discuss Adam's request for a mate. And now, for the the second time after his "birth," Milton's God puts Adam to sleep. During his second dream, which is roughly analogous to the story in *Genesis,* Eve is created. Adam sees during his second sleep, with the internal sight of Fancy, everything that happens to him: the removal of the rib; the wide wound streaming with cordial spirits, or warm blood; the second creature as she emerges under God's hand; the healing of the wound; the sweetness flooding his being at the sight of her. Then he awakens and finds her nearby, "Such as I saw her in my dream" (VIII, 482). This is the passage of Book VIII cited by Walter

Jackson Bate in the biography as the one Keats had in mind when he wrote to Bailey: "The Imagination may be compared to Adam's dream—he awoke and found it truth."

Randall is fascinated by both of Adam's dreams, the dream of the erotic counterpart and the dream of the new earth, in both of which John Milton stresses the quality of flowing: first as the earth presents its "liquid Lapse of murmuring Streams" and a fragrant, smiling aspect that "o'erflow'd" Adam's heart; then as Eve is created during his warm swoon when he can see and feel the sweet flowing of blood from his side. To the dream of the earth, in her title poem of *Adam's Dream,* the poet adds the secular perspective of the astrophysical cynic ("Mountains crumble, planets cool"), and the announcement that man's arrival is a blot on paradise:

> When Adam woke,
> when Adam woke,
> all the silver waters broke,
> all the beasts stood up to mourn,
> and the maples and the thorn
> laid down their leaves
> when time began.
>
> Silver cities rise and fall
> for Adam's dream.
> Mountains crumble, planets cool
> for Adam's dream.
> Adam's neighbor, Adam's son
> watch the sea swing up and down,
> roast and shiver, spit and turn
> for Adam's dream.
> ("Adam's Dream," 1, *AD* 48)

Although Randall's earth is fluid, too, in its way, the waters "roast and shiver, spit and turn" and all the silver waters break. The unified undine imagery in Milton is severed into hard, atomic, lifeless bits by an Adam whose dream sounds like a five-year urban renewal plan.

The erotic dream of Adam is correspondingly confounded by the fact that (as in "Variations: The Puritan Carpenter" in 1965) the speaker of this suite of poems is both male and female—or, more often, a female who cannot sympathize with or touch Adam's misguided, deep enchantments. The woman is witness and sufferer, but not heroic center: "Once I lay / where Adam stood. / Day's eye, night's lid. / And dreamed a dream out of my side / and woke and it was blood" (*AD* 49). Again in poems #6 and #8, the woman's desire to empathize with the firstborn Adam's consciousness leads into labyrinths out of Celtic lore by the Brothers Grimm: "Between two dreams, / bloody and rare, / my heartways cross. / A shade hangs there"; "At the root of Adam's tree, / woundmaster, grow me. / Ditchdrought, hailstone, / blood rot, stranglevine" (*AD* 51, 52). Finally Eve must embody her desperation in direct questions and still further images:

> When the nerve of day is struck,
> Adam, what shall be my light?
> Who shall take it from my side?
> Will it breathe? And will it bleed?
>
> Shall I know it for my mate?
> Shall I fear it? Shall I get
> breed that couples in the dark?
> ("Adam's Dream," 7, *AD* 51)

After destruction of the earthly paradise, what recourse? what light? what to believe in? The two dreams tangle unmercifully here. The "it" that needs to be taken from the speaker's side ("what shall be my light? / Who shall take it from my side?") is connotatively woven from an irrational shimmer of meanings. The "it" is Adam's rib, to be sure; also the spear in Christ's side, if the nerve of day is struck; but the urgency for its removal also suggests the birth-labor of ideas, Minerva driven from the bone of Jupiter, also the parturition of incestuous offspring ("Shall I know it for my mate?…Shall I get / breed that couples in the dark?").

The title poem of *Adam's Dream* thus energetically promotes associations that it cannot dispel, or choose among. It is frequently a sign of pre-emergent thought in Randall's work that beautiful and striking lines do not yield viable interpretations. "I think," she says in another letter, "that I sometimes use music to temper confusion." But in this particular volume, the confusion of Christ with Adam with Eve with Zeus with the lateborn poet is achieved under the erotic sign of mating, breeding, coupling—a sexual darkness. And indeed I suspect that much of the trembling, diffuse energy of this book is owing to the experience of a consuming dark Eros, whom Iris Murdoch calls "the Black Prince":

> I tried to find you in the tongues of my body,
> along the walls of my heart
>
> …
>
> Then I tried how my tongue would speak you or how my hand
> would feed you, how my blood would clear and run
> with your color.
> ("**Loving 2**," *AD* 35)

The woman in "His Wife Wounded" has a wound in her throat "stretched wide as summer," "twisting, so that no words might come out" (*AD* 31). The poet-speaker of "As Theory" says she confounded her own simplicity "'for a man / who would not hear a wonder / in the old common tongue'" (*AD* 36). The poem "Letter" addresses an absent one: "The heat is terrific. The storms are terrible…It will not change here…Have you found a new face / in your foreign desert?…Your empty parking-slot and unkempt yard / image you like a mold. I can fill them in / with the old features. I do not feel love loosening" (*AD* 38–39). In another poem a blood-streaked lily given her by an old lady farmer scents her room "like a live smoke" during a fiery summer when the crops pale, her father sickens, and her passion enfeebles her: "When I tried to make love, I wept" (*AD,* 29). And, returning again to the imagery of the wound in both Eve and Adam, one of two paired political poems in the book mingles social with sexual guilt:

> My own sight
> gutters when it must
> spot its familiars: lust,
> missed duty and willed waste,
> false manner, murdering dream,
> affection bound and beaten.
> Fear, when the man splits wide
> of his wars, and the fleshed side
> shows its infection…
> ("**September 1, 1961**," *AD* 75)

The new Adam of appetite and injustice has given form to a grotesquely diseased body, part Grail King, part Christabel, and the landscape is peopled by his/her goblins and nightmares—"familiars" of a failed magician.

In one of her few essays, on the contemporary British novelist Iris Murdoch, Julia Randall reminds her readers of the Christian belief, discussed by Virgil and Dante in *Purgatorio* XVIII, that "although every love kindled within us arises of necessity, the power to arrest it is within us, and that we are judged according as we use this power to garner and winnow good and evil loves" (*The Hollins Critic,* February 1976). Comforting and tidy, if true; but what if something is not quite right here? Randall now addresses one of the central and frightening themes of Murdoch, most bleakly presented in *The Time of the Angels:* "But what if desire is a machine, and the power to arrest the machine is *not* within us? What if love (physical love at any rate) is simply the destroyer, a destroyer that theology has no power to circumvent, psychology no power to appease?"

It is no surprise that Randall merely brushes her shoulder against this elegantly packaged rhetorical question, before moving off to sprightlier considerations. Her image of a Black Prince as the destroyer who cannot be appeased is powerful, but, given her background and predilections, literary and liturgical, repellent to her; hence the extent to which such a force appeared in her own poetry would be the extent to which its existence would need to be masked, postponed, wilfully transmuted. *Adam's Dream* is perhaps the uneven record of a deflection, if not an abnegation, of her subject.

The two visions of Milton's Adam in *Paradise Lost* do not, of course, necessarily pair off with the conversational, discursive poems of Randall on one hand, or with her hieratic, compressed lyrics on the other. But the two subjects, the beautiful creation and the perfect erotic complement, are definitely her favored subjects, expressed impurely in the "difficult" runes and enticing concealments of *Adam's Dream.* In *The Farewells,* however, the elegiac mood brings both the fading vision of an earthly paradise and the lost loves into unaccustomed harmony. Furthermore, the harmony so justly and amiably alternates the two modes that it emphatically recalls by negation what must have been their earlier isolation as the reticent and the voluble. The verse in *The Farewells* is more candid, as if to say: What I earlier teased into the poems by implication was not worth concealing. At the same time, the verse is itself stronger in its knitting-up by interior rhyme, line-break, and dramatic syntax, allowing Randall to treat her political (especially environmental) and personal losses alike with convincing passion, anger, and the high remorse of a great natural tragedienne whose most astonishing gestures are the simplest to execute.

"A Farewell to History" is a clear salute to the fellow of her flesh, and a leavetaking. With a sigh of relief, the poet names what she has outgrown the patience for, from reproduction caryatids to discussions that begin with God "and end up breaking teeth." The 140 lines of "Album Leaves" comprise six suites, or tableaus, one of "Kenneth making stew / at 13 rue de Savoie":

> "You've
> got to build it on the meat." Indeed you do.
> It was too cold to keep your feet
> on that floor. When the chauffage failed, we took a stall at the Comique
> and jogged home out of breath
> across the Pont-Neuf.
> How shall I use that death?
> **("Album Leaves," 5, FW 28)**

The question, how to use that death, has been answered (by name, by anecdote, by admission that this "death" was once breathless, giddy, and alive) by the time it is posed in words. The words themselves represent a compromise between the ordinary and the "poetic" (that is, rhyme, alternating measure, alliteration, elegance of syntactic management). With their own colloquial pressures, the ironic emphases of conversation ("Indeed you do," "that floor," "chauffage" = heat, "Comique" = Opera comique, "jogged") flatten the little explosions of rhyme and euphony (from the more overt "thirteen," "meat," "feet," "Comique," to the less, "stew," "rue," "You've," "do," "too," "Neuf," "use"), which one nearly fails to hear with the waking senses. But that "nearly" is enough to distinguish what we hear from prose.

More active counterpoint, in the following passage from "The Trackers," negotiates line and line-break in a fashion peculiar to Julia Randall, who employs rhyme not only to bind together bits of unlike phrases that happen to fall on the same line of verse, but also to control the speed with which the line is read. Even out of context, three lines from this passage, "day, into jay," "windrow. And Hershfield's low," and "Sinai is silent," illustrate the isochronous effect of intralinear rhyme across lines of varying length and continuity. The first will tend to drawl out between the rhyming syllables "day" and "jay," in order to make the interval commensurate with the curtailing of the longer second interval between "windrow" and "low." In context, however, still finer and more numerous consonances and rhythmic pegs measure lines, link line-ends, define syntactic phrase ("waking/day," "wren…bent/windrow"), and catch the least like elements in a net of off-beat, accidental likeness, as masculine "strings" hitches forward to its feminine echoes in "waking" and "stuttering." Randall is speaking about a pack of hounds who run through her woods:

> …but they cannot feast
> on my pawky bones, on my breast
> strings, for the prize is sped
> from my arms into waking
> day, into jay
> scream, and the house wren
> stuttering into the bent
> windrow. And Hershfield's low
> Sinai is silent.
> (FW 24)

Musically, these new poems are at once more relaxed and more direct. So also syntactically the poems now, more unequivocally than before, forge relations between actor and object, and, as a result, thematically the poems can manage to be more casual without relinquishing nuance. The bird in "The Kingfisher, February" is both literally present on Long Green Branch and a symbol of the divine breaking into time. In "The Trackers," the lover has been loosed into dream, pursuing the poem's speaker, catching up, establishing the new terms of an old combat. But these new terms are planted in the literal (laurel, oak, Hershfield's Hill) and end there at morning; the hounds' fearsome acceleration upon their prey (note how they *round* the oak roots) is channeled into spontaneous daybreak:

> Hounds I have never seen run in my dream
> down schist and shale where I have never been
> on Hershfield's Hill, bursting the laurel cover,
> rounding oak roots. I hear them over and over.
> Some farm a mile away
> must loose them. There is nothing there by day.
>
> And what do they sing, with their bell voices,
> soft eyes, strained haunches
> unleashed in the night wood?
> Dream-blood, dream-blood.
> …

And I
fall, piecemeal—
tooth, tongue, nail—but they cannot feast
on my pawky bones, on my breast
strings, for the prize is sped
from my arms into waking
day, into jay
scream, and the house wren
stuttering into the bent
windrow. And Hershfield's low
Sinai is silent.

Just as, in "The Trackers," Randall views the demon lover through this local, domestic lens, so throughout *The Farewells*, by way of making peace with her more enduring loves, she reduces the parts played by earlier mentors. Wallace Stevens, for example, is audible only in a passing reference to Mt. Chocorua in "Album Leaves" and in the first stanza of "Hardwood Country," which echoes his "Large Red Man Reading": "poet and peasant in the glow of things / reading of earth and sky the finite rhymes" (*FW* 22). W. B. Yeats shrinks back into a place-name as a little bird calls "along the shadowy groves at Coole / bidding the sycamores farewell. / Farewell" (*FW* 15), while his Crazy Jane figure shifts eastward two degrees to become Jill, Randall's open-eyed Muse "who keep[s] an undegraded eye / and tongue to tell a master by" (*FW* 63). William Wordsworth, who played such a prominent role, by name and by influence, throughout *The Puritan Carpenter,* is present only in the small corner of this second tableau of "Album Leaves." I suspect that the stumbling rhymes of "were," "wicker," "Schopenhauer," and "picture" are intended to smarten up or counteract, with their mild jaggedness, the lilting triple meters that alternate with the classic Wordsworthian iambs into which Randall easily falls beginning with the third line:

Views. Remember Elephant Rock,
domed poll and back
rising above the tide? From one blue glass
on Aunt Louisa's table, I can get
completely around her house. I still end up
at the Harvard Classics—brave new names they were,
then: Aristotle, Schopenhauer.
Girl in a wicker chair, a scene of the self. "The picture
of the mind revives again," but only the picture.
The mind is here with us, composing, quarrying
old summer silences. The tide
rises and falls.
   (**"Album Leaves," 2, FW 26**)

Randall "answers" the line from "Tintern Abbey" with an opposing and uncooperative rhythm, "but *ON*ly the *PIC*ture"—two amphibrachs that sullenly face the beautifully modulated but actually rather plain remark of Wordsworth's, "The picture of the mind revives again," which in context weeps a little for what it has lost:

And now, with gleams of half-extinguished thought,
With many recognitions dim and faint,
And somewhat of a sad perplexity,
The picture of the mind revives again...
   (**"Tintern Abbey," 1798, 11. 58–61**)

Not only does Randall muffle its iambics in her reply, she also distorts the shape and emphasis of Wordsworth's line by splitting it across the line-break, thereby forcing it to stress the flimsiness of mere *appearance* in light of real mental work.

This is not what he meant, as Randall the Professor well knows. Her misconstruction implies her decision to take the "picture" as something alienated from the original stream of feeling. Images of her family, in the real as well as the mental album she has kept, are all too easily summoned; but these images are mute, and the beaches now deserted:

> …we waded, spoke
> words that were histories without a book
> to save them, unless we
> are the book we cannot read,
> dark documents of seasons with the dead.
> **("Album Leaves," 2, FW 26)**

Julia Randall would finally quarrel with the constitutive strength of recollection in tranquility, hinting at the irretrievability of language and meaning from the past, the difficulty of making it anew in the present. Equally difficult is the effort to *affirm*. Dedicated to her younger brother and composed in the leafless clarity of January, 1976, "Album Leaves" closes with these words of poignant relinquishment:

> How to bless—
> we don't know that. Of suffering
> we know something: the child's cry
> of separation tunes us till we die. Of sacrifice
> this little: brothers all, who lay
> leaf over leaf, to leafless clarity.
> **("Album Leaves," 6, FW 29)**

These notes—the child's cry of separation from the womb, home, belovedness; the "tuning," schooling, trimming, and constriction of yearning by our experience of solitude; the laying of the leaf of the present over the leaf of the past as year rises on bleak year; and the elegiac identification that extends from her to us, "brothers all"—these are the choruses of Randall's new song. Family clay is startled to reclamation by the approach of death, as she wrote in "Maryland," but even in life the nearness of pain and loss returns all of us to the family sod, tunes all of us to one voice, "a dream of dying," she writes in "The Soloist," "alien / to our last blood, so unoriginal to the end, / 'Father' (it cries), 'and friend'" (*FW* 48). We crave the clichés of companionship and familial caress to the extent that we are driven by our solitudes. To the extent, however, that we are driven by our frictions, we try to escape the heavy parent, the draining friend. However prodigal the child, the father who has ever eluded him has the last word whenever he opens *his* mouth:

> Aging, I found a father in my face
> and did not love him, rusty man
> that he was, not even for childhood's sake.
> And then my tongue, his make
> and rebel, trimmed my youth
> and age of fable. Then it spoke
> home truth.
> **("The Prodigal Enters Heaven," FW 58)**

Randall is not alluding to any hereditary determinism but to the inevitable reduction, under life's harrow, of two important relationships, to which we must ultimately respond with reverence.

One of these is the gift of living things, which are nevertheless being destroyed even as we breathe: "Oh loud / companionable light, what air / shall we inspire when you are mute?" (*FW* 66). Across landscapes that are by turns ravaged and precariously reclaimed, dying and momentarily smothered in blooms, a little bird flits, warbling. He begins in the first poem of *The Farewells,* in the shadowy groves at Coole. He screams as jay and stutters as house wren in "The Trackers." He flutes his five quick notes as Papageno in "The Bird Who Sang Mozart"—and indeed a dove-tailed Mozartian delicacy and reserve have been a crucial inspiration for the new harmony Randall has devised to link the old stylistic poles of prose and ballad. The bird appears again, majestically, as the angelic kingfisher, endangered by the practices that convict us of irreverence to the created world: "My diver, what dread beings, / or brotherly, die daily to our sight?" (*FW* 75).

And as these last lines from "The Kingfisher, February" suggest, the second important relationship life reduces us to is analogous to the first. The natural world we must mourn harbors the human one we must constantly lose as the self struggles to winnow its good loves from the chaff of remorse. In the poem that cunningly draws so many of her themes to a close, Sophocles' blinded Oedipus moves out of life, accompanied by birdsong (in *Oedipus at Colonus* the birds are a feathered choir of nightingales). Kithairon is the mountain where Oedipus had been abandoned by his father Laius with a stake through his feet. It is not far from Thebes, where he eventually ruled in his father's stead. Now, as then, the choir is the same, as is the passage they perform: *our* music, self-time, but perfected and unearthly. The only king who didn't desert Oedipus in a worldly sense was Theseus; but on an eternal view, the only loyal king was Zeus, who brought Oedipus his death:

A Farewell to Music

There is a time for meeting lords of time,
as father, brother, lover, muse, and friend,
in single combat; times when the mind,
learning itself like muscles, separates
thighs, fingers, diaphragm,
substance and dream.

This is self-time, the oracle that speaks
decision at the crossroads doubly heard,
once in the sequence of the royal bed,
once in the right-of-way cleared by the sword.

Last, at Colonus, when the catalogue
is near complete, and we forget
whose *Grosse Fugue* this is—Mozart,
Beethoven?—and the performer,
whoever he is, repeats the ingenious
dove-tailed design, at last there come
the rooks to silence him, the shelter
of this old grove, this sacred nine
moving like music in the stream,
one choir that rose on Kithairon
abandoned of all kings but one.
(*FW* 47)

The movement implied by the title, *The Farewells,* namely the reduction of the human actor to the last few realities of any importance, solves the problem mentioned earlier of overly thor-

■ **BOOKS BY JULIA RANDALL**

The Solstice Tree. Baltimore: Contemporary Poets Series, 1952.

Mimic August. Baltimore: Contemporary Poets Series, 1960.

Four Poems. Roanoke, Va.: Tinker Press, 1964.

The Puritan Carpenter. Chapel Hill: University of North Carolina Press, 1965.

Adam's Dream. New York: Knopf, 1969.

The Farewells. Chicago: Elpenor Books, 1981.

Moving in Memory: Poems. Baton-Rouge: Louisiana State University Press, 1987.

The Path to Fairview: New and Selected Poems. Baton-Rouge: Louisiana State University Press, 1992.

---

ough, and too precipitate, rhetorical closure in the poems. Now each poem from its inception is immersed in the long process of anagnorisis or recognition, by the performing consciousness, of the laws of our particular being and the Force that has included us in a great fugal composition. Julia Randall has found the right concentration and the proper unified dramatic embodiment for her double dream of fading love and diminished paradise, in poems that affirm what they must leave. And she has found the proper register for her voice. Poems like "A Farewell to Music" distinguish her as one of our few serious lyric poets.

Mary Kinzie
February, 1983

UPDATE

Julia Randall has since published two more books of poetry, *Moving in Memory: Poems* (1987), and *The Path to Fairview: New and Selected Poems* (1992). She also co-edited, with Louis D. Rubin and Jerry Leath Mills, *The Algonquin Literary Quiz Book* (1990).

"Julia Randall writes the sort of canticle that only good sinners can write, a praise of created things that seems, because of its secularization, to rise more spontaneously and with a completely open lyricism" (*Virginia Quarterly Review*). Although some critics have found her work imitative, too aware of poetry as literature, most, like critic Robert Wallace, appreciate her "wise" and "astonishingly pure" evocations.

The Path to Fairview: New and Selected Poems spans more than forty years, including both the earlier, "somewhat self-absorbed reflections and . . . more authoritative, outward-looking later work," according to *Publishers Weekly.* "Randall's most engaging poems capture the pleasure of isolated moments, especially as they feed the imagination. . . ."

Volubility, Exile, and Cunning: The Fiction of Frederic Raphael

Cleanth Brooks used to talk sometimes about how literature was "diagnostic." He never claimed it was of any therapeutic use, either because he didn't like polemical poetry and fiction, or, more simply, because, as a man of good sense, he knew that poems and novels don't fix anything. But, as he suggested, they can tell us a great deal about ourselves, if we know how to ask the questions with the right tact and circumspection. I was reminded of his remarks when I came across what I take to be a crucial passage in one of Frederic Raphael's novels. He writes, toward the end of *Like Men Betrayed,* of the condition of exile:

> His mind is calm. He is like a husband, long deceived, who has decided on practical steps. He will no longer sit at home under a burden of anguish, pretending to know nothing of what eats his heart. He has a scheme; he has accomplices who are not exactly certain of his motives but who will certainly arrange that things go smoothly. Vengeance was his dream; action displaces it. It is not the only motive which now stimulates him; there are also the pleasures of secrecy and of surprise. It is he who is the deceiver now. A plot makes every movement of the plotter significant. He might be detected at every moment; every moment when he is not is a minute triumph. Freedom is deception. The future has a shape now; the new diary is not a succession of empty leaves but is marked with crucial, if innocent-looking, appointments. The exile feels fully grown at last; he is leaving the scenes of his childhood; he will be distant from those who would write off his present opinions as the obvious fruit of a past they can trace only too easily; he turns his back on those who mutter that the apple never falls far from the tree. He breaks out like a figure in a tapestry from the stitching which makes him a mere shadow in a landscape. He will no longer be goaded to indignant pain by the sound of prattling passers-by in the main square who parade unaware of the oppression under which they live.

As is the case with many of Raphael's paradoxical observations, one's first reaction is to the sheer wit of the conception, and only later does there come an appreciation of its uncomfortable or merely melancholy truth. Raphael has other versions of this particular view of imposture and dissimulation as conditions for a heightened, intensified kind of life. In *Heaven and Earth*, for example, he talks about the existence of a spy:

> What a strange pleasure there must be in having a cover story, something false to which it becomes a duty to remain true! Every action must be satisfying at that point; nothing you do must be sincere, everything is a fake for a genuine purpose.

Raphael's life has been one in which exile, or at least calculation of one form or another, has been a given. Born in Chicago, educated at Charterhouse and St. Johns, Cambridge, a nov-

Frederic Raphael

Frederic Michael Raphael was born August 14, 1931, in Chicago, Illinois, but was educated in England at Charterhouse and received his M.A. from St. Johns College, Cambridge, in 1954. In 1955 he married Sylvia Betty Glatt. Raphael is known as a writer of novels, short stories, film scripts, screenplays, biographies, and translations. He has been a contributor to periodicals and a fiction critic since 1962. He has worked at the *Sunday Times* and is also an author for the Independent Television Network and of radio plays for the British Broadcasting Corporation. Raphael is a member of the Royal Society of Literature.

Raphael won the Lippincott Prize in 1961. In 1965 his critically acclaimed screenplay *Darling* won the British Screenwriters' award for best original screenplay, the British Film Academy award, and an Oscar from the Academy of Motion Picture Arts and Sciences (United States). He received another Oscar nomination in 1966 for the screenplay *Two for the Road*. He was also named Writer of the Year by the Royal Television Society in 1976. Raphael has lived in Britain, France, and Greece, and has con-

veyed the atmosphere of foreign places in his writing. Having written more than twenty novels, numerous screenplays, and translations of Greek plays, Frederic Raphael comments, "For me, the novelist is, above all, the historian of conscience." ■

elist of great distinction who is, however, better known for his screenplays (*Darling, Two for the Road, Far from the Madding Crowd*), an Anglo-American Jew who lives now mostly in France, he is more sensitive to the stitching in the tapestry because it has always been a matter of conscious effort to seem to be one of "them" (whoever they are). It was, when he was a schoolboy, much easier to blend in. And in his curious way, he excelled at blending in, becoming more English than the English. Classically trained, as the upper-level civil servants used to be, he writes a dandified prose that flaunts low-frequency words likely to send even high-brow readers to their large dictionaries. And as these occasionally arcane words suggest, he is proud of what he takes to be the privileges of exile. Earlier in *Like Men Betrayed*, he has a not particularly sympathetic character remark:

Shall I tell you the real weakness of Karl Marx? He was an exile twice over. A Jew and an exile. A man without a country, living outside even the country he was born in. How could such a man present a whole picture of the world, of the springs of human action, how? And Freud the same, of course. The emphasis on the family because the country meant nothing to him. Introspection as landscape. The inclination they both had to look back, to argue from piety, wasn't it a kind of nostalgia for an Eden they never knew? They dismissed boundaries because they had never known them. They never had a language of their own. I'm not gloating, I'm not judging, but isn't it the truth?

By extension, Raphael's idiolect is the language Englishmen ought to speak but don't. His English is too good, like that of the Hungarian in *My Fair Lady*, or like that of Nabokov. Or Auden (an Englishman but defective, gay, and, finally, an American citizen living in Italy and then Austria).

Raphael has written books about Somerset Maugham and Lord Byron, who are an odd pair but who were both defective Englishmen. In *Somerset Maugham*, Raphael observes:

> It has been said that Philip Carey's club-foot, in *Of Human Bondage*, was a metaphor for his stammer or, as Francis King proposes, for his homosexuality. Is there not another possibility? As early as his forties, when the book was written, Maugham may have become aware of the paucity of his natural gifts, in comparison with the great writers in whose footsteps he made so lame a showing. His many successes in the theatre gave him kudos and made him rich, but he was irked by the demands of managers and by the limitations imposed both by public expectations and by the Lord Chamberlain's grotesque prudery and officious piety.

If it is not a great leap from Carey's lameness to Maugham's lamenesses (the stammer, the homosexuality, the irksomeness of the theatre), it is only a small step from Maugham's difficulties to Raphael's—one substitutes the movies for the theater, and the Jewishness for Maugham's various kinds of outsiderishness.

> The oddness of Maugham lies in the unobtrusive singularity of his circumstances: he was a rare bird without being an exotic one. How many writers are of truly Anglo-French culture?…In England…he was obliged to an imposture: he learned, as boys will, to mimic those around him the better to avoid the fate of the painted bird in the flock of dun sparrows. He had to affect that emotional indifference which goes with the stiff upper lip. He had, even on the Champs Elysées, diverted his *petits camarades* with nervous precociousness. To create a diversion is both to amuse and distract; it is a very apt term to apply to the activities of those who seek to avert adverse comment on their singularity by entertaining their companions. The "story-teller" is, in nursery terms, both a teller of fibs and a source of amusement; Maugham deflected and attracted attention by the same means. His ability to embroider the truth with plausible patterns became, as it does with writers, second nature.

When Raphael describes his own outsiderishness, as he does in an essay called "Why I Became a Writer" (written for BBC Radio and collected in *Cracks in the Ice*), he is aggressively, or distractingly, amusing:

> I was born in Chicago, at a time and in a place where Cicero brought to mind not the great Tully but the little Caesar known as Al Capone, who ruled the city from the fortress suburb of Cicero. My father was British, my mother the American daughter of a Lithuanian mother and a German father, whose name was Mauser. In my ambitious innocence I always thought that he would prove to be a fugitive sprig of the great gunsmiths. He was an indefatigable inventor, forever taking out patents which either ruined him in their development or were stolen from him by plausible associates. My paternal grandparents had long lived in England. Raphaels are to be found in the annals of the Bayswater Synagogue at the beginning of the 18th century and I have no reason to suppose that the name was not in even earlier records. My grandmother, who detested being Jewish, always said that the family was one of the first to return to England when Cromwell revoked the expulsion of the Jews.

He makes his feelings about his own Jewishness crystal clear:

> I lost my American accent. Who wanted to be different from the herd? I learnt to be British, I suppose, with no very different zeal from that with which I learned to be a classical scholar. I took on colour. I was less cunning than scared: scared of being different. Yet juggle as I might with my accent, I could never, of course, escape the crucial difference between myself and the chapel-going mass: I was Jewish. …My schooldays [at Charterhouse] were leaden with dread. I feared the word Jew itself, the mere mention of it in a reading from the Bible, as if it were the pointing finger of damnation. I had no belief, merely that endless fear. I suppose that I had friends, but I had no feelings of closeness, least of all, I fear, with other Jews—there clearly were one or two—in the school. I sought to impress my elders, the schoolmasters, with my wit and my intelligence. I was a clever boy. I do not think that I was especially likable. Fear is not attractive and I was often frightened.

There are various possible reactions to such fear, but Raphael's was, as he tellingly puts it, to learn "to be British…with no very different zeal from that with which I learned to be a classical scholar." Indeed, he conflated British-ness with classical scholarship, adopting the aggressive academic style and making it into a weapon he could brandish with ever greater effectiveness at Cambridge and then in the "real world" of intellectual and artistic life in London. His habitual trope as a novelist is the paradox, which, while it has a legitimate use in fiction as a means toward a satisfying re-vision, can also be a demonstration of the author's wit and, therefore, a manifestation of a kind of aggression.

In a characteristic passage in *Like Men Betrayed*, Raphael writes:

> The Marshal greeted him [Papastavrou, a general who has beaten the Italians] as effusively as a Byzantine emperor would a successful commander whom he had resolved to blind at the first opportunity. He offered the general any post in the Cabinet which he might care to name, a large pension and a huge grant of land. The Old Man even went so far as to ask if he had any suggestions for constitutional reform. The general refused both pension and grant. He declined to make any political proposals. The Marshal was appalled; he feared the general had some bee in his bonnet. And so he did; he requested that the funds offered to dull his ambitions should be devoted to the region whose sufferings he had witnessed. He asked to be made provincial governor and requested that certain of his officers and men, who could not be demobilized owing to the state of the war, be drafted to assist him. The use of the army for the improvement of the condition of the people aroused the deepest suspicion both of the notables and of people whose campaigns had been less brilliant than the general's. For his own personal use, the Cabinet would have voted any amount of money the general demanded; his selflessness was blatant extortion. They discussed having him assassinated…

This kind of defiant wit has its own tradition in British literature that runs from Byron (lame and an exile) through Oscar Wilde (gay and an exile), but it has affinities with Jewish humor which tends to be self-mocking. Of Stephen Hellman, Jewish lawyer in *Heaven and Earth*, a young woman whom we later discover to be his daughter remarks:

> He's got every damned book practically that was ever written on the subject [the Holocaust], hasn't he? Hitler and…That's why he can't take anything that happens in the present really seriously: even when he's being serious about it, there's something sarcastic—something remote—about him. He's waiting for something to go wrong so that he can join his ancestors, really be one of them. The world's a joke to

him, but essentially a Jewish joke: when you laugh, it's because it hurts, and especially because it hurts him. It's a vanity in him and all his acquisitiveness comes from it, don't you think so?

It is almost a coincidence that the style of much of the world's serious business is accessible only through such aggressive exercises of wit. Pamela, the protagonist's wife, says to her husband, "We shall never be honest. We shall never never never be honest. No matter what happens, no matter what has happened or will happen, we shall never be truly what we truly are," and Gideon, her husband, jokes, "The economy couldn't support it," adding:

> There aren't words enough. Because you're right: "on the contrary" is the heart of the matter. To be true we should have to accept that the false and the true are endlessly and necessarily confused. We should have to accept that plus is a form of minus, that everything that is also is not and everything that is not most certainly is, and that everything we say to each other depends on what we don't say and that what we don't say is present in our acts and what we dare not act is present in our speech, or in its silences or in its pacing, and that all the world's a stage, and what has been said before needs to be said again.

It may be true, or have a truth in it, but what it mostly seems to be is display, which is, in Raphael's work, an aggressive assertion of intelligence in which he is too intelligent to put much trust. All that dazzling linguistic display and it does no good, either to his narrators or, in the literary world, to Raphael, himself. A wordsmith, he has a deep distrust of words, and he cites, in one of his essays ("The Necessity of Anti-Semitism") Paul Valéry's paradox, *"la profondeur de la surface,"* upon which he comments: "Deep down, we might gloss him, language is superficial."

California Time, a novel he published in 1975 and one for which I have particular admiration and fondness, is a dazzling display of obsessive *jeux de mots* to which his characters are driven by the irrationalities of their setting, the movie business in La-la land. Their manic yammer is a distraction, but those who have minds out there tend to be distracted. There seem to be no rewards for paying attention, only punishments.

Here are a couple of sample passages. The first salvo of the book's opening is:

> It will be remembered that during his transatlantic flight Victor England watches a Western. The camera, panning the prospect, discovers a panning prospector. He shakes his sieve and there is the gleam of pay dirt. He stops, stoops, and picks out the gold on his palm. He looks around nervously. In the west, they collect percentages with a gun.

At home, there is England's wife, Fleur:

> She never rose until noon. She hoped that by leaving half the day on her plate she might diet her way to a reprieve from time's acid punctuality. She put out whatever reminded her of the caustic tick of reality. She had devised a way of both looking and not looking at things; to wince was to wrinkle. She was like one of those meticulous ephemeral insects whom the mere shadow of a hostile presence was enough to ball into immobility. Her unflinching terror at the smallest natural shock had given her a reputation for fearlessness.

Or, to suggest something of the scale of Raphael's arabesques, later on, at a Hollywood party:

> Somebody asked, hey wasn't this the house where they found that actor after he had been cut in a thousand pieces or something? The silence said yes and was luckily lanced by the doorbell and a crowd of welcome welcomes and happiness to be

there! The woman who had been too loud about the murdered actor tried again, pianissimo behind the piano, with a director whose work did well in Persia and places. It was true, he told her, pulling focus through a straight-up martini without the olive, that a once romantically silent star had screamed his last in the Canadian pine library while a bunch of motorcycle kids tried new ways to make him talk. At first the director was blinking SOS across the room to any woman who knew Morse, but pretty soon the golden cross between his questioner's best breasts got his casting vote and he warmed to his cruel task. He gave her the inside details about torture and mutilation amid the rare, red, rarely read books in the den where the old lion met his Daniels. The special effects soon had the gold cross between the woman's matching teeth and her thrilled thighs sighed together like lovers doomed to part.

What makes this demonic spritzing tolerable is its irrelevance to the real business of the novel, which is a contemplation of the irrational behavior of Dame Fortune. Hollywood's stars and executives (but not its writers) are our heroes and demigods, screens for our projections, vessels for our psychic investments. To be "in" or "out" there is not at all subtle. One can look at the grosses of one's last picture, or the sums one's agent is asking for the next. The executives know, and the bankers, and even the headwaiters and hotel managers. One need not be Jewish to be chosen (although that doesn't hurt). It is not absolutely essential even to be talented or intelligent (too much intelligence can be troublesome, actually, which is one of the novel's mordant admissions). What the public or the fickle gods or the finical camera's lenses decide from moment to moment is who is photogenic and who isn't. These people are public faces and when they lose face they die.

Raphael's plotting is as playful as one might expect of a veteran screenwriter. Thus, in *California Time*, Ramon Verdugo, the manager of La Mission (whose name, in Spanish, means *executioner*) is mortified and, literally, dies, when a couple comes into the Bonne Auberge, the hotel's chic restaurant. The lady is in her "double breasted birthday suit," which is to say she is completely nude. She is not the problem, though; it is the man, who is dressed but isn't wearing a tie.

Victor England, the protagonist, hearing about this goes to his suite to lie down for a nap. And intruding, Raphael tells us:

> Victor England ought to be collapsing under the force of the hard arts practiced against him, but instead he disdains to "print" or register them. To be a director, it has been said, is a neurosis not a profession (the words are those of a writer cheated into bitchy riches); a director can select what he wants from life and edit into "the real" (or the reel). What we are witnessing throughout *California Time* is an explosion of conventional expectation, an assault on the proprieties both in life and (the same thing?) in art. ...Victor England has survived because he does not learn and is not altered—the very negation of the morality by which the novel has been made metaphysically respectable, that of trial by circumstance. The maze that has been constructed to bait and abet him serves neither to contain nor to flummox. How much has really happened to Victor England of all the events with which his name has been connected? It may be that he has dreamed them all. It may be that they never took place, or that he misunderstood them ...All that one can say is that they have a certain status. They have been paid for, the definitive Californian justification.

The fun of that novel—and it is, indeed, great fun—is that it is at the same time knowing and helpless. The very geology of Los Angeles is uncertain, and there is no real distinction, in the movie business, between truth and dreams. Dreams, after all, are what they buy and sell, and appearances are the only reality.

Talent may be burdensome but it can be a kind of comfort. As Victor England broods:

> Talent was always the best insurance. Someone would always want you again for what you had done before. To get him for less than they had promised struck them as a victory. Let it be so: being somebody's trophy meant you always had a case. What if he had to live on only twice what a prime minister made? The simple life had its attractions, so long as they didn't include simplicity.

■ ■ ■

At this point, a little candor may be in order. Part of what draws me to Frederic Raphael's work and career is that he is a clearly excellent novelist, a man who has performed brilliantly over and over again and who, in any reasonable culture and society, would be acknowledged as an ornament and valued for his wit and vision. But in these sorry times, he is a writer who can't get his work published in the United States—the land of his birth and the largest market in the world for Anglophone literature. I know this because for some years we had the same agent. And I find in his tribulations a kind of comfort. As long as Raphael has difficulty placing his novels, I can tell myself that it isn't my fault that I haven't been able to sell mine. It's the publishers', or the market's, and I can wave my arm and blame them.

In a recent note to me, Raphael said something fairly close to what he had put into Victor England's head: "Don't cry for me, etc. I am, I suppose, buoyed up by a very small vanity which promises that, *malgré tout*, ah shall prevail. Rage is a good additive but a poor basic fuel. *Nuch!*"

And, in the long run, he may yet prevail, even though in the long run we are all dead. He has published twenty-two novels, four collections of short stories, three biographies, six collections of essays, and, with Kenneth McLeish, various translations from the Greek and Latin. Such recent books of his that American publishers have failed to snap up (*A Double Life, Old Scores, The Latin Lover and Other Stories*) are almost as easily obtainable as they'd be if they'd come out here. The Internet allows one to browse the lists if not the actual shelves of Blackwell's or The Internet Book Shop (www.bookshop.co.uk) in Oxford as easily as those of Amazon. Or, for out of print titles, there is Moe's Books in Berkeley. As bookselling comes lurching hesitantly out of the nineteenth century, actual book publishing may be about to change in such a way to allow "midlist" authors, like him and like me, to survive and even flourish.

A Double Life and *Old Scores*, two of his latest novels, appeared from Orion in London in 1993 and 1995 and have not yet found an American house (let alone home). These works about France in the aftermath of the war (which is to say the defeat and the occupation and, more often than the French are comfortable about admitting, the collaboration) are rather darker than some of the earlier books, but there are familiar themes that reappear. Early in *A Double Life*, Guy de Roumegouse, the narrator who is a retired diplomat, recalls that:

> During the war, I had occasion to travel with false papers. I was surprised at how easily, and with what abundance of fictitious detail, I was able to bore the police. My untrue self came more easily to me than my real character; I liked him rather better than the person whose experiences I had in fact had. I was able to be so artlessly garrulous about his life that the Germans handed me back my phony credentials before I had given them a quarter of my cover story…Could I have been equally plausible in giving an account of my actual existence?

That the impostor is a creator of fictions and therefore a kind of novelist is fascinating to Raphael, but he pursues the issue relentlessly. For him, all self-awareness involves a degree of imposture, an imposition of will on what ideally should be spontaneous, natural, and authentic. "Know thyself" is not an instruction designed to make us comfortable. In *Old Scores*, we have a variation on the same theme which announces itself on the opening page:

> My sister was the pretty one. As far as our parents' self-esteem was concerned, Pansy and I represented the good and the bad news. When Mickey and Toni parted, Pansy's charm and beauty promised them both, separately, that they had some compensation for their marital disaster. My quite good 'A' levels and subsequent university career led only to apprehension; although she did not say so, I suspected that Toni feared that a graduate daughter might also prove a harsh judge…
>
> Taking myself to be a sort of worthy disappointment made me more dutiful than my sister. I elected to pose as the sane one. There was a spice of concealed accusation in my regular memory for birthdays and in my apt selection of Christmas presents. Pansy was lovely; I, it seemed, was loving.

Then, in case we've missed the significance of "to pose as the sane one" and the crippling qualification of "it seemed," Raphael has Rachel Raikes, his protagonist, tell us:

> Being clever, or clever*er*, offered me the satisfactions of blameless duplicity; I was a deceiver without being dishonest. Heart and head were, in my case, very communicative partners. Having decided to be Pansy's trustworthy, reliable and thoroughly decent sister, there was something more than a little wilful in my virtue.

In both these novels, there is a sense of France as a place so rich in guilt and suffering that even honorable men and women are tainted by it. France, however, is only one more convenient venue for Raphael's general view of how life is in the world. In *Like Men Betrayed*, Greece offers the same occasion for witty disgust and the consideration not only of the guilt of the innocent but even of the innocence of the guilty:

> The Minister's house is watched by a single figure in a pale blue rain cape, rather crumpled, and a waterproof beret. He salutes the Minister, who allows his driver to pull up at the curb because the limousine is too wide for the chained gateway. How easy it would be to kill him! One could be abroad before suspects were even listed. Is there any sense in such an assassination? And is not its possible senselessness part of its attraction? One would have the amusement of seeing the newspapers attempt to fit it into a pattern, a new terrorist policy. The Minister has a kind of innocence. Is it that which one wants to rape? He walks so unostentatiously from his car (finding time to bend and salute the chauffeur, whose wife has had a little girl that very afternoon) and keeps his ears down in his astrakhan collar; these spring evenings can be deceptive. He wears gloves and grey spats. How little of him shows, especially with those thicker spectacles! So much paper-work! He is scarcely a man at all. He is like one of those insects which bleed a blanched liquor when they are split and to which one would like to apologize for having doubted their animal status…. The Minister's puny appearance, his dutiful precision, these minuscule attributes are more depressing than the screams of the tortured. Torture, one's humanity cries out, cannot continue; it demands revenge and challenges men to wrest the iron from the executioner's hand…It is more difficult to go fiercely into action against the petty, the prim, the pale. There may be glory in assassinating a tyrant, but his painstaking minion?

The villains are not the French or the Greeks or the Spaniards, it turns out, but language, which is unreliable and illusory, and then, beyond that, intelligence itself. The Philistine's old taunt—If you're so smart, why aren't you rich?—may lack a certain elegance but is not an irrelevant question. More pointedly, and painfully, one might ask, If you're so smart, why don't you understand anything? Why isn't the life you lead richer, more satisfying, or more authentic?

Roumegouse, in *A Double Life,* remarks—as he is being hauled off to be examined at the local Gestapo headquarters!—on the curse of intelligence and imagination. He finds it a character flaw that he is not absolutely terrified and observes:

> Even at this dark hour, there was in me an inability wholly to inhabit my time. What might in others be a source of imaginative strength was, and is, for me a failure to engage with the world. I cannot bring all my strength, of mind or body, to bear simultaneously: some part of me always manages to escape.

A few lines later, he offers his doubts about the most basic assumptions of Western, or at least of Cartesian, thought:

> It is a tradition, of which Descartes is our national instance, to suppose that the mind is rarer and more durable than the body. The perishability of the flesh, like the scandal of shit, leads philosophers to think that we should be happier and nobler if we were purged of our carnal shell, but is it necessarily the case that our thoughts or feelings, dispensed from practical considerations, are the better part of ourselves or even that they could be sustained, in any recognisably personal form, without the vulgar envelope of the body?…If I were in a more coherent contact with myself, I should almost certainly have lacked that capacity for anaesthesia (it has nothing in common with courage) which enabled me to watch myself being taken into the tall grey building which housed those whose business it was to terrorise me in the interests of a cause which all but a few must have known was as good as lost. They were, in some sense, already dead themselves: they had power, but no hope.

Whether a less intelligent Raphael would be "in a more coherent contact" with himself is at least a plausible question. There can be no doubt, however, that such a person would be very much more commercially successful as a novelist. Which is both a joke and a pity.

■ ■ ■

Raphael's new novel, *Coast to Coast*, published by Orion in May, is an odd book in several ways. For those who know Raphael's screen work, it is a re-make of *Two for the Road*, but without Stanley Donen's cheer or the breeziness that Audrey Hepburn and Albert Finney brought to the rather slick story of the marriage of the successful architect and his wife, which we see in intercut glimpses of three motor trips through France. In *Coast to Coast* the architect is now a writer of television sit-coms, and the itinerary is from Massachusetts to L.A. (in a Type-E Jaguar, yet), but the donnée is the same and the marriage, here too, is in deep trouble.

Remakes are very Hollywood, of course. They are a way of wringing more money out of something that has gone well. In Frederic Raphael's version, though, they can be a way of reclaiming what started out as his own vision and then got transformed into something else and usually less interesting. One of Raphael's novels is, in fact, the "novelization" of *Darling*, which is a weird thing to do (and almost as weird a thing to claim to have done). But unlike most novelizations of screenplays, this was a chance for the screenwriter to restore those scenes he'd liked but had lost in the collaborative process. The publisher didn't much care what was in the book. What they were selling was the tie-in, the chance to have Julie Christie's face on the cover, a souvenir of the experience of the film. Of those who bought the book—a paperback original—only a small number would have read it all the way through, and only a few of them might have noticed that there were scenes in the novel that hadn't been in the picture.

■ BOOKS BY FREDERIC RAPHAEL

novels

Obbligato. London: Macmillan, 1956.

The Earlsdon Way. London: Cassell, 1958.

The Limits of Love. London: Cassell, 1960, Philadelphia: Lippincott, 1961, London: Fontana, 1989.

A Wild Surmise. London: Cassell, 1961, Philadelphia: Lippincott, 1962.

The Graduate Wife. London: Cassell, 1962.

The Trouble with England. London: Cassell, 1962.

Lindmann. London: Cassell, 1963, New York: Holt Rinehart & Winston, 1964, London: Fontana, 1989.

Darling. New York: Signet, 1965.

Two for the Road. London: Jonathan Cape, 1967, New York: Holt Rinehart & Winston, 1967.

Orchestra and Beginners. London: Jonathan Cape, 1967, New York: Viking Press, 1968.

Like Men Betrayed. London: Jonathan Cape, 1970, New York: Viking, 1971.

Who Were You with Last Night. London: Jonathan Cape, 1971.

April, June and November. London: Jonathan Cape, 1972, Indianapolis: Bobbs-Merrill, 1972.

Richard's Things. London: Jonathan Cape, 1973, Indianapolis: Bobbs-Merrill, 1973, New York: Macmillan, 1975.

California Time. London: Jonathan Cape, 1975, New York: Holt Rinehart & Winston, 1975.

The Glittering Prizes. London: Allen Lane, 1976, Hammonsworth: Penguin, 1976, New York: St. Martin's Press, 1977, New York: Viking Penguin, 1979.

Heaven and Earth. London: Jonathan Cape, 1985, New York: Beaufort Books, 1985, New York: Penguin Books, 1987.

After the War. London: William Collins, 1988, New York: Viking Penguin, 1989, London: Fontana, 1989, New York: Viking Penguin, 1990.

The Hidden I: A Myth Revised. New York: Thames and Hudson, 1990.

A Double Life. London: Orion Books, 1993, London: Phoenix, 1994, North Haven, Conn.: Catbird Press, 2000.

Old Scores. London: Orion Books, 1995, London: Phoenix, 1996.

Coast to Coast. London: Orion Books, 1999, North Haven, Conn.: Catbird Press, 1999.

short stories

Sleeps Six and Other Stories. London: Jonathan Cape, 1979.

Oxbridge Blues and Other Stories. London: Jonathan Cape, 1980, Fayetteville: University of Arkansas Press, 1984.

Think of England. London: Jonathan Cape, 1986, New York: Scribner's, 1988.

The Latin Lover. London: Orion, 1994, London: Phoenix, 1995.

(One of the producers did read it, did notice, and asked, "Freddy, where did those terrific new scenes come from?" He was happy to be able to reply that they'd been in early versions of the script but had been cut.)

Coast to Coast exists in a kind of afterglow of *Two for the Road*, the similarities being enough to remind us of that other "road" picture and therefore to call our particular attention to the differences. This story of Marion and Barnaby Pierce is darker, even, at times, nasty. Their aches are sharper, their betrayals more deeply wounding. And Pierce, being a writer of comedy, can spout Raphael's aggressively clever patter so that the novelist can show off and, once again, demonstrate how verbal brilliance is almost totally irrelevant to the business of living and useless if not actually counterproductive. At one point, he gives us this exchange:

"I never thought saying things was too courageous," Marion said, "I think *not* saying things is what takes courage sometimes."

"It gives you very tight lips though."

"My problem is not your problem. My problem is not you. My problem is me. My problem is the history of men and women until now. Big one, right? What makes me think I can lick it? Nothing whatsoever. It's just sometimes you have to go to bat knowing that."

All His Sons. North Haven, Conn.: Catbird Press, 2001.

essays

Bookmarks. London: Cape, 1975, London: Quartet Books, 1975, Scranton, Pa.: Salem House, 1978.

Cracks in the Ice: Views and Reviews. London: W. H. Allen, 1979.

The List of Books: An Imaginary Library (with Kenneth McLeish). New York: Harmony, 1980, London: Mitchell Beazley, 1981.

Of Gods and Men. London: Folio Society, 1992.

France: the Four Seasons (with Michael Busselle). New York: Cross River Press, 1994, North Pomfret, Vt.: Trafalgar Square, 1996, London: Pavilion Books, 1996.

The Necessity of Anti-Semitism. Manchester: Carcanet, 1997, New York: St. Martins, 1997.

Eyes Wide Open: Working With Stanley Kubrick. New York: Ballantine, 1999.

biographies

Somerset Maugham and His World. London: Thames & Hudson, 1976, New York: Charles Scribner's Sons, 1975, *revised and expanded:* London: Cardinal/Sphere Books, 1989.

Byron. London: Thames & Hudson, 1982.

Popper. London: Weidenfeld & Nicolson, 1998.

translations (with Kenneth McLeish)

The Poems of Catullus. London: Jonathan Cape, 1978, Boston: David R. Godine, 1979.

The Serpent Son (The Oresteia of Aeschylus). Cambridge: Cambridge University Press, 1979.

The Plays of Aeschylus (2 vols.). London: Methuen, 1991, Portsmouth, N.H.: Heinemann, 1991 and 1992.

Euripides: Medea. London: Nick Hern Books, 1994, New York: Theatre Communications Group, 1996.

Euripides: Plays Six. Portsmouth, N. H.: Heinemann, 1997.

Sophocles: Ajax. Philadelphia: University of Pennsylvania Press, 1998.

screenplays

Nothing but the Best, 1964.

Darling, 1965.

Far from the Madding Crowd, 1967.

Bachelor of Hearts, 1968.

Two for the Road, 1968.

A Severed Head, 1971.

Daisy Miller, 1974.

Rogue Male, 1976.

The Best of Friends, 1979.

Richard's Things, 1981.

Oxbridge Blues, 1984.

Women and Men: Stories of Seduction, 1990.

La Putain Du Roi, 1990.

Eyes Wide Shut, 1998.

He drove for a while, and then he said, "You could just as well say that there isn't *anything* that doesn't require courage sometimes. Including cowardice. Particularly that even."

"One day," Marion said, "you'll maybe reflect on why it is that you save so much of your cleverness for saying those kinds of shitty things only to *me*."

"And writing shitty comedy. For money. I don't need to reflect. I know."

"And then you can go on—but only if you seriously want to—to ask yourself why all your real feelings are so angry and why you save them for when we're alone. Whereas…"

"Aw-aw."

"…when there are people around, not including the children however, you are Mr. Considerate Sweetie-Pie, as seen on TV."

"I'm only nice when I'm faking it is that what you're saying. Which is truly cute of you. Not kind. Cute. And shitty."

It is a sad, appalling, even shocking book. We may suppose that the anger Pierce feels about television producers is not unrelated to Raphael's own feeling about some of the moguls and demi-moguls he's worked with. The hurts that husbands and wives can expect from their children and from each other are universal (and, one is tempted to add, paramount and twentieth century). To these, Raphael brings his spate of words, brilliant, perfectly useless, but fascinating.

David R. Slavitt
February, 1999

UPDATE

Since this essay appeared, Frederic Raphael's novel *A Double Life* and his novella-story collection *All His Sons* (2001) have been issued in the United States. *The Dictionary of Literary Biography* describes Raphael, who is known for his high standards, thus: "His interests are never shallow, his technical ability has continued at the highest level, and his vision of contemporary society is tempered by wit and a wry self-knowledge. . . ."

Publishers Weekly called *A Double Life*, set in Nazi-occupied France, the "brilliant and wrenching story of a man whose emotional response mechanism has been terminally misdirected." *All His Sons* contains some stories originally written for BBC Radio. *Booklist* praised the "cosmopolitan, sophisticated fiction" about people in film and literature and *Publishers Weekly* called it "cynical and wise," "a darkly funny meditation on truth, heritage, race and loyalty."

Scientist of the Strange: Peter Redgrove

■ **I**

In the early 1950's, British poet Peter Redgrove was an Open and State Scholar in Natural Sciences at Cambridge when, with Philip Hobsbaum, he helped to found that well-known poetry workshop called "the Group." As a young scientist, Redgrove ventured upon his poetic experiments with a certain amount of trepidation, because the major literary personage at Cambridge, F. R. Leavis, was known to frown on such hybridism. Nevertheless, the Group's method appealed to Redgrove's scientific mind. The author of a poem was not allowed to discuss it with the others, at least not at first, but must sit listening to them get it right or wrong. This procedure was just like introducing an unknown element into a carefully prepared solution!

From this early "laboratory" work, Redgrove has gone on to write more than a dozen volumes of poetry, including four that were selected as choices by the prestigious Poetry Book Society. In addition, he has collaborated with his wife Penelope Shuttle, also a poet, on a number of novels and a psychology book entitled *The Wise Wound*.

In a sense, Redgrove's aim as a poet has been to imagine and fully participate in the world that he first studied with the detachment of a scientific observer. And there is a religious dimension to this process. He has symbolically killed the fastidious scientist in himself to prepare for the rebirth of the thinking *and* feeling poet, whom he calls the "scientist of the strange." For Redgrove believes that science has been mistakenly conceived as an instrument of power rather than of powerful participation. In subscribing to the so-called objectivity of science, we have cut ourselves off from our own feelings and sensations, and therefore the means of experiencing ourselves as part of nature's shifting patterns. Consequently, all that pertains to this realm, which includes a great deal of our own nature, has become strange to us. The poet's healing task is to help us recover our wholeness and our place in the whole.

In transforming himself from scientist to scientist of the strange, Redgrove has been inspired by a discipline that lies halfway between the "hard" sciences he studied in his youth and the humanistic endeavor of literature, namely psychology. His poem "The Idea of Entropy at Maenporth Beach," which represented an important turning point in his career, was dedicated to the Jungian analyst John Layard, with whom he trained. The notion that man strives to fulfill his capacities for feeling, sensation, and intuition, as well as thought, also derives from Jung, although Redgrove evidently felt the need for such development long before he encountered Jung's terminology. And, of course, psychoanalysis is the science, if we will accord it the label, that deals with the strange or uncanny contents of the unconscious. Nevertheless, in this brief essay on a poet who himself deserves to be less of a stranger on this side of the Atlantic, I have chosen to concentrate on Redgrove's own symbology. By tracing his metamorphosis through a number of poems, I hope to convey the essential flavor of a remarkable writer.

Peter Redgrove

Peter Redgrove, poet, novelist, and playwright, was born January 2, 1932. He was educated at the Taunton School in Somerset, England and at Queen's College, Cambridge, where he was Open and State Scholar in Natural Sciences and became a founding editor of the literary magazine *Delta*. In 1961 he won a Fulbright Award; in 1962 he became a Gregory Fellow in Poetry at Leeds University; and he served as the resident author and senior lecturer in complementary studies at the Falmouth School of Art in Cornwall from 1966 to 1983. Among Redgrove's numerous honors and awards are the Guardian Fiction Prize for his first novel, five Art Council Awards, and election to the Royal Society of Literature in 1982. He has since won the Cholmondeley Award from the Society of Authors (1985) and a Leverhulme Emeritus fellowship (1985-87).

Redgrove has also trained as a Jungian analyst and has practiced as a lay analyst since 1969. ■

■ II

The drama of this theme can be felt in the mutual reverberation of two poems from his first major book, *The Collector* (1959): the title poem and "Lazarus and the Sea." "The Collector" is not quite in Redgrove's own voice, just as its protagonist is not really a full person. The poem's faintly Audenesque ironies pin down a specimen of naturalist who "chose / Observations made to stir him in default of love." His own "senses still," he looks on at the spectacle of men and nature "with reasonable curiosity," and is even "interested" in the illness that finally kills him.

The subject, however, seems to have infected the style. It is as if Redgrove, while projecting where the scientific method alone will take him, were still collecting other poets' mannerisms. The verse is clever and pointed but lacks a characteristic force:

> And thus the beauty and terror of his life
> Moved him mildly. This living landscape where before
> He failed, was absorbing, with the horny rocks and the
> Mist that glittered like a skin,
> And with reasonable curiosity he saw
> Crows fall from the sky...

Obviously, the collector's reactions to "the beauty and the terror" are inadequate, but the reader may also be tempted to ask: From what vantage point does the poet himself see this situation? Is he simply a collector of collectors?

The answers to these questions are provided by another poem in the volume, "Lazarus and the Sea." While "The Collector" is spoken by an omniscient observer, "Lazarus and the Sea" is a dramatic monologue. The emphasis is different from that in the Biblical story, where the joy of resurrection is the central concern. Here the stress is on the experience of death and dissolution itself, because like nothing else it teaches one about "the beauty and the terror":

> I could say nothing of where I had been,
> But I knew the soil in my limbs and the rain-water
> In my mouth, knew the ground as a slow sea unstable
> Like clouds and tolerating no organisation such as mine
> In its throat of my grave…

If "The Collector" is about the dangers of detachment, this is participation with a vengeance. This is Prufrock really come back from the underworld, and not just fantasizing about it. In fact, the whole poem could be viewed as an unfolding of Eliot's lines: "I am Lazarus, come from the dead, / Come back to tell you all, I shall tell you all."

What *is* the insight that the poet/persona gains from this baptism in the elements of earth and water? It is not so much a bare statement as an idea fledged out in sensation: the feel of what it is like to be woven into the pattern of a world that is changing, where even "the ground" is "a slow sea unstable / Like clouds." The scientist has elected to experience the nitrogen cycle! The style, too, has profited from this vigorous participation. The poem begins, for instance, with an assurance and urgency missing from "The Collector": "The tide of my death came whispering like this / Soiling my body with its tireless voice." And whether consciously or not, these lines contain a sea-echo of Whitman's great initiatory poem, "Out of the Cradle Endlessly Rocking": "Whereto answering, the sea…Lisped to me the low and delicious word death."

The title poem of Redgrove's next book, *The Nature of Cold Weather* (1961), advances the drama. At the end of "Lazarus," the protagonist was ironically "uprooted" from his death and returned to his "old problems and to the family." Now the poet-scientist will perform another experiment in merging with the elements. This explains the pun in the title. He will search for both the nature, or characteristic qualities, of cold weather and for nature itself in the phenomena of cold weather. At first, the subject seems unpromising. What possibly could be learned from the *nature morte* of the cold? But then we may remember the injunctions of Wallace Stevens in "The Snow Man," which tell us that one can gain a knowledge of reality only by having "a mind of winter." Only such a mind can behold "Nothing that is not there and the nothing that is."

In this group of twenty-one poems, Redgrove resourcefully adapts his form to the theme, which is a variation on the death-and-rebirth ritual of "Lazarus and the Sea." Each of these small poems is like a nugget of ice, an imagist scene of winter:

> The moon stares for an instant, then a cloud lays
> Flat on her mouth like a finger;
> Over the acres of ground-leaves,
> The spiking darts that were trees,
> Again she steals upon them with her red.

But "imagist" is a misleading term in this context if it implies merely a visual appreciation. As we would expect from the author of "Lazarus," these poems implicate all the senses, including touch:

> And my fist that strikes it
> Cracks in a leaf-net,
> Pain as if crushed
> Leases the nail-quicks.

Imagism also implies poetry that lacks dramatic development; however, there is a definite drama here, beneath the surface of the ice one might say. Redgrove is attempting to experience nature on its own terms, undistorted by ordinary human perspectives. The poems, therefore, are like the experimental notations of a scientist as this "absolute zero" is approached. And for a brief period toward the end of the series, Redgrove is actually able to look through the snow-man's eyes:

> *O, what beauty in the ice-rose,*
> *The heels and skews,*
> *The bevels, ramps and biases of snows,*
> *The glass thorns, the grey flat eyes.*

In this sense, the poem is another death, a dying into nature, like the one described in "Lazarus." At the same time, it involves a symbolic killing of the cold, objective scientist in himself, who is identified with the "giant" of the ice that personifies the winter.

Redgrove therefore enjoys a two-fold victory in this poem. He is able to merge with natural forces, even under the most inauspicious conditions, and he also links the spirit of winter with the numb and frozen scientist in his psyche. This permits him to celebrate *"The breakup of the giant…"* with the delicious sensuousness of a pagan religious ritual:

> First the houses burn his fingers
> Flushing up brown soil along his arms,
> His whiteness smutches, and the pricking comes intense,
> Freckles and patches, wens and mud-craters
> Where those beautiful declivities shone,
> And long before, his eyes broke, and he is blind…

The melting described here, which is a great easing of the spirit, continues into the last poem of the book, "Mr. Waterman," a comic prose-poem whose fluidity contrasts with the tight imagistic verses of the first part of "The Nature of Cold Weather." This combination of science-fiction and sit-com is rendered in a form often used by Redgrove, one that Philip Hobsbaum has called the "interrupted monologue." Such a monologue is largely spoken by one person but occasionally interrupted by another character or characters.

In this case, a psychiatrist is interviewing a patient with a very peculiar complaint indeed. His pond is developing a personality and becoming more and more intrusive:

> It was getting playful, obviously, and inventive, if ill-informed, and might have got dangerous. I decided to treat it with the consideration and dignity which it would probably later have insisted on, and I invited it in as a lodger, bedding it up in the old bathroom. At first I thought I would have to run canvas troughs up the stairs so it could get to its room without soaking the carpet, and I removed the flap from the let-ter-box so it would be free to come and go, but it soon learnt to keep its form quite well, and get about in macintosh and galoshes, opening doors with gloved fingers.

The comic inventiveness of the poem is closely allied with the personification of the pond itself, which symbolizes a new-found freedom of imagination. The speaker, on the other hand, is ridiculously mundane in contrast to his irrepressible genii. He is struggling for his normality, and in wanting to keep this passionate Mr. Waterman at arm's length, especially from his wife, he is another version of the mild-mannered protagonist of "The Collector":

> …I dread the time (for it will come) when I shall arrive home unexpectedly early, and hear a sudden scuffle-away in the waste-pipes, and find my wife ('just out of the shower, dear') with that moist look in her eyes, drying her hair: and then to hear him swaggering in from the garden drains, talking loudly about his day's excursion…

In some respects, this poem is a brilliant reversal of "Lazarus and the Sea." The end of that poem was an anticlimactic return to "old problems," after being torn away from an elemental union. "Mr. Waterman," however, shows the elements intruding boldly into the normal family, creating some new problems. The imaginative perceptions that seemed so precariously achieved in "Lazarus" now humorously threaten to overwhelm the speaker:

> ...I thought I might ask him to join the river for a spell...But...he might not be able to free himself from his rough dirty cousins, and come roaring back as an impossible green seething giant, tall as the river upended, buckling into the sky, and swamp us and the whole village...

The use of a psychiatric interview as a frame for this monologue is a nice touch as well. It ironically suggests the clinical, detached perspective that is actually being undermined by the dynamic of the poem. Also, the fact that the next patient to be interviewed will be Mr. Waterman himself hints that these two characters are really different aspects of the same person: the virginal collector and the emerging scientist of the strange.

■ III

The ghost of "The Collector" has been laid, at least temporarily, in "The Force," which is the title poem of Redgrove's 1966 volume. If the misguided scientist needed to study nature as an array of specimens, the poet here has a jaunty and clear-eyed understanding of the creative forces at work in the world, and of our access to them:

> At Mrs. Tyson's farmhouse, the electricity is pumped
> Off her beck-borne wooden wheel outside.
> Greased, steady, it spins within
> A white torrent, that stretches up the rocks.
> At night its force bounds down
> And shakes the lighted rooms, shakes the light;
> The mountain's force comes towering down to us.

The obviously allegorical name—Tyson means to tie or harness the sun's power—is not didactic but just part of the general fun. The cosmic and the domestic accommodate each other easily in these lines, with the former not in any way diminished by the latter. And the "farmhouse" is almost like a fairytale cottage, where Redgrove's Lazarus could live happily ever after in tune with his vision of the elements. Mrs. Tyson's "backyard" is neither closed off nor imprisoning; on the contrary, it is open to the "loosened torrent" of a stream that comes from "an overflowing squally tarn." It, too, is part of the elemental dance in which:

> ...Sun
> Pulls up the air in fountains, green shoots, forests
> Flinching up at it in spray of branches

Nothing blocks or dams the water, and force is not feared but easily used.

The minister in "The Sermon," which appears a little later in the book, is actually preaching about this "force," although the word he uses for it is "God." This poem is another one of Redgrove's interrupted monologues, with the congregation providing a suspicious, literal-minded antiphony. One could say that, in their collectivity, they represent the feeble spirit of the collector. The minister, however, who is one of many eccentric and appealing parsons in Redgrove's poetry, is a version of the scientist of the strange. Disconcertingly unorthodox, he sees God in a celebration of life and sex:

> Appetite for life, friends…in all your pantings, your teemings, your pantings, the
> green roofs of your fields, the juices of the laid grasses, the soft beds of feather hay
> in the sun and of haymaking feathers in the night-time, in all of these you may
> sometimes meet God—in the city's symphony of bedsprings on spring nights under
> the peppery sky twirling with stars, in the white soft babies waited on hand and
> foot, in the bedrooms and in the bedsprings…

To which the congregation replies nervously:

> We don't understand at all. Didn't he make us? Isn't he above and beyond us? Does-
> n't he live in heaven, out there? If he's infinite how does he get into our houses?
> How does he know what goes on down here?

They are confused and frightened by the notion of a God who, like the "Mountain's force" in
the earlier poem, can come "towering down to" them. The minister keeps putting them off with
the phrase, "But I was coming to that," but his explanations only raise them to a higher pitch of
alarmed resentment: "We've had enough. This is blasphemy. You are Antichrist."

> This outcry of theirs inspires him to a culminating statement:
> What I am asking you to do, friends, IS to carry on before it is too late, before we
> are all snatched back to God from whom we came…I am asking you, friends,
> whatever it all means, whoever is right, whatever explanation we use—to—carry
> on, so *some* good can come of it, to carry on, to experiment, as I am doing, good
> my dear sweet world, to carry on, to carry on…

Redgrove plays ironically with the phrase, "to carry on," which could mean either do as you
were doing before, or act wildly. Actually, the minister is saying both things at once! On the one
hand, he is telling them to do what they are already doing: have sex and make babies. But at
the same time, he wants them to participate so fully in life that its strangeness and wildness are
revealed. He wants them not to live a detached, observing existence, like the collector, but "to
experiment" and open themselves to feelings and sensations. This whole sermon, in fact, could
be taken as a gloss on Keats' exclamation: "O for a life of sensations rather than of thoughts!"

Part of the drama of Redgrove's work, however, comes from the persistence with which the
freewheeling experimentalist is haunted by the more orthodox scientist. There is a particularly
nasty visitation in "The Haunted Armchair" from *Dr. Faust's Sea-Spiral Spirit* (1972). This unin-
terrupted monologue, with its obsessive repetition, is like a miniature Beckett play. Particularly
reminiscent of that playwright are the sense of timelessness and limbo, and a voice that is very
much disembodied despite its concern for the body:

> I want it not to go wrong. I want nothing to go wrong.
> I shall guard and hedge and clip to the end of my days
> So that nothing goes wrong. This body, this perfect body
> That came from my mother's womb undiseased, wholesome,
> No, nothing must go wrong…

This is the voice of a man who is desperate not to be soiled by life. The epigraph is a quote
from the Biblical parable of the servant who "hid his lord's money" rather than using it to gain
more (Matthew 25). Clearly, the speaker of the poem is in the same position as the servant in
the gospel story. Rather than spend himself in living, he wishes to guard himself from life by
remaining pure and untainted.

The poem seems to be spoken by a more extreme version of the naturalist in "The Collector." He was at least curious about his world, while the interests of this speaker do not extend
beyond the borders of his own body. Redgrove is showing us a more virulent form of the dis-

ease of detachment whose symptoms he first delineated in the earlier poem. This character is collecting only himself:

> I rinse my eyes with the sterile saline; I close, I pull the thick curtain,
> I close the door and lock it, once, twice, thrice, I sit, I lie, I sleep
> > in the great armchair,
> And I sleep. Sleep, sleep, is the preservative, cultivate sleep, it keeps
> > me perfect.

He treats himself as though he were a taxonomic specimen, being prepared for a long museum life. But it is also true that this poem gains in power over the earlier one by having the character speak directly.

Several writers, including D. M. Thomas, have interpreted the end of this poem as a recantation, a realization on the speaker's part that he has been wrong. They see the evidence for this point of view in the verb "grants," which supposedly signals a release:

> How much time have I seen withering? Did I come here today?
> Suddenly everything grants me withering. Shall I sit here again?
> The body is gone. I sit here alone. A Nothing, a virgin memory.
> A grease-spot. A dirty chair-back.

In my opinion, they are misreading these final lines, which only confirm the whole direction of the poem. The character fades into nothing, a "Haunted Armchair" only, "A grease-spot." Ironically, he *has* kept himself pure in one sense, becoming "a virgin memory," but only because he has done and accomplished nothing. While he thinks of himself as pure in this way, he has really become a spot of grease, the essence of dirtiness.

Just as "The Collector" was a dialogue with "Lazarus and the Sea," "The Haunted Armchair" is answered by "The Idea of Entropy at Maenporth Beach," which appears earlier in the Dr. Faust volume. As the title suggests, this poem was written with Wallace Stevens' "The Idea of Order at Key West" in mind. Redgrove has commented that he finds the chaotic music of the sea in this Stevens poem more interesting than the woman's song. This response might be expected from an author whose Lazarus willingly forsook his own body's "organisation" for nature's more comprehensive patterns. It is easy to understand why Redgrove would naturally distrust an "Idea of Order," believing that it might lead to the rigid, self-protecting and -defeating order exemplified in "The Haunted Armchair." In this, he resembles A. R. Ammons, who from the beach at "Corsons Inlet" renounces small and easy orders in favor of a "large view" that sees "no / lines or changeless shapes." Perhaps this consciousness of—in Ammons' terms—"enlarging grasps of disorder" is what distinguishes Redgrove and Ammons, two postmodernists, from Stevens, the great modernist. One can even speculate that in "The Haunted Armchair" Redgrove has unwittingly shown how postmodernist writers are haunted by the all-encompassing systems of their modernist forebears.

Like its prototype, "Lazarus and the Sea," "The Idea of Entropy at Maenporth Beach" is about a ritual of baptism in the elements of earth and water. The persona in this instance is a woman, as is Stevens' persona. When the poem begins, she is wearing a white dress, the symbol of purity. However, her attitude toward purity is diametrically opposite to that of the character in the armchair: "It was a white dress, she said, and that was not right." Her immersion in the mud is seen as a fructifying and life-giving process:

> Who is that negress running on the beach
> Laughing excitedly with teeth as white
> As the white waves kneeling, dazzled, to the sands?

Clapping excitedly, the black rooks rise,
Running delightedly in slapping rags
She sprinkles substance, and the small life flies!

While Lazarus was painfully "uprooted" from his burial, the woman in this poem rises of her own accord and is able to use her renewed contact with the elements of earth and water. Her willingness to submit herself to this initiation is liberating: "And in their slithering passage to the sea / The shrugged-up riches of deep darkness sang." These lines can refer to both the mud itself and to the "riches" of the unconscious, which have been freed by this act of participation.

Of course, without the act of participation called reading, the premises of this poem are liable to seem absurd. The poem is like a strange religious ritual, with only the religion omitted! A woman dressed in white immerses herself in the mud by the seashore and then runs around delightedly. How are we supposed to take this? Redgrove is fully aware of the danger involved here. The "Entropy" referred to in the title is not only an idea, a component of the theme; it encompasses the very risk that we have been talking about. The fact that the actions described in the poem could be viewed as ludicrous is part of Redgrove's flirtation with the notion of disorder.

What saves the poem is that the poet's delight and good humor are ubiquitous, as much in the description of the mud as in the actions of the woman:

The mud splatters with rich seed and ranging pollens.
Black darts up the pleats, black pleats
Lance along the white ones…

. . .

The mud recoils, lies heavy, queasy, swart.
But then this soft blubber stirs, and quickly she comes up.

The reader is not being preached to but playfully invited to come on in, the mud's fine!

These two poems demonstrate the same symbolic constellation that we saw in *The Collector*: the death of a pristine "scientific" character and the rebirth of a character who plunges into the earth itself to gain strange insights. And this rebirth has a strongly religious dimension. One difference, however, is that in this later version, the poems are more exuberant and assertive, and the rebirth more optimistic.

It is obvious why Redgrove regards "The Ideas of Entropy at Maenporth Beach" as a turning point in his poetic career. This poem represented his boldest attempt yet to participate in the disorderly richness of nature and the unconscious. It is significant, too, that a woman performs this ritual, both standing in for the poet and showing him the way. This muse figure reappears again and again in the Dr. Faust book. She is, for example, one of the "Young Women with the Hair of Witches and No Modesty" who initiates him into the mysteries of water, always a favorite element:

I used to see her straight and cool, considering the pond,
And as I approached she would turn gracefully
In her hair, its waves betraying her origin.
I told her that her thoughts issued in hair like consideration of water,
And if she laughed, that they would rain like spasms of weeping

This is simultaneously an initiation into water's looseness, multiplicity, and richness of contradiction: "…she loosened her hair in a sudden tangle of contradictions, / In cross and double-cross, surcross and countercross." She is the means by which the formerly virginal and detached young scientist is transformed into a scientist of the strange.

This theme is stated quite explicitly in the poem "The Youthful Scientist Remembers":

…I had envisaged
Some library of chemistry and music
With lean lithe scores padding the long pine shelves,
Plumage of crystal vials clothing strong deal tables;
had thought that the stars would only tug at me slightly,
Or sprinkle thin clear visions about me for study—
Instead you point at that flower, your dress fits like a clove.

The young scientist had imagined that the study of nature would be relatively uninvolving, a subject of "interest" as the collector might have said. He describes his vision in terms of music, a clean art that, as Auden once observed, does not involve the sense of smell. The "crystal vials" are pictured as "Plumage" because the scientist thinks his discipline is a lofty enterprise, related to the flight of birds, and certainly not something that would root him in the earth. However, these fantasy plans are disturbed by a woman whose clothes are stained with mud and who is described in plant-like terms. She is the one who gives him an alternative vision of nature:

After a day's clay my shoes drag like a snail's skirt
And hurt as much on gravel. You have mud on your jersey,
This pleases me, I cannot say why. Summer-yolk
Hangs heavy in the sky, ready to rupture in slow swirls,
Immense custard: like the curious wobbly heart
Struggling inside my pink shirt. Spring is pink, predominantly,
And frothy, thriving, the glorious forgotten sound of healing…

These images conjure up a medium that is dense, viscous, disorderly, and sexual, compared to the "lean lithe scores" of the chemistry laboratory he had dreamed about. Although the youthful scientist is confused by the change that has come over him, this confusion is a source of pleasing wonder rather than dismay.

▪ IV

The appearance of this muse figure gives a powerful impetus to Redgrove's work. She becomes the midwife who facilitates the birth of the scientist of the strange. From this point on, the poetry radiates a new energy, as if a repression had been lifted. The book that benefits the most from these developments is *The Weddings at Nether Powers* (1979). The title, and Redgrove has always has a flair for titles, suggests that things have come together in the unconscious which till then had been kept asunder. It also celebrates the poet's marriage to nature, especially those aspects of it, characterized by mud and darkness, which had previously been feared and despised. Since this volume is very much concerned with symbolic marriage and poetic rebirth, it is no accident that the first poem is entitled "The Visible Baby." The collector might have been repelled by a squalling, needy little baby. But the scientist of the strange is able to look right through the child as if it were transparent, watching the earthy forces of nature actively working:

I can see the white caterpillar of his milk looping through him,
I can see the pearl-bubble of his wind and stroke it out of him,
I can see his little lungs breathing like pink parks of trees,

I can see his little brain in its glass case like a budding rose;

There is no sense of disgust here at all. Instead, the lines glow with warmth and wonder. Lazarus is now a proud father, and the mysteries that he almost had to die in order to see are now clearly visible to him in the child that he strokes and burps. In other words, the domestic situation that once stood opposed to the elemental vision of nature is now one with it, which union is still another connotation of the marriage referred to in the title.

There is a characteristic of Redgrove's style in this book that might confuse an uninitiated reader. I am alluding to his tendency to plunge right to the heart of a poem in the first lines, rather than carefully building up to a climax. Sometimes these initials statements are not even complete sentences:

Cloth woven on a loom whose spindle-weights
Are made of the sliced bones
Of forefathers and foremothers.
(**"The Looms of the Ancestors"**)

His first meal after the resurrection,
Everything around him ready to open, to give up its dead.
(**"Undressing Food"**)

The bowling down the hill of blazing wheels
At the time of solstice, mother of grasses:
(**"Drunk on the Moon"**)

Redgrove has compared this procedure to tuning into a radio station. As you spin the dial, the first things you will hear will only be approximate and you must keep tuning to understand what is being said. He has also compared it to the practice of meditation, where you first present yourself, almost bluntly, with a subject for meditation and then proceed to elaborate on it. I would only add, in terms of the theme that we have been discussing, that Redgrove's new confidence in his ability to see into the heart of natural processes leads him to dive immediately into his subject with no preliminaries. Therefore, what may temporarily seem obscure to the reader derives from the poet's increasing assurance.

The poem "Guarded by Bees," which I will quote in its entirety, begins in such a way and also demonstrates how Redgrove has been able to link his own tranformation to a prophetic vision of society:

The pornographic archives guarded by bees
Who have built comb in the safe; iron doors
From which the honey drips; I sip a glass
Of bee-sherry, yellow and vibrant; I came here
Past the old post-office, boarded up,
From within the cool darkness sun-razored
I heard the hum of bees; my friend tells me

That the radioactive cities of the future
Will be left standing for euthanasia,
They will be kept beautiful though all the trees
And lawns will be plastic. Those who wish to die
Will drift through the almost-empty streets,
Loiter through the windows of the stores,
All open, all untended, what they fancy they can take,

Or wander through the boulders of Central Park, its glades
To hear the recorded pace and growl in the empty zoo-cages,
And consider the unperturbed fountains of water,
While it, and they, are rinsed through and through
As the pluming spray by sunlight, with killing rays,
Lethal broadcasts, until they can consider no more.
Germs over the whole skin die first, the skin after,
Purity first, then death, in the germless city that amazes
The killed lovers with its pulsing night-auroras.

I reply I would prefer a city constructed of OM,
A city of bees, I want this disused city
Converted to a hive, all the skyscrapers
Packed with honeycomb, and from the windows
Honey seeping into the city abysses, all the streets
Rivers of cloudy honey slipping in tides,
And the breeze of the wings as they cool our city.

This would be my euthanasia, to be stung by sweetness,
To wander through the droning canyons scatheless at first,
Wax thresholds stalagmited with honey-crystals
I snap off and munch, and count the banks
That must brim with the royal jelly…

And some wander through the sweet death, city of hexagons
And are not stung, break their hanging meals off cornices
In the summer-coloured city, drink at the public fountains
Blackened with wings drinking, and full of wonder
Emerge from the nether gates that are humming
Having seen nature building;
                others stagger

Through the misshapen streets, screaming of human glory,
Attended by black plumes of sting,
With a velvet skin of wings screaming they're flayed.

The first two phrases, of course, are not sentences but images, carrying the reader into the poem willy-nilly. What are these "pornographic archives guarded by bees"? Their meaning will become clearer as the poem continues. Nevertheless, the whole poem is somehow present in this picture of a human structure (the safe) that has been preempted by the natural world (bees). This lightning beginning conveys a sense of sweetness and danger, overflowing richness and sexuality. We do not have a speaker until the third line, and the location alluded to in the fourth line is uncertain. Is it an apiary where metal safes house the hives? The "old post-office," which is "boarded up," may have started the poet thinking about his friend's description of "the radioactive cities of the future," which will also be abandoned. Or it could be that his friend is with him and telling him this in person. Still another alternative might be that the "iron doors / From which the honey drips" are only imaginings conjured up by the sound of the bees in the post-office. The important point is that the poet's mind is vibrating at these frequencies when he remembers or hears about future cities.

The second stanza of the poem is simply the wish of the character in "The Haunted Arm-chair" writ large. Redgrove is saying that this is where our desire for mastery, fear of involve-

■ BOOKS BY PETER REDGROVE

The Collector and Other Poems. London: Routledge, 1959.

The Nature of Cold Weather and Other Poems. London: Routledge, 1961.

At the White Monument and Other Poems. London: Routledge, 1963.

The Force and Other Poems. London: Routledge, 1966.

New Poems 1967: A P.E.N. Anthology of Contemporary Poetry. edited by John Fuller, Harold Pinter, Peter Redgrove, London: Hutchinson, 1968.

Penguin Modern Poets II. with D. M. Black and D. M. Thomas, London: Penguin, 1968.

Work in Progress. London: Poet and Printer, 1969.

Dr. Faust's Sea-Spiral Spirit and Other Poems. Boston: Routledge, 1972. London: Routledge, 1972.

Three Pieces for Voices. London: Poet and Printer, 1972.

In the Country of the Skin. London: Routledge, 1973.

The Hermaphrodite Album. with Penelope Shuttle, London: Fuller D'Arch Smith, 1973.

The Terrors of Dr. Treviles. with Penelope Shuttle, London: Routledge, 1974.

Lamb and Thundercloud: Totleigh Barton Poems. London: The Arvon Press, 1975.

Sons of My Skin: Selected Poems 1954–74. Edited with an introduction by Marie Peel, Boston: Routledge, 1975. London: Routledge, 1975.

The Glass Cottage. London: Routledge, 1976.

Miss Carstairs Dressed for Blooding and Other Plays. London: Marion Boyars, 1976.

From Every Chink of the Ark: New Poems American and English. Boston: Routledge, 1977. London: Routledge, 1977.

The Wise Wound: Menstruation and Everywoman with Penelope Shuttle. London: Gollancz, 1978. New York: Richard Marek, 1978. Harmondsworth: Penguin Books, 1980.

New Poetry: An Arts Council Anthology. edited by Peter Redgrove and Jon Silkin, London: Hutchinson, 1979.

The God of Glass. London: Routledge, 1979.

The Sleep of the Great Hypnotist. London: Routledge, 1979.

The Weddings at Nether Powers and Other New Poems. Boston: Routledge, 1979. London: Routledge, 1979.

ment, and hatred of nature will lead us. There will be such "purity," engendered by "Lethal broadcasts" of radiation, as no creature will be able to bear. Yet the physical structure of the city will remain intact—as it would, for example, after a neutron-bomb attack—a collector's item for a nonexistent posterity. The haunted chair of the previous poem has become a haunted and ghostly city of "almost-empty streets," ironically full of available consumer-goods. By the end of the stanza, even the germs have been eliminated and only a light-show remains (what could be purer?) for a vacant audience.

The rest of the poem is Redgrove's answer to this negative vision, an answer that he has been preparing through all the poems we have read, from "Lazarus and the Sea" through "The Idea of Entropy at Maenporth Beach." This is the same cityscape described by his friend; however, Redgrove has "converted" it "to a hive." The human structures have been overrun by the looser and richer orders of nature, represented by the bees, just as in the first image the bees "built comb in the safe." There are definite religious implications to this surrender of human control. Redgrove describes the new city as being "constructed of OM," which is a reference to both the humming sound of the bees and to the sacred syllable OM in the Hindu religion. While the city in the second stanza is apparently silent, except for the recorded sounds of the zoo animals, the "city of bees" is vibrant and resonating. In Yoga, the syllable OM is believed to be an aid to meditation, so that existence in this environment is like a perpetual meditation. The descriptions in this final section of the poem are, indeed, uncanny, as befits a scientist of the strange. They are strange to us, however, because we have imposed our artificial constructs on the world and therefore do not recognize what should be familiar. This passage is one of Redgrove's most powerful images of "nature building," which is the very opposite of nature dominated and studied by man.

The Beekeepers. London: Routledge, 1980.

The Apple-Broadcast and Other New Poems. Boston: Routledge, 1981. London: Routledge, 1981.

Cornwall in Verse. edited by Redgrove. London: Secker & Warburg, 1982.

The Facilitators, Or, Madame Hole-In-The-Day. London: Routledge, 1982.

The Working of Water. Devon, U.K.: Taxus Press, 1984.

The Man Named East and Other New Poems. London: Routledge, 1985.

The Mudlark Poems and Grand Buveur. London: Rivelin Grapheme Press, 1986.

Explanation of Two Visions: Poems. Leamington Spa, U.K.: Sixth Chamber Press, 1986.

The Black Goddess and the Sixth Sense. London: Bloomsbury, 1987.

In the Hall of the Saurians. London: Secker & Warburg, 1987.

The Moon Disposes: Poems, 1954–1987. London: Secker & Warburg, 1987.

The First Earthquake. London: Secker & Warburg, 1989.

Poems, 1954-87. New York: Penguin, 1989.

The One Who Set Out to Study Fear. London: Bloomsbury, 1989.

Dressed as for a Tarot Pack. Devon, U.K.: Taxus, 1990.

Sex-Magic-Poetry-Cornwall. Worcestershire, U.K.: Crescent Moon Publishing, 1992.

Under the Reservoir. London: Secker & Warburg, 1992.

The Cyclopean Mistress: Selected Short Fiction, 1960-1990. Newcastle upon Tyne, U.K.: Bloodaxe, 1993.

The Laborators. Devon, U.K.: Taxus, 1993.

My Father's Trapdoors. London: Jonathan Cape, 1994.

Alchemy for Women: Personal Transformation Through Dreams and the Female Cycle. London: Rider, 1995.

Abyssophone. Exeter, U.K.: Stride, 1995.

Assembling a Ghost. London: Jonathan Cape, 1996.

One's place in this second city depends entirely on one's attitude. Although Redgrove mentions "euthanasia," those who show a humble acceptance of and joy in the processes of nature do seem to escape death, emerging "from the nether gates." They participate in this city with all their senses, feeling "the breeze" of the bees' wings, hearing their "humming," seeing "the public fountains / Blackened with wings drinking," and tasting the delicious "honey-crystals." However, there is a special hell in store for those who insist on human lordship, "screaming of human glory." The "velvet skin of wings" that enwraps them is a real nightmare image. Like any return of the repressed, this vision combines elements of extreme sweetness and extreme danger.

For Redgrove these stanzas are a penetration into the heart of a mystery "Guarded By Bees." If we cannot see how we are part of creation and instead claim authority over it, we will be stung to death, though not literally by bees of course. Our own psyche will revenge itself upon us, causing us to destroy ourselves and other living creatures with the sting of deadly radiation.

"The pornographic archives," therefore, are the documents of a civilization that has brought us to this pass. They represent the knowledge we have pursued in an attempt to dominate nature rather than find a place in its patterns. These documents are the false honey of a society that values scientific objectivity over feeling and sensation. And they are "pornographic" because they distort true knowledge in the same fashion that pornography distorts sexuality. However, Redgrove's symbols are characterized by a wise ambivalence, and the meaning of the archives is transformed by their new guardians, the bees, just as the city itself is changed. In this way, what was once obscene becomes a sacred text, reflecting the love that builds all things.

Philip Fried
October, 1985

UPDATE

Since this essay was written, Peter Redgrove has published the following books of poetry: *The Mudlark Poems and Grand Buveur* (1986), *Explanation of Two Visions: Poems* (1986), *In the Hall of the Saurians* (1987), *The Moon Disposes: Poems 1954–1987* (1987), *The First Earthquake* (1989), *Dressed as for a Tarot Pack* (1990), *Under the Reservoir* (1992), *The Laborators* (1993), *My Father's Trapdoors* (1994), *Abyssophone* (1995), and *Assembling a Ghost* (1996). He also has published several works of fiction and non-fiction.

Although better known in his home of Great Britain than in the United States, Redgrove still draws an appreciative audience. With his scientific and psychoanalytic background, "nature poet" Redgrove brings a depth and range of knowledge to this writing that is uniquely his own. "Redgrove's poems are lush, imagistic, and exuberant," states *Contemporary Authors*, "presented in a language that blends the visionary with the scientific." According to *Encounter*, they are evidence of the "imagination allowed to work, on its own principles, to capacity, to a fullness of utterance, [in order] to achieve a necessary condition of expression." An essay in *British Poetry since 1960: A Critical Survey* states that Redgrove "has tried to do something quite new in English poetry, to fuse the traditional feeling for Nature with a knowledge of the biological processes and the theories of the structure of the universe," and *Equivalencias* has called him "the leading exponent of contemporary mystical verse."

"I think every person has a central poem," Redgrove once told *Poetry Review*. "I don't know what else to call it. The word poem is better nowadays than using the word spirit or soul."

Critics typically respond—usually favorably, sometimes less so—to Redgrove's "use of prolific imagery, the transformations which take place in his poems, and the otherworldly atmosphere they create," stated *Contemporary Authors*. His work, in its lushness, is sometimes found to be overdone and overwhelming. *The Kenyon Review* commented on Redgrove's "keen sense of the numinous": "[He] reveals the radiant auras, the envelopes of energy surrounding common things," the review stated. "When his strategies fail, they produce little more than a blur, a screen of mist between the reader and the object. But when they succeed, as they often do, we find ourselves in a world akin to that of Turner's paintings or Blake's visions."

"There is no poet writing in Britain with a more ebullient imagination than Peter Redgrove," wrote the *Times Literary Supplement*. "Everything he sees is transformed by that imagination."

David Adams Richards: Canada's "Independent" Intellectual

One thing most graduate students in Canadian English classes know is Northrop Frye's oft-printed summation of Canadian literature, specifically that "There is no Canadian writer of whom we can say what we can say of the world's major writers, that their readers can grow up inside their work without ever being aware of a circumference." Frye continues: "If no Canadian writer pulls away from the Canadian context toward the centre of literary expression itself, then at every point we remain aware of his social and historical setting." Upon examination, Frye's two statements seem contradictory, not of each other but within themselves. Growing up inside of anything *requires* demarcation and periphery, for "inside" is understandable only if its opposite, "outside," is knowable, the opposite term's absence as meaningful as any presence. But the point is not to argue the theory willy-nilly; rather, to test whether Frye's remarks about our literature are still valid as artistic measures. In my view, they never were; in my view, they reflect a colonial bias the stigma of which remains entrenched in the Canadian ethos. By extension, the inference that art should extinguish the particular for the universal seems ludicrous, the sort of pronouncement that cultural elitists like Eliot and Woolf were fond of making. Are readers of Faulkner and O'Connor not aware of Mississippi and Georgia; are readers of Hardy and Lawrence not aware of Wessex and Nottingham? Do Faulkner, O'Connor, Hardy, and Lawrence, the great regionalists, not occupy "the centre of literary expression"? What, then, limits "social and historical setting" from being a means to that center? And what exactly admits the particularities of these great regionalists to universals?

In Frye's two statements, we witness what has been a sad truth about Canadian literature (and, indeed, Canadian culture) for the last century: the consensus, seeded and confirmed by our critics (Frye the greatest among them), that what is Canadian is second-rate. Eliot's fierce Anglophilia is but the blueprint that critics like Frye followed, critics who believe that for Canadian literature and art to evolve to a world stage it must cease being Canadian, must deny its "Canadian context." This, of course, as we know from Edward Said, is the great lie of cultural imperialism, and it is a lie that Canada, wedged uneasily between two cultural monoliths (Britain and the U.S.), has ceded to. That we had little choice in the matter is noteworthy if inconsequential. The fact remains that Canadians have been rewarded for looking elsewhere for excellence in art, music, and literature—and that this "elsewhereness," espoused by our second-greatest critic, Hugh Kenner, has informed the creation of art and literature in this country. Even critics from our own regions, none finer than Nova Scotia's R. J. MacSween, fell prey to this "elsewhere" poetic. Assessing the world-class poet from New Brunswick, Alden Nowlan, MacSween wrote: "The only complaint from this reader is that Nowlan seems always to hunt in the territory which is already his own. It would be wonderful if he were to enter a land of volcanoes and wizards." Volcanoes and wizards? There is not a volcano or wizard in Faulkner, O'Connor, Hardy, and Lawrence, all writers who MacSween admired tremendously, all writers who hunt in territories of their very own. There is, however, a sense of "awayness" in their hinterlands, a

David Adams Richards

Born in Newcastle, New Brunswick, in 1950, David Adams Richards is a novelist, poet, playwright, screenwriter, essayist, and short story writer. Raised in a middle-class family, he was the third of six children. His love of writing developed at the age of fourteen, when he read *Oliver Twist* by Charles Dickens. In 1969 he entered St. Thomas University in Fredericton. There he studied English literature, attended informal writing workshops, and wrote his first book of poetry, *Small Heroics*. Before completing his degree, he left St. Thomas to pursue his writing career full-time. In 1971 he married Margaret McIntyre.

In 1974 his first novel was published. His first three novels, which form a trilogy, together with a collection of short stories trace the intersecting lives of working-class characters. In 1986 he received a short-listing for Canada's prestigious Governor General's Award for *Road to the Stilt House* and the Canadian Book Information Centre's award as "One of Canada's Ten Best Fiction Writers." In 1988 the first book of his second trilogy, *Nights Below Station Street,* won the Governor General's Award. Two other major awards followed (the Canadian Authors Association Award and the Canada-Australia Literary Prize) for the second novel in the trilogy, *Evening Snow Will Bring Such Peace*, and he won another Governor General's

Award in 1998 for *Lines in the Water.* Two of his novels have been made into films from his screenplays, and Richards' original screenplay, *Small Gifts* (1994), has also aired several times on CBC TV. He has also published nonfiction and has served as writer-in-residence at the University of New Brunswick, the University of Alberta, and Hollins University. Richards currently lives in Toronto. ■

sense that confers legitimacy by virtue of difference. While regions from away constitute literary landscapes, then, regions from home, if we are to believe the experts, rarely do.

I would be manipulative of the truth if I implied that the young Faulkner, O'Connor, Hardy, or Lawrence experienced anything different in their times. Fact is, they experienced much the same thing. Reeking of the familiar, their works were similarly dismissed. The foulest smells always seem to issue closest to home, at least in the estimation of home-bred critics.

■ ■ ■

At the university—the place where [Wheem] had staked his whole life—his amorality had become moral; and he had treasured this intellectual comfort. All of a sudden people were

*saying how moral, how comforting he was to women and he, in his three-piece suit, began
to believe this also. It didn't matter if it was true. Only that it didn't have to be true if people believed it.*

Hope in the Desperate Hour

■ ■ ■

I establish this bias as a way of introducing David Adams Richards, though I admit being
uncomfortable in introducing a writer through the detritus of his critical reception. To
appreciate Richards, however, is to understand something of that reception. Richards is
unique in Canadian literature for the drubbing he has taken at the hands (and feet) of critics, the vast majority of whom have been urban, academic, and miles removed from the
social periphery which Richards inhabits and explores. When I say Richards is unique, I
mean he leads all other Canadian writers in the abuse he has taken. And when I say he
inhabits and explores a social periphery, I mean to say that, as an Atlantic Canadian artist,
he exists outside of the ideological engine-room of our nation, both culturally and geo-
graphically. His sensibility is working class, rural, and anti-intellectual, the consequence of
which has been his labeling as "literary regionalist" by critics and appraisers from away. But
if Richards is a mere regionalist, then so is Chekhov; not a bad thing to be a regionalist,
which is the secret we in the hinterlands are not telling, the secret that time alone will con-
fer as excellence.

The reception of Richards' 1996 novel, *Hope in the Desperate Hour*, is indicative of what I
am saying about his critical reception. The following reviews come from Canada's largest-circulating mainstream media—from *Maclean's* magazine, our national weekly, and from our two
most-read dailies, *The Montreal Gazette* and Toronto's *The Globe and Mail*.

Entitled "Beautiful Losers," the *Maclean's* review begins,

> …the novels of David Adams Richards are an acquired taste. One of the country's
> best writers, he is not among its most popular for the simple reason that his books
> are so often sad.… [Richards] ferrets out the tragedy in the lives of marginal people.

The Montreal Gazette review, sinisterly entitled, "If Not For Dysfunction, These Losers Wouldn't
Function At All," also takes a personal affront to Richards' fictive cast and landscape, portraying
the author again as a rat ferreting out misery in a human landfill:

> Like much of Richards's fiction, *Hope in the Desperate Hour*…assembles the usual
> collection of chronic losers and low-rent dreamers. When they aren't abusive, they
> are unreliable.… There are so many doomed points of view drifting in and out of
> the narrative it may be hard to find your way.… You may also be tempted to ask
> why you should bother.

The third review, from *The Globe and Mail*, starts to sound familiar, a tawdry concord that has
clear ideological overtones:

> …a sky has lowered a storm and anyone who hasn't been afflicted by scandal,
> shame, rejection, marital collapse, police investigation or medical calamity is about
> to get their due.… For desperation in this abundance, time isn't measure
> enough.… [Richards sets a] standard for unsentimental observation of the blighted,
> eternally straitened lives of people trying to do right and ending up, most of them,
> wronged. In Richards' novels there's always some abstract smell in the air, "of
> evening," or "of snow." It's rank tragedy, more like.… The promise of hope notwith-
> standing, the inevitability of despair hangs heavy.

The constant in the review segments above is a direct and undisguised frontal attack against Richards' working-class people (against the majority of New Brunswickers), an attack that, if mounted outside the presumed "make-believe" world of fiction, would bring the swiftest penalties imaginable, those reserved for an enlightened "zero tolerance." Canada's new intellectualism holds, then, and paradoxically, that we must empathize with the working-class in real life, but in fiction, obviously, we are free to despise them. (Does this discrepancy in tolerances say anything about enlightened attitudes? You bet it does!) The diction alone betrays the sour taste left in the mouths of the culturally elite who, in Richards' work, must suddenly contend, not at arm's length but face-to-face, with the recipients of their social welfare. To translate their prejudice, that which is presented as "official mainstream verdict" in our largest-circulating print media, Richards is not "popular" because his books are "sad," focusing on the "inevitability of despair"; he is not popular because he writes about the "marginal"—what *The Globe and Mail* reviewer patronizingly refers to as "the good people of New Brunswick"; and he is not popular because his characters are "losers" who "smell" bad and whose "dreams" are tantamount to "dysfunction." Such judgment, full of the prejudice of center and privilege, smacks of the worst kind of colonial, satisfied dismissal. Yet it is tolerated; indeed, the sum of this criticism informs our national consciousness. And Richards, who has confronted these attitudes directly in his work, has paid the price accordingly.

If scorn alone were the only criteria for greatness, Richards would be our greatest writer. However, when scorn as critical reception is added to the remarkable quantity and quality of his literary output, Richards has no equals in Canada; he *is* our greatest writer, for whom scorn is a reflection, albeit twisted, of the freshness of his vision. So precocious is that vision that critics, who sense their own tolerances and ideals being challenged, respond to his work with anxiety and rancour. And just as Henry James and F. R. Leavis, the greatest critics of Hardy's time, dismissed the "poor little" Dorsetshire writer not only as "factitious and insubstantial" but so insignificant as to hardly bear mentioning in *The Great Tradition*, so have Canadian critics dismissed Richards, pushing him outside of what has been deemed the safe and proper sphere of literary attention. In both cases (for Hardy and Richards), it is anxiety, discomfort, and awe expressed as dismissal. As I have written elsewhere, Richards is the most admired and berated and misunderstood Canadian writer of the century.

Humans are savage in the absence of precedent. Thus, our most celebrated artists are rarely championed in their lifetimes; instead, veneration usually goes to the popular, as two of the three Richards reviewers above openly admit.

■ ■ ■

It felt good to be in the hayfield again. The day was hot. Across the river the reserve sat blinded in the heat. The slanted roofs, the smoke from the far-off dump. A dry road led through its centre, and now and then a car silently travelled that road. In the late afternoon he went down to the river to sit and drink a bottle of beer. A salmon rolled in the rip just out from him.

Hope in the Desperate Hour

■ ■ ■

Though I have chosen—again, with reservation—to enter Richards' work through the fallout of his critical reception, I now move from effect to cause, examining the raw material of Richards' artistic vision, that which has made the Canadian critical establishment so uncomfortable and defensive. To begin, Richards' literary output has established him as a writer who must be taken seriously; in fact, few Canadian writers in the last twenty-five years have been as prolific as Richards, who published his fourteenth book last fall. Another problem (the fundamental one as I see it) that Richards' work presents for the critical establishment is an unprecedented consistency of moral vision. His first published volume, a collection of poems entitled *Small Heroics* (1972), documents early in his writing career the concerns that dominate his mature work. In its title, the collection announces Richards' preoccupation with that which is outside the literary mainstream, whether it is "angered dogs / Who behind hedge rows / Bark at flakes" ("Barren Man") or old women who "Strain out excrement in pain / And think of tired things" ("An Old Woman"). Appearing next to what traditionally has been considered non-literary subject matter is also Richards' concern in this collection with the constancy of suffering. The "small heroics" of bees hopelessly but valiantly defending their hive against a human's extermination ("Small Heroics") is presented as on par with the inconsequence of human misery:

There is a certain Harmless
Walking on the road
A beggar in the morning
Wading spring water
Collecting bottles as he goes;

Before his time another
Existed exactly the same
Collected refuse in a ditch
A wet sack making him lame.
"Traditional"

Though the subject matter of *Small Heroics* does not include the "volcanoes and wizards" that for some constitute appropriate literary attention, the feel for emotional suffering, lived experience, dusty roads and salmon rolls, and the resilience of the human spirit in Richards' first published work is remarkable, especially when one considers that he was only twenty-two when the collection appeared. Such precocity, as Dylan Thomas's self-destructive boozing confirmed, is always a dangerous thing, both to its host and to those subjects it implicates in its gaze.

■ ■ ■

You do not always know how things happen. They just do, and then in hindsight and with reflection, you have the feeling of an epiphany—of some kind of justice in the faintest measure in all things, all events.

Hope in the Desperate Hour

■ ■ ■

From the time of his first published volume of poems and first fictional trilogy, Richards' work has focused both on the downtrodden and on the motives of so-called liberal humanist interventions to alleviate suffering. Whether disenfranchised or empowered, his characters are good and bad, heroic and cowardly, spontaneous and calculating, their deeds and actions often speaking in opposition to what they are allowed to think of themselves based on what others say about them. The reckless John Delano in *The Coming of Winter* is a good example of this incongruity between actions/instincts and words. Dismissed as self-serving by most of the characters in the novel (and, indeed, most of the readers looking into it), John struggles throughout the narrative not so much to come to terms with the accidental death of his best friend, but to find a way of providing for his best-friend's girlfriend, a result of John's struggle is less important than the struggle itself, which is manifest at best as a fuzzy abstraction in John's unconscious mind. Booze and his own worst tendencies only defer a resolve that his instincts and his loyalty to his dead friend cannot deny: "He kept glancing from side to side as he drank but more often glancing up the road toward her place, her home as if he knew in himself he must see her now."

Such subtlety of intentions is what characterizes Richards' work, giving it the power that only a disciplined and spare fidelity to truth can convey. What Richards is interested in exploring is not a showy, angst-ridden emotionalism but the quiet insecurities, perplexities, and loyalties that constitute a life. Many times his characters admit that they don't even know the reasons for their own actions, as Arnold does in *Road to the Stilt House* when he says, "I can never tell you why I got the tattoo on my back. I never know why I smell gritty stove dirt in my blood, or why I falsely told the RCMP officer I blamed Canada for my own lost mistakes." Equally perplexed by his own motives, Joe Walsh, too, is paralyzed by uncertainty:

> The worst of it was that he had no faith in himself concerning this [job]. If he did not do the job he would be looked upon as ridiculous. If he looked ridiculous perhaps Rita would think it was because he had quit drinking and had gone strange. If he did not do it he would feel less than himself, and yet, once he had done it, he felt something would happen that could make him regret it.
>
> *Nights Below Station Street*

The outcome of Joe's dilemma, like the outcome of John's and Arnold's (like the outcome of Tracy McCaustere's in *Hope in the Desperate Hour*) is not the focus of Richards' effort. Instead, the allowance for uncertainty that Richards gives his characters is a passport to their freedom— to succeed or fail on their own, without their creator's intervention. And, usually, the stakes are not as spectacular as success or failure; usually, the stakes are much more subtle: struggling to overcome personal weakness and fear, confronting the private demons of alcohol and violent upbringings, and battling the various attitudes that seed inferiority. As Sheldon Currie writes, the kind of subtlety of the unconscious that Richards employs, as well as the personal agency he gives his characters, is not the stuff of popular fiction, nor is it for the faint of heart:

> All Richards' work requires close attention, a healthy tolerance for ambiguity, and an ability to get along without cheap novelistic tricks: silly sex, needless violence, fashionable ideas, *au courant* dialogue, and romanticized characters. And more than anything else the reader needs to bring the kind of intelligence and imagination necessary to discover meaning without the author's intervention, as well as the wit and sense of humour to see the comic in the tragic and vice versa; these are troubled waters, these Miramichi River stories, complex and profound, simultaneously comic and tragic, [not] for the inexperienced or the inattentive....

That Richards' imagined world takes work (in the form of concentration) and a good deal of lived experience (in the form of emotional maturity) admits his art to the realm of the serious, where manner and motive, humor and compassion, attain spiritual dimension. And though he has evolved technically from his first fictional trilogy, Richards is rare in that his aesthetic emerged fully formed. The combination of Richards' high moral seriousness and what he assumes to be his reader's commitment, in kind, to his exploration of the triumphs and absurdities of the human heart, removes his work from a popular ground. Inattentive readers, as Currie correctly suggests, can easily miss the point.

■ ■ ■

His father would stand with his shirt out weaving back and forth, his right fist cocked a little, back against the wall, and the dry earth, the smell of hay, tumbling with the crickets and the smell of summer and all the world jostling in trumpets of song—a mentally unfit melancholy man along a road with a little boy by the hand. Then you know truth. You don't know it before then. (This is what he could not tell Vera, of course.) You don't know it before then.

For Those Who Hunt the Wounded Down

■ ■ ■

A lack of compromise to the sloth of contemporary tolerances is only one aspect of, and actually incidental to, Richards' work, even though that sloth is writ large in his critical reception. Much more deliberate in Richards' program is a preoccupation with the social constructions of normalcy. Consequently, his work often challenges and interrogates what we as educated, middle-class readers assume to be "normal" and "expected," with the result usually being the private admission that our assumptions are not only false but damaging to those they implicate. To read Richards carefully, then, is to be constantly surprised into self-discovery and reassessment, exactly those discoveries that we as educated moderns like the least.

Richards' treatment of the presumably delinquent Jerry Bines in *Road to the Stilt House* and later in *For Those Who Hunt the Wounded Down* provides abundant evidence of the surprise of subverted expectation. When he is introduced in the first novel, Bines is a small-town thug, ruthlessly preying upon the defenseless Arnold, whose fear of Bines is focused on "coarse and steel-toed" boots that he'd seen "kick a wounded deer to death." Implicated in the theft of jewelry and clothing from the churchyard vault, suspected in the murder of a Norwegian sailor, and given to terrorizing Arnold at will, Bines has little to redeem him in the first novel in which he appears, except the brief suggestion at the end that he is a fulfillment of others' worst fears:

> The police did no favours for Jerry Bines, and he did no favours for them. It started long ago with the police. They did no favours for him, for a long time. When he went to jail...they knew he was a bad apple. They knew that from day one, and treated him accordingly. One day led to the next and soon he was being locked up during exercise. Soon he was let out of his cell only to shower.

Leaving only that unexplored suggestion that Bines is not the sole author of his fate, Richards closes the novel with a promise that "The road, sooner or later, will tell us everything. We only have to wait." And so, like Arnold, who also knows the truth that the road will tell, we wait, a wait that is almost ten years. Two other novels are published, a new trilogy cemented. Bines reappears in the final book of that trilogy, in *For Those Who Hunt the Wounded Down*, his presence held in abeyance as if to challenge the casual reader's span of attention (as if, as well, to show critics like Frye that it *is* possible to grow up inside his fiction).

When Bines is again introduced, he is attended by all the fabulous rumor and gossip of a bad reputation, and we, safe like the townsfolk in the novel, revel in his badness: that "he was the only man to ever come over the wall at Dorchester;" that he was "the kind of man who if he can't beat you with his fist would get a brick." Catching us unaware, however, are a series of less fantastic insights about Bines that only fragments reveal: his love of children, his protection of the innocent, his forgiveness of human weakness, his tenderness toward a sick son, and, most remarkably, his genuine desire for reform. When we exit the subterfuge of communal myth-making and gossip and enter Bines' own consciousness, we discover a personality and spirit that our expectations cannot accommodate. But Richards doesn't let us off that easily. To further unsettle our assumptions about the tidiness of character and class, Richards introduces a foil for Bines, a personality whose well-intentioned, middle-class motives mirror our own. A social worker specializing in child welfare, Vera is a character we recall from an earlier novel, *Nights Below Station Street*. As her introduction in *Nights* indicates, she is rather hapless and pathetic, given to trends and low self-worth:

Vera was tall and thin, and she wore a pair of granny glasses with golden frames and big long flowery dresses…. Vera had affected a sort of British accent from a year at Oxford…. As a little girl Vera had read all of Jane Austen. She began writing poems, and they had a poetry group at noon hour in the school. She was interested in all kinds of things. (Nevin [her boyfriend] hadn't read anything but because he grew a beard everyone assumed he had.) Vera always seemed to be alone. Ralphie would watch her coming up the lane, as a schoolgirl carrying her books in her arms, with her big round glasses fogged up and snow falling on her hair. Because she always ate oranges the boys used to call her sucker. And she was always looking for new friends. And there was a great deal of silence about her.

When Vera reappears in *Wounded*, her motives, like Bines', are revealed. She has since divorced Nevin "for mental and emotional cruelty, and [speaks] calmly about this," and she seeks out Bines as a malleable ground for her pop psychologizing:

It wasn't that his story interested her so much. But he fitted a pattern that she had concerned herself about over the last four or five years. And she had convinced herself that she could expose this pattern better than anyone else, show his kind of male violence, show the broader scope of such violence and how it "impacted" on children and women. "Impacted" being the new word of choice for her at this moment.

When entered, Vera's own consciousness reveals a cold-hearted ideologue, whose covert and unreflexive violence is much more insidious than that ever carried out by Bines. What is remarkable about both characters is not the opposite path of their trajectories across three novels, but our own desire as middle-class readers to assign them qualities neither deserves: Bines doesn't deserve our condemnation any more than Vera deserves our admiration. In fact, opposite trajectories may not even exist; the more likely probability is that Bines always tended toward moral goodness and Vera toward moral corruption. Quick to judge, however, we assume what we've been taught to assume. As Richards has written elsewhere, "If one of my characters had a car up on blocks in his back yard, he must be *illiterate*, and probably *slept* with his sister."

What is at stake in Richards' later work, then, is a wholesale examination of the motives and perceptions of liberal humanism, especially when "impacting upon" interventions to alleviate the suffering of the downtrodden. Why is it, Richards is asking, that progressive ideology as active, often disruptive, intervention goes unquestioned? Why is it that enlightened attitudes and their attendant "isms" pass for models of social justice? Why is it that the educated middle class suddenly has a monopoly on social concern, and that social concern is immediately assumed to be the hallowed (and nonpartisan) business of a few? As Father Billy says at the close of *Road to the Stilt House*: "'Meddling has killed them, legislation has destroyed their house; how can anyone be legislated to have honour, to love or hope for goodness, when there is triumph in the social worker's face and pride in the schoolmaster's eyes?'" The result of such narrow and self-serving attitudes, Richards illustrates, is a further hunting of the already-wounded, and so Vera's eventual book on Bines, entitled *The Victims of Patriarchy (and Its Inevitable Social Results)*, is in the end not about Bines and how he "shook your hand" but about Vera, just as all middle-class interventions ultimately serve the middle class. In telling truths about ideology that are not only unfashionable but that implicate those who have taken out student loans to pay for their moral positions, Richards has attracted the wrath of those who chart our ideological ground.

■ ■ ■

God calls on man not to be comfortable but to be great.

Hope in the Desperate Hour

■ ■ ■

If we are to marshal the evidence of Richards' assessment via the inference of his critics' wrath, we must not only conclude that his subject matter is deficient of literary merit and his social satires unworthy of advanced ethics of correctness, but that the role of the artist in society is to affirm rather than interrogate social and ideological truth. Fortunately for all of us, Richards has dispelled these myths in his work, showing us an opposite way. But to suggest that his path has been easy would have been to do him an injustice, for, like all great artists, he has not only had to deal with the lading of his genius but with the intolerance of those along the way. I have therefore called him in the subtitle of this article, Canada's "independent" intellectual, choosing C. Wright Mills' term as a descriptor. Himself an uncompromising intellectual, Mills wrote the following about the responsibility of the intellectual in the twentieth century:

> The independent artist and intellectual are among the few remaining personalities equipped to resist and to fight the stereotyping and consequent death of genuinely lively things. Fresh perception now involves the capacity continually to unmask and to smash the stereotypes of vision and intellect with which modern communications swamp us.

Along with only a handful of other writers and public intellectuals in our mass-society, Richards is worthy of Mills' highest calling.

Robertson Davies—like Frye, a Canadian well-known to American readers —wondered aloud in the first book of his Deptford trilogy whether or not Canadians would recognize a saint if one were presented to them through selfless action. Based on the neglect of Mary Dempster, his saint in *Fifth Business*, he concluded that we would not. In David Adams Richards, Davies' hunch is again confirmed—mind you, not because Richards is any kind of saint, but because his books, which are modern-day morality plays, have been systematically neglected and dismissed. I say "systematically" to reflect both what has gone on and what Richards has identified as the calculation of dismissal as opposed to the spontaneousness of good will.

As Walker Percy has written, it is rare that adults are treated to a fresh vision; it is rare that they can recapture "the loss of the creature." Well, the good news that I bring is of a writer so accomplished, and so outside the literary mainstream, that reading him is to read again for the first time. As John Moss has observed, "It is difficult to imagine prose more elliptical and precise…. Richards writes with such integrity, in ways sanctioned…not by precedent or convention but by an utter conviction in the truth of what he does, that the genius of his art makes…a vision of the human condition that excites and appalls with stunning force." In an age of abundant confusion over morality—an age in which, writes Richards, many mistake "being nice for being good, being compliant for taking a moral stand"—the fiction of David Adams Richards takes considerable risks in documenting the only kind of truths which have (and will) outlive sophistry: truths of charitable intention, of self-sacrifice, of courageous action, of humility, and of that fierce human capacity to remain hopeful, often against all the evidence and all the odds. Though some Canadian critics, I am ashamed to admit, have shown little tolerance for anything but new-age morality in their literature, many Canadian readers, distrusting the critical establishment, are starting to take a second look at a writer whose quantity and quality of literary production is unmatched in Canada today.

■ BOOKS BY DAVID ADAMS RICHARDS

Small Heroics (poetry). Fredericton, N.B.: New Brunswick Chapbooks #17, 1972.

The Coming of Winter. Ottawa: Oberon Press, 1974.

Blood Ties. Ottawa: Oberon Press, 1976.

Dancers at Night (short stories). Ottawa: Oberon Press, 1978.

Lives of Short Duration. Ottawa: Oberon Press, 1981.

Road to the Stilt House. Ottawa: Oberon Press, 1985.

Nights Below Station Street. Toronto: McClelland & Stewart, 1988.

Evening Snow Will Bring Such Peace. Toronto: McClelland & Stewart, 1990.

For Those Who Hunt the Wounded Down. Toronto: McClelland & Stewart, 1993.

A Lad from Brantford & Other Essays. Fredericton, N.B.: Broken Jaw Press, 1994.

Hope in the Desperate Hour. Toronto: McClelland & Stewart, 1996.

Hockey Dreams: Memories of a Man Who Couldn't Play. Toronto: Doubleday, 1996.

Lines on the Water: A Fisherman's Life on the Miramichi. Toronto: Doubleday, 1998.

The Bay of Love and Sorrows. Toronto: McClelland & Stewart, 1998.

Mercy Among the Children. New York: Doubleday, 2000.

David Adams Richards is one of our best-kept cultural secrets. He won't be for long. If ever there has been a Canadian writer whose body of work and constancy of human care deserve Nobel consideration, Richards qualifies. His life's work has been the documentation of a pure and simple spiritualism. The lifeblood of a people has been his sacred trust. Many have grown up inside his work, delighted by the familiar and knowing with certainty that someday soon the fictional Miramichi will be as well known as Yoknapatawpha. It is certainly as richly conceived and presented, as carefully cherished and protected.

Tony Tremblay
October, 1999

UPDATE

David Adams Richards has since written the novel *Mercy Among the Children* (2000), which won Canada's prestigious Giller Prize for fiction. It has met with mixed reviews, however. "Readers with sufficient fortitude for unrelenting misery and despair will find rewards in a harrowing and powerful novel," wrote *Library Journal*. *Publishers Weekly* called it "stark and affecting," and predicted a larger U.S. audience for Richards. "The dogged narration takes some time to acquire dramatic tension, but eventually its unflagging rhythm becomes addictive. . . . Richards shows how powerfully the novel can operate as a mode of moral exploration—a fact sometimes forgotten in the age of postmodern irony."

Gabrielle Roy: Granddaughter of Quebec

■ I

I don't know why the works of Gabrielle Roy aren't better known in this country. It isn't that we don't read French novels, or Canadian novels. Most of us read *Maria Chapdelaine* in youth, and many of us are now reading Margaret Atwood. It is true that French-Canadian books are hard to come by; my bookseller in Cambridge (Mass.) told me to write Blackwell's in Oxford (Ox.) for books published in Montreal (no luck). But our neglect of the first woman elected to the Royal Society of Canada, and the first Canadian to win the Prix Femina, must have other causes. Perhaps she is not modern? Neither is Isaac Bashevis Singer. Perhaps she is not experimental? Neither is Robert Penn Warren. Perhaps she is not feminist? Neither is Eudora Welty. Perhaps she has a bad press? But her first novel, *Bonheur d'Occasion (The Tin Flute)* was a Literary Guild selection with an initial printing of 500,000. Her Canadian bibliography, both in French and English, is enormous, and I gather that she is taught as a classic in the schools, and is considered the founder of a truly Canadian literature.

Gabrielle Roy, the youngest of eleven children, was born in 1909 in Saint-Boniface, the French suburb of Winnipeg. Her maternal grandparents were farmers who left Quebec in the 1890's. Her father was one of two million Quebeckers who left at the turn of the century to work in the textile mills of New England. Via Wisconsin he worked his way north to Manitoba, where he became a government agent who helped to colonize immigrants, mostly in Saskatchewan. Educated in Catholic schools and at the Winnipeg Normal Institute, she taught school for seven years—"les plus belles années de ma vie." In 1937 she left for Europe, where she briefly studied drama in London, toured France, and started contributing to French and Canadian journals. Forced to return by the war, she settled in Montreal and reported, largely for the *Bulletin des Agriculteurs,* on the social and economic life of the Province of Quebec, and on the peoples of Canada. *Bonheur d'Occasion* was published in 1945, and since then there have been some eight books. Mme. Roy is married and lives in Quebec.

I have stolen the title of my essay from the *Dossiers de Documentation sur la Littérature Canadienne-Française* (Editions Fides, Montreal, 1972). (The literary critic begins in enthusiasm and ends in research.) But my working title, in bad French, was "Gabrielle Roy: Chère Maître." Gabrielle Roy has nothing in common with Henry James except mastery and a deep concern with emerging national character. Her one short-term expatriate, Pierre Cadorai of *La Montagne Secrète,* dies of homesickness. Casting around for helpful comparisons, I thought of Flaubert—but Roy has sympathy. Of Willa Cather—but Roy has subtlety. Of Katherine Mansfield—but she has force. Of George Eliot—well, yes, but hardly canoeing down the Mackenzie. Finally I paused at Chekov, and was rewarded when my research heard her say

Gabrielle Roy

Gabrielle Roy was born in 1909, in a suburb of St. Boniface. The youngest of eleven children, she became a teacher, but left home for Europe, to study acting, at twenty-eight. Within a year she quit acting and began to freelance travel pieces for Quebec newspapers. She left Europe at the advent of the blitzkriegs and returned to Montreal to write, continuing her freelance work and later writing regularly for *Le Bulletin des Agriculteur,* the Quebec farm periodical. Her first book, *Bonheur d'Occasion,* was published in 1945. Quickly translated into English as *The Tin Flute,* it became a Literary Guild selection, won the Governor General's award for Canadian fiction, and the Prix Femina in France. The winner of many of the most prestigious literary awards in Canada, Roy was the first woman elected to the Royal Society of Canada, and she was the first Canadian to win the Prix Femina. She won two more Governor General's Literary Awards, the most recent for *Enchantment and Sorrow: The Autobiogra-*

phy of Gabrielle Roy, which was awarded posthumously in 1988. She died in 1983. ■

I lived part of my life under the secret charm of a nouvelle that I read when very young.... For a long while this early reading penetrated my thoughts, fashioned in me, so to speak, a way of seeing, of observing and grasping the real.... A nouvelle of Tchekov, *The Steppe*.... Perhaps my penchant for uniting landscapes and states of mind (*âme*) dates from this time.

In the following introduction to Roy's work, I have grouped the novels and tales without regard to chronology: The City, The Plain, and the Territory are my categories, transected by the Innocence/Experience or Garden/City theme (vide Hugo McPherson, "The Garden and the Cage," *Canadian Literature,* summer 1959). This grouping seems to be the commanding one, though other groupings suggest themselves. If we followed Marc Gagné's excellent study, *Visages de Gabrielle Roy* (Montreal, Beauchemin, 1973) we should have I: Man, Society, and Progress; II: Cosmology; III: Aesthetics; and IV: the Moral and Religious Problem. Or as my high-school history teacher used to say: Time, Space, and Significance (Miss Ramsdell did not think highly of Aesthetics). But any model is a *modus operandi,* built to be discarded as soon as it has served its purpose.

■ II

The City, in *Bonheur d'Occasion* and *Alexandre Chenevert,* is Montreal; in the former the French working-quarter of St.-Henri, which looks from the docks and the railroad-tracks up toward the more affluent and more English Westmount. *Bonheur d'Occasion* is untranslatable. *Occasion* means chance, or caught-on-the-fly, or bargain. Happiness is a sometime thing. The tin flute of the English title refers to the toy six-year-old Daniel, dying of leukemia, so much desires, but which the family cannot afford. The story is set in the last years of the Depression; Azarius Lacasse, a truck-driver, is often jobless, and the family, held more or less together by the courage of the mother, Rose-Anna, moves from one squalid lodging to another. The eldest daughter, Florentine, a five-and-dime waitress, becomes pregnant, is deserted, marries another boy, and clings to her hopeless ambition of a life less destitute than that of her ever-increasing family. Ironically, the war comes to save them all. Azarius and Florentine's young husband enlist. The book is both compassionate and angry (though not in tone). It was denounced in a Montreal pulpit and sold to Hollywood. Though in every sense a novel, it marks the transition, I think, from Gabrielle Roy journalist to Gabrielle Roy artist.

Alexandre Chenevert, white-collar Montrealer, is no less spiritually frustrated than the Lacasses. Like them, he is numberless. The more wonder that he can be made interesting, without benefit of plot or platform or literary hi-jinks. The novel is realistic, but its realism is touched by both humour and poetry. A sympathetic, unsentimental, unself-conscious imagination penetrates it; *otherwise,* in its clarity of observation and of style, it is very French.

The first two chapters, for instance, give us a night of insomnia and a day in the cage—the teller's booth at the Banque d'Economie de la Cité et de l'Ile de Montreal, for which Alexandre Chenevert, aged fifty-two, has worked for thirty-four years. He is a frail, nervous, repressed, methodical little man; the father of two dead blue babies and one unhappily married daughter. Why should we be concerned about him? It is the question Dr. Hudon and l'abbé Marchand, the hospital priest, ask themselves. Because, with his narrow life, his financial worries, his terminal cancer at fifty-four, he represents suffering humanity? But both men deal with that every day, professionally, and even statistically—much as we deal with the four Ozark children murdered and the fifteen Ugandans shot. Through his patient Chenevert, the physician discovers that he *is,* in fact, interested in suffering; that he is one of the sufferers. And the chaplain discovers that, in fact, he is *not;* that he is unable to offer the sufferer anything more than routine clichés about the soul's salvation.

Chenevert, whose favorite work of art is *The Keys of the Kingdom,* and who derives his information from the media, is obsessed by man's inhumanity to man. The Jews, the Chinese, the Hindus keep him awake night after night. When Gandhi is assassinated, he fasts. But he knows that he is powerless:

> Cependant, lorsque Alexandre pensait que l'on pourrait
> faire la guerre sans son consentement, dans son dos,
> pour ainsi dire; lorsqu'il pesait at calculait que son
> petit argent si péniblement gagné pourrait
> contribuer à tuer quelque inconnu, achèterait
> des bombes, de ces armes meurtrières dont la seule
> idée l'empêchait de dormir; alors, au moment
> d'adresser son chèque au Receveur général, Alexandre
> se serait souhaité le courage d'aller plutôt en
> prison. Mais l'héroisme en ces temps n'était plus
> accessible; bien avant, on l'eût mis à la raison.

He feels powerless to find the truth:

> Alexandre vivait à l'âge de la propagande. Prenez
> un comprimé d'aspirine. Aspirine s'épelle:
> A-S-P-I-R-I-N-E. Je répète: A-S-P-I-R-I-N-E.
> Achetez un pain de savon Lux. Il faut détruire

l'Allemagne. Il faut remettre l'Allemagne sur
pied. Il mousse.

Chacun savait bien pourtant que le savon Lux
ne moussait pas plus qu'un autre. D'un bout à l'autre
de la vie, l'homme entendait un interminable prêche,
et devait se demander: Est-ce vrai? Est-ce faux?

In the cafeteria line at the North-Western Lunch, Alexandre sees the files of souls at the
Last Judgment. He reproaches his colleague Godias for being happy in a tragic world. And yet
he cannot admit to Dr. Hudon that he is unhappy himself; he has not the right.

Les malheureux, c'étaient ces pauvres gens qui
n'avaient pas de pays, pas assez à manger…Il
eut envie de demander au docteur s'il avait lu, lui
aussi, la semaine dernière, dans l'*Echo,* que trois
hommes sur quatre, sur notre planète, étaient
sousalimentés. Non, il ne se voyait pas le droit
d'être malheureux.

On Hudon's recommendation, Chenevert takes a brief wilderness vacation in a primitive
cabin at Green Lake. Here is peace and plenty, flesh, fish, and fowl, and a friendly dog to whom
he gives a name—albeit the wrong one. He dreams at first that he has been asked to add up the
exact numbers of Chinese, but someone appears and throws his accounts into the lake. He
sleeps at last.

He leaves, nevertheless, before his fortnight is up, after trying in vain to communicate his
happiness to his wife and the editor of his newspaper. He is disturbed by the thought that the
faith of his backwoods landlords, the Le Gardeurs, is based on security—or, in short, upon
inequality on earth. But he does not leave without his vision.

La grande affaire, c'était que le Lac Vert fût et
qu'Alexandre l'eût vu de ces yeux. Après, il en
garderait toujours la possession. Croire au Paradis
terrestre, voilà ce qui lui avait été indispensable.

The Earthly Paradise is one necessary belief, and its complement is the belief that we do not
live and die for nothing.

…la passion du Christ n'avait pas ému
complètement Alexandre. N'y avait-il pas eu des
milliers d'hommes qui avaient souffert autant
sinon plus que le Christ, pour des motifs
dérisoires: des frontières, des histoires d'huile,
d'intérêts; parce qu'ils étaient Juifs? Parce qu'ils
étaient Japonais? Et combien d'hommes, s'ils avaient
eu la possibilité comme Jésus de racheter les autres
par leur mort, n'eussent pas longtemps hésité. Mourir
sans profit pour personne, là était la véritable passion.

If dying for nobody's sake is the true passion, Alexandre does not succeed at it. His dying
touches the doctor, the priest, Godias, his longtime clients at the teller's booth, even the flip-
pant bank secretaries. And he feels in their sympathy with his suffering some reflux, perhaps,
of that which he has so long and so fruitlessly poured out on strangers.

To call Conqueror Greenoak Roy's "crucified Canadian" is perhaps taking things too far, for the novel has as much in common with the comedians Beckett and Kafka as it has with the Catholics Greene and O'Connor. The ingenuity of the book is that it is a portrait, though we are loath to recognize it, of a man like ourselves: one who craves the dimension of love in a world of pipelines, placebos, and propaganda. One who can subscribe, finally, neither to creed (Marchand) nor to reason (Hudon); one who gazes from his bus in bewilderment at "chalets en simili-brique, en simili-pierre—dans un pays riche de beaux bois," and at the electrified Christ on a Hydro-Quebec pole: does he light up automatically, or does somebody have to pull the switch?

■ III

Like *Alexandre Chenevert, La Montagne Secrète* concerns the inner journey, but this time the external one starts at the Green Lake and ends in an unfamiliar city. The setting, except for the final scenes in Paris, is in fact the Garden—and what a strange forbidding Garden it is, from the Mackenzie across Saskatchewan and Manitoba to Ungava and Labrador: Canada North, already perishing with the caribou before our eyes.

By waterway across this land, and living off it physically and spiritually, comes Pierre Cadorai, l'Homme-au-crayon-magique, the man with language. Trapper, fisherman, woodsman, Pierre is of uncertain descent. All we know is that his father dealt in skins, and once traded a moth-eaten top-hat to an Indian chief for the best pelts of the season—a startling image of the divine relationship. For a few days Pierre befriends Nina, the little waitress at Fort-Renonciation, and sketches her in her man's shirt and red socks against "le vaste horizon tout pénétré de cris d'oiseaux de mer." And he "thought in spite of himself that he ought to have done her nude, shivering with cold, in this sort of terrestrial paradise."

For two years he traps and fishes with the Dane, Steve Sigurdsen, making hundreds of pencil and crayon sketches on rough paper or wood: the cabin, the snowshoes, the dogs, the frail spring foliage. In the summer, at Great Slave Lake, he is able to order paints for the first time. Then, "pour se connaître mieux, se mieux accomplir," he sets off alone by canoe, hunting his food and paying for an occasional vegetable by tacking sketches to a cabin door. Ten times over, the packet of work that he carries with him is lost to savage weather or savage water. He is nearly blinded by snow; he winters with Indians; he is briefly a miner at Flin-Flon. He arrives finally at Ungava (the northernmost part of Quebec, between Hudson's Bay and Labrador), and here at the end of summer he comes across the mountain which is to obsess him. Nameless and unknown to any human eyes but those of the Eskimo Orok, who warns against its sunset splendor, it is for Pierre the secret goal, the life-giver, *La Resplendissante*. Hour after hour, day after day he draws its every aspect, ignoring the approaching winter and his diminishing supplies. One evening he catches sight of an ancient bull caribou and pursues it to its death. The body warms him through a blizzard. The mountaintop has disappeared. His camp has been savaged by a bear. Weeks later he arrives gangrened and exhausted at Orok's village, a few sketches clasped to his breast.

Here he is discovered by Père Le Bonniec, who insists on arranging a show in Montreal and eventually a fellowship for study in Paris. There Pierre is happy only on the banks of the Seine, where he hails a canoeist, Stanislas, who turns out to be an art student able to get Pierre accepted by his own instructor. Pierre is most successful at drawing the animals in the zoo. In trying to render the streets and landscapes of France, he feels quite consciously the anxiety of influence. He dies in his windowless, woodstove-overheated garret, not at all à la bohème but in the endeavor to recapture his north woods existence. His penultimate work is a self-portrait; he is sketching the mountain once more when he expires.

Such are the simple elements of this story, as lightly drawn as Cadorai's sketches. It is left to us to be surprised by the bare reality (old Gédéon, a Klondike relic, does not at first recognize his own likeness), or to draw further implications. One is reminded of that steamy journey to the heart of darkness, if only by contrast to this icy voyage to the heart of light.

In the arctic Eden, man is not yet fallen. Those who meet—Pierre and Nina, Gédéon, Steve, Orok—are brothers and sisters. They suffer bodily privation, they must kill to eat, they survive in a hostile or at best an indifferent Nature. Yet even here the worm of imagination is at work, and his image is communicated by Pierre across a continent. What is the worm, and what is his message?

The worm, as we have always known, is either God in man, or man against God. Orok watches Pierre sketching the mountain:

> A cet homme Dieu devait parler mieux qu'à Orok.
> Il n'y avait pas à en êre enyieux. Dieu parlait à
> qui il voulait. Du reste, ce n'était pas toujours
> souhaitable d'être celui à qui Dieu parle. Ne
> s'expliquant pas nécessairement avec clarté, Dieu
> était néamoins mécontent de n'être pas compris…
>
> —Que l'Homme-au-crayon-magique, dit-il, prenne garde
> à la montagne. Elle n'aimait peut-être pas sortir de
> son mystère et du silence; elle lui en voudrait
> peut-être de faire son image.

The mountain has two things to say to Pierre:

> Il se peut qu'aucune ne soit comme moi. Cependant,
> personne ne m'ayant vue jusqu'ici, est-ce que j'existais
> vraiment? Tant que l'on n'a pas été contenu en un regard,
> a-t-on la vie? A-t-on la vie si personne encore ne nous
> a aimés?
>
> Et par toi, disait-elle encore, par toi, enfin, Pierre,
> je vais exister.

The artist is charged to give God a real existence, but *par le mauvais temps,* when the mountain withdraws into the clouds, he is reproached:

> Depuis des siècles je suis ici à attendre. Je n'existe
> vraiment que quelques semaines par année, au plus fort
> de l'ete, lorsque mon front sort enfin des brouillards
> et de l'infinie solitude. Je n'existe qu'un moment,
> lorsque je suis belle et calme. Et toi qui m'as vue ainsi,
> tu n'as pas su fixer l'instant, la splendeur, l'exceptionelle
> splendeur qui est ma vérité.

Just before the blizzard which nearly overcomes him, the mountain asks Pierre, "Quel est ce fou qui ose me croire peut-être indulgente?" At the end of his forces, Pierre looks up and sees the single caribou "aux énormes bois, tel un arbre sur sa tête." He wounds but does not kill it before he runs out of ammunition. He pursues it in the dusk through the mountain defiles, finally racing it eye-to-eye, hatchet in hand. "Ecoute, frère," says Pierre, "je n'en peux plus…J'ai faim. Laisse-toi mourir." The caribou is finally, brutally killed; Pierre eats and weeps—"pleurait sur cette création, son inimaginable dureté." In this familiar version, God absconds but sends a comforter.

Oddly enough, it is Père Le Bonniec who suggests that the artist is the rebel against human destiny. How does it happen, he asks, that the best things accomplished in this world are acts of protest? "To create, isn't that to protest with one's whole soul? Unless…unless there is a secret collaboration."

And in his feverish dying dreams of the mountain, once more resplendent and perfect as it has never been in his renditions, Pierre thinks, knows, that his vision is his own work. The imagined mountain has very little to do with the mountain of Ungava. What he has taken from it, he has dissolved in his own interior fire and reshaped into art. So who has succeeded best at creating the mountain, God or Pierre? God, or man against God, or perhaps a secret collaboration?

Whoever he is, what does the worm say? Here, too, we have contradictory inklings which perhaps are reconciled among the stars. On shipboard for France, Pierre reads Shakespeare and is struck by Hamlet's charge to Horatio:

And in this harsh world draw thy breath in pain,
To tell my story.

To tell my story. Is that what it was all about? A self-portrait? But the strange self-portrait has, almost, the horns of the caribou/Christ. So whose story is it?

On his first morning in Paris, Pierre visits the Louvre, where he is struck by Ghirlandaio's *L'Homme à la Verrue* (Man with a Wart, or Old Man with his Grandson). He remembers Le Bonniec's insistence that the artist works for an audience—not for fame or gain, but simply for communication.

> Pierre voyait un viellard au visage affligé d'un nez
> monstrueux, triste de se voir laid devant le regard du
> petit enfant adoré qu'il tenait dans ses bras. Mais, à
> cause de ce tendre amour dans les yeux du viellard, l'enfant
> le trouvait beau et lui souriait dans le ravissement. Et
> le viellard devenait beau, en effet, par les yeux de
> l'enfant. Et Pierre…se demandait si c'était ce qu'
> entendait le Père Le Bonniec lorsqu'il parlait du double
> regard qui est peut-être le moment de la naissance de la
> beauté. Fait étrange, voici que devant ce petit tableau il
> pensait a sa montagne, belle, mais seulement à qui savait
> la voir.

The *double* take is beauty—even for the solitary voyageur, who wishes still in the heart of Paris to *donner la parole aux bêtes*. Not to *name* the beasts, but to express their lives, to give them speech—as Rilke has given them speech, as Cézanne has given speech to rocks and stones and trees. The One Life within us and abroad—to express that *is* to tell the story. Else the nightingale were a mere noise, and Keats a sod.

■ IV

Somewhere between the Garden and the City lies the Frontier. It may be way up in the northwest (*La Petite Poule d'Eau*), where, because she persuades the province to send a schoolteacher to her island family, Luzina Tousignant loses them one by one to the civilized south. Or in the northeast (*La Rivière sans Repos*), where the white man's impact on Inuit life is dramatized by Elsa Kumachuk's struggle to bring up her half-white son. Or it may be as near as the back streets of Winnipeg—la rue Deschambault, three steps from the prairie. It is inhabited, sparsely enough, by a motley crew: Slavs and Scots, Hungarians and Dutch, Italians and Chinese.

Father Joseph-Marie (*La Petite Poule d'Eau*) finds twenty languages insufficient for two or three hundred parishioners in Saskatchewan. The overwhelming impression is one of distance from home. Sam Lee Wong, on the Manitoba prairies, thinks he remembers hills, but he does not know from where. *Levavi oculos*—onto the taiga and tundra, onto the endless wind- and fire-driven plains.

One of my favorites among the "Frontier" group is *La Route d'Altamont,* which like *La Rue Deschambault* is semiautobiographical. Christine's father, like Gabrielle Roy's, is an *agent colonisateur;* the grandparents are pioneer homesteaders from Quebec. These are stories of the generations, of the neighbors in St. Boniface, of the "little Ruthenians" and their gardens at the end of the world. But that is as good as to say "Tintern Abbey" is about a family walking-trip.

The title story of *La Route d'Altamont,* for instance, is a meditation on time, space, memory, and identity. It is dominated by plains, cut in a checkerboard pattern by roads leading, apparently, nowhere. The contrasting human vision of Christine and her mother during their annual fall visit to Uncle Cléophas' farm is of circles and hills. Christine does not at first know that. A third-generation native, she loves the open land without secrets. Her mother is reminiscing about the hills of Quebec, which she has not seen for sixty years. Christine takes a "wrong" turn at an unmarked crossroad. Suddenly they are in a chain of little rocky hills, and the mother, transfixed, communes with them, while Christine watches puzzled.

> Je me demandais tout simplement ce qui pouvait retenir
> si longtemps ma mère en plein vent, sur le roc; et si
> c'était sa vie passée qu'elle y retrouvait, en quoi cela
> pouvait-il être heureux? En quoi pouvait-il être bon, a
> soixante-dix ans, de donner la main à son enfance, sur une
> petite colline? Et si c'est cela la vie: retrouver son
> enfance, alors, à ce moment-là, lorsque la viellesse l'a
> rejointe un beau jour, la petite ronde doit être presque
> finie, la fête terminée.

For two years mother and daughter keep the secret of the hills. Then they learn one evening from Cléophas that the tiny hamlet, Altamont, was founded by Scots highlanders. He says there is no road there. A Norwegian harvest laborer is describing his native mountains and fjords.

> Par ces soirs de souvenirs et de mélancholie, bien des
> fois nous avons retrouvé ainsi, à de rêveuses distances, des
> horizons perdus.

The lost horizons are not only those of the past, but those of the future. The mother is free to rejoin her youth, for all her life-choices are made. Always identified with her father, the dreamer who moved the family west, and herself possessed in youth of the migratory instinct, she becomes more and more like her proper mother, whom she never entirely understood.

> Ah, c'est bien là l'une des expériences les plus
> surprenantes de la vie. A celle qui nous a donné le jour,
> on donne naissance à notre tour quand, tôt ou tard, nous
> l'accueillons enfin dans notre moi. Des lors, elle habite
> en nous autant que nous avons habité en elle avant de
> venir au monde. C'est extrêmement singulier. Chaque jour,
> à présent, en vivant ma vie c'est comme si je lui donnais
> une voix pour s'exprimer.... On se rencontre, on finit
> toujours par se rencontrer, mais si tard!

■ BOOKS BY GABRIELLE ROY

Bonheur d'Occasion. Montreal: Société des Éditions Pascal, 1945.

The Tin Flute (tr. Hannah Josephson). New York: Reynald & Hitchcock, 1947, Toronto: McClelland & Stewart, 1947.

La Petite Poule d'eau. Montreal: Beauchemin, 1950.

Where Nests the Water Hen (tr. Harry L. Binsse). New York: Harcourt, Brace and Co., 1951, Toronto: McClelland & Stewart, 1951.

Alexandre Chenevert. Montreal: Beauchemin, 1954.

The Cashier (tr. Harry L. Binsse). New York: Harcourt, Brace and Co., 1955., Toronto: McClelland & Stewart, 1955.

Rue Deschambault. Montreal: Beauchemin, 1955.

Street of Riches (tr. Harry L. Binsse). New York: Harcourt, Brace and Co., 1957, Toronto: McClelland & Stewart, 1957.

La Montagne Secrète. Montreal: Beauchemin, 1961.

The Hidden Mountain (tr. Harry L. Binsse). New York: Harcourt, Brace & World, Inc., 1962, Toronto: McClelland & Stewart, 1962.

La Route d'altamont. Montreal: Editions HMH, coll. L'Arbre, #10, 1966.

The Road Past Altamont (tr. Joyce Marshall). New York: Harcourt, Brace & World, Inc., 1966, Toronto: McClelland & Stewart, 1966.

La Rivière Sans Repos. Montreal: Beauchemin, 1970.

Windflower (tr. Joyce Marshall). Toronto: McClelland & Stewart, 1970.

Un Jardin au Bout du Monde. Montreal: Beauchemin, 1975.

Garden in the Wind (tr. Alan Brown). Toronto: McClelland & Stewart, 1977.

Cet été Qui Chantait. Québec and Montreal: Les Editions françaises, 1972.

Enchanted Summer (tr. Joyce Marshall). Toronto: McClelland & Stewart, 1976.

Ces Enfants de ma vie. Montreal: Stanké, 1977.

Children of My Heart. (tr. Alan Brown). Toronto: McClelland & Stewart, 1979.

Fragile lumières de la terre: Écrits divers, 1942–1970. Montreal: Éditions Quinze, 1978.

Fragile Lights of Earth: Articles and Memories, 1942–1970 (tr. Alan Brown). Toronto: McClelland & Stewart, 1982.

La détresse at l'enchantement. Montreal: Boréal Express, 1984.

Enchantment and Sorrow: The Autobiography of Gabrielle Roy (tr. Patricia Claxton). Toronto: Lester & Orpen Dennys, 1987.

Le temps qui m'a monqué: suite inédite de La détresse et l'enchantement. Montreal: Boréal, 1997.

But when Christine, the last of her many children, decides to quit her teaching job for Europe—les Alpes, les Pyrénées—and for writing, the mother, deeply hurt, fails to recognize the family resemblance. There is a last visit to the Altamont hills. The magic is all gone. The mother insists they have lost their way, though of course it was only when they were lost that they found themselves.

> Qu'est-ce qui manquait donc à notre promenade
> d'aujourd'hui? Les collines? Ou peut-être le regard?

Le regard. We are back again at the Ghirlandaio, back not at involuntary memory (though that, too) but at involuntary happiness, involuntary love, involuntary beauty—momentary in the mind, but immortal in the flesh.

■ V

To have expressed in words the secret connections between Garden and City, hill and plain, youth and age, pioneer and pilgrim—such is the work of Gabrielle Roy. She has "given the regard" to her vast open-ended country—"beautiful, but only to those who know how to look at it." Like Virginia Woolf, she sees the novel not as a succession of events, but as "a succession of emotions radiating from some character at the center." The mistake of the amateur writer is to think that the emotions are, in themselves, valuable to art. An opposite mistake is to think that the object irradiated can be known in itself, without taking into account the organ of perception. Art, if not consciousness itself, begins in a mysterious cooperation. But beneath this world of "fitting and fitted," of internal and external, subject and object, seems to lie some universal unchanging underground, where, as Edwin Muir has it, all our most precious experience takes place. None of us exists wholly in the world which others see, and upon which our daily life is necessarily based. We exist also in that underground where the artist, when his regard is deep enough, can take us; where the life of men and beasts and stars is indivisible. Gabrielle Roy's books will appeal to proponents of the One Life in Canada and abroad.

Before her death in 1983, Canadian writer Gabrielle Roy published two more novels: *Un Jardin au Bout du monde* (1975), tr. *Garden in the Wind* (1977); and *Ces Enfants de ma vie* (1977), tr. *Children of My Heart* (1979). She also published a collection of her writing in *Fragiles Lumieres de la terre: Ecrits divers 1942-1970* (1978). Before her death, she also contributed to *The Penguin Book of Canadian Short Stories* (1980). Her autogiography, *Enchantment and Sorrow: The Autobiography of Gabrielle Roy*, was published posthumously (1988), as was her memoir, *Le temps qui m'a manque: Suite inedite de la detresse et l'enchantement* (1997), and one of her most popular children's books, *My Cow Bossie*, reminiscent of the work of Laura Ingalls Wilder, was reissued in 1988. Roy's first novel, the award-winning *Bonheur d'Occasion*, was made into a feature film in 1983.

Although Roy never gained a wide reading audience in the United States, she was greatly respected in her native Canada. Sometimes compared to Willa Cather, she wrote compassionately of the struggles of the people of rural Manitoba, where she grew up. The mix of cultures in the northern Canadian woods, and the struggles endured by the many disadvantaged people there—of which she was one—provided Roy with rich material for her novels. "Roy's experience has taught her that life offers an endless series of storms and mischances, wrote *Canadian Literature*. "She records their plight with a tolerance and compassion that rests not on patriotism, humanism or religiosity, but on a deep love of mankind . . . and a sense of wonder and of mystery is always with her." The *Journal of Canadian Fiction* agreed: "Roy immerses us directly in the suffering of her characters: we feel, we think, we live with them. The appeal is directly to the heart."

Canadian Forum suggested that what connects Roy's work is "people's lifelong struggle to understand the integrity of their own lives, to see their lives as a whole, and their need to create bridges of concern and understanding between themselves and others. . . . It is this very tension, and the success that she has demonstrated in dramatizing it, that makes Gabrielle Roy unique among Canadian writers."

Julia Randall
December, 1977

Faith and Practice: The Poems of Mary Jo Salter

Among the many intricate gestures that connect the four books of poems by Mary Jo Salter, one might isolate for brief inspection some of her uses and considerations of the words "original" and "originality." In her first and second books, *Henry Purcell in Japan* (1985) and *Unfinished Painting* (1989), the word occurs in splendid poems, though it does not suggest that its later appearances will be especially worth watching for. "Welcome to Hiroshima," from the first book, treats calmly of what some have thought unspeakable, presenting harsh details from a museum dedicated to the atomic blast, and noting "questions of bad taste, how re-created / horror mocks the grim original."

"Armistice Day," one of several poems occasioned by Salter's mother's art—she was a painter—and her death, begins, "Have I shown you these before?" This is very much in the middle of things; the persona reveals herself gradually as Salter, speaking to her daughter about her mother, but just at the beginning the fragility of originals, and the durability of copies, gets brief but resonant treatment. "These" are photographs of charcoal sketches ("snapshots of / the originals") Mrs. Salter made of wounded soldiers, and then gave to them, during World War II:

> And I suppose
> We're better off to have the photos, if
> the way this paper they've been pasted on
> has yellowed now is any indication.
> What always strikes me, though, is how much life
> she seemed to draw from them, these sorry boys
> turbanned in bandages....

That turn on the phrase "drawn from life" is an example of Salter's unusual interest in wordplay; she drops surprising puns into solemn contexts often enough to suggest that she forgoes many more opportunities than she takes; rarely but memorably, she can test even my tolerance for the clash between solemnity and playfulness, as when, in "'Late Spring,'" about a Chinese painting, she refers to grains of rice as "paddied cells."

In *Sunday Skaters* (1994), the major poem is "The Hand of Thomas Jefferson," which I will discuss in detail later. Here it is enough to notice that the great "Hobby" of Jefferson's later years was the University of Virginia; the Rotunda, and its resemblance to the Capitol, give Salter a chance to muse on the nature of originality and copying:

> They say the nation's Rotunda fills—
> he trembles like Adams—with the light of Trumbull's
>   paintings of revolution, and more
>
> copies made for the cause. He'd have the men
>   who come to his university

Mary Jo Salter

Mary Jo Salter was born August 15, 1954, in Grand Rapids, Michigan. She grew up in Detroit and Baltimore, and was educated at Harvard and at Cambridge University. She is the author of four collections of poems, one of which, *Unfinished Painting*, was the Lamont selection for the year's most distinguished second volume of poetry. She is also an editor of *The Norton Anthology of Poetry* and has served as poetry editor for the *New Republic*.

Her many awards include Guggenheim, N.E.A., and Ingram Merrill Foundation fellowships; an Amy Lowell Poetry Travelling Scholarship; the Witter Bynner Foundation poetry prize; and the Lavan Award from the Academy of American Poets. She shares with her husband, the writer Brad Leithauser, the Emily Dickinson Chair in the Humanities at Mount Holyoke College, where she teaches poetry and poetry writing. ■

> understand this: originality
>   is knowing what to copy, and when.

Finally, in *A Kiss in Space* (1999), there is "Alternating Currents," another long poem to be taken up presently, in which the surprising idea is advanced that Braille can represent the *Iliad* in the original, and Helen Keller considers the question what originality could possibly be. For Salter, it consists in part in making one's own distinctive way through a richly varied anthology of received poetic forms.

In Salter's poems a central tension is that between the urge toward the good, in both life and art, and something else: there is not only the playfulness bordering at times on minor mischief, but also the calm acceptance of darker sides of being human in the world. Many of Salter's poems are, overtly or indirectly, expressions of faith in traditional Christian values, if that phrase may be taken calmly. At the same time some of those poems, and many others, play with the language and with poetic conventions in an apparent effort to push at, or pull the rug from under, the very conventions Salter seems in most ways to respect. Others, like "Welcome to Hiroshima," move steadily on terrifying ground.

Henry Purcell in Japan is a first book of quite unusual maturity, not only in terms of craft, but also in terms of attitude. A better word might be "outlook," since outward is the usual direction of Salter's gaze. She had what it took to learn real lessons from the likes of George Herbert. There are a few graceful love poems here, and some references to a first pregnancy, but the details of personal life are not dwelt on in this book. The personal in these poems is, rather, a matter of resonances, the sympathetic vibrations between the matter observed and the noticing voice. "Refrain," a villanelle with slant-rhymed second lines, opens thus:

Never afflict yourself to know the cause,

said Goneril, her mind already set.
No one can tell us who her mother was

or, knowing, could account then by the laws
of nurture for so false and hard a heart.

The poem stays exclusively with *King Lear* until the refrain lines come together at the end:

The King makes a good fool: the Fool is right.
No one can tell him who his mother was

when woman's water-drops are all he has
against the storm, and daughters cast him out.
Never afflict yourself to know the cause;
no one can tell you who your mother was.

The last-minute arrival of the second person gives these lines the sound of a moral at the end of a fable. Spoken in most poetry workshops, that sentence would not be taken as a compliment, or even as mere description. The end of the poem is an unobtrusive but effective example of Salter's willingness to attempt what is widely warned against.

Many formalist poets consider the opportunity for such attempts one of the primary motivations for working within the tradition. As J. V. Cunningham said nearly forty years ago, "…the problem of form is how to get rid of it. But to get rid of it we must keep it; we must have something to get rid of." Throughout her poetry, Salter makes stanzas both regular and varied at once: consistent length, nearly regular meter, and rhyme schemes that shift sometimes to the point of uncertainty about what the rhyme scheme is.

"Luminary" is an early but durable example; it is a kind of riddle, in that it never names its subject, which is the moon. The first stanza sets up more than it at first seems to:

Just *how* did she come to be there—
shining hugely, inches above the street,
like the answer risen from a question?
In a moment's movement, between
long rows of houses with an air
of subjects at attention,
she settled all her weight
on a great, invisible throne

The only full rhyme is *there / air*, but it seems easy enough to work out the other pairs. However, *question / attention* and *between / throne* have an interdependence that echoes, for example, *one / expansion* in Donne's "Valediction: Forbidding Mourning." This slight instability is enriched in the following two stanzas, as the arrangement of rhyme pairs is varied:

For hours the traffic, like the one-
way tide of her desire,
was drawn into that signal stare.
Yet as she rose she dwindled; what
had seemed the dazzling crown
of a sun-descended sovereign
contracted to a pillbox hat
morning would pull down.

Retiring rather late that night,

> although still a queen, she fit
> into the grid of one windowpane
> the size of a chessboard square.
> And with room to spare—
> enough to allow a pawn
> among the advancing stars to share
> the spot she rested on.

In the second stanza, it is no longer easy to be sure how to pair *one, crown, sovereign*, and *down*, even though two of them are full rhymes. The uncertainty arises partly from the altered rhyme scheme: in the first stanza, there are no pairs in the first four lines; in the second stanza there is one. Things seem to sort out as we move into the third stanza, where *sovereign* is most audibly answered in *windowpane*. Within this third stanza, however, *windowpane* either is not paired or, with *pawn* and *on*, is part of a triplet, like *square, spare,* and *share*. Against these faint suggestions of disorder the stanzas end with slant but solid rhymes, three words it is a pleasure to say aloud: *throne, down, on*. Meanwhile, the metrical patterns of the stanzas also shift constantly, without quite obliterating the impression that most of the lines tend toward iambic trimeter or tetrameter.

In my view, controlled unpredictability gives this poem both steadiness and liveliness, but some kinds of control are in the eye of the beholder. I have encountered people deeply expert in the craft of verse who are capable of flat declarations that, for example, Richard Eberhart can't get away with rhyming "avidity" and "stupidity" in "The Fury of Aerial Bombardment" because triple rhymes should be reserved for humorous effects. Such people tend to be equally certain that shifting rhyme schemes and unstable metrical patterns are important violations of the verse contract. What makes for pleasant surprise is a matter of opinion.

"At City Hall" at first seems simpler, but in terms of rhyme its four-line stanzas are irregular over a range between two pairs and no rhymes, though in many cases the end-words in rhyme-less stanzas echo end-words in other stanzas. The poem recounts, in third person, a young couple's acquisition of a marriage license. Its tone is light at the outset:

> "What kind of license you looking for?"
> the woman lounging behind
> the counter asked. What *kind?*
> A question so disarming the groom
>
> (just outvoicing the dusty carriage
> wheels of ceiling fans)
> conceded ignorance. "Don't mind
> him," the bride said. "A marriage
>
> license." Across the room,
> the only sign—and it was huge—
> was lettered, simply, DOG LICENSES.

"Huge" rhymes either with nothing else in the poem, or with *marriage / carriage*. It doesn't matter. With secure deftness, the poem moves on to the bride's hesitation above the blank marked "Married Name," that raises questions "not to be resolved // by closing time," while the groom pauses over the infant footprint on the bride's birth certificate, coming to grips with the realization that she "had once // been living, evidently, / only for minutes…"

> Asked now to raise
> right hands, to swear they knew

of no impediment,

> he set down his tennis racket;
> their eyes, for an instant long
> to be remembered, gravely met
> in the sweet embrace of fear.

The faintness of the possible end-rhymes with *long* and *fear*, and the distance back to them into parts of the poem not quoted here, make the last sentence and the final stanza a small miracle of formal versification: increasing metrical stability, the tensions of the final clause, and internal slant rhyme bring the poem to a rare firmness of closure.

The third and final section of *Henry Purcell in Japan* is called "Japanese Characters," and opens with the poem of that title. The six poems in the section occupy twenty-one pages; these are substantial items, including the title poem of the book. They arise from an extended sojourn in Japan, when Salter's husband, the writer Brad Leithauser, was employed at the Kyoto Law Center. "Japanese Characters" and the final poem, "Shisendō," are cast in iambic pentameter, somewhat irregularly rhymed; the former is 143 lines, and the latter 127, so each has room for a gradual accretion of impressions, and then their subtle transformation.

"Japanese Characters" is intellectually rigorous, without sacrifice of music or emotional richness. It takes up one complex example of the ways in which our knowing depends on our saying. It begins by stating a difficult problem:

> To look into a word as through a window
> and address the thing itself: a simple wish,
> and one calling me to a simpler time—
> yet when can that have been? Life before English?

Before one acquires language, one looks into a word without having any idea what it is; certainly it is not a window. In any case, in Japan, surrounded by unfamiliar ways of naming things, of which some are familiar and others are not, the speaker (this poem, like fewer than half of the poems in this book, is in the first-person singular) confronts her fear and enchantment, and the slow accretion of meaning around brush-strokes that are rarely painted exactly the same way twice. The contrast between these characters and "typecast, upstanding Roman ABC's" is mysterious:

> How is it that the straitened Japanese,
> living by Muzak and the megaphone,
> tossed from such boats of reference stay afloat
> with strokes on their letters fluent as a stream,
> always familiar, never quite the same?
> A mystery even when, some damp weeks later,
> these start to take on clues of…character.

The last third of the poem introduces an amateur astronomer who "spotted a nova no one else had found." He attributes his discovery to luck, even though

> "I know the sky quite well"—a vivid claim
> suggesting a nightly rummage through its shelves
> of scorpions and saucepans….
>
> . . .
>
> The universe
> observes, it seems, the old misspeller's curse:
> You have to have things down to look them up.

...

Just as new words, once never seen, appear
on every page as soon as known, the sky

prints images upon the clouded eye:
distinguish these, and others will come clear.

The convergence of the universe of stars and the characters that name the universe, occurs easily, as if it were a matter not of the poet's will, but an inevitable development from the observations made.

"Shisendō" is more of a tourist's poem, a lecture-walk through a pavilion in Kyoto called, in English, The Hall of the Hermit-Poets:

...here in the northeast hills, first you must climb
until Kyoto shrinks within the palm
at the base of one long, narrow arm of street
to reach the spot where Ishikawa Jōzan
retreated from the feudal wars, and built
the hermitage whose gate now stands ajar.

The speaker of this poem is primarily a voice addressing a "you," but there are three references to "us"; the first specifies that the speaker is among those "visitors who return at every season." Still, it is the barrier of language that is of interest here: the gradually clarifying pane through which a culture is becoming more clearly defined. The tour proceeds at last to the room whose walls are decorated with paintings of the "thirty-six ancient Chinese hermit-poets":

Most of them hatted, wispily bearded, old,
they sit patiently in brilliant folds of cloth
cut from the long bolt of time. Above their heads
fall poems in a few scrawled, simple lines.

This cascade of wittily echoed *l*'s gives way to the recognition that the builder of the pavilion must have known these poems by heart, "But for us

It's enough to know each letter's packed with secrets,
like the *shi* of Shisendō, or "poetry":
composed of two linked characters—a "tongue"
jangling like the clapper on the bell
of "temple"— it rings but half a change
on the word for "word" itself: "tongue" joined to "leaf."

Among these considerations, there is a rich evocation of the life of Ishikawa Jōzan, the man who built Shisendō, a soldier and a scholar of the Tokugawa period. The lore of the poem is lightly presented, so a world begins to exist in which the Western imagination can meet at least the feel of the poems on the walls, however vague the denotations remain.

"Henry Purcell in Japan" is a superb embodiment of the between-cultures feeling of these half-dozen "Japan poems." It is also a handsome final expression of another important theme in this collection, which has to do with the speaker's faith, in the more or less traditional Christian sense. The first poem in the book, "For an Italian Cousin," declares the speaker's "kind of faith, at least," and "Facsimile of a Chapel" is a brilliant characterization of the struggle between belief and skepticism. In that poem, the speaker comes upon a chapel in a corner of a museum:

As it always does when I forget
I'm not really a Christian, my heart

flew to my knees. I was praying,
once again, for the soul
of my grandmother.

The speaker goes on to ask, "What consecrates a place?" and notes the difficulty of sensing a holy presence in this museum. One senses the magnificence, not of the Creator, but of the Curator. Is God everywhere, or nowhere? Still, she acknowledges her place in this complex scheme:

Yet knowing of my share,
and knowing I'd never happen, in my own
century, on a place better to look,
I pulled up a chair.

"Henry Purcell in Japan" describes a couple of Japanese funerals, emphasizing the speaker's feeling of being foreign. People are assembling at a private house as she passes:

As I walked by they stared at me—
not angry, not stirring or saying a word,
but as if they expected me to concede
I didn't belong there.
At home once more, she listens to a choral performance of Henry Purcell:

Rejoice in the Lord alway,
they sang; *And again I say rejoice*!
How explain to anyone the joy
of that single missing "s"—a winding path

down into a heritage so deep,
so long a part of me it seems
the very state of God?

The tensions between English chapels and Shinto shrines, the living and the dead, are not to be reconciled, perhaps, though the poem ends with a reconciliation between grief and joy:

Yet at home in my random corner
on truth, with no choice but to play
the world sung in a transposed key,
mine was another mourner's voice:
And again I say rejoice.

That duality—joy/grief, quick/dead, light/dark—is central to Salter's second book, *Unfinished Painting* (1989). Dedicated to the memory of her mother, who died before she turned sixty, the book has a predominantly elegiac tone. The title poem and two or three others, including a longer sequence at the end of the book, arise from Salter's mother's death; the second section is a sequence of nine parts called "Elegies for Etsuko," made for a friend in Japan who killed herself when she was twenty-eight. Yet among these poems there are also love poems and one or two meditations that provide opportunities for Salter's unusually serious playfulness.

"Unfinished Painting," in fact, maintains this balance. Its topic is a portrait of Salter's older brother, painted by their mother; it is reproduced on the jacket. The poem itself makes only a two-word reference to Mrs. Salter's death: "Like, too, the image he's retained / of the sun in her, now set.… " It is concerned with various convergences of joy and self-doubt, and demonstrates once again that the painting's being unfinished is one of the things about it that speaks most beautifully of the time from which it came. The third and fourth stanzas are wittily descriptive:

Drawn as if it might reveal
the dotted hills of Rome, a drape
behind him opens on a wall
she'd painted with a roller once.
       Everything made at home—

she made the drapes, she made the boy,
and then, pure joy, remade him in
a pose to bear his mother's hope:
the deep, three-quarter gaze; the tome
       he fingers like a pope.

Between the dedication page and the concluding section, the book gives this poem a poignant context. The five poems at the end of the book, "Dead Letters," take up the challenge of the mail that continues to arrive, addressed to Salter's deceased mother; in moving detail, yet reassuringly conversational tones, the poems recall small moments of joy, triumph, defeat, and hope. At the end, Salter speaks of plants she took from her mother's room, or received from her when her own daughter was born, and tries, nearly a year later, to keep alive. One of the powers that keeps these poems afloat is the tone of acceptance that accompanies the grief:

You too were one to note
Life's artful correspondences.
But I can't let them go,
not yet; and granted time to tend
a growing tenderness, I send

more letters, Mother—these despite
the answers you can't write.

These poems gain power, too, from being preceded by the intensely moving series of poems arising from the suicide of Etsuko Akai. They range through sadness and anger, as well as joy in the recollections of a friendship. Here is the seventh of the nine poems, in its entirety:

Once, in Kyoto, we gossipped past the temple
graveyard where you'd lie, on to the shrine

where you wanted us to buy two paper dolls:
featureless, pure white, the kind a child

cuts in hand-holding chains across a fold.
An old priest had us sign them both for luck.

I wrote across the heart, you down the spine,
then quaintly (so I thought) you drew two smiles...

That was before you snapped your pretty neck.
Happy you may have been, but never simple.

Not all the poems are in the second person; the sequence begins with a third-person setting of the scene; the third poem is a third-person-limited entry into the troubled mind of the subject; and the ninth draws on many old traditions, and makes its strong contribution. It opens with a nod toward Salter's ambivalence about prayer:

On the master list we keep
imagining the scribes still keep

religiously, up there in space,
of every human life, let
them not neglect to fill the line
for Etsuko Akai, who's gone
      from Earth at twenty-eight.

In the impossible blue dark,
let all the bearded saints and
rainbowed angels sorrow can invent
take her, who never made her mark,
and gladly mark the day for love
not of what she might have been,
      but what she humbly was.

The tension between faith and belief seems to recede from the final stanza, but not Salter's sensitivity to the power of context. Doubt and belief are still at odds; "invent," in the second stanza above, is echoed in "inventory" below. The last line admits and even celebrates the futility of some wishes:

Since they will all be there for ages,
let them in their inventory
preserve in lucent, gilt-edged pages
those things I would myself record:
such as the way she'd tell a story—
she'd race, and trip, and laugh so hard
      we'd ask her to start over.

Salter's work has from the beginning included a few longer poems that somewhat noticeably exhibit many characteristics of the essay. Most recently, *A Kiss in Space* includes "Alternating Currents," a poem in four parts adding up to over 350 three- and four-stress lines. According to a note at the back of the book, the poem "was born from a remark by the playwright Suzan-Lori Parks that both Sherlock Holmes and Alexander Graham Bell had assistants named Watson." The note goes on to mention "the most useful books [Salter] consulted for the poem" —eight books about Holmes, Conan Doyle, Bell, and Helen Keller, who comes into the poem by way of her encounters with Bell.

Of course every good poem has time invested in it, but most of that investment has been unwitting. The poet has an experience that does not at first seem to be material for poetry, but days or weeks or decades pass, and the perception or the memory connects with others as emotional states vary, and at last the poem occurs. There is seldom a reasonable way to list the books that have helped in this process. Naturally enough, "Alternating Currents" has a great many qualities that have nothing to do with the soundness of Salter's research.

The four sections of the poem approach somewhat gradually the intersections they hint at. The first, titled "Reading in the Dark," is concerned with Helen Keller, Alexander Graham Bell, and Annie Sullivan, Keller' teacher. It begins in a hotel at Niagara Falls, where Bell helps Keller to feel the vibrations the falls create in a windowpane. So the flow and force of water grow from a feeling in a hand to a concept in the mind (and a recurring image in the poem). The end of the section illustrates aspects of the poem's form and strategy:

At her fingertips, the Braille
armies of words amass: she scans

The Iliad in the original.
(What is original? She hasn't
dared to ask since, at eleven,
a story she had thought she thought
up wholly by herself had proven
to be the tale of a "plagiarist.")
Sometimes she is just as glad
not to tire Teacher, and will work
late into the night—but then,
she writes to kindly Mrs. Hutton,
"one wearies of the clash of spears
and the din of battle." No one hears
the punctured pages turning as
she soldiers on alone, the blind
reading the blind: the lovely Helen
following Homer in the dark.

The form is pleasantly difficult to pin down: lines of four stresses, with here and there a line that might have three in other contexts, and rhyme that turns up according to no pattern I have discovered. The style of the poem modulates easily between the conversational and the elevated, absorbing the risky puns, for example, into the stately last sentence above. By the end of this section, neither of the two Watsons has been mentioned.

The second section, "The Final Problem," takes its title from the Sherlock Holmes adventure in which Conan Doyle killed his hero—or so he thought, until in response to public clamor he contrived a resurrection. As devoted readers of the Holmes stories recall, the great detective met his end on a narrow path above the Reichenbach Fall in Switzerland, where he had gone in full knowledge that there he would have a chance to rid the world of Professor Moriarty, "the spider in a vile / network of radiating evil." Salter's tireless alertness to connections ranges from the incidental observation that Conan Doyle was an oculist, to end-word juxtapositions such as "vile" and "evil." In such a rich context it is almost possible to overlook the reappearance of waterfalls.

Here, from the first section, is part of Helen Keller's nightmare, in which she sees her teacher as a "quarrelsome tormentor,"

driving her to "an abyss, a perilous
mountain pass or rushing torrent."
Once "I saw her robed in white
on the brink of Niagara Falls."
Her costume appeared to be an angel's.
When she dropped into the whirlpool,
Helen, frantic, dove in to pull
Teacher from danger; the figure wrestled
out of her arms and swam to shore
untwinned. And this—the unthinkable
thoughtlessness of one who loved her—
was the purest terror.

And here is the passage retelling the "death" of Holmes, in the second section of the poem:

Face to face
at last, detective and nemesis—

their twin defiance heightened by
the pointed altitude of the Alps—
peer at each other in a bliss
of imminence. The great men tumble
in a wrestler's grip together
down the Reichenbach Fall—unseen
by Watson, who runs up too late.
Yes, that's very good. He'll call
helplessly down the abyss
to hear nothing but his staggered voice
crack open on the cliffs in echo.

The last word is *echo*: twinned figures wrestle above an abyss, and fall. Meanwhile, "unthinkable/thoughtlessness" is an enjambment few poets could have managed.

"The Final Problem" moves on to consider the mystery of Conan Doyle, whose gullible nature seems in many ways unsuited to the task of inventing Sherlock Holmes, a genius of logical analysis plagued with boredom and addiction. The section ends with an image of Holmes's indoor pistol-shooting.

This brings us to the third section, "Hearing Shadows," which opens with the news of President Garfield's having been shot. Alexander Graham Bell has developed an instrument, an "induction balance," with which he might be able to help doctors locate the bullet. Salter's explanation of this device is perhaps cursory and, as she says in her note, "probably highly unscientific," but one does understand that it is something like an audible sonogram, and that its results are somewhat inconclusive. In its way, so were those of the bullet:

The autopsy
reveals the bullet had always lain
too deep for a safe extraction—
which hadn't, in fact, been necessary.
A death caused mostly by infection:
Doctors' unwashed hands.

The fourth section, "A Tangled Skein," opens with a quotation from *A Study in Scarlet*, the novel in which Holmes and Watson first appear. It is the moment when Watson finds a statement in a magazine article and, unaware that Holmes is its author, pronounces it "ineffable twaddle." The statement is that

"'From a drop of water…
                                    …a logician
could infer the possibility
of an Atlantic or a Niagara
without having seen or heard of one
or the other.'"

Finally, we are reminded at the end of the poem that something other than logic can be at work here; Annie Sullivan decides how to go to work with her new pupil:

Keep talking. From a drop of water,
a single word, a Niagara
untangles in their hands.

Before that happens, Salter declares her own lines "tangled," but available for the spirits she has summoned to be in touch with one another, that they may consider, in Holmes's words,

"the scarlet thread of murder" that runs
"through the colourless skein of life."

Among the engaging details recounted here is Bell's gradual disenchantment with the telephone, his annoyance with its tendency to interrupt his dinner, and its uselessness to his wife
("the winningly named / Mabel, the original / Ma Bell"), who is deaf:

> She writes to us
> instead, an essay on the art
> of lipreading. A misnomer. The kiss
> of unheard word with thought must come,
> she says, by marking body clues
> (eyebrows, hands); on the lexicon
> of context; and, since very little
> is ever understood at once,
> on empty-headed readiness
> to miss a detail. You can feel
> your way back to the blanks.

This passage, like many another in this resourceful poem, makes an illuminating way of
considering the differences between direct current and alternating current, whether of water,
electricity, or the play of thought and word.

The intricate textures of historical or imagined lives—and who can say, at certain points of
intersection, which is which?—have received brilliant treatment in many of Salter's poems. Her
third book, *Sunday Skaters* (1994), ends with a section titled "Two American Lives." The first of
these is Thomas Jefferson's, and the second Robert Frost's. These are ambitious subjects, perhaps, but where skill and curiosity are well-matched, the writer, at least, can stop thinking
about ambition and press on.

In "The Hand of Thomas Jefferson," a spirited alertness to possibility seems perfectly suited to an exploration of three extended moments in the life of a man whose serious playfulness,
perhaps more than his ambition, propelled him to majestic and enduring achievements. The
settings of the poem's three sections are Philadelphia, 1776; Paris, 1786; and Monticello, 1826.
The first and third sections are naturally centered on July 4, the date of the Declaration and of
Jefferson's death (and John Adams's) fifty years later. The drafting and wrangling over the Declaration, and the slavery issue, are mingled in the first section with a fine note on Jefferson's
restless scientific curiosity. The morning of the fourth, he had bought a thermometer, and
throughout the day recorded some temperatures:

> The apex came at one in the afternoon:
> seventy-six, the aptest of temperatures.
> Jefferson must have held up to the light
> his instrument, and read it like a vein
> pulsing with the newborn body's powers.
> "The earth belongs to the living," he would write—
> out of his hands, henceforward into ours.

The dignified cadences of this section are modulated in the second part toward a much
more nearly conversational style. In sixteen stanzas of nine lines each, this section takes up the
widowed Jefferson's ministry to France, during which he became infatuated, apparently, with
Maria Cosway, the Italian-born wife of an English painter. The hand of Salter's title is broken in
this section:

> hopping a fence, head over heels
> for her, he trips and falls. The wrist
> of the hand that wrote the Declaration
> has snapped, the right one, never to be set
> properly again.

Wrists will come up again, forty years later, as the aged Jefferson and Adams exchange accounts of ailments. But as the relationship with Maria trails off and Jefferson prepares to sail home, he poses for a painting by John Trumbull, who had introduced him to her:

> Omniscient men at a table
> have signed a Declaration. The crippled hand
> of its author healed, the handsome
> face a decade younger, his heart made whole
> once more, Martha's eternal husband,
> he is painted into the simpler role
> posterity will assign him.

The tension in this section between the characteristics of prose and of verse is unusual even for Salter. Though her work rarely sounds much like Richard Wilbur's, she is interested in some of the same kinds of shapely stanzas that have engaged him, and she is similarly acrobatic in balancing attention to sentences and to lines. However, her facility can rarely give the verse forms a slightly cursory sound, so that the prose impulse, on which they feel as if they have been imposed, still trudges on. The greater risk of this facility is that easy conversational verse might sometimes seem to trivialize a matter of more moment than the sound seems to account for. Such moments occur in most verse; they are scarce enough in Salter's.

"The Hand of Thomas Jefferson" concludes with a leisurely and touching section of 180 lines, in envelope quatrains. It begins with a consideration of the two days a year that Jefferson opened the White House to the public—January 1 and July 4—and by occasion moves on to the remarkable coincidence of the date of his and Adams's deaths:

> Second, the fourth of July—the nation's date
> of Independence that fell
> just at mid-year (a mathematical
> boon he was born to appreciate)
>
> held within itself, more secretive
> than he, another message so
> cryptic his own Creator alone can know.
> We never guess it while we live.

As Jefferson sinks toward his final hours, he has a moment of recognition that his daughter is coming up the stairs to take his temperature. This account of the poem necessarily brings the opening and closing thermometers much closer together than they are in the poem; the rounding-out is entirely satisfying.

As Robert Lowell did a few years earlier, Salter finds irresistible the connection to be made between Robert Frost and Coleridge's "Frost at Midnight." This meditation on a poet's relationship to his art and his family draws heavily and convincingly on work that has been done on Frost's life since the rather demonizing job Lawrance Thompson made of it. But among Salter's pleasures here is also making the connection between two poems, when she quotes Frost thus: "The most inalienable right of man / is to go to hell in his own way."

■ **BOOKS BY MARY JO SALTER**

Henry Purcell in Japan. New York: Alfred A. Knopf, 1985.

Unfinished Painting. New York: Alfred A. Knopf, 1989.

Sunday Skaters. New York: Alfred A. Knopf, 1994, New York: Alfred A. Knopf, 1996.

A Kiss in Space. New York: Alfred A. Knopf, 1999.

for children

The Moon Comes Home. New York: Alfred A. Knopf, 1989.

I opened with a glance at some of the links between Salter's books as they are formed by the word "original." I might close with the observation that there are others, and that looking at all of them would involve a great many more of the shorter poems than I have emphasized here. For example, there are in *Sunday Skaters* a number of poems arising from Salter's sojourn in Iceland; these converse rewardingly with the earlier poems set in Japan. For another, "The Moon and Big Ben" in *Unfinished Painting* recalls "Luminary," and might remind us in passing of Salter's charming book for children, *The Moon Comes Home* (1989). Finally (for now), in the Paris section of the Jefferson poem, "A hammer in the architect's heart / pounds when a manned balloon clears a tree, / rising from the Tuileries." This is very near the end of *Sunday Skaters*; "Fire-Breathing Dragon," the first poem in *A Kiss in Space*, recounts a ride in such a craft:

> no glass
> between us and the world we clear
>   of nailed-down roofs and trees that appear
> in the breeze to be tethered balloons.

At this point in Salter's career, the longer poems appear to culminate in the superb achievement of "Alternating Currents." Yet Salter continues in shorter poems to balance an exquisite combination of generosity, good humor (and occasional bad humor), and an amazing gift for defining fleeting impressions that find their way into memorable, engaging, life-enriching poems.

Henry Taylor
February, 2000

Lillian Smith: Walking a Trembling Earth

■ I

"The South is in trouble" becomes the refrain of *Killers of the Dream*, Lillian Smith's psychological tract against racial proscription. The nature of that trouble has to do with the guilt of slavery and the restless turning which guilt has bred in the Southern mind. It is a stalwart and secret trouble. It is a trouble as awesome and endless as the flat, curving landscape of Smith's native middle Georgia.

> We who were born in the South…identified with the South's trouble as if we, individually, were responsible for all of it. We defended the sins and sorrows of three hundred years as if each sin had been committed by us alone and each sorrow had cut across our heart…. We knew guilt without understanding it and there is no tie that binds men closer to the past and each other than that.

Killers of the Dream is a courageous book. Its entrance, in 1949, into the mass consciousness was an event for the cause of racial equality and—as a result of Smith's feminist perspective—women's suffrage. The book, along with her novel *Strange Fruit*, represents Miss Smith's most distinguished work and is still considered an important text with a formidable audience in cities and universities today. Smith simply had the courage to tell the truth as she saw it. This is in itself an achievement rarely accomplished or even attempted.

Her honesty is both the strength and weakness of *Killers of the Dream*. While the writing is marked by an eloquent style, the book is disorganized. Her soul-searching is sometimes tedious. She returns to the same themes and statements again and again, as if hoping to intensify the power of her ideas through repetition. The effect is often to create the impression of someone trying to replace historical reality with legend: she symbolizes broad and complex questions. In fairness to Miss Smith, one must admit it may well be that much that is historically true of the South cannot be learned from what is known to us as its "history." Southern history has a reputation for being somewhat discreditable and, as C. Vann Woodward puts it in his *The Burden of Southern History*, "faintly ridiculous." In literature this reputation was in large part earned by the "historical" novels of post-bellum, anti-Negro authors such as Thomas Dixon, whose most famous book *The Clansman* was adapted into the motion picture *The Birth of a Nation. Killers of the Dream* constitutes a search for a new system for assessing the Southern heritage, a new arrangement of the mechanisms of the Southern dilemma. The result of the search is Smith's own myth about the South, and she clearly picks psychology over history.

> The unraveling out of what had been woven so tightly was usually a slow process. One thread at a time came loose. Then another. Sometimes a great hole was torn by a quick stabbing experience. However it happened, it was not long before the lessons taught him as a Christian, a white man, an American, a puritan, began to contradict each other…. The ideas, denying each other, we could bend to with rela-

Lillian Smith

Lillian Eugenia Smith was the seventh of nine children born to Calvin Warren and Anne (Simpson) Smith. Born on December 12, 1897, she lived with her family in Jasper, Florida, until 1915 when her family moved to Clayton, Georgia, and Smith enrolled in Piedmont College in Demorest, Georgia. Although she attended Piedmont for one year only, her education also included a total of four years at Peabody Conservatory in Baltimore, Maryland, and one year at Teachers College, Columbia University. Interspersed with her education were experiences such as serving as the head of the music department at Virginia School, Huchow, China, from 1922 to 1925 and assisting her father in the direction of Laurel Falls Camp for girls which she then owned and directed for 25 years after her father's death. In 1936 Smith, with the help of friend Paula Snelling, established, as editor and publisher, a magazine originally entitled *Pseudopodia*, and then *North Georgia Review* and *South Today* respectively. A strong advocate for civil rights and racial equality, Smith was a member and former vice president of the American Civil Liberties Union and a member of the advisory board of the Congress of Racial Equality (Core) from which she resigned in 1966 because of the increasing militancy of the organization. As an author, she was a member of the Author's Guild and P.E.N. Her various

awards and honors include: honorary degrees from Oberlin College, Howard University, and Atlanta University; the Page One Award in 1944 for *Strange Fruit*; the Constance Skinner Lindsay Award in 1945 for *Strange Fruit*; the Southern Award in 1949 for *Killers of the Dream*; a citation from the National Book Award Committee for a "distinguished contribution to American letters"; and the Rosenwald Foundation Fellowship for two years. Lillian Smith died of cancer on September 28, 1966. Her manuscripts, as well as the complete file of *South Today* and related materials, are now preserved in the library of the University of Florida. ■

tive ease. By practicing intellectual deafness we could keep ourselves from hearing, or hearing simultaneously, the antiphonal choruses of white supremacy and democracy, brotherhood and segregation, love and lynching....

What is remarkable is that Lillian Smith created in *Killers of the Dream* a work that is simultaneously expressive of what she both loves and hates about the South. This feat may be the effect of her peculiar vantage point. She was, after all, a reconstructed Southerner who stayed in the South. Miss Smith was a Southern lady by birth and breeding. She traveled widely. Once she lived on New York City's Brooklyn Heights for eight months, but she always kept her mountaintop home at Clayton, Georgia. She knew the county house crowd and country politics intimately. One of her brothers was a county politician. She was at once a product of the South and a citizen of the world, a twentieth century woman. One trademark of her writing where the description of her homeland is concerned—its sight and sound, its denizens and their ways—is a sensory verisimilitude that is very powerful.

■ II

Lillian Eugenia Smith was born in Jasper, Florida. After her father's naval stores failed due to wartime disruptions when she was eighteen years old, her family moved from Florida to Clayton, Georgia. Memories of that Jasper childhood were to provide material for chapters in *Killers of the Dream* and *Memory of a Large Christmas*. She was to turn the questions concerning race, sex and sin generated in her Deep South childhood into a literary enterprise which would make her voice heard worldwide.

She began reading in earnest at age ten in her family library. She encountered Shakespeare, Milton, Hawthorne, Dickens and Tennyson. By the time she entered Piedmont College at Demorest, Georgia, she had read sufficiently to be admitted to an advanced English Literature tutorial. In one year she reviewed English Literature from *Beowulf* to the twentieth century. She left Piedmont after one year and returned to Clayton to help her ailing father with the new family enterprise: The Laurel Falls Camp for Girls.

Lillian Smith was of a generation of Southern girls who attained a level of independence and spontaneity unknown to their mothers and grandmothers. She came out of the Jazz Age when women bobbed their hair, shortened their skirts, rolled their silk stockings at the knees and smoked cigarettes in public. Debutantes were doing scandalous new dance steps, drinking gin from the infamous hip flask, rebelling at the universities. A "new woman" had emerged in the South and the United States. It had become the fashion for magazines like *Ladies Home Journal* to advocate marriage *and* careers for their readership. Well-bred women were working among the Negro poor and fighting sweatshops. They were taking their own education seriously and striving for political equality with men. An increasing number of girls attended college in the South. Women were becoming lawyers and doctors, newspaperwomen and businesswomen, librarians, teachers, social workers and political activists.

Lillian Smith was financially independent from the age of eighteen to the end of her life. She had worked to support her term at Piedmont, the small Southern school (there were only thirty-five students in the college division) run by Congregationalists from New England. At age twenty she became the principal of the Laurel Falls Camp for Girls on top of Old Screamer Mountain. This was a role she was to fulfill, often in absentia, for the next twenty-three years. During a time when most girls did not attend even the cinema unescorted, Miss Smith took herself to China.

When she was twenty-four years old, after working her way through three years of study at the Peabody Conservatory of Music in Baltimore, she accepted a position as head of the music department at a Methodist mission school in Huchow, China. During her three years at the mission school for wealthy Chinese girls, Smith was able to observe the struggle for racial and social equality within the context of a foreign society. She happened to arrive in China at just the right time to witness great social upheavals brought on by the long, democratic yearnings of the Chinese people. These yearnings became manifest in the Kuomin-Tang Declaration of 1924, which called for freedom from imperialistic domination and for racial egalitarianism, the equalization of land ownership, and the regulation of capital. The young Smith, through her China experience in the early twenties, began to formulate her political consciousness. It was at this juncture that she became troubled by the institution of exploitation called colonialism, and when she returned to Georgia in 1925, she started to see the subordinate and superordinate roles of blacks and whites respectively through new eyes.

> I left the South and went to China. I lived three years in Chekiang province and there I saw the same old segregation I thought I had left behind. I collided in China with white colonialism. I heard the same old story but now it had a new accent, a

sharper rhythm, different imagery. Somehow, it seemed more cruel because it was, to me, a new cruelty. Old cruelties never bother us much. It was, perhaps, a critical moment in my life: when my interior world finally began to reach out and tie itself to my external world. However that may be, the first time I saw a Chinese coolie brutally lashed on Nanking Road—in broad daylight—by a British policeman, my mind tore wide open.

The years following her return to the American South brought again for Lillian Smith the responsibility of family business. She ran the girls' camp and traveled back and forth to Florida to help run the family's hotel. She spent a year studying at Columbia University. In 1930 her father died and she returned home again to assume the care of her invalid mother. Yet amid her tremendous responsibilities during this period of her life, Smith found time and courage to claim a writer's work and title.

With a friend, Paula Snelling, she co-founded a small literary magazine and review, *South Today*, the first white liberal magazine in the South. She wrote a novel on her experience in China. This early novel, however, was rejected by the publishers she sent it to as "shocking" and "revolutionary" material. She wrote three other manuscripts during this period which were never presented for publication. These projects all burned in a fire in her study in Clayton in 1944. After the death of her mother in 1938, Smith took up traveling. She spent several months in Brazil, where she began work on *Strange Fruit*. She received Rosenwald Fellowships to travel and study in the Southern United States. Later she would travel the Western United States and India.

■ III

In 1944 Lillian Smith was accorded fortune and renown through the publication of *Strange Fruit*. Within one year the novel sold more than 650,000 copies and caused a literary furor. It was hailed and damned by turns. Orville Prescott in the *Yale Review* heralded Smith's first published novel as "a very considerable achievement." In one of the most favorable reviews of the book, Struthers Burt summed up his evaluation of *Strange Fruit* for the readers of the *Saturday Review of Literature*: "Twenty years ago had a well-brought up and well-placed Georgia woman like Lillian Smith written 'Strange Fruit,' she would have had an unhappy time in her own community. As it is, I believe Georgia will be greatly interested in her novel, argumentative but receptive, and in the final analysis, proud that a major new novelist is a native Georgian. For 'Strange Fruit' is a major novel whatever else you may think of it." Other reviewers found the work "intelligent," "wise" and "important." Still others found it in violation of good taste. For many, the book constituted an affront because a "daughter of one of the South's oldest families" had written this indictment against racial segregation, exposing segregation's most intimate and inhuman aspects. The reviewer for the *Christian Science Monitor* found the book unacceptable due to its use of "uncouth speech" and depiction of "licentious behavior." The novel was banned in Boston because of its obscene language and banned in certain Southern towns—by "gentleman's agreement"—because of its themes of miscegenation and lynching. Three months after its publication, the United States Post Office banned *Strange Fruit* from the mails. According to Smith, Mrs. Eleanor Roosevelt talked to President Roosevelt on behalf of the novel. The ban was lifted within a few hours.

Strange Fruit is a tale about the fate-crossed love affair between a well-to-do white boy, Tracy Dean, and the colored Nonnie Anderson. The novel reports on the Southern town of Maxwell, Georgia, its evangelism and prejudice, its hypocrisy and wild injustice which lead

Nonnie's older brother to murder Tracy, and the institution of mob rule which leads the town to mutilate and burn an innocent Negro for the crime.

The book's title is composed of the two words Smith had used in an early article for *South Today* to describe Southern white culture as a "strange fruit" of racism. Among Negroes, the expression had long since come to stand for the lynched body swaying from a tree on a rope. The jazz artist Billie Holiday had in her repertoire before the publication of Smith's book a song called "Strange Fruit," written by poet Lewis Allan. The song is a lovely and bitter protest against racisim and mob rule in the American South:

> Southern trees bear a strange fruit
> Blood on the leaves and blood at the root

In her 1956 autobiography, Miss Holiday states that Lillian Smith once told her the song inspired her to write the famous novel. This might be only another show business legend. Smith was calling her manuscript *Jordan Is So Chilly* until its acceptance at Reynal and Hitchcock in New York. The publishers suggested she find a different title, and after consideration Smith offered: *Strange Fruit*. The title was printed courtesy of Edward B. Marks Music Corporation, the publishers of Holiday's protest song. Smith's and, ultimately, her publisher's choice of a title for the book may have been less of a tribute than an attempt to foster identification between a white writer's first novel and the Northern liberals and intellectuals that had already made something of an icon of Billie Holiday and her music. This I think at least bears a little on the actual situation surrounding the naming of the Smith novel.

It is true, the novel's content could not have been better fitted to suit the times. When the book appeared in 1944, the protest-centered novel was already comprising a special genre in literature. The war of the forties inspired a great democratic sentiment among Americans, and not since the Reconstruction Era had the federal government taken such an active role in the removal of racial barriers in our nation. Brave stands had been taken in the United States against segregation in schools, churches and interstate travel. The war against Hitler had called into question the whole concept of master racism. Roosevelt's Executive Order of June 25, 1941, had created a Fair Employment Practices Committee empowered to see that hiring under government contract in American war plants was conducted without regard to race, creed or national origin. Four years after *Strange Fruit* came out, a decision handed down by the California Supreme Court held a statute forbidding miscegenation unconstitutional. This is not to suggest, of course, that foiling Hitler meant that the American Negro was ushered at last into a Promised Land. The wartime riots in black communities were notorious. Yet, as critic Robert Bone has pointed out in his study *The Negro Novel in America*, after World War II, our social climate was distinctly favorable to the Negro's cause.

Lillian Smith received the Constance Lindsay Skinner and the Page One Award for her novel. Her publishers were awarded the *Publishers Weekly*–Ad Club Prizes for the *Strange Fruit* advertisement campaign. Smith swiftly became a national celebrity. She was called on as a spokesman for civil rights in much the same way that Harriet Beecher Stowe, transformed by the success of *Uncle Tom's Cabin* into public heroine, became linked with the Abolitionist movement of the nineteenth century.

Strange Fruit's white lover is a shy, mother-dominated young man, torn by love and his "duty" as a Southerner. Smith's negress is wise and passive. Though she has been to Atlanta and graduated from Spelman College, the prestigious black woman's college, Nonnie Anderson returns to Maxwell and takes a job as a nurse to a white family's retarded son. Tracy Dean drops out of college after one year. (He had been in the army, but he failed at that too.) His mother wants him to join the church, marry and become a solid citizen. He has returned to Maxwell and his sexual relationship with Nonnie, which began when he was twelve years old and she was six. While in the war and army in Marseille, Dean realized:

> He had never thought in his life of dancing with Nonnie, never had wanted to dance with her, but now he thought: We could dance here. That was all; but the words turned a key, suddenly opening his memories. She had been something you tried not to think about—something you needed, hushed your mind from remembering. Now she was here. All the little things—filling his mind. Voice inflections...odd way she said the word *down*...brushed up her hair above her temple...vein that throbbed there when she was tired...sudden quick way she would lean forward when excited, though her voice would stay low. She wasn't a Negro girl whom he had in a strange crazy way mixed his whole life up with. She was the woman he loved.

This realization, however, fails to sustain him once he has returned to his home town, and he returns to the night moves of his love affair with Nonnie Anderson. Urged by his parents, he becomes engaged to a white woman and takes up the practice of religion. But Nonnie soon is pregnant with his child. The town preacher, suspecting Dean's problem, tells the boy to pay some good darky to marry the Anderson girl. Tracy pays his houseboy, who seems the most obvious choice, $100 dollars. He then visits Nonnie by the Big Swamp at night to tell her his plan. The inference is that he will continue to have access to her sexually after the marriages are made. He leaves her with a bag of money and starts out on the footpath from "colored town" back to the white district. Nonnie's brother, Ed, who has heard the whole tale in a barroom earlier that evening, meets Dean on the path and shoots him dead. Ed escapes from the county, using the money Dean left for Nonnie. He is gone from Maxwell before the body is found on the path from colored town and the manhunt begins. The houseboy is suspected of the crime and lynched, because he is the one who finds Dean's body. Despite the fact that there is no real evidence against him, he is sacrificed because in this Southern town when a white man is murdered by a black man, a black man's death, any black man's death, is required.

In the novel's concluding section, the editor of the local newspaper prepares the editorial which will appear the morning after the lynching. Smith uses this opportunity to editorialize the events of the novel and state a major theme of the work: More than a national crime, lynching is a ritualistic compensation in the South. Smith achieves this statement through the voice of her newspaper editor.

The lynching occurs at the climax of a week-long religious revival in Maxwell. The revival has been building momentum since the beginning of the novel. "It takes a long time to get a revival going," one of the townspeople remarks in the opening chapter. The lynching, the central event in the novel, thus arises out of the religious fervor generated in the town. In this way passion and violence are married. "Hush," a white woman tells her child solemnly as the black man burns, "they're lynching a nigger. Don't you wan to see 'em burn a nigger?"

By weaving such expressions as "all Maxwell thought...," "the town knew...," "Maxwell lay white and empty," "Maxwell, Georgia slept," throughout her narrative, Smith personifies the place of her novel. Though the Maxwell, Georgia, of *Strange Fruit* is spun—by her own admission—out of Lillian Smith's memories of the legends and landscape of Jasper, Florida, it is more than a specific geographic location. Maxwell could be any Southern town; it stands for every Southern town. Its characters are types found in any small Southern community, representing a cross section of their milieu. Smith's portrait of a town is one which grows into an archetype. There is "colored town" and "white town" within Maxwell divided by the Big Swamp. The Swamp is also an important region in the spiritual landscape of Dixie. In a speech written for Paris radio in the late fifties, Miss Smith described that region as follows:

My earliest memory of the American South, which is my home, is of an earth that trembled: the ground beneath my feet never seemed quite firm.

The street of the small town on which I lived was quiet and serene. It sheltered its upper-class white children in spacious homes.... But not far away was the Big Swamp—the "trembling earth" the American Indians called it—and I was aware of the existence of this swamp from my earliest years. I knew in that limitless place—as without dimensions to a child's eyes as is a dream—there were strange things unfamiliar to Main Street: Its dark waters were full of secret, slow movements of creatures one never saw and its earth trembled if you stepped on it: that earth was green and beautiful and luxuriant with tangled growth,...and though the ground was firm and strong enough to bear the weight of trees, it trembled when a child stepped on it. I was told there was no solid foundation of rock under its surface but only mysterious waters which flowed from an unknown source to an unknown destination, and I believed it. And this belief and these images crept slowly to the center of my imagination and took root there.

As I grew older, as I saw more and learned more and asked more, I felt the moral earth trembling beneath my pressing questions. And again, I was aware of mysterious and unplumbed currents flowing below the thin human reason and again I saw the movement in those dark water's of forces, threatening and cruel and eternally fascinating. But I knew, also, that those waters nourished the flowers and the great trees beyond it, and I could not forget this.

Nonnie Anderson and the Big Swamp are unifying images within the novel. Both exist at an intersection of the focus of the town. Nonnie appears in the novel's first sentence:

She stood at the gate, waiting: behind her, the swamp, in front of her Colored Town, beyond it, all Maxwell.

She is linked with the swamp by her frequent "visits." She has visited the swamp since her early childhood. She tells Tracy that she "hears" the swamp, that it says to her, "come here, come here, come here."

Her rich beauty exists at an intersection of black and white aesthetics. The blood of these two peoples runs in her veins.

White boys whistled softly when she walked down the street...for Nonnie Anderson was something to look at twice, with her soft black hair blowing off her face, and black eyes set in a face that God knows by right should have belonged to a white girl.

Physically, she is as lush as is the earth and full. For Tracy, she is the figuration of the solace his mother, his sister, and his white fiancée cannot give him:

And whatever he wanted she would give him. That was Non. Her body—or a drink of water. It'd all be the same. And she'd give it like a swamp bay lets you smell its sweetness.

Her image haunts each of the novel's 371 pages. She appears at the end of the book, lacing her shoes to return to work with Maxwell's other colored women the morning after the lynching. She has, like Maxwell, Georgia, endured the explosion of terror, and she will continue to endure, carrying Dean's baby inside her until his seed has fructified, producing yet another kind of "strange fruit."

More than a story based on a town's private legends, *Strange Fruit* is a public dream about racism, originating in the nightside of the American imagination. The book was called an attack on the South, a tract against lynching, and, by certain Spelman women who said a Spelman girl would never behave like Nonnie Anderson, a libel against Negro women.

In an article for the *Saturday Review of Literature* called "Personal History of *Strange Fruit*: A Statement of Purpose and Intention," Lillian Smith wrote:

> I thought of my book as a fable about a son in search of a mother, about a race in search of surcease from pain and guilt.... It seems to me a book about human beings journeying across deep chasms and down into forbidden areas, but journeying also back to childhood, always back to the room where they were born, seeking to find, wherever they travel, that which they left there, so long ago.

This concern with the past was not new to the movement of Southern literature. The Southern character in fiction is almost always haunted by the ghosts of the past. Faulkner's Gavin Stevens in *Intruder in the Dust* asserts: "The past is never dead. It's not even past." T. S. Stribling, whose novels influenced those of William Faulkner, introduced the notion of a "chain of wrongs and violences" out of which a human life is molded. The writing of Thomas Wolfe reflects an understanding of how the traumas of childhood can continue to shape an individual throughout his entire lifetime. It is true, the renaissance in Southern literature owed a debt to the thinking of Sigmund Freud.

IV

Killers of the Dream was published in 1949. Smith was still a national figure. Her name still carried with it the aura of her first book's success. She had written a dramatization of *Strange Fruit* for the Broadway stage which critics generally agreed was a significant though flawed work. Her use as a storytelling device of the flashback and stream of consciousness writing, which made the novel so engaging, worked against her faithful stage adaptation. The *Time* magazine review of the play called Smith an "unconverted novelist." She traveled to India as a member of the Famine Commission and guest of the British government. She worked on another novel, *Julia*, which she was to keep locked away in a bank safety box never to be read or published because of its "highly personal nature."

Killers of the Dream can be read as a personal memoir and as a subtext to *Strange Fruit*. The themes of the novel are provided with more depth in the second book. It also contains much exposition regarding the inner life of the South, as well as personal experiences some strands of which entered her story. The world of Smith's fiction is given new dimension by the nonfiction work. The same search for origins is taken up in both books.

In each of the four parts of *Killers*, the first sentence contains the word *children* or *childhood*. In much of the book the reader has the overwhelming sense of being urged backward toward some first state, toward a revelation of the way things are through a showing forth of what has been. The *childhood* of the book is not only an individual childhood. It is both a collective childhood and a metaphor for what Smith herself has called the "uncovered moment" and the "unfound door." One thinks of Amanda Starr's declaration in Robert Penn Warren's novel, *Band of Angels:* "You live through time, that little piece of time that is yours, but that piece of time is not only your own life, it is the summing-up of all the other lives that are simultaneous with yours."

Lillian Smith does present her own childhood in the book and quite beautifully. She writes:

> I was born and reared in a small Deep South town whose population was equally Negro and white. There were nine of us who grew up freely in a rambling house of many rooms, surrounded by big lawn, back yard, gardens, fields, and barn. It was

the kind of home that gathers memories like dust, a place filled with laughter and
play and pain and hurt and ghosts and games.

Smith's father was an important man in their town, an employer of hundreds of black and
white laborers. He owned the water works, the ice plant and the turpentine still. He was also a
religious man who once kept the Smiths kneeling at family prayer while the "fire siren at the
mill sounded the alarm that his mill was on fire." The siren grew louder and louder and yet
"with quiet dignity he continued his talk with God while his children sweated and wriggled
and hearts beat out of their chests in excitement."

In *Killers of the Dream* Smith portrays her mother as a woman shy with words, an insubstantial Southern lady who in a way that was never truly articulated but was none the less real
rejected Lillian as an infant and handed her over to the care of a Negro nurse. The black nurse
came from the backyard beyond Mrs. Smith's flower garden. Her own home was a tiny cabin
wallpapered with sheets of newspaper. This woman became Miss Smith's "colored mother" and
provided the child with the depth of nurture her "white mother" could not.

The occasion of Smith's becoming the charge of a mammy or psuedo-mother is expanded
on by the author in a discussion of the whole psychology of the mammy-child reciprocal in the
South:

> Because the white mother has always set up right and wrong, has with authority
> established the "do" and the "don't" of behavior, his conscience, as it grows within
> the white, Southern child ties its allegiance to her and to the white culture and
> authority which she and his father represent. But to the colored mother, persuasive
> in her relaxed attitude toward "sin," easy and warm in her physical ministrations,
> generous with her petting, he ties his pleasure…. He begins to admire more and
> more the lovely lady who is his "real" mother. He is impressed by her white beauty,
> her clothes and grace and charm…. But when he is miserable, he creeps away and
> crawls up in old black arms, every curve of which he has known by heart since
> babyhood, and snuggles against a cotton dress that is ragged maybe but will always
> smell good to his memory…. Sometimes he wants to stay in her lap forever; but he
> slips away shamefaced, remembering that his "mother" is not "fitten," as she says
> herself, to sit in the living room and eat at the table with the rest of the family.

The nature of this relationship, Smith maintains, creates in the Southern child a dual conscience of "what is done and what isn't,…Madonna and whore; Mother and nurse; wife and
prostitute; white consciousness and colored pleasures; marriage and lust;…belief and act."

Smith's relation with her own mammy is effectively employed to depict the strain put on
whites by, on the one hand, living within such an intimate proximity of the blacks and, on the
other, denying black humanity in order to advance white supremacy. She thus draws a diagram
for seeing how white supremacy not only divides the races but how it divides the white child's
heart as well. All of this facilitates a richer reading of the relationship between the lovers in
Strange Fruit and makes plain what Smith meant in 1945 when she described that novel as a
"fable about a son in search of a mother."

In addition to the race issue, *Killers of the Dream* also addresses the suffrage of Southern
white women. Smith presents the women of her homeland as a subjugated, "culturally stunted"
people.

> The little ghost women of small Southern towns…swishing softly into church,
> sometimes singing in the choir, slipping like their carefully made custards down
> the dark maw of life.

■ **BOOKS BY LILLIAN SMITH**

Strange Fruit. New York: Reynal and Hitchcock, 1944.

Killers of the Dream. New York: Norton, 1949; Garden City, New York: Doubleday, 1963, 1978.

The Journey. New York: World Publishing Co., 1954; New York: Norton, 1965.

Now Is the Time. New York: Viking Press, 1955.

One Hour. New York: Harcourt, Brace, 1959.

Memory of a Large Christmas. New York: Norton, 1962, 1980.

Our Faces, Our Worlds. New York: Norton, 1964.

The Winner Names the Age: A Collection of Writings. New York: Norton, 1978.

How Am I to Be Heard?: Letters of Lillian Smith. Chapel Hill: University of North Carolina Press, 1993.

The white women of the South, Smith contends, are possessed of an emptiness which they come to accept as natural to their existence as women. This great, gnawing emptiness becomes in their lives synonymous with "female trouble," prodding them to visit the doctor's office as regularly as the church "to moan their misery." Smith describes the pedestal of Sacred Womanhood to which the old colonels' oratories elevated Southern women as ultimately having the effect of debasing women and making of them psychic children.

Smith celebrates the forming of an Association of Southern Women for the Prevention of Lynching in 1930 as a significant point in the advancement of Southern women. She sees this event as emblematic of white women's rejection of their implicit and instrumental role in the white *man's* institution of racism.

> They said calmly that they were not afraid of being raped by black men; as for their sacredness, they could take care of it themselves; they did not need the chivalry of a lynching to protect them and they did not want it.

These ladies took out after the Ku Klux Klan and socialized with colored women as sister Christians engaged in a common cause.

Lillian Smith identifies the "killers of the dream," in the book's last section, as the killers of the spirit of idealized democracy. The dream is the sanctity of life. Smith asserts in *Killers of the Dream* that the white man's burden is not the black man nor any other oppressed group, but his own childhood. The book is a fine sociological-psychological analysis, an exploration into the psychic content and workings of its Southern author and the South itself, an effort to bring what is hidden into the light in order to help provoke courage and healing.

Smith died of cancer on September 28, 1966, in Atlanta, Georgia.

Don Belton
June, 1983

The Dark Train and the Green Place: The Poetry of William Jay Smith

■ ■ ■

Over a long period during which American poetry has seen a series of wavering takeovers of styles, eligibilities and objectives, William Jay Smith has been writing poems which, without yielding to the tumblers and the barkers, have never put him out of touch with the avant-garde. He has gone on writing poetry to the best of his distinguished ability, as it has pleased him to write it, neither nervously nor defiantly. And when he has struck out in a new direction, it has never been because he was beckoned to.

Looking back, it is obvious that his sort of tough scepticism had much to do with his interest in the Spectra Hoax; and his small book on that exhilarating rip-off was a good barometer of his natural poetic climate.

Assuming the reader's familiarity with that bastard of the fancy of Witter Bynner and Arthur Davidson Ficke (and in any case, lacking the space for recapitulation), it is necessarily only to say that its birth—over several bottles of good whiskey and a bellyful of contempt for what its perpetrators saw as the Neo-Fake in poetry—the invented school of Spectra writers, headed and guided by its two mythical but gaudy founders, Emanuel Morgan and Ann Knish, resulted in a wide and instant vogue, often in amazingly knowledgeable places. Ficke and Bynner set out to prove their conviction that anything which combined inscrutability with pomposity in judicious proportions would be irresistible to those whose nervous bandwagonism amounted to a literary tic. Interestingly enough, it was in general the aficionados rather than the lumpen-proletariat among readers who accepted the worth and validity of the work. While a number of newspapers denounced the effusions of the two elusive poets as pernicious nonsense (though in most cases they did not question the poets' physical existence), it was again and again experienced editors and poets who hastened out on the doomed limb. When that limb ultimately broke, it was largely from the swollen intricacy of its ramifications.

There were bruised feelings, a few long animosities, and much jostling to get to the rear of the room. But from the point of view of this article, the most interesting thing in the entire instructive story is the irreducible grain of poetic truth and release—originally unsuspected by the hoax's authors—incorporated in the mass of fakery, and Smith's understanding of that grain's nature.

The link between Smith's own work, and his consideration of the Spectra Hoax, is his ability to sift and recognize; never to be frozen in a paralytic hostility. He knows so well the fascination of nonsense rhymes, of the sinister jingle, the street-ditty, the games-song. But his basic attitude was fairly well defined when he wrote, in 1961, of the Spectrists, "Their antics, of course, seem mild in comparison with the belches, sexual grunts, and general incoherent exhibitionism of the 'new Poetry' today." His humor is the basis for his success with children's poetry, and his preoccupation with death is closely related to his humor.

William Jay Smith

William Jay Smith was born in Louisiana in 1918. Educated at Washington University and the Université de Poitiers, he attended Oxford University as a Rhodes scholar, in addition to graduate work at Columbia University and the University of Florence.

He taught creative writing, children's literature, and French, English, and American literature at Columbia University, Williams College, and Hollins College (now Hollins University, where he became professor emeritus after 1980). He has been writer-in-residence at Arena Stage, poetry consultant to the Library of Congress, and a member of the Vermont House of Representatives.

Throughout his distinguished career, Smith has received many awards and honors, including two National Endowment for the Arts fellowships, two National Endowment for the Humanities fellowships, the Gold Medal of Labor (Hungary), an Ingram Merrill Foundation grant, a California Children's Book and Video Awards recognition for excellence, a medal for service to the French language from the French Academy, a Pro Cultura Hungarica medal, and the René Vásquez Díaz prize from the Swedish Academy.

He is a member of the Academy of American Poets, the Authors Guild, PEN, the Authors League of America, and the National Institute of Arts and Letters. ■

In an interview with poet Elizavietta Ritchie for the magazine *Voyages,* during his period as Poetry Consultant to the Library of Congress, Smith commented that "any humorist has a tragic sense," and quoted Laurence Olivier's statement that any fine comedian could play tragic roles, but that the reverse was not true. Humor being based profoundly on the sense of proportion, it is natural that it should contribute to an understanding of "the dark underside of things" spoken of by Smith, as well as to the lightheartedly comic—if such a thing exist in the purest sense. Hesse's remark that "humor is a crystal which grows only in deep and lasting pain, and after all belongs to the better products of mankind…" is apposite to Smith's work; and perhaps one of the reasons for the calibre of both Smith's and Roethke's children's verse (though their poems could not be more different in texture and approach) is both poets' sense of the value of the outrageous in children's poetry. Children have a vivid and instinctive knowledge of evil and violence, but no understanding of its working and roots. They simultaneously protect and please themselves by receiving the bland and ferocious statement. There it is, without confusing comment. The tuffet-crashing spider, the blind and tailless mice, the cradle pitched from the broken bough, are instinctively accepted.

In his poems for children, Smith's own awareness of violence and the outrageous leads straight into a hilarity and exhilaration which give the poems much of their success. They employ the kind of splendid non-sequitur which appears so logical and alive to a child.

In the major body of Smith's poetry, development has always sprung from, and returned to, his basic convictions, and above all, his understanding of the spontaneous characteristics of his poetic gifts. By preference and by temperament, he is a poet of elegance, craft, and wit, the first and the last having a dark underside. His command of form is brilliant, but he has evaded the danger of being hag-ridden by his own capabilities. With rare exceptions, it is only the recent poems which allow a passionate personal emotion its head. Up to that point, any passion has been in the infusion of intensity, of seeing, of hearing, rather than as a discretely identifiable element.

The early poems, circa 1946, already show the categories and manner which will be explored and developed, but never abandoned. In general it seems to be the uncertain and ultimately enfeebled poets who continue to try on a tentative series of totally differing masks. Even the voices of the early and late Eliot share an unmistakable timber, at the end of a very long journey. It is in exploring his own poetic nature rather than in exchanging it for an annual model that the valid poet grows and varies.

■ **II**

In "The Note on the Vanity Dresser," the characteristic imprint is already there.

> The yes-man in the mirror now says no,
> No longer will I answer you with lies.
> The light descends like snow, so when the snow-
> man melts, you will know him by his eyes.
>
> The yes-man in the mirror now says no.
> Says no. No double negative of pity
> Will save you now from what I know you know:
> These are your eyes, the cinders of your city.

The echoes of word off word, and line off line, the austere pun, the delayed-action image, the monosyllabic elegance, all are there. For the good poet, categories are slippery things, but in understated ways they do declare themselves. The awful thing, lightly said, is there too.

> You shipped him off address unknown
> You shipped him off beyond endurance
> I cannot reach him on the phone
> He left me all his life insurance.

And the desperate jingle:

> O I feel like the kinks in the paws of the Sphinx
> O I've got those negotiable knees.
> On goes the phone with a tone all its own:
> P-lease! P-lease! P-lease!

Tentative categories in the Smith *oeuvre* are: the poems for children; the poems of magic, radiant or sinister; the poems of formal delight; and the poems concerned with death—by far the majority. Constantly these categories merge, overlay, borrow. But these basic concerns form the poetry's texture.

There is little magic knocking around in the poems of most of Smith's contemporaries, and the *frisson* has been replaced by the brutally-engendered recoil; though Donald Justice, for one, can often give a fine twilit chill. Smith's poems of this genre (magic; sinister), are not limited to, but include: "Hotel Continental," "Elegy, Cupidon," "The Barber," "At the Tombs of the House of Savoy," "The Ten," "Interior," "Processional" and "Still Life;" (and magic; radiant), "Lion," "A Green Place," "On the Islands Which Are Solomon's," "The Peacock of Java," and "Quail in Autumn."

The poem of sinister magic often involves a figure baroque and mysterious; but its mysteriousness, its baroque quality, comes usually from the transformation of a mundane object: an old man, a barber, a snowman. There is nothing quite so frightening as the familiar which turns to you a stranger's face; the truism, no longer safe. It is a device which has fascinated Alfred Hitchcock visually. In "Cupidon," the mystery is left in the hands of the uneasy climber up those winding stairs.

> "To love is to give," said the crooked old man.
> "To love is to be poor."
> And he led me up his accordion stair,
> And closed his iron door.
>
> "To love is to give." His words like wire
> Dragged the ocean floor.
> "Throw ten of your blankets on the fire,
> Then throw ten thousand more."
>
> His room was the prayer on the head of a pin,
> As clean as a diamond cut
> Was the iron door which opened in
> And would not open out.
>
> "To love is to give, to give, to give.
> Give more and more and more."
> And the wind crept up his accordion stair,
> And under his iron door.

The proportion of monosyllables is vital. Nothing destroys the suggestive like amplification; the freedom to be frightened is curtailed by every qualifying word. The theme of outgoing, the images of closure and entry, are enormously effective. The prayer shrunk to a freak, the accordion which opens and closes; the iron door, shut, penetrable. The thin words are cold and meager: *wire, pin, cut, out, in, wind, crept.*

In "Cupidon" the threat is universal. In "The Barber," though its taproot is wide, the focus is particular.

> The barber who arrives to cut my hair
> Looks at his implements and then at me.
> The world is a looking-glass in which I see
> A toadstool in the shape of a barber chair.
>
> The years are asleep. A fly crawls on the edge
> of a broken cup, and a fan in the corner whines.
> The barber's hands move over me like vines
> In a dream as long as hair can ever grow.

The poem has all the terror of stasis; it melts into the image of immobility and death, of days netting the years, of moss inching up the gravestone. The mirror is before, and the barber behind. Mirrors are one of the recurrent Smith images, and there are few objects more intractably eerie.

Sometimes the poems of sinister magic are also overtly the poems of death, as in "Elegy," "At the Tombs of the House of Savoy," or "Still Life."

It is more difficult to write the poem of radiant magic. If one has the gift, as Smith eminently has, of conjuring the dark, the ominous element itself will give an impetus to the poem. The radiant is rarer, and once conceived, more difficult to communicate. Only the most supremely unimaginative lack contact with the sinister, even though that contact, usually through the camera or newspaper, will be more likely to belong to the sinister brutal than to the sinister magic. To achieve a contemporary poem of the radiant magic is a mind-boggling task. The question is not that the era is worse, argue that how you like. It is that the worst is forced upon our consciousness, saturates our nerve-ends, and attacks, as at our most vulnerable point, our attempt to communicate truth in aesthetic terms.

A poem starting as ordinarily as

The lion, ruler over all the beasts,
Triumphant moves upon the grassy plain…

ends in a magic secret:

He gazes down into the quiet river,
parting the green bullrushes to behold
a sunflower crown of amethyst and silver,
a royal coat of brushed and beaten gold.

In reverse, this mirror is no less magically revealing than the barber's. The invitation to "A Green Place" is not given by a naturalist:

Where shy mud-hen and dainty porcupine
Dance in delight by a quivering pawpaw;
Dance by catalpa-tree and flowering peach
with speckled guinea-fowl and small raccoon.

We will question these secret animals in a moment. There is, on Solomon's islands, a "swift, black bird which on wild pepper feeds." The poet calls it:

Hop to my hand, dark beauty, stripped of song.

There is the

…Peacock

of Java, which brings, even
To the tree of heaven, heaven.

There are the small quail which

…dart up, through shafting sunlight fled.

Like brightness buried by one's sullen mood
The quail rise startled from the threadbare wood.
A voice, a step, a swift sun-thrust of feather
And earth and air come properly together.

It is the background, the things of daily earth which, lacking the things of sun and air, are threadbare and sullen. The quail shafting through sunlight, the lion, gold and amethyst, silver in his dewy ruff, the shy mudhen and dainty porcupine, the Java peacock, design for an emperor's tapestry, are *speechless*. This is the key. Hop to my hand, dark beauty, *stripped of song*.

Verbal things are entangled in the soiled nets of the daily human experience. The radiant images are speechless; are themselves only; are free. They shine in their silence, and we cannot find their fault. To achieve them in the words of a poem is something which cannot possibly be learned. The Ark's Dove, Peter's crowing Cock, the Garden's Serpent, are images of power and alteration. In every radiant poem of Smith's, there is a bird or beast; though never as a stock symbol.

The magic in nursery rhymes is both radiant and sinister, though far more often the latter. Smith's magic poems, and his poems for children, are siblings of his sense of strangeness. The difference is that the children's poems are gentler and merrier; gentler and merrier also, one might add, than the chopper with his taste for heads, or the death-watch of the fly.

It is extraordinary how often Smith's poetry has been discussed without emphasis on its preoccupation with death. The passing shadow of death shades words, phrases, lines, in many of the poems in which death is not the poem's core; such poems, for example, as "Two And One," or "Evening At Grandpoint," or "Of Islands," or "Chrysanthemums." Perhaps this is to some extent true of most good poems; they are set in, or against, the sense of death. But there is a group of Smith's poems in which death is the true protagonist, or such an important guest that he dominates the host poem. The extraordinary thing is the consistency of approach within the variety of result. Death is never a *subject;* it is a presence, a timing, a destination, a watcher. The list would be a long one. Against death's vastness, the details of life and motion stand out, distinct and precise. "Persian Miniature" gives the sense of history, of a dark force; but above all, of the constancy of death's presence. It is full of the hour-glass sense. "The sands are moving. I have seen them move."

> Ah, all the sands of the earth lead unto heaven,
> I have seen them rise on the wind, a golden thread.
>
> The sands of the earth which enter the eye of heaven,
> Over the graves, the poor white bones of the dead.
> Over the buckling ice, the swollen rivers,
> Over the ravened plains, and the dry creek beds
> The sands are moving. I have seen them move.
> And where the pines are bent, the orient
> Grain awaits the passage of the wind.
> Higher still the laden camels thread
> Their way, beyond the mountains, and the clouds
> Are whiter, than the ivory they bear
> For Death's black eunuchs. Gold, silk, furs
> Cut the blood-red morning. All is vain.
> I have watched the caravans through the needle's eye,
> As they turn, on the threshing floor, the bones of the dead,
> And green as a grasshopper's leg is the evening sky.

It's a remarkable poem; bland as a glaze; elegant; unreconciled. The echoes are dry as sand: *thread, thread; bones, bones; dead, dead.* The color-contrasts are violent: blood-red, white, gold, green: all bound towards black. "The orient grain awaits the passage of the wind.... " but the true grain which will be threshed is the bones, the poor white bones of the dead. And it is seen so clearly, so coldly, in such detail; from some terrible distance, through a small cold eye. Miniature, indeed.

Set that poem beside an even briefer poem, "At the Tombs of the House of Savoy."

> Turin beneath, on the green banks of the Po,
> Lies ringed with bright sunlight, with peaks of snow,
> While here in the dark this death's-head wears a crown.
> The dead look up, and Death on them looks down,

And bares his teeth, his bone-white haddock eyes,
Which take the casual visitor by surprise
And follow him intently on his round
As fishbone-fine his steps through vaults resound.

Despite their relationship, the contrast between the two poems is strong. Here the view is immediate, not distant. The observer is now the observed. Outside is the poster city; here, right here, is the omnipotence of death. Forever the dead stare on Death, who stares straight down on them from above—hostile, unwinking, with bared teeth and bone-white haddock eyes. The final line is a total success, in itself and in its relationships. Death has picked the flesh of the visitor's steps, they are fishbone-fine, under the related gaze of the haddock eyes. The eyes are "intent," they are waiting for something—for the ending of the tiny sound of the fish-bone-fine steps intruding temporarily on the hollowness of the vaults. The tiny fretting of the line's first half—"fish," "fine," "steps," hushes in the huge finality. The last heavy words fall like a dead weight, like the slamming of a stone lid: "…through vaults resound."

For all their differences, the two poems have in common, beside their chief concern, something germane to all this category of Smith's poems. This is the attitude, the visual and emotional attitude, toward death. Death is seen as a Webster–Tourneur figure, macabre, insistent. This is not the sorrow of death, but its horror, its implacable hostility. It is not seen through the eye of love, or loss, or passion. This is not "queens have died young and fair…," or, "There would have been a time for such a word." This is the sharply conceived, predatory figure of the ancient shape, the grimmest reaper.

Just as Smith's love poems are elegant, stylized, at one wry remove, so his poetry's encounter with death is in universal, almost heraldic, terms; less a lament for loved flesh and blood—including one's own—than an embossed glimpse of the pale horse's rider. It is pointless to ask whether the method produces the emotional climate, or the emotional climate the method. One of the most impressive aspects of Smith's poetry is this heraldic, this embossed, quality, the lovers

Where, on one elbow, rousing by degrees,
They stare, a sheet loose–folded round their knees,
Off into space, as from Etruscan tombs…

Time (actually death, in his aspect as time) is forever galloping across a dying world; the camel train, on its vain journey; El Tiempo, scouring the plain. It is all part of Smith's intense identification with form, with mortality as an artifact. In his essay on the poetry of Elizabeth Bogan, his largest measure of admiration is for her poetry's shape and form, the shell shape, the shape of a musical instrument, the outward image of her inner experience. Up to the most recent poems, even his most natural and realistic figures have about them this archetypal gloss. In two of his best short poems, horses' hooves mingle in an image of departure into time. The hooves of the rodeo-rider's horse (*Dark drum the vanishing horses' hooves…*) mingle with the sound of hooves as El Tiempo scours the prairie:

Time after time after time after time comes El Tiempo
Galloping on upon the prairie, time
After time after time after time after time at a terrible tempo,
Galloping on to the end, he ends in time.

Although there are several congenialities which draw Smith to the writings of Jules Laforgue, whose prose and poetry he has translated, the latter's preoccupation with death is certainly prominent among them, and accounts for much of the excellence of the translations.

Smith says, "Behind everything Laforgue wrote was the awareness of death." For Laforgue, the moon was an image of death, watching over the antics of his clowns:

Tattooed upon their pure white hearts
Are the maxims of the moon.
"Brethren, let us think of death:"
Is their bacchantic watchword.

■ III

In his *Voyages* interview, Smith stressed that it is the preoccupation with words, single or in phrases, rather than with ideas or concepts which originally triggers his poems; and it is his control of language which makes his translations so fortunate. He writes excellent prose, a thing surprisingly rare among poets; and reading his translations of Laforgue's poems, for example, one sees how he is able to reproduce that painter's eye of Laforgue's, that passionately accurate seeing of detail, color, shape, the true *look* of things. When he writes, of babies, "…their nostrils wide, their eyes glazed by the future…," two sorts of observation mesh. Laforgue said of Corbière that he had "an incurably indelicate ear." Smith and Laforgue share the delicate ear and eye.

1966 marks a deep division in Smith's poetry. It was then that he published *The Tin Can and Other Poems*, and a new direction had been taken. It was a direction which was to he followed in the *New & Selected Poems* of 1970. In *The Tin Can* there are very few of the brief and compact poems, the lyrics, which have been Smith's characteristic speech. There are a few glittering visitors front the old country, such as "Quail in Antumn" and "Fisher King," and a few poems which blend the approaches of the past with those of the future—"Morels," and "The Woman on the Porch." But the character of the poetry is altered. There is a series of long poems, at once looser and more massive in structure. The title poem is especially significant, since it deals with Smith's own aesthetic. It opens with, and sustains, long, carrying stanzas, often of two or three lines, which run with a raised fluctuating tension to a distant period. An epigraph explains that the Japanese use the word "kanzame" or "tin can" to mean going into hiding. "When someone gets off by himself to concentrate, they say, He has gone into the tin can."

The poem's protagonist has come
        …here to the tin can in mid–winter; to a sagging New England
farmhouse in the rock–rooted mountains, where wind
rifles the cracks.
Here surrounded by crosshatched, tumbling stone walls, where
the snowplow with its broad orange side–thrust has outlined
a rutted road.

Where the dimly cracked gray bowl of the sky rests firmly on the
valley and gum–thick clouds pour out at the edges.

Where in the hooded afternoon a pock–marked porcupine–
quilled landscape fills with snow–swirls, and the tin can settles
in the snow.

I have gone into the tin can, head high, resolute, to confront
the horrible black underside of the world.

Here Smith's control of form has strain put upon it, and responds well. In the poem's second section, he blends physical presences with those of the imagination, and both with memory, skillfully and vividly. The dark underside is there:

And always the face, the woman's face, brooding over all, rising
from the earth beside me, disembodied; always the woman
clean and classic as sunlight, moving about the room, sifting
the dirt, watering the shadowy flowers, polishing the spotted tin.
I hear her speak softly! and there she is again beside me and again
the face turns, a small bat–face, and the lips draw back in a red
wound and shriek; and the room is filled with the smell of mould and money.

It is an impressive poem—to a writer, a fascinating one; but it is far from wholly success-ful. The fairly lavish use of exclamation points does not set off true explosions, and in certain stretches of the poem, there is a sense of point–proving. Yet it is a memorable piece of work, and—more important—it leads, via "The Angry Man" and "Fishing For Albacore," to Smith's most distinguished poem, "What Train Will Come."

"The Angry Man" is a less ambitious but more fully achieved poem than "The Tin Can." Its surrealism functions. Its images of "monsters of the mind's making" convince. Readers of the Lawrence Durrell description of the slaughter of bats with a bullwhip may be troubled by that recollected image imposing itself on the poem's final section; but the section itself is a created and logical response to the earlier part of the poem. In "The Angry Man," Smith has come into control of his new territory.

"Fishing for Albacore" is a separate, distinct pause. It is a poem almost totally without fail-ures or soft spots, accurate, alive, easy in its motion, vivid. And yet, in spite of its undertones, it seems on rereadings and in retrospect a brilliant, acutely observed piece of description. Just that.

"What Train Will Come" is something else.

Here the deft touch, the miniaturist's eye, the formalist's joy in discipline have been less abandoned than absorbed into a naked report of a vision of destruction. We have had so many visions of destruction—facile or genuine—in current poetry (what else are card–carrying poets permitted to write about?) that it will perhaps give the measure of the poem's force to say that its impression on the reader is as strong as though it were the first of its genre read. It may be that Smith's established reticence, his distrust of the undisciplined, above all, his sense of the formal distance between the artist and his creation, make the contrast of these last poems with his earlier work peculiarly effective.

The subway, deep under the earth's surface, dirty, violently lit and violently dark, echoing and silent, routine, under the eye of violence, is the perfect metaphor for the poem. A scrawl from subway graffiti is the epigraph:

What train will come to bear me back
across so wide a town?

What train will come runs through the poem at intervals, like the sound of wheels distantly approaching along a buried track, in an approach which may be dreaded as much as hoped for. *What* train? The sound is a drum, a pulse; and the poem rolls off on its own dark track, through war, and the memory of private war, with no surety of escape and no motion but that of descent.

The radiance is gone, is behind, or above, in that "green spot" for which the child of mem-ory has longed as he stared at the sordid wreckage of a tornado. Wreckage, in the poem, is also the wreckage of gentleness and of human lives; even of destinations.

Perhaps one of the reasons for the importance of the direction taken by Smith's recent poems is the emergence of roots. There is no touch of regional roots in Smith's earlier work;

■ BOOKS BY WILLIAM JAY SMITH

Celebration at Dark. New York: Banyan Press, 1947; New York: Farrar, Straus, 1950; London: Hamilton, Hamish, Ltd.

Sirocco (translation of Romualdo Romano). New York: Farrar, Straus, 1951.

Calendar of Salusbury Correspondence (editor). Mystic, Connecticut: Verry, Lawrence, Inc., 1954.

Typewriter Birds. New York: Caliban Press, 1954.

Laughing Time (for children). Boston: Little, Brown and Co., 1955.

Valery Larbaud: Poems of a Multimillionaire (translation). New York: Grove Press, 1955.

Boy Blue's Book of Beasts (for children). Boston: Little, Brown and Co., 1957.

Poems, 1947–1957. Boston: Little, Brown and Co., 1957.

Puptents and Pebbles: A Nonsense ABC (for children). Boston: Little, Brown and Co., 1959.

Typewriter Town (for children). New York: E. P. Dutton and Co., Inc., 1960.

The Spectra Hoax. Middletown, Conn.: Wesleyan University Press, 1961.

Herrick (Introduction). New York: Dell Publishing Co., Inc., 1962.

What Did I See? (for children). New York: Crowell-Collier, 1962.

Ho for a Hat! (for children). Boston: Little, Brown and Company, 1963.

The Golden Journey (for children, with Louise Bogan). Chicago: Reilly and Lee, 1965.

If I Had a Boat (for children). New York: Macmillan Publishing Co., Inc., 1966.

The Tin Can and Other Poems. New York: Delacorte Press, 1966.

It Rains—It Shines (for children). Eau Claire, Wis.: Harvey House, Inc., 1967.

Poems from France. New York: Thomas Y. Crowell, Inc., 1967; New York: Apollo Editions, 1972.

Mr. Smith and Other Nonsense (for children). New York: Delacorte Press, 1972.

A Rose for Katherine Anne Porter. New York: Albondocani Press, 1970.

New and Selected Poems. New York: Delacorte Press, 1970.

---

and obviously a poet with regional roots is a different matter from a regionally rooted poet. Louisiana, Missouri, Washington, Virginia, New York, Vermont, France, Italy, England, shaped a highly uncolloquial tongue. The strongly developed sense of the formal and an unusually impersonal tone worked against the manifestation of personal emotional roots. The combination made for a somewhat dangerous sense of detachability. Now, in the latest poems, the work is striking strongly into the depths and background of personal experience, incorporated and transformed. It is an added and needed strength. In his *Voyages* interview, Smith quoted the last line of a poem called "Tulip: Magnificence Within a Frame." That, he said, is what poetry should have. Originally the frame was a strongly and artfully designed structure. In the last poems, it is less a frame than a body, an intricate, unpredictable body, housing life.

■ IV

In the case of most poets, pure lyric poetry belongs to their youth, if indeed it ever belonged to them at all; this is a truism. But Smith's lyricism had always a preserving salt of wit and irony, and there is no reason to believe that the list of its accomplishments is closed. Certainly this particular poet is going to be governed, not by what is "appropriate" to the poet of the seventies, but by the monsters and magic of his own mind's making. It seems doubtful if the images of desolation and horror will totally control his poetry's future. We credit his truth when he says,

There are real things of beauty here
and sorrow is our praise.

Josephine Jacobsen
February, 1975

Two Plays By Charles Bertin: Christopher Columbus and Don Juan (translations). Minneapolis: University of Minnesota Press, 1970.

The Pirate Book (translation of Lennart Hellsing, for children). New York: Delacorte Press, 1972.

Poems from Italy. New York: Thomas Y. Crowell, Inc., 1972; New York: Apollo Editions, 1974.

Selected Writings of Jules Laforgue (translations). New York: Grove Press, 1956; New York: Evergreen Books, 1957; London: Calder, 1957; Westport, Conn.: Greenwood Press, 1972.

The Streaks of the Tulip; Selected Criticism. New York: Delacorte Press, 1972.

Granger's Index to Poetry, Sixth Edition (editor). New York: Columbia University Press, 1973.

Venice in the Fog. Greensboro, N.C.: Unicorn Press, 1975.

Verses on the Times (With Richard Wilbur). Gutenberg Press, 1978.

Journey to the Dead Sea (Illustrated by David Newbert). Omaha, Neb.: Abbatoir, 1979.

The Tall Poets. Palaemon Press, 1979.

Mr. Smith. New York: Delacorte, 1980.

The Traveler's Tree, New and Selected Poems (Illustrated by Jacques Hnizdovsky). New York: Persea Books, 1980.

Army Brat, A Memoir. New York: Persea Books, 1980.

Army Brat: A Dramatic Narrative for Three Voices (play based on Smith's memoir). Produced in New York City, 1980.

A Green Place (Illustrated by Jacques Hzindovsky). New York: Delacorte, 1982.

The Key. New York: Children's Book Council, 1982.

Plain Talk: Epigrams, Epitaphs, Satires, Nonsense, Occasional, Concrete, and Quotidian Poems. New York: Center for Book Arts, 1988.

Journey to the Interior. New York: Stone House Press, 1988.

Collected Poems, 1939–1989. New York: Macmillan, 1990.

Birds and Beasts (Illustrated by Jacques Hzindovsky). New York: Godine, 1990.

The Cyclist. New York: Stone House Press, 1995.

The World Below the Window: Poems 1937–1997. Baltimore: Johns Hopkins University Press, 1998.

Here Is My Heart: Love Poems (Illustrated by Jane Dyer). New York: Little, Brown, 1999.

Around My Room (Illustrated by Erik Blegvad). New York: Farrar, Straus, 2000.

The Cherokee Lottery: A Sequence of Poems. Willimantic, Conn.: Curbstone Press, 2000.

Hey Diddle, a Riddle. Delray Beach, Fla.: Winslow Press, 2002.

UPDATE

The long list of William Jay Smith's works has many new titles, including, most recently, *Journey to the Interior* (1988), *Collected Poems, 1939–1989* (1990), *The Cyclist* (1995), *The World Below the Window: Poems 1937–1997* (1998), *The Cherokee Lottery: A Sequence of Poems* (2000), and *The Girl in Glass: Love Poems* (2002), and, for children, *Here Is My Heart: Love Poems* (1999), *Around My Room* (2000), and *Hey Diddle, a Riddle* (2002). He also has served as editor and translator of many more volumes in that time as well.

"I am a lyric poet," Smith once told *Contemporary Authors*, "alert, I hope, as my friend Stanley Kunitz has pointed out, 'to the changing weathers of a landscape, the motions of the mind, the complications and surprises of the human comedy.' I believe that poetry should communicate. . . Great poetry must have its own distinctive music; it must resound with the music of the human psyche."

His poetry, written for both adults and children, follows the tradition of Frost and Stevens, and he uses traditional rhymed metrical-stanzaic forms "with a personal style that transforms his subject matter into a memorable reading experience through a lively wit and a writer's eye perceptive enough to make the reader see more than he thought his vision couuld accommodate," according to the *Dictionary of Literary Biography*. "[He is] one of the premier writers who are influencing the voices only now beginning to be heard."

Smith continues to be well read, and receives unqualified praise for his work. In his most recent book of poetry, *The Cherokee Lottery*, Smith—who is part Choctaw—tells the story of the forced removal of the five civilized tribes in the eastern U.S. to the Oklahoma Territory by way of the Trail of Tears. Using several different voices, Smith's work is "visual, humane, unforgettable," wrote *Booklist*, with a haunting style: "Many of the poems appear in the book's signature stanza, a lopey, three-line, roughly pentametric form that sounds sometimes reportorial, sometimes Shakespearean, sometimes both at once."

His collection *Around My Room*, an illustrated selection of his poems for young children, is "characterized by infectious rhyme schemes and verse forms" that are "attuned to the playful language of preschoolers and, like those of Mother goose, roll trippingly off the tongue," wrote *The Horn Book Magazine*. "As all good poetry should, the enchanting collection gives readers a new point of view."

Poetry reprinted from *The World Below the Window: Poems 1937–1997*, published by the Johns Hopkins University Press, 1998, and copyright 1998 by William Jay Smith.

The Poetics of
W. D. Snodgrass

■ **I**

Born in Wilkinsburg, Pennsylvania, in 1926, W. D. Snodgrass began his undergraduate career at Geneva College in 1943–44. After his freshman year he entered the U.S. Navy and served until 1946, when he returned to college and married Lila Jean Hank. He stayed in school only briefly; then, in 1949, he entered the University of Iowa, where he took his B.A. in 1949, his M.A. in 1951, and his M.F.A. in 1953, the same year in which he was divorced from his first wife. It was the breakup of this marriage that he chronicled in a sequence of poems which became the title series of his first book, *Heart's Needle*. The collection appeared in 1959 and won both the first award in poetry of the Ingram Merrill Foundation and the Pulitzer Prize in 1960.

While he was at Iowa, Snodgrass began to write a very personal, very lyrical kind of poetry. Snodgrass' subjects were those which were closest to him and to most readers—family, personal environment, the everyday happenings behind which there often exists something so meaningful that the average person is unable or unwilling to confront it, let alone write about it. Snodgrass felt that it is the poet's job to write about these things. His poetry was a continual stripping away of the surfaces of our world, and a simultaneous exposure of the mental and emotional reasons behind our actions and reactions. Most of the poems in *Heart's Needle* struck a balance between feeling and sense, as in the first stanza of "Song":

> Observe the cautious toadstools
>   still on the lawn today
> though they grow over-evening;
>   sun shrinks them away.
> Pale and proper and rootless,
>   they righteously extort
> their living from the living.

The poet said what he had to say boldly and lyrically. His verse was polished without seeming slick, like stone tiles worn by the passage of the living. For the most part Snodgrass worked with strict metrical nonce-forms, but he found considerable freedom within their limits; the current of his thought ran swiftly and strongly beneath the surface of his lines, no matter what subject motivated him: divorce, marriage, loss, love, return.

His work had personality and craftsmanship; often he touched a responsive chord in the reader. As in "A Cardinal," one could hardly gainsay him when he ended,

> We whistle in the dark
> of a region in doubt
> where unknown powers work,

W. D.Snodgrass William

De Witt Snodgrass is a poet, critic, essayist, and translator. Born in Wilkinsburg, Pennsylvania, in 1926, he attended Geneva College and the State University of Iowa. He taught at Cornell University, Syracuse University, the University of Rochester, and Wayne State University, as well as at the University of Delaware, where he has been distinguished professor emeritus since 1994. Snodgrass has won numerous awards, including a *Hudson Review* fellowship in poetry, the first $1,000 award in poetry of the Ingram Merrill Foundation, an N.E.A. grant, and a Guggenheim fellowship. In 1960 Snodgrass won the Pulitzer Prize in poetry for *Heart's Needle*. He also won first prize for translations of Romanian letters from the Colloquium of Translators and Editors in Siaia, Romania (1995) and a nomination for the National Book Critics Circle Award in criticism category (2001) for *De/Compositions: 101 Good Poems Gone Wrong*. ■

as watchmen in the night
ring bells to say, Watch out,
I am here; I have the right.

In various of his early poems the narrative first-person "I" was not merely the poet speaking of himself subjectively, but the persona of the poet speaking for Everyman in the real and terrifying world, out of despair and into human joy. Here, in this first book of poems, was a man's life shown to the bone, and one knew it was not made of whole cloth. Many readers were deeply moved by *Heart's Needle*, including the present writer, who wrote an undergraduate "Letter to W. D. S." when the book was published (a poem that was the beginning of a long friendship and which was included in my *Awaken, Bells Falling* [1968]):

> *Letter to W. D. S.*
> Christ, you made me sad
> with your love tunes gone awry,
> the bitter root twining mossily
> among the pages of a songsheet tossed to
>
> wind down the wind and
> moulder in a lost cranny
> of some meadow. I'm not used to loss,
> though aware of it, as one is aware of
>
> cancer. A woman
> I knew, wrinkled like blown snow,

died of a wild part of herself which
ravened its own life. Her children, grown to seed

themselves, kept locks on
their tongues, but their hearts' faceless
prisoner snarled at the world behind
portcullises of eyes. Like those striped lines of

yours, that scourge of ink
and pillory of paper.
Why did you flay yourself there, in the
marketplace? Was it because sorrow shown is

simpler than covert
loneliness? All of us are
alone. The world we blow through is cold.
Snow fetters our sorrow. Still we flute and fife.

But not every poem in the book was flagellant. Not the least of Snodgrass' qualities was his sense of humor, unique among the members of the so-called Confessional School, if one does not count John Berryman's bitter clowning. In the poem titled "These Trees Stand…" Snodgrass acknowledged the humor of his last name in the refrain, "Snodgrass is walking through the universe." Readers will not appreciate the full import of this line unless they know the etymology of the poet's name, but will respond merely to its sound. It is, in fact, two words compounded: *grass* and the past participle of the archaic English verb, "to snid" or mow; thus, "Snodgrass" means "mown lawn" or "cut grass." The third and final stanza of this poem begins, "Your name's absurd, miraculous as sperm / And as decisive."

∎ II

"April Inventory" from *Heart's Needle*, like many lyrics before it, sang its confession, and no distinction would have been made between Snodgrass' work and traditional lyric poetry if it hadn't been for two things: the new subject matter of broken marriage together with the problems attendant upon divorce, the everyday frictions of home life in conflict with infidelities of the mind and of the heart; and the fact that John Berryman and Robert Lowell were influenced by his work and began writing their own confessional poetry.

"April Inventory" became a standard anthology piece of rueful good humor as it examined the position of the aging teacher-poet among the co-ed flowers of the campus. It was and is wistful, nostalgic, and funny, yet it made the necessary observation and comment as well, even as it sang: one of the traditional ways in which the best egopoets capture and hold the attention of the reader is through lyricism, a fact that has largely been forgotten in the age of the "personal poem" that ensued in the wake of Lowell's abandonment of metrical form and the subsequent triumph of the prose poetry of the Beats and the Black Mountain poets.

"April Inventory" is in many ways typical of Snodgrass' early production, and a close examination of the poem will reveal many of Snodgrass' early devices and strategies. One notices immediately on the typographical level, simply by the layout of its lines, that this is a verse mode, not a prose mode poem, and it is stanzaic rather than strophic; the poem is sixty lines long arranged in ten sestet stanzas.

It is soon clear to the reader that the sonic level is strong. Scansion shows that the poem's general prosody is accentual-syllabics; specifically, normative accentual-syllabics. All lines are the same length; the meter is iambic tetrameter. The rhyme scheme is *ababcc*, but there is linked rhyme between stanzas 1 and 2, 5 and 6, and 7 and 8, so that the complete rhyme scheme is much more complicated. Some of these are falling rhymes, specifically the *l* rhymes in stanza 5 (where they first show up) and in the following stanza 6, where the *m* rhymes also fall, the *p* rhymes in stanza 7, the *r* rhymes in stanza eight, and the *v* rhymes in stanza ten, closing the poem. Snodgrass utilizes metrical variations in a craftsmanly way to provide sonic interest:

> The green catalpa tree has turned
> All white; the cherry blooms once more.
> In one whole year I haven't learned
> A blessed thing they pay you for.
> The blossoms snow down in my hair;
> The trees and I will soon be bare.[6]

The first line of the poem is acatalectic—that is, perfect iambic tetrameter, but the second line opens with a spondee substituted for the first foot (*all white*). The next two lines are acatalectic, but a trochee is substituted for the third iamb in line five (*down in*). The last line of the first sestet is perfect again.

Thereafter substitutions occur relatively frequently, often of spondees or trochees for the prevailing iambs, as in the first foot of stanza two, line three (whole line 9), where a trochee substitution occurs. In the first foot of the next line (10), a demotion occurs in the first syllable of the first foot. This line also contains a w-glide elision ("grad*ua*lly") and a caesura which compensates for a missing unstressed syllable just after the elision:

> The trees have more than I to spare.
> The sleek, expensive girls I teach,
> Younger and pinker every year,
> Bloom gradually, out of reach.
> The pear tree lets its petals drop
> Like dandruff on the table top.[12]

In the first line (13) of stanza three there is a promotion—by means of rhetorical emphasis—of a syllable, "so," to the level of a secondary stress in foot three, and there is another spondee substitution in foot one, line three (15). The English language hates three unstressed syllables in a row, and as a result "with" in line sixteen takes a promotion to secondary stress, thus giving it rhetorical emphasis—both teeth *and* hair are falling:

> The girls have grown so young by now
> I have to nudge myself to stare.
> This year they smile and mind me how
> My teeth are falling with my hair.
> In thirty years I may not get
> Younger or shrewder or out of debt.[18]

The last line of this stanza substitutes two trochees in the first two feet (*younger*, *shrew*der).

> Stanza four is acatalectic throughout:

> The tenth time, just a year ago,
> I made myself a little list
> Of all the things I'd ought to know,
> Then told my parents, analyst,
> And everyone who's trusted me,
> I'd be substantial, presently.[24]

The first line (25) of stanza five puts rhetorical stress on the word "one," but its position in the line, between two strong stresses, counteracts the emphasis; the result is a promotion only to secondary stress, which tends to make the reader aware that the last word of the line, "about," is likewise rhetorically emphasized: "I haven't read *one* book *about* a book." In the last line (30) a trochee is again substituted in the first foot (*Get* the de*grees*):

I haven't read one book about
A book or memorized one plot.
Or found a mind I did not doubt.
I learned one date. And then forgot.
And one by one the solid scholars
Get the degrees, the jobs, the dollars.[30]

There are other substitutions in stanza six: a spondee in the first foot of the third line (33), *"one lovely girl"*; a trochee in the first foot of the next line (34). *"Lack*ing," and a trochee in the third foot, "a source-*book* or." In the next line (35) there is a promotion in the first syllable of the second iamb ("I showed *one* child"), and in the last syllable a secondary stress is forced upon the preposition "of" at the end of the line (syllable 8) by means of its position where a strong stress ought to occur in the meter, and because it rhymes with "love" in the next line (31) which, though the previous line (30) was end-stopped with a period, is nevertheless an enjambment. The effect of this construction is to invoke sarcasm and thus emphasize the stereotype being set up:

And smile above their starchy collars.
I taught my classes Whitehead's notions;
One lovely girl, a song of Mahler's.
Lacking a source-book or promotions,
I showed one child the colors of
A luna moth and how to love.[36]

In the next sestet another promotion is forced by overstressing through alliteration in the second line (38) syllable one, foot two: "to *bark back,* loosen love and crying"; notice that "loosen love" is also an alliteration:

I taught myself to name my name,
To bark back, loosen love and crying;
To easy my woman so she came,
To ease an old man who was dying.
I have not learned how often I
Can win, can love, but choose to die.[42]

In the fourth line (40) of this stanza there is another substitution of a trochee for an iamb in the third foot (*"Man* who"), and in the next line (41) a rhetorical emphasis promotes the unstressed syllable in the second iamb ("I have *not* learned")—had the poet written "haven't," there would have been no promotion, no deviation from the norm.

Stanza eight repeats this phrase in the first line (43): "I have not learned there is a lie," and alliteration with the rhyme-word in the first syllable of the next line (44), "Love shall be," forces the substitution of a trochee in the first foot. "Loves" in the fourth line (46) of the stanza is both a repetition and a continuation of the alliteration; thus, the first foot of this line is a spondee, *"Loves only..."*:

I have not learned there is a lie
Love shall be blonder, slimmer, younger;
That my equivocating eye

Loves only by my body's hunger;
That I have forces, true to feel,
Or that the lovely world is real.[48]

By this time in the poem the falling rhymes have become prominent, and the effect of the spondee and trochee substitutions, together with the repetitions and the promotions, is giving the poem a considerable feeling of metrical variation and a concomitant sense of acceleration, both metrical and rhetorical. The return to acatalexis in the last two lines (47 and 48) of this stanza merely emphasizes this sense, for it causes the poem to pause suddenly. To use a metaphor from boxing, Snodgrass has been jabbing faster and faster, peppering the reader with softening-up and setting-up blows. Now he has used a combination and stepped back before he delivers the haymaker.

Stanza nine returns to the metrical norm, including rising rhyme, except for a rhetorical promotion of the first syllable of line three (51), "my," and another of the second syllable in the first foot of the fifth line (53): "There *is* a value underneath." In the second syllable of foot three of the following line (54), a preposition is promoted because of its position in the line: "The gold and silver *in* my teeth," which has a rhetorical effect:

While scholars speak authority
And wear their ulcers on their sleeves,
My eyes in spectacles shall see
These trees procure and spend their leaves.
There is a value underneath
The gold and silver in my teeth.[54]

Another rhetorical promotion takes place in the second syllable of the second line (56) of the last stanza: "We *shall* afford," and in the same spot in the next three lines as well, (57): "There *is* a gentleness"; (58): "That *will* outspeak," and (59): "There *is* a loveliness exists," so that the four middle lines of the last stanza are a series of grammatical parallels that serve the rhetorical function of delivering the climactic knockout blows:

Though trees turn bare and girls turn wives,
We shall afford our costly seasons;
There is a gentleness survives
That will outspeak and has its reasons.
There is a loveliness exists,
Preserves us, not for specialists.[60]

The major genre of "April Inventory" is the lyric. The minor genre is the "confessional" poem, or perhaps it would be more accurate to say that it is a humorous lament with a didactic point. In any event, it is a poem with its levels in balance, and this equilibrium is mirrored in the qualities of character that show through the poet's lines. He is complex—funny and intelligent, suffering and indignant, disdainful and confused, logical and sympathetic. Although Snodgrass in these early poems set aside the narrative and dramatic genres of the academic formalists, he was nevertheless still utilizing some of the favorite New Critical techniques and approaches of that school.

■ III

Of all the so-called "academic poets" of the period, Robert Lowell was perhaps the paradigm. His *Life Studies* appeared in the same year as *Heart's Needle,* but it jettisoned much more than merely restrictions on personal privacy. Metrics and rhyme, mythological and literary allusions, even intellectuality and extended metaphor went overboard. Waves of confessional guilt, personal angst, and prurient intimacy gushed over the bows of the ship of literature, breaching the hull, and there was no longer even song to carry the interest of the reader over the reefs of boredom and through the cloying Sargasso of dysfunction.

Inasmuch as Snodgrass was a student of Robert Lowell and John Berryman at the University of Iowa, it was perhaps a foregone conclusion that the three poets would be seen as forming the core of a "school" of personal poetry. One of the earliest people to use the expression "Confessional Poets" was Donald Justice, a student in the Iowa Workshop himself at the time, and later a teacher there. In a Brockport Writers' Forum interview of the early 1970s Snodgrass acknowledged his debt to Lowell and mentioned a remark of Randall Jarrell: "Snodgrass, do you know you're writing the very best second-rate Lowell in the whole country?" But the fact is that Lowell was writing a much looser and less interesting second-rate Snodgrass.

An early interest of Snodgrass' was in translation. With Lore Segal he translated, from the German, Christian Morgenstern's *Gallows Songs* (1967), which chronicled the adventures of Palmstrom, an unearthly, even fey creature who innocently falls afoul of life in many ways but emerges essentially undamaged. (I would like to acknowledge at this juncture, many years after the fact, that these poems gave me the inspiration and impetus to write my own series, *Pocoangelini: A Fantography* [1971], and I owe Messrs. Morgenstern and Snodgrass a debt of gratitude.)

After Experience appeared in 1968, and *Remains* in 1970. Although the writing of this latter collection antedates the publication of the former, it appeared later in a limited edition under the anagram pseudonym "S. S. Gardons"—the poet still fooling around with his surname— because the chapbook is comprised of those pieces Snodgrass felt were too personal and familial even for the original confessional poet to publish while the people with whom the poems are concerned were still living. A new edition appeared in 1985, and the collection was also included in *Selected Poems 1957–1987* (1987).

Some of the better known poems from *After Experience* are "The Lovers Go Fly a Kite," the title poem, "'After Experience Taught Me...,'" and "A Flat One," an elegy that considered the subject of death through the quotidian examination of a cadaver, late a patient in a hospital where the poet had given care:

> Before each meal, twice every night,
> We set pads on your bedsores, shut
> Your catheter tube off, then brought
> The second canvas-and-black-iron
> Bedframe and clamped you in between them, tight,
> Scared, so we could turn
>
> You over. We washed you, covered you,
> Cut up each bite of meat you ate;
> We watched your lean jaws masticate
> As ravenously your useless food
> As even thieves at hard labor in their chains chew
> Or insects in the wood.

One night observe that if the poet can sing of such things, no subject is unpoetic; all that's necessary is the talent and the technique with which to sing it.

The last part of the book consisted of translations from the French and the German, but a few poems that preceded the translations were written in "free verse." Although in his later work Snodgrass began to move away from traditionally rhyming and metering poems—a phenomenon that overtook his generation as the 1960s progressed into the '70s, but which now in the '90s is reversing itself among the younger generation with the advent of "Neoformalism"—his balancing of the levels of poetry has continued to be characteristic of Snodgrass' work in all his books of lyrics including *If Birds Build with Your Hair* (1979), *The Boy Made of Meat,* subtitled "A Poem for Children" (1983), and *A Locked House* (1986), though not in *The Führer Bunker.*

The Führer Bunker: A Cycle of Poems in Progress, which appeared in 1977, was a departure from the poet's earlier lyrical approach. In fact, it was a return to earlier New Critical precepts and a turn to dramatic poetry. Snodgrass wrote in an "Afterword," "All the figures in this cycle were actually in the places, doing and saying pretty much the things these poems show." The poems are monologues, not songs or first-person narratives. Each character speaks in his or her own voice; there is thus a strong documentary element in these poems about Nazi Germany during World War II and a much greater range of approach as well. Some poems are written in prose, others in verse, yet others in a mixture of the two. There are even a few—those that are speeches by Heinrich Himmler—that are spatial poems written on graph paper, one square allotted to each letter or space.

A good example of a quasi-verse speech is that of "Eva Braun," Hitler's mistress. Dated 22 April 1945, the poem begins with an epigraph: *"(Hitler's mistress received no public recognition and often felt badly neglected. Her small revenges included singing American songs, her favorite being 'Tea for Two.' Having chosen to die with him in the bunker, she appeared quite serene during the last days)."* The poem begins with the opening of the song: "Tea for two / And two for tea," as though Braun had been murmuring it to herself, and then she says in a soliloquy, almost in an aside to the audience (the reader),

I ought to feel ashamed

Feeling such joy. Behaving like a spoiled child!
So fulfilled. This is a very serious matter.
All of them have come here to die. And they grieve.
I have come here to die. If this is dying,
Why else did I ever live?

The next verse from the song follows this strophe which can be scanned as very loose iambic pentameter blank verse, though some might argue that it is actually only lineated prose. Henceforward, strophes will alternate with lines from the song, and the soliloquy will end with the last lines of "Tea for Two."

This strategy is very clever and rather experimental. Snodgrass manages to characterize Eva Braun at the same time that he advances the narrative and provides the reader with an intimate glance into one possible version of history. Even in his rendition of a female character Snodgrass can be quite convincing:

No friends or relations
On weekend vacations

That I, I above all, am chosen—even I
Must find that strange. I who was always
Disobedient, rebellious—smoked in the dining car,
Wore rouge whenever he said I shouldn't.
When he ordered that poor Chancellor Schuschnigg
Was to starve, I sent in food.

We won't have it known, dear,
That we own a telephone, dear.

■ **BOOKS BY W. D. SNODGRASS**

Heart's Needle. New York: Knopf, 1959.

After Experience. New York: Harper, 1968.

Gallows Songs. Ann Arbor: University of Michigan, 1967.

Remains (under the pseudonym S. S. Gardons). Mount Horeb, Wis.: Perishable Press, 1970.

In Radical Pursuit. New York: Harper, 1975.

The Führer Bunker: A Cycle of Poems in Progress. Brockport, N.Y.: BOA Editions, 1977.

If Birds Build with Your Hair. Berkeley: Nadja Press, 1979.

The Boy Made of Meat. Concord, N.H.: William B. Eweert, 1983.

Six Minnesinger Songs. Burning Deck Press, 1983.

Heinrich Himmler: Platoons and Flies. Pterodactyl Press, 1985.

Selected Poems, 1957–1987. New York: Soho Press, 1987.

W. D.'s Midnight Carnival (with Deloss McGraw). New York: Artra Publishers, 1988.

The Death of Cock Robin. Cranbury, N.J.: University of Delaware Press, 1989.

To Shape a Song. Berkeley: Nadja Press, 1989.

Snow Songs. Berkeley: Nadja Press, 1992.

Each in His Season. Rochester, N.Y.: BOA Editions, 1993.

Spring Suite. Berkeley: Nadja Press, 1994.

After-Images: Autobiographical Sketches. Rochester, N.Y.: BOA Editions, 1999.

De/Compositions: 101 Good Poems Gone Wrong. St. Paul, Minn.: Graywolf, Press, 2000.

I who joined the Party, I who took Him
For my lover just to spite my old stiff father —
Den Alten Fritz — and those stupid nuns.
I ran my teachers crazy, and my mother—I
Held out even when she stuck my head in water.
He shall have none but me.

The effect of the sequence of poems is cumulative. When one is done reading it, one experiences the effect of having finished reading a novel or a play. The feeling is compounded by the simultaneous sense that one has been reading exceptional poetry, for Snodgrass is always aware of the language and its music.

Even when Snodglass appears to be writing lineated prose poems he is in fact maintaining his wonted balance of the levels of poetry. One good example is "Old Apple Trees" from *If Birds Build with Your Hair*. It is built upon an extended metaphor that begins immediately with a pair of similes: "Like battered old millhands, they stand in the orchard— / Like drunk legionnaires, heaving themselves up,…" The conceit is carried forward over the whole poem as the narrator imagines a night on the town among real people like the old trees which, when he returns home, he sees as now historical and universal, both as trees and people, "…the rough trunks holding their formations / Like elders of Colonus, the old men of Thebes / Tossing their white hair, almost whispering,…" In fiction this would be called a circle-back ending, but here it is a return to the origins of the poem both literally and figuratively, with a greatly amplified power of allusion and overtone.

Some people might call these lines "free verse" (that is, line-phrased prose: during this past thirty years we have forgotten that verse is metered language, according to the *O. E. D.*, and prose is unmetered language), but, like "Eva Braun," it is in fact a form of blank verse: variable, unrhymed iambic lines tending toward pentameter. Merely to look at the poem laid out is to see that most lines are nearly of a length, except toward the end of the poem where they narrow down to approximately tetrameter length. Such lines as, "No man should come here except on a working pass" or "Till even the belly dancer leaves, disgraced" are clearly based in meter.

The *Selected Poems* ends with the chapbooks *A Locked House* (1986), and the title poem of *The Death of Cock Robin* (1989), which is subsumed under the title *The Kinder Capers* (1986) together with a poem titled "Darkling." Reading through these poems by one of our finest contemporary poets, I find myself thinking how interesting it would be if some of the others of Snodgrass's generation, those who moved away from the formal lyric, were to return to what they did so well thirty years ago—just for a visit, perhaps—to see whether maturity hasn't added a quality of depth to their ability to sing, as it has done in the case of this poet, who never abandoned his Muse.

Lewis Turco
June, 1993

UPDATE

W. D. Snodgrass has since published four volumes of poetry, *To Shape a Song* (1989), *Snow Songs* (1992), *Each in His Season* (1993), and *Spring Suite* (1994). He also has written a memoir, *After-Images: Autobiographical Sketches* (1999), and a book of criticism, *De/Compositions: 101 Good Poems Gone Wrong* (2001), and published two books of translations, *Selected Translations*, (1998), and *Five Folk Ballads* (1999).

Snodgrass is often called one of the first "confessional" poets, one whose work deeply affected the world of poetry. These days, however, most critics seem to think that Snodgrass's best poetry is behind him. *World Literature Today* attacked *Each in His Season* as "a series of mostly long-winded, sometimes wicked verses which at their best border on parody but never quite achieve it," and concluded: "Some writers add to their reputation by further works; some would be better advised to rest on their laurels."

In the Everlasting Present: The Poetry of Elizabeth Spires

Elizabeth Spires will soon publish her fifth book of poems. In it she continues to practice—in the senses both of rehearsal and of professional pursuit — a poetic art of unusual largeness, grace, persistence, and ease in the company of great forerunners. Her poems are those of a person very much in the world, open to a variety of places and relationships, alert to all we have in common, especially love, mortality, the passing of generations, and the roughly equal mysteries of sleep and waking. The consistency and unity in her work are surprising not only because the work is so good, but also because Spires was still in her mid-twenties when she started publishing the poems collected in her first book.

In this latest collection, along with the qualities her earlier poems have led us gratefully to expect, there is a new inclination to trust simplicity of observation and statement. *My Mother's Doll,* for example, opens with the speaker's brief account of finding in her late mother's living room a rag doll "tall as I was," recalling its particular way of keeping the children company, and deciding to leave it in its accustomed chair as the apartment is closed for the winter:

I imagined you sitting in darkness all winter,
the blinds drawn, only the dust to keep you company.
Did your heart beat faster when you heard the hum
of the refrigerator? When a letter fell through the mailslot?
Or did you lapse into a sleep deeper than my own,
cold, dark, profound, where winter passed in a dream
and you, in your solitude, were nothing, *no one,*
because she wasn't there to speak your name?

The somewhat ordinary use of "I imagined" will have its effect enlarged and deepened at the end of the poem, but here it is important to notice not only that the inanimate doll takes on additional human characteristics, but also that the use of "my own" in the fifth line above enables the speaker and the doll to share the profundity of the winter sleep, and the paradox of a dream of nothingness. This is one of the many ways in which Spires probes at the boundaries between sleep and waking, dream and consciousness. For her, the two states may constitute a duality for the purposes of "discussion," but that they are in various important ways inseparable is a frequently recurring theme in her poetry. As Paul Eluard said, "There is another world, but it is in this one."

The poem's concluding two stanzas move out of the perfect tense into the present ("this summer") and the future, as the speaker returns to open the apartment and waltz around the room with the doll for the amusement of her own daughter, "my daughter / who barely knew my mother." The poem ends:

When we leave, I'll straighten your blue dress,

Elizabeth Spires
Elizabeth Spires was born in Lancaster, Ohio, on May 28, 1952 to Richard C. and Sue Wagner Spires. Her father worked in grounds maintenance; her mother was a real-estate broker. Spires earned a B.A. from Vassar College in 1974 and an M.A. from Johns Hopkins University in 1979. Among her numerous awards are two National Endowment for the Arts fellowships; two Pushcart Prizes, 1981 and 1995; a Guggenheim Fellowship in Poetry, 1992; the Whiting Award, 1996; and the Witter Bynner Prize in Poetry, from the American Academy of Arts and Letters in 1998.

She has taught English at Washington College, served as poet-in-residence at Loyola College, and visiting professor in Writing Seminars at Johns Hopkins University. She is currently professor of English at Goucher College. Spires married Madison Smartt Bell, a novelist, in 1985, and they have a daughter, Celia Dovell. They live in Baltimore, Maryland. ■

comb your mop of hair into a neat page boy.
Then I'll put you back in the chair until the next time
because I cannot imagine it empty,
cannot imagine this room without you.

Despite the direct simplicity of their diction and tone, it is hard to take the last two lines literally. The power of the speaker's imagination has already been demonstrated. The narrative is clear enough: the speaker has never experienced the doll's absence from this room, and is determined not to do so. The last two lines are not so much a declaration of inability as an outright refusal. At the same time, they gently suggest the difficulty, not of imagining, but of actually experiencing, the mother's absence from the room.

Though "My Mother's Doll" is thoroughly comprehensible and complete in itself, it also has its place in the developing sequence that is Spires' work up to now. Her poems respond with unusual richness to being read as a continuous larger work. An aging pupil of the New Criticism will remind himself that whatever autobiographical narrative seems to arise from such a reading is fictional to some indeterminable extent, and may therefore be thought of as entirely fictional. Recurring images and thematic concerns in Spires' five books weave a bright thread of artifice into the succession of chronologically predictable stages of a life — childhood, early love, later love, motherhood, bereavement, consolation — and make these five collections amount to considerably more than an engaging assortment of fine poetic responses to crucial moments.

"Tequila," the opening poem in Spires's first book, *Globe* (1981), combines with the title poem to establish a tension between autobiography and imagination that does not slacken as Spires's work develops. "Tequila" is placed in a prefatory position in *Globe*, before the first of the book's three numbered sections, and, though it is in the first person, it has the diction and tone of a fable, beginning with a vague if powerful setting:

> I live in a stone house high in the mountains,
> close to the stars . . .
>   Last night, a little lonely,
> I went to the bar in the valley
> where the regulars tell their stories,
> one about a man with a runaway dog,
> who stood by his door each night calling
> *Tequila, Tequila.* Nobody
> knew how long his grief would last
> or what he did when his house went dark.

The ellipses are part of the poem. They hover above a perilous balancing act between tonal expectations, but if there is a famous joke about a man with a dog named Tequila, this speaker appears not to have heard it. (The poem predates by a couple of decades the notorious Chihuahua, seeker of Taco Bell.) After three sentences of speculation about how the man spends his nights, the poem continues:

>   Nobody should
> go near a man who wants to be
> that lonely. Nobody does.
> Bragging, I told them I'd go back
> to any year in my life
> and live it over. I lied
> and said nothing had ever scared me.
> They looked at me, all husbands and fathers.
> The stars will blind you, they warned,
> the ghosts in the alley
> will blow smoke in your eyes and steal
> your money. I nodded, pretending to know.

Even in this stylized context, the warnings of the men have the arbitrary flavor of invented local superstition. If we did not know that the author of the poem is a woman, would the phrase "all husbands and fathers" make us think so? The speaker has fallen among would-be protectors who lack her awareness that one of the things they share is ignorance—of another man's pain, the sources of fear, what comes next. Someday, she thinks, she will leave with a few belongings, by the only road, "the one that leads / everywhere":

>   And though I'm not friendly,
> I'll leave a note on the door,
> black writing on a white square, cryptic
> and small, so the regulars can make up
> my story: *Gone to find Tequila—*

Between the ellipses near the beginning and the dash at the end, the poem shows how a life can be imagined, how a road often leads away from the opening proposition. The title poem, which is the first poem in the first section, suggests how the road circles back on itself.

The first half of "Globe" is a recollection of playing in a small apartment under the supervision of a middle-aged baby-sitter who didn't want to take the speaker outside. The child contented herself with making card houses, coloring, and lurching about in an old pair of her mother's shoes. Into this bearable boredom comes the deliverer:

> Enter my father at 5:15, dark and immediate,
> finished with his shift at the factory.
> He was hiding something behind his back.
> He turned as I circled him,
> keeping whatever it was out of sight.
> *Close your eyes and hold out your hand—*
> I touched a globe slotted on top for coins,
> my hand shadowing the continents
> like a cloud thousands of miles wide.
> He put my finger over the state where we lived,
> then handed me his loose change to fill the world with.

The images of the pair revolving like part of the solar system, and of the hand over the continents like a huge cloud, are not only lovely, but also a pointer, like the phrase "dark and immediate," to the consciousness of an adult narrator looking back. It happens that the rest of the poem is on the following page:

> Memory's false as anything, spliced in the wrong parts,
> queerly jumping. But better than forgetting.
> We walked out into the soft light of October, leaves
> sticking to our shoes like gold paper.
> I was four years old and he was twenty-five,
> same age as I am writing this.

A very slight increase in the diction's informality here brings the child into the foreground again, despite the sophistication of the thought. The phrase "But better than forgetting" and the last line are the child responding to the adult, even though in the last line the child-adult is writing the poem. As a recollection of a rich moment between a young father and his small daughter, the poem has its fair share of memorable power and charm, but another of its strengths is in its understanding that being true to what one remembers is sometimes a matter of having to write fiction.

The remainder of the book's first section is mostly in this mode: the lyric or meditative potentialities of a moment seemingly recalled from actual experience. About halfway through the section, "Flashback" quietly throws a nearly invisible net of rhyme over the irregularly metered stanzas. It is probably not difficult to read the poem a time or two without noticing that it rhymes, so effortlessly do the line-ends move in synchrony with the elevated free verse Spires uses in the majority of the poems in this book:

> All afternoon the night falls
> on our bodies like thin, invisible nets. It's July;
> albino fathers, filled with unrest,
> run up and down the beach awkwardly tossing beach balls
> against the wind. The ocean pushes against the sky,
> flattens it into a blue plate hovering above
> our heads. Arms interlaced, we lie
> in the sand, young and "almost in love,"
> languid somnambulists on the verge of waking.
> I rouse myself, put my ear to your chest,
> and hear waves breaking . . . .

The second section of *Globe* is chiefly given over to poems that take the speaker/author out of herself, sometimes into the imagined selves of invented or historical characters, sometimes into figures depicted in works of art. In almost every instance, a central concern of the poem is the oppression of a woman. "Widow's Walk" is the brief monologue of a whaling captain's wife; its languorous near-complaint would perhaps be too mysterious without the help of the powerful epigraph, which quotes an observation Crevecoeur made on Nantucket: "A singular custom prevails here among the women. . . . They have adopted these many years the Asiatic custom of taking a dose of opium every morning; and so deeply rooted is it, that they would be at a loss how to live without this indulgence." There is a monologue spoken by Elizabeth Siddall, wife of Dante Gabriel Rossetti, in whose coffin he deposited poems, only to recover them by exhumation several years later.

The power in these poems is often in their understatement. Some of the situations are inherently melodramatic; Spires is alert to the pitfalls, and manages to move swiftly from horror to black humor and back again, as in "Yeoman Murdering His Deformed Wife with a Sickle (Kuniyoshi)," the third poem under the title "After Three Japanese Drawings." In the first half of the poem, the man's unhappiness is displayed. Then,

> In early spring, after a winter of rain,
> they stood in the garden arguing. He reached
> for the sickle meaning only to cut off her hand.

[Here the poet briefly invites us to reflect that the man seems to have considered this a relatively harmless intention.]

> But she screamed. Travellers were passing
> on the bridge not far from where they stood.
> Alarmed, he swung the sickle again and again
> till she was quiet under him.

There is an eerie calm in these poems, as if the speakers had somehow come to terms with the wrongs done them, or were taking some consolation from this chance to tell how it was.

The final section of the book is in some respects the most ambitious, and in some others the least successful, strong as it is. Many of the poems have their foundations in the story of a relationship that has failed, or ended, anyway. Too often, they are stripped down to essentials, perhaps to avoid the sentimentality of confession. Still, they are not so far reduced as to deny themselves such opportunities as this image from "The Hill," the second part of a six-part sequence called "Letters to the Sea":

> But now you touch me as a widow's grief
> touches a mirror: unclouded silver
> changing to ocean without center or shore.

Globe launched a poet whose accomplishment was already extraordinary, the limits of whose promise would be hard to discern.

Swan's Island (1985) contains poems and groups of poems that may have arisen from the end of a relationship and the beginning of another, but that somewhat accidental aspect of the work is less important than the continued subtle explorations of a woman's roles, of the use and place of rhyme, and the possibility of conversation with poems by earlier practitioners. The title poem, four pages in medium-short lines of free verse, is an account of aspects of a solitude, a month on an island off the coast of Maine, in a one-room cabin that makes the speaker think of monks. The poem's first line is "The island's dark tonight." The poem's shape and concerns do not demand that we recall Arnold's opening line, "The sea is calm to-night," for there is no second person addressed until near the end of the poem. The days pass, and the speaker becomes accustomed to the way they do, learning to make primitive semaphore exchanges with lobstermen, and then learning that the knowledge thus gained is of little use. At the end of the poem, though, the echo of Arnold has some relevance; there is someone it would be good to be true to:

> *Swan's Island.* A world
> existing side by side with yours,
> where love struggles to perfect
> itself, and finally perfect,
> finds it has no object.
> The waking dream's intact—
> the world continues not to change,
> and staying the same, changes us.

The way the constant world changes its inhabitants is spectacularly demonstrated in "Storyville Portraits," a sequence of six poems based on photographs of New Orleans prostitutes in the first few years of this century. The photographer was E. J. Bellocq (1873–1949), who lived in or near the fabled red-light district and made fine photographic portraits of many of the women there. The plates were discovered by Lee Friedlander in the 1950s; he printed them with great care and expertise, and published them in 1970. Those with the *sang-froid* to read a few paragraphs on the subject by Susan Sontag may turn their browsers to http://www.masters-of-photography.com/B/bellocq/bellocq_articles2.html, where several of the photographs Spires addresses are also reproduced.

The poems are similar in form: each is roughly two dozen lines, give or take a line or two here or there, with a stanza break near the middle. The first parts tend toward description, the second parts toward speculation, toward conclusions that require imagination, though it is imagination closely loyal to the observations and to the photographs. In the second part of the fifth poem in the sequence, we begin to feel how the six women become one woman:

> Tired of the pose, her left hand
> moves, blurring the slow exposure,
> ring flashing out, fingers slowly dissolving.
> Body and soul, thought and emotion, the present
> moment and hereafter: two sides of a coin
> spinning so fast distinctions are useless.

But the erasure of distinctions requires the distinctions to be there in the first place. Here is particularity again:

> Her eyes invite, *defy*, any hand
> to touch her, knowing the soul,
> intact, *whole*, subsists entirely
> on the meager rations of the physical,
> that flesh is permeable to Time,
> her visible hand a claw of light and shadow,
> as, alone and strangely generous,
> she shares the slow death of her body with us.

In the end of the sixth poem, Spires strengthens the conclusion that we are not these women, and that we are. The woman in this picture holds a dog in her lap:

> She is happy
> perhaps, but not in a way we know,
> and probably she doesn't stop
> to think so as she holds the dog's
> body, the corporeal husk,
> a shield, an offering to us,
> believing, as she must,
> *There is no life but this one.*

The noticeable repetitions of the *us* sound constitute a formal feature it would be easy to make too much of, but it is there. Spires does not use rhyme in a way that makes it seem frequent in her work, and yet it is. She is fond of assonances like this one, and of internal rhymes that evade the reader who glances down the right edge of the poem seeking patterns. A way of thinking about it further presents itself in "Clue Sestina"—which, being a sestina, manages form without actually rhyming—and "'Ever-Changing Landscape,'" a longer poem in free verse describing and meditating on one of Maryland's, if not the country's, most engaging places, the Ladew Topiary Gardens.

"Clue Sestina" arises from the board game; why didn't someone think of it sooner? Here is the opening stanza, along with enough of the second to get to the end of a sentence:

> One of us will die in a room
> of this drafty mansion though I accuse nobody.
> The truth, they say, is seldom black and white.
> My idiosyncratic "sense of form" permits me to note,
> however, certain departures, omissions in the story,
> for instance, the disturbing fact that Miss
>
> Scarlet, chronic insomniac, was miss-
> ing this morning from her bedroom.

Though I am strongly prejudiced in favor of regular meter in sestinas, I admire the steady sense of line in this one, in which lines vary in length quite considerably, but always somehow manage to seem like reasonable departures from the iambic pentameter which does assert itself in five of the seven stanzas. This reasonableness is admittedly in the eye of the beholder; it would be easier just to lay it down that there is always a lazy clumsiness about unmetrical sestinas, and to declare that this one would have been better if the line lengths had been regularized. But Spires's poetic project includes a restless curiosity concerning the relationships between formalism and the absence or near-absence of meter. She writes mostly free verse, strictly speaking, but the vast majority of her lines have an authority that it is easy to associate with metrical writing.

"Clue Sestina," to be sure, is in part a *jeu d'esprit*, but anyone who has tried to write both formally and amusingly has discovered how hard that is. In several ways this poem reveals that Spires has this on her mind. Having decided, for example, that one of the end-words will often be the "Miss" of "Miss Scarlet," she accepts that each line ending thus will be heavily enjambed, and so even when she does not use "Miss / Scarlet," she uses the end-word as an occasion for a hard enjambment, as in the first line of the second stanza, quoted above. She rolls easily with the corollary, which is that in each stanza a line is likely to begin with "Scarlet." She also plays with our expectations of the line-ends, using "conservatory" and "Colonel Mustard, an old Tory" where the first stanza has led us to expect "story."

As the poem moves toward its close, more of the lines are longer, perhaps more hospitable to a small adjustment of the tone, which will admit a last sentence of spooky darkness. Professor Plum enters at the end, admits that he has been away all day with Miss Scarlet, and then

> He looks around the room,
> smiles, takes out a white revolver. "Our little story
> ends, I'm afraid, on a tragic note. You'll never find Miss
> Scarlet. Death is a very small room in which to hide a body."

The first-person speaker who refers in the first stanza to "my idiosyncratic sense of form" uses the first-person pronoun twice in the second stanza:

> I took the secret passageway to the conservatory,
> relieved, when I got there, to find no body.

This person, whoever it may be, henceforth withdraws, but not before having made an overt statement about form and the desire to search for gaps, not to say loopholes, in the accepted boundaries of a game or a craft or a world.

The Ladew Topiary Gardens near Monkton, Maryland, created on his farm by Harvey S. Ladew (1887–1976), are world-famous; they feature such extravagances as a topiary horse and rider jumping over a wooden gate, in "pursuit" of a topiary pack of hounds and a topiary fox. Topiary, the art of training and trimming shrubs and other plants into recognizable non-plant shapes, is almost too good an example of the convergence of nature and art:

> The easy certainty of nature
> opposed to the artifice of topiary,
> the hills' "ever-changing dream"
> juxtaposed with swans and unicorns
> that have to be constantly
> pruned and clipped to keep them
> recognizable, unchanging.

The phrase in quotation marks, echoing the title, comes from a bit of Ladew's old-fashioned whimsy. In a garden house called the Tivoli, there is a picture window with a gold frame around it, and a label below: "'Ever-Changing Landscape' by Harvey Ladew." This passage, though, comes late in the poem, following a leisurely description of the place as the speaker wanders through it, late in the season, the clipping suspended for the winter. The speaker uses the first-person plural most of the time, but uses the singular once when stating an opinion. The impression that "we" are two people is reinforced by a profile of Spires in *Ploughshares* (Winter 1999–2000), where it is stated that in 1985 Spires married the novelist Madison Smartt Bell at Ladew Topiary Gardens. Back in the poem, in the Tivoli,

> Already it's late afternoon,
> the view from the window
> darkening like an old oil painting,
> hills flattening to shadow,
> rain taking the edge off
> everything. Time *is* fleeting,
> a platitude I think Ladew
> would agree with. In a minute,
> regretfully, we'll leave the Tivoli,
> the empty-headed jardiniere,
> and the view, all intersecting.
> Nature will have its way.
> The topiary, left unclipped
> all winter, growing into
> what it wants to be.

It is not actually necessary to bring in biographical notes from elsewhere to see this poem as, at least in part, a love poem. The two poems immediately preceding it are more traditional love poems, and the first of them, "Two Shadows," is "For Madison." It is quiet, unassuming, and fully and wonderfully achieved. It looks back as well as forward, taking account of inevitable change, and centering on a single recollection; it is short enough, and splendid enough, to quote in its entirety:

> When we are shadows watching over shadows,
> when years have passed, enough to live
> two lives, when we have passed
> through love and come out speechless
> on the other side, I will remember
> how we spent a night, walking the streets
> > in August, side by side,
> following two shadows dressed in long gray coats,
> unseasonable clothes they didn't seem to mind,
> walking so easily, with easy stride,
> merging for a moment, then isolate,
> as they led us to your street, your door,
> and up the steps until, inside,
> love became articulate: eye, lip, and brow.
> When we are shadows watching over shadows,
> we will not speak of it but *know*, and turn
> again toward each other tenderly,
> > shadow to shadow.

John Donne, in "Air and Angels," treats his familiar theme of the necessity to embody the spirit; this is the second half of the first stanza:

> But since my soul, whose child love is,
> Takes limbs of flesh, and else could nothing do,
> More subtle than the parent is
> Love must not be, but take a body too;
> And therefore what thou wert, and who,
> I bid Love ask, and now
> That it assume thy body, I allow,
> And fix itself in thy lip, eye, and brow.

Spires has already begun her conversation with Donne earlier in this collection, in a stark and dreamlike poem called "Bread and Water," about a period of separation between the speaker and an addressed "you." "The long year after you left," it begins, and characterizes the ensuing loneliness. Attempting a geographical cure, the speaker took a trip south one winter:

> Walking the beach in January, I came upon
> a mermaid, ribs hollowed out, one sandy arm
> thrown over her face, who lay on a strip
> of no-man's-land, tail curved in an ache
> toward the water. The next day she was gone,
> erased by the tide.

The directness of the statement here invites a literal reading, but soon enough it is clear that this apparition is a sand sculpture—another fine convergence of artifice and natural forces. At this point the speaker recalls Donne's "The Ecstasy":

"A great prince in prison lies,"
wrote Donne. I understood but would admit
to no one. Although I ate, I starved,
denied. My room: my cell.
My ration: bread & water.

Spires' book, *Annonciade* (1989) continues the great conversation with predecessors, and deepens and extends her range. The opening poem, "The Beds," is a sumptuous daydream based on the changing bed display in a store window in London, and reminds us that the images of bed, sheet, and pillow, as well as brief mentions of sleep and waking, are abundant in Spires's work, often with the effect of suggesting that the traditional binary distinctions are less than the whole truth. The beds in the shop window are never slept in, but often changed, and attended by tired clerks. At the end of the poem, as the day's shoppers head home, the moonlight offers an opportunity for an extended simile that almost makes us forget the moonlight it describes:

It drapes itself casually across the beds,
like the misplaced towel or bathrobe
of a woman who has just stepped out for the evening,
wearing new evening clothes, made up so carefully
she can't be recognized, who secretly knows
she will not be coming back until morning
to sleep, if she sleeps then,
in the perfect bed of her own making.

At the far end of the book, "The Woman on the Dump" takes as its epigraph the last line of Wallace Stevens' "The Man on the Dump," and works, as the older poem does, the metaphor of detritus as the world, but it is very much its own poem for all that. At the heart of the divergence between them, perhaps, is that the Stevens poem contains the sentence "One rejects / The trash," and Spires includes in her account of the woman's care for the objects in the dump the phrase "rejecting / nothing."

There are several poems in *Annonciade* with more grace and largeness than Spires had exhibited in her first two books, but the title poem, and a prose narrative immediately following it, are in a class by themselves, a pair of superb achievements. To do them anything near justice will necessitate slighting others, but they require attention. "Annonciade" is in about 160 lines of pentameter-based free verse. As it opens the speaker is waking, the morning sounds detailed, the setting gradually revealed, first as La Maison de Repos, then the Midi, "Mountains and blue air and the sea," "the azure coast." The bed image, so steadily recurrent in Spires's work, appears in the first twenty lines. The "brilliant / light of the Midi," the speaker says,

changes white
shadowed sheets on the crumpled bed
into a still life of desire and absence.

At first, the speaker is plural, but at the end of the first verse paragraph becomes individual:

these things I see as I steady myself
at the window, still wanting to be alive.

It becomes clear in the next paragraph that the speaker is a patient at a sanatorium, one of the luckier ones, not yet in a wheelchair or in need of constant help. The description of the patients' sense of themselves and their place is quietly harrowing:

It is at breakfast that the curtained ambulance
sometimes slips away, delivering one

from our midst to health or oblivion.
A place at the table is empty, a face
gone forever, but nothing is said
to note the absence of the missing one.
Our silent circle contracts, or grows
larger to accommodate a new arrival
who pauses, uncertain, in the door,
unsure of what will happen next, waiting
to be politely questioned or ignored.

On a hill above the sanatorium looms the Annonciade, a former monastery that has become a museum, though the faithful still come to climb,

in ones and twos, the 500 worn stone steps
of the Chemin de Rosaire, one old soul
all in black holding her rosary
as she climbs, counting the beads and steps
that take her, one by one, to heaven.

The long verse paragraph that includes this passage makes clear distinctions between such believers as the old woman described above, and "the fallen-away / and sightseers" who cross themselves or genuflect "out of almost-forgotten habit." This phrase is wonderfully open to quite opposite meanings: habit nearly abandoned, or habit ingrained beyond consciousness. Meanwhile it also evokes a nun's attire. Spires is keenly alert to such opportunities; near the end of the paragraph, after describing pilgrims who used to come when the monastery was active, it is announced that "the old order's gone."

The poem continues with a meditation on the state of the patients, reduced to mere symptoms or afflicted body parts, awaiting prognoses. It ends with an old but still scary thought:

How can such suffering be chance?
Surely the spirit chooses its affliction
and makes it manifest, watching itself
fall and retreat from the world to atone,
as holy hermits did, for some secret
failing only its own heart knows.

The final verse paragraph begins in the afternoon, when fatigue and fever tend to be at their worst, and daydreams most extravagantly discouraging. Spires inserts a line of extreme light-verse technique - two identically-metered and rhymed half-lines—in the midst of the speaker's fantasy of recovery and departure:

        I will rise
from this pallet of rest and recrimination
and step nakedly back into the world,
pulled down the mountain's winding road
to the lit auberge where the concierge
will calmly greet me, asking no questions,
knowing my journey was difficult.

Soon the speaker adopts a rhetorical stance, beginning two sentences with a syntactical turn that contains both unusual certitude and the interrogative: "Then will I take my place," "Quietly will I sit there." The cock that crowed in the poem's third line comes back to "[betray] its desire for dawn," and for a moment the speaker will "briefly belong / to the world." The poem ends with a brief vision of unity,

> as if Earth
> and Heaven had joined in a solitary moment
> of love, the deceived and deceiving
> eye, as it falls to sleep, feeling
> strange intimations of happiness.

The boundary between illness and health is wide and vaguely demarcated; these states are perhaps unusually appropriate for an attempt to detect the unity behind, above, or below the dualities by means of which we often perceive what happens and what is.

The speaker of "Annonciade" is more clearly fictional, distinguished from the poet, than that of "Falling Away," the three-and-a-half-page prose piece that immediately follows the poem. One thinks briefly of the much longer "91 Revere Street," the apparent memoir that takes up a section of Lowell's *Life Studies*. "Falling Away" begins, "Memory: I am sitting at my desk in sixth grade at St. Joseph's Elementary in Circleville, Ohio." Subsequent details of age and preoccupation with poetry seem to put this piece in the category of memoir, but that it is in a book of poems suggests that this is perhaps not the first place in which to seek facts about Spires' life.

What does happen in the piece is partly a function of its placement; we have just seen the "fallen-away" grouped with the "sightseers," and this account of a time at a Catholic school, where hell and eternity fail to submit to their impossible analyses, ends with a dream in which the narrator is back in the classroom, but as a teacher, in an empty classroom, where the dualities still seem to hold:

Standing in the dark hallway, I'm thinking how I'll finally see through the keyhole into that polarized world of good and evil, guilt and absolution, that even a fallen-away Catholic can't escape. After all, I have all time. Have all eternity.

How and where one has "all eternity" is a matter of faith, but Spires's fourth book, *Worldling* (1995), finds ways of rejoicing in the knowledge that in this world, life comes to an end. The situation at the heart of the collection is the birth of the poet's daughter, Celia. The book is divided into two sections, the first of which takes its epigraph from Hannah Arendt, who in *The Human Condition* says that what makes humans mortal is their ability to see an individual life as a straight line with a beginning and an end, cutting across the arcs of natural life's cycles. "The First Day," about the morning following the child's birth, ends with the speaker making a note to herself:

I picked up the pen, the paper, and wrote:
I have had a child. Now I must live with death.

Two poems at the end of the section place the speaker and her family at the beach. "Fisher Beach" recounts an afternoon of expected beach activity, including the husband/father's brief swim out far enough to make the speaker hold her breath without realizing it, and watching three children write their claim to presence in the sand in letters almost too big to see, and stick figures representing each of the three of them. Their caption is "TRURO AUGUST 1 WE WERE HERE!" immediately following the speaker's observation that these words and date "defy, or underscore, the transience of our stay."

"On the Island" is set at a place like Martha's Vineyard or Nantucket, accessible by ferry for stays whose length tends to divide people into day-trippers, seasonal regulars, and year-rounders. From the outset, partly set up by the preceding poem, it delicately invites an allegorical reading:

One ferry arrives as one is pulling out.
July was a high point, hot, bright and buttery.
August is huge and blue, a glittering gemstone
curving dangerously at either end into what precedes
and follows it. The ferry begins as a small white point
on the horizon and gradually enlarges into an event
we don't know whether to dread or impatiently wait for.

The poem's central event is a grandmother's happily determined swim with a couple of granddaughters whom she challenges to keep up with her. While she is still out in the waves, the inbound ferry sounds its horn, and the speaker ponders briefly the possible fates of those who must ride it in order to leave. Some of them will never return, and some will do so throughout their lives. Meanwhile,

The ever-widening wake of the inbound ferry
cannot shake the resolve of the woman in the waves.
She follows it out, waving her arms wildly
as she goes, not in distress, oh no,
but simply to give the ones going away a good goodbye. . . .
. . . and they, not yet caught up in the life ahead of them,
wave back at her. They wave back.

The remarkable thing about this poem is not merely that it succeeds as a kind of allegory, but that it does so without insistence, with great subtlety and delicacy, even though it uses such heavy equipment as the ferry. Spires' gift of observation is that she can look closely and deeply at the same time.

The second section of *Worldling* has a wider range of departure points—women in a sauna, waking from a nap, three poems about other poetic voices—but the strength of the underlying theme of mortality is not muted, even in such a poem as "'Something Happens,'" a tribute to William Meredith and the gallantry with which he has met the effects of the stroke that took most of his ability to speak and write:

I am getting better.
Something happens.

Poetry provides no rescue.
Yet I'll say these words while I can.
Something is happening to us all.

This is immediately followed, almost as if to clarify, by an imagined letter from Samuel Johnson to his deceased wife; he expresses his gratitude that he will soon join her.

The book closes with "Life Everlasting," another poem of more than usual length—just over 140 lines—and of truly rare economy, given what it manages to do. It is at once an account of reading a book to a child, a discussion of the book, and a meditation on the great subject the book essays. The book is Natalie Babbitt's *Tuck Everlasting* (1977), a widely praised novel for younger readers in which the protagonist confronts the question whether ageless eternal life would be a gift or a curse. The reading prompts the listening child to say, "Mother, promise never to die!" The speaker recalls being young enough to have chosen to drink the waters of immortality, and then considers the dawning of her conviction that mortality is preferable. As the speaker finishes the book, the child falls asleep, so there is unresolved doubt about how much of the ending the child has heard:

■ BOOKS BY ELIZABETH SPIRES

poetry

Boardwalk. Cleveland, Ohio: Bits Press, 1980.

Globe. Hanover, N.H.: University Press of New England, 1981.

Swan's Island. New York: Henry Holt, 1985.

Annonciade. New York: Viking, 1989.

Worlding. New York: Norton, 1995.

Now the Green Blade Rises. New York: Norton, 2002.

for children

The Falling Star. Columbus, Ohio: C. E. Merrill, 1981.

Count with Me. Columbus, Ohio: C. E. Merrill, 1981.

The Wheels Go Round. Columbus, Ohio: C. E. Merrill, 1981.

With One White Wing. New York: Simon & Schuster, 1995.

Riddle Road: Puzzles in Poems and Pictures. New York: Simon & Schuster, 1999.

The Mouse of Amherst. New York: Farrar, Straus, 1999.

I Am Arachne. New York: Farrar, Straus, 2001.

The Big Meow. Cambridge, Mass.: Candlewick Press, 2002.

> But sleep now.
> And I'll sleep too, to wake with you,
> wake to the everlasting present of our life.

Maturity of vision, technical skill, and pure nerve have very rarely combined with such success. "Life Everlasting" is a consoling splendor that stands firmly on its own as an actual masterpiece; it also gathers great power from the poems that lead up to it.

As noted at the beginning of this essay, Spires' fifth collection, in preparation under the title *Now the Green Blade Rises*, moves out from the death of the poet's mother as the major landmark on the path these poems have made. Not surprisingly, then, the mother's presence, as in "My Mother's Doll," is stronger here than in the earlier four volumes. The child and the husband/father also appear, of course. There is an intensification of awareness that time is fleeting, as if in later middle age the speed of a lifetime's passage is more noticeable. The poem called "1999," for example, moves rapidly between two views of a hundred years: it is a short time, and, because we won't see the end of it, an incalculably long time.

This sense of rapid passage is balanced, however, by a couple of poems concerned with an older friend, who is revealed in notes to be the poet Josephine Jacobsen. The more ambitious of these is "Two Chairs on a Hillside," a dialogue in which the first speaker has most of the seventy lines, the second offering brief prompts and responses amounting to a total of maybe fifty words. It is not clear for most of the poem who the second speaker might be; the first speaker describes, in fabulistic terms, a relationship between two people, gradually revealed to be women, one older than the other, the speaker the younger. They are described as having spent whole seasons in two chairs on a hillside, wintering through until spring thawed their garments, experiencing and sharing loss such as widowhood, that alters everything.

At last the second speaker asks a question indicating that the speakers are a couple; the first speaker characterizes them as on the way to a state the pair of women glimpsed:

> "Each night I stand here looking up. The chairs are proof
> of what I've told you. Can you see them up there?
> Two empty chairs no element can change, as fixed
> in their relation as any starry constellation—"
>   "As we are?"
> "No, as we will be someday. We aren't complete
> in what we are yet. We're in the middle of a story

we'll tell twice over, each in our own slant way.
We've written half the pages, but half remain.
To be done, if at all, out of love—"
                              "How do you know all this?
                              Who told you?"
"I was one of the two."

The faintly stilted language, and the departures from realistic narrative, are reminiscent of the longer dialogue poems of Robert Frost, such as "West-Running Brook." The verse form, and then the diction, and, in the case of Spires' poem, certain narrative details, lift the poem out of the realm of the notational, and stand it where it is free to prophesy. That Spires is able to do this convincingly sets her well apart from her contemporaries. Some of her work is as good as we have had in the past fifty years.

Henry Taylor
April, 2002

The Waiting Dark: Talking to Mark Strand

■ **I**

It is dark and I walk in
It is darker and I walk in

In mid-career, a year or so before the publication of his *Selected Poems* (1980), Mark Strand began publishing humorous stories in the *New Yorker*. They acted as a relief perhaps from the sameness of dark tone that stamped his poems—although his poems were often marked by wit, a certain dry humor that may be a distinctive feature of his voice, and that laces the dream-like, haunting, impressionistic nostalgia that characterizes a great many of his poems. For example, the poem I like best, "Keeping Things Whole," handles serious paradox with a playful tone—although when I remarked how funny it is, Strand demurred:

> — It's a paradox. I wouldn't put that in the class of humor. It's a paradoxical situation: wherever I am, I am what is missing. I mean, in effect it simply says, I suppose, in the end, that the world can get along very well without me, and in fact that my being there is…an interruption. The presence of consciousness is altering, disturbing, isolating…

> — But then the wonderful throw-away humor of "We all have reasons for moving. / I move to keep things whole."…

> — It's rather jaunty, you're right.

With that concession, the conversation moved on to the stories, but I wish I had pressed the question of the poem a moment longer. The seriousness of the subject was not in doubt, but it may be that the handling appears more complex—more humorous—to me than it does to its author. A similar subject, a paradox of negative definition—absence is presence—is handled with more solemnity, and less charm, in "The Guardian":

The sun setting. The lawns on fire.
The lost day, the lost light.
Why do I love what fades?

You who left, who were leaving,
what dark rooms do you inhabit?
Guardian of my death,

preserve my absence. I am alive.

It seems to me that "Keeping Things Whole" is a far better poem precisely because of its humor, the complexity of its tone.

Mark Strand

Mark Strand was born in Summerside, Prince Edward Island, Canada, on April 11, 1934. He received his formal education in America, with a B.A. (1957) from Antioch College, a B.F.A. from Yale University (1959), and his M.A. from the University of Iowa (1962). His extensive teaching career has taken him to the University of Iowa, Mount Holyoke College, Columbia University, the University of Washington, Yale University, the University of Virginia, California State University, Fresno, the University of California, Irvine, Brooklyn College Princeton University, Brandeis University, and Johns Hopkins University. Strand has also spent time outside the United States as a Fulbright fellow at the University of Florence (1960–61) and as a Fulbright lecturer at the University of Brazil, Rio de Janeiro (1965–66).

His writings have won wide acclaim. He has received an Ingram Merrill Foundation fellowship, a Rockfeller Award, and a Guggenheim fellowship, an award from the National Institute of Arts and Letters, and a fellowship from the Academy of American Poets. In addition to his many previous honors, more recently he has won grants from the National Endowment for the Arts, a MacArthur Foundation fellowship, the Bobbitt National Prize for Poetry, an

appointment as U.S. Poet Laureate by the Library of Congress, the Bollingen Prize for Poetry from Yale University Library, and both the Pulitzer Prize and *Boston Book Review* Bingham Poetry Prize for *Blizzard of One: Poems.* ■

In a field
I am the absence
of field.
This is
always the case.
Wherever I am
I am what is missing.

When I walk
I part the air
and always
the air moves in
to fill the spaces
where my body's been.

We all have reasons
for moving.
I move
to keep things whole.

Earlier, in a letter, I had asked him about the inspiration for the poem. He replied: "'Keeping Things Whole' came out of nowhere. I was playing cards with Don Justice and the idea came to me. I told him to wait a second while I went out to the kitchen, and I jotted the poem down. It came out whole. I never changed a word. The game we were playing was cribbage. It was about 11 at night." Poetry's play and the play of the poets are nicely attuned in this anecdote. I might cite it as evidence of a serio-comic mixture of tone at the root of the poem. But in any case, the very division of our responses to the poem may illustrate the difficulty of a critical description of Strand's style.

Thinking of the fiction as a clue, a new approach, I asked him about the stories, but first, since the stories entail a more complex texture of writing, and in view of the fact that Strand comes to poetry from painting (he was a student of Joseph Albers at Yale), I asked whether the spare style of the poetry derives in any way from minimalism in art.

— No, he replied, it derives from insecurity to write more complicated sentences. I mean I think I began with such uncertainty as a writer that I clung to the simplest formulations, verbal formulations, that I could, in order to stay out of trouble. And it took years and years for me to gain confidence enough to write in a more compli-cated fashion. These stories would've been unthinkable years ago—though my turn of mind hasn't changed or altered so much. It wasn't suddenly that I discovered a funny-bone in my body and began writing this sort of fiction. I could never string together enough sentences that I was sure of before...

— To handle Nabokovian humor.

— Yeah. Even now I leaf through Nabokov to find sentences I like, to write versions of them—you know, when I'm stuck, and want a shot in the arm....

The story "True Loves," for example (*The New Yorker*, December 31, 1979), is reminiscent of *Lolita* in tone and erotic subject, though the humor is broader, closer to slapstick, and the texture of the writing less dense. In the developing picture of his work the stories are comic relief—relief from solemnity, from the lyric oddness that is the defining characteristic, perhaps, of Strand's individual poetic style—relief from the severely minimal diction, the disarming tone but high compression, the startling speed of the typical Mark Strand poem. Consider "The Marriage," for example:

The wind comes from opposite poles,
traveling slowly.

She turns in the deep air.
He walks in the clouds.

She readies herself,
shakes out her hair,

makes up her eyes,
smiles.

---

* Linda Gregerson, in *Parnassus*, {Fall/Winter 1981}, has written the best account of the development of Strand's style through *Selected Poems*. My concern here is less with chronological development than with the essential voice that permeates all of Strand's work. I take his work, including the fiction, to be all of a piece.

The sun warms her teeth,
the tip of her tongue moistens them.

He brushes the dust from his suit
and straightens his tie.

He smokes.
Soon they will meet.

The wind carries them closer.
They wave.

Closer, closer.
They embrace.

She is making a bed.
He is pulling off his pants.

They marry
and have a child.

The wind carries them off
in different directions.

The wind is strong, he thinks
as he straightens his tie.

I like this wind, she says
as she puts on her dress.

The wind unfolds.
The wind is everything to them.

The combination of simple diction, surreal time and journalistic concreteness of detail makes this a good example of what Strand has called (in an interview with Wayne Dodd and Stanley Plumly) a "new international style." "I feel very much a part of a new international style that has a lot to do with plainness of diction, a certain reliance on surrealist techniques, a certain reliance on journalistic techniques, a strong narrative element, etc.… "

In contrast to the speed and compression of "The Marriage," the story "True Loves" is absurdly expansive, romping through a succession of marriages and infatuations, marriages *as* infatuations, all over the globe: Machu Picchu, the New York subway, Hollywood, Australia, Nova Scotia, Belgrade, Venice, Rome. Strand, the quintessential New Yorker, is nothing if not cosmopolitan, a citizen of the globe, debonair, Nabokovian, smart. But also wandering, lonely, lost. Lost, melancholy in many of the poems; jovial, recreational in all of the fiction. I asked him if he had been to any of the exotic places in "True Loves." "Oh, I've been to all of them," he said. "I did it as a kind of travel guide. I did it as a kind of joke."

Currently at the University of Utah, where besides creative writing he teaches European as well as American literature, Mark Strand has taught at a number of universities across the United States and has spent Fulbright years at the University of Florence and at the University of Brazil. He has published a number of translations from Spanish and Portuguese, most recently a series of poems from the Portuguese of Carlos Drummond de Andrade. He was born in Summerside, Prince Edward Island, Nova Scotia, but he is an American, and he studied at Antioch, Yale, and the University of Iowa. He lived for a number of years in New York City, particularly in the art world. In our conversation he remarked: "When I'm West I feel very…Eastern most of the time. When I'm East, it's clear that I've been living in the West for a few years, and I don't really know what's going on." It is a genuine restlessness, a penchant for wandering, that blossoms in "True Loves."

The phase of the fiction may signal a change in the center of gravity of his work. There was, to be sure, always a narrative impulse, but it was curtailed, parabolic, or sometimes a touch too portentous, as in "The Untelling":

> I felt myself descend into the future.
> I saw beyond the lawn, beyond the lake,
> beyond the waiting dark, the end of summer,
> the end of autumn, the icy air, the silence,
> and then, again, the windowpane.

There was, just as surely, a considerable lightness and humor among the poems, for all their predominant dark. In "Courtship," for example:

> There is a girl you like so you tell her
> your penis is big, but that you cannot get yourself
> to use it. Its demands are ridiculous, you say,
> even self-defeating, but to be honored somehow,
> briefly, inconspicuously in the dark.
>
> When she closes her eyes in horror,
> you take it all back. You tell her you're almost
> a girl yourself and can understand why she is shocked.
> When she is about to walk away, you tell her
> you have no penis, that you don't
>
> know what got into you. You get on your knees.
> She suddenly bends down to kiss your shoulder and you know
> you're on the right track. You tell her you want
> to bear children and that is why you seem confused.…

Conversely, among the stories, "The Tiny Baby," for all its comic beginning, ends in an enigma as heavy and dark as many of the poems. The story of the tiny baby, hardly a story at all but a hyperbolic image, a caricature perhaps of something like the "viable fetus" in recent abortion controversy, plays with the sentimentalities of the fatuous mother ("she kept the baby in her purse so she wouldn't lose it") until suddenly the tiny baby has become the smallish woman who is "watching the street for a sight of her favorite hairdo," and who is left, in the end, with the darkly ambiguous thought that "Death will not have me."

Even "Mr. and Mrs. Baby," though in keeping with the title it is a light spoof throughout, has, as good humor must, a serious core. Strand commented on the characters:

> — I just thought of them as Americans, a people who have never grown up. I mean
> we are a young country, we behave like youngsters.… we are, well, consumers in
> the way teenagers are consumers. We are lost.

Lostness, emptiness, uncertainty: the central theme of Strand's work is elusive.… or is elusiveness itself. Elusiveness as a motif may be the link that unites the two sides, the light and the dark. Among the poems it is present in "Darker," "The Untelling," "My Mother on an Evening in Late Summer," and "Where Are the Waters of Childhood?"—examples of the graver mood—as well as in the comic "Eating Poetry," "Marriage," and "Courtship," for example. The surreal humor of "The Tiny Baby"—"She told the sitter, 'The baby's in the living room, but it's real small. It you don't see it, don't worry'"—may be a way of moving beyond ordinary discourse, a way of creating, like "the feel of not to feel," the feel of unknowing, of the elusiveness of meaning, of the uncertainty of human *being* itself.

We discussed surrealism as an influence. I remarked that his work is characteristically gentle, whereas I thought of surrealism as something frenetic. Strand replied:

> — Well, it's supposed to be shocking. It has this destructive element. Surrealism is a way of overthrowing the tyranny of the previous order. I never felt the need to overthrow anything.

Thinking of Kafka and his father I asked about a story in which the father, a failed writer, dies and returns transmogrified into a fly, and then a horse, and finally a beautiful woman:

> — The father in that story, "More Life," is not real?

> — No. He's a composite figure. He has elements of my father, but then there are elements of me and elements of other people. A lot of it is just made up. A situation that's rather bizarre, far-fetched, but one that has a certain psychological truth. It's one of the justifications, I suppose, for surrealism that no matter how far-fetched the externals are, there is an element of reliable.... well, there is evidence of the truth that is hard to perceive and deliver in a less shocking and curious manner.

> — Your writing is never bitter. It's gentle incongruity....

> — Well that's good.... I'm not bitter. I'm not angry. You know, it probably is a terrific shortcoming, but I feel rather lucky as a writer. I mean, I have no complaint. I have complaints about society, but society on the other hand is treating me rather well.... I'm very often unhappy but my unhappiness does not constitute complaint. It has to do with being human. Being human isn't being happy all the time; being human is not just knowing that someday you're going to die; it has a lot to do with monitoring yourself. It has a lot to do with self-consciousness. And I think being one's own best witness is not often a case for joy.

As he said in connection with "Keeping Things Whole," "the presence of consciousness is altering, disturbing, isolating.... " But when we are alone, truly alone, like Meursault at the end of *The Stranger*, the freedom to celebrate being in the world may rise like a tide of light, an illumination both secular and numinous, a dawning:

> I have carried it with me each day: that morning I took
> my uncle's boat from the brown water cove
> and headed for Mosher Island.
> Small waves splashed against the hull
> and the hollow creak of oarlock and oar
> rose into the woods of black pine crusted with lichen.
> I moved like a dark star, drifting over the drowned
> other half of the world until, by a distant prompting,
> I looked over the gunwale and saw beneath the surface
> a luminous room, a light-filled grave, saw for the first time
> the one clear place given to us when we are alone.
> (**"A Morning"**)

The luminous room, the light-filled grave, is the void, is the waiting dark made clear and inviting, once and for all.

If the romantic affirmation of "A Morning" seems too easy, seems even with its understatement to claim too much, consider another late poem, "For Jessica, My Daughter." Here the central question is posed with disarming, translucent directness.

> Jessica, it is so much easier
> to think of our lives,
> as we move under the brief luster of leaves,
> loving what we have,
> than to think of how it is
> such small beings as we
> travel in the dark
> with no visible way
> or end in sight.

He recalls ecstatic or mystical moments

> when the body's bones became light
> and the wound of the skull
> opened to receive the cold rays of the cosmos,
> and were, for an instant,
> themselves cosmos…

But now he discards in candor the overblown vision and offers, instead, merely the poem, "a sheet of paper," against the dark:

> But tonight
> it is different.
> Afraid of the dark
> in which we drift or vanish altogether,
> I imagine a light
> that would not let us stray too far apart,
> a secret moon or mirror,
> a sheet of paper,
> something you could carry
> in the dark
> when I am away.

Never was the virtue, the artifice of artlessness more skillfully directed, more touchingly employed. The archaic simplicity of the theme and the plainness of the diction join in perfect song. It is as moving as it is unpretentious. It is a measure of the temper of our time.

Philip Cooper
October, 1984

UPDATE

Mark Strand has since published many more books, including *The Continuous Life* (1990), *Reasons for Moving, Darker, and the Sargentville Notebook* (1992), *Dark Harbor: A Poem* (1993), *Blizzard of One: Poems* (1998), *Chicken, Shadow, Moon, and More* (2000), *The Weather of Words: Poetic Invention* (2000) and *The Story of Our Lives; with, The Monument and The Late Hour: Poems* (2002). He also has edited and translated several volumes, has written for children, and has published numerous works of fiction and non-fiction.

One of the leading contemporary poets in America, Mark Strand is known for his "precise language, surreal imagery, and the recurring theme of absence and negation," according to *Contempo-*

■ BOOKS BY MARK STRAND

Sleeping with One Eye Open. Iowa: Stone Wall Press, 1964.

Reasons for Moving. New York: Atheneum, 1968.

New Poetry of Mexico, editor and translator with Octavio Paz. New York: Dutton, 1970.

Darker: Poems. New York: Atheneum, 1970.

The Contemporary American Poets: American Poetry Since 1940, editor. New York: New American Library, 1969. New York: New American Library, 1971.

Eighteen Poems from the Quechua, translator. Cambridge, Mass: Halty Ferguson, 1971.

The Story of Our Lives. New York: Atheneum, 1973.

The Sergeantville Notebook. Rhode Island: Burning Deck, 1973.

The Owl's Insomnia: Selected Poems of Rafael Alberti, editor and translator. New York: Atheneum, 1973.

Elegy for My Father. Iowa: Windhover Press, 1973.

Texas, by Jorge Luis Borges, translator. Austin: University of Texas Humanities Research Center, 1975.

Souvenir of the Ancient World: Selected Poems of Carlos Drummond de Andrade, editor and translator. New York: Antaeus, 1976.

Another Republic: Seventeen European and South American Writers, editor. New York: Ecco Press, 1976. New York: Ecco Press, 1977.

The Monument. New York: Ecco Press, 1978, New York: Ecco Press, 1979.

The Late Hour. New York: Atheneum, 1978.

Selected Poems. New York: Atheneum, 1980.

Planet of Lost Things. New York: Crown, 1982.

Mr. And Mrs. Baby and Other Stories. New York: Knopf, 1985.

The Continuous Life. New York: Random House, 1990.

Reasons for Moving, Darker, and the Sargentville Notebook. New York: Knopf, 1992.

Dark Harbor: A Poem. New York: Knopf, 1993.

Blizzard of One: Poems. New York: Random House, 1998.

The Weather of Words: Poetic Invention. New York: Knopf, 2000.

Chicken, Shadow, Moon, and More. Chappaqua, N.Y.: Turtle Point Press, 2000.

The Story of Our Lives; with, The Monument and The Late Hour: Poems. New York: Knopf, 2002.

rary Authors. In his career of more than 30 years, the former Poet Laureate has won the respect of critics and the devotion of many readers—something that he has said still surprises him.

A *World Literature Today* review of his Pulitzer Prize-winning *Blizzard of One* called him "one of the most successful of living poets," and noted that "he has been associated with a kind of surrealism that is typical of Latin American writers such as Octavio Paz, who often got their surrealism earlier in Paris."

In *Chicken, Shadow, Moon, and More*, according to *Booklist*, Strand "writes with deceptively offhanded elegance and wit that belie deep and haunting emotions and an acute attunement to the beauty and inexplicableness of life." His poems in this collection are "lean yet lyrical," the review stated, "and always the language is exact, musical, and transcendent." *Library Journal*, however, took exception: "[T]he lines Strand comes up with are mostly cliched . . ., cute . . ., or simplistic . . ., although every so often there is a good surrealist image of the sort we are used to finding in Strand's poetry."

Publishers Weekly called Strand's most recent collection of essays, *The Weather of Words: Poetic Invention*, a "charming miscellany." *The Antioch Review* called it "marvelously eclectic": "Savvy and elegant as a poet, Strand is even more readable discussing poetry. . . . Strand doesn't pretend to offer answers; he simply discusses." In his introduction to *The Best American Poetry 1991*, he notes, "It may be that something beyond 'meaning' is being communicated . . . not knowledge but rather some occasion for belief, some reason for assent, some avowal of being." One of the finest lines in the book describes how the last lines of poems "release us back into our world with the momentary illusion that no harm has been done."

Hollis Summers, A Poet in Passage

"Already I am beginning to feel stupid and lonely because your answers are so covered and well-dressed. Is it necessary to wear a hat and gloves with you? Well, Is it????" So ends a letter by Anne Sexton to Hollis Summers in 1960, which in many ways points up a dilemma poetry faces in our day. In the body of the letter, Sexton bewails Summers' lack of response to her baring of "soul" and his refusal to come from behind his "gentle mask."

The dilemma suggested by Sexton's comments is the dichotomy between the "let it all hang out" school of modern romanticism and the "well-dressed" or what I would like to call the neo-baroque tradition we have seen since the first decade or two of our century. The term baroque comes from the Portuguese *barroco*, which names an irregular pearl. The musicians, artists, and poets from the late sixteenth through part of the eighteenth century grew out of the classicism of the Renaissance, which became the restraining "pearl," while the emotions erupted into the spontaneity of a lovely and strange gem. In much of our finest poetry we see a restraint and implosion; on the other hand, to extend the metaphor, much of our poetry just kicks out the grain of sand, leaving nothing for the mollusk genius.

While for the poets of the seventeenth century the restraining influence was the classicism of the preceding age, at least part of the neo-baroque tendency in our age is gentleness, suggested by the phenomenon that much of our finest poetry comes from the gentlemanly tradition of the southern part of our country—one thinks of John Crowe Ransom, Allen Tate, and Robert Penn Warren, among many others. The restraint of the code, like classicism, produced a well-ordered, albeit powerful, poetry that still influences, despite developments from every direction in the stream of our poetic literature.

Hollis Summers is a Kentuckian, gentle (and his gentility is no mask), baroque, and powerful, and the irritants that produce his poetry are given to us as celebrations. (It is interesting to note that he chose seventeenth-century poetry as his area of concentration while working on a creative writing Ph.D at Iowa State.) A parallel in Summers' work might also be made to what critic Wesley Trimpi calls Ben Jonson's "plain style." This style, Trimpi says, is "unspecialized," a "styleless style, whose models are the familiar letter and the urbane conversation, [which] is by definition incapable of prediction." Trimpi says that Jonson was concerned that style should "subserve a subject matter of sufficient importance with clarity and distinction." It is a style that "claims the experience as the writer's own but which, at the same time, recognizes that it is relatable to the experiences of others and that the relationship might be valuable."

Much of this applies to Summers, save that he cannot be said to have a "styleless style," since his style often does, indeed, call attention to itself, particularly with regard to tone. In this he is not unlike Jonson's contemporary Robert Herrick, who, in addition to learning and adapting what he learned from Spenser, Donne, and Jonson, was always very careful to make sure

Hollis Summers Born in

1916 in Eminence, Kentucky, Hollis Summers was
educated at Georgetown College, Middlebury College,
and the State University of Iowa, where he received
his Ph.D. He taught in several universities, but mainly
at Ohio University. Among his honors were College of
Arts and Sciences Distinguished Professor of the Year,
1958–59, and the *Saturday Review* poetry award for
1957. He was a Danforth lecturer (1963–64) and a
Fulbright lecturer (1978) and participated in various
writers' conferences, such as those at Breadloaf, Antioch, and Morehead. Georgetown College awarded
him a D.Litt. (1965) and he received a National
Foundation of Arts grant in 1975. He won the Nancy
Dasher Award for best creative work by an Ohio
professor in 1986 and garnered the 1987 Helen
Krout Most Outstanding Ohio Poet Award, presented by the Ohioana Library. Summers also received a
grant from the Fund for Advancement of Education,
a *Saturday Review* poetry award, and a grant from

the National Foundation of Arts, and he was named
Distinguished Professor at Ohio University. He died
in 1987. ■

his readers were aware of the tonal quality of his verse. There is yet another quality that Summers shares with Herrick. Elsewhere I suggest of the seventeenth-century poet what might well
be said of Hollis Summers:

> What separates Herrick from his predecessors (the Elizabethans, Metaphysicals,
> and neo-classicists) is his tone and his concept of the poet, a concept not articulat-
> ed until Wordsworth. Herrick saw the poet as a man who is set apart from the rest
> of men because he is more highly endowed with what is present in other men;
> because of this, the personality of the poet becomes an extremely important ele-
> ment of the poetry.... He is a man "speaking to men" of his delights, discontents,
> and beliefs, informed by what he was…[a man whose] sensibilities were the same
> as those of other men, with the requisite extra "enthusiasm," "tenderness," and
> "greater knowledge of human nature." The poetry, then, places self above the idea,
> or even the poem, on the basis of what might be called an epiphany of the poet.

The modernists were Summers' predecessors, and, unlike many of his contemporaries, he
has not rejected them, any more than Herrick did his. Rather he is a part of the tradition T. S.
Eliot speaks of. Herrick developed for our literature the concept of the poet's personal
epiphany, which began a line that runs through Wordsworth, Whitman, and e. e. cummings,
among others. While there is wide diversity among these poets and each of necessity possesses
an individuating tone and style, the essential parallel among them is the self-epiphany tradition, of which Summers is a striking example in our own time.

In his second book, *Seven Occasions*, Summers articulates his approach to poetry and demonstrates his concern for order, an order which, like the *barroco*, is the basis for wide-ranging human celebration. Divided into seven sections of seven poems each, the book tends to suggest many of the possibilities of the mystical number: seven is symbolic of perfect order; completeness; the union of three and four; the reconciliation of the square with the triangle; the basic series of musical notes, colors, and planetary spheres (and the gods corresponding to them); the seven deadly sins and their inverse virtues; and, finally, pain.

A six-line epigraph to the book indicates the direction of the poet's work, or, to a large extent, the direction of lyric poetry itself:

One face waits and the other watches
The chariot approach; and the other waits
While the one face sees it depart;

And even Janus must turn to catch
The moving present chariot
Carrying his two-faced heart.

The poem suggests a complexity of time and space, certainly, but also a complexity of attitudes (suggested by Leonard Ungar, by the way, to be a distinguishing feature of seventeenth-century metaphysical poetry) in that Janus' heart shares the coming and going of his head, which moves to catch the moment. And the moment is the important aspect of lyric poetry, at least of the poetry of Hollis Summers.

Extending the definition, "Seven Occasions for Song," the title poem of the book, is couched as a "speech on singing birds" (creatures that often show up in the poet's work). Though Summers makes his "speech in words, / Balanced on a cushion instead of a wing," he affirms he knows "why birds sing." They sing, first of all, to sing, demonstrating "their sense / That sense involves a gut's mystique, and sound / Means melody." The fact that they flock around each other is to assure an audience. Some birds sing their names, defining their identity, "Until, alone, they feel like a seminar." But those who "trill brilliantly for sex," need, I think, to be characterized by the rest of the stanza:

Employing a hundred kindred arts and tricks
Of dancing, rhetoric, and politics;
Fearful of remaining virginal wrecks
They sometimes sing their hearts out protesting
Love, loathing music, and hearts, and nesting.

The fourth occasion for song is the need of the young and old for comfort—"They seek a small song breathing / Like sleep, before dawn, after night." "Some shout aggression," a definition of power, anger, and ego, while some birds are "trembling wary sentinels, / Skilled at reading a shadow's portents," and "they cry, 'Beware,' and 'hide.'" Finally, some sing as a protection after danger: as if "song could forestall / Death, they sing a ceremony of infinite / Sky and a quiet tree and a day long / As life, shining, utterly fit for song." They sing a celebration.

But in the final stanza, the reasons for song are unified,

And seven occasions become one occasion
And every bird sings from seven throats
His seven heavenly sins of every season;
Knowing he sings with only human vision
Composed of human measures and human notes
He finally sings for no final reason.

Having clearly indicated in the first stanza that he is writing as a human being and as a poet, and that he knows why birds sing because he "owns a tree and an anthology," Summers is summoning Janus of the two faces and two-faced heart, knowing the necessity for turning his head to face the moment. He is singing "for no final reason," except that, like Tennyson's linnet, he must.

This, I take it, is the essential object of Hollis Summers' poetic career—to understand the "gut's mystique" which is "sound" and "melody," to communicate with the flock, to identify and define himself, to achieve the unity of pleasure and its attending pain in conjugality, to seek comfort, to understand aggression and fear, and to create through ceremony a talisman to forestall death.

The vision of Janus, who "must turn to catch the moving present," tends to inform the body of the poet's work, and unlike Picasso, who worked with the image in just one phase of his career, Summers develops the image throughout his work in terms of maturing or aging— I'll use the word "passage"—rather than striving to find new directions; his direction has always been that of catching singing birds mid-flight, knowing the approaching and the departing as well as the moment of the turn, although there has been a development in his poetics as well. In his earlier work, one is aware of a strong concern and delight in the traditional forms of verse (couplet, quatrain, sonnet) and even an imitation of George Herbert's shaped "Easter Wings" in "The Trial" (*The Walks Near Athens*). In some later poems the delight in formal verse remains, but at times the rhythms find different shapes in the use of line, though without losing the tone of restraint that is the basis of Summers' neo-baroque flights.

While the Janus motif emerges one way or another throughout Summers' work, a look at specific instances suggests the continuous concepts of passage. Love in all its manifestations is a dominant theme, and marriage as an arena for love fascinates Summers, particularly the marriage that endures for "whatever reason."

In "A Kind of Song" (*Seven Occasions*), as a couple metaphorically travels a highway, the woman looks backwards and "never cared what she was seeing"; she "Perpetually cricked for looking back / At what she had stopped being / Miles ago…" while her husband "never knew where he had been" or if anyone followed; his vision was "far before him / Clear at the edge of the next horizon." The irony in the final stanza develops from things mechanical:

> I suppose a song could be made for an age
> Of serviceable windshield wipers,
> And serviceable rear view mirrors,
> Allowing often enduring marriages.
> I would not lament the standard equipment
> Of motor driven lovers
> In moving fellowship.

The gentleness and restraint of Summers' tone is to be seen in what might be called a poetic word ("lament") followed by the auto industry's "standard equipment," which, of course, suggests the binding aspect of man's and woman's unifying physical characteristics, and they become "motor driven" as they manage a "moving fellowship." The exploitation of such extended meanings and dichotomies of tone is the baroque pearl of much of his poetry.

The concept of "serviceable" mechanics can develop into an awareness of human differences, or a conscious love that does not depend on "standard equipment." In "The Separation," whose context supplies the title for *Sit Opposite Each Other*, the differences can develop a unity through conscious love. In the opening stanza, the poet suggests that "When riding on trains in any country /…arrange to sit opposite / The person you love, taking travel." The reason for this arrangement is the different perspectives of the lovers:

One of you views the about to happen
The other what is leaving,
Knowing that if you sat together
You would still make different journeys.

But the admission of the separation of sensibilities unifies, in the best Donnian sense, those sensibilities:

Opposite, two people admit two sceneries.
If, later, seen landscapes become important,
You can try to merge the fields and mountains
Sensing, at least, you have traveled together.

The poem assumes a didactic tone throughout until the last two lines. Summers begins the final stanza by suggesting that making such arrangements is possible, and that it is of the utmost importance to remember to do so. But, aware of the constant presence of the "motor driven" aspect of life, he turns to himself and his message with irony:

I should not need to be telling this.
I should not need to remember.

The Janus concept moves from poem to poem in at least one other instance in the work of Summers and suggests the evolving sensibility (or passage) with regard to love and sex—the two faces, and the turn of the head to understand the "two-faced heart." In "King's X" (*The Walks Near Athens*), Summers again examines a moment of experience, enlarging it to the cosmic—though on the way understanding the intensity of the mundane. Dealing with the brevity of sexual gratification and its letdown, "The moment after the moment of love / Makes false the moment" because "petty compromise replaces / Revelation." While the house and the baby that needs tending proclaim public sex, the intimacy is private. The necessity of "following fashion" to "prove...unity" means they "let the gas man in / And prove the utter lie of poetry." The lovers must tidy up after passion, as we do after the ultimate death, and make "Another reckoning with time, / Another winter, another spring."

After about two decades Summers writes "A Bed Revisited" (*Occupant Please Forward*). Since the poem illustrates several aspects of the evolution of his poetry, it is worth reproducing in its entirety:

Once I wrote, "The moment after the moment of love
Makes false the moment."
The words are long enough ago and I am old enough
To quote myself.
I was talking about sex, neither pure nor simple,
But purer and simpler
Than an easier word like love. I talked about breathing,
Shouting, "Now, now, now."

And so I still shout, still relish the movement of a mouth
Melting the moment of the moment.
I probably knew the moment after the moment made true.
I know now.

The theme of the poem is, of course, the difference between a mature love and a younger love that achieves its intensity through sexuality. While "King's X" laments the "petty compromise" that replaces "Revelation," "A Bed Revisited" sees the relationship between the moment of ecstasy and the mundane as being part and parcel of one another. What we have in the two poems is the continuum of the Janus image made flesh, as it were, containing the voice of the same man modified by experience. Without self-consciousness, the older man glosses the younger by filling in the orgasmic "Now, now, now," while the younger man might have felt this too great an exposure which would make "false" his "moment." But the symbols of this moment, the symbols of public sex, are the house and baby; this is the continuum of love that after passage leads to a fuller insight into the totality of sex, both public and private.

■ ■ ■

In a retrospective of Summers' fiction, Carol C. Harter says, "At the same time that he asks rhetorically, 'Isn't everything autobiographical?' Summers claims: 'You can't tell anything the way it is.' This apparent contradiction is manifest in Summers' early novels.... " It would seem, however, that when one is dealing with artistic expression, one doesn't deal with the way "it is" but with what is most true, real, and believable, which constitutes at once the poetic voice and faith. Later Ms. Harter tells us that Summers at a writers' conference told of his grandmother's constant question: "Aren't you ever going to learn to control your voice?" It is the control of voice that defines the "epiphany of self"—by which I mean something not unlike a transfiguration, a baroque enough way of suggesting such a concept.

If Herrick is the beginning of a line of poets who define the poetic personality, a word should be said about the ramifications of this sort of poetry in the twentieth century. First, since the nineteenth century, the narrative has been taken over almost completely by the novel and short story (a few notable exceptions exist, of course) and as indication of this, we find many writers working in both forms. Summers is one, and, of course, Robert Penn Warren has won the Pulitzer in both forms. Poetry has become almost entirely lyrical. The nature of our culture and growing longevity has changed the notion of the poet as a young man and has allowed the possibility of a fairly long career. This is of utmost importance for a poet such as Summers, whose work is about ordinary life, not in the Wordsworthian sense, but in the modern domestic sense: the world of marriage, children, travel, job, cocktail parties, aging, and the anticipation of death. He is perhaps in direct contrast to what has been called the suicide school, among whom is counted Anne Sexton, who had so much difficulty dealing with conventions and, perhaps, the possibility of a complete life.

We have had, so far, six collections from Summers. We view through his poetic sensibility those things most men encounter from the middle thirties to their sixtieth year. We have, really, no youthful poetry from Summers, and so we meet in the first of his books what might be called early maturity, a world view of patient irony, where he is not startled by life but intensely interested in it and greatly desirous of celebrating it.

In his first book, *The Walks Near Athens*, 1959, the poet's youth and education are behind him and he is settled with his family and professing English at Ohio University. Besides his stanzaic imitation of Herbert, we find something of a literary cast to many of the poems. In "On Looking at Television's Late Movies," for example, he ironically notes that while in celluloid immortality, in which "Smiling dead actors" pose "Love and, yes, age, / And yes, death.... / In the water where Keats wrote I have read / Permanence.... " In "Girl with the Top Down" the image is of Enobarbus, as a golden-haired girl "moves in her jeweled barge down the bright street / Her lips parted as if she smiled a word / Like *sin*." The modern queen of the Nile is likened to "an actress / Dancing naked in Cinemascope" and is ultimately juxtaposed to another girl, "Waiting for a bus, smiling as if she preferred / Waiting virtuous in the sun on her own two feet." And in his elegy "Once Upon a Time," on F. O. Matthiessen, he encounters suicide, puzzled but with a sense of the depth of pain experienced by the "Christian,

Socialist…undone/ With the wearily twirling world…. " Summers focuses in on the care the critic took with his glasses after he removed from his pocket the letters "written to the world he loved." He took

> From his eyes the glasses which were able
> With his mind's help to look
>
> Deeply at the world, a task
> For brave men. Then he stepped through air
> Sightless in April. Do not ask
> About his glasses. Do not ask where.

Perhaps the poem from this first book that best suggests the prevailing tone of self-irony throughout his poetry is an eight-line lyric, "If I Were Twenty":

> If I were twenty and in love with love
> This night of clouds and circled moon and air
> That moves as intimate as hands, I know
> My heart would beat with wondering, aware
>
> A miracle was breathing, now, close
> within the dark, whispering the start
> Of present music and an opening door.
> But I am far past twenty. Quietly, heart.

Seven Occasions, published when Summers was forty-eight, defines, as I have suggested, his program for poetry, and contains one of his rare long poems, "The Tree"—a retelling of the third chapter of Genesis. In its way as baroque as Milton's poem (but certainly of another character), it is a whimsical epistemological study that sets out to decide which fruit it was that the pair tasted and asserts from knowledge gained in a dream, that it was a fig—a symbol of growth and of sexual unity, both vaginal and phallic. The serpent, in his temptation, "Spoke only information," while Eve repeats, half listening, "I need, I need," until the tempter vanishes, asserting that "knowledge is the fruit of knowledge." When Adam tastes, the pair celebrate "Their first human communion of deceit," and time begins:

> With the taste of fig Adam and Eve kissed
> Darkly naked. God and I moved.
> I tried to watch His expression as He slipped
> From the withered apple where he'd hidden. Love,
>
> Perhaps, or agony, or even fear?
> I have found it difficult to name expression
> In daylight, much less dream….

The sin of man is a mixture of all seven occasions for song—the poem appears in the seventh section, where the bird "sings with only human vision / Composed of human measures and human notes…"—and the poet knows

> …I would need to tell this story joking
> Before I acknowledged knowledge as love. "We sold
> Our souls for information." I think it was Adam who spoke,
> But I cannot be sure….

Adam and Eve do not take "their solitarie way" through the garden; rather, Summers finally asserts that

Knowledge is a fig, and I am a dreaming lover
Learning. I give you, with love, my word.

What is important in the Summers worldview is a wry honesty about deceit (one finds him often asserting, "I lie a lot"). In the penultimate poem, in this second book, about imagined retirement, "On Accepting the Gold Watch," he finds that he cannot resign with a condemnation of the culpability of those he leaves behind because

I know I leave too many fingerprints
On fabric, flesh, and document
Now to stand among you claiming either
The luxury of amnesia or innocence.

In his next book, *The Peddler, and Other Domestic Matters* (published in 1967, when he was fifty-one), Summers views the idea of retirement from another angle—how one behaves at the gathering of colleagues where the plaque, with the "tribute" ironically "Bitten into the convention-al shield screwed as a gift / To the conventionally slick square of wood," is presented. In "Notes for a Man Invited" the plan is to make those younger colleagues who are ill at ease a bit more comfortable, which can be done "A little only by a final act of final arrogance." He understands the conventions of such ceremonies, while his younger colleagues cannot grasp moving to "another space / Lying in directions unutterably undiscovered." This is the knowledge of passage, a fuller understanding of conventional deceit, which tells the truth of the retiree's sensibility:

They are also unsure retiring ever means
Another word for grace, becoming another way of grace.

Since Summers has yet to retire, we see here again the movement of the two-faced head. With children mostly grown, a better income, sabbaticals, and the like, travel becomes an increasing-ly important occasion for his poetry, and the mid-life passage continues to engage his concerns on many levels. In "Discovery" he examines the dead world of Pompeii amid tourists, but in examining this death in stasis, he discovers life:

But once in Pompeii, at dusk,
Alone alive I
Walked in a garden alive
And found blackberries
And picked and ate blackberries.

In other poems in *The Peddler*, Summers finds surreal sameness in the waitresses, service station attendants, and lavatories at freeway plazas as in "Bridge Freezes Before Road Surface"; this generality in people and places leads him to sensations of dislocation and to reflections that when younger, "the whole/ World fitted in a nutshell /…I did not know a man could not / Remember the feel of his skin" ("The Brotherhood").

Occupancy of a house over a number of years is something of a continuum, changing slowly, at times imperceptibly, and Hollis Summers at the beginning of his fifties catches the progress of a home in the moment of the poem. In "The Exchange," the tables in the house begin changing from place to place; where a bed "had once seemed permanent," is a table set for dinner; certain articles of furniture find their way to neighbors' houses, and even the living things are exchanged:

…the maples turned to apples;
The privet hedge replaced itself with laurel.
and then the pets: our Siamese for a mongrel.

The poem has a surreal cast since the memory ties all exchanges to the moment, but the poet comes back to tap the meaning of time and memory, with a suggestion of ultimate finality:

> But we endured, and glad I am we did…
> We have all settled into our altered neighborhood.
> and now, outside, a moon shines like a gold thimble
> I remember, the first memory of all.
> The house is determined to collect ourselves.
> The hillside trembles.

Summers published two more books in his fifties, *Sit Opposite Each Other* (1970) and *Start from Home* (1972), and the tone changes to some extent as he grows into these years. His subject matter, while still that of the birds and Janus, deals essentially with home and travel. Indeed, his wife, Laura, has commented that while they have never been much to use a camera either at home or abroad, they didn't need to because the poems serve as a family record. The concept of traveling with a loved one was suggested earlier in the discussion of "The Separation," from which the poet derives the title for the book published when he was 54. In the first poem of the volume, "If Time Matters," he suggests that it does, so "take a plane," but "If time is even more important, go by ship." One has the time to

> Consider the importance of any small mystery,
> A cup of tea, or a piece of paper.
> A plane, too, is like a jail,
> But it does not hold a place named *Jail*.
> Ships do, as truly as does the Vatican.

In "Flagship, Tourist Class" he captures the boredom of walking the decks, the often foul weather, the need to "write letters, / In both directions, home and where we go to, / Weaving small webs for holding on." But to while away the hours, talking is better—about home, work, children, Christmas, flowers:

> …we always say we prefer
>
> Traveling Tourist Class where you get to know
> Interesting people, all the while alert
> To snatch a glance through the No Admittance doors
> Where the opulent, no doubt, also wait for Bingo.

What we have in these poems are, if you will, sensitive snapshots unavailable to film, yet we do find the visual as fixed as it would be on the emulsion. In "More Nuns," the poet tells us that his Baptist background leads to his surprise "to come upon / Nuns on every single travel." On this day he sees four sisters

> With five prancing loud nymphets
> In bathing suits of flowered net,
> The nuns were habited.

The poem ultimately deals with a way of behavior, of, perhaps, a religious humanity, wherein the nuns accepted the nearly nubile girls for their animal spirits and suggests that perhaps this is more religious than the Puritanism of either Roger Williams or a Baptist lady missionary he once knew.

Two other poems in this book pointedly suggest a feeling or theme that tends to run through a major portion of his work, which is the "I-Thou" concept of Martin Buber. In "The

Relations" the poet looks on the street where he lives and renders the existential moment (significantly without punctuation):

> Around the shaggy sun
> All the sky staggers
> Down Congress Street
> Missing none of the houses
> Every tree says
> Look at me
> Nothing relates to anything
> Everything says see

And, in dealing with relationships among people, "How to Get Along in the World" becomes somewhat didactic, though by the end of the poem, one feels that Buber's dictum that "All reality is an activity in which I share without being able to appropriate for myself" is realized:

> Even should no music sound
> Wave to the girl who circles round
> And around on a merry-go-round;
>
> Wave to the boy who waits in the back
> Of an open truck;
>
> Wave to the man on top
> Of any mountain.
>
> They have mounted
> On, in, up,
> Not because the thing stands,
>
> Not for any reason save
> Waving
> Being waved to.
>
> Smile and wave.
> Say, I have seen you,
> I see you.

In *Start from Home*, published two years later, domesticity is generally celebrated; Summers sees family as a continuum, with all the paradoxes of love. In the poem "Family," the poet recalls his mother insisting that they hold hands as they cross the street—"We will die together." The family "was the unit / Of almost everything: / Religion, politics—whatever words." The child worried about the flies that rode home from a family picnic:

> I was sentimental.
> I still want families to stay together.
> I killed the homeless flies, before we reached our house.

In "Traveler," the poet sums up the nature of being away from home. After defining the alienation one finds on the highway because of the traffic and wanting communion with those who tailgate him, he avers that "the speeders get wherever earlier":

> But I know that people are ugly in airports, on docks,
> Leaving, and I know they are beautiful coming home.
> That is all I know about traveling.

The nature of a long love in contrast to various other carnal arrangements is celebrated in "Confession." At the outset, the poet and his wife, with "a temporarily unmarried friend," visit a pornography store where the friend "purchased houseslippers shaped like breasts / Whose erect nipples were conditioned to squirt liquids." Another time, with "temporarily married friends" they, apparently in Amsterdam, look at the whores in windows who "Called to suggest / Various watered arrangements." They also have attended a party where "almost everyone / Skinny dipped in a muddy lake / Before making at love." The Freudian water imagery shows up in every instance in quiet grotesqueness, but carnality is not merely instances of sexuality, nor is it exclusive of the rest of love:

Once,
A thousand times,
We, only smiling,
Rowed, clothed, married,
A lake together.

But carnality is a matter of passage as well. Babies are tended "the moment after the moment of love," but the babies grow up. In "The Adjustment" Summers talks of his maiden aunt who at seventeen bought herself a wedding ring, vowing that she would always wear it and never marry; she "boasted /…'No one on earth will ever see my body nude, / Not ankles, arms, nor throat.'" Her death was "modestly lamented,"

And now my lovely unmarried daughter wears the ring,
A locket bobbing between her breasts,
The while displaying her thighs and arms.
I suppose one must become accustomed to inheritances.

Home is also one's professional life, particularly if one be a professor, and Summers in the poem "Home" defines his university in Athens, Ohio, where "The University sits on a Hill /…facing another hill and the mental hospital." The juxtaposition of the two institutions is played throughout the first half of the poem, where "The confined sick shuffle the university grounds; / The college young strain by the hospital ponds." In so doing, "The mad sometimes fall into the university pool. / The yearning young sometimes forget to take their pills." "Pills" is a typical Summers play on words, suggesting that on both hills problems occur when the pills are ignored, and he follows the opening with what one might take to be the nature of university social life, which encompasses, ironically, the two institutions:

We are having company again.
One must attach no symbolism to the names of our guests,
The Inchoates, the Ethnics, the Ordinances, and the Jubilates.
The Jubilates own a wailing wall apiece;
The Inchoates teach both Logic and Philosophy,
Posting charts on everything on all their bathroom walls;
The Ethnics honestly love Mankind and whip each other;
The Ordinances sleep with their maid as well as their dog.
We keep having each other for dinner.

Summers' most recent book, *Occupant Please Forward*, appeared in his sixtieth year in 1976 and takes another step of the passage, one that is perhaps less marked by bemused irony and is more intense with regard to aging and the pain of anticipation. In "Golden Age Festival" he projects himself into an outing where the festivities ("Festivities is their favorite word") are held in a warehouse because of rain. A young lady spoke on cosmetics and nutrition, some "old fools" tried to dance when "they played records on a Victrola" (the old trade name is important to the tone), prizes were given for "The Oldest, and the Longest Married." They ate the picnic lunches each had brought and finally were taken to their own street corners on a bus. The tone of the poem is not unlike the reportage of mundane facts of an outing that one would find in a grade school report—about his lunch: "Mine was very good, a hard-boiled egg and a tuna sandwich"—and when the speaker gets off the bus,

> The rain hadn't stopped and it was cold.
> At least the cold of the warehouse was dry.

Particularly poignant is the identification, rather than detachment, of the person in his late fifties.

We find very few tears in the works of Summers; indeed, tears do not often fit the restrained emotional impact that is part of what I have called neo-baroque—they hide. In "Manual for the Freeway," however, the poet in his mock-didactic manner, admonishes the reader not to look at passing drivers because freeways are for being alone, and if by chance one catches another motorist's eyes, it should not be acknowledged:

> Should you smile
> The other driver
> Assumes
> You ridicule.
>
> Should you nod
> The other driver must run you down.

After all,

> Where else can a person go to cry?
> Where else can a person go?

After some thirty years of marriage, Summers develops an extended metaphor which eschews the road of life metaphor for one that is more apt; in "The Tunnel" he defines the dim light of uncertainty in advancing passage. After naming the signs one finds on entering a tunnel about speed, sun glasses, lights, and staying in lane, the couple, "who have traveled long together," realize that

> The world is full of signs
> For married people;
> And we are used to tunnels,
> Faint walls and ceilings,
> Funeral parlor light;
> We are customed to obey.

But the difference in this tunnel is that the poet doesn't find the "curve of light / Promising other tunnels' ends," and though the taillights of other cars are missing, he decides that

> The tunnel probably ends;
> We must drive alone together
> Even if no sign says
> Tunnel ends.

With late middle age often comes lethargy, and in the poem "Energy," the poet is about his usual wry self-irony, self-amusement. While the piece needs no explication, its entirety is necessary:

> He had planned to compose a monograph
> On potato washing as a cultural tradition;

Fascinated by monkeys and children on television,
He meant to comment lengthily on;

And he intended to say fully that predators,
Eagles, for example, make gentle parents;

And he was determined to write on sex at Disneyland
Because he'd had it at.

Four volumes would have proved sufficient
For the story of life.

But it was always Tuesday, and always February
Out of ink and raining.

Contemplating human extension, Summers in "Immortality" defines the process of making dandelion wine, telling us that it can be drunk after six months, but it is better to wait a year, and that in the following spring, the fermentation will begin again in the bottles. As with procreation, nurture, and settling, the wine ferments again, but we should not be alarmed because "Dandelions remember; / They will settle after other dandelions bloom." And in "The Mocking Birds," a bird not really accounted for in "Seven Occasions for Song," Summers says, "I suppose I love the mockers finally," though he has "championed the message birds / Who know their own names / And call out for audience."

But were they the last of us,
The mockers would still sing nameless,
Mocking at most the nature of silence
At least themselves
Still nesting.

"Please Forward," one of the title poems of this collection, deals with the inevitability of his house coming into another's possession. He focuses on the sun parlor with a piano and flowers and the need to close it off for the cold season; after all, he has other rooms in which "To sort papers / And write letters." He consoles himself in having been blessed, as others have not, with a sun parlor with music and flowers. But in "Memo from a Patron of the Arts," the first two stanzas suggest a jaundiced view of the arts, though the sensibility for beauty prevails with a response that does not suggest immortality but vitality:

I am tired of poems about paintings,
And sculptures on classical subject,
And theme music made for famous people;

I am gut-weary of our applauding
The incest of the arts, mistaking a poem
For shelter, a dance for love, a photograph for food.

Still, hungry, I have had erections
All over, in libraries and galleries,
Still.

■ ■ ■

We have had six volumes of Hollis Summers' poetry, containing some 350 poems that define what I have called the epiphany of the poetic personality. His work is autobiographical, though of the sort that Samuel Johnson recommends:

The mischievous consequences of vice and folly, of irregular desires and predominant passions are best discovered by those relations which are levelled with the
general surface of life, which tell not how any man became great, but how he was
made happy; not how he lost the favour of his prince, but how he became discon-
tented with himself. (*The Idler,* No. 80)

It is poetry from a gentleman's voice, a poetry that demonstrates restraint and is subtly passionate in terms of what I have called baroque, derived from the poets of the seventeenth century
and those of the first half of ours. It is a poetry of passage, some twenty-five years of modifying
sensibility.

It is, ultimately, a poetry that one lives with, perhaps at different levels of understanding at
different times of one's life (we all share to some extent the Janus experience) as one lives with an
intimate friend, knowing his basic sensibility and identifying with his passage through the world.

It is almost a decade since *Occupant Please Forward,* though Summers continues to write
and publish in magazines. We certainly need another book to continue the relationship. One
poem in particular suggests the continuance of the poet's poetic passage, a long work of some
250 to 300 lines, "Brother Clark," which appeared in the 1980 Spring issue of *Ohio Review*.

The poem tells in third person the story of an early pubescent boy with spots on his lungs,
who is confined to bed for several months. Visiting him is a deacon from the Baptist church
where his father is the new minister. Though the mother shakes her head, Brother Clark is
asked by the father for "a word of prayer," which turns out to be fifty-seven minutes of self-
indulgent orison, clocked by the boy who had been given a watch, "a reward for having been a
patient patient." For the rest of the first twenty-two sections, we move back and forth between
the prayer and details of the boy's growing sensibility, which tend to project a life. He is somewhat confused by various religious persuasions through the black maid's staunch Methodism,
which can't abide the Baptist faith, and the liberal Episcopal background of a neighbor, Mrs.
Roland, who dances, smokes, and drinks cocktails; he thinks about a girl named Claire; he is
troubled by the "boys in Rest Rooms, easy with their bodies" and "He told himself secrets"
about his own developing body; he grows concerned with the prayer, which leads him to fears
of death. Brother Clark's prayer moves in and out of the boy's thoughts while the boy is struck
by the man's right cheek that was "eaten yellow and purple with cancer." When the prayer was
not about Brother Clark himself,

> "I have confessed the cause of my cancer,
> the lusts of my flesh, my rotting soul,
> I have repented and Thou hast cured...,"

the boy felt that Brother Clark "was telling God on him" and was filled with a child-like fear of
God and notions of death and an afterlife. By the twenty-third section, the boy had recovered
and was well enough to attend Brother Clark's funeral, which lasted only twenty minutes at the
church and ten at the graveside. Brother Clark died at 57, as "many years as he prayed minutes
over me." In the 24th section, the poem's amused and indulgent reflection on the boy from the
third person, moves into the first person for a summation of the child's projection:

> It is hard to know how old I was or am.
> Sixty is six times ten.
> Twelve goes into sixty.
> The tables add and multiply,
> divide, subtract.
> For years Brother Clark has known

■ **BOOKS BY HOLLIS SUMMERS**

poetry

The Walks Near Athens. New York: Harper, 1959.

Someone Else (poems for children). New York: McGraw-Hill, Lippincott, 1962.

Seven Occasions. New Brunswick, N.J.: Rutgers University Press, 1965.

The Peddler, and Other Domestic Matters. New Brunswick, N.J.: Rutgers University Press, 1967.

Sit Opposite Each Other. New Brunswick, N.J.: Rutgers University Press, 1970.

Start from Home. New Brunswick, N.J.: Rutgers University Press, 1972.

Occupant Please Forward. New Brunswick, N.J.: Rutgers University Press, 1976.

Dinosaur (chapbook). Athens, Ohio: Rosetta Press, 1977.

After the Twelve Days. Ashland, Ohio: Ashland Poetry Press, 1987.

novels

City Limit. Boston: Houghton, Mifflin, 1948.

Brighten the Corner. New York: Doubleday, 1952.

Teach You a Lesson (co-author). New York: Harper, 1956.

The Weather of February. New York: Harper, 1957.

The Day After Sunday. New York: Harper, 1968.

The Garden. New York: Harper, 1972.

Other Concerns and Brother Clark. Athens: Ohio University Press, 1988.

Helen and The Girls: Two Novellas.. Baton-Rouge: Louisiana State University Press, 1992.

short stories

How They Chose the Dead. Baton Rouge: Louisiana State University Press, 1973.

Standing Room. Baton Rouge: Louisiana State University Press, 1984.

other books

Kentucky Story (a collection of short stories edited with James Rourke). Lexington: University Press of Kentucky, 1954

Literature: An Introduction (textbook). New York: McGraw-Hill, 1960.

Discussions of the Short Story (edited). New York: Heath, 1963.

---

all there is to know of nothing,
Heaven or Hell,
my parents, Mrs. Roland, Todd, Claire,
the others.

Older now than Brother Clark ever became
I wait for his prayer to end.

God, blessed Jesus, Lord, have mercy upon us.

Robert McGovern
June, 1987

UPDATE

After poet and novelist Hollis Summers died in 1987, two books came out posthumously: *Other Concerns and Brother Clark* (1988) and *Helen and The Girls: Two Novellas* (1992).

The Kentucky-born Summers, who began his writing career with fiction, was widely regarded, and better known, for his poetry. As a poet, wrote *Prairie Schooner*, "Hollis Summers' dominant trait is a quiet clarity. His effects recall the painter Andrew Wyeth's steady melancholy, his whimsical affection for the mundane, and his strong shadows. . . . Summers allows his forms a full display; their structures glow with vitality. Miller Williams, writing in *Saturday Review*, suggested that Summers has an easy hand; he employs the devices of both conventional poetry and contemporary language without awkwardness."

Leaving home and returning home are central to much of Summers's poetry and fiction. "Isolated and often despairing, Summers's fictional characters frequently develop acute awareness as they travel away from familiar, orderly, and comfortable surroundings," stated the *Dictionary of*

Literary Biography. "They are tested and test themselves in Mexico or Malta; but the crucial tests ultimately occur in the most mundane settings: a quiet Ohio living room, a Kentucky bedroom."

Summers also received favorable reviews for his novels, especially *The Weather of February* and *The Day After Sunday*, the latter of which was considered by many to be his finest. After reading *The Day After Sunday*, Jessamyn West wrote to Summers's editor: "If any word of mine can bring the pleasures of this book to other readers, I'll be glad to shout them." Summers set his story in Kentucky, and "creates a totally controlled, brilliantly structured novel about an ordinary family whose daily lives—mundane, pleasant, and comfortable on the surface—mask emotional trauma, psychological imbalance, and spiritual despair," according to the *Dictionary of Literary Biography*. In a review of the novella collection *Helen and The Girls*, *Publishers Weekly* stated: "Summers . . . handles familiar, universal themes here with compassion, never sinking too far into sentimentality."

Reviewer Warren French once wrote: "Hollis Summers, who knows this country like Antonioni knows Rome, has captured the feeling of emotional starvation in a land of physical plenty with a skill that leaves a critic at a loss for words."

Between Past and Present: Characters Finding Their Way in Gladys Swan's Fiction

Meant to describe two new members of the carnival troupe, these lines from Gladys Swan's *Carnival for the Gods* apply equally well to the entire procession of dreamers and drifters, losers and malcontents she has created in her novel and two collections of stories (the more recent of which, *Of Memory and Desire*, appeared in August 1989 from LSU Press).

What do these characters look for? Some look for homes. Some for security. Some look for what they missed in their youth, through abuse, neglect, or naiveté. Some look to succeed, in whatever limited way they've redefined success. Some simply took to find their way, "suspended between past and present," stranded at the halfway point along the road from youth to old age. But most of all, they look to avoid the final catastrophe of a failed life.

These themes, already present in her novel *Carnival for the Gods*, and her first collection, *On the Edge of the Desert*, appear again in the new collection, *Of Memory and Desire*.

The tone of the new collection is set in several stories dealing with abuse or neglect in childhood, especially the aftermath, the effect on the adult person. For example, in "July," Julio is forced from his home as a young boy, then rescued from the streets by an old man—an itinerant handyman. They travel the Southwest together in the old man's truck. The old man gives young Julio the anglicized nickname "July," teaches him to make money and get along in the world. But he also controls him, keeps his money and doles it out a little at a time. By the time the narrative takes place the old man has turned senile, roles have gradually been reversed, and July is now the caretaker.

Initially July is concerned with survival, not success. Then their truck breaks down on a desert road, and they take refuge in a nearby cafe. A pretty, ambitious waitress awakens July to the idea of success. She forces a confrontation with the old man, causing July to "discover what he had never known before."

> He wanted something to happen…wanted a change…wanted to put his arm around the girl…He wanted to be off and never look behind him. He had a life. Right now.

Even before he meets the waitress, though, we sense the young man's initial stirrings of freedom. He stands by the side of the road, their truck broken down, and realizes there's nowhere to

Here they were, just another pair among the number she had seen, in the procession of all the broken, illformed, misbegotten things headed out of the world and onto the road, moving from town to town, never calling any place their own. They were her family, if you could call it that—they were her fate.

■ GLADYS SWAN, CARNIVAL FOR THE GODS

Gladys Swan

Gladys Swan was born in New York City on October 15, 1934. She received her B.A. from what is now Western New Mexico University and her M.A. from Claremont Graduate School. Swan has been a teacher on the middle school level, assistant professor, then associate professor at Franklin College in Indiana, and a member of the faculty in the Vermont College M.F.A. program, as well as writer-in-residence at the University of Texas at El Paso and Ohio University. She has received the Lilly Endowment Fellowship, the Distinguished Service Award for Literature from Western New Mexico University, and a Fulbright Fellowship to serve as a writer-in-residence in Yugoslavia. She has received the Indiana Arts Commission Master Fellowship in Literature. Swan presently lives in Columbia, Missouri, where she is a member of the faculty at the University of Missouri at Columbia. ■

go: he's trapped by the natural surroundings, the sun beating down, a mountain peak just over his shoulder. Here he experiences a communion with nature that is almost sexual.

> …the mountain seemed to enter him, the cloud pouring down over him, the bluff forming inside him…he was struck by the land, as something to possess and wound him…He breathed deeply, felt something in him rising to the surface, strong and full. He looked out as if it had suddenly been given for him to rule over the empire of summer…

At this moment July first senses himself as having power, able to get the upper hand with the old man and in his life as a whole. In the end, July turns his back on the old man, lets him wander off, then absconds with all his money.

"Lucinda" is one of the most riveting stories of the new collection. (It appeared in the anthology *The Best of the West 2*.) Lucinda is the young daughter of Pilar, the main character of that story. Pilar, product of childhood abuse, is driven from home, takes refuge in a Mexican whorehouse, then at age 14 is salvaged from that occupation by Alex, a sort of redneck U.S. drug dealer. Alex travels the country carrying out his deals while "keeping" Pilar in an apartment in New Mexico. Pilar is content waiting for Alex's unscheduled returns home, moving with him when things get hot, tolerating his interest in other women, hanging on to her fragile life, willing to accept the relative security of being "kept" in this way. Her need to preserve this security intensifies after the birth of her daughter, Lucinda, who becomes the center of Pilar's life, her reason for existence.

Pilar never learns the meaning of success, only security. She is awed by the amount of money involved in Alex's deals, can't imagine what anyone would do with so much. She asks only for simple things, and those usually for Lucinda. Her nightmare is not one of failure, but of traveling somewhere, she knows not where, alone.

Waking from the nightmare, feeling her husband slipping away, the security of her life vanishing, Pilar goes outside.

> A bank of clouds extended over part of the city, but beyond it the sky was a rich blue, so filled with light that everything stood out against it with a sharpness that made it seem caught there forever in utmost clarity. The dark blue mountain closest and the pink mountain farther away, so clear, so bright it was like looking at a picture. For a long time she did not move.

The story ends with Alex setting off on yet another trip: destination not specified, time of return unknown; Pilar content to wait, unquestioning, strengthened by her determination to nurture Lucinda and the fortification she seems to draw from the land, her nature surroundings.

In this story Pilar's friend Sarah (Sally) functions as an alter ego. Sally has a lot of the qualities Pilar needs, to feel more at home in the society, to feel comfortable even with her own husband. Unlike Pilar, Sally is fluent in English, has travelled and moved around, is familiar with Los Angeles, where Pilar's husband, Alex, has done business. Even though as members of the *narrative audience* we wouldn't trade Pilar, with all her simplicity and richness, for Sally's prosaic imitation of a contemporary woman, Sally nevertheless is attractive to Alex, an object of envy to Pilar. In this sense Sally embodies Pilar's needs and aspirations, her goals and ideals. (Such use of characters is seen in other of Swan's stories.)

The haunting tale "Of Memory and Desire" tells how an unnamed boy and an old recluse nicknamed "Goat Man" scratch out a living on land near a southwestern town. As the town expands, a young man looking to get ahead, "Chico" Benevidez, discovers Goat Man pays no taxes on the property, has no deed. Benevidez, we learn, developed his intense wish to succeed as compensation for growing up in a dysfunctional home, running away as a child. He uses his position in the county tax office to defraud Goat Man and the boy of their farm. He gets away with it, even though in the process Goat Man is burned to death in his own house. No one knows for sure what happened to the boy, though occasionally he pops up here and there. (Including in *Carnival for the Gods* and the last scene of "On the Eve of the Next Revolution.")

This story also deals, metaphorically, with the ravaging of the land. Goat Man and the boy (representing the conservators of the land) live simply, in a log cabin, in harmony with the land, taking only what they need, leaving the natural surroundings intact. But in the end, they are no match for the greed and ambition of Benevidez (representing the untamed economic growth of the twentieth century). Benevidez is an apt figure for greed and untamed growth. He lacked the civilizing influences of a normal childhood, yet in the emotional hunger of his youth developed a clear idea of what he wanted to achieve.

For him, success is having a civil service job, owning land, being respected. He is driven principally by the wish to overcome the poverty, neglect, and shame of his childhood.

> Already [Chico Benevidez] had a burning desire and a terrible energy. If he had his dreams, they were no more powerful than his hatreds, his sense of the unfairness of things. Yet he could see himself in some other place, rich, with men working for him. In spite of everything, there must be a way. He could look around and see that people had lifted themselves up, gotten jobs, made money. True, there were families that never made it up out of the mud, never had a decent shirt on their backs.

But he would do it. You had to keep your eyes open, bide your time, and grab your chance when it came along.

Important in each of these stories is the landscape, the natural surroundings, the characters' sense of place. In an interview in *Writers' Forum 16*, Swan described the importance of place in her own life, especially at the age of 10, when she moved from a small Delaware town to the Southwest.

No doubt the contrast between a flat green stretch mostly of farmland and the mountains of New Mexico had initially to do with that…It was a complete shock, the difference in landscape and culture. I was torn from my roots, from what I'd taken for granted, and forced into another set of accommodations. I didn't really belong anywhere, and that gave me a vantage point outside not only what I knew but what I was observing.

In "Getting an Education," Crystal Munsinger is not displaced, is not abused as a child, does not live in poverty. She grows up, goes to college. A neighbor, Findlay Brightwood, teaches her in college. Her reaction to Brightwood is the substance of the story, the metaphor for Crystal's education.

Crystal's education is not motivated by ordinary notions of success—through no fault of her mother's! Mrs. Munsinger's idea of success is clearly spelled out for her: "the first member of the family to go to college…the importance of an education had been impressed upon her ever since she could remember." For Mrs. Munsinger,

the title of doctor, lawyer, congressman called up an immediate awe: anyone who had a profession was a superior being. Education spelled opportunity. Crystal knew that her mother would be overjoyed to see money and social position come her way. But in any case, [her mother] wanted her to be a teacher so that she could be somebody in the world and not have people look down on her.

But for Crystal this isn't enough. In college—and after—she hungers for truth. "How was it that people's lives took a certain direction, that they were what they were?" She believes she has the answer, then realizes what she learned is only a minute fraction of the whole.

It was like so many fragments of glass that the light shone through, first one way, then another. And each time you took out the collection to add another piece, you found that the light had shifted and nothing was the same.

And yet, Crystal thought, you might add the pieces, but perhaps through it all, curved like a snake or the bed of a river, something was being created, so that after a time you were looking at a strand, a connection, a pattern.

Crystal's education (the "Education" of the title) is that she comes to see a pattern in all the fragments, or at least comes to *hope* such a pattern will emerge, even when it comes to Brightwood's startling demise. When she wishes for Brightwood that he might, in the end, have been permitted to discover "any sense in the world," we hear the plaintive cry of a young woman whose education has brought her a long way but nevertheless left her without a real solution. In fact, has taught her there *is* no solution.

In "The Ink Feather" a young girl is abused by her older brother's anger and tyranny, neglected and unprotected by a depressed and complaining mother. The girl does her best to avoid her brother and work around her mother's moods. She uses her imagination to erect a protective cocoon of fantasy around herself, performing surgery on her dolls, retreating into the fantasy world of her wraithlike playmate, Mary Jane. Then, in the final moment of the story, the girl defies the mother and brother, leaves the house without permission, returns and vandalizes the brother's desk and office, spilling a defiant blot of ink on the rug in the shape of a feather.

In previous stories ("Lucinda," "July," "Of Memory and Desire") abused children leave their dysfunctional homes, at least in some sense escape the pattern of abuse. The children reach adulthood, and the stories tell of how their later lives are affected. In "The Ink Feather," however, Willa's only escape is into her own fantasy life, taking "flight from what was too much to bear." (The quote, a line from Swan's earlier story "Flight," states a theme seen in perhaps four of the stories from her first collection.)

"The Ink Feather" contains another striking example of duality of characters in Willa and her playmate, Mary Jane. Mary Jane's face appears at a window, or pops up from behind a bush or a fence. She appears to have the freedom Willa longs for. She seems a necessary psychological complement to Willa, helping Willa cope with her life at home. In fact, Mary Jane has the qualities of an "imaginary playmate," and we aren't certain whether she's real or not, given Willa's propensity to operate out of her imagination. Regardless, Mary Jane is to Willa in *this* story what Sally is to Pilar in "Lucinda."

Relationships of this type abound in Swan's earlier collection. "Decline and Fall" is the story of Evvie Skyler, a middle-aged librarian who revisits her decision as a young woman to stay behind while her older sister follows the love of her life. The story suggests that the older sister's life, though ended in tragedy, might well have been a more fulfilling choice for Evvie. The denouement of "In the True Light of Morning" centers on a conflict between the Rev. Ira Jack Dodgett and Burl Canady. First Burl almost kills Ira Jack (symbolic of Ira Jack's early propensity toward sin); then Ira Jack almost kills him, but stops in time.

> It seemed that he and Canady as well were caught in the grip of a dark and hideous error. He might as well be choking in the clutch of his own terrible ignorance.

As Jung would explain to us, Burl Canady is truly Ira Jack's dark side, come back to haunt him. Ira Jack, by sparing Burl Canady's life, comes to "own" his dark side. Something of this duality can also be discovered in the high-voltage relationship between Orlie Benedict and Gaunt Partner in "Flight." "Your partner in misery," Orlie calls himself to Gaunt Partner.

Returning to the new collection, "Reunion" and "On the Eve of the Next Revolution" continue themes found in Swan's first collection. They are midlife stories, stories of men returning to their homes of origin, literally for Jarvis in "Reunion," metaphorically for Sol in "Revolution." Truly these men are "suspended between past and present."

Jarvis has bounced around from job to job, city to city. By most standards his life is "unsuccessful." He returns for a family reunion, hoping to search out his roots, to evaluate from whence he came, perhaps to see where it all went wrong. He finds reminders of past mistakes, of failures. He speaks of his failed marriage.

> You come to the end of such things and finally you call them by their true name— failure. It's like living with fading eyesight or a loss of hearing—all happening so gradually you don't notice, till one day the world is in shadow and no birds sing. Then you know only what is lost, not how to get it back.

For Jarvis success is not the issue. He wishes to escape failure, especially the ultimate catastrophe of a failed life.

Seeing the habits and patterns engulfing those left behind while he wandered the country, he decides to move on.

> I thought of those who were staying behind, visited by rain and snow and all the varying weathers of experience. I could have stayed with them, under the illusion

of safety; but it was too late for that. At least I knew where I had gotten my restlessness. I'd held it down for thirty years—now I was a leaf in the wind.

It is a recurring theme in Swan's fiction: the despair associated with stasis, the hopefulness of moving on. (Certainly a very *Western* theme, for those who like to classify her in that genre.)

But moving on for what? His sister tells him: "There is nothing in this world worth chasing…Spend your energy chasing around and all you get is a little pool of tears." But Jarvis abhors this attitude. In his old room, he draws inspiration from a drawing he made as a child: a man with wings. "A good way to get past your mistakes, I thought. Fly beyond them." In finding the picture, he's found himself, his psychological roots.

At the same time his favorite niece leaves her family, abandoning a relatively safe existence to avoid being trapped and smothered in the small-town atmosphere of her home. Her moving on is a mirror of Jarvis's aspirations, and he takes vicarious comfort from this. At the end Jarvis still has no fixed goals, but he has hope: for his niece, for himself. For him, hopefulness is its own reward, and that's where he differs from his family.

"On the Eve of the Next Revolution" is the story of Sol, an American veteran of the Spanish Civil War and 1930's and 1960's idealism. Sol returns not to his *family* roots but to the roots of his idealism, visiting Felipe, a former comrade in arms in Mexico. He finds Felipe still mouthing the same slogans they'd fought for together, years before. But issues once important to Sol as a social activist now confuse and disillusion him.

> He was like a spectator watching an old movie: it was strange to look at himself then, and now also to see Felipe, who still held a pure faith in the old ideals. Quite astonishing after so many years to see a man who burned with the same fire, spoke with the same words—"Bourgeois Decadence," "Elitism"—hated the Church and American capitalism with the same passion.

He wants to feel he's made a difference in the world, but is ambivalent about the causes he's fought for. He is financially set, but worries there is no home for his idealism. "Was there a place for an old idealist…?" he asks. Or was there "nothing left for him but to rot?"

He also is disappointed over his offspring, an older son and daughter leading empty lives, and a sensitive but confused younger son about to enter college.

Sol has achieved financial success, now wishes only to be reassured that his life hasn't been wasted. "To ask for some tangible proof that he hasn't wasted his time…Was that asking too much?"

Eventually the story comes down to Sol and the younger son, Steve. On a hillside they come across a herd of goats as they walk home across the Mexican countryside. The incident is described in one of the most stunning passages in Swan's work.

> The ridge beyond them, touched by the dying sun, was set ablaze and the clouds above glowed with the color. The breeze had dropped; everything was quite still, as though awaiting a blessing. Then came a rustling, very faint at first, as though a light rain were beginning, and Sol looked up, expecting the first drops. But the rustling increased, and a flock of goats appeared from over the rise and flowed down the slope. Warm brown, sleek black, white, dappled, with sharp, delicate faces and slender legs, they passed, their small hoofs on the dust making the hush-hush of rain in the leaves. A boy walked barefoot alongside. He glanced up at the strangers, but gave them no sign.

With a look and a smile Sol and his son share the pleasure and excitement of the experience. This mutual experience crystallizes what Sol was unable to articulate for his son, "as though he had caught a sudden glimpse of some possibility of the imagination." It resolves the central issue of the story. At least *this* will live beyond him: the appreciation of life and nature, the sensitivity he sees mirrored in his son.

Like Sol in "Revolution," the heroine of "Black Hole" wishes to preserve something intangible. She is Helen, 53 years old, pregnant from a brief liaison with a stranger. The story is told from the point of view of her daughter and son-in-law. Helen has decided to take the emotional and medical risk of going through with the pregnancy, not from any moral or religious conviction, but hoping somehow to preserve the rare experience of this liaison: the magic of the meeting, the coming together, the conception. At the end, the birth of the baby is unresolved, but the birth of Helen's new realization of her own life is accomplished, even blessed by her son-in-law. Like Sol in "Revolution," Helen needs to know that something in her *current* life is worth preserving, worth framing; that there's a chance "for something that till now never existed."

Also like Sol, and like Jarvis in "Reunion," Helen is "suspended between past and present," a theme found in at least half a dozen stories in Swan's first collection. "Losing Game" tells of a man returning to search for his father. Evvie Skyler's poignant revisiting of her life choices in "Decline and Fall" (cited earlier) certainly belongs on this axis. "Rest Stop" is the painful journey of three generations of a family to return home in an automobile after struggling to make ends meet in another city. In "The Wayward Path" an elderly woman lives in a town for years but never feels she has found a home among the town's people. At the end she entertains delusions they are stoning her as a witch. "In the True Light of Morning" (cited earlier) tells the story of Ira Jack Dodgett, an itinerant, self-proclaimed minister of God. In the story he tries to help a man return home, finds it burned out, and realizes he himself is no better off. Rachel, in "On the Edge of the Desert," returns home to a dying mother, "suspended between life and death, and she stood suspended between past and present."

How do these earlier Gladys Swan characters react to finding themselves at this precarious overlook on the road from youth to old age? Rachel is able to take solace in her image of the desert flowers, their "continuity of form, of life holding onto its precarious existence by preserving the precious water." Jason Hummer in "Losing Game" is able to take comfort in imagining his father has given him his paternal blessing as he moves on. But in these stories the characters like as not come out of the experience filled with terror (like Ira Dodgett, at the end of "In the True Light of Morning"), or despair and confusion (like Papaw at the startling denouement of "Rest Stop"), or vivid delusions of persecution (like Sibyl Gunther in the last scene of "The Wayward Path").

For these latter characters, their worst fears have been realized: their lives *have* been wasted. Among all of Swan's fictions, their stories most closely fit Edward Engelberg's model in *Elegiac Fictions,* his recent study of the motif of the unlived (wasted) life. He says:

> The mixture of memory and desire perfectly describes the emotional stress of the observer of waste: what memory there is will be disjunctive; what desire there is will be frustrated.

It is of interest that Engelberg cites T. S. Eliot's reference to memory and desire in the opening lines of *The Waste Land.*

> April is the cruellest month, breeding
> Lilacs out of the dead land, mixing
> Memory and desire, stirring
> Dull roots with spring rain.

Meanwhile, Swan's source for "memory and desire," given in the epigraph to the collection bearing that title, is the more hopeful line of Stendahl's: "It is always somewhere in the stirrings of memory that desire is born." And for Swan's characters, in general, the future represents hope more than futility or despair. Certainly Jarvis ("Reunion"), Sol ("On the Eve of the Next Revolution"), and Helen ("Black Hole") feel they *can* avoid the failed life.

The tendency toward hope rather than despair energizes the characters of Swan's forthcoming (1991) collection, *Do You Believe in Cabeza de Vaca?* These characters are a far cry from those cited in Engelberg's study, are even more hopeful than characters in Swan's first two collections: for example, the despairing and confused Evvie Skyler and Beulah Grenebaum from *On the Edge of the Desert,* or Fannie Wasserman or the frightened Willa in *Of Memory and Desire.*

In the upcoming collection, relationships are increasingly important to the narrative personae. In her first two collections Swan draws relationships between characters and their alter egos (Sally and Pilar, Ira Jack Dodgett and Burl Canady, Evvie Skyler and her older sister, Willa and Mary Jane, Orlie Benedict and "Gaunt Partner"). In her forthcoming collection the relationships are often with younger people, representing hope for the future. In "Tooth," a college janitor invests hope in an undergraduate he befriends. Daniel, of "In the Wilderness", reaches out to the woman friend of a man he knows. The narrator of "Rabbit in the Moon" has hopes for her four-year-old son.

In "The Turkish March," the narrator is hounded by the fractured piano-playing of a neighbor's granddaughter, until the girl becomes ill, and he actually longs for her to resume. Life (even the imperfect life, the "unlived life"—in the case of the granddaughter, "the unpracticed life") is more important than perfection.

Here hope is the watchword, even for the narrator of the powerful title story, "Do You Believe in Cabeza de Vaca?" She refuses to surrender to the past. She shows how fabrication can be used to reverse failures in our past, how fiction overcomes history—or at least, makes it tolerable.

The narrator of "The Rabbit in the Moon" longs for an old partner, but her desire is tentative.

> You think you put somebody behind you, but then something opens up—a life you start to imagine. The things you thought you'd got past wanting.

And she maintains her perspective: "Maybe I could go back if I thought you could go forward." Above all, she retains hope: "The future—somebody's got to reinvent it. Maybe it'll come to me..." She, as well as anyone, expresses in her closing lines the brand of hope found in these new stories: "I figure it this way: You take what you can get. You dream. You lie low."

There is a kinship between this woman and Alta, the heroine of *Carnival for the Gods*. What prevails in both women is the desire—the *need*—to take control of their own lives, rising above failures caused by old loves. Alta not only *feels* she can avoid the failed life: eventually we see her do it.

Before that, however, she too contemplates a wasted past, as in the first chapter of that novel, included in the new collection as a story. Here the carnival is broken down in the middle of the desert. Alta's life reaches a new low. Her rebound eventually provides the force behind the novel.

Once again, fear of the failed life generates the energy for change. "This is my life," Alta thinks. "This is time leaking away, as it has been doing year upon year."

In *Carnival for the Gods* (the novel) Alta seizes control from her husband, Dusty, whose wild dreams and misguided schemes have held her hostage, without a home, without any realistic hope for the future. She sets a new course for herself and the members of Dusty's traveling carnival, eventually leads them to a sort of promised land, where they are transformed into their ideal selves by participating in the ultimate carnival.

The surrealistic novel embodies in the ultimate sense the theme of "characters finding their way." These characters are seeking not just the next town, not just the next phase of their lives, not just their own ideas of success. They seek redemption itself.

The novel is, in fact, a metaphor of life and redemption. The characters are happy as long as they are preparing for a show, the carnival intact. The show makes them work together, brings out the best they can do. For them the carnival provides a chance for real redemption. This is consistent with Judaeo-Christian tradition, which says man is on earth only to fulfill God's will. In *Carnival*, man is on earth to perform in a carnival for the Gods.

The troupe's final show is ended by a hotel fire. But the fire doesn't symbolize their ruin: instead it is a cleansing fire, a purgatorial, reparatory fire, that frees the characters to travel on to the next stage of their redemption.

According to Swan, her new novel, *Ghost Dance: A Play of Voices*, also deals with "a set of characters in search of something to give dimension to their lives, a renewal of energy and direction, a new set of potentials." The treatment will be more realistic than *Carnival*, "even though the action moves into another territory before it's over."

Returning to the recent collection, "Land of Promise" and "Sirens and Voices" continue the theme of characters suspended between past and present. "Land of Promise" is the story of Fanny and Moe. They move to the desert with their two children to accommodate Moe's respiratory ailment. But they both change. Moe loses his drive and ambition, loses interest in his marriage, drawn instead to the beauty and simplicity of the natural surroundings. Fanny becomes an exile, bitter over lost opportunity, full of anxiety about their survival, yet afraid to go back. "It is a terrible thing to leave your home," she says. Fanny longs for the past, for her old home, sees her life in the West as a failure; Moe is satisfied with the academic knowledge of the rocks and surroundings he has gained in his wanderings: "these were all his riches." At the end Moe is trapped by guilt over Fanny's death, over his neglect of her. It is "his gift, or perhaps his curse, to wander the land and never have a home."

Like earlier stories, "Land of Promise" ends with a nature epiphany.

> [Moe's] gaze wandered off to the horizon, where the blue of the distant peaks faded into the inner shell of sky streaked with pink and ivory, far beyond the reach of the eye. It was like a dream. And it seemed as though he could stand there forever listening to the crickets intoning their summer chant, singing of earth and the mountains, of all the things that would never die.

"Sirens and Voices" is the story of Bobby Carmody and her husband, Herman. Bobby embezzles from the men who defrauded her after the death of her father. To her it is occult compensation. Herman is a befuddled spectator in this story, unable to figure out what is driving Bobby, unable to know how to react to the people and events he encounters.

In a sense "Sirens and Voices" and "Land of Promise" are companion stories in that both involve incompatible couples. In "Sirens and Voices," Bobby and Herman counteract one another, not unlike Fanny and Moe in "Land of Promise."

"We were doing all right," says Herman, satisfied with the status quo. "Is that all you can think of?" counters Bobby, impatient to plan their next vacation, begin the next elaborate home decoration project. For her, "home" is an evolving idea. She sees a house with more and finer trappings, elaborate material furnishings; perhaps even an alternate home in Florida, or at least regular vacations there. To Herman, however, "home" means security. Bobby's shenanigans baffle and terrify him, reminding him only of the risk of losing it all.

> Now when he came home in the evenings and stood before the blue house it seemed scarcely real. He stood looking at it as though it might vanish in an instant, go up in a puff of smoke.

As we have seen earlier, a feature of Swan's style is the "nature epiphany"—a moment when the main characters form a communion with nature, with the sun, or a mountain, or a tree, and nature seems to speak to their difficulties. Often these moments seem to occur in "that mysterious ground where Dionysus shakes hands with Apollo," which Swan wrote of as fiction editor of *Intro 12*. Such moments appear regularly in the stories discussed, as well as in her first collection. For example, in "The Peach Tree," near the end of the story, with snow covering the ground and the bushes, the blue and green sky contrasting with the mountains, Beulah Grenebaum celebrates the winter.

> The cold was sharp to breathe as a hound's tooth, but each breath left the sting of ecstasy. A single crystal with an inward spark kept back from the cold: what was it that made life seem a luxury even in this bitter weather?

And at the end Beulah likens the structure of the peach tree to that of the duality of the person, a theme touched on earlier.

> The tree is bare now,...whose twigs and exposed branches made an intricate web against the sky, following the trunk till it entered the snow. And beyond? She tried to imagine how the roots lay in the frozen ground, and saw the woody crown descending and dividing into branches and diminishing into fine hairlike fibers. It was as though...the roots formed an image of the tree itself, a nether tree, that in its descent into the depths and the darkness left her to surmise what hidden life?

The pattern varies in other stories. "On the Edge of the Desert" *begins* with such a scene, as Rachel returns to see in an entirely new light the land where she grew up. Ira Jack Dodgett is not able to gain *solace* from nature at the conclusion of "In the True Light of Morning." Instead, a sunrise "the color of fire or the color of blood" fills him with terror, "as though the world were to be drowned or set ablaze." and in "Rest Stop," the family stops at a clearing where they hope at last to rest and be refreshed by nature, but instead they find the area polluted, infested with flies, unusable.

Swan spoke of these "nature epiphanies" in the *Writers' Forum 16* interview. She said "the land the natural world, seems to me the underlying source of meaningful values." She decried "the materialization and exploitation of the landscape."

> No doubt there will always be a tension between man's technology and his environment, but we've stripped the landscape of spirit, and suffered the consequences. Even so, I think the spiritual aspect still exists as potential. For me the wilderness is the undifferentiated landscape to which you can return to put yourself in touch with the forces, both creative and destructive, that shape our lives. To those who are receptive, a mountain, a tree can speak. That's a good deal of what *Ghost Dance* is about.

So here they are, "suspended between past and present," stranded along the road between youth and old age, searching for homes, striving to avoid failure. How do these characters resolve their difficulties? In "July," the title character does it by betrayal. In "Reunion," Jarvis does it by moving on. In "Rest Stop," Ruby does it by shooting her husband. In "Flight," Orlie Benedict does it by gentle persuasion. But often as not, Swan's characters are like the rest of us:

■ **BOOKS BY GLADYS SWAN**

On the Edge of the Desert. Urbana: University of Illinois Press, 1979.

Carnival for the Gods. New York: Vintage Books, 1986.

Of Memory and Desire. Baton Rouge: Louisiana State University Press, 1987.

Do You Believe in Cabeza de Vaca? Columbia: University of Missouri Press, 1991.

Ghost Dance: A Play of Voices. Baton Rouge: Louisiana State University Press, 1992.

A Visit to Strangers. Columbia: University of Missouri Press, 1996.

News from the Volcano. Columbia: University of Missouri Press, 2000.

they can't always make things turn out the way they'd like, so they compromise, acknowledge the truth, revise their attitudes, make the best of the situations they're in. Like the narrator of "Rabbit in the Moon," they take what they can get, they dream, they lie low.

Often, in their difficulties, these characters look to the land, to nature. What they find are not answers. Instead they find lights, colors, clouds, breezes, smells, feelings, textures; the hush-hush rustling of a herd of goats; the "dark exultation" of a "feather drawn by the ink;" a bowl of fresh cherries; the smell "of things growing in the soil, reaching for their summer;" the sight of a coyote escaping through the woods; the "sound of voices and the smell of chili"— stuff that does not give them answers, but nevertheless comforts and reassures them; that helps them continue along the road from youth to old age; that enables them to find their way.

Ed Weyhing
December, 1990

UPDATE

Novelist and short-story writer Gladys Swan has since published three collections of stories, *Do You Believe in Cabeza de Vaca?* (1991), *A Visit to Strangers* (1996), and *News from the Volcano* (2000), and a novel, *Ghost Dance: A Play of Voices* (1992).

Swan once wrote for *Contemporary Authors,* "What I am trying to communicate through my fiction is a way of perceiving, a way of knowing and responding to experience that goes beyond the intellect of the rational mind. What some people have been ready to call 'mood' in my stories is to my mind that area of sensibility evoked by image and which is the province of imagination, intuition, and feeling. My efforts in my stories have been to explore what seems to me a largely neglected area of the psyche, particularly in modern America."

She travels a good deal, too, especially to Europe. "Travel is of most importance to my work," Swan continued in the same essay. "Not only is it fruitful to see how other people respond to their surroundings and create a certain culture in relation to them, but traveling takes one out of the structures he is accustomed to and forces him to look with a different eye. Good literature should do the same."

In a review of her story collection *Do You Believe in Cabeza De Vaca?,* *Publishers Weekly* praised "the author's ability to convey entangling emotions," about "lives in varieties of disrepair." The same publication gave an appreciative critique of her next volume of stories, *A Visit to Strangers*: "Each of these 13 short stories has a haunting, raw and melancholy tone as Swan's characters twist painfully at the end of their emotional tethers. . . . Not for the faint of heart, these stories may be serious and even dour, but they are also distinctive and, above all, memorable." *News from the Volcano,* however, got a mild review. "Swan portrays America's troubled desert Southwest. Hers are memorable pictures—though they often strain for significance," wrote *Publishers Weekly.* The characters—amid their "dusty mesas and towns," convenience stores, and truck stops—"try and often fail to fend off the bleakness of their lives and their landscape." The novella contained therein, "Gate of Ivory, Gate of Horn," got the best review of the book: "a moving look at the dilemmas of a family and of a region."

Her most recent novel, *Ghost Dance*, "mixes past and present, reality and illusion, in a powerful, if fragmented narrative," wrote *Publishers Weekly*. "Swan has an acute eye and writes with strength. Although her ultimate message of rebirth and redemption is partly shrouded in hazy mysticism, she calls forth the Native American past and evokes the fantastic in the midst of the ordinary."

The Meditative Eye of Charles Tomlinson

■ **I**

Charles Tomlinson's poetry tempts one to adjectives like "restrained," "modest," "exquisite," "moral," "patient," and "attentive." He is the most fastidious and observant of poets, scrupulously probing into the world around him, continually noticing the fluctuations in that world's appearance. He has a physical and metaphysical concern with the shimmer and glamour of surfaces and for him, as for Ruskin and Stevens, "the greatest poverty is not to live in a physical world." By now all readers of Tomlinson's poetry must know that he is a painter as well as a poet, and indeed he brings to his poems a painter's sensitivity to the importance of exteriors. He shares with some of the painters he most admires (such as Constable and Eakins) an attentiveness to physical detail, an objective concern with the shadings and shadows of landscape, a wonder before the natural object, a fidelity to the nuances of light and darkness. A moral sense informs Tomlinson's respect for the Other—both human and nonhuman—and much of his work investigates the complex relationship between the observer and the observed. The poems not only see, they are about the difficult and creative act of seeing. This in turn leads him to investigate the paradox of a dual allegiance to the shaping imagination and to the splendors of the unshaped natural world.

In the measure of his interests and in the measured way they are presented in the poetry, Tomlinson has some clear American prototypes and analogues. American connections are very much to the point since no other English poet has been more deeply influenced by, or attentive to, American poetry. Tomlinson's carefully noticed moral landscapes have much in common with the blocked observations of Marianne Moore (in Miss Moore's exemplary case one uses the word "poems" advisedly and only for lack of a more appropriate word) and the sharply focused "machines" of William Carlos Williams. His concern with the shifting relationship between appearance and reality is reminiscent of Stevens, but the austerity of his presentation has more in common with the Objectivists. In fact, one of the paradoxes, indeed one of the pleasures of reading Tomlinson's work, involves watching how the extravagant painterly sensibility of, say, a Stevens can be tempered by and reflected through the stringent imaginings of, say, a Zukofsky. But although Tomlinson has deep affinities with Stevens and Moore, Pound, Williams, and Zukofsky, Bishop, Bronk, and Oppen, he is very much his own poet and has created his own singular body of work. When his *Selected Poems* are published later this spring [1978]I believe we will begin to see just how solid and definitive that body of work actually is. To my mind Charles Tomlinson is one of the most astute, disciplined, and lucent poets of his generation. He is one of the few English poets to have extended the inheritance of modernism and I suspect that his quiet meditative voice will reverberate on both sides of the Atlantic for a long time to come.

Charles Tomlinson

Alfred Charles Tomlinson was born in Stoke-on-Trent, Staffordshire, England, in 1927. He was educated at Queens College, Cambridge, and London University. He has traveled in the United States on a fellowship with the Institute of International Education. He was a visiting fellow at Princeton University and taught at the University of New Mexico in Albuquerque as a visiting professor of English literature. From 1956 until 1992, he served on the English faculty at the University of Bristol. He and his wife, Brenda, live in Gloucestershire, England. ■

■ II

Tomlinson's first pamphlet, *Relations and Contraries* (1951), is weak and wholly derivative in uncharacteristic ways. The title resonates throughout Tomlinson's work, but only one poem from the book, somewhat chastely entitled "Poem," survives into the *Selected Poems*. It is with *The Necklace* (1955) that Tomlinson finds his characteristic subject and theme, although not quite his most natural manner, and it is here that any reading of the work must begin. Written under the elegant sign of Stevens (in what Stevens calls "the Italy of the mind"), *The Necklace* is a book of jewels and flutes, irised mornings and olive twilights. It does not quite escape its Stevensian echoes (Tomlinson's jewels are both more precious and more delicate than Stevens' wild diamonds) but the poems do sometimes swerve away from Stevens' influence and at such moments Italy becomes a plainer, barer, and altogether less Romantic and chimerical place. The weather, like the tone, is often slightly chilly in Tomlinson's finest poems, "the air / is unfit for politicians and romantics." His most decisive poems have edges and outlines, the sharp sculptural clarity of crystal. But most important is the fact that *The Necklace* declares the subject and the aesthetic of Tomlinson's work: the art and act of seeing, of noticing relations and contraries, of making space articulate. The poem "Aesthetic" is an early Ars Poetica.

> Reality is to be sought, not in concrete,
> But in space made articulate:
> The shore, for instance,
> Spreading between wall and wall;
> The sea-voice
> Tearing the silence from the silence.

Marking the voice between silence and silence, sighting the expanse of shore spreading between wall and wall; these are cognitive and creative acts, the way to search for and, hopefully, to discover reality. Tomlinson attends to the concrete in all its particularity, but the poems continually tell us that, for art, what matters is not the single object but the object in relationship to other objects, the tissue of relations that hold together the world.

The relationship between the voice (or in the case of the painter, the hand) and the eye is a complex one. No poem is more central to Tomlinson's early work than "Thirteen Ways of Looking at a Blackbird." (Donald Davie first noticed the centrality of Stevens to the development of Tomlinson's art in his perceptive introduction to *The Necklace*. Tomlinson himself comments on the "dialogue with and departure from" Stevens in his preface to the 1966 reprinting of the book.) Tomlinson's "Nine Variations in a Chinese Winter Setting," "Eight Observations on the Nature of Eternity," "Suggestions for the Improvement of a Sunset," and "Observation of Facts," all tell us, in one way or another, that our sight is provisional, that "Six points of vantage provide us with six sunsets." "Flute Music" relates that

> There is a moment for speech and for silence.
> Lost between possibilities
> But deploring a forced harmony,
> We elect the flute.
>
> A season, defying gloss, may be the sum
> Of blue water beneath green rain;
> It may comprise comets, days, lakes
> Yet still bear the exegesis of music.

The music's difficult job is to create a harmony (unforced), to gloss a season (which defies gloss), to govern "the ungovernable wave." It must translate the provisional world in all of its fullness (what we see) into the language of consonant forms (what we hear).

> Seeing and speaking we are two men:
> The eye encloses as a window—a flute
> Governs the land, its winter and its silence.

It is the supreme exegetical function of art to circumscribe the moonlight, to speak of the unspeakable, to embody in song the diversity and economy of the phenomenal world. The flute must move "with equal certainty" (and fidelity) "through a register of palm-greens and flesh-rose."

Such work demands a delicate balance: it eschews an extravagant Romanticism; it shuns "a brittle and false union." Tomlinson's aesthetic of quiet attentiveness stands in a calm Wordsworthian light; it also stands at the opposite end and indeed takes as its enemy—at the moment somewhat unfashionably so—the grandiloquent and frenzied propulsions of, say, a Shelley. It refuses the projection of the self onto a mute natural world. "Through Binoculars" speaks of a saving normalcy and tells us "Binoculars are the last phase in a Romanticism." A later poem, "Farewell to Van Gogh," announces that, despite Van Gogh's "instructive frenzy,"

> The world does not end tonight
> And the fruit that we shall pick tomorrow
> Await us, weighing the unstripped bough.

But it is not until he takes the lucid step into his first full-scale collection, *Seeing Is Believing*, that Tomlinson's anti-Romanticism deepens into a profound mediative stance.

■ III

In *Seeing Is Believing* (1958) Tomlinson extends his subject and finds his characteristic voice. One has the impression of an exact and chaste mind registering the felicities of the thing seen, taking cognizance of the world's "spaces, patterns, textures." The poems begin with the visible, with the particular, but in the act of looking there is already what he will later call "a grasping for significance." From Ruskin he has learned that the work of art demands "First the felicities, then / The feelings to appraise them." So the particular radiates outwards, growing into meaning; the meaning inheres in the relationship between the thing seen and the eye seeing. And it is a very delicate human instrument that can translate the nuances of the visible into the rhythms of the spoken. There are any number of such correspondences between sight and sound in *Seeing Is Believing*: the slow, bulky movement of oxen in "Oxen: Ploughing at Fiesole," the clean, paring motion of "Paring the Apple," the momentary looming of clouds in "A Meditation on John Constable." Here is how "The Atlantic" precisely replicates the unfolding of a wave.

> Launched into an opposing wind, hangs
>   Grappled beneath the onrush,
> And there, lifts, curling in spume,
>   Unlocks, drops from that hold
> Over and shoreward. The beach receives it,
>   A whitening line, collapsing
> Powdering-odd down its broken length;
>   Then, curdled, shallow, heavy
> With clustering bubbles, it hears
>   In a slow sheet that must climb
> Relinquishing its power, upward
>   Across tilted sand.

In an interview (*Contemporary Literature*, Volume 16, No. 4, Autumn 1975) Tomlinson summarized the implications and the ethical basis of his own celebration of particularity. It is a celebration that hinges on the engagement of the eye, the contemplation of an object that, in the simple privileged status of its being, draws us into the pressures of a relationship and, in so doing, saves us from the false engagements of isolation. Tomlinson writes,

> In my own case I should add that the particular, rather than existing in its own isolate intensity, means first of all the demands of a relationship—you are forced to look, feel, find words for something not yourself—and it means, like all relationships, a certain forgetfulness of self, so that in contemplating something, you are drawn out of yourself towards that and towards other people—other people, because, though the words you use are *your* words, they are also *their* words; you are learning about the world by using the common inheritance of language. And once you are moving on into your poem, rather than "isolate intensity," you are aware of belonging among objects and among human beings and it is a great stay for the mind, this awareness. And a great chastener in that you realize that you in your *own* isolate intensity would be an egotist and a bore.

And so the "labour of observation" is also the human labor of speaking to men. In the same interview Tomlinson tells us that "The celebration here is not only a celebration of objects, but of the forms of language we choose to articulate the sense of objects bodied over against us." Thus the poet's dual allegiance to the texture of the world and to the texture of the word.

Tomlinson's finest poems argue by arguing nothing; they illustrate by the simple example of their making. Certain visual artists (usually realists of one stripe or another) are for him exemplary presences; their formidable job is to detail the exterior world in all the manifestations of its complexity while, simultaneously, mapping the region of their own interiors. Cézanne at Aix confronts the same mountain "each day / Immobile like fruit." His difficult task is to transcribe the present moment, the looming mountain "there / In its weathered weight." "A Meditation on John Constable" tells us that

> Art
> Is complete when it is human. It is human
> Once the looped pigments, the pin-heads of light
> Securing space under their deft restrictions
> Convince, as the index of a possible passion,
> As the adequate gauge, both of the passion
> And its object. The artist lies
> For the improvement of truth. Believe him.

But Tomlinson's poems tell us again and again that we may only believe the artist when the work appears as an adequate gauge "of the passion and its object," with equal fidelity to both.

■ IV

A Peopled Landscape (1963) and *American Scenes* (1966) develop and extend Tomlinson's central theme while adding a new dimension to his work. As the work progresses that theme finds its way closer and closer to a full articulation. Its announced intention is to save the appearances, to treat a landscape "where what appears, is." In a recent memoir Tomlinson restates his basic principle as such: "that one does not need to go beyond any sense experience to some mythic union, that the 'I' can be responsible only by relationship and not by dissolving itself away in ecstacy." (Tomlinson's memoir, "Some American Poets: A Personal Record," in *Contemporary Literature*, Volume 18, No. 3 (Summer 1977) pp. 279–304, is particularly useful for an account of his literary relations to America.) The moral imperative of that theme is to approach the Other with a hard, contemplative eye, to caress and embody, to render and enact, always remembering the Stevensian proposition that "a fat woman / by Rubens / is not a fat / woman but a fiction." In a similar way William Carlos Williams categorically proposed "No ideas but in things" without forgetting that the writing is always of words. Tomlinson's finest poems, like Williams', are verbally rooted in a physical locality. His work proposes, as Marianne Moore's does, "a moral terrain where you must confront nature."

The references to Williams and Moore are appropriate since they are the guiding presences in much of Tomlinson's work. In *A Peopled Landscape* and *American Scenes* Tomlinson's flirtation with America (and with American poetry) is blown into a full-scale love affair. It was through the services of Hugh Kenner that *Seeing Is Believing* was published in America well before it found an English publisher (a neat reversal of the Frostian formula), and it is not surprising that Tomlinson first found an American audience and home. While remaining English in character, his work is essentially tuned to the homemade (the word is Kenner's) visual aesthetic of the most scrupulous American moderns.

These books illustrate Tomlinson's "dialogue with the spirit of the U.S." in a number of ways. On a personal level they recall his first visit to America and his subsequent year-long sojourn in New Mexico. Thus many of the poems are physically rooted in American territory, particularly in the Southwest. Of greater significance is the fact that those poems which return to Tomlinson's own region do so with a new philosophical disposition to the local that in part derives from Williams and Moore. Many of the poems in *A Peopled Landscape* also employ the triadic stanza (staggered tercets) that are so readily associated with the poems of Williams's maturity. Poems like "Up at La Serra" and "The Picture of J.T. in a Prospect of Stone" are English in idiom ("Picture" of course recalls Marvell's famous poem of a similar title) but are formally characteristic of American modernism. (Olson's projective verse essay is also of relevance here.) To my mind Tomlinson never quite shapes the triadic stanza to his own hand (except perhaps in his imaginative translations of Machado) and after *A Peopled Landscape* few poems in tercets appear. But the experimentation with Williams' form introduced a new flexibility into Tomlinson's line, a new sense of ceremonious and sometimes hesitating motion and, consequently, his newfound sense of rhythmic possibility infused and energized the major blank and free verse poems of the three volumes that follow *American Scenes*.

A Peopled Landscape and *American Scenes* also introduce a notable new element into the landscape of Tomlinson's poetry: people. Seashores and mountains are generally the major characters in a Tomlinson poem, but increasingly over the past fifteen years he has turned his scrupulous eye to field hands and weeping women, Hopi Indians and desert motel owners. To be sure the task remains the same: "to obliterate mythology," to treat the human element with the same watchfulness, care, reticence, and respect that one accords to nature. An earlier poem ("Paring the Apple") warns us that "There are portraits and still-lifes / And the first, because "human" / Does not excel the second." And yet the introduction of people into Tomlinson's peopleless universe does bring with it a welcome note of lightness, warmth, wryness, and humor. Here one may find Mr. Brodsky, an American "whose professed and long / pondered-on passion / was to become a Scot"; Chief Standing Water who reads Madame Blavatsky and overcharges for hotel rooms; Homer Vance, the old Hopi doll-maker who died "beating a burro out of his corn patch"; and even Roy Rogers makes an appearance in Barstow, for it was here that he spent a night in a motel "at that execrable junction / of gasoline and desert air." These characters prefigure later presences like Carlos Trujillo, who killed a mountain wolf "so that birds should have meat," and the three bums—one female, one drunk, one mad—of "Terminal Tramps." There are also somewhat pastoral figures who appear in "Return to Hinton" and "The Hand at Callow Hill Farm." That farm hand, for example, seems to enact characteristic Tomlinsonian virtues.

> Silence. The man defined
> The quality, ate at his separate table
> Silent, not because silence was enjoined
> But was his nature. It shut him round
> Even at outdoor tasks, his speech
> Following upon a pause, as though
> A hesitance to comply had checked it—
> Yet comply he did, and willingly:
> Pause and silence: both
> Were essential graces, a reticence
> Of the blood, whose calm concealed
> The tutelary of that upland field.

For Tomlinson, "pause and silence," and "a reticence of the blood," are essential virtues. The locale may be Taos, Fiascherino, or Bristol, but the qualities he admires remain the same. And of course the world remains "a presence which does not present itself" whether one engages the deserts of New Mexico, the pebble beaches of Italy, or the manscapes of England. It is also in the fortunate condition of things that men are as much a part of nature as mountains and seashores, that seashores may share their sliding surfaces with poems, that poems may share their modest insights with men.

■ **V**

The Way of a World (1969) and *Written on Water* (1972) continue Tomlinson's delicate negotiations with the world. Negotiations (the title of the first section of *American Scenes*) involve interchange, balance, a healthy and sustaining respect for the Other. The chief negotiations of these two books are with water and time, each with its possibilities, recurrences, and contingencies, each with its merciful gifts and merciless denials. "Swimming Chenango Lake" is the major poem of Tomlinson's maturity, the central poem of his central theme; in it we see a mind of acute delicacy returning to its first concerns, asking and modifying its recurrent questions. The poem begins, as so many Tomlinson poems begin, with an observer reading the water's appearance.

> Winter will bar the swimmer soon.
> 　　He reads the water's autumnal hesitations
> A wealth of ways: it is jarred,
> 　　It is astir already despite its steadiness…

Over a third of the poem studies, in careful hesitating rhythms, "the geometry of water," but at a certain moment the eye must recall its dependence on the body, the swimmer must entrust himself to the lake.

> 　　But he has looked long enough, and now
> Body must recall the eye to its dependence
> 　　As he scissors the waterscape apart
> And sways it to tatters. Its coldness
> 　　Holding him to itself, he grants the grasp,
> For to swim is also to take hold
> 　　On water's meaning, to move in its embrace
> And to be, between grasp and grasping, free.

Between grasp and grasping the swimmer encounters "the all but penetrable element" learning that water is "a possession to be relinquished / Willingly at each stroke."

> Human, he fronts it and, human, he draws back
> 　　From the interior cold, the mercilessness
> That yet shows a kind of mercy sustaining him.

And so the swimmer moves through a non-human element, above and yet inside its "tiny shatterings," establishing his relation to a world that sustains and yet is alien to him. The careful swimmer knows enough to respect the water, acknowledging its murky depths, knowing it also as the necessary element of his movement. There can be no reduction of relations: the water is, simultaneously, merciless and merciful.

In a way all of the sea poems in *Written on Water* (Section 1 is called "Sea Pieces"; Section 2 "By the Middle Sea") comment on this poem. Most aptly, "On Water" tells us that the sea "confers / as much as it denies: / we are orphaned and fathered / by such solid vacancies:." It is through our dealings with water; it is by contemplating the meaning of what we are not that we might yet establish our right relations to the exterior world and hence might also discover both what we are and what we might be. That meditation carries its burden of responsibility. The world makes its own silent demands. The cold hills in "Appearance" draw us "to a reciprocation," asking "words of us, answering images." Those answering images are the poet's art.

As water confers and denies, so does time, emptying us with its paucity and filling us with its fullness, asking our consent. "In the Fullness of Time" (a letter to Octavio Paz) tells us that "the day goes / Down, but there is time before it goes / To negotiate a truce in time." That truce involves a commitment to the quotidian world, to what Randall Jarrell calls "the dailiness of life." In the evanescences of daily air one may discover that

> It is the shape of change, and not the bare
> Glancing vibrations, that vein and branch
>   Through the moving textures: we grasp
> The way of a world in the seed, the gull
>   Swayed toiling against the two
> Gravities that root and uproot the trees.
> **("The Way of a World")**

For the Augustan poet with his modest and hesitating sense of the slow arc of day and night, the shape of change may have its own seemly aspect. Time asks our consent,

> And how should we not consent? For time
>   Putting its terrors by, it was as if
> The unhurried sunset were itself a courtesy.
> **("In the Fullness of Time")**

The unhurried sunset that is itself a courtesy: there is no more appropriate embodiment of Tomlinson's cordial and courteous sense of his own relations to the world.

This is perhaps the appropriate moment to register my dissatisfaction with the poems when they descend from a saving normalcy into an argumentativeness with suicides and romantics. Tomlinson's sense of courtesy, ritual, ceremony, and tradition sometimes leads him to political and antirevolutionary poems ("Prometheus," "The Assassin") which are heavyhanded and moralizing in their pronouncements that "He who howls / with the whirlwind, with the whirlwind goes down." It is too often an unsympathetic set of opinions that keeps telling us how much a Genet missed of the world, how little a Van Gogh understood sequentiality. We are a little too often reminded that "The times / spoiled children threaten, what they will do." And yet, perhaps I am mistaken, for Tomlinson's political notions sometimes root down to another layer of feeling. From its initial complaint, "Against Extremity" deepens like a coastal shell into a kind of prayer.

> Against extremity, let there be
>   Such treaties as only time itself
> Can ratify, a bond and test
>   Of sequential days, and like the full
> Moon slowly given to the night,
>   A possession that is not to be possessed.

There can be no doubt that these lines come from the same cautious hand that has also written, convincingly, "I have seen Eden."

There is a concise conjoining of the watery imagery and the theme of sequentiality in the "Written on Water" section of "Movements." This is the final section of the penultimate poem of the volume and, as if to complete the arc begun a book earlier with "Swimming Chenango Lake," the poem states

> "Written on water," one might say
> Of each day's flux and lapse,
>   But to speak of water is to entertain the image
> Of its seamless momentum once again,
>   To hear in its wash and grip on stone
> A music of constancy behind

    The wide promiscuity of acquaintanceship,
  Links of water chiming on one another,
      Water-ways permeating the rock of time.

And so the shudder and glimmer of water and time, the shape of change and the waves of constancy. Each day returns another sunset, yet "Six points of vantage provide us with six sunsets." The obligation is to move around the world noticing both the vantage points and the sunsets, scrupulously looking at that precise point where water meets sky. And as soon as one looks the whole man is invested. For we don't see with our eyes, but in some area well behind the retina. And we never see quite the same sunset because we are never quite the same person looking. The prose poem "Skullshapes" makes this quite clear.

> One sees. But not merely the passive mirrorings of the retinal mosaic—nor, like Ruskin's blind man struck suddenly by vision, without memory or conception. The senses, reminded by other seeings, bring to bear on the act of vision their pattern of images; they give point and place to an otherwise naked and homeless impression. It is the mind sees. But what it sees consists not solely of that by which it is confronted grasped in the light of that which it remembers. It sees possibility.

What is, what was, what might be. The world in its fullness may evade rendering, but "the mind is a hunter of forms," and the struggle for articulation is a necessary one. That conjoining of what one sees to what one remembers, that shaping of possibilities and contingencies to the exigencies and restraints of language, that act of making may be called art, that zone of interchange is the imagination.

■ VI

Since *The Way In* (1974) is readily available, only a few of its poems will appear in the *Selected Poems*. But some of the poems that do appear—"The Marl Pits," "At Stoke," "Foxes' Moon," "After a Death"—are among Tomlinson's best. *The Way In* is a book of returns to the manscapes of England, to English elements and seasons. It is, in some ways, a more personal book than any of Tomlinson's others; in "The Marl Pits" the poet breathes "familiar, sedimented air"; in "At Stoke" he speaks of the first single landscape of his childhood. The poem also speaks (implicitly) of the journey to other landscapes (Italy, America) and of the gradual way home.

  I have lived in a single landscape. Every tone
      And turn have had for their ground
  These beginnings in grey-black: a land
      Too handled to be primary—all the same,
  The first in feeling. I thought it once
      Too desolate, diminished and too tame
  To be the foundation for anything. It straggles
      A haggard valley and lets through
  Discouraged greennesses, lights from a pond or two.
      By ash-tips, or where the streets give out
  In cindery in-betweens, the hills
      Swell up and free of it to where, behind
  The whole vapoury, patched battlefield,
      The cows stand steaming in an acrid wind.
  This place, the first to seize on my heart and eye,
      Has been their hornbook and their history.

Most of *The Way In* speaks of a region tamed and handled, manmade, diminished. The poem "Foxes' Moon" presents "night over England's interrupted pastoral." And "After a Death" brings us to a place where "Verse…turns to retrace the path of its dissatisfactions." And yet this patched landscape has its own kind of fullness, its own "language of water, light and air." These churches, wards, midlands, and marl pits have their own kind of insistence; they call the meditating eye to a personal answering song.

The Way In is a gentle book of coming home, of witnessing and remembering, of negotiating with the regions of one's past. I feel certain that when these poems are stacked together with the new poems that will appear in a book to be called *The Shaft*, they will further demonstrate Tomlinson's unique moral imagination and deep reflective range. The poems in *The Shaft* continue to balance loss and metamorphosis, constancy and change, sunsets and dawn. They speak quietly of a singular past, but of even greater significance, they continue to encounter "the moment itself / abrupt in the pure surprise of seeing" ("The Gap"). No poem speaks more appropriately of Tomlinson's saving and graceful sense of the world than "Rhymes" which tells us

> Word and world rhyme
> As the penstrokes might if you drew
> The spaciousness reaching down through a valley view,
> Gathering the lines into its distances
> As if they were streams, as if they were eye-beams:
> Perfect, then, the eye's command in its riding,
> Perfect the coping hand, the hillslopes
> Drawing it into such sight the sight would miss,
> Guiding the glance the way perfection is.

Charles Tomlinson's coping hand continues to probe into the surfaces around us, to guide us on a pleasurable and measured journey into the natural world. We may not ever arrive, but his life's work certainly helps us to glance, however imperfectly, "the way perfection is."

Edward Hirsch
April, 1978

UPDATE

Since this essay appeared, Charles Tomlinson has published more than a dozen volumes of poetry, including: *The Shaft* (1978), *Selected Poems, 1951–1974* (1978), *Airborn/Hijos del aire* (with Octavio Paz, in English and Spanish) (1981), *Notes from New York, and Other Poems* (1984), *Collected Poems, 1951–1981* (1986), *The Return* (1987), *Annunciations* (1989), *Selected Poems* (1989), *The Door in the Wall* (1992), *Jubilation* (1995), *Selected Poems, 1955–1997* (1997), and *The Vineyard Above the Sea* (2000). He also published another volume, *Eden: Graphics and Poems* (1985), for which he produced the artwork.

For more than forty years, Tomlinson, an artist as well as a poet, has proven himself a master of his craft, and is admired for his breadth of knowledge, technical skill, and painterly imagery. Although regarded by many as a major talent, he has never been seen as such in his native England. This may be due in part to his international sensibility: he is also a translator fluent in French, Italian, and German, he frequently writes about his extensive travels, and he has looked to America both for subject matter and poetic mentorship, especially the modernists. Critics in England "get [a] wild smell of [William Carlos] Williams off his work," suggested the *New York Times Book Review*.

Although *World Literature Today* criticized Tomlinson's *Selected Poems, 1955–1997* for giving the reader more expectation than fulfillment, it stated that the collection has "a certain

■ BOOKS BY CHARLES TOMLINSON

Relations and Contraries. Aldington, Kent, U.K.: Hand and Flower Press, 1951.

The Necklace. Eynsham, U.K.: Fantasy Press, 1955.

Solo for a Glass Harmonica. San Francisco: Westerham Press, 1957.

Seeing Is Believing. New York: McLeod, 1958.

A Peopled Landscape. London: Oxford University Press, 1963.

Poems: A Selection (With Tony Connor and Austin Clarke). London: Oxford University Press, 1964.

American Scenes. London: Oxford University Press, 1966.

The Poem as Initiation. Hamilton, N.Y.: Colgate University Press, 1968.

The Matachines: New Mexico. Cerillos, N.M.: San Marcos Press, 1968.

To Be Engraved on the Skull of a Cormorant. London: Unaccompanied Serpent, 1968.

America West Southwest. Cerillos, N.M.: San Marcos Press, 1969.

The Way of a World. London: Oxford University Press, 1969.

Words and Images. London: Covent Garden Press, 1972.

Written on Water. London: Oxford University Press, 1972.

The Way In. London: Oxford University Press, 1974.

In Black and White (graphics). Manchester, England: Carcanet, 1976.

The Shaft. London: Oxford University Press, 1978.

Selected Poems 1951–1974. London: Oxford University Press, 1978.

Airborn/Hijos del Aire (With Octavio Paz). London: Camden House, 1981.

Some Americans. Berkeley: University of California Press, 1981.

The Flood. London: Oxford University Press, 1981.

Poetry and Metamorphosis (lectures). London: Cambridge University Press, 1984.

Notes from New York, and Other Poems. London: Oxford University Press, 1984.

Eden: Graphics and Poems. Bristol, U.K.: Redcliffe Press, 1985.

Collected Poems, 1951–1981. London: Oxford University Press, 1986; as *Collected Poems* (expanded), Toronto: Exile Editions, 1989.

The Return. Oxford: Oxford University Press, 1987.

Annunciations. Oxford: Oxford University Press, 1989.

The Door in the Wall. Oxford: Oxford University Press, 1992.

Jubilation. Oxford: Oxford University Press, 1995.

Selected Poems: 1955–1997. New York: New Directions, 1997.

William Carlos Williams & Charles Tomlinson: A Transatlantic Connection (With William Carlos Williams). New York: Peter Lang Publishing, 1999.

The Vineyard Above the Sea. Manchester, England: Carcanet Press, 1999.

American Essays. Manchester, England: Carcanet Press, 2001.

edited by charles tomlinson

Marianne Moore: A Collection of Critical Essays. London: Prentice-Hall, 1972.

William Carlos Williams. London: Penguin, 1972.

command of language that is impressive . . ., and an air of presenting a miracle in words if one will just trust him enough to see him through." The same publication noted his "unpretentious" recent book, *The Vineyard Above the Sea,* for the "subtle verbal music in his phrases that leads one on from poem to poem." In the title poem, he describes an Italian landscape near a village called Corniglia with "the sort of loving detail a native of the place might envy," Throughout, his descriptions are imagistic, concrete, supple, and brief, and he "packs his short poems with intensity, forcing the reader to take them slowly and think his way through them." While the book may be limited, "it has the understated dexterity that is manifest in all of [Tomlinson's work]. . . . [A]s a poet he has been consistently compelling for over forty years, and that is a record few could match."

Belonging
Nowhere,
Seeing Everywhere:
William Trevor
and the Art of
Distance

∎∎∎

At the age of sixty-five William Trevor has written some twenty books of fiction that for range of effect—philosophical density, exactness of style and idiom, variety of character, comic depth, and tragic intensity—have been unequaled among contemporary writers of English fiction since the death of Patrick White. Trevor is a precise workman, as befits the sculptor that he was in early life; his fiction does not sprawl and heave and occasionally founder as does that of, say, White or Faulkner; and because he does not take huge risks and gamble his literary capital on big, ambitious, and complicated novels such as *Riders in the Chariot* and *Absalom, Absalom!*, he probably won't win a Nobel prize despite the considerable measure of his achievement. Trevor has earned continuing recognition in Ireland and England, including a C.B.E.; but he remains relatively neglected in the United States, despite having been awarded a Bennett prize by the *Hudson Review* in 1990 and having regularly appeared in the *New Yorker* and *Harper's* for some years.

In the thirty years of his publishing career Trevor has never lacked an audience. *The Old Boys* (1964), his first novel, was a Book-of-the-Month Club selection, and it won the Hawthornden prize in England.

As a writer one doesn't belong anywhere. Fiction writers, I think, are even more outside the pale. Because society and people are our meat, one doesn't really belong in the midst of society. The great challenge in writing is always to find the universal in the local, the parochial. And to do that, one needs distance.

∎ **WILLIAM TREVOR (1993)**

No one has had a closer vision, or a hand at once more ironic and more tender, for the individual figure. He sees it with all its minutest signs and tricks—all its heredity of idiosyncrasies, all its particulars of weakness and strength, of ugliness and beauty, of oddity and charm; and yet it is of his essence that he sees it in the general flood of life, steeped in its relations and contacts, struggling or submerged.

∎ **HENRY JAMES, "TURGENEV" (1897)**

The ensuing years have brought more honors and a growing critical recognition, but it puzzles me that Trevor's star is not in a still greater ascendant. One reason is that he isn't a flashy writer, nor a self-promoter. And he hasn't reached his proper audience in this country partly because the English dramatizations of his fiction have seldom, if ever, been broadcast on PBS.

Trevor's second collected stories (1992) did make a great impression in the U.S. The *Times Book Review* ran a long and brilliant piece by Reynolds Price in February 1993. This big book, which contains about ninety stories, deserves a place on the same shelf of short fiction with Frank O'Connor and Elizabeth Bowen, Ernest Hemingway and Eudora Welty, A. E. Coppard and V. S. Pritchett. Now that Miss Welty and Sir Victor have quit publishing fiction, Trevor stands as the best writer of short fiction in the English language. ("The modern short story deals in moments and subtleties and shadows of grey," he has written. "It tells as little as it dares.")

William Trevor

Born William Trevor Cox in 1928 in County Cork, Ireland, the author had his early education in provincial Irish schools and attended Trinity College, Dublin. At one time he considered a career as a sculptor, and he won a sculpture competition, Irish section, in 1953. Since he turned to writing, he has won many distinctions, among them the Hawthornden Award, the Royal Society of Literature Award, and the Whitbread Award. In 1972 he won a Society of Authors traveling scholarship, and he was awarded the Allied Irish Bank Prize for Literature in 1978. A year later he was made Commander, Order of the British Empire. Trevor has also won the following awards: the *Sunday Express* Book of the Year Award and the Whitbread Book of the Year award (both 1994), both for *Felicia's Journey*; the Lannan Literary Award for Fiction (1996); and the *Irish Times* Literary Award for Fiction (2001) for *The Hill Bachelors*. In 1999 his story *Felicia's Journey* was adapted as a film by Atom Egoyan.

Married and the father of two sons, he makes his home in Devon. ■

No one in his right mind would argue that, say, John Updike is William Trevor's equal; and his countryman John McGahern, who has occasionally rivaled Trevor in such superb stories as "The Country Funeral," is much more uneven in his short fiction, which hiccoughs from sketches and anecdotes to fully realized stories. McGahern's collected stories (1992) include only a dozen or so works that measure up to Trevor's consistently higher standard and achievement.

This brings us to the matter of William Trevor's nationality. There would be little question of where his real sympathies lie, even had he not settled the matter. "I am Irish absolutely to the last vein in my body." Ireland, he continues, is "the country you put first, the country you feel strongest about, the country that you actually love." But, he adds, "If I had stayed in Ireland…, I certainly wouldn't have written. I needed the distance in order to write."

William Trevor began his writing career with two splendid comedies about London—*The Old Boys* (1964) and *The Boarding-House* (1965). These were struck in the vein of Jonsonian humor that runs through Dickens to the early Waugh. Trevor hasn't abandoned this mode, which in his hands never descends to caricature; but he has moved a great distance from it in the succeeding decades. The reason that his characters have grown more complex and sympathetic may be inferred from an observation he made with asperity to Stephen Schiff when Schiff was writing about Trevor for the *New Yorker* (January 4, 1993). (This piece is itself Jonsonian in its maker's delineations of Trevor's physiognomy.) "The thing I hate most of all is the pigeonholing of people…. I don't believe in the black-and-white; I believe in the gray shadows, the murkiness, the not quite knowing, and the fact that you can't ever say 'old spinster' or 'dirty old man.'" (What Trevor has said of Pritchett's characters applies equally well to his own: "As real people do, they resist the labels of good or bad; they are decent on their day, some experiencing more of those days than others do.") Although many figures of this kind—apparent stereotypes—appear in both *The Old Boys* and *The Boarding-House* and although they are flat characters for the most part, their portraits, limned thirty years ago, do not violate the axiom that Trevor has recently declared, for he has followed it from the beginning.

To say, for instance, that any of the unmarried women in *The Boarding-House*—Nurse Clock, Rose Cave, Gallelty, Miss Clericot—is simply or only a spinster is to do great violence to Trevor's delicate portraiture, especially the characterization of Nurse Clock. The same applies to the more numerous cast of aging men, from Studdy, a petty blackmailer and thief; to Major Eele, whose taste for pornography far outruns his impulse for romance; to Tome Obd, a mad Nigerian; to Mr Scribbin, whose only delight is listening to records that reproduce the sounds of trains. This teeming cast of eccentrics and misfits, male and female, could comfortably and believably have appeared in Jonson's *Bartholomew Fair* or Dickens's *Bleak House*.

Trevor, like most first-rate writers, often takes risks that would stop a lesser and more finicky artist in his or her tracks. In *The Boarding-House* he has written a novel without a protagonist—unless, and mark this, that figure is the owner of the boardinghouse, William Wagner Bird, who is the presiding intelligence in this novel (through the agency of his journals—and through his ghostly presence). What is remarkable about that, you may be thinking. The oddity is that Bird dies in the opening scene of the novel. He leaves the boardinghouse to Nurse Clock and Mr. Studdy, who are enemies and are completely unalike and greatly at odds. But for a long period they are forced to become confederates to circumvent Bird's will and change the boardinghouse into a toney nursing home—after they have sacked most of the boarders. Studdy, a wretch and a parasite, is the closest figure to the novel's antagonist. After absorbing a few setbacks, he comes off nearly scot free as the action ends. Mr. Obd, after being thwarted in his protracted courtship of an English woman and having experienced Blakean visions of his late landlord, kills himself and very nearly incinerates all the other boarders. The comedy turns very dark and ends in pathos, which is the way a story or novel by Trevor usually concludes, regardless of how light-hearted or hilarious its action has been earlier.

One lingers in considering a character like Studdy because, as Trevor has said of Pritchett's similar figures, "from their modest foothold on the periphery they rarely inaugurate events, and influence their own destiny through occasional, glancing swipes." It is such people who fascinate Trevor—seemingly ordinary folk who become uncommon when he takes a long hard look at them and reveals their natures to us. The flat characters of the early novels have much in common with the more complicated and complex people who regularly populate the stories because as Trevor develops as a writer he accomplishes what he says of the good story—that it "economically peels off surfaces." He hit his natural stride by the seventies as the stories reprinted in *The Ballroom of Romance* (1972), *Angels at the Ritz* (1975), and *Lovers of Their Time* (1978) abundantly demonstrate. In such first-rate stories as "In Isfahan," "Angels at the Ritz," "Matilda's England," and "Torridge" Trevor shows his mastery of the form. "He manages to stuff a short story with as much emotional incident as most people cram into a novel, without ever straining the tale's skin," Schiff shrewdly remarks.

The complexities and complications of Trevor's characters have tended to multiply and thicken as the years have passed. Consider, for example, *Mrs. Eckdorf in O'Neill's Hotel* (1969), which naturally proceeded from *The Boarding-House* and is a darker and richer version of the same experience. Reduced to its essentials and oversimplified, that experience involves the overlapping lives of people living on the margins of society—and thrown together in the urban version of a drydocked ship of fools. In a boardinghouse or a hotel like O'Neill's the sad voyage of life for a long-term resident may not end until insanity or death has done its work.

Trevor is still more fascinated with the effects that a boarding school exerts on its masters and pupils, as *The Old Boys* makes plain. None of the old boys in that novel has grown up; and the protracted adolescence of Jaraby, Sole and Cridley, Nox, Turtle, Ponders, and the others is at first amusing but becomes pathetic. This theme regularly recurs in Trevor's fiction: sometimes, as in "A School Story," "Torridge," and "Children of the Headmaster," it is the principal theme propelling the action; on other occasions, as in "Going Home," "The Grass Widows," and "The Third Party," the boarding-school theme is more nearly a leitmotif, a matter playing in the story's background, not generating its action, as the principals endeavor to struggle through the day and find a modicum of satisfaction.

Within the boarding school lurk many possibilities that illumine the complications of life in the wider—and, one might presume—the more responsible world of action and liability. But the preoccupations of boys often carry over into mature life—or what passes for it, as a story such as "Torridge" dazzlingly reveals. (Schools are incubators for infantilism and protracted adolescence.) Torridge, an unlikely butt but one all the same, has been endlessly patronized and satirized and belittled by three of his fellow students. Years later, when these "normal" chaps get together with their families for a regular reunion, one of them impulsively invites Torridge. It turns out that he, who volunteers that he is homosexual, is also the most nearly normal and human of the whole sorry lot of old boys. His series of revelations about the school leaves the other men and their families deeply shaken. "The silence continued as the conversation of Torridge haunted the dinner table. He haunted it himself.... Then Mrs. Arrowsmith suddenly wept and the Wiltshire twins wept and Mrs. Wiltshire comforted them. The Arrowsmith girl got up and walked away, and Mrs. Mace-Hamilton turned to the three men and said they should be ashamed of themselves, allowing this to happen."

Here, as usual, the quiet understated style of Trevor secures the dramatic point better than a gaudier and more assertive prose would. It would be instructive to dwell upon Trevor's exact idioms of conversation and of description, the way that he marks his characters with conversational tics (Torridge keeps saying "As a matter of fact" as he reveals one unpalatable fact after another in rapid-fire succession), the simple but precise diction, the occasional clinching metaphor, the representative items and details. Let us consider this descriptive passage from the same story: "Mrs. Arrowsmith was thin as a knife, fashionably dressed in a shade of ash-grey that reflected her ash-grey hair. She smoked perpetually.... Mrs. Wiltshire was small. Shyness caused her to coil herself up in the presence of other people so that she resembled a ball. Tonight she was in pink, a faded shade. Mrs. Mace-Hamilton was carelessly plump, a large woman attired in a carelessly chosen dress that had begonias on it. She rather frightened Mrs. Wiltshire. Mrs. Arrowsmith found her trying." Note how easily and exactly the description moves into drama, which is to say that Trevor here shows us not merely three women together but a geometry of relations.

We are reminded of the old-fashioned novelists like Dickens and Hardy, but such a Victorian novelist would be much more lavish and pile up far more details. Trevor's details are those of the sculptor and painter that he once was: they are chosen to be representative, not comprehensive or exhaustive. He is so sure of himself and so practiced and easy in his execution that he can deliberately repeat such commonplace words as *ash-grey* and *carelessly*. And even here, in a passage that would seem neutral, humor creeps in, with Mrs. Wiltshire's ball-like dimensions contrasting with the carefree plumpness of Mrs. Mace-Hamilton upholstered in her frumpy dress patterned with begonias. It is the formidable Mrs. Mace-Hamilton, not her vulnerable counterpart, who reproves the three old boys and bullies, one of whom is her husband.

Homosexuality of every stripe appears in Trevor's fiction. We are not surprised that it is especially important in the stories and novels about public schools, but it threads its way through much of his other fiction as well. For instance the old commander in *The Children of Dynmouth* (1976) is a repressed homosexual, and the antagonist of this novel, who is but an adolescent boy, realizes this fact although the commander's wife has not. This is one of Timothy Gedge's most startling revelations as he inveigles himself into the lives of the citizens of Dynmouth, including those of Commander and Mrs. Abigail; and having no identity or life of his own, Timothy spies upon various families. Timothy, however, is not a reliable observer, for he thinks that he witnessed a murder which in fact was an accident—or, more probably, a suicide.

When the Anglican priest in Dynmouth, Quentin Featherston, puts together everything of significance involving Timothy's knowledge and his delusions about what he has witnessed, including the rogering of his own mother, Featherston explains to one of Timothy's victims, Kate, a younger child: "There was a pattern of greys, half-tones and shadows. People moved in the greyness and made of themselves heroes or villains, but the truth was that heroes and villains were unreal. The high drama of casting out devils would establish Timothy Gedge as a monster…But Timothy Gedge couldn't be dismissed as easily as that…. [He] was as ordinary as anyone else, but the ill fortune of circumstances or nature made ordinary people eccentric and lent them colour in the greyness. And the colour was protection because ill fortune weakened its victims and made them vulnerable." (Timothy, who always wears yellow, is the victim of bad luck and is very vulnerable.) But Kate, the strong and intelligent little girl, does not believe the priest. Before we too dismiss Featherston as a sentimental psychologist or sociologist, we should remember that his beliefs about human nature are close to Trevor's own. Such sympathy as Featherston's enables this author to respond to every shade of humanity and inhumanity, including homosexuals, voyeurs, obsessed and demented souls, misfits and failures of every kind and station, and outright criminals (blackmailers, arsonists, thieves, murderers).

Such a figure appears in "Gilbert's Mother" (*Harper's*, May 1993). In our advanced times he would be called dysfunctional, but that is not the half of it. Gilbert, who has murdered several young women, could be an older version of Timothy; but Timothy is estranged from his mother while Gilbert has been cosseted by his. (Both characters have lost their fathers at an early age.) This story turns on the mother's dawning awareness of her son's criminality as he has gone from car theft to murder. Gilbert is an English version of the Son of Sam—and a thief and arsonist as well. Gilbert's nervous mother agonizes about whether she should report him to the police, but we—and she—know that she will not. "No one would ever understand the mystery of his existence," she thinks, "or the unshed tears they shared."

Murder of a different sort drives the action of both *Fools of Fortune* (1983) and *The Silence in the Garden* (1988), both of which devolve from the continuing sectarian violence in Ireland from the Easter Rising until the present day. Trevor reveals the barbarities of the Black and Tans as well as the IRA; but, far more important, he also reveals the festering psychic wounds that senseless barbarity leaves in its wake. "Vengeance breeding vengeance." Such, too, is the theme of "Attracta," one of his most powerful stories: indeed Pritchett thinks it the best in *Lovers of Their Time*. Attracta, an elderly Protestant schoolmistress whose life has been all but ruined by her parents' accidental deaths in an ambush—and by her reflecting upon their deaths and those of a young English couple in Belfast—gradually but inexorably runs off the rails. The Englishman, a soldier, is decapitated by his murderers, who send his head through the post to his young bride, who, until the package arrives, knows not of his death. She, having gone to Belfast, is raped by his murderers and kills herself. As the story ends, Attracta has lost her livelihood for trying to awaken her charges' moral awareness. The story powerfully conveys "what is going on in the backs of the minds of all the people in the town, of whatever faction: of how all, except one or two bigots, are helplessly trying to evade or forget the evils that entangle them," as Pritchett perceives. Attracta, in contrast, sees in a moment of searing revelation: "In all a lifetime I learnt nothing. And I taught nothing either." The pathos is wrenching and recalls similar moments in *Fools of Fortune* and *The Silence in the Garden*, neither of which succeeds so well as "Attracta."

In both novels and elsewhere (as in "Beyond the Pale") Trevor seems off his form when he becomes enmeshed in the coils of the troubles endlessly unfolding in Ireland, as Bruce Allen has complained in "William Trevor and Other People's Worlds" (*Sewanee Review*, winter 1993). Although Allen overstates his case, one is inclined to agree that Trevor is at his best when he writes about "the individual at war with himself, his nearest and dearest, his community, and what, in a more innocent time, we might have called his soul."

In any event most readers will agree that William Trevor's essential country is the Irish village. "An Irish village on market day in a…Trevor story can come to life with the crowding abundance of Dickens's London," as Reynolds Price observes. I do not agree, however, with Price that Trevor's stories of London life tend to be shallow and vapid. He writes persuasively about London as well as Dublin and various foreign places, especially Italy. As is by now well known, Trevor grew up in a long succession of small towns and villages in Ireland, where his father worked as a bank manager; and he knows this life with minute exactness. He seems even more sympathetic to and at home with farms and farming communities than with the small town, as one of his best stories, "The Ballroom of Romance," demonstrates vividly.

The irony of Bridie's situation is that she is stuck with her father, a crippled widower, when she would like to be in town. In the town she talks with old acquaintances who are married or working. "'You're lucky to be peaceful in the hills,' they said to Bridie, 'instead of stuck in a hole like this.'" But Bridle is trapped in her narrow round, just as they are. "The Ballroom of Romance" illustrates Pritchett's acute insight that "Trevor quietly settles into giving complete life histories, not for documentary reasons, but to show people changing and unaware of the shock they are preparing for themselves." In this situation Bridie is more self-aware than the usual figure in Trevor's fictive world. As the story closes, she sees herself marrying Bowser Egan, even though "he would always be drinking" and would be "lazy and useless" and profligate. It is a bleak revelation about a life teetering on the edge of defeat; yet we admire Bridie for her steadfast loyalty to her father and for her ability to deal with life's privations and reversals, of which she has confronted more than her share. This Saturday night will be her last at the Ballroom of Romance: now she will wait for her father to die and Bowser Egan's mother to die and Bowser himself to court her at last, not merely run into her at the dance hall on Saturday night.

In Trevor's fiction, romance is ordinarily this bleak and unrewarding. The artificiality of dance halls and the snatched moments within them, whether in the city ("Afternoon Dancing") or the country, is frustrating for all concerned. Seldom does romance flower there or anywhere else in Trevor's world; and rarely does romance, no matter how urgent, have its way for more than a summer's day. That is but one moral of "Lovers of Their Time," my favorite of Trevor's many splendid stories. Norman Britt and his lover, Marie, carry on their affair of some years in the grand second-floor bathroom of an opulent railroad hotel. "Romance ruled their brief sojourns, and love sanctified—or so they believed—the passion of their physical intimacy. Love excused their eccentricity." But, finally, the romance grinds to a halt: Norman returns to his promiscuous wife, and Marie marries another man after she and Norman have lived with her mother, who treats Norman as a boarder. In the background we hear the jejune songs of Elvis Presley and the Beatles "celebrating a bathroom love." The unnatural romances adumbrated in "Office Romances" are even harsher—and in "Mulvihill's Memorial" still more wretched. And in Trevor seldom does romance flicker more than occasionally in even the best marriages, as "Mr. McNamara,"; "Angels at the Ritz," "Mags," and *The Children of Dynmouth* reveal with chilling finality. The respite from the taxing realities of single life that marriage seems to promise evaporates quickly, so quickly in fact that in Trevor's fiction marriages often go unconsummated even though they may quietly continue, like so many bad habits, for years until a reversal occurs.

In "Mags" a middle-aged couple painfully discovers that the wife's childhood friend Mags, who has come to help her with the children and stayed until death, has consumed their marriage, leaving little besides her own dowdy clothes. Mags, the "innocent predator," has changed their marriage forever. In *Reading Turgenev* (one of the paired novels of *Two Lives*) the young wife is driven to madness by her cold unmarried sisters-in-law and her inept husband, and romance for her is but a sad interlude with her cousin, a dreamer who dies early after living a life of fantasy. The woman herself gradually retreats into fantasy and then is institutionalized. Yet that is not the whole story: the other side is that Elmer Quarry and his sisters believe they were nearly poisoned by that young woman, Elmer's trying wife, Mary Louise—and that they, for all their failings, are far from being wicked. In the end we sympathize with them, particularly Elmer, whose many domestic frustrations have made him an alcoholic. He continues to coddle his wife as she returns to live in his attic and persists in her singular love affair with the memory of her cousin Robert. *Reading Turgenev* is Trevor's most acute study of madness, but that subject runs through much of his fiction, beginning with *The Boarding-House* and *Mrs. Eckdorf* and running through "The Raising of Elvira Tremlett" to this new novel. Madness in Trevor's fiction could easily be the subject of a Ph.D. thesis in English literature—or, better yet, in abnormal psychology.

The failure of romance, the theme of *Other People's Worlds*, need not always lead to madness. Julia Ferndale, a likeable widow, is bilked by Francis Tyte, a smooth confidence man, after their wedding when in middle age she foolishly risks all for love. Francis is by no means an innocent predator, even though he is another of Trevor's halfhearted villains and parasites. Julia sensibly cuts her losses and returns to her good life in a village. The startling contrasts between the village life of Julia and the seedy world of Francis, a member of the homosexual demimonde in the city, are as strongly presented as nearly anything that Trevor has published. This novel stands, with both parts of *Two Lives*, as one of his best, which is to say one of the most ambitious and fully realized. The early novels are far more limited, and some of the later ones, particularly *Fools of Fortune* and *The Silence in the Garden*, are too cramped and crowded within the narrow space that Trevor allows himself. The reader who wants to sample William Trevor's fiction might well begin with *Angels at the Ritz* and *Other People's Worlds*.

My unabashed advocacy of Trevor's fiction (which extends to his other writing, especially *A Writer's Ireland*) is seldom tinged with negative criticism such as I have just declared. I do wish that he were less casual about his titles. *Reading Turgenev* is a silly title for a novel otherwise so artful and subtle, and his editor should have said so. *Mrs. Eckdorf at O'Neill's Hotel* is merely descriptive, and many of his stories bear such mechanical titles. I am bothered by his run-on sentences: save for these comma splices, his punctuation neatly registers the nuances of his insight into suffering humanity. Obviously I am not the person to carp about William Trevor but the one to celebrate his tender and ironic depiction of character caught in the vise of circumstance.

The critics of the future will investigate William Trevor's characters, situations, places, and themes; they will linger over the subtleties of his unvarnished prose, the old-fashioned and innovative techniques that he employs, including the great chances that he takes (such as sudden and

■ BOOKS BY WILLIAM TREVOR

A Standard of Behaviour. London: Hutchinson, 1958.

The Old Boys. London: The Bodley Head, 1964, New York: The Viking Press, 1964, Harmondsworth: Penguin, 1965.

The Boarding-House. London: The Bodley Head, 1965, New York: The Viking Press, 1965, Harmondsworth: Penguin, 1966.

The Love Department. London: The Bodley Head, 1966, New York: The Viking Press, 1967, Harmondsworth, Penguin, 1968.

The Day We Got Drunk on Cake. London: the Bodley Head, 1967, Harmondsworth: Penguin Books, 1969.

The Girl. London: French, 1968.

Mrs. Eckdorf in O'Neill's Hotel. London: The Bodley Head, 1969, New York: The Viking Press, 1970, Harmondsworth: Penguin, 1970.

Miss Gomez and the Brethren. London: The Bodley Head, 1971, New York: The Viking Press, 1972, Triad/Panther Books, 1978, 1984.

The Ballroom of Romance. London: The Bodley Head, 1972, New York: The Viking Press, 1972, Harmondsworth: Penguin Books, 1976.

A Night with Mrs. da Tonka. London: French, 1972.

Elizabeth Alone. London: The Bodley Head, 1973, Harmondsworth: Penguin Books, 1973.

Angels at the Ritz & Other Stories. London: The Bodley Head, 1975, New York: The Viking Press, 1979, Harmondsworth: Penguin Books, 1979.

The Children of Dynmouth. London: The Bodley Head, 1976, New York: The Viking Press, 1977, Harmondsworth: Penguin, 1977.

Lovers of Their Time & Other Stories. London: The Bodley Head, 1978, New York: The Viking Press, 1979, Harmondsworth: Penguin, 1980.

The Distant Past. London: The Bodley Head, 1979.

Other People's Worlds. London: The Bodley Head, 1980, New York: The Viking Press, 1981, Harmondsworth: Penguin, 1982, New York: Viking Penguin, 1991.

Beyond the Pale. London: The Bodley Head, 1981, Harmondsworth: Penguin Books, 1981, New York: The Viking Press, 1981.

The Stories of William Trevor. Harmondsworth: Penguin Books, 1983, New York: Viking Penguin, 1989.

jolting shifts in point of view and in time); they will wonder about his religion and politics; they will speculate about the unhappiness of his parents and wonder if that wound drove him to bend the bow of his art; they will ask themselves if his natural mode is the story or the short novel or the novel (I cannot answer this simple question); they will marvel that a traveler has learned foreign cultures and customs so well and ask how Trevor can write almost as surely about, say, Umbria as London or an Irish village; they will chronicle the use of Irish legend and history in his fiction; they will scratch their heads about the names he assigns to his figures, major and minor; they will try to discover the sources of his art and, in doing so, they will be forced to consider Henry James, F. M. Ford, Joyce Cary, and Elizabeth Bowen among many others; they will make weather almost as heavy of his use of popular culture, especially films and music; and they will have to measure his range as a man of letters—as critic, editor, and dramatist as well as fictionist.

Few, if any, of them will be so intelligently responsive as the best of his critics to this point, critics who include not only those I have cited, especially V. S. Pritchett and Reynolds Price, but Elizabeth Spencer, Graham Greene, and still others who have responded to him with great sensitivity and insight. Consider Price once more: "Trevor's vision is deeply, but though never entirely, comic. However bleak the present and future of a given human life, the salient nearness of a vital ongoing world of rocks and fields, ocean and shore, will throw an enormous inhuman yardstick up against that one sad life and let us see the unreadable smile of time and fate." Let the last word be Pritchett's: "As his master Chekhov did, William Trevor simply, patiently, truthfully allows life to present itself, without preaching; he is the master of the small moments of conscience that worry away at the human imagination and our passions."

George Core
October, 1993

Fools of Fortune. London: The Bodley Head, 1983. Harmondsworth: King Penguin, New York: Viking Penguin, 1984.

The News from Ireland and Other Stories. London: The Bodley Head, 1985, Harmondsworth: Penguin Books, 1987, New York: Viking Penguin, 1986.

The Silence in the Garden. London: The Bodley Head, 1988, New York: The Viking Press, 1988, New York: Viking Penguin, 1989, Harmondsworth: Penguin.

Nights at the Alexandra. New York: Harper & Row, 1987.

Family Sins and Other Stories. London: The Bodley Head, 1990, New York: The Viking Press, 1990, New York: Viking Penguin, 1991, Harmondsworth: Penguin, 1991.

A Writer's Ireland. London: Thames & Hudson, 1984.

Scenes from an Album (play). Dublin: Abbey Theatre, 1981.

Two Lives: Reading Turgenev; My House in Umbria. London: The Bodley Head, 1991, New York: Viking Penguin, 1991, New York: Penguin Books, 1992, Harmondsworth: Penguin, 1992.

The Collected Stories. London: The Bodley Head, 1992. New York: Viking Penguin, 1992.

The Oxford Book of Irish Short Stories (ed.). New York: Oxford University Press, 1989, New York: Oxford University Press, 1991, Oxford: Oxford University Press, 1989, Oxford: Oxford University Press, 1993.

Excursions in the Real World (memoirs). New York: Knopf, 1994.

Felicia's Journey. New York: Viking, 1994.

Juliet's Story. New York: Simon & Schuster, 1994.

Outside Ireland: Selected Stories. New York: Penguin, 1995.

After Rain. New York: Viking, 1996.

Death in Summer. New York: Viking, 1998.

Ireland: Selected Stories. New York: Penguin, 1998.

The Hill Bachelors. New York: Viking, 2000.

Three Early Novels. New York: Penguin Putnam, 2000.

UPDATE

The prolific William Trevor has since published many more books, among them *Juliet's Story* (1994), *Felicia's Journey* (1994), *Outside Ireland: Selected Stories* (1995), *Marrying Damian* (1995), *After Rain* (1996), *Death in Summer* (1998), *The Hill Bachelors* (2000), and *Nights at the Alexandra* (2001).

"Trevor's short fiction has been praised for its delineation of character, especially its portrayal of ordinary people—the lonely, the alienated, the victims of society—as well as those who, at the extreme, are pathological evildoers," according to the *Dictionary of Literary Biography*. "His stories have been called tragicomic or darkly comic; they create a wide range of effects from nostalgia for lost love to sardonically bitter commentary on evil. Trevor's artistic vision, however it may be interpreted, is rooted in his compassion for human suffering." He has been compared to Muriel Spark, Anton Chekov, and Andre Malraux, but most often to James Joyce. "Yet like Joyce before him," wrote *Washington Post Book World*, "Trevor is entirely his own writer, with his own uncompromised vision of human limitations made accessible by a rare generosity toward his characters and their blighted lives."

After so many books and so many years of writing, Trevor is still tremendously popular with readers and admired by critics, and his readership is growing.

The stories in *After Rain*, "very powerful, tragic tales, truly beautifully written," are marked by their sometimes painful honesty, according to *Quadrant*. "Every one of Trevor's stories is a tragedy. In each case, the protagonist could have chosen another direction, and the outcome would have been quite different." In a review of *Death in Summer*, *Booklist* wrote: "Writer of some of the most elegant, burnished fiction in the English language, Irishman Trevor submits a tightly structured tale about three deaths occurring within a small circle of strangely interconnected people and within a short period of time."

The Hill Bachelors explores "the quiet lives of characters caught between desire and circumstance," wrote *Book*. "Set throughout the Irish countryside, Trevor's stories contrast his characters' emotional struggles with Ireland's harsh, sprawling beauty, offering readers a collection both gorgeous and heart-rending, seamlessly paced and defiantly hopeful." *Commonweal* stated simply, "*The Hill Bachelors* gives strong support to the growing consensus that William Trevor is one of the very best writers of short stories alive," and added, "It is rare to find such themes—such difficult happy endings—so convincingly treated in modern English."

Postscript: Since I wrote this essay in May, two books by and about William Trevor have been published. Suzanne Morrow Paulson's *William Trevor* appears in Twayne's Studies in Short Fiction series. Part 1 is devoted to her readings of various stories; and although the critic cannot resist indulging herself in such foolishness as gender codes and intersubjectivity, the commentaries are usually helpful. Part 2 contains two good interviews and a little criticism by Trevor himself; in part 3 some sound criticism of his fiction is reprinted, but such hands as V. S. Pritchett and Elizabeth Spencer are missing in action. The bibliography is solid and useful.

Trevor's *Excursions in the Real World* appeared in London bookshops in August; it will be published in the U.S. by Knopf. This collection contains some of the superb pieces that have been seen recently in the *New Yorker,* especially "Field of Battle." Most of these occasional essays are struck in the reminiscent mode, but there are a few critical pieces such as a wonderful celebration of Somerville and Ross. The most memorable pieces are the sketches of actual people that constitute the bulk of the book—such personal reports as "Miss Quirke" and "Old Bull." Trevor is not so good an essayist as a maker of fiction, but his essays are well worth reading and rereading, especially for the insight they afford into his fiction—and, less often, in this retiring man's own temperament and life.

A Certain Slant of Light: The Poetry of Lewis Turco

Lewis Turco has been called a "poet's poet," and that is truly what he is, a craftsman who weighs each word in the palm of his mind, knowing which word will work, and which word will not. The effect of a Turco poem is, "These words and no others." The individual poems are invariably of high quality, a quality especially remarkable when one considers the virtually complete range of formal approaches that Turco employs. His is a virtuosity which only Auden, perhaps, among poets, can match. When Turco writes a series of poems, as he has often done (beginning with *The Sketches* in 1962), and as he has done in these books, the effect easily exceeds the sum of the parts.

■ I

To discuss *The Inhabitant* (1970) is to do the book an immediate injustice, like translating into the fragmentation of language the meaning of an experience which has meant what it has meant. The book should be read like a novel, beginning with the first poem, "The Door," and expanding with the Inhabitant as he haunts his rooms looking for the self that became—before he was aware—his own ghost. Lewis Turco's *The Inhabitant* emerges from the consciousness of a man searching the rooms of his house, listening to the footfalls of his heart until, in the last poem, "The Dwelling House"—a modern allegory of Creation—he gradually unwinds himself from his dream and walks naked through his city, knowing that "in each eye he saw the image folk saw in his." That final reflection of and from the eyes of humanity is the Inhabitant's inheritance from the myriad reflecting surfaces and reflective rooms of his house.

To open the doors of this house is to enter rooms animated by their own life. Suddenly the word *livingroom* takes its stress on the last syllable, as its "Lamps dimly recall old shadows in the various corners." This is the dimension we expect—and sometimes find—in poetry, the reverberation beneath the seemingly simple surface. In "The Livingroom" the Inhabitant confronts his former self, the young skull beneath the aging flesh, his youth reflected to him, in the imagery of death:

> He watches the skull grow upward on its stem of spine; he waits
>> till it is tall as a lily, and the chairs wait, the couches
>>> roar quietly.

In "The Attic" the Inhabitant visualizes "mirrors reflecting upon solitude." Life may move below the attic, but the attic itself is alive:

> The mathoms listen until, downstairs, carpets swallow the
> noises of living, until the furniture absorbs motion.

Then the machine clicks on: the clock dial begins to turn; dust

Lewis Turco

Lewis Turco was born on May 2, 1934, in Buffalo, New York. He served four years in the U.S. Navy before receiving his B.A. from the University of Connecticut in 1959. He then received his M.A. from the State University of Iowa. Turco has been the recipient of such prestigious honors and awards as an Academy of American Poets Prize, a Breadloaf poetry fellowship, a resident fellowship at Yaddo, and an award from the Poetry Society of America. He has also won the *Silverfish Review* Chapbook Award for *A Family Album* and the Cooper House Chapbook Award for *Murmurs in the Walls*.

Turco was the founding director of both the Cleveland State University Poetry Center and the Program in Writing Arts at the State University of New York at Oswego, where he taught until 1996. ■

feeds the cogs. It is making things, making them slowly,
out of the debris of afternoons and the streetlamp suicides
of evening moths.

Downstairs, the Inhabitant senses "a vague weightfulness overhead," but only his pet understands, "and, now and then, the cat acts strangely." Things are alive up there, in the dust and the dark.

"The Cat" receives a poem of its own, imaged as "lethal but sensual," an inoffensive pet that echoes the malevolence of its wild relatives. This cat is "a familiar of houses," *not* of witches, "a domestic that keeps accounts," but that touches the edge of darker metaphors, realized in "The Couch," which "waits against / the wall like some / old lion couching in gloom." The familiar fuses with the image of a huge cat, hungry behind the jungle flowers—but the metaphor cannot be paraphrased, must be felt as it evolves within the poem.

"The Hallseat" holds in breathless mimesis the process of autumn,

the golden oak fading the
paper fading behind a
spotted mirror

and holds the past within its impress:

only in the seat itself
where certain moments repose
forgotten now…

The hallseat must sit against its wall and wait for someone to tumble into memory.

"The Photograph" suggests that "it is unwise / to trap a moment such as this / in a frame gilt or / otherwise," yet captures the inexplicable process of growing old in a way that can only be felt deeply within the relationship between the poem and its reader. To quote it in bits and pieces is to try to trap a moment, to lie about the way it means.

"The Glider" on the porch, reminiscent of so many summers past, becomes a vehicle towards another dimension, "for now the / glider vessel of summer / first starship insubstantial as / its voyage enters the wind," brushing the edges of evening, of eternity. But while he is sitting on "The Porch" the Inhabitant listens to sirens "wiring the afternoon—stitching it with steel to the approaching darkness." At the scene of the accident, a child, uninhibited by adult dishonesty, cries, "See his bones!" The poem—which William Meredith called a schizophrenic piece among "flawless poems"—flushes time through the intersection of time's ending for this body "who lay like a sack of winter in the center of a summer street."

The Inhabitant is a sequence of acceptance, finally. Standing in "The Summerhouse" the Inhabitant gazes at his family through the windows, as though he were looking into an aquarium, and accepts the dark imagery of summer, sad, sustaining: This is what there is. It is enough: the nightwind, the windows

> alight in the livingroom, the flowers of the garden touching
> toward the summerhouse, the neighbors on their porches, the
> road rolling outward into the darkness under streetlamps
> moth-haloed and the nighthawk's wing and call.

And he accepts in "The Study" his own alienation from his creativity and self, having merely projected himself into objects, like the lamp, the poem's prime metaphor: This is where the Inhabitant lives. These things are his—

> these books, this music upon which the lamplight falls, upon
> which he too, once, threw a radiance now eaten by wires tapping
> the sources of silence and desuetude.

In "The Garden," however, the Inhabitant thrusts against time, using words as runes to spin the world the other way around, back to that primal instant "in that garden / again wearing only these / the tongue's / jewels the ear's / riches eyes like amethyst." This moment of the garden is realized in a different way when the Inhabitant moves into his yard with "the Scythe" "to / whittle / the congregation" of milkweed stalks "into / a large circle then slowly / a smaller one scything / in spirals the / bees moving / always / toward the center." The Inhabitant and his alter-ego, "The crescent blade with its snath / handle," close in with the cutting edge of time towards an ultimate confrontation with the bees. But for once, the Inhabitant controls snaky time and leaves the "bees drinking / one

> nightcap of nectar before dust cut
>   into the still green air
>   and the Inhabitant leaned
>   on the snath
>   against his
>   blade.

But "The Guestroom" holds the Inhabitant's constant guest, Death, and in the poem the Inhabitant becomes his guest. In "The Basement"—which is a domestication of the legend of Orpheus and Eurydice—there hides a doll for which the Inhabitant's daughter cries. The father finds it, but finds as well his own sense of decay and corrosion poised against the timeless world of the child.

The Inhabitant hears only the keening of silence through time, as he weaves his life in and out of dreams. He dreams of that impossible She in "The Bedroom"—"He was without that dream of absences which grasp and do not grasp, wishless to keep her midnight hues: blue and stone, magnificent, where nothing ever ends." He comes, however, to "the moment of waking, already remembrance," and "Too late he has found it to be one more dream." He rises, remembering sleep and dream on an impossible sea, brooded over by the presence of that she who "clothes the night with a curved phrase."

The critic of *The Inhabitant* can only touch the surface of that which has touched him deeply. The poems pulse with life, reflect the angles of day and night, light linked by the consciousness of a single man, and become an allegory of all solitary inhabitants of the flesh. We, like "The Portrait of a Clown," find our "lips...at the edge of something," always on the brink—of what? Truth? Life? Ourselves? Merely the next moment within our walls?

The house chews at people, drinks time, endures, even as transient inhabitants eat and drink within its living walls. Appropriately, one of the Inhabitant's consistent metaphors is of weaving. The texture of the poems is rich; its effect upon the reader is deeply woven. Like our own experience these poems are threaded of the many moments of time below and beyond the narrow loom of the present.

Conrad Aiken, one of the twentieth century's finest poets, when he read *The Inhabitant* wrote Turco a letter which was used, with Aiken's permission, on the cover of Turco's next book, *Pocoangelini: A Fantography and Other Poems* (1971): "*The Inhabitant* is the best new poem I've read in something like thirty years—profoundly satisfying to me, speaks my language, such a relief to have WHOLE meaning again, instead of this pitiable dot-and-dash splinter-poetry or sawdust cornflakes which we usually get." Referring to Turco's earlier *Awaken, Bells Falling* Aiken continued, "And you're *all* good. You give me courage to *read* again, and even to believe again in myself. So you see how handsomely I'm in debt. Thank you! You should be, and will be, better *known*." The reason Aiken responded thus is that the door to the poem

> "once opened
> the visitor must remain in
> that place among the
> Inhabitant's couches and
> violets must be that man
> in his house cohabiting
> with the dark
> wife her daughter or both."

■ II

American Still-Lifes (1981) is divided into three sections: "Twelve Moons," "Still Lifes," and "Autumn's Tales." "Twelve Moons," as one might infer, contains as many poems as moons. "Still Lifes" consists of a prologue, twenty-seven poems, and an epilogue. "Autumn's Tales" is nine poems long. Immediately we perceive the architecture of the collection.

"Twelve Moons" is a guided tour through the months of a northern climate. Our primary focus is on what the Amerindian moon reveals from month to month on the landscape beneath. The poems are woven in a language upon which a human observer does not intrude. Instead, the intensity of observation insists on *our* response. We are not told what or how to "think" about the poems; we must tell *them* what *they* mean. For me, living in a northern climate, they mean the re-creation of my own myth of the seasons, as I observe what the moon shows of a land that deals in extremes. The closest analogues I know in American literature are Henry Adams' wonderful description of New England contrasts at the beginning of *The Education*, and Thoreau's magnificent swing through the seasons in *Walden*. Turco's work is always original, and always aware of its heritage—one reason for the resonance of the poems.

"Twelve Moons" proves a feeling of natural process occurring away from and regardless of "men…in their villages / dreaming themselves awake." The images of the poems are the vesture of archetypes that exist prior to man and may perhaps survive beyond life. The sound of "footsteps in the earth" or the wakening of a boat may disturb the process, but only temporarily, we infer. Fish, bird, deer are viewed within a precise shading of light or shadow, clearly at times, and at other moments "through a glass darkly." The ideal stance of man towards all of this would seem to be "to climb / under the cloud and bright song." But, at the end, in "Hunting Moon," men wait:

> Snow nearly hard as hail
> rustles through the bare branches
> and settles among the leaves
>
> at the roots of the forest.
> In its den of earth
> a bear dreams of berries,
>
> of fish gleaming in the shallows.
> A herd of deer
> shifts edgily in a clearing,
>
> the young bucks shivering.
> From a distance
> a jay cries
>
> across the gray air.
> They are in the wood,
> the band of men,
>
> downwind and quiet.
> The wind begins to rise.
> The snow starts to flake and drift.

Predators enter the woods. We sense the invasion of man upon the woodlands of life itself. These poems represent a subtle retelling of "The Fall of Man" played through the prism of twelve separate months. The sequence represents a chronology, a "history," and, perhaps, a negative teleology. If the poems imply the fragility of life, however, we infer the permanency of the nature that underlies its living manifestations.

■ III

"Still Lifes" seems also to represent a kind of "history," but here the poems are too subtle, too partaking of whatever "art" may be, for the clumsy non-art form known as "literary criticism." My response must be impressionistic, and even more subjective than is most criticism. What I feel, however, is language charged with a repressed consciousness, as if one's unconscious were invited upward to do the "interpreting."

The colonial village over which the articulate and descriptive "camera-eye" begins to rove is deserted, as indeed the "lost" colony of Roanoke was found to be when the British relief expedition at last managed to get through. In fact, the second poem in the sequence, "The Colony," after the prologue, "Landscape," ends with a near-quote from the journal that describes what the would-be rescuers found at Roanoke:

> Rising out of the summer woods

there is a column of smoke
beginning to fade into the sky where,
now and then, a tern or oriole

stitches stillness with a call
and emptiness with a curve of plumage.
The palisade stands open.
The living quarters yawn shadow

into the heat. The fires are cold,
their ash white and fine as snow
on the bare places in the grass.
The blacksmith's tongs lie where they were left;

a water barrel has rolled,
dry as the August wind,
into a corner of the compound.
The woods stand close,

but in them there is no echo —
only the needle rustle of the pines.
The bark on the log paling

has not begun to show moss,
but one of the chief trees or posts
at the right side of the entrance
has the bark taken off,

and five feet from the ground
in fair capital letters is graven
CROATOAN without any cross
or sign of distress.

What has happened here? Why are the fires cold, the colonial utensils rusting? An Indian raid? The Plague? One gets the eerie feeling that some antique version of the neutron bomb has wafted through this structured but uninhabited "society." An occasional footprint, the impress of hoof and wheel in snowfall as the poems press on through the 17th, the 18th, the 19th centuries, but "If anything moves it is a naked branch," as in "The Maple Works." The poems move, as this one itself says, "out of the unknown toward the forsaken."

We seem to be on Keats' urn, where the little town is emptied, "and not a soul to tell / Why thou art desolate, can e'er return." Nature seems to represent stasis, invisibility, when contrasted with more basic process: "peeling wood /…musts to lichen near the gate" of "The Tollhouse." "Musts," of course, conveys "necessity" within its duplicity. "The bell rings twice," but we feel its summons as a result of the wind's will, and that the echo melts unheard into twilight. But even the wind is implicit in "The Tollhouse," which ends with a magnificent metaphor. The dark river that cleaves the earth together in daylight, cleaves it asunder at night. Even the villagers who come to "The Mill" "in mufflers and shawls" seem to be "shadow," ghosts of a former time who brood over New England before the camera eye moves south and west over the rest of America. The poems, like "The Stockyard," inhabit "a memory / of slow passage."

And we move on in time as well, to "The Observation Tower" near which there is a car in which "a radio plays the blues," to a world of "streetlamps," a modern church with all the paraphernalia of Sunday-school, "garages…by a gravel drive" belonging to the parsonage beside "The Church," to bathrooms in the houses of the epilogue, "Prothalamion," "where men stand behind glass to gaze into glass, / to feel an edge of steel against hair and flesh."

The mirrors suggest what may be happening—we reflect on the infinite regress implicit in the mirrors and realize, perhaps, that we have found a window into the past. The wraith of former times haunts the present with a way of life, and the lives that followed that way, merely physically erased from the American landscape. The effect of the sequence cannot be described, but I'll make an effort:

As people move into this world of the poem, we recognize, reflexively and reflectively, the presence of people in the earlier poems of the deserted places which suddenly come alive with the activity seemingly suspended in that former time. We recognize, as Hartley says, that "the past is another country—they do things differently there." What we have in "Still Lifes" is, as the final poem says, "a wedding of moss and streets." Whatever seems to be gone continues to lurk above, around, beneath the macadam poured over "deep-down things," as Hopkins calls them. Even more implicit is that modern man and woman could disappear more completely than have the inhabitants of the history that drifts through the present. We recall the "column of smoke" with which the sequence begins at Roanoke.

That I must be impressionistic about the sequence argues Turco's brilliant success. The poems insist on response, even if the response is inadequate. "Poetry," after all, as Frost wisely says, "is what evaporates from all translations." Most modern poetry is delivered already evaporated. But not these poems, this poem, "Still Lifes." I leave it to readers to discern in my response a possible line of approach, but I leave it to them, more importantly, to develop *their* response to the suggestive depth and culminating impact of the poems.

■ IV

The last nine poems, "Autumn's Tales," portray a snowstorm approaching a modern town; they are snapshots taken over a few minutes of time, beginning with close-ups of a neighborhood and then trucking back for longer shots, each poem—each "frame"—showing both the landscape and the development of the storm until, in the last wide-angle "Vista" shot, the camera-eye loses sight of the village in the full fury of a blizzard and the falling night.

"The Neighborhood," with its repetition of "settle" and its variants, has the effect of a sestina. That effect asserts a powerful gravitational pull to the poem's "meaning" down into its fine ironies. As "free" as the poem may seem to be, it works precisely because Turco knows the form underlying what the poem "says," the form that releases the poem into its feeling of "freedom." The final two stanzas of "The Trees" create a wonderfully complex metaphor that makes of the sky at once an ocean and a ship, and of a kite an emblem of the earth's slow-roll into darkness:

a kite, worn thin by scraping
against the sky, rustles
along the prow of night:

It is a figurehead of tissue,
of soft wood, its ragged tail
caught in shadow, pulling darkness.

While the craftsmanship is magnificent, it is the servant of a transcendent effect.

At the end of "The Street" (as it were), "the curbs of vision" pick up the specificity of street *per se* and suggest the limitations on our ability to see anything beyond what we can see from our defined perspective. A neat duplicity of language, itself seemingly a limited quantity until

Turco gets hold of it, *suggests* limitations, both physical and emotional. "The Fences" become at once snow-laden walls and a force that "will cut through dusk / as though they were knives with white edges." The magic that metaphor is created for dazzles us with its sleight-of-word. And at the end—a reminder of Wordsworth's "The Prelude," as "The hills rise over the valley, / and the river is lost." Twilight moves in finally, as it has encroached all along, to give this book an ending as effective and as "realized" as is the last page of a fine novel.

■ **V**

The Shifting Web: New and Selected Poems (1989) is a beautiful book—crafted and printed with the fine eye that Turco gives to such matters—and full of the superbly crafted poems for which Turco is celebrated. Turco makes other poets (all but a few) look like people trying to write poems. It is a treat to revisit many of these poems, to read the new ones, and to savor the range and depth of this splendid collection.

No explanation for a poem exists, poetry being what evaporates from all translations, as Frost said fifty years ago. In Turco's case, diction and detachment are crucial elements. His choice of words reflects his interest in language, and his contribution to the language rests in his specific and image-bearing Anglo-Saxon verbs and nouns. His words "play"—they balance alternative but complementary meanings within the alert ear. Even in highly personal poems, and there are some here, Turco creates a brooding presence beyond the personal voice, giving us an identity to inhabit as we experience a daughter leaving home, as in "A Daughter Moves Out," a son suddenly grown taller than his father, as in "Corral," or a chapter of love on which the book must be shut in a trunk, as in "Attic Poem," all from the final section of "New Poems."

The final piece, "Poem," is an invitation to read what has gone before. The wind stirs and begins to move again across the words, touching them as if they were strings (to borrow the old simile). The poems I have come to know are here: "Burning the News," from *Awaken, Bells Falling* (1968), one of the great anti-war poems in the language; "Pocoangelini 26," in which the hero takes fifty-one strikes before connecting with his imagination; "The Attic" full of the dusty mathoms that will never be used again but which will be thrown away only when the old house is sold or torn down; poems from "Bordello," each one a technical *tour de force* and a moving dramatic monologue, and a section from *American Still-Lifes* which begins in colonial mystery and ends in the still living of modern mundanity, plus monsters like "Fetch" from *A Cage of Creatures* (1978) and "Werewind" from *A Maze of Monsters* (1987), and on and on....

I will not rob the completeness of each poem by slicing out fillets. The poems here are completed works, each with its woven integrity. Those who wonder what poetry is all about and whether it is worth bothering about should read *The Shifting Web*. This book is what poetry is all about. Turco translates his words into our experience. He weaves us into his shifting web of words.

Much of Turco's work, like that of his older contemporary craftsmen—Louis Coxe, Richard Eberhart, and Howard Nemerov spring to mind—will find its way into whatever future lies before us. The qualities that tend to make Turco's work "too good" for contemporary celebrity will earn him several precious pages in anthologies yet unborn. The sensitive reader, however, educated to what poetry is and is not, should be reading him now. Turco will reward that experience, as the reader finds that his perceptions are honed, his imagination is challenged, and his awareness of language, world, and life are immeasurably enhanced.

Herbert R. Coursen, Jr.
April, 1991

■ BOOKS BY LEWIS TURCO

First Poems. Francestown, N.H.: Golden Quill Press, 1960.

Awaken, Bells Falling: Poems 1959–1967. Columbia; University of Missouri Press, 1968.

The Book of Forms: A Handbook of Poetics. New York: E. P. Dutton, 1968.

The Inhabitant. New York: Mathom, 1970.

The Literature of New York: A Selective Bibliography of Colonial and Native New York State Authors. New York: Mathom, 1970.

Pocoangelini: A Fantography and Other Poems. Northampton, Mass.: Despa Press, 1971.

Poetry: An Introduction Through Writing. Reston, Va.: Reston Publishing Co., 1973.

The Weed Garden. Orangeburg, S.C.: Peaceweed Press, 1973.

A Cage of Creatures: Poems. Potsdam, N.Y.: Banjo Press, 1978.

Seasons of The Blood. New York: Mathom, 1980.

American Still-Lifes. New York: Mathom, 1981.

The Compleat Melancholick. Saint Paul, Minn.: Bieler Press, 1985.

The New Book of Forms: A Handbook of Poetics. Hanover, N.H.: University Press of New England, 1986.

The New Book of Forms (expanded edition), Hanover, N.H.: University Press of New England, 1986.

Visions and Revisions of American Poetry. Fayetteville: University of Arkansas Press, 1986.

A Maze of Monsters. Livingston, Ala.: Livingston University Press, 1987.

Dialogue. Cincinnati: Writer's Digest Books, 1989.

The Shifting Web: New and Selected Poems. Fayetteville: University of Arkansas Press, 1989.

A Family Album. Eugene, Ore.: Silverfish Review Press, 1990.

The Public Poet: Five Lectures on the Art and Craft of Poetry. Ashland, Ohio: Ashland Poetry Press, 1991.

Murmurs in the Walls. Oklahoma City, Okla.: Cooper House, 1992.

Emily Dickinson, Woman of Letters: Poems and Centos from Lines in Emily Dickinson's Letters. New York: State University of New York Press, 1993.

Legends of the Mists. Kew Gardens, N.Y.: New Spirit, 1993.

A Book of Fears. West Lafayette, Ind.: Bordighera, 1998.

Shaking the Family Tree: A Remembrance. West Lafayette, Ind.: Bordighera, 1998.

The Book of Literary Terms: The Genres of Fiction, Drama, Nonfiction, Literary Criticism, and Scholarship. Hanover, N.H.: University Press of New England, 1999.

The Green Maces of Autumn: Voices in an Old Maine House. Dresden Mills, Maine: The Matham Bookshop, 2002.

UPDATE

The versatile and productive Lewis Turco—poet, playwright, children's author, short-story writer, and critic—has since published several creative works: *A Family Album* (1990), *Murmurs in the Walls* (1992), *Legends of the Mists* (1993), and *A Book of Fears* (1998); and the nonfiction *The Public Poet: Five Lectures on the Art and Craft of Poetry* (1991), *Emily Dickinson, Woman of Letters: Poems and Centos from Lines in Emily Dickinson's Letters* (1993), *Shaking the Family Tree: A Remembrance,*(1998), *The Book of Literary Terms: The Genres of Fiction, Drama, Nonfiction, Literary Criticism, and Scholarship* (1999). He also has edited *The Life and Poetry of Manoah Bodman: Bard of the Berkshires* (1999).

"Those who frequent the small world of the little poetry magazines know Lewis Turco as a champion of the classical virtues of form and craftsmanship," according to an *Agora* review, although Turco has said that he hopes to be known for other things as well. He once told *Contemporary Authors*, "Although people believe—because my name is associated with *The Book of Forms*—that I am interested only in traditional ways of writing, such is not the case. I am as interested in experimental writing as in any and all other aspects of the subject. In fact, most of my own poems are written in unrhymed syllabic verse. . . . I'm one of those writers who loves to write; I'm never happier than when I'm working on a project. . . . I'll try anything."

His willingness to experiment is evident in his 1993 tribute to one of America's favorite nineteenth-century poets. *Emily Dickinson, Woman of Letters* is a collection of poems created from lines of Dickinson's letters arranged by Turco in poetic form, and sometimes bridged by Turco's own words. The controversial project was viewed as highly original if nothing else. "The effect is to create a number of new poems which seem to be written in the famous poet's voice," wrote *Contemporary Authors*. The *Emily Dickinson International Society Bulletin* commented, "The book is a curious one, bound to raise conventional eyebrows," and stated that readers "will eerily hear Dickinson's voice . . . for the poems themselves are based on her words." A review in *Nineteenth-Century Literature* praised Turco for staying "well clear of greeting-card banality, retaining Dickinson's verve, haunted complexity, and resonance without clarity." And *Eclectic Literary Forum* found the book to be "an unusual contribution to Dickinson scholarship . . . and a strong addition to Turco's own work—a creative homage to another poet."

Home at Last, and Homesick Again: The Ten Novels of Anne Tyler

On television, a woman whose house has just been flooded for the third time in nine years says she thinks she can move back in next week. I am baffled. "Why," I ask, "do they *stay* there? Why don't they move?"

"Because," says my friend, "it's home."

I have trouble with this. On leave now, I leap across regions, trailing boxes of books. So "home" is for me a mystery more observed than undergone. For many others, too, "home" and "family," here and now, are meanings in the midst of change.

Yet as most reviewers have pointed out, home and family are two of Anne Tyler's favorite themes. Anne Tyler's books tell of staying at home or running away or coming back home or making a new home or failing to. Usually, house and family—place and persons—fit together, to be a home: the rigid Pecks' rigidly contiguous houses in Roland Park (*Searching for Caleb*); the Tulls, their lives divided between row house and restaurant (*Dinner at the Homesick Restaurant*).

The novels too have family traits; they share memory and history and genes. Their richness of physical texture, and their distinctive characters, draw a reader to celebrate the multiplicity and variousness of experience, to share Caleb Peck's "delight in noise and crowds." But nearly every novel has its Daniel Peck as well as its Caleb. Daniel's urge is to pull it all back together, to search for the wandering Caleb. In the spirit of Daniel Peck, then, let me suggest some patterns I have found in Tyler's blessed profusion.

I think Tyler's texts concern themselves, through the metaphor of home and wandering, with the issue of personal psychic growth. In *The Reproduction of Mothering* (Berkeley, 1978), Nancy Chodorow describes early growth as a painful and a paradoxical process: the infant "achieves a differentiation of self only insofar as its expectations of primary love are frustrated." At best, the person matures with both a sense of a separate self and a sense of basic relatedness, the memory of "primary love." But each sense may remain vulnerable to the other: "merging brings the threat of loss of self" and "separateness…threatens…the infant's very sense of (related) existence." Even though we emerge from the experience of these first fierce paradoxes, as adults we carry their traces and retell their story. For Tyler, "home" signifies the trace of that "sense of oneness," and wandering the trace of autonomy. The intensity of these longings is apparent in her characters; the struggle for both autonomy and intimacy structures her plots. Tyler's recurrent metaphors complement the plotting: for example, "strings" suggest merging, and "foreignness" suggests separateness. Some characters move out of symbiotic love; they become able to love another person who is different and separate. Others never make it away from home.

Tyler's interest is not limited to the growth of a central consciousness. Although family may serve as a metaphor for one person's several alternatives, Tyler is also concerned with

Anne Tyler Born October 25,

1941, in Minneapolis, Minnesota, Anne Tyler spent
her childhood living in various Quaker communes
throughout the Midwest and South, then settled in
Raleigh, North Carolina. At age sixteen, she entered
Duke University as a Russian major (B.A., 1961).
Although encouraged by novelist Reynolds Price to
pursue her writing, Tyler continued her graduate
studies in Russian at Columbia University. In 1963
she married Taghi Modarressi, a psychiatrist from
Iran, and they currently reside in Baltimore. Tyler's
novels have received many prestigious awards and
nominations: American Academy and Institute of
Arts and Letters (1977), National Book Critics Circle fiction award nomination (1980), and American
Book Award nomination in paperback fiction
(1982), all for *Morgan's Passing;* and for *Dinner at
the Homesick Restaurant,* National Book Critics Circle fiction award nomination (1982) and Pulitizer
Prize nomination for fiction (1983). Tyler received a
National Book Critics Circle fiction award and a
Pulitzer Prize nomination for fiction (both 1985),
both for *The Accidental Tourist,* and the Pulitzer
Prize for fiction (1988) for *Breathing Lessons.*

Tyler, a member of the American Academy and
Institute of Arts and Letters, has also edited (with
Shannon Ravenal) *Best American Short Stories 1983,*
and contributed short stories to *The New Yorker,
Antioch Review,* and *Southern Review.* ■

family as a community of persons in relationship. Freud, says Janet Malcolm, called
human relations "tragic"—"because we cannot know each other." For Tyler, they are tragi-
comic. We can at least know that we do not know. In her first novel, *If Morning Ever
Comes,* point of view is largely limited to the protagonist Ben Joe Hawkes. But even there,
Tyler uses dramatic irony to explore the reality of multiple consciousnesses. In *Dinner at
the Homesick Restaurant,* that early amused and affectionate sense of irony has grown into a
moving sense of the tragedy as well as the comedy of the paradox at the heart of the family.
As they fatally miss one another, the Tulls will inevitably do more damage than they heal.
In all her novels, Tyler's characters and her families continually express their conflicting
urges toward wandering with Caleb into the (object-) world and staying at home in hopes
of bliss with Daniel. Frustrated in both, they often find themselves, when home at last,
homesick again.

Tyler's novels present a meditation on mutability. How can identity persist if someone
changes? Daniel Peck clings to the vision of immutability. Hoping thus to beat time and death,
such characters ironically sacrifice growth. Daniel's grandson Duncan Peck, clings to the vision
of change, so he stays on the road. But for Duncan, change itself becomes the constant. It is
through characters like Morgan Gower in *Morgan's Passing* that Tyler reaches her own vision of
the compatibility of permanence and change, of identity and growth.

Finally, in her fiction Tyler raises issues particular to art. Images of art and types of artistry pervade her novels: cooking, childbearing, photography, fortune-telling, acting, puppetry, circuses, and (most recently) writing itself. With these images, she explores the nature of fantasy and its relation to what we conventionally call the real. In *The Tin Can Tree,* there is the photographic but evanescent image of dead Janie Rose; in *Earthly Possessions* there is photographer Charlotte Emory's magical realism and her father's ironically more subjective "objective" realism. Tyler makes the issue central to her plot in two novels about artists, *Celestial Navigation* and *Morgan's Passing.* In these, she plays with questions of illusion and awareness in both the aesthetic process and the process of psychic growth.

The plot of *If Morning Ever Comes,* Tyler's first novel, unfolds to Ben Joe Hawkes his illusions about his family and himself. And it shows—a theme Tyler will sustain—the apparently accidental, almost quirky way in which marriages (hence families) are made. Ben Joe, a Columbia law student, comes home, then (to his surprise) goes back to New York with a bride. Shelley Domer is different from him in nearly every way, but she loves him unswervingly and her character meets his deepest need. Tyler's scenes brilliantly capture the gaps between Ben Joe's and Shelley's thought processes, the differences between their readings of the same world. The novel also depicts the links between the two, shaped out of their intuitions about what they deeply want. At the center of the novel is a family that is homesick. Bound together is need—Hawkeses always seem to come home when the world wounds them—yet they find their needs badly met at home where habitual ways of relating and an insular view of the family keep them from reality and growth. In Ben Joe's, as in later Tyler families, the illusion of family self-sufficiency means a kind of isolation from the "world": Ben Joe's disturbing desire for his sister expresses the family reluctance to seek satisfactions outside its borders. Although it seems to offer both oneness and autonomy, this illusion suppresses differences between family members. For the Hawkes family, a habitual failure to communicate directly and plainly has kept the family tuned to one another's hidden messages and chary of crasser outsiders' ways; thus they have, at least superficially, bonded more closely together. Long on charm and manipulation, they are short on honesty and depth.

Two women outside this island help Ben Joe. Lili Belle, his dead father's mistress, helps him shake the rigid boundaries with which he has perceived her as "home's" antagonist. And Shelley tells him the truth about her feelings and about herself. Thus Ben Joe, like his father, finds the capacity to risk committing himself to someone outside the home.

Like Ben Joe Hawkes, Joan Pike in *The Tin Can Tree* (1965) is "homesick, but not for any home she'd ever had." She feels temporary and distanced, as a substitute mother for her cousin Simon, a potential wife to James Green, and only a hander, not a binder (or "tier") of tobacco. But the families she observes are themselves fixed in repetitive patterns. Simon, whose sister Jamie Rose has died, believes that "unliving things last much longer than living." Yet his mother's inertia and silence, instead of monumentalizing Janie Rose, blight Simon. And James's courtship of Joan never deepens or grows.

Appropriately, breaking away effects awareness and change. When Simon runs away, his mother comes out of her trance and into the present again. Joan leaves on the bus, until her fear of the "world" reveals itself to her as love for young Simon, and she goes back, never even missed. And when James goes back to his original home, he recognizes that the home he had defiantly left "for good" does not even exist; "no one seemed to be as [he] remembered."

In *The Tin Can Tree,* Tyler meditates on the meaning of art for the theme of permanence and change. Photography and family stories capture the evanescent, are a way "of remaining." The dead child Janie Rose may be the liveliest and most memorable character of all. It is the picture of Janie Rose in one of James' photographs that occasions the novel's reflections of the "remaining" quality of art. For Janie isn't *in* the picture even as a clear image—she's a tiny set of dots in a faraway car—until viewers, who remember her habit of playing "grande dame" in that car, put together the image. Even so, the image still comes and goes to their eyes, vulnerable to their receptivity and imagination and faith. Art can apparently transcend time, then; but it is in time as well, and so depends upon its viewers, its listeners, its readers.

A Slipping-Down Life (1970) takes its characters and setting from the version of 1960s pop culture to be found in small-town North Carolina. Evie Decker lives with her distant, "reasonable" father and Clotelia, their black maid. Evie is fat and lonely; she is in the fringest of outgroups at high school. She listens to the radio constantly. On impulse in a restroom at a concert, she carves the name of a local rock star, "Drumstrings" Casey, on her forehead. They marry; Drum turns out for a while to be surprisingly homey. But his failing career and dissatisfaction with Evie's looks send him into depression and adultery. Meanwhile, practical Evie works at the library. When her father dies, Evie, pregnant, "squares her corners as if she were a stack of library cards" and goes home to her father's house; Drum does not follow.

Drum defines himself as an artist, an original. But his one musical idea, "talking out," consists of an incoherent collage of phrases he hears spoken. Drum never talks *himself* out; his art is simply "hauling in words by their tails." After Drum fails as a star, he plays the blues at home; this domestic art is original, more expressive. But Drum accepts the sixties ideology that, denying the value of privacy, made the public the only reality. Like Drum, Evie feels she has to make a mark in the world to be real; she does so by carving his name on her forehead. And the public consumes her act: at the high school, she too is a celebrity.

Despite their investment in publicity, the privacy of stubborn, unlikely love—a Tyler hallmark—creates a family and a home for Evie and Drum. But at the end of the novel, Evie gives birth to herself, belatedly, by separating herself from Drum: she "felt something pulled out of her that he had drawn, like a hard deep string." Evie has fed on Drum from the start, when she eagerly listened as he played on the radio. In this novel the "string" of that symbiosis is severed, to allow the chance for autonomous growth.

Evie becomes herself by leaving her husband's home; Elizabeth Abbot in *The Clock Winder* can never be herself in her father's house. A minister who cares more about creating a public identity than recognizing home truths, he rejects Elizabeth because of her belief in reincarnation. She drifts to Baltimore where she lives with the Emersons. A born fumbler at home, Elizabeth away turns out to be a paid and effective handyman. The Emerson family, though as imperfect as her own, is imperfect in ways more congenial to Elizabeth's own unconventional self. Widowed Mrs. Emerson has always been "taken care of." She dresses impeccably, wears heels and gold bracelets, and, a southern lady, holds in her stomach, even at home. Now she tries to keep ruling the roost after the children have flown, with a dictaphone. Her children include Andrew, in New York, who is probably psychotic; calm Matthew; Timothy, in medical school; Peter, the youngest, in college; Mary, with her husband and children in Dayton; Margaret, in her second marriage in Chicago; and Melissa, a fashion model in New York.

Tyler's treatment of Mrs. Emerson develops a narcissistic character first seen in James Green's brother Ansel and later to be reincarnated as Morgan Gower. Mrs. Emerson perceives herself as unjustly deprived of attention and affection, so she demands it constantly; yet, paradoxically, her incessant self-involvement (perfectly symbolized in her use of the dictaphone, which never answers back) makes it impossible for her to perceive others accurately and to get what she wants. Tyler's treatment of this narcissistic figure gains in complexity and compassion with Mrs. Emerson. Her unpleasant manipulativeness, so like Ansel's, now unfolds as need. In a scene told from her point of view as she suffers a stroke, we see the "single, narrow-boned girl that had been looking out of her aging body all these years." Yet Tyler is unswervingly unsentimental about the stubbornness of human limitations. Mrs. Emerson remains irritating and demanding in her relations to her children and, by that route, to the reader. When Peter is in Vietnam, she, "secure in her sealed weightless bubble floating through time…keeps writing to ask if he has visited any tourist sights."

On the other hand, Elizabeth learns—painfully—to acknowledge reality. After participating, unwittingly, in Timothy's death, she severs her connection to the Emersons, saying "I don't want to be relied on," and nearly marries a man her father has chosen. The scene with Timothy repeats itself years later. This time the crazy brother Andrew has the gun; in revenge for Timothy's death, he aims at Elizabeth. "But she [has] been through this before; she [knows] now that it [is] something to be taken seriously…" Andrew does in fact shoot her. But Tyler, the story's plotter, confirms Elizabeth's choice. The shot is harmless as a bee sting, and Andrew says, his spell broken for the moment, "Oh Elizabeth. Did I hurt you?"

In *Celestial Navigation* (1974) Jeremy Pauling, afraid of the world, has retreated into the narcissism of Ansel Green and Pamela Emerson. But unlike them, Jeremy, an artist, has a gift of vision. His tremendous sensitivity seems to require tremendous external stability; the cost of this immobility is the absence from his art, and his life, of depth and roundedness, of connectedness to a social world. Jeremy "lives at a distance" and navigates by the stars.

Things change when Mary Tell moves in as a boarder: Jeremy falls in love. Mary Tell responds, for her own good reasons. When babies come, Jeremy's art, too, grows from collage into sculpture; at first he had felt "presumptuous using up so much vertical space." But then their purposes cross. Intending to be sensitive to his fears, Mary protects him and thus cuts off Jeremy's chance to grow more confident; Jeremy, though he is "slaying dragons" in overcoming his fears, believes to "keep her respect it [is] necessary that she never even guess it." Jeremy begins to retreat from his family, into the order and boundedness of his art. And when Mary finally leaves with the children, he moves into a shared fantasy with another boarder, Olivia. The novel ends with Jeremy in full retreat from a world he now renders confidently in "great towering beautiful sculptures" but in which as a person he can only whisper and creep.

Anne Tyler said at one time that of her novels she liked *Celestial Navigation* the best; a reviewer has said that Jeremy comes closest to expressing Tyler's own self-perception as an artist. Tyler has further said she intentionally brackets herself into two, artist and woman; it's as though Jeremy and Mary—the names are nearly anagrams—are in one body. So it can be helpful to read the novel as Tyler's most direct fictional exploration of the tensions between artist and woman as well as those between the desire for a separate self and the desire for union.

Jeremy and Mary experience both sides of these conflicts. Jeremy's artistic vision makes him a very separate self, oblivious to the conventions of social relations. Yet in his symbiosis with his mother he has almost entirely "merged" with her. In loving Mary and the children as "other" selves and in confronting his terror of leaving the block, Jeremy shows signs of resolving the conflict. Mary, as Jeremy perceives, merges with her children; she believes "the deepest pieces of herself [are] in those children and every day they scattered in sixty different directions and faced a thousand untold perils." So Mary takes it as her task to become more independent, especially of men's views.

The tragedy of the novel evolves inevitably from each character's newfound "strengths." The conflict is adumbrated early when, despite his terrors, Jeremy wants to come to the hospital to be with Mary when one of their children is born. But Mary, eager to be self-sufficient and, she believes, sensitive to his fears, wants him to stay at home. He stays at home. But later, when

Mary wants them to marry, Jeremy simply makes himself, in his studio, unavailable. In the final critical scene, when Jeremy has journeyed alone to find his family, he pushes further than he knows how. He insists on navigating the bay waters, with the children, to air out some sails. But Mary, aware of both his need to do this and his incompetence, chooses the children over him. In so doing, she chooses "the deepest pieces of herself," but also trusts her own lone judgment rather than acceding to a man's. His navigation mistrusted, Jeremy's response is, once again, to withdraw.

He makes it to the sailboat, but when he gets there, the boat only goes round and round in "wider and faster circles," while he sits there alone. At the end, his life at home is reduced to dependence on Miss Vinton to navigate him even through his own Baltimore block. Once again, he is living at the extreme of separateness that comes from his artist's vision, and the extreme of merging that comes with his infant's relationship to a woman.

Again in this novel Tyler uses the metaphor of strings to depict the relationship to home. If he tries to "set out on a walk" Jeremy must "ignore the strings that stretched so painfully between home and the center of his back"; in their bubble, Olivia says "no strings snagged us to the rest of the world." The lure of that imaginably perfect state of being—the bliss of merging, the self in unimpeded relation to someone else—lies at the core of homesickness in many Tyler novels. Sometimes the fantasy broadens to include the rest of the family, which then sees itself as a self-sufficient unit that can survive without the "outside world." Ben Joe Hawkes, Mrs. Emerson, and Jeremy Pauling are all driven by this fantasy, and all saved from it for a time by relationships with outsiders.

It is that feeling of family wholeness that Daniel Peck, who is looking for his brother Caleb (lost since 1912), wants in *Searching for Caleb*. Tyler's Baltimore Pecks have isolated themselves for five generations by stiffly valuing the virtues of politeness, suppression of feeling, and submersion of idiosyncrasy. Their credo is "avoid the new"; they have roped in outside genes for reproduction, but then driven the breeders—Margaret Rose, Sam Mayhew—away. But now they are struck with some embarrassingly exuberant immigrant German genes of one first generation marriage, genes that keep inducing travel.

It is to Daniel's credit that he won't take the Peckish route of simply denying Caleb's reality. Daniel, in fact, rescues his grandniece Justice and sends her to the "outside world" of school. But in searching for Caleb he looks to stop time, to retrieve an imagined past of wholeness, to repair loss. He dreams the romantic dream of timeless wholeness, of a "small town" where "I would know everybody in it and none of them would ever die or move away or age or alter."

This family's habit of irrationally endorsing utterly conflicting values informs the youngest family of Pecks as well. A married couple who love to travel, Duncan and Justine are first cousins who have chosen to marry safely within the family; they have the ultimate "self-sufficiency": sex within the family. Justine and Duncan produce a daughter, Meg, who is pure genteel Peck.

Compounding the ironies is the discovery that the wandering Caleb has spent his life literally or figuratively bound and tied to others. For years in Storyville he was "Stringtail Man," tied to White-Eye, a blind black guitarist, with a long rope. Even in the nursing home, he is tied to his best friend. Yet however tied Caleb is, he is not tied to Pecks. Caleb celebrates the union of difference, as his relation with White-Eye most clearly shows.

Like Daniel, Justine searches for a happier past by searching for Caleb. When she finds him, she doesn't want to keep him, for a very Peckish reason: he's journeyed too far from the family, she feels; he has lost his connection. Her search has failed. Only when Caleb, having vanished again, sends a Peckish bread and butter note does she perk up. For through this she learns that travel doesn't mean only loss, that change doesn't mean the end of identity. Finally acting on the "rule" she's held as a fortune teller for years—"always change"—she, not Duncan, makes the decision to join Alonzo Divish's traveling circus. Completing the novel, Justin and Duncan resolve the Peck contradictions to their own satisfaction through a sort of art. Alonzo's circus, Habit-Forming Entertainments, will offer them both permanence and change, identity and variety, home and lots of travel.

There are more varieties of art and artmaking in this novel than ever. Music, cooking, fortunetelling, the circus—all suggest both the earthliness of art, its interwovenness with daily experience, and its distinctiveness, as expressive form, from daily experience. Caleb's music is integral with the world. In New Orleans, "the solitary strains of his music had a curious trick of blending with street sounds—with the voices of black women passing by or the hum of the trolley lines or a huckster's call. First you heard nothing; then you wondered; then the music separated itself and you stood still with your mouth open."

In this novel, art rather than the family offers the image that resolves the conflict between merging and separation. Of all Tyler's insular families, the Pecks most obviously cut themselves off from the mainland. (They even cut off Sulie, their lifelong black maid, who retaliates by keeping for decades the secret of Caleb's disappearance.) The only Peck of the next generation is Meg; the family has, from a small beginning, flowered and then closed, shaped, notices Justine, like a diamond. The image is much like Jeremy's, in *Celestial Navigation:* "His life, he thought, was eye-shaped—the tight pinched corners of childhood widening in middle age to encompass Mary and the children, narrowing back now to this single lonely room." Such images suggest the sterility Tyler sees in merely "staying at home" when that means denying the reality of the outside world, the "other." Daniel's last words are, "Well, I had certainly hoped for more than *this* out of life." Caleb has lived his life.

In *Searching for Caleb,* Tyler created a family who habitually turn inward in a delusion of self-sufficiency. In *Earthly Possessions* (1977), Tyler turns this notion inside out, to explore a character who believes—falsely—that her family and her earthly possessions tie her down, imprison her, keep her from the new and the strange, keep her, metaphorically and literally, from travel.

Charlotte Emory has always yearned to travel. As a child, she felt imprisoned in her home with a grotesquely fat mother and a withdrawn father. Instead of running away, she is kidnapped by a mad woman, apparently a war refugee. Charlotte as an adult believes she "enjoyed" her horrifying journey and models herself secretly after this damaged woman, stripping herself mentally of all attachments to people and things, prepared for a forced march. When she's kidnapped again as an adult, by a thief behind her in the bank line, Charlotte learns that traveling can be confining, that earthly possessions can be liberating, and that she will do plenty of traveling in her psychic journey with her husband, the familiar stranger Saul.

Paralleling Charlotte's growth to awareness is a shift of tone. At the beginning, Charlotte's voice is wry, humorous, distanced, self-deprecating. By the end, it is richer, more various, and more deeply felt. And it is in part through the process of narrating (itself a form of travel) that Charlotte learns she has been wrong in certain crucial assumptions. Charlotte tells the reader two juxtaposed past tense stories, one of travels with Jake the bank thief, the other of growing up. In the telling of each she revises her memory, her history, and thus her understanding of herself.

Charlotte's tone as she begins her story is jocular and clever, confident and breezy: she introduces her mother as "a fat lady who used to teach first grade" and lards her own speech with TV clichés. But, we later learn, this is a tone she studiously acquired when she "gave up hope…I loosened my roots, floated a few feet off, and grew to look at things with a faint, pleasant humorousness." Similarly, Charlotte's early memories are later revised. At first she tells us that her mother had not believed Charlotte was her true daughter. Actually the fears were Charlotte's own: "that I was not their true daughter, and would be sent away…[and] that I *was* their true daughter and would never, ever manage to escape to the outside world." Near the end of the novel, her mother gives Charlotte a photograph to burn. It is of a little girl; Charlotte is now only "almost sure" of her own memory that her mother searched through hospital records for her "true" blonde daughter.

In the final section, the only one told in the present tense, we hear a voice tutored by the immediate past, the long past, and the telling of the tale. Charlotte accepts that she distorted the truth, but sees those distortions as simultaneous blurrings and expressions of truth. To see her mother as not her "true mother" expressed the truth of her own feelings. As a visual artist, Charlotte photographs people who costume themselves whimsically. Comparing her pictures to her father's supposedly more realistic work, she has always felt guilt. Now, she says their "borrowed medals may tell more truth than they hide." And, she thinks, her minister husband Saul's congregation is "suspended in a lens of his own, equally truthful, equally flawed."

Thus in the novel an initially passive and unreliable narrator becomes active and reliable. In her forced march with Jake chained into a moving island of a car, she finds travel more isolating than home, and Jake less of a stranger to her than her own husband Saul, whose "leathery, foreign smell…[had] called up so much love." To meet new people, then, she goes back to her family; to free herself of "earthly possessions," she accepts the reality that "nobody's ours": to travel, she goes home. Even Jake the thief, more insistent a wanderer and more alone than Caleb Peck, eventually sees that he is running only from himself. As Charlotte tells Saul, "We have been traveling for years, traveled all our lives, we are traveling still. We couldn't stay in one place if we tried."

Readers seem to like or dislike *Morgan's Passing* (1980) because they like or dislike Morgan. As an utter narcissist, Morgan can be infuriating. His wife, Bonny, understands him as "real only in the eyes of others;" he loves costume and lies and roles. But Morgan develops an interior, too. He is, by the end, capable of not just fantasy and projection, but of insight and love for someone different. For Morgan, that person is Emily Cathcart Meredith. Emily (like Anne Tyler) grew up in the rural South as a Quaker. She marries Leon Meredith, to leave home and "join the world," and she becomes an artist, making puppets and puppet shows. But she is, despite her marriage, emotionally alone.

Tyler dramatizes Morgan's move out of narcissism subtly and with a clear eye to the zigzag process of change. Originally Morgan is so needy and so self-involved that he is at once "never truly happy if he [feels] that even the most random passing stranger [finds] him unlikable" and certain that his hand is "so repulsive" to two women on a bus that they are "babbling utter nonsense just to keep from thinking about it." Morgan projects his own wish to be carefree and unattached onto Emily and her husband. He cannot hear Emily when she says they are "not who you believe we are." He loses interest in his own children when they quit thinking he is "so wonderful." But Morgan reveals to the Merediths, as he has to no one else, his actual life and his true feelings. Then he "combines his worlds," inviting the Merediths to his home. And he begins to separate his "playacting" from his true feelings: "Let's stop fooling, Emily," he tells her. "I love you."

Emily's relation to art is different from Morgan's in the same way the direction of her growth is different. She has almost never dramatized herself; dressing always the same, austerely, in leotards, her imagination plays upon the world instead of her self, as her manipulation of puppets and marionettes suggests in contrast to Morgan's self-costuming. For her, reality weighs all too heavily on art. When she reinvents Beauty and the Beast so that the beast remains a beast, she quickly calls her version the "more authentic" one.

But her sense of reality is also a gift to her as an artist. She is capable of dialectal relationships with her creations; her puppets, each a "distinct personality," seem to take on lives, even expressions, of their own, relatively free from the imprisoning projections of an artist like Morgan. If her strength is that she is as "uncurtained as her windows," her lack is that, Emily denies herself fictions of her self. Emily yearns to find life more "interesting" than it seems to her to be. Thus Emily's growth comes as she allows herself to "just…get out of [her] life sometimes," to "make things more interesting than they really were." Emily, who has always manipulated her puppets and marionettes with ease, now feels herself drawn to Morgan, "this completely other person," by "strings that pulled her, by ropes." So it is appropriate, then, that Morgan learns to work the strings on a marionette; at the end of the novel, as "Leon Meredith," he is Emily's co-puppeteer.

Morgan suffers with the Peckish anxiety that change is death: "I wish she'd stay this way forever," he says of his daughter Gina. For Morgan, life feels like a series of snapshots rather than a home movie. It's not really paradoxical that he has so many different costumes himself; they are as discontinuous in space as his children seem to him in time. How, he wonders, can a person persist over time as an identity, without either ossifying or losing all connection with the past? Yet Morgan grows, he experiences the paradox, and having experienced it, he accepts its reality as a mystery, and changes his mind about the importance of comprehensibility. "So much lacks logic," he says. Both Morgan and Emily come to love images of art that suggest permanence in change, change in permanence. Emily likes a photographic image of Wilbur Wright, tense with potential yet "suspended forever," and she sees Morgan this way. And Morgan has his own Grecian urn: "There was something about [Emily] running that seemed eternal. She was like the braided peasant girl in a weatherhouse, traveling forever on her appointed path, rain or shine, endearingly steadfast."

The idea behind the title of *Dinner at the Homesick Restaurant* (1982) has been around for a good while in Anne Tyler's fiction. In *The Clock Winder*, Mary Emerson says to the maid Alvareen, as she brings in an apple pie, "Now aren't you an optimist. Have you ever known this family to make it through to the end of a meal?" In *Searching for Caleb*, Caleb as a chef makes the "comfort foods that every man turns to when he is feeling low," and works in a cafe that he's made to look like the "kitchen in the home of a very large family."

If *Morgan's Passing* focused on characters who grew out of limited ways of imagining and of loving, *Dinner at the Homesick Restaurant* returns for a hard and unequivocal look at some people who remain stuck in family patterns of mismatched needs and strengths. The Tulls compulsively reenact old failed efforts to cure their homesickness. Yet they mostly manage, if not to return home at last, some creative accommodation, as adults, to the irretrievable stunting of their lives. After the flamboyance of Morgan and the steadiness of Emily, the cruelty of the Tulls—conscious and unconscious—harks back to Tyler's earlier fictions, to the cross purposes and double binds and misreadings and misuses her characters have perpetrated on one another since the beginning. *Dinner at the Homesick Restaurant* offers not only the clearest vision yet of damaged and damaging people, but it dramatizes in unencumbered and revelatory scenes the processes of the family dynamic through which the damage is perpetuated. As one reads, each such scene holds like a bulb the chance for growth and change. Yet each inexorably freezes into the patterns of the family. Because Tyler chose for her structure a series of self-contained chapters, each focused on one family member's point of view, the reader is schooled in caring for each flawed character. So the effect of those lucid revelatory scenes is to produce, in the reader, the deepest sense so far in Tyler of irony that is both understood and felt. Tyler shows a family repeatedly botching up what could be, with the difference of a hair, moments of intimacy and love. And she shows the resiliency and creativity, even in these conditions, of human beings.

A recurrent Tull memory connects them, illustrates their differences, and suggests Tyler's vision of the intricate web of experience and memory that makes a family. In the country for a family outing, Pearl Tull is shot (neither seriously nor intentionally) by an arrow from a new archery set her husband Beck has brought. The shot comes from a bow held by her oldest son Cody. In her memory, Pearl blames Beck, more particularly because the wound gets infected when he is gone. Cody remembers himself as feeling angry and jealous of his brother Ezra, his mother's favorite, and blames Ezra. When Beck thinks of it, he blames Pearl—in fact family life itself—for ruining his plans. No one tells anyone else how he sees the episode. Nevertheless, the family's deepest assumptions are focused on this scene. It's after this happens that Beck leaves for good, explaining decades later that he could not handle the "grayness," the "half-right-and-half-wrongness" of family life: the very ambiguity that lies at the heart of this scene, and of the novel's structure and meaning.

Given their various needs and lacks and strengths, each Tull develops so predictably as to suggest that Tyler here (at least until the novel's end) relinquishes a bit of the faith in change, however slow and small, that informed her earlier work.

Pearl, whose point of view opens the novel, appears to the reader as a strong and honest woman whom Beck's disappearance has wounded in ways that in turn wound her children. We know that she still thinks of and cares for her children because we are in her mind; but the children don't. Pearl misses Beck's cherishing, his smell, even an intimacy she rarely lets herself remember. She determines to replicate the experience by imposing a fantasy of closeness and a goal of self-sufficiency on her remaining family. And she becomes bitter. After Beck leaves, she becomes a "nonfeeder"; her creativity turns into destructive abuse, verbal and physical. Now lacking not only a husband but any adult friends at all, she expects her children to have grownup capacities and intents. From babyhood, she feels, Cody was "absent," "batt[ing] her away"; Jenny was "evasive" and "opaque"; and Ezra was "mild and confused," the "only one who would let her in." With these perceptions of her children's intentionality she turns to them as a helpless or enraged child herself, looking for an adult. In dying, she at last searches for her own self again. Restlessly rehearsing her past, she finds in her girlhood journal that moment of perfect past happiness which, as she reads and remembers it now, can let her rest, home to herself at last. It is 1910:

> Early this morning, I went out behind the house to weed. Was kneeling in the dirt by the stable with my pinafore a mess and the perspiration rolling down my back, wiped my face on my sleeve, reached for the trowel, and all at once thought, Why I believe that at just this moment I am absolutely happy.
>
> The Bedloe girl's piano scales were floating out her window, and a bottle fly was buzzing in the grass, and I saw that I was kneeling on such a beautiful green little planet. I don't care what else might come about, but I have had this moment. It belongs to me.

Each of the children accommodates to Pearl, both competitively and cooperatively. Cody, for instance, reenacts with great ingenuity and variety his fundamentally simple and impossible effort to achieve closeness with his mother by destroying her love for Ezra, whom he believes she prefers. Yet, at crucial moments, he will protect Ezra—from getting lost in a crowd, from a woman who doesn't appreciate him—so deeply connected are Cody's envy and his love. At one time Pearl, anxious and worried about a photograph of Ezra drunk, turns to Cody as to a trusted adult. Cody, open to this offer of what seems to him honesty and intimacy, tells the truth: he set up the photograph. Then Pearl—feeling betrayed—turns on Cody, and tells him he has been "mean" since the day he was born. Cody, betrayed in turn, retreats, without apparent feeling, to his task. It is a task that suggest both his need and his adjustment to deprivation: he is sneaking a look at his father's letter to Pearl. Later, he destroys Ezra at Monopoly. Inevitably, Cody will go on to steal Ezra's fiancee, will see Ezra enviously even in his own son.

Ezra seems to Pearl the one most likely to meet her need for closeness, since he will "let her in." The irony is that she loves him for what is in fact Ezra's weakness: his incapacity to assert and defend himself, to keep danger "out." Hence for Ezra to grow, to move into competence and a separate self, would mean the loss of his mother's love. It's a plot he acts out clearly with Mrs. Scarlatti. When he designs her restaurant in his own vision of a good fit between feeder and fed, Ezra loses her love. As with Cody, a moving scene shows Ezra exposing some deep feelings to his mother ("I'm worried I don't know how to get in touch with people"); as with Cody, in her own need for him to listen to her, Pearl can't hear him. She calls his words "nonsense." Ezra retreats to his own pattern of response, sticking around his mother after this, dutifully hearing her own piece.

Finally, Jenny—perhaps the most detached and determined of the three, with her ambition and her discipline—tries to put the family behind her entirely, marrying out, moving away, and, as a doctor, caring for children as her mother could not. None of this works as she hopes. With a man, her goal had been an "innocent protective marriage," safe from the abuse she had known in her first home. Yet in her three marriages, she seriously misjudges each man. In the last marriage, she herself is the "protective" one. She marries a man whose wife has deserted him and his "flanks of" children, even a baby who "was so little and so recently abandoned that she turned her head and opened her mouth when [Jenny] held her horizontal." Because of them she has no time to talk to her husband Joe, no time even to think any more. Her chapter title, "Dr. Tull Is Not a Toy," suggests, her harassment at the hands of the children she treats. Of the three young Tulls, the most vividly abused by Pearl was Jenny. As a single parent, in a terrible period, Jenny beats and tortures her own child Becky. That Jenny has her reasons (as had Pearl)—fatigue, loneliness, memory—doesn't obviate the sense that this is an inevitable repetition of family damage. Abused as a child and abusive as a mother, now she receives abuse from children. Yet, touchingly, it is Pearl who finally comes to her to "put the world in order again"; Ezra and Cody follow. The damage and the healing are so deeply connected as to sustain the pattern that keeps the family together.

That sense of inextricable love and hate, creativity and destruction, appears in the Tull family meals at Ezra's Homesick Restaurant. Designed to supply needs not filled at Ezra's own home, in his restaurant the food matches the hunger. But at the restaurant, because of their conflicts, the Tulls never finish a meal. These broken meals keep the diners unsatisfied and coming back for more; Ezra, whose need is to feed, keeps arranging dinners again. At the end, though Pearl is dead and Beck (who is back for her funeral) threatens to leave before the "dessert wine," there is a hint—barely a hint—that this one meal will be not only consumed but consummated.

If so, the Tulls may be home at last without being quite so homesick this time. The moments of intimacy may for once go full term, freeing Cody and Ezra and Jenny, even Luke and Beck, from repetition, and founding family connectedness on a basis that is healthier than the denials and damage of the past. Maybe. There's one good sign in Luke. Like some other Tyler children, he has the courage and honesty to speak out. To his father, he says, "How come you go on hanging *on* to these things, year after year after year?"

The Accidental Tourist retrieves from *Earthly Possessions* the metaphor of the forced march. Like Charlotte Emory, Macon Leary travels, but under duress. Passive, he is nevertheless mobile—at the will of others. When he must leave the familiar comforts of home, Macon spends his energy trying to replicate those comforts abroad, so as to avoid the perils of travel: the new, the strange, the foreign. Brilliantly, Tyler assigns him the profession of writing travel guides for people like him—businessmen away from home against their will, who want king-sized Beautyrest mattresses in Madrid, a Taco Bell in Mexico City, Chef Boyardee ravioli in Rome. To do his job, Macon is, of course, forced to travel.

The novel begins with a scene of travel. Macon and Sarah, his wife, are coming home from a failed beach vacation. Their efforts to talk end up, habitually, in the same cul de sac: Sarah blames and criticizes Macon, and Macon withdraws. Macon is actually static, or in retreat, in both his marriage and his identity. Ethan, his son, is dead, "murdered in a Burger Bonanza his second night at camp." When Sarah decides to leave him, Macon responds, at first, with relief. Now he can have the system, the order, he longs for. He does his laundry by "treading the day's dirty clothes underfoot" while he showers; for breakfast, he eats popcorn from a popper hooked to a timer next to his bed. But the craziness and failure of his systems look him in the face (who can say what enables this moment?): he hears himself telling a stranger, the grocery clerk, about his anguish—and his Byzantine basement arrangement breaks his leg. Suspecting that he has "engineered his injury…just so he could settle down safe among the people he'd started out with," he moves into his grandmother's house, where he grew up. Two brothers and a sister have already returned; as children, "none of them ever stepped outside without obsessively noting all available landmarks, clinging to a fixed and desperate mental map of the neighborhood."

The accident that sends Macon on a journey that he finally, willingly, chooses has to do with his irascible Welsh corgi Edward. Macon wavers between indulgent identification with the dog and anxiety at his increasing violence. One day, in a hurry to catch a plane, he takes the dog to his regular vet to be boarded and is turned away; Edward bit the attendant. He locates the Meow-Bow, which will take Edward in, and where Muriel Pritchett works. Frizzy haired, wildly dressed, Muriel is a dog trainer, a single mother, and determined to get involved with Macon.

It is the relationship that she develops with Macon that forms the core of *The Accidental Tourist*. Unlike passive, proper Macon, Muriel is feisty, tenacious, self-respecting. Muriel trains the dog by refusing ever to allow him to beat her in their power struggles: Macon is horrified when she yanks Edward into the air by the chain collar and lets him dangle, as punishment. Nevertheless, Macon slips into living with her, slips into caring about her son, and slips into liking the neighborhood itself. Singleton Street, working-class, ethnic, is new and foreign to his bland home and past; yet he loves "the surprise of [Muriel], and also the surprise of himself when he was with her. In the foreign country that was Singleton Street he was an entirely different person."

But the crisis remains. Still an accidental tourist there, Macon is not willing to make a choice to stay with Muriel, and is easily seduced into returning home with the familiar Sarah. Predictably, they fall into the familiar conflicts: his passivity, her discontent. The crisis comes in Paris, where Macon is on a job. To his horror, he sees Muriel on the plane. Determined as ever, she has called his travel agent and booked an identical trip for herself. Macon freezes up; his back goes out, and he can't move at all.

Sarah flies from home to take care of Macon and his job. In Paris, she tells him of her desire to have a second honeymoon and another child, and complains that he could have "taken steps" to prevent Muriel's coming to Paris if he'd wanted. Macon reflects on the accidental quality of his life: "His marriage, his two jobs, his time with Muriel, his return to Sarah—all seemed to have simply befallen him. He couldn't think of a single major act he had managed of his own accord."

In the morning, he "negotiates the journey" out of bed, gets dressed, and packs to leave. Of his own accord, he has decided to go back with Muriel. In the cab, he feels "a kind of inner rush, a racing forward. The real adventure," he thinks, "is the flow of time…" Like agoraphobic Jeremy Pauling, whose desire to find his family moves him out of his block, Macon is no longer an accidental tourist. But unlike *Celestial Navigation,* which ends with Jeremy's failure, *The Accidental Tourist* ends with hope. In this novel, going home to Muriel represents not repetition and stasis, but growth and change. It is the best kind of travel there is.

The psychoanalyst most recently embraced by literary critics, Jacques Lacan, argues that the conflict between the desire for the bliss of perfect union and the principle of reality of separation is irreconcilable. In this he is congruent with Nancy Chodorow's perceptions. Lacan goes on to argue that this split structures the very subject, the "self," that seeks a way out of it. Impelled to seek a blissful "home" in the imaginary, we will inevitably be homesick when we (think we) find it: it does not exist. Preoccupied with similar questions, Anne Tyler chooses narrative as her medium. Perhaps because of the possibilities offered by time, plot, metaphor, and character, her emerging reflections on the subject differ from Lacan's in their interest in and emphasis on process. In time, her novels suggest, lies the possibility of moving into neither "pure" union nor radical isolation, but a kind of maturity that accompanies acknowledgment of and submission to the real. Her characters travel from homes where everything stays the same to homes that admit change, variety and surprise; they move from (false) Eden to (real) earth. Of them all, Macon most clearly chooses to abandon his illusion that home means either safety or imperishable bliss. For that reason, he may be able to be content, to be at home without feeling homesick again.

Anne G. Jones
April, 1986

UPDATE

The prolific Anne Tyler has, since this essay appeared, written five more best-selling novels: *Breathing Lessons* (1988), *Saint Maybe* (1991), *Ladder of Years* (1995), *A Patchwork Planet* (1998), *Back When We Were Grownups* (2001). She also has written a children's book, *Tumble Tower,* illustrated by her daughter Mitra Modarressi (1993), and a screenplay based on her novel *Breathing Lessons* (1994), and edited, with Shannon Ravenel, *Best of the South: From Ten Years of New Stories from the South* (1996). In 1988 *The Accidental Tourist* was made into an Academy Award-winning film, starring William Hurt, Kathleen Turner, and Geena Davis. In 1994 *Breathing Lessons* was made into a Hallmark Hall of Fame television movie (for which Tyler co-wrote the script) and starred Joanne Woodward and James Garner.

Tyler's main theme, as described in the *Dictionary of Literary Biography,* "is the obstinate endurance of the human spirit, reflected in every character's acceptance or rejection of his fate and in how that attitude affects his day to day life. She uses the family unit as a vehicle for portraying 'how people manage to endure together. . . .'" Tyler once told the *New York Times Book Review,* "Reading Eudora Welty when I was growing up showed me that very small things are often really larger than the large things. . . ."

Tyler's early work got a lukewarm reception, and was even called dull. Today, however, her books are received with enthusiasm. In a review of *A Patchwork Planet, International Fiction Review* wrote: "[the quilt]'was made up of mismatched squares of cloth no bigger than postage stamps, joined by the uneven black stitches of a woman whose eyesight was failing. Planet Earth, in Mrs.

■ BOOKS BY ANNE TYLER

If Morning Ever Comes. New York: Knopf, 1964, New York: Berkley Publishing Corp., 1985.

The Tin Can Tree. New York: Knopf, 1965, New York: Berkley Publishing Corp., 1983, Boston: G. K. Hall, 1984.

A Slipping-Down Life. New York: Knopf, 1970, Boston: G. K. Hall, 1985, New York: Berkley Publishing Corp., 1985.

The Clock Winder. New York: Knopf, 1972, New York: Berkley Publishing Corp., 1985.

Celestial Navigation. New York: Knopf, 1974, New York: Berkley Publishing Corp., 1985.

Searching for Caleb. New York: Knopf, 1976, New York: Berkley Publishing Corp., 1985.

Earthly Possessions. New York: Knopf, 1977, New York: Berkley Publishing Corp., 1985.

Morgan's Passing. New York: Knopf, 1980, New York: Berkley Publishing Corp., 1985.

Dinner at the Homesick Restaurant. Boston: G. K. Hall, 1982, New York: Knopf, 1982, New York: Berkley Publishing Corp., 1983.

Best American Short Stories 1983 (Co-Editor), New York: Houghton, 1983.

The Accidental Tourist. New York: Knopf, 1985.

Breathing Lessons. New York: Knopf, 1988.

Anne Tyler: Four Complete Novels (contains *Dinner at the Homesick Restaurant, Morgan's Passing, The Tin Can Tree,* and *If Morning Ever Comes*). New York: Avenel Books, 1990.

Saint Maybe. New York: Knopf, 1991.

Anne Tyler: A New Collection (contains *The Accidental Tourist, Breathing Lessons,* and *Searching for Caleb*). New York: Wing Books, 1991.

Tumble Tower. New York: Orchard Books, 1993.

Ladder of Years. New York: Orchard Books, 1995.

A Patchwork Planet. New York: Knopf, 1998.

Lubb Dup. Chicago: Sara Ranchouse Publishing, 1998.

Back When We Were Grownups. New York: Knopf, 2001.

Reunion en el Restaurante Nostalgia. New York: Random House, 2001.

Un Mundo Roto. New York: Random House, 2001.

Alford's version, was makeshift and haphazard, clumsily cobbled together, overlapping and crowded, and likely to fall into pieces at any moment.' The patchwork quilt, long an emblem of women's work, is an appropriate symbol for Tyler's novels: chronicling sequences of realistic and apparently random events, they move imperceptibly towards a remarkable revelation."

Back When We Were Grownups, Tyler's most recent novel, has won the customary praise from critics and readers alike. A *Publishers Weekly* review lauded the story of Rebecca—widow, mother, grandmother, and caretaker—who, at 53, decides she has grown into the "wrong person" and sets out to find the life she lost: "The ease of [Tyler's] storytelling here is breathtaking, but almost unnoticeable because, rather like Rebecca, Tyler never calls attention to what she does. Late in the novel, Rebecca observes that her younger self had wanted to believe 'that there were grander motivations in history than mere family and friends, mere domestic happenstance.' Tyler makes it plain: nothing could be more grand."

Despite Tyler's famously private life—she does not teach, lecture, or do readings, and seldom grants interviews—she is one of the best-known and best-loved novelists writing in America today.

This Intersection Time: The Fiction of Gordon Weaver

At the core of the fiction of Gordon Weaver is a fascination with the mystery of time. And what he seems to find within that mystery is the key to identity: that identity is determined by time in its survey of a man's life.

Of course, all writers must deal with time implicitly or explicitly, with the processes it embodies of generation and annihilation of individuals, eras, cultures, with its delimitation of individual identity in the context of a life-span and a culture. Our era's transfer of power from an anthropomorphic god to impersonal processes of biology and physics, the displacement of God's wrath by nuclear fission, of the permanence of man's biological preeminence by a long, diverse evolutionary process leading to an unknown conclusion, has perhaps resulted in a particular consciousness in this century's fiction of man's powerlessness to time, the perishability not only of an individual or of his cultural context, but of his species, of the planet which bred the first germ of his appearance.

Time is a prominent concern of many major modern and contemporary writers, each of whom deals with it in his own particular fashion: Joyce with its psychological simultaneity, Eliot with its mystical dimensions, our temporal enslavement "at this intersection time," our liberation at "the still point of the turning world"; Wolfe, Steinbeck and others investigate time via broad family tapestries, Fitzgerald via the return of a changed person to a changed place. Barth, Fowles, and Boyle revive forms of the past to house contemporary psychological realities; Huxley, Orwell, and Barth create landscapes of the future as projections of the consequences of our present. Coover, Barthelme, and Hawkes play with temporal-spatial distortions to create new perspectives of existence in a zone of timelessness, while Beckett, John Gardner, and John Fowles treat time as the French existentialists do, as a *"salle d'attente,"* similar to Calvino's railway station metaphor in *If on a Winter's Night a Traveller:* an "illuminated limbo suspended between two darknesses…" where fiction and fact (i.e., fictional fiction and fictional fact) are fused like man and goat.

Weaver's approach to the process of time is via the moment, the point of temporal intersection. In his own words, Weaver's technique is "…to settle on a given moment in a character's life, to stop that moment in time, examine it, see its implications…," to examine "…how experience *means* to people…" rather than "…how it can be described from without, 'objectively.'"

In over two decades of publishing, Weaver has been remarkably constant in his pursuit of this vision. His six books of fiction and eighty magazine stories are a gallery of such moments, a frieze of characters suspended in different aspects of time's triptych of dimensions. His first published story, "When Times Sit In" (1962), is about a man fleeing time's flux; his most recent, the award-winning novella, "The Eight Corners of the World" (*Quarterly West,* fall-winter 1984–85), deals with one man's attempt to gather the heap of broken moments of his life into a coherent whole.

Gordon Weaver <small>Gordon</small>

Weaver was born on February 2, 1937, in Moline, Illinois. He received his B.A. from the University of Wisconsin-Milwaukee (1961), his M.A. from the University of Illinois (1962), and his Ph.D from the University of Denver (1970). He was an instructor in English at Siena College (1963–65); then an assistant, associate, and full professor of English at the University of Southern Mississippi (1970–75). He was also director of the University's Center for Writers (1972–75). He has been professor of English at Oklahoma State University since 1975, where he served as department head until 1984. He is a member of the Associated Writing Programs and an adjunct faculty member of the Vermont College creative writing program. Among his many honors and awards, he has received a Woodrow Wilson National fellowship (1961–62), the St. Lawrence Award for Fiction (1973), and a National Endowment for the Arts fellowship in creative writing (1974). Weaver married Judith Gosnell in 1961; they have three daughters. He currently lives and works in Stillwater, Oklahoma. ■

Between these two, we find an array of characters consuming and being consumed by the moment: conmen photographers who peddle the timeless moment in a snapshot ("Fantastico," 1972; "The Eight Corners of the World," 1984); fathers sifting through the rubble of the past to find in their memory of *their* fathers "a meaning worth the living" for their own sons (*Give Him a Stone,* 1975); failed men whose lives have progressed on the warp of a moment's misperception ("Getting Serious," 1980; "Whiskey, Whiskey, Gin, Gin, Gin," 1983); men locked into the past (*Circling Byzantium,* part one, 1980), the present (*Circling Byzantium,* part two, 1980; "The Parts of Speech," 1984), and the future (*Circling Byzantium,* part three, 1980).

Weaver's moments determine identity. They are crucial not necessarily because of any dramatic occurrence, but because of some spiritual-psychological charge for the character (as in *Give Him a Stone* when Oskar Hansen, Jr., sees his estranged father approaching the house and recognizes how much the man has aged), by some configuration of emotion and weather and event and mere physical perception (as in *Circling Byzantium,* when young Batterman is walking home behind some friends from an afternoon's swim and becomes aware that he exists at the center of time, that time's procession, as his own with it, is inevitable and unimpeachable), or by illuminating the point at which quantitative change becomes qualitative change (as in *Count a Lonely Cadence* with its description of the sergeants who wake up one day with no enthusiasm left for who they were or thought they had been; in this, Weaver's first book, we see already the seed of the time/identity theme, although that novel would seem to have been more consciously focused on the theme of individual alienation).

These moments are seen through the tunnel of years in microscopic clarity; time stops at its center and "becomes (*is!*) arranged on a frozen continuum as solid as sculpture." And: "All this I know, then-now, in this sweltering and pulsing fraction of time that I make, in writing this, forever."

Here the child Oskar sees that his father is a man who has been "reduced" and glimpses the secret of time: "that people age, that a man…will see the time when he is less than he was, and in that knowledge, torment himself with yearning for that former self. He cannot recover losses, cannot abide self-awareness, never hope to arrest the certain path of his future." This passage gives some hint of why Weaver's stories so often derive from characters who are "losers"—the overweight, bankrupt, prisoners, spastic, alcoholic, the shards of broken homes. Again, in Weaver's own words, "Failure seems to me the lot of most men, in any endeavor. We all fail in view of our mortality. We'll never beat the world, but we *can* find terms, within ourselves, and in our particular contexts."

The way in which Weaver's characters confront these facts give further access to this time/identity mystery, viewed always from a moment of narration which is eternal as sculpture, as a painting, a snapshot. But the picture caught by human perception is fallible. In the title story of *Getting Serious*, the narrator relates an incident from his youth upon which the bulk of his future experience is based: "My world, in this time of my beginning, is no more or less than my vision of it, and this picture is my vision, this time and place, these people…" The twist here is that this "vision," upon which the narrator bases his future actions or, in any event, which furnishes the psychological-emotional reality from which he is motivated to action is *mistaken;* he does not see beyond the deceitful surface of his surroundings. The child's vision does not penetrate the posing vanity of the adults whose "heroism" so impresses him. Hence he models his adulthood after the flair of a liar. Again, in "Whiskey, Whiskey, Gin, Gin, Gin," a child perceives the drunken happiness of his brother as genuine and sacrifices his life in pursuit of that artificial joy.

Sometimes Weaver's subject and theme meld, and the access and approach to time is as direct and directly philosophical as T. S. Eliot's, as in *Give Him a Stone* where the narrator, a now adult Oskar Hansen, Jr., addresses his own son about the life of the grandfather whom the boy has never met:

> What I make for you is the mystery of a life, mystery if only because all ends in death, all stories end abruptly in death. Son, if we can make a life for my father, then we make the meaning of his death. Believe in this, and we can surely believe in ourselves. He was my father, you are my son, and I stand between you to tell this lie that it might make us true. I trespass fact that you and I might know what we cannot know…We imagine what we can never know, and if we can, if we *will* believe, then we can live as he died, in a peace with the mystery of our ends in death. We will have made a meaning, you and I, worth our living…

The meaning which is made of the life of the father in *Give Him a Stone* becomes all the more credible, moving, and tragic in the face of that life's erosion by time. By every measure, Buck Hansen, Sr., is a failure, a man who has been "caught and engulfed" by "dirt, time and circumstance," a common man with hubris, thus a tragi-comic figure. He fails out of high school for a refusal to render an apology for an impetuous insult to the principal, breaks up his family and loses his fine house because he cannot resist bragging about his mistress, marries again to a woman dying of cancer, only to join up with another woman who is in league with her brother to fleece him of the financial backing Hansen hopes to finagle from them. He is a man who "could not accept…that nothing was sufficient beyond its moment. And this knowledge scalded him." (This, itself, is a specific concern we see repeatedly in Weaver's fiction—in the "happy hour" motif, particularly in "Whiskey, Whiskey, Gin, Gin, Gin," "Nigger Sunday," and in the black-comic scalding of Christianity in "Haskell Hooked on the Northern Cheyenne".)

Thus, Buck Hansen wolfs Mexican chili for breakfast, only to find himself, an hour later, hunched over the steering wheel, suffering heartburn. Yet it is this very appetite which moves him forward in time. "It is not chili for breakfast, not nostalgia for a place (the Mexican restaurant) he knew back before the world went to hell and gone; it is appetite! For one more day, he has made himself believe. A man who believes, lives. A man who lives, hungers, and he who can hunger *must eat!* He has made himself live another day in a world that no longer needs or wants him." He was a man who "would not submit (to time's insufficiency), and that is something, after all."

Indeed, it is that refusal to submit, that hubristic rashness, which will give him the gumption to steal his nine-year-old son for a few days to take him on an automobile tour from the Twin Cities to Chicago, to Indiana, to Long Island, trying to salvage his life which is in default both emotionally and economically, to reclaim some intimacy with his boy, to imprint himself upon the child.

The facts of the journey, of course, must be embellished, enlarged, interpreted from the narrator's present moment in time, many years later, as he relates the tale to his own son. Thus he must "trespass fact that you and I might know what we cannot know." This is quite ingenious. The voice is thus not a fiction writer, but is anyway writing fiction, achieving for the novel a further dimension—one that we see not infrequently in Weaver's fiction, though rarely so fully developed as here—the dimension of the open framework through which we glimpse from time to time the writing of the story, the painting of the picture, the close-up on the snapshot, the freeze-frame display, though what these freeze-frames display is not the blurred instant of athletic triumph, but the triumph of imagination, the clarity of created meaning beyond fact.

This technique has the effect of grinding the gears of time to a halt, and with this our own priorities are willing to pause, with Buck Hansen's, for example, as he steals his son. Hansen's character is quintessentially American—one of the worse sorts of American, the gross blowhard bigot overweight salesman bully, a character ripe for the acid of a Sinclair Lewis or a Dan Greenburg (e.g., *Going All the Way*). Yet this vulgar blowhard comes so poignantly alive as to earn our respect, and we are led to experience our own humanity in a place we did not know that it existed—in this most American heart of the heart of the country. Buck Hansen, after all, is an American hero, an American father-failure, a big man suffering our national fate, fighting time, fat, bankruptcy, appetite, the loss of war-generated riches, the post-war slump, the inevitability of decay and death, the built-in destructive element of the capitalist legend we pursue. And, remarkably, the book makes us know the dignity and strength of this man, the indefatigible resilience, the power to do. Hansen is pursued throughout the book by a collection agency bloodhound, a man much younger than himself and of more modest appetites and abilities who learns something about Buck Hansen and, presumably, about America. He learns that Hansen is not what he expected: not a respectable, buttoned down, establishment man who has had a turn of bad luck, but that he is what he is, a corpulent blowhard, a bull, a raw force.

I believe that in the character of Buck Hansen we come close to an American spirit. Here we have a man who got rich on the war, selling a machine that made a part of a machine which manufactured a machine for the war effort, a man who looks with disgust at his bloated 49-year-old body as he strips to bathe, who struggles futilely to win himself back from fat and decay. Yet still there is in him a core of dignity, integrity, character, the power of affection for his son, for his dying wife, which enables him to come to terms with his disgrace and win our respect. The last we see of him, just after he has returned his son to the boy's mother (in a good new blue suit), he is knocked down by his oldest son; Buck rises and daubs his lip and exits with greater dignity than he has had at any previous moment in the novel. His act of foolishness has, in a sense, achieved more than anything else he has done in his life, has finally calmed him with enlightenment, enabled him to give his son enough of himself with which to create a life and a meaning "worth the living" for his son and grandson both. The book is an object lesson on the function of fiction, on its importance for our survival, and one that is apropos in this time of the disintegrating family. Buck Hansen is a truly American character, his story a truly American one—how many thousands, millions of times a year does this story take place, do overweight, middle-aged men in moral and economic dissolution flee in broken-down cars, often with court orders and collection agencies close behind, back into the rubble of their past to try and find the lost ends of their dignity and meaning as human beings.

We see a similar picture of America, though from yet another angle, in Weaver's award-winning short story "Hog's Heart." Here a younger (even heavier) man comes to the end of his life prematurely, realizing that he has devoted himself and all of his energies to a sport at which he was good, but never quite good enough. As a player he was severely injured early in his career and taken on as coach by his alma mater, where he is still a local hero. Yet as a second-rate coach, he is not able to whip his second-rate team into victory and dishonors himself by hiring a non-collegiate professional place-kicker from Cuba, a black man who cannot even speak English and for whom he must forge academic credentials, to help save his and the team's name by beating "somebody big-timey" at the big game of the year. The overweight Hog develops heart palpitations, believes that he is dying. The story follows his attempt to leave order in his life, to make peace with his family and himself, to transcend the bullying of his athletic director, and the shame of his dishonor. Here, again, we see a man whose course in time is awry, twisted from the early emphasis on football away from the farm of his origin. When he visits his parents on their farm, he hears his father recall how young Hog used to lift a calf every day to build himself up for football—the sport that would deliver them all from poverty to affluence. There is some touch of mythic-Biblical proportion to this image of the boy lifting the calf—a suggestion perhaps of the sacrifice, perhaps of the sacrifice of Hog himself, of American vitality spent on non-serious pursuits. Hog does succeed in delivering his family from poverty, but at the cost of his life and honor, regaining his dignity only at the moment of supreme loss. Here we have another tragi-comic figure, and again one who moves us as a human being and not as a satiric emblem.

A mistaken course also steers the passage through time of the narrators in two other fine examples of Weaver's short fictions: the title story of *Getting Serious* and the yet uncollected "Whiskey, Whiskey, Gin, Gin, Gin."

In "Getting Serious," the narrator's image of manhood is shaped by the event of Captain Guy Roland of the Army Air Corps returning from the war, an event frozen in his mind like a snapshot ("My world in this time of my beginning, is no more or less than my vision of it, and this picture is my vision, this time and place, these people...") Guy Roland, however, is a phoney; a fact which escapes the boy's perception of him as he watches from afar the glittering exploits of the returned "hero," driving a flashy car full of flashy women, sporting the flashy decorations on his uniform, telling flashy stories. The narrator grows up and goes off to his own war and is wounded and goes on to his own life and fails, touching back from time to time at this scene of his beginning, only to realize at the last that this man upon whom his images of glory and brightness were founded is dead, metaphorically dead. Roland's wartime adventures never led him further than a cozy post down south, his ribbons were purchases from the PX, his battlefield souvenirs purchased. We see Roland at last as a drunken, pathetic figure, a waste of a man. The narrator leaves again, liberated finally from this enchantment with the false hero, a man who has been broken by life, but serious enough not to have cheated himself of the enlightenment which follows the ruin.

In "Whiskey, Whiskey, Gin, Gin, Gin," the narrator's early views of happiness are of drunken people, or at least of people drinking: his father in a bar room, his brother home from the

Navy and falling down laughing with drunkenness. He believes in their happiness, in the lure of the "happy hour" with its clinking ice cubes and cocktail peanuts. He pursues such hours, and their illusions strip him of his initial success in life as husband, father, trial lawyer. But life is, after all, an inevitable progression of loss:

> Anyone, everyone is born into a family. I have a father, mother, brothers, and my life with them remains with me, a part of me, forever. My family is broken by divorce, a world war, death, distance, time. It could make a man nostalgic. Sad. I think of them, remember, and might be sad, but I drink. Not to forget. I drink. I fill my glass with ice, vodka that looks like purest water, drink. And I remember: father, mother, brothers, myself as I was then. And I am not sad. A man is born into a family, and they die, separate, that is the way it is. There is no reason for sadness, no point in nostalgia. I fill my glass, drink. It is clear, cold, pure…

I repeat, for effect, one line from the above quote: "My family is broken by divorce, a world war, death, distance, time." This sentence surely could describe the life of many a postwar American—perhaps, in a sense, describe the state of the American post-war spirit, of the American family and America as a family. (Why *do* we drink so much?) The genius of this story, as with much of Weaver's fiction, is its consistent success in evading moralisms or, no mean task, explanations. It is a picture of a phenomenon, a sharply focused picture of a situation which does not attempt to simplify with explanations. "I fill my glass, drink. It is clear…" Here we have the phenomenon. A confused man drinks to seek clarity.

In "Parker's Dream," another as yet uncollected story, we again see a man confounded by reality who finds order beyond the real—here, in his dream life. As his daily life becomes more confused and distressing, his dream life becomes richer and more orderly and full of harmony. All the dead of his past reassemble into a kind of parade of beauty in his dreams. Those who are incomplete in his daily life become whole in his dreams, the withered arm of a colleague is healed, the sad become happy, his alienated children return to the bosom of the family. Finally, inevitably, Parker, the TV man, comes to prefer his dream to his life. As reality's nettles reach to snag him, he is sublimely indifferent, for he is dreaming.

Theme and subject, of course, are two separate things. While the theme of time can be found in much of Weaver's fiction, his subjects are as varied as his characters. They are mostly middle-class, midwestern, middle-aged men, but not exclusively so, and even within that general description there is a good deal of variety. We have stories of army yard-birds ("Wouldn't I?"), of murdering policemen ("If a Man Truly in His Heart"), alcoholic lawyers ("Whiskey, Whiskey, Gin, Gin, Gin") a genius spastic ("Finch the Spastic Speaks"), an overweight student ("Macklin's Epigraphic Loss"), a divorcee suicide ("The Cold"), a Black car-washer ("Nigger Sunday"), an old man waiting to die ("Waiting"). We have a middle-class man who manifests an insanity which is nothing less than literal Christianity; he sells what he has to give to the poor, only to be advised by a priest that he ought to seek psychiatric counseling ("Haskell Hooked on the Northern Cheyenne").

In Weaver's third novel, *Circling Byzantium* (1980), however, time is both theme *and* subject.

That novel is divided into three parts, each from the point of view of a different character focused in a different direction in the triptych of time, all three of whose paths intersect on a single point—with regard to the selling and development of a lakeside resort in upstate Wisconsin. (We have seen this resort and lake elsewhere in Gordon Weaver's fiction and find that it is, in fact, modeled on real experience of Sylvercryst Resort, Silver Lake, Wautoma, Waushara County, in north Wisconsin—a place where Weaver spent his summers from the ages of four to fourteen or fifteen. The lake resort is, of course, a natural point of focus for such a story, as natural as the waters of Ibsen's *Enemy of the People*. Each of the three main characters in the novel is governed by a fixation on a different aspect of time, and the relationship of each to the lake and what they wish to do with the lake is governed by that fixation.

The focal character in the first part, Leland Spaulding, Jr., lives in the past, in memories of his father and his mother and the happiness he knew as a child before his father was killed in the war. He views the present with a bitter eye, a bitter man, tiresome in his tireless complaining, yet when he turns his eye inward to the past, to his childhood, suddenly we see a different person, one of gentle, homely sensibility. His view of the future is one of resistance. He wishes to block the development of the lake resort, to preserve the past. Ironically, the past he wishes to preserve is the future which the father he so venerates once sought to block.

The second part character, Horse Batterman (who owns the resort and sells it to the developer), lives in the present, at "the center of time," a place where he has dwelt ever since he was a boy and had a vision of sorts, while walking home from an afternoon swim at the lake, a vision of the foolishness of trying to resist or overpower or route time's inexorable, inevitable progress. There is a joy in his passivity to time, a mythic grin of acceptance. Yet his fate is substantially altered by the activity and advice of the character on whom the third part focuses, the developer, a self-made man who buys the resort and builds it into a money-making venture, and is infuriated that Batterman is capable of *enjoying* the fruits of his insights and efforts, of being happy with them, while he himself is not, for Batterman lives in the now, while he himself lives in a world not yet realized. This character is looking always to the future, working always to make a success which ironically he is incapable of taking pleasure from in the present. His motivation is essentially a negative one, a drive from squalor toward economic power and freedom, and this very drive leads him to the loss of his wife and children, the loss of his present and finally of his past as well, turning his personal history into a joke—a "Polack joke," which is the title of the last part of the book.

Each of these characters has been touched by war: the first lost his father to World War I, the second lost his chance to be a football hero as well as fifteen months of his life as a P.O.W. to the Korean conflict, while the third was excused from World War II because of fallen arches which gave him the opportunity to lay the groundwork for his "success," always sacrificing his present for the future.

As in *Give Him a Stone*, the narration takes us into the center of time's mystery, lets us pace our way around it, examine it, and circles us back to where we started at the beginning of the book, knowing something more about the place. One easily thinks of T. S. Eliot in Chapter IX of *Give Him a Stone* and in the middle part of *Circling Byzantium*, the section titled "At the Center of Time." In the latter we have the circle of the title reflected in the book's structure, in the former as we reach the end of the father and son's flight, the last of all illusions of finding a backer to reclaim the life which has gone to pieces on Buck Hansen, the narrator says, "It remains only that we complete the circle, finish, return to the point of our beginning..." One thinks of Eliot's "...and the end of all our exploring / Will be to arrive where we started / And know the place for the first time."

Another piece in which time appears as both theme and subject is a story titled "Nigger Sunday" (originally published as "Suds' Sunday" in *Perspective*, Spring 1965) from his first collection, *The Entombed Man of Thule*. Here we have a man, a car-washer named Suds, who has lived all his days in anticipation of Sunday's pleasures, pleasures so ephemeral that he watches with barely suppressible alarm even as he lives them, as the long hard work and anticipation of the week leads to their arrival and vanishing, leaving Suds again unsatisfied with the insufficient moment to face the Sisyphus stone of Monday and his hopes for the next Sunday. There is a particularly arresting quality to this story in its presentation of time's swirling maelstrom of illusion in a precision of detail which makes its movement comprehensible.

A favorite metaphor for the moment and for the writer's task in portraying it is the snapshot and the photographer, reflections not only of the frozen moment, but also of the art of fiction in general and of Weaver's technique in particular. Irony is a strong factor here, the apparent objective realism of the photograph being so heavily subject to distortion, misrepresentation, interpretation. The key "snapshot" memories of "Getting Serious" and "Whiskey, Whiskey, Gin, Gin, Gin," for all their seeming clarity, reflect—in Weaver's own words—"…moments when, for all his intense perception, he [the narrator] failed to see the truth which might have made him live differently, turn out differently."

In the dozen years between the Barcelona photographer of "Fantastico" (1972) and the Japanese Foto Joe of "The Eight Corners of the World" (1984), this irony grows considerably more complex in its relationship to individual, cultural, and world history. Fantastico is a man whose bastard birth leaves him nameless and thus affixed in the present, without a past; falling prey finally to the yearning for a future (children), he falls in love with a prostitute; he snaps her picture and tacks it to the wall of the Texas Bar, tells her, "…in a thousand years when you are dust, even then some *turista* will come to the Texas Bar for an *aperitivo*, and on the wall he will see you as beautiful as you are today, and may likely lament your death, even then, a thousand years from now." A deception of sweet yearning, an irony of bittersweet proportions. The deceptions and ironies perpetrated by Foto Joe in the Texas Bar of post–World War II Eta Jima as an ex-Japanese military officer/ex-undergraduate at Oklahoma A&M, and alumnus of Native Land Loving School of Japan, thriving already in the assumed identity of the victor, are considerably more black-comic, diabolical and multilayered.

We see a clear progression in Weaver's work, clearly traceable developments, steepening of mystery, expanding of structure. The seeds of ideas in stories develop through collections and grow to novels. Themes touched only in passing in earlier pieces reappear later to be explored more deeply. The photographer of "Fantastico" develops over a dozen years into a transformed producer of low-budget high-yield martial arts films; the missed opportunity of making contact with the "other" in "Salesman from Hong Kong" or the momentary transfiguration of a child playing war, putting on a German helmet ("The Day I Lost My Distance") reappear on a much larger scale in "The Eight Corners of the World" where the two cultures war and blend and presumably (though the novel is still only in progress) resolve themselves in the truth which can only be reached via the trespass of fact.

In *About Fiction*, Wright Morris asserts that the first of the fictions the writer must create is his reader. Gordon Weaver describes the reader to whom he addresses himself as one with a superior level of response to which he must write up, lest he fail to grow as a writer.

His most recent productions—the fragments of his novel-in-progress ("The Eight Corners of the World") which have been published and the remarkable long story, "The Parts of Speech" (*Kenyon Review*, summer 1984)—would seem to indicate that this method of growth functions well. I have already touched upon the former work and would like to concentrate the remainder of this essay on "The Parts of Speech," which seems to me a "major" short story (if such a classification exists, as I believe it ought) and perhaps a harbinger of what we may expect from Gordon Weaver in the second two decades of his career as a creator of fictions.

"The Parts of Speech" is a ten or twelve thousand word story divided into three distinct parts bracketed between a brief preface and even briefer epilogue, the whole work launched by a tantalizing epigraph from Peter Taylor's "Daphne's Lover." The story is narrated by a fiction writer. Of its three main parts, the first two purport to be "true," the third a fiction based upon a third-hand anecdote received by the narrator at the end of part two.

The story is about identity as fiction and as lie and about the consequences of this, about the lives that are fed to this process. A young woman comes to die, to be killed in the process of a lie, a deceit—or perhaps as the result of a series of lies or fictions in which she herself is a participant.

In the preface, the narrator identifies himself as a creator of fictions, considers briefly what that entails, and explains the structure of the story to come, a mixture of two parts "truth," one part fiction.

In the first part, we see the narrator as a sixteen-year-old high school transfer student hiding the pain of his insecurity in the garb of an impenetrable, self-imposed anonymity. However, his protective isolation is threatened by the invasion of an English teacher who never asks her students "to speculate as to the relationship of literature to life," but who insists that they participate in a daily flash-card drill on the parts of speech. The narrator has never learned this aspect of grammar. As the drill works toward him, he dreads what he knows can only be the penetration of his shell of aloofness, that by which he survives in this alien school. But he is saved. The girl behind him, Cynthia Von Eschen, whispers the correct answer to him, allowing him to preserve his anonymity—a girl who "seemed to embody, as naturally as light or air or motion itself the impenetrable anonymity" which the narrator has made for himself through "unblinking alertness and unstinting effort." The whispering of the saving answer becomes a daily ritual and is the only contact the narrator ever has with this anonymous, plain, isolated girl.

In the second part, ten years later, the narrator learns that the girl is dead.

In the third part, he presents his fictional account of her death, told from the third person point of view of a Chicano soldier who is an habitual liar. The Chicano creates a false identity for himself as a war hero with which to seduce women, comes upon Cynthia, now a college student and still steeped involuntarily in the anonymity which makes her victim to the created identities around her. In the course of his deceit, as a result of it, she is scalded to death, unconscious with drink, in a bath tub.

The epilogue addresses itself to the meaning of the story: "…the truth…is real only in the *substance* [my italics] of the language that embodies it…if a fiction works, the lie is well told, then it becomes real, the truth again because the reader is not who he was any more when he believes something new." (This idea is echoed from nearly ten years earlier in "The Two Sides of Things" from *Such Waltzing Was Not Easy.*)

The lie that kills Cynthia, in a sense, perhaps, begins with the fiction of the narrator's pose which would not permit him to respond to her act of friendliness and compassion and leads her via her continued loneliness to the situation which causes her death. She, too, of course, was partner to the lie which "saved" the narrator from exposure in his guise of aloofness; to an extent she was also a voluntary victim of the false hero's lie. Stepping back further from this structure, we see that this intricate construct of lies is itself presented to us by a fictional fiction writer within a fiction which he informs us is built of a mix of truth and fiction.

In the epilogue, we are told that the goal of the fiction writer, the driving desire, is to make "real things which last." And though fiction is identified as a lie, it differs from the lie in that its words embody substance, it builds on elements of truth and on the "solid little foundation building blocks" of language and grammar to create what is real and enduring, while the lie seeks to create only illusion and deceit.

Thus, identity is fiction or identity is a lie. Fiction is realer than fact, an arrangement of fact and imagining, a trespass of fact to something real enough to endure. The lie is a solitary, ill-founded guise behind which men hide in weakness, continually subject to exposure, living "in rather than upon their imaginations," prey to "the immediate, excruciating present," where "yesterday [is] a figment of memory, tomorrow a shifting unreliable rumor."

The lies and fiction by which we live are serious matters. Each present moment is the link between past and future, each generation the vital link in a culture's survival. Every man is charged to make of his past a viable fiction for the future, "a meaning worth the living." Of our fathers we shape meanings for our sons.

Still there is the unidentified, perhaps unidentifiable element with which a writer creates his fictions (and presumably with which a man creates his identity): there is "skill, imagination, and an unknown of which [he is] a little bit afraid," an unknown which the writer is sometimes "not entirely certain…is a wholly good thing."

With this stroke, it would seem, Gordon Weaver has dropped the floor and raised the roof-beams of his future work. Here would seem to be a link of powerful promise between his fiction's past and future, a point to which his past twenty years of effort has inexorably led him, a point from which his forthcoming novel will no doubt proceed to bring an ever more complexly sharpened focus upon the Chinese box of identity and the heap of broken images of our time.

Thomas E. Kennedy
February, 1985

UPDATE

Gordon Weaver has since published several books of fiction, including *Morality Play* (1985), *A World Quite Round* (1986), *The Eight Corners of the World* (1988), *Men Who Would Be Good* (1991), *The Way We Know in Dreams: Stories* (1994), *Four Decades: New and Selected Stories* (1997), and *Long Odds: Stories* (2000). Weaver, the editor of *Cimarron Review* since 1989, also has won many of the top fiction prizes for his work.

"Gordon Weaver writes fiction mostly about middle- and lower-middle-class, middle-aged, mid-western men: football coaches, professors, lawyers, television producers, insurance sales-men, alcoholics, bar owners, soldiers, fathers, sons, and brothers," wrote the *Dictionary of Literary Biography*. "At the core of his fiction is a fascination with the mystery of time, and what he seems to find within that mystery is the key to identity."

In a review of *The Way We Know in Dreams*, *The Review of Contemporary Fiction* called Weaver "a deceptive writer": "Although he usually writes in an apparently simple manner, he troubles us with his metaphysical and epistemological questions. The title of his new collection of stories provides a clue to his underlying concerns. How do we know things? . . . Perhaps the best stories in this carefully arranged collection are those in which Weaver's heroes—who are often failures in daily life—are unsure of their positions."

Four Decades: New and Selected Stories, according to a *Booklist* review, challenges our views on middle-class life and examines characters whose existence has been shaped by "an inexplic-able, arbitrary fate": "In some stories, however, Weaver gives the break from middle-class life a more positive, purposeful turn, driven by a vision of alternative social possibilities, of a sort many of the bleaker protagonists in the other stories cannot fathom." A *Studies in Short Fiction* review called Weaver a "major talent" and remarked, first, on the fact that there were only twelve carefully chosen stories in the book (a surprising paring from such a long career), and, second, that "these stories evidence the tight thematic focus tethering this writer's work for forty years: the role of memory and fiction as twin constructs of the self." The review conclud-

■ BOOKS BY GORDON WEAVER

Count a Lonely Cadence. Chicago: Henry Regnery Co., 1968.

The Entombed Man of Thule. Baton Rouge: Louisiana State University Press, 1972.

Give Him a Stone. New York: Crown Publishers, Inc., 1975.

Such Waltzing Was Not Easy. Urbana: University of Illinois Press, 1975.

Circling Byzantium. Baton Rouge: Louisiana State University Press, 1980.

Getting Serious. Baton Rouge: Louisiana State University Press, 1980.

The American Short Story, 1945–1980: A Critical History (editor). Boston: G. K. Hall, 1983.

Morality Play. Kirksville, Mo.: Chariton Review, 1985.

A World Quite Round. Baton-Rouge: Louisiana State University Press, 1986.

The Eight Corners of the World. Chelsea, Vt.: Chelsea Green, 1988.

Men Who Would Be Good. Oak Park, Ill.: Tri-Quarterly/Another Chicago, 1991.

The Way We Know in Dreams: Stories. Columbia, Mo.: University of Missouri Press, 1994.

Four Decades: New and Selected Stories. Columbia, Mo.: University of Missouri Press, 1997.

Small Defeats. Huntsville, Tex.: Texas Review Press, 1998.

Long Odds: Stories. Columbia, Mo.: University of Missouri Press, 2000.

ed: "What Gordon Weaver offers in *Four Decades* is a rich, impressive testament to a lifetime crafting fictions, and a thoughtful exploration of the fictive life."

Long Odds: Stories received a cautious review, however, from *Publishers Weekly*: "Although frequently on target in their criticism of middle-class complacency, these 11 stories about men bewildered by contemporary mores often take their critiques too far. Weaver dwells on humankind at its most embittered and alienated—not a bad practice in theory, but one-dimensional when pushed to excess. . . . The stories mix emotional accuracy with an unsettling tendency toward overgeneralization; Weaver pities his characters for their confusion, and yet these artfully composed stories may suffer from an overdetermination bordering on fatalism."

A Bad and Green Dream: Bruce Weigl's Many Voices and Landscapes

Bruce Weigl is known primarily as a Vietnam War poet. It is probably more accurate to say that Weigl is the paradigm of the Vietnam combat veteran poet; his poems represent the finest poetic achievement from that debased experience. Yet even without his war poems, Weigl has produced enough sustained and varied poetry to be considered a significant writer in any genre. Weigl is not merely a paradigm of the Vietnam War poet, he's a model of how a contemporary poet writes. This is a writer whose violent, compulsive memories are the emotional and literary standards of a period. Besides his war poems, Weigl, when he writes in the tradition of a James Wright, is also a working-class poet from the industrial Midwest. But perhaps most important of all, he is a poet of sexual darkness, his erotic poems as shame-riddled and guilt-infested as any that Theodore Roethke or Robert Lowell wrote. Finally, these darker moments in his poetry are as explicit about rough male-to-male sexuality as the innovations of John Rechy, Hubert Selby, Jr., and John Wieners. Long after the Vietnam War fades from memory, readers will come back to Weigl's erotic poems that ultimately harken back to Walt Whitman, that great progenitor, and the flip side of America's puritanical ethos, its Cadmus epiphanies. Still, there is only one place to start with Bruce Weigl's poetry, and that is Vietnam.

Defenseless villages are bombarded from the air, the inhabitants driven out into the countryside, the cattle machine-gunned, the huts set on fire with incendiary bullets: this is called pacification.

■ GEORGE ORWELL IN "POLITICS AND THE ENGLISH LANGUAGE" (1946)

Ezra Pound wrote that poetry to be good should be at least as well written as good prose. Perhaps his observation is nowhere more true than with the literature of the Vietnam War. This was a war that produced more prose about itself than anything else, and might eventually, if it hasn't already, manufacture more words than any war ever fought. John Clark Pratt's *Vietnam Voices* (1984), an anthology of war writings, had a bibliography that was nearly twenty pages long, and that list could easily double by century's end. Vietnam War poets must not only match up to good prose, their poems must be at least as well written as some of the novels and memoirs about the war, no easy challenge for anyone. But where does the poet Bruce Weigl fit in all this writing? Because so many of the Vietnam War poets share qualities in common with the prose, often I find myself applying Pound's observation about poetry and prose more rigorously than I might with other poets. Partly this is due to the fact that all these writers, no matter what forms they choose to write in, share a common language of war in the battered landscape of Vietnam. Their voices are not measurably different for the same reasons, nor are the images and emotions of this world perceptibly varied in prose and poetry. But I think it also can be said that the Vietnam War poets who are up to the challenge of the prose often excel beyond it.

The best poetry of the Vietnam War, like the prose, concerns itself with narration, dramatic effects, characterization, and moral fervor. This is not a self-reflexive poetry, not a language-

Bruce Weigl

Bruce Weigl, born in Lorain, Ohio, in 1949, earned a B.A. from Oberlin College, an M.A. from the University of New Hampshire, and a Ph.D. from the University of Utah. He is the author of several collections of poetry and the editor or co-editor of collections of critical articles, most recently *Charles Simic: Essays on the Poetry* (University of Michigan Press). Weigl's poetry, essays, articles and reviews have appeared in such magazines as *The Nation, Tri-Quarterly, The Western Humanities Review, The American Poetry Review, The Southern Review, The Paris Review, Antaeus,* and *Harpers.* For his work Weigl has been awarded the Pushcart Prize twice, a prize from the Academy of American Poets, nominations for the Lamont Poetry Prize and the William Carlos Williams Prize, a Breadloaf fellowship in poetry, a Yaddo Foundation fellowship, and a National Endowment for the Arts grant for poetry. Weigl has taught at the University of Arkansas, Old Dominion University, and in the writing pro-

gram at the Pennsylvania State University from 1986 until 2000. He is past president of the Associated Writing Programs. ■

centered verse or an experimental one. A direct response to harsh, raw experience, it depends, like the prose, on realistic details. The poets seem less interested in beauty and truth than in being correct and honest, and most important, being authentic about the experiences of war. While the prose generally disturbs, it does not shock the way the poetry does, and when the poetry does this, I am reminded how rarely poets' voices truly startle.

The affinities between the prose and poetry of the Vietnam War inevitably lead me away from Ezra Pound to the great arbiter of prose decorum, George Orwell. In "Why I Write," Orwell says there are four great motives for writing: sheer egoism, aesthetic enthusiasm, historical impulse, and political purpose. He writes of "a desire to seem clever," and he goes on to say that this impulse comes from a "desire to share an experience which one feels is valuable and ought not to be missed." Vietnam War poems are rarely attempts at being clever, though the poets are more inclined to verbal inventiveness than the prose writers. Something which Philip Caputo wrote in his memoir *A Rumor of War* should be kept in mind, though; imagination is the last thing a soldier needs in combat. To take this perception out of the theatre of war and into the arena of literature, specifically into the cabaret of poetry, consider Wallace Stevens's remark that in a catastrophe the imagination is replaced by observation.

Invariably war writers have a desire to share experiences which they feel are valuable and ought not to be missed. This seems true no matter what the political disposition of the writer. I once heard this impulse summed up at a Vietnam War conference by an oral historian who said that the classic war story begins: "Shit, I was there. I know." It is, as Orwell suggested, an historical impulse that is often tinged with political purpose.

These thumbnail observations about war writings generally, Vietnam War writers specifically, and the differences between the poetry and the prose are presented as background for Weigl's war poems. As I said at the outset, he is more than just a war poet, true; yet one needs to understand his poems about the war before the rest of his work can be appreciated. The war poems are the point at which one enters into the working class, the morally introspective, and the erotic poems. War is what made this working-class kid a poet. Let's not begin in Ohio, then, but at Quang Tri in Vietnam, in a steamy jungle, where life and death, sex and beauty, all get speeded up. A poem like "Temple near Quang Tri, Not on the Map" gives off a sense of experience, of being there, as the other poems about the war do—I think of poets like W. D. Ehrhart, Yosef Komunyakaa, and Walter McDonald, all of whom have written memorably about Vietnam—but Weigl's poem in Quang Tri casts a spell with its ineluctably tragic rhythms. This immediately illustrates what differentiates this poet from virtually all other Vietnam War writers; the concision of the poetry makes the dramatic impact of the narratives even more emotionally charged than one would encounter in a story or novel. Less really is more in Weigl's universe. Sometimes, in just a page, Weigl is capable of creating the tense contradictions of a moral universe full of elaborate interior worlds whose corners are supported by fear, discovery, healing, and pain. Sometimes, too, in his most powerful poems, he severs the moral cord, setting the reader adrift into proscribed nightmare landscapes bereft of grace and the civilizing touch. Weigl then puts the reader into a frontline experience, terrifying and real. Prose just is not equal to the lyrical explosions and the bleak epiphanies that Weigl's poems regularly deliver.

Even though the poem about Quang Tri reads best as literature, it also provides a terrible sense of the history of this war. Weigl describes how the jungle at dusk reveals "ivy thick with sparrow." (To any historian or combat soldier, this detail allows them to date what time in the war the event occurs. In the later years, as the war ground on and on, birds were a rarity because of bombardment, and ivy no longer existed because of defoliants such as Agent Orange.) A squad of American soldiers comes upon an old man muttering to himself in a small jungle temple. The commanding officer (CO) ignores the old man because the area appears "clean," not booby-trapped or hiding Viet Cong or their material; it seems to be "friendly," which is to say— not hostile. But then the old man's face becomes visible, his eyes "roll down to the charge / wired between his teeth and the floor." The poem ends: "The sparrows / burst off the walls into the jungle." The last two lines of this poem once again suggest the difference between vicarious and actual experience, between imagining things and writing about what one knows. As ordinary as those two lines seem when they are isolated from the rest of the poem, they show how veracity of experience is as telling a poetic detail—Pound's rhythm of experience—as diction. Like the eye of a storm, there is a kind of imploding silence which precedes the concussive explosion from a bomb. The birds sense it and fly away before they are caught in the explosion's arc; soldiers are not fleet-footed or swift-minded enough to do the same. I find these innocuous lines quite chilling because Weigl has seen to it that I understand just what it is he is saying and feeling here. Maybe because we have come to expect a certain kind of surrealism in the juxtaposition of poems and images in a volume, Weigl's use of cause and effect strikes me as extraordinary. This is not imagination but observation, the authentic echo from experience; we are in the midst of the catastrophe for which Wallace Stevens required observers—good journalists, in other words—more than inquisitive scribes (the poets).

Cause and effect are not pretty, abstract ideas about the external universe in Weigl's hands; they are as grim as bad luck, as scary as incoming rounds at a base camp. What effect does an old man wired to a charge in the jungle have on the psyche? "Surrounding Blues on the Way Down" answers that thorny question, being one of a handful of great poems produced by the war. At the outset of this essay I alluded to the fact that Weigl was not merely a Vietnam War poet, but that he was a paradigm of such a poet; "Surrounding Blues," "Temple near Quang Tri," and several other Weigl war poems are the reason why the claim about him can be made. A three-stanza work, Weigl's dramatic arc is so taut that the poem reads like a three-act play, with, just as the Quang Tri poem had, a set-up, complication, and resolution of action. Here is the exposition, the protagonist introduced, a young soldier barely in country, the rain-black clouds opening like orchids. He did not hate the beautiful war yet, this eighteen-year-old says.

The dramatic confrontation comes about between the older, more experienced soldier and an old Vietnamese woman—what the Americans called a mama san—bent over her sack of flowers at the roadside. The older soldier hits the brakes on the jeep, spinning the tires backwards in the mud. Weigl writes that the soldier did not hate the war, "but other reasons made him cry out to her." She smiles her betel-black teeth at them. Push and pull, conflict and tension, this is a dramatic moment as striking as any found in a novel or play; the confrontation is as inevitable as intersecting lives in a Greek drama. Call it Fate. Call it Destiny. The Vietnamese called it the Will of Heaven. Hegel wrote that tragedy occurs when two rights collide, but Weigl has chosen the terms of a morality play to evoke his sense of tragedy. This is the collision between right and wrong, good and evil, American soldiers and innocent-seeming Vietnamese non-combatants (if such a person existed in this guerrilla theatre without a specific area of operation and an undefined enemy who more often than not wore civilian clothes). Even here, the irony of this moment cannot be overlooked; a good, professional American soldier would find any Vietnamese person suspicious back then, even an old woman at the roadside; she could be Viet Cong. But Weigl thinks like a soldier with a dramatic flare and a moralist's agenda, and he resolves this conflict with violent resolution. He describes how the young soldier sat in the jeep while the older American slammed the woman to her knees, "the plastic butt of his M16 / crashing down on her."

Anyone could write a line about a soldier abusing an old woman, but only a soldier would make sure the gun was an M16; probably only a writer would think to mention the butt of the M16, too, or maybe even a poet might do that. But it is only Bruce Weigl who adds that word "plastic" to the line, making it vividly horrible and horribly vivid. The *plastic* butt of his M16 crashes down on her. When was the last time a poem made you cringe? Or when was the last time a poem was propelled by such rage and craft? A reader of poetry nearly all of my life, I can't recall ever feeling this way about a poem, though I might have experienced it reading prose such as Hubert Selby's *Last Exit to Brooklyn* when Tralala gets gang-raped. Yet poetry, as Pound said, in order to be effective, needs to be at least as well written as prose. Here is such an instance.

In one of Weigl's domestic poems entitled "Hope," a similar narrator waits passively as Joe gets out of his car and kills a dog at the roadside. Substitute the passive reader for that observer in the jeep, and you begin to understand why Weigl's poetry makes one uncomfortable; the feelings in his poems are as raw and messy, emotionally speaking, as life itself. He also makes clear in other poems that Vietnam was a world in which violence would be done to you if you didn't do it first. Human qualities such as desire, compassion, and the imagination are worthless attributes in a war zone. A tour of duty in Vietnam provided the worst indignities, including the possibility of being killed, but it also included smaller degradations to break the human spirit. Weigl's poetry chronicles how war assaults the senses, even the nose; he graphically evokes the latter experience in "Burning Shit at An Khe," when the narrator climbs down into a literal shithole with a rake and matches, ready to burn the fifty-five-gallon drums filled with human offal.

As powerfully evoked as the poem at An Khe is, it gives no clue to the tragic rhythms which Weigl is capable of registering on the page. The shit detail replicates experience into poetry, but experiences like those described in the temple poem at Quang Tri lead to ones in a later poem like "Surrounding Blues on the Way Down": showing how one violation of human dignity leads to another, how a booby-trapped temple causes an old woman to get smashed by the plastic butt of a rifle at the roadside. For that reason, Vietnam War poetry differs from other contemporary writing in that it often shows how things are done—an old strength of Imagism—but it also shows us why, which is the old strength of moral philosophy, of essayists and homilists. Why men fight wars is not answered, but once they are in combat, a poet like Bruce Weigl explains why one thing leads to another in a combat zone, the push and pull of tragedy, but also that dramatic condition of choice, how even the most innocuous choice may ultimately lead to one's undoing or even death.

When I picked up *Song of Napalm* (1988) several years later, I was curious to see how these poems had aged, and also to see whether I still believed my bravura remarks about his writing that I had made in an earlier long essay about the literature of the Vietnam War. I also wanted to see what Weigl had written after his first trip back to Vietnam in 1985. *Song of Napalm* reads like a selected poems, but with exceptions and important exclusions. The book is not a selected poems per se; rather it is a selection of Weigl's war poems. It omits some of his finest poems—"The Life Before Fear," "Hope," and "Killing Chickens"—set in working-class neighborhoods of the industrial Midwest, usually Weigl's hometown of Lorain, Ohio. But the absence of Weigl's domestic poems does not lessen *Song of Napalm*. His war poems read, as I have already said, like mini-dramas, and have enough poetic resonance for any reader. The book also presents an occasion to bring his war poetry to a wider audience and to publish new poems that were written after he visited Vietnam again in 1985. These new poems are nearly serene, certainly without dramatic effects or violence; they read more like meditations, quiet observances of survival rites, chronicling such actions as wandering into Old Hanoi, oil lamps glowing in small storefronts and restaurants

> where those, so long ago my enemy,
> sit on low chairs and praise the simple evening.

Yet Weigl is not merely an observer providing journalism with line breaks and meters. When he asks a farmer questions, the man points to a stone and stick house that survived the American carpet bombings of North Vietnam, and he concludes that there are questions which people who have everything ask people who have nothing "and they do not understand" ("Dialectical Materialism"). Yet as moving as some of these newer poems are, this collection is about those older poems, some of which are quite simply the best poems ever written about war. One could easily imagine his work becoming a kind of coda to the poetic sensibility explored in Paul Fussell's monumental book about World War I poetry, *The Great War and Modern Memory* (1975), which delineated the awful trench warfare from 1914 to 1918 and the literary voices—Siegfried Sassoon, Robert Graves, Edmund Blunden, David Jones, Isaac Rosenberg, and Wilfred Owen—who "remembered, conventionalized, and mythologized" it. Besides the Quang Tri poem and "Surrounding Blues" and, to a lesser extent, the An Khe shit-burning detail poem, the volume also includes a war classic such as "The Last Lie," and a more humorous war poem, "Girl at the Chu Lai Laundry." All these poems are pared-down, hard-edged, written in a passionate open-verse style.

It reminds me that George Orwell also cautioned against overelegance, declaring that "the inflated style is a kind of euphemism." Bruce Weigl cannot be accused of euphemism; he writes as much from observation as imagination, and, yes, the poems are as good, are better—good being the enemy of better—than nearly all the prose, and certainly all the movies about the Vietnam War. I am likewise reminded of another Orwell maxim: "The great enemy of clear language is insincerity." Weigl manages to be authentic and sincere; his language is as clear as unadorned emotion itself, and as charged as the lingering imagery of war which so many soldiers live with on a daily basis, not with the luxury of memory, hardly objective remembrance of things past, but with the ballistic recognition of a first action, which finally is what a flashback is, theatre's illusion of the first time, albeit in technicolor, not externalized, but playing nightly in the mind, and at horrible pitch and spin, old experience appearing as if it were first experience. If these poems labor under a burden, it is not an artistic one but an ethical one. Guilt and shame suffuse every stanza, perhaps right down to the syllables. Weigl is not a bleak poet, but he is merciless, more on himself than others, and his poems, while full of the light of artistry, are really as morally dark as tunnels in nightmares, as emotionally lacerating as a thick strap across the back. Besides the guilt of war, his lines are filled with imagery about sex's shamefulness, a world in which men rape each other as often as they violate women. A sense of the forbidden accompanies even the most ordinary gestures.

> You think you're far away from me
>
> but you're right here in my pants
> and I can grab your throat
>
> like a cock and squeeze.

This sad, sad poem is like a bad dream, circling and circling with its analogies and extended metaphors into a world of sex and death, a world like the jungle itself and that awful war. "The Soldier's Brief Epistle" ends with lines declaring that the enemy did not cry out, "and he was very difficult to kill."

Because Bruce Weigl refuses to forget these experiences, he makes us remember who we are, that beyond our own geographical and human borders, there is an uncontrollable savagery imbedded in the American grain. Certainly no poet in my own memory comes close to the level of violence that is found in Weigl's writing, yet the violence is never gratuitous, never merely pornographic. Like any dramatic detail, it is there to illustrate a point, to complicate, to unmask, reveal, illuminate an experience, and to move an action forward into resolution. Weigl's poems illustrate our deepest, most troubled emotions. Even children aren't immune to the raging, out-of-control forces in these poems. Consider "The Last Lie" in which another miserable convoy is on the move. A guy on the back of an open truck raised a can of C rations at a child.

> He didn't toss the can, he wound up and hung it
> on the child's forehead and she was stunned
> backwards into the dust of our trucks.

I have often heard Vietnam combat veterans say, decades after their tours of duty, that all they learned to do was kill and heal, heal and kill. Now they wanted the healing to stay, and the killing to go. I have also heard it said that the two nicest words a veteran can hear are: Welcome Home. (Weigl's poem "Anna Grasa" reminds me that the poet was welcomed home by his family, and, however difficult that homecoming was, perhaps that reception is what saved him where other veterans despaired completely and were lost.) In his most recent book, *What Saves Us* (1992), Bruce Weigl now writes of the healing and the welcoming. Keep in mind, though, that the welcome mat is at the back entrance, and the healing is slow and painful. These poems, in many respects, are less public than his other poems. They are clotted at times with introspection, marbled with an old rage now tranquilized by time, family, social obligations and commitments, and maybe even by tranquilizers and drugs; these are denser, more daring testaments. But it is also a synthesis of Weigl's major obsessions: the war, shameful sexuality, and the working poor.

As in some of his later poems in *Song of Napalm*, Weigl finds himself back in Vietnam. The time is the early nineties. The men, so often occasions for violence, whether Americans or Vietnamese, are absent; here the poet communes with a lady, not a succubus, but a living, breathing human being, this Vietnamese woman who seems to make him breathless. Her name is Miss Hoang Yen, and because of her, "I am unable to sleep." The poem is entitled "Her Life Runs Like a Red Silk Flag," and immediately Weigl shows how much the conditions and occasions for his poems have changed. But he also shows something I once heard the novelist Pete Dexter talk about so articulately. Every writer eventually comes upon a place that puts chills down the spine, and Dexter said that you then need to write about that place. Dexter's place was Milledgeville, Georgia, where he lived as a small child, but had never been back until, fully grown and on a newspaper assignment, he returned. The feeling he got from the place eventually became his novel *Paris Trout*. Lorain, Ohio—which, incidentally, besides being Weigl's hometown is also Toni Morrison's—might be one of those spine-tingling places for Bruce Weigl; still, nothing compares to Vietnam. This is how that place in Southeast Asia affects the man, now a renowned poet and university professor, no longer that soldier boy in the killing fields, but a responsible adult. An old woman brings cake on a blue place and smiles her betel black teeth at him, but—says the poet—he does not feel strange here.

And yet he does feel strange.

When he was a soldier in Vietnam, his most often used word to describe the experience was "miserable." In "Girl at the Chu Lai Laundry," he refers to his "miserable platoon" moving out; in "The Last Lie," he writes about "the miserable convoy." Misery has been replaced by the slow healing, the welcoming home (Vietnam being the home away from home). But underneath the healing and welcoming lie the hurt and pain of Vietnam, the humiliations (theirs and ours), the indignity, the cruelty, the shame, and guilt. The next line finishes that poetic thought in a complicating way. He writes that he did not feel strange in the house that "my country had tried to bomb into dust." A blank verse line never sounded so thick and tortured as that one! It makes Robert Lowell's adjectivally dense confessional poems, by comparison, seem guiltless, even airy and light-hearted. Holding his hand, Miss Hoang Yen says he is not to blame, but the poet disagrees. If you doubt these observations, listen to the three lines right after she tells him that he is not to blame:

With the dead we share no common rooms.
With the frightened we can't think straight;
no words can bring the burning city back.

They part on Hung Dao Street, "with her eyes / she told me I should leave." By now many familiar Weigl images merge and define the poem's moment. He cannot sleep, thinking and praying about her, and he says that he ached for her and for himself. Then come the birds, not exploding off a temple as they did in Quang Tri a lifetime ago. This is a softer moment. "Some birds sang morning / home across the lake." What a lovely image! The poem ends with images from another time, perhaps not even a time but an artistic moment like a Vietnamese painting. "In small reed boats / the lotus gatherers sailed out / among their resuming white blossoms."

The lotus might make other people forget; all Bruce Weigl can do is remember. Or maybe it is not so much ordinary remembering as that Weigl is obligated—by himself if by no one else—never to forget. It is a kind of curse, this collective memory that demands recollecting in order to heal the community at large; it is a kind of martyrdom in poetry if you will. This last memory—the obligation never to forget—seems to be the kind under which Bruce Weigl operates. His poems are about having a conscience, about being conscious, alive and there—about never forgetting.

Even in the act of love-making with a beautiful woman, the poet cannot leave what he calls "the killing ground." A poem such as "The Loop" begins with a jay in the trees in the flyway, but immediately a "God of the great nothing" hovers over them. In between, "the woman of the green year" entwines him in a borrowed bed, "summer tearing / apart from the inside," he rolls her nipple between his lips "like a bullet" from "a bad and green dream." Later, he experiences the smell of a Vietnamese woman's hair on a train. Then, the old war never far away, he envisions a necklace of human ears, one of the more awful things that soldiers did in combat. From love to this: back to the war again. And yet one must and does get on with a life after Vietnam as the title poem suggests; only, as Weigl writes, what saves us is never what we thought it would be.

It is the night before going off to his first tour of duty as a young American soldier in Vietnam, and the poet, a wordless young man, finds himself with a girl in the back seat of his father's car at the empty lot of "the high school / of our failures." He thinks she owes him something, and that something is her young body; he lifts up her skirt and pulls her cotton panties up as high as she can stand. He says that he is on fire and Heaven is in sight. But in the midst of their heat, she stops abruptly and offers him her crucifix to take with him. But, as he says, we are not always right about what saves us. He thought that dragging "the angel down that night" would save him. Instead, he went to war with her crucifix, rubbing it on his face and lips "nights the rockets roared in."

Besides the war and its veterans, besides the shame and guilt of sex and nearly everything else—this is a poet who suffers from the sin of being born—Weigl is a first-rate working-class poet, and his working people often are immigrants. His miniature dramas of these people are like tiny icons in words. In an early poem, he could write touchingly of his immigrant grandmother Anna Grasa. Another dark, yet wonderfully funny poem of these immigrants and their tumultuous rooms occurs in "Shelter." Again, the scene is set for this tragi-comedy: amid the crucifixes and dried palm leaves and the lavender smell of his grandmother's Sunday black silk dress, his family comes home after church. The emotional honesty, not only of the images themselves but the very cadence of the lines is so refreshing. They have come into grandmother's house "as a family," and then the after-thought—"after church." Once again, Weigl is strongest as a dramatic poet, his moral commentary most effective when he first entertains and moves us before, as Brecht would say, he changes our lives. The poem has that classic three-act structure of set-up, complication, and resolution. The set-up occurs with the arrival of the family at the grandmother's home. The complication occurs in the crowded kitchen, among the dandelion salad, blood sausage, black bread, and dark wine. There the aunts and uncles and their children mingle. The poet wants to say something—he tries to say something—but "the air is suddenly wrong." And isn't that the essence of all dramatic situations: the air is suddenly wrong. This is the complication: his grandfather swears too loud; his brothers only laugh. The women shush them, telling them to eat, "but something's cut too deep this time." Suddenly, the air is wrong; then something's cut too deep this time.

Put another way: in purely dramatic terms—*something happens*. Choices are made, ineluctable choices, propelling the action in a certain direction; in this case, into the tragicomic rhythms of these displaced immigrants. The children are shooed outside, and from behind a tree of "drunken plums," the young Bruce, always the keen observer, watches his grandfather wave a pistol in the air, and the uncles reach for it as a shot explodes through the low ceiling and the bedroom floor where his sister sleeps "and lives on." The poem's end almost reads like a folktale, so simple and yet so freighted with the emotional charge of a dramatic resolution.

It also reminds me of remarks that Chekhov made about how he constructed his own plays: "People are having a meal, just having a meal, but at the same time their happiness is being created, or their lives are being smashed up." It also reminds me, even though I called it tragi-comic earlier, which I think it is, that there is also melodrama and even bathos here. The young Chekhov often had a character produce a gun on stage and then not always do the most dramatic thing with it; shooting that gun is often too obvious, dramatically speaking, as witness Chekhov's jubilant remark after *The Cherry Orchard*, and how there is "not a single pistol shot in it."

Sometimes, though, as Weigl makes clear, the gunshot is the most dramatic moment because the action arrives at its grimmest humor by that sound. It is heightened by the fact, as they wrestle the gun from the grandfather, that the sister sleeps in the room above and that the bullet goes through the ceiling and into the room where she sleeps. Dramatic, melodramatic, tragi-comic: "Shelter" manages to be all these things in under forty-five lines. That is poetic concision, but it is also dramatic construction, leaving out more than you put in, finding the actions, along with the images, which propel these motivated characters into their ultimate choices, thus revealing themselves in the process. In other words, something happens.

In the second part of *What Saves Us*, Bruce Weigl repeats what he has done so well from book to book, which is to take the ordinary and make it tremble with remarkableness, even an illuminating kind of terror. His erotic poems are always underpinned with guilt and shame, those old cornerstones of a good working-class Catholic upbringing in America. Family poems, while loving and full of gentle observations amid the harsher realities he renders, are never sentimental. He'll make a love poem out of the dross of war or make a war poem sensual and erotic. His poems are nothing if not earthy; their raw physicality can even be frightful, whether about men or women. Consider "For the Luminous Woman in the Trees," which commences this section of the book in which the narrator enters a cemetery with a girl for the purpose of having sex with her. They will not make *love* in this poem; they will *fuck*. Remember, this refined poet minces no words. His companion in the cemetery is equally droll. "She wanted to eat stars, she said / but settled for me." Their kisses, he writes, are evil, a "slaughter of lips." Then comes another one of those revelatory moments that Weigl uses so effectively to stretch a poem into naked reality: "Into rage we squandered our desire." Rage is in this poem because rage is how they—not just the soldiers but all the baby-boomers—squandered their desires in the wet grass where they hammered their hips together "exactly like dogs."

The poems in *What Saves Us* are not such ground-breaking, seminal works as *The Monkey Wars* (1985) and *A Romance* (1979) were, but rather more subtly and thoroughly explore Weigl's already established obsessions: the war in Vietnam, working-class Ohio, male violence (and violation), and a polymorphous-perverse assortment of shame-infected lusts—toxic guilts in equally toxic Lorain! Occasionally these familiar terrains, situations, and characters render up epiphanies as happens near the end of "The Third Person." Mill stacks and open-hearths are evoked:

on the street of filthy bars
where the fathers walked
from one century into the next
in black fly ash masks of despair.

Sexual encounters, though graphing the same geography of emotions as earlier poems, are less veiled, more directly uttered, those to men, even out of the closet, and explicit.

I come back in my mind
to the man who made me suck his cock
when I was seven, in sunlight, between boxcars.

Still, the last line of this poem, while not what many readers might expect the poet's response to be, might also be a coda for all Weigl's experiences as translated into the explosive passions of his poems: "Say it clearly and you make it beautiful, no matter what."

■ BOOKS BY BRUCE WEIGL

A Sack Full of Old Quarrels. Cleveland, Ohio: Cleveland State University Poetry Center, 1976.

Executioner. Tucson, Ariz: Ironwood Press, 1976.

A Romance. Pittsburgh, Pa: University of Pittsburgh Press, 1979.

The Giver of Morning: On the Poetry of Dave Smith. Editor. Houston, Tex.: Thunder City Press, 1982.

The Imagination as Glory: The Poetry of James Dickey. Edited with T. R. Hummer. Urbana, Ill.: University of Illinois Press, 1984. Reprinted by Madison Books.

The Monkey Wars. Athens, Ga: University of Georgia Press, 1985.

Pushcart Prize XI Anthology: Best of the Small Presses 1986–87 Edition. Contributing Editor. New York: Pushcart Press, 1986.

Song of Napalm. New York: Grove Atlantic, 1988.

What Saves Us. Evanston, Ill: Triquarterly Books, 1992.

Poems from Captured Documents. Translated with Thanh Nguyen. Amherst, Mass.: University of Massachusetts Press, 1994.

Charles Simic: Essays on the Poetry. Editor. Ann Arbor: University of Michigan Press, 1996

Sweet Lorain. Evanston, Ill.: Triquarterly Books, 1996.

After the Others. Evanston, Ill.: Northwestern University Press, 1999.

Archeology of the Circle: New and Selected Poems, New York: Grove, 1999.

The Circle of Hanh: A Memoir. New York: Grove, 2000.

This thought reminds me of that great war writer Isaac Babel, a figure of infinite wisdom and contradiction; after all, Babel was a Jewish Cossack—a Jewish Cossack, for Crissakes!—who wrote so well about Christ and Christianity. His beautiful paragraphs often masque the bloody truth—a single horrifying image usually—buried amid that lovely heap of words. This happens in virtually every story of *Red Cavalry*, one horribly revealing line being the point of all those gorgeous words; it is the point of everything Babel does, making and revealing, pasting up and tearing down, almost as if his paragraphs always contain a vanishing point where the lines of perspective converge and where the eye naturally wanders if the reader is alert enough to these tendencies in his writing. This vanishing point in the perspective of Bruce Weigl's poetry invariably brings the reader to a greater truth in the poet's work. Take the poem entitled "The Hand That Takes," the longest poem in the new collection. Suddenly, in the midst of all those words, there is a startling revelation, a great dramatic discovery comparable to a "recognition" scene in a classic Greek tragedy. "I have loved war," Weigl writes. *I have loved war*. The simplicity of that remark should not deceive anyone into thinking it a throw-away line, an aside, nothing of consequence. Once again I think of how Isaac Babel leads everything in a paragraph to that one phrase or image which springs the entire passage into a recognition. *What Saves Us*, as I read it, becomes braided around that utterance, that combat soldier's dichotomy: kill'em/heal'em.

Finally, to evaluate the poetry of Bruce Weigl, one needs to ask a darker question about the literature of the Vietnam War, and that is: what purpose does any of this literature serve beyond its documentary values? The Vietnam War still brings out strong feelings in people, and yet what does this have to do with poetry? I have never seen the so-called hawks convince the so-called doves of a single thing about this experience, nor have I seen the doves change the mind of a single hawk. War does not lend itself easily to literary persuasion or even discussion. That is to say, literature will never change the spin someone wants to give the war, no matter how convincing the argument. But where does that leave the poetry? Where does that put a poet like Bruce Weigl? I find myself not wanting to come up with a facile answer, but I do think this poetry extends the definitions of what poems are, and what they do to our lives. Unlike movies about the war which seem only to calculate the easily observable details of surfaces, this literature chronicles the interior world of the mind and body, the exterior world of the senses (however brutalized) by war. What really is so remarkable about the best of this poetry is how it locates music in such utterly debased human experience, a world so absent of caring and tenderness, yet capable of incredible passion and discovery. The idea that a combat soldier would write poetry about that experience years later still flabbergasts me; I find the incongruity beautiful and illuminating. But when the novelty wears off, I still return to Ezra Pound's dictum about poetry and prose. Most Vietnam War poets labor under the burden of prose, and most of these poets do not hold up well by comparison to the prose. Bruce Weigl, however, is the exception. In his writing, not only do we find a poet equal to the war's prose, but someone who surpasses nearly all the prose writers with what Robert Stone calls his "impacted, precise verse." Vietnam War prose to be good should be at least as well written as Bruce Weigl's poetry.

Michael Stephens
April, 1994

UPDATE

Bruce Weigl has since published several books, including the poetry collections *Sweet Lorain* (1996), *Archeology of the Circle: New and Selected Poems* (1999), and *After the Others* (1999), as well as *The Circle of Hanh: A Memoir* (2000).

Known best for his powerful, eloquent poems about the Vietnam War, in which he fought, Weigl also often writes about growing up in the steel town of Lorain, Ohio. *The Southern Review* called the poems in *Sweet Lorain* "strong and fine, full of the right kind of daring," and described those in *After the Others* thus: "One enters a Weigl poem, feels an unsettling tremble, then walks on without really knowing if it's over, or if anything has been resolved."

A Passion Equal to All Hope: Theodore Weiss

■ **I**

Theodore Weiss' poetry is among the most demanding (which is not necessarily to say obscure) currently being written, not because it is erudite, far-ranging, uncompromising, and oblique, as it certainly is, but by virtue of the poet's *modus operandi* of reconciling fragments through the fashioning of multi-faceted wholes. His rich thematic diversity, various but specific characterization (for his work abounds in real people), and accelerated interplay between objects and notions, all combine to keep the reader in an intensely mobile state, as befits a poetry of the "demeanors of the mind."

Although I propose to indicate a number of Weiss' recurrent motifs, one, fragmentation, must be mentioned at once; for much of his poetic method, as well as his obliquity, stems from this theme. More than a theme, it is the underlying structure, the form and sign, by which passion may be brought to equal hope. We are still some distance from "all hope," but that will come in the plenitude of time and the completion of the poet's life-work.

Ideal phenomenalism, in its zeal to reduce material to patterns made up of sensa and the gaps between, has left the physical world in fragments. Hume and most idealism since, including the "unsensed sensa" of Russell and recent linguistic phenomenalism, has been content to ratify this view, merely revising it enough to conceal the extent of disintegration. The problem faced by Weiss, and perhaps faced more critically by him than by any other of our contemporary American poets, is: how to reconstruct a world in shambles in such a way as to fill in the gaps in sense patterns, so that pterodactyls and antarctic rock, never seen by man, may nevertheless exist? What is the continuant that constitutes the world whole? Weiss, whose approach is similar to phenomenology's, recommends the intent examination of immediate experience, a recourse to Husserl's *"Zu den Sachen"* (to the things), whether the things be flowers or weeds, memories, concepts, words or poems. The *intention* (in the phenomenological sense of the word) to follow such a course is, in fact, the sought-after continuant. (This should not be confused with WCW's "no ideas but in things," an untenable, even an unintelligible crotchet.)

Now Weiss, in thought and language radically opposed to his only world in ruins, must notwithstanding present the appearance of fragmentation, for the texture of object-gap-object-gap is the result of centuries of a false metaphysics of perception, of what Husserl and others have termed "psychologism," and that is how his readers behold reality; indeed, that is how Weiss himself will see it when his intentions and attentions flag. Yet fragmentation has to be presented only to be made whole and continuous once more. Consequently his very language must find the tropes and syntax to enact the twin drama of destruction and reconstruction, wounding and healing, division and integrity. Weiss addresses several strategies to this end.

One such strategy is prolepsis, the figure of anticipation, whose building blocks look random but fit securely and handsomely. Others are dislocation and disassociation. It is tmesis, however,

Theodore Weiss

Theodore Weiss was born in Reading, Pennsylvania, on December 16, 1916. He was educated at Muhlenberg College, where he received his B.A. degree in 1938, and at Columbia University, where he took his M.A. degree in 1940. The following year he married Renée Karol.

He has held numerous professorial positions. He has taught English at the University of Maryland, the University of North Carolina at Chapel Hill, and at Yale University. He was assistant and associate professor of English at Bard College and lecturer at the New School for Social Research in New York from 1947 to 1966. From 1961 to 1962 he acted as visiting professor of poetry at Massachusetts Institute of Technology and was lecturer for the New York City Young Men's Hebrew Association from 1965 to 1967. Poet-in-residence at Princeton University from 1966 to 1967, he taught English and creative writing there from 1968 until 1987 and has been professor emeritus since then. He has been editor and owner of the *Quarterly Review of Literature* since 1943.

Theodore Weiss was a member of the Wesleyan University Press Poetry Board from 1963 to 1968. Since 1964, he has been an honorary fellow at Ezra Stiles College and at Yale University. He was the recipient of a Ford fellowship in 1953, the Wallace Stevens Award in 1956, a National Endowment for the Arts grant in 1967 and 1969, and the Ingram Merill Foundation grant in 1974.

Weiss has been honored as a reader at the White House (1979), a participant in the International Poetry Conference in Struga, Yugoslavia

(summer, 1980), as a guest of the city of Jerusalem, Mishkenot (1980), and as a Guggenheim fellow (1986-87). He also has won, among other awards, a Shelley Memorial Award from the Poetry Society of America (1989), a PEN Club Special Achievement Award (shared with his wife, Renée Weiss, 1997) for publishing the *Quarterly Review of Literature*, and the Oscar Williams-Gene Derwood Award from the New York Community Trust (1997) for the body of his poetic work

He was awarded a Doctor of Letters degree at Muhlenberg College in 1968 and at Bard College in 1973. ■

that provides Weiss with his most dramatic and persistent means of division and re-integration. Tmesis: welding together fragments; a cutting. A familiar example is Hopkins' "brim, in a flash, full," constructed from *brimful in a flash*. Tmesis admits of a texture as tightly woven as Pindar's Greek or Horace's Latin, and permits syntactic elements to avoid or combine with whatever other elements the poet finds significant, a property not common to the rigidity of English grammar. Moreover, and more importantly, tmesis divides insofar as it introjects a middle between parts of a conventional phrase (as in the example from Hopkins) or word (as in "ungoddanneddependable"). Its division is purely formal; its re-integration is meaningfully formal. To experience the entire range of tmesis we should extend the figure to include stanzas, set similes, divigations, comic subplots in tragedies, etc. Nor is it limited to the verbal arts. You can discover tmesis in the laterally recessive space between the foot-soldier and the gypsy madonna in Giorgione's *The Tempest*, in the miscellanea embedded in certain Gaudi façades, the gigue in Bach's C major suite for violoncello. Or compare it to that binary structure in which the human trunk is intromitted between outstretched arms—any crucifixion or person doing his daily exercise will do.

A mattersome property of tmesis is its two-fold directional mobility. Its poles, although stretched apart by the intruded matter, exert pressure against both sides of the middle: the stretching can bind or alienate the terms; the pressure can be a grave threat or a subtle caress. It behooves the craftsman either to maintain the terms in tension or to control the degree of stretch and pressure according to what is appropriate to form and content. Weiss is past-master of this aspect of his art, and his utilization of it is ubiquitous; it is everywhere in lines and phrases, but can extend to embrace total poems. Dramatic enjambment is its preferred linear means, comma and dash its characteristic punctuation. Dashes set Weiss' world between something more intimate than parentheses, more binding than brackets, more present than the blank spaces of a Dickey. Dashes circumscribe Weiss' phrases with the zero phonetic value of silence; reading them is like tiptoeing over mined ground, confronted at every moment with the threat of fragmentation. But it must be remembered that dashes, if disjunctive, are also conjunctive.

I would like to cite, chiefly as exempla, but for the pleasure in it, too, some varieties of local tmesis in Weiss:

> I huddle in our room,
> waiting for the words, struck countless times,
> to open, let the genie, burnt-match black
> and hot with incense, treasure, out: let me,
> Eden-deep and sweeping-past-desire, in.
> **"The Visit," II**

> Had I only
> his book's good company, that company
> it kept waiting, perfect, on him,
> humble the world, I'd lord it truly.
> **"Caliban Remembers," I**

> The will—whether the Will of Avon
> or the Passaic's goose—is here
> **"A Midsummer Nightmare"**

> Like something
> mattered out of air, a smile—
> did it reflect the morning
> songs that once enlightened?—
> would flicker, then go out.
> **"The Dance Called David"**

Tmesis, then, the characteristic mode of Weiss, is simultaneous fragmentation and unification, a passion equal to hope.

■ II

His first book, *The Catch*, was not published until 1951, when the poet was 35. It should be mentioned that Weiss had other irons in the fire. He was and is a diligent teacher, and since the early forties he and his wife, Renée, have edited *The Quarterly Review of Literature*, a journal that has served as university, laboratory, church, and home to several generations of young writers. He has also engaged in critical labors. Even though I highly regard Yvor Winters, both as poet and critic, I was stimulated by Weiss' lambasting, courageous, brilliant, youthfully brash, of the crusty, kinky criticism of the Californian. But at the age of 35, Weiss, already a mature poet widely published in literary magazines, decides that it is time to issue a first book. Thus it is not surprising that so many of his techniques, themes, and central symbols are already established in *The Catch*. Nor will his future work be one of radical changes that give the impression of false starts; rather he will develop, broaden, deepen, consolidate. And he will meet earlier selves in later poems, like Shelley meeting himself in the garden.

To make a catch you need a hook, so Weiss at the outset provides us with "The Hook." Here we are immediately plunged into his sea of the imagination with its waves of passionate minds, his own, his students', and that of the overbrimming sculptress. It is a paeon to hope, a fusion of passion and hope. But all the while the artist is refining his craft of juxtaposition and tmesis, deftly transforming scenes from cafeteria to quarry to sea, from inner to outer: a revelation of order within the seemingly fragmentary. Every future triumph will be such a catch. "A Brown Study" might well have been titled "a study in suspensions," for it involves suspension within suspension. The poem is a swirl of transformations held still in the mind while fragments of studies for still-lifes (a brown fruit, shards of a rising Venus, and a pineapple) are brought into unity. Here Weiss has gleefully hooked a full reel of Shakespeare-an rhetoric:

> a pomp that holds
> the world together worm to star,
> orders bedlam in the sky...

Indeed, the poles of Weiss' language are the Swan of Avon and the Passaic Goose, Shakespeare and William Carlos Williams, and the effort at fusion is here—and in his most recent book, *Fireweed*—in progress. More than two disparate ways of speaking are at stake, however; here are two epochs (with many more between), two worlds, two sets of moral values. Sometimes Weiss' syntax buckles under the stress and urgency (as in the first stanza of his marvelous "The Dance Called David"), but almost never his diction. In "Cataract" he gathers and ties together, by means of the outrageous gesture of a pun, the image of the beholder's eye and the conflicting elements of fire and water. Weiss has the delightful temerity to load his puns with meaning till they groan more obstreperously than any irreverent reader possibly could. "The Dance Called David" is surely the most beautiful poem in this first book, superior to "As I Forget," a later poem also dedicated to the poet David Schubert (1913–1946). It is a lyrical phenomenology of compassion and love reconstituting the fallen world of time. Delicately and fittingly, it is enrolled under the auspices of Dante. But "Shades of Caesar" is the most ambitious poem in *The Catch*. Weiss' erudition is enormous, and he is not too timid or squint-eyed to employ it, here or in any other appropriate place. "Shades of Caesar" avails itself of this erudition to view the city's desecration from the vantage of the academic community. While observing the loves of Caesar-Cleopatra and Odysseus-Calypso merge in the troubled waters of the Nile and "the lordly Hudson" (I believe Weiss' use of the adjective precedes Paul Goodman's), the reader experiences the collapse of the heroic dimension. Seeds of Weiss' masterpiece, "Caliban Remembers," are to be found embedded in this poem.

Despite the breathtaking successes of this first book, his second, *Outlanders*, is clearly an advance. Symbols and lemmas are developed not only within each poem but also from poem to poem in a more deliberate manner than in the earlier book; there is a greater cohesiveness and unity achieved. One such lemma is "the state of weeds," and, by means of poetry's reflexive nature, here turned explicit, the state of poems. In the singable opening poem, the book's title is defined as weeds, their persistence and pride in lowliness. This theme is expanded in the next poem, "Barracks Apt. 14," under the motto "All must be used," i.e. unto the least fragment. The corollary to this statement is that nothing must or can be lost, flowers and weeds must be reintegrated in the same garden. The junk that demands reintegration is nature's and man's, whether of the dump-garden or of the mind. Yet, as the next poem, "The Greater Music," makes clear, only Orpheus the poet can perform this reintegrative act. "The Greater Music" is attended by a delicate train of inner and off-rhymes, as befits orphic song. As though he were saying it for the greatest music, the wholly integrated occasion, Weiss rarely indulges our ears with rhyme. This omission, since it implies that his other efforts are secondary, not "the greater," seems to me a basic defect: the poet has sacrificed his most reverberating string to a hierarchy of value judgments that is, after all, putative and only argumentative. Be that as it may, the "state of weeds" theme is continued in "A Local Matter," "A Working Day" (which invokes the Thoreau who sat out the disunion of things), and the old woman working in her garden of "The Generations" (a situation to which he will later return with splendid results). "Homecoming," on the other hand, suggests that there may be a limit to the process of reintegration, a hint that if carried far enough it could become undifferentiated, inhuman. The stoicism that Weiss associates with Odysseus recommends that over-integration be resisted with courage. Stoicism, it should be indicated, is in itself a major Weissean theme, and usually appears accompanied by joy. Except for Richard Wilbur and the Spanish Jorge Guillén, Weiss is perhaps the most joyous poet now celebrating in America. But the stoical attitude requires courage, too, and a stance of bear-the-world-and-it-will-bear-you. For instance, "A Local Matter" proffers stoicism as an equilibrium of pain and joy. Upon the mouse's and chestnuts' pain and death, such inconsiderable local matters, depend the seasons and other such cosmic matters, which in turn lead to the quest for an appropriate grief and the acceptance of death. Yet joy preponderates in the very music of a passage like the following:

> Now in the lute-time,
> soon brute, of the year I
> slouch down, the silky lounge
> of one in perfect health
> (hear the chestnut
> gayly crying in its country fire).
> I lounge as I wait the advent
> of one all sinew and strain,
> the lunge. Like a string tautening
> to the discords of precisionist
> pain, I fit: come, windy
> dark, like all the kingdoms
> of the north and within the gates
> of my Jerusalem set your sundry
> singing thrones!

Weiss' fascination with Leopardi, the most pessimistic of poets, and a giant among the Stoics, originates in a dialectic of grief and joy, with stoicism their antidote. Consolation Weiss will offer, but seldom to himself. Of Leopardi he once wrote:

> Believing life in its common ills as in its
> end essentially unhappy, he fully understood

the common need of consolations. Yet he despised this need (especially as it feeds on
the deceits of reason, little more than a form
of anesthesia) and the failure of almost all
of us to live in denial of it.

Weiss rings still other changes on fragmentation. "In This Tower" differentiates between fragments and differences, the first requiring the effort to make it whole, the second with wholeness already inhering in its nature. This is how it begins:

As the sycamore makes one thing
of the wind, and the birch another…
as these roses, four kinds of roses,
related in scent, yet as different
as their colors, make in the vase
out of their difference one fragrance

so in your moods by the gamut
of glances, the narrow yet infinitely
many diapason of breath, you make
one sundry thing of the air.

In reference to the above lines I should like to point out that the contemporary disdain for the simile (and especially the set-simile) is merely superstitious and is based on the groundless supposition that metaphorical identity is somehow truer and more poetic than similitude. Both tropes have appropriate functions. In Weiss' brilliant set-simile similitude is the appropriate figure to convey the theme of differences.

In the opulent scene-painting of "An Egyptian Passage" he describes two disparate worlds, and, by a thrilling change in point of view, the poet "sitting on a polar star," recomposes the world in a visual-spatial epiphany. Weiss' version of St. Francis occurs in "Descent," and characteristically he is "pining to compose the world." But primarily this poem is a lament for loss of belief in a golden Orphic Age. Because love can partially restore this age, self-consolation does not cheapen sentiment. Richard Howard, in many respects an astute commentator on Weiss, woefully and implacably undervalues him as a love poet, whether that love be domestic or an aspect of agape.

Two more poems in this second book deserve singling out, "The Great Yea" and "The Fire at Alexandria": the first for its fervent optimism in regard to the university and community of scholars, a theme to which he returns again and again (spectacularly in "Two for Heinrich Bleucher"); and the second for its startling transformation of symbols in a little miracle of fusions: sparks from his earliest poems becoming words and words becoming a pentecostal fire that burns not only the lost but the preserved. God's holy fire indeed!

■ III

In 1962, the New York University Press published Weiss' longest single poem, *Gunsight*, extending to 55 pages. Nothing in his work thus far had prepared his audience for such magnitude, complexity, and ambition. Nor had the poet overreached himself. The protagonist (or, better, the center of consciousness) of *Gunsight* is a young soldier who is experiencing (the only proper word for his complex of reactions) surgery under ether. Into his consciousness, clouded and distorted by the anesthetic, throngs a phantasmagoria of voices, distinct and typographically signaled, that are simultaneously the same and the other ("the same is the other," Weiss has written elsewhere), or, as he wrote in still another connection, "all things communicate invisibly, exchanging their fluids and messsages." Thus are the Weissean themes continuant throughout the fabric of his work.

There is another voice, too, auctorial, a narrator's or the poet's, a voice distinctly Shakespearean, whereas the phantasmagoria usually sounds like the Passaic goose. But even in the auctorial voice, even in the lines that serve as introduction, penetration into the wounded consciousness is profound and pervasive, for the poet will make no false and self-limiting claims to objectivity. So adroit is Weiss' handling of this polyphony of voices that the need for tmesis is obviated, and it is so coherent and dramatically textured that mere isolation of a word or phrase (sometimes repeated from pages earlier) can return situations and notions to us without confusion, blending them into new situations and notions.

As the poem is built on particular voices, it also displays a scheme of varying temporal levels: the operating table is both past and present. Memory hearkens back to a childhood hunting expedition which blurs with soldiering episodes and exploits, his wound, and the operation itself, all accomplished through polyhonous (rather than syntactic tmesis and multi-referent syntax and diction. When hunting-soldiering imagery begins to merge with recollection of first love, lyrical rhymes crop up:

> (we'll lip to lip in mastery
> enlarge the airs our senses sing,
> the hanging gardens fingers bring)

or:

> In coil-
> ing warmth we lie that love, untoil-
> ing, forage in us, finding, share
> its raptures in our blended air.

or, subtly phasing out the dense music:

> Our honey-suckled kiss
> plunking us, we blithely crest
> the tide; like a sprig in the beak
> of a dove we, soaring, wake.

The above citations represent "the higher music" as exemplified in the poem of that title; but the rhymes are also emblems of duality, the paired words completing the paired lovers. The primal beloved, however, is soon fragmented into the many light-loves who are little more than names and "horror in such white hands," the hands simultaneously referring to those of the surgeon. The soldiering episodes that follow explore phases of a young soldier's experience—boozing, brawling, his lusts (in relation to which the last of the quotations above is echoed distortedly:

> (we crest the tide,
> high on a jaunty world-wide
> spring in a bird's beak)

and will reappear in other distortions), escapades, training and battle ordeals. Throughout this phantasmagoria of voicings and temporal levels the struggle between consciousness and anesthetic possesses moral overtones of the stoic theme, and provides, literally and figuratively, a feat of endurance. The alert reader will recall his passage on Leopardi which relegates consolation and the deceits of reason to "little more than a form of anesthesia."

Amazingly, Richard Howard considers *Gunsight* to be without literary and classical references. This is so far from being true that the poem's crisis is a grand, commanding *katabasis* closely modeled on those of Homer and Virgil, and outdistancing Eliot's, Pound's, and even Crane's, in significance and ordinary, everyday application. In it the narrator-poet is transformed into a Tiresias-like figure, a boding tension: "...hear one / who knows and so can speak for all the dead." And, indeed, this section bristles and sparkles with references to Homer, Virgil, Dante, and, if my reading is correct, the tragedies of Shakespeare. In Hades the anesthetized dream encounters a soldier companion, Frank ("a wound for mouth"), and, very movingly, the dreamer's own mother. Her speech, though interrupted by her son's importunings and other ghostly voices, is awesome in its mingling of tenderness and sweet anger to get at a truth available only to prophetic poetry. From this encounter to the conclusion, Weiss' tone becomes increasingly redemptive. There are setbacks, of course; setbacks are in the nature of things; but on the whole an unconsoled endurance is its own redemption.

One feature of *Gunsight* is that it can be profitably read in different ways, each providing new perspectives. Experiment with reading only the wounded soldier's lines, then add the various voices in italics, and, finally, the narrator-poet's lines. It is instructive to confront the success of Weiss' voicings with the failure of James Dickey, in *The Zodiac*, to give voice to his Marsman's drunken speeches. Dickey's failure can be attributed to the lack of distance between the poet and his character: there is no room for focusing or situating moral force. Whereas Weiss' moral force is evident in every word.

Weiss' next book, *The Medium*, elaborates on what the poet is able to redeem through art and love. The title poem takes a stand, not unopposed, since Weiss inhabits actuality and not an illusive world of dreams, on language as the medium of love. "White Elephants" redeems an old Hudson Valley manse, the white elephant of American slang being transformed into a sacred emblem through a pun's sleight-of-mind. Such transformations are apprehended as action on the moral plane, which in "The Moral" reveal that value can be grasped even from failure, for nothing is lost and all is used. As our poet says:

Whatever has happened, diverse ravishings
that love to bask in balmy weather
of a scream, the passionate failures,
the perfect despairs, these never fail us.

The most ambitious poem in *The Medium* is "Two for Heinrich Bleucher." Here Weiss returns to the ideas, so often twinned in his mind, of exile and the university as a viable community of scholars. Weiss, himself a teacher, is careful to distinguish among kinds of teaching. I would recommend this poem as required reading for all who contemplate adopting the profession. And yet the poem leaves me just a trifle uneasy. I would blame the complication of roles inherent in the teacher-scholar-exile tmesis, and possibly the introduction of Socrates stretches the poem further out of shape and debilitates idea as well as landscape. The poem's nobility remains intact, despite my quibbles.

■ IV

The Last Day and the First (1968) seems to me Weiss' most accomplished book so far, and one among its poems, "Caliban Remembers," his crowning achievement. The realism of *Gunsight* is that of the play of intersubjectivity, whose true hero is the many, not the one. "Caliban Remembers" is the precise opposite insofar as it isolates and compresses realism into a single consciousness. If there is a multi-consciousness in any way operative, it derives from a quartet composed of Weiss and the poem's three great predecessors, Shakespeare, Browning, and Auden. Richard

Howard sees the debt to Shakespeare and Auden, but only "permanent dispossessions" from Browning. I am not altogether certain I know what Mr. Howard means; I am certain I do not agree with what I think he means. Weiss conceives of Caliban as a composite which he must break down without dispossessing any of the resulting fragments. In fact, Weiss' language in this poem is a tribute to and a contemporary preservation of Browning's. The modern poet alters the Victorian's worldview, nothing more, nothing less. "The Tempest" is an extraordinary tmesis whose poles are the newly forged myth of Ariel and Caliban; "Caliban Remembers" is a mythic tmesis, similarly extraordinary, whose poles are Caliban's consciousness and his bodysense, with the world in between at full stretch and pull. Here is a short example:

> Witch she,
> not my poor mother, I tweaked as ever,
> as a jay its secretest feather.
> And most, blood at the heart hopping,
> dare I speak out her name.

(It will be seen, of course, that "most" and "dare," without the intervening proximity of "blood…hopping," could never have been brought into so significant a nexus. There exist, after all, ways of getting around a petrifact but beautiful tongue: take it deep, deep into your mouth.) Here all elements of the tmesis are coterminous if not undifferentiated; and there is no malignant, witchy mother-goddess. Then Caliban soliloquizes (the form is soliloquy, the circumstance is the hero fishing, with "The Catch"—Weiss' first poem!—as defining term of the fishing symbol) thus:

> God I, the sky my gliding.
> earth, everything in it my subject,
> far below.

From this godlike situation of the *cogito* dominating nature's object world, Caliban meditates to a state wherein his consciousness is united with the world, subject and object no longer standing over against each other, but participants each in each. That is to say, Cartesian doubt is redeemed in phenomenological affirmation. As Prospero abandoned his wand, Caliban, now part Ariel, renounces possessive magic and the prevalent powers in order to immerse himself in the flux of efts and ooze, like William Carlos Williams baptized in the filthy Passaic. This work, the finest long poem in decades and entirely *sui generis*, is haunted by tutelary spirits. It is a pity that Weiss has not fully come to grips with the complementary figure of Ariel, though there are traces of him in the poet's gardeners of soil and university, as well as in Caliban.

The eminent successes in *The Last Day and the First* are so many that I will only discuss two more. "Mount Washington" is a somewhat rambling but not overlong piece in the tradition of "The Prelude." Its theme, which will be recognized as a recurrent one in Weiss, is obliquely and succinctly stated in the epigraph borrowed from Emerson's "Thoreau":

> At Mount Washington, in Tuckerman's Ravine,
> Thoreau had a bad fall…As he was…
> getting up…he saw for the first time…
> the *Arnica mollis*.

Were "Mount Washington" fifty times longer, given its frisky delight in language and reminiscence, its proposity-punishing puns ("eidel/weiss"), its relevant-to-all-things erudition, it would be too short. The author's delight is infectious. The second poem is "Wunsch-zettel" (meaning a Christmas wishing-list), another of Weiss' tender, compelling scrutinies of women gardeners; but this one recapitulates the others (including teachers, scholars, exiles, stoics) in a character of near-tragic joy, near-tragic because she is without the starkness of, say, one of Yeats' personages. Weiss' compassion is too detailed for tragedy in joy. A fascinating extension of tmesis is employed to suggest her accent and at the same time play it down so the stoical aspect of exile can be disclosed.

After the triumphs of *The Last Day and the First*, his next volume, *The World Before Us* (1970), marks time. The poet sits way back, invites his soul, experiments tried themes in new combinations, and performs the satisfying feats of reworking the fire-words and fishing symbols in the recollected light of "Caliban Remembers." "The Youngest Son," a rendition of the prodigal son that is more contemporary than Rilke's or Gide's, introduces regular stanzas and some end-rhyme into his work. "Yes, But…," in which Frost's certainty is set against Williams' uncertainty and Weiss manages to discover strength even in the latter (everything used, nothing lost), must be singled out, as well as the Muiresque horror of "A Certain Village."

■ V

With *Fireweeds* (1976), Weiss' most recent book, relaxation is over, tmesis returns, and the scholar-poet, perhaps reinvigorated upon completion of a long study of Shakespeare's early comedies and history plays, rides the crest of his intellect. In this book Weiss has need for all his courage and wit, for here he most specifically and forthrightly confronts our times and our evils; and yet there are high—I almost wrote lavish—praises given, too. All in all, *Fireweeds* does not contain his best poems, perhaps, but it is his ripest book. The title conjoins two ubiquitous Weissean symbols: the sparks and fire of words, i.e., the Word as pentecostal sacrament, and the weeds that must not be lost. It might be argued that the contents of this book tend to be wisdom-poems, not quests for wisdom, and at least two of them, "The Storeroom" and "A Charm Against the Toothache," approach his major work.

"The Storeroom" and "Another and Another and…" continue, augment and consolidate the Odyssean adventure in the stoic mind of the poems, while "As You Like It" contradicts Auden's contention that people are indifferent to the great event. Cockily, Weiss presents his Mrs. Gudgeon, an English charwoman, as taking from experience whatever she can use, and concludes:

>   This is the greatness
> of each creature,
>   the mouse at the Feast
> of the Gods, one crumb doing for it
> what heaped-up platters cannot do for Them.

Even the critic Harold Bloom gets his come-uppance in "An Everlasting Once," though good-humoredly and without malice. Weiss can afford to take time out for little tasks like that.

He praises the English language in "The Cure" and the saving grace potential in evil in "A Stroke of Good Luck." Words are a burning house, an apotheosis of fire, in "Rushlight," while in "A Place To Be," another for Heinrich Bleucher, now grown old, sparks from the earliest poems flare up with renewed vitality:

> And if the fire's flagged to embers,
> though at times still flaring up,
> revealing remnants of the various sights,
> those mighty ruins, which it reveled in,
> this unexpected, final something else
> intensifies your worth.

■ BOOKS BY THEODORE WEISS

poetry

The Catch. New York: Twayne, 1951.

Outlanders. New York: Macmillan, 1960.

Gunsight. New York: New York University Press, 1962.

The Medium: Poems. New York: Macmillan, 1965.

The Last Day and The First: Poems. New York: Macmillan, 1968.

The World Before Us: Poems. 1950–1970. New York: Macmillan, 1970.

Fireweeds. New York: Macmillan, 1976.

Views and Spectacles: Selected Poems. London: Chatto & Windus, 1978.

Recoveries: A Poem. New York: Macmillan, 1982.

A Slow Fuse: New Poems. New York: Macmillan, 1984.

From Princeton One Autumn Afternoon: Collected Poems of Theodore Weiss, 1950–1986. New York: Macmillan, 1987.

A Sum of Destructions. Baton-Rouge: Louisiana State University Press, 1994.

Selected Poems. Evanston, Ill.: TriQuarterly Books/Northwestern University Press, 1994.

prose

The Breath of Clowns and Kings: A Study of Shakespeare. New York: Atheneum, and London: Chatto and Windus, 1971.

Gerard Manley Hopkins: Realist on Parnassus. (Reprint of 1940 Edition), Folcroft, Pa.: Folcroft Library Editions,1976.

The Man from Porlock: Engagements, 1944–1982 (essays). Princeton, N.J.: Princeton University Press, 1982.

Thus poem after poem in *Fireweeds*—no falling off, no embers, a burning house rather than a flaring up (though, like Marianne Moore, he must be permitted his modesty), weeds and flowers still carefully tended, swan and goose luxuriating together, a sacrament of words. This is "the passion equal to all hope," not merely to hope, and, no matter how his surroundings fragment, it shows no sign of weakening. Veteran readers of Weiss may be congratulated for bringing their own passion to bear on the difficult hope in the man: he is their mirror, and in it they too are reconstituted whole.

Robert Stock
April, 1979

UPDATE

Theodore Weiss has, since this essay was written, published six volumes of poetry: *Views and Spectacles: Selected Poems* (1978), *Recoveries: A Poem* (1982), *A Slow Fuse: New Poems* (1984), *From Princeton One Autumn Afternoon: Collected Poems of Theodore Weiss, 1950-1986* (1987), *A Sum of Destructions* (1994), and *Selected Poems* (1995).

Weiss, known for his ability to write on a range of deep human experiences—including war, spiritual enlightenment, and man's place in the universe—once told *Contemporary Authors* that his primary motivation for writing is "to entertain, extend others, and to keep myself company," and he listed his influences as "Browning & Hopkins; Stevens & Williams; and things seen, heard, thought." Weiss also commented that his writing process is "too mysterious, too hidden to describe briefly."

His recent work continues to have an appreciative audience among readers and critics. *Booklist* addressed *A Sum of Destructions* thus: "Weiss is a master at making each poem whirl, tornado-like, to its end. He can start with a slow, dreadful building up whose stillness implies forthcoming violence, then break into staccato language, and follow the outburst with the relief of surviving. . . . Like a home owner glancing fearfully out the window at an increasingly darkening sky, Weiss sees quite clearly and with the realization of potential loss."

"One feels the poet pulled along by his vision, and his verse continually rising to its demands," a *Nation* article once observed. "Weiss neither spurns sublimity nor refuses the homely particular. There is a rare splendor to his work."

Exorcizing the Demons: John Edgar Wideman's Literary Response

In his socio-literary classic *The Souls of Black Folk* (1903), W. E. B. Du Bois characterized African-Americans as being in possession of a double-consciousness in which "one ever feels his twoness—an American, a Negro; two souls, two thoughts, two unreconciled strivings; two warring ideals in one dark body." The notion is a persistent one in the annals of African-American literature. James Weldon Johnson through his narrator in *The Autobiography of an Ex-Coloured Man* (1912), makes the further observation that this psychological condition reflects a "dual personality" exacerbated in the psyche of a black man "in proportion to his intellectuality." According to that analysis, the condition assumes an even greater significance in direct proportion to an individual's capacity to comprehend his predicament.

If the narrator in Johnson's novel is correct, then we should be especially concerned about what life has consisted of for a person such as John Edgar Wideman. Raised in the predominantly black, inner-city community of Homewood in Pittsburgh, Pennsylvania, Wideman would later win a scholarship to attend the University of Pennsylvania, where he would become an All-Ivy League basketball player in addition to being Phi Beta Kappa. But it was the winning of another important distinction that catapulted him into the international spotlight. In 1963 he became only the second African-American to win the prestigious Rhodes Scholarship. Prior to that year, the only African-American ever to have received the award was Alain Locke in 1907.

When Wideman won the scholarship, *Look* magazine covered the story in an article, "The Astonishing John Wideman," where the awardee was credited with having stipulated that as far as he was concerned, "being Negro is only a physical fact." He elaborated:

> "If there were something I wanted very badly that being Negro prevented me from doing, then I might have the confrontation of a racial problem, and I would be driven to do something about it.... But so far, the things that I've wanted to do haven't been held back from me because of my being a Negro. So the problem is not my own problem, not something I feel I have to cope with or resolve."

He was saying, in so many words, that race was not an issue for him. And perhaps, during his college years, he was someone who could afford this luxury. Many on the UPenn faculty considered him a genius; fellow students likewise regarded him highly. Maybe he was just one of those rare individuals who would have succeeded in spite of any obstacle.

Then there is another way to interpret Wideman's statement, as Chip Brown, in a 1989 *Esquire* article, suggests when he says that "to page through the paean is to study a time capsule on race relations circa 1963: the monochrome white students with their pre-skinhead haircuts, the unquestioned assumption that assimilation is a one-way street and black shall bend to white." How does a young black man respond to his place in a college setting that is overwhelmingly white? How does he respond when he is the star athlete, Pharisee (treasurer of the

John Edgar Wideman

John Edgar Wideman was born June 14, 1941, in Washington, D.C., but grew up in Homewood, a Pittsburgh ghetto where many of his books are set. He attended the University of Pennsylvania on a basketball scholarship and was selected as an Oxford University Rhodes scholar, only the second black to receive this honor. In 1984 Wideman was awarded the PEN/Faulkner Award for Fiction for *Sent for You Yesterday*. Wideman also received a National Book Award nomination (1984) for *Brothers and Keepers*, the John Dos Passos Prize for Literature from Longwood College (1986), the Lannan Award (1991), and PEN/Faulkner Award and American Book Award, Before Columbus Foundation, (both 1991), both for *Philadelphia Fire*. He also received a MacArthur fellowship (1993) and an honorary doctorate from the University of Pennsylvania.

Wideman taught English and directed the Afro-American studies program at the University of Penn-

sylvania from 1966 to 1974. He taught English at the University of Wyoming, 1974–1985, and since then at the University of Massachusetts at Amherst. ■

senior men's honor society), and recipient of a scholarship to Oxford University. *People* magazine, in 1985, quotes Wideman as having said, "I believed in the whole Horatio Alger thing." And why shouldn't he have believed in it? He had come from inauspicious beginnings; his father at various times had been a waiter and a trash collector. The son applied himself, strove to be something better. Why shouldn't he believe in the dream? Why couldn't he be, first and foremost, an American?

Interestingly enough, just one year after the *People* article, Wideman agreed to an interview with Kay Bonetti which appeared in *The Missouri Review*. In this latter interview he expressed a different position than what he had said earlier with regard to how he perceived himself within the Horatio Alger framework. Now he was contradictorily maintaining, "I was never simply somebody who bought the American dream, the Horatio Alger myth. I was always somebody who had ghosts, who had demons." Which John Wideman should be believed? And what exactly was the nature of those demons? Excessive guilt? A sense that he was running from his roots in the Homewood community?

In the *People* article, Wideman's wife, Judy, offered additional insight into her husband's dilemma. She declared:

"In the 60s, there was a gradual willingness on John's part to look at himself and his background. It was painful, difficult for him to do. In order to achieve the things he'd done, he'd had to look away. The difference between where he was and where his family was was very difficult for him to reconcile."

Upon his return to the United States, Wideman accepted a professorship at his alma mater and set about the task of becoming a writer.

It has become fashionable among some critics to conclude that located within the context of the author's first three novels (*A Glance Away,* 1967; *Hurry Home,* 1970; and *The Lynchers,* 1973) is evidence that he was trying to adjust his work to meet the standards of a mainstream white literary tradition. In *Glance,* we certainly do see elements of James Joyce and T. S. Eliot. Wideman's Robert Thurley, for example, is just another version of Eliot's J. Alfred Prufrock who mourns "I grow old…I grow old… / I shall wear the bottoms of my trousers rolled." Thurley is an elderly professor whose limited hopes hinge on the prospect "that life would continue to be played out in half-light, in pleasant bodily fatigue" even as he waits for the musical sounds and "knew the oboe was the sound of death."

Home is the continuation of a modernist style of writing consisting of stream-of-consciousness technique and Joycean-type reliance on dashes to distinguish between different speakers. In one memorable scene our protagonist, Cecil Braithwaite, accedes to a shoeshine boy who wants to shine Braithwaite's shoes without receiving any payment. But once Braithwaite's shoes are shined, the boy appeals to a nearby crowd of blacks and insists that Braithwaite is attempting to exploit him. The collective voice of the crowd, referring to Braithwaite as magistrate, demands:

— Pay the boy, magistrate…
— How much do you want.
— We want you, magistrate….
—I've done nothing wrong.

Someone punches Braithwaite in the face as he stumbles along, with the mob crowding in on him to exact further punishment. The episode is reminiscent of Kafka's Joseph K. who, in *The Trial* (1925), is awakened by two strangers who drag him off and accuse him of having committed a crime of which he is unaware.

While *Lynchers* is generally regarded as the last novel written in Wideman's early phase, it has also been suggested that it marks the beginning of a major shift in emphasis on the part of the author. James W. Coleman remarks, "The world that he creates is less dominated by white literary vision than that in *A Glance Away,* and he focuses on life in the black community much more here than in *Hurry Home.*" Indeed *Lynchers* is quite different from either of Wideman's earlier works. One is taken aback by the chronological listing of lynchings, beatings, and various other types of assaults by whites against blacks. That list enumerates 116 incidents that took place in the relatively short period between 1867 and 1871. But the message Wideman means to deliver has to do with the building up of animosities over a much longer period of time to the point where four young black men have resolved to turn the tables, so to speak, and conduct a lynching of their own. It will be a modern-day lynching, and the victim will be a white policeman.

Willie Hall, the leader of the conspiracy, explains how the killing will make an important statement to society's privileged classes. The lynching will serve as a refutation of the complacency that had allowed those upper classes to believe they could exist quietly, insulated from the horrors of inner city life. The lynching will be a warning: "No, the flunkies you pay to keep us within bounds are not enough. We must show how the cops are symbolic…. We will lynch one man but in fact we will be denying a total vision of reality." The improper vision of reality that Hall alludes to is the one portraying America as a place where all is well while in actuality society is on the verge of upheaval. Killing the policeman will itself cause upheaval, but this way, there is a good chance that a large amount of control will be in the hands of Hall and those who are like him. Hall urges:

Do you believe what we're seeing this morning?…Do you see the next step? How vulnerable the lies are that hold this mess together as it stands. Do you realize how we have all the evidence we need to expose the lies, to shatter the arbitrary balance and order. Nothing but an alley between two alien forms of life. The whites are just a few paces away living in a manner which makes a mockery of our suffering. Two people in a fifty thousand dollar town house…. And babies on this street sleeping in drawers, on the floor…. It's an alley we can cross, we can cross in numbers. Nothing in the world can stop us if we decide the barrier is not there anymore. If we all die at least the lie will die with us.

In these times of governmental budgetary crises and private industry layoffs, many whites have also been made to suffer. There is the urge—especially when executives are nonetheless thriving economically—to say that the issue has more to do with class distinctions than with matters of race. Actually, both class and race are important factors. But as one listens to statistics, the racial factor assumes a frightening dimension—infant mortality twice as high among blacks, unemployment twice as high, and a prison population so filled with black men that it has almost become euphemistic to acknowledge that there are more young black men, between the ages of 18 and 25, in jail than there are attending college.

Wideman has always been deeply concerned, in his writing, with those very issues. In a 1988 interview, he made it clear "there was no game plan at the beginning which was scuttled for another game plan somewhere in the middle. There is always back and forward and testing." He pursued creative writing, in large part, due to opportunities he saw for experimentation. In *Lynchers,* even with its racial themes, one still sees the Joycean use of dashes as a means of distinguishing between speakers. Furthermore, stream of consciousness technique continues to be employed to convey an ambiguity that pervades racial issues the author is intent on examining.

A close analysis of *Home's* Cecil Braithwaite reveals Wideman's alter ego. Braithwaite was the "first of his race to do, to be, etc." Wideman is giving us a glimpse of his years at UPenn. Since, by 1973, many more black undergraduates were attending historically white institutions than was the case during his undergraduate years between 1959 and 1963, the author has updated the social phenomenon and made the institution a historically white law school where, even in the early 1970s, the percentage of black enrollment was still painfully low. A surrealistic chorus of blacks taunts Braithwaite:

> Real is Cecil, real were those fine white men your classmates and what they do and what you will do as practitioner of the law. Nothing good comes without sacrifice. Christ paid for our sins. Let *them* pay for their own. Don't you know *they'll* only drag you down, eat you up, Cecil. Being one of *them* is as impossible, frankly, as is being one of us. That's fact, it's written. I kid you not. Just look at the realities of the situation.

Much of *Home* is devoted to the protagonist's psychological journey in search of himself while the author is simultaneously engaged in a probing intellectual search of his own.

■ ■ ■

Wideman's search runs him head-on into the circumstances of his younger brother, Robby. In a *60 Minutes* interview conducted in 1985, the younger brother recapitulated events surrounding the first time he ran afoul of the law. John was summoned in from Philadelphia to "take him upstairs and…talk to him." The brothers went to Robby's room, but nothing was resolved. "We couldn't talk," explained Robby, "because our worlds were so different."

What had happened between the time when John had grown up in Homewood and the time, 10 years later, when Robby came along? Describing how the community was when he was a boy, John, in that *60 Minutes* interview, made the following assessment:

"The community itself was much more closely knit. It was much more like a small town, a small Southern town…. if I went out on the street, somebody on some porch, Mrs. Ellis, would be checking me out. If I went too far, or did something I wasn't supposed to do, she certainly would tell my mother. The crime was petty-ante stuff, and usually not directed with any kind of brutality or viciousness inside of the community."

The community had changed. Adult support mechanisms were no longer as strong as they had been in the past.

However, it should also be considered to what extent sibling rivalry was a factor. In the collection of reminiscences entitled *Brothers and Keepers* (1984), Robby confides, "Wasn't nothing I could do in school or sports that youns hadn't done already. People said, Here comes another Wideman. He's gon be a good student like his brothers and sister…. I was another Wideman, the last one, the baby, and everybody knew how I was spozed to act." Robby had a choice: He could go along with the program of high achievement or strike out in a different direction.

John would later come to understand his brother's agony. Sprinkled throughout *Glance* are episodes that convey what it must have been like having an older brother who excelled in everything. Eddie Lawson—as much a major protagonist as Robert Thurley—recalls being teased and thinking, "My brother was the worst …because he was my brother and different because he was bigger, stronger and was loved." Perhaps those impressions are not justified. But in the younger brother's mind, the impressions become the reality.

Eddie is fixated on his older brother who "grew fast and rank, a strong hard-handed boy whose shoes had to be left outside at night. Huge, smelly things Martha would carry dangling like fish from their strings, holding her nose but laughing and loving the ritual." The shoes signify communal effort. The brother, Eugene, is John Wideman, who shoveled snow off the courts so that he could practice basketball through the winter. The sister's role was to make sure that his shoes were left outside overnight so they would be aired out and ready for use the next day. She facilitated John's efforts as did his parents in struggling to provide a home for the developing star. All that might have been left for other family members to do was simply watch and perhaps contemplate as Tommy (Robby) does in *Hiding Place* (1981) when he ponders how he "could have played the game. Tall and loose. Hands bigger than his brother's. Could palm a ball when he was eleven." But it would have been difficult to have been better than John. Difficult, in fact, to have been half as good as the older brother.

So Robby sought avenues by which he might make his mark in music. But he failed, once again, at what for anyone would have been a difficult proposition. "If that cat hadn't fucked us over with the record," Tommy rationalizes in *Hiding*, "we might have made the big time." It becomes clearer what sort of pressure the younger brother was responding to, a pressure that had been building for quite some time. Robby, in *Brothers*, expounds on his need to fantasize:

> When I was a very little child, oh, about six or seven, I had a habit of walking down Walnut and Copeland streets…. As I walked I would look at the cars and in my mind I would buy them, but they only cost nickels or dimes. Big ones a dime, little ones a nickel, some that I liked a whole lot would cost a quarter. So as I got older this became a habit. For years I bought cars with the change that was in my pocket, which in those times wasn't very much.

The danger here is evident, for those cars represent the unattainable. A child's game developed, as Robby goes on to say in *Brothers*, into "a way of looking at things—an unrealistic way—it's like I wanted things to be easy, and misguidedly tried to make everything that way, blinded then to the fact that nothing good or worthwhile comes without serious effort." This realization came late for Robby. School, for him, ceased to be a viable means to achievement, and instead he turned to the streets for his answers, answers that included fast money, drugs, and the prospect of meeting with a too-early death.

While still in Philadelphia, as UPenn's first black tenured professor, John wrote an essay for *The American Scholar* entitled "Fear in the Streets" (1971). In this essay he remarks on the dehumanizing consequences of having to live in a decaying inner city. Referring to such an existence as being in a "metaphysical cage," he further reflects that its "filth, violence and brutality—the streets lined with uncollected garbage, the bloody emergency wards, the direlicts and addicts—are an epiphany validating the worst things the black man has heard about himself." The answer for Wideman was to leave and exchange Philadelphia for the University of Wyoming in Laramie. "I'd come west," the author confesses in *Brothers*, "to escape the demons Robby personified."

Meanwhile, Robby was becoming more and more immersed in a life of crime to the point where one fateful day in November, 1975, he and two friends robbed a used car dealer who also was known to moonlight as a "fence" for stolen goods. What Robby describes in *Brothers* takes on the dimensions of a turbulent blur: An agreement that the fence will buy a truckload of stolen televisions from Robby and his two friends. Only, there are no televisions. The stipulated televisions become a ploy to get the fence to bring money. On the night when the deal is supposed to be consummated, the fence tenders cash, saying, "Okay. Here's the money. Where's the TVs?" Sudden chaos ensues. The robbers demand, "Throw down your money on the ground." A wind blows the cash everywhere. Robby is frantically chasing it. One of the robbers, Michael Dukes, fires a warning shot. The fence is not hit but falls down and then scuffles "to get up again.... looked like he was digging in his clothes for something." Dukes fires again, this time fatally wounding the fence. Robby never fired a shot, but he nevertheless was involved in the perpetration of a crime in which a man's life was taken. So he was sentenced to life in prison without the possibility of parole.

Even as he "escaped" to Wyoming, John Wideman was aware of the precariousness of his unique situation. Just how far removed could he allow himself to be from his brother's tormenting situation? True, John had come along during the patient, more tranquil 1950s, whereas Robby grew up 10 years later. There was that all-important difference. Yet, in the *60 Minutes* interview, Robby's words became ominous as he talked about black males who "wanted to be able to believe in our country and believe in the things that we were being told, but the contradictions were there and the majority of all the guys that I grew up with are now either in jail, they're dead, they're in the streets strung out on drugs and, you know, that—that says it there, that very few of us made it through. Very few of us made it through." When a 34-year-old man looks around only to discover that the majority of young men he grew up with are either dead, in jail, or on drugs, then something is terribly wrong. One wonders if there has come into existence a new type of slavery that, though different in many respects, is just as overwhelming and brutal.

This is what the author must have been pondering during the eight-year lull between *Lynchers* in 1973, and the next two books, *Hiding Place* and *Damballah*, both of which first appeared in 1981. The latter two works are his first installments of what has come to be known as *The Homewood Trilogy* (the third installment, *Sent for You Yesterday*, would appear two years later) in which he sought to determine what had made previous generations of blacks so much stronger. Using the rich heritage of his own family, he offers us models such as the elderly Aunt Bess who, in *Hiding*, berates the fugitive Tommy and proclaims, "Life's hard. Didn't nobody never tell you? Didn't nobody never hold you up and look in your eyes and tell you you got to die one day little boy and they be plenty days you wish it be sooner stead of later?" She wants him to be aware that times were rough for blacks long before he was born, yet they managed somehow to survive and occasionally prosper. They kept hope alive for future generations in spite of the presumed insurmountable odds.

In "Lizabeth: The Caterpillar Story," one of twelve stories in *Damballah*, we are presented with John French, Wideman's maternal grandfather, encountering his little daughter who has just eaten a piece of a bug. The daughter, Lizabeth, is Wideman's mother when she was a child. Freeda French, John French's wife, was supposed to have been watching the girl. "What did she eat?" the grandfather demands. "What you saying she ate? You supposed to be watching this child, woman." Freeda gives her husband what is left of the caterpillar and he "measures the spiraled length of caterpillar…strokes its fur…seems to be listening or speaking to it as he passes it close to his face." He is calculating what he must do. Then he swallows the caterpillar and reasons, "I got the most of it then. And if I don't die, she ain't gonna die neither." We are witness to a powerful love.

Wideman broadens the theme of family love when, in *Yesterday*, he shows us Albert Wilkes, who was adopted by the socially conscious Mr. and Mrs. Tate. Wilkes grows up to be an extraordinary piano player, specializing in the blues, but then one day he shoots a white man. The chain of events is ambiguous, best conveyed nonetheless in a conversation between Freeda and John French as they discuss the profound implications of the fugitive Wilkes' return. Calling him "a doomed man," Freeda expostulates:

I know he shot a white police, and they gon hunt him down till they get him.

Wasn't no policeman. Was a white man coming after Wilkes cause Wilkes been messing with the white man's white woman.

Found him dead in his uniform.

Wilkes knew what that white man after. Uniform didn't make no nevermind.

Lord saith vengeance is mine.

Ain't no vengeance to it. Man come to kill Albert Wilkes. Albert Wilkes got his shot in first. Lord didn't say nothing about standing still and dying just cause some peckerwood decide he needs you dead.

It should be noted, at this point, that the author is no longer using Joycean dashes to distinguish between speakers. Moreover, stream of consciousness technique has given way somewhat to clearer commentary and a clearer dialogue. But Wideman does not altogether eliminate the stream of consciousness technique that had been so much a part of his earlier works. In fact, as Freeda and John French discuss Wilkes' situation, their conversation becomes one voice telling the story of the whole black experience.

A similar function is served through Ralph Ellison's portrayal of Jim Trueblood in the novel *Invisible Man* (1952). Trueblood commits incest with his daughter. At the point of penetration he realizes he was trapped in the impossible position of "having to move *without* movin'." And yet, in the telling of his story, he urges, "When you think right hard you see that that's the way things is always been with me. That's just about been my life." As we ponder the extreme poverty of the Trueblood family—a grinding poverty that forced the two parents and their daughter into the same bed to stay warm—we are made to reconsider the extent to which Trueblood may or may not be morally culpable. When we learn that penetration occurred while Trueblood was in the midst of a dream about an unattainable white woman, we ponder his life even more. It is easy to argue that Trueblood has committed a heinous crime. Yet, it is equally possible to view Trueblood's plight as symbolic of how black Americans as a whole have had to find a way to make the most out of extraordinarily difficult circumstances.

Trueblood actually earns a living better than he had ever been able to do before, now telling his story for money. He becomes a vital cog in the survivalist culture of which the blues is a key ingredient. *Invisible* has been called a blues novel, and in an essay entitled "Richard Wright's Blues" (1945), Ellison defines blues as "an impulse to keep the painful details and episodes of a brutal experience alive in one's aching consciousness, to finger its jagged grain, and to transcend it…by squeezing from it a near-tragic, near-comic lyricism." Just as we had been able to do in the case of Trueblood, we must consider, when it comes to Wilkes, all the mediating factors. Did the white woman love Wilkes? Were she and the policeman married? Did the policeman approach Wilkes as an officer of the law or did he approach Wilkes as a jilt-ed lover in the heat of passion? Such details would have helped greatly in our evaluation of Wilkes as he shot the white man. But in such a case, what are the odds of achieving legal jus-tice? Wilkes must flee; the year is 1927. He is a black version of the ballad character, Tom Doo-ley, who must hang down his head and cry because he, not knowing the Civil War was over, had shot a Union soldier. Dooley flees but then finally is compelled to come home where he, as will be the case with Wilkes, must be killed as a consequence. Flight had preserved a certain victory, and with the hero's death, the onus is upon the community to capture victory through the words of a song.

Yesterday is just one of many such "songs" that in a way vindicate Robby Wideman, for Wilkes personifies a black essence of which Robby can partake. *Reuben* (1987), John Wideman's next novel, serves to vindicate the author himself. In *Home*, Braithwaite had graduated from law school and was so uncertain of who he was that he could only thrash about in life, doing odd jobs. But *Reuben* provides us with a different kind of lawyer who can reconcile his white main-stream education with the all-black community from which he was spawned. He lives and works in an "old wreck of a trailer" where he functions as a one-man legal services operation.

> Nobody else in Homewood would do what Reuben would do for the little bit of money he charged.… Peace bond, bail bond, divorce, drunk and disorderly, some-thing somebody stole from you, somebody catching you stealing from them, child support, a will…for as long as anybody could remember Reuben had been per-forming these tricks for the poor and worse than poor in Homewood.

Thus Wideman resolves the dilemma of the black intellectual. He must, in some form or fash-ion, return to the black community and aid in the quest for survival.

■ ■ ■

One would have thought that fate had been unkind enough through the process of events that led to Robby's imprisonment. However, that was before the author's youngest son stabbed his room-mate in a hotel in Flagstaff, Arizona. The two boys, Jacob Wideman and Eric Kane, were part of a small group who camped regularly in Maine. It was August, 1986, school was out, and the group decided to travel back west, inadvertently ending up in Flagstaff. By the time they made it to Uni-versity Inn in that town, they were frustrated and exhausted. Three of the boys checked into one room; Jacob and Eric checked into another. Time passed and in the wee hours of the morning, Jacob plunged a knife into Eric's heart, killing him, and leaving a world to ask why?

There is a haunting passage in *Brothers* where the author ponders what the seeds were that led to Robby going wrong. The paradoxical conclusion drawn is that "the more you delve and backtrack and think, the more clear it becomes that nothing has a discrete, independent history; people and events take shape not in orderly, chronological sequence but in relation to other forces and events, tangled skeins of necessity and interdependence and chance that after all could have produced only one result: what is." One might interpret that as meaning certain events are unavoidable. But it also seems to be saying there are some things still within our control.

Jacob was three years old when the family moved to Wyoming. Never in his life did he have to undergo the hardships that, for example, a child of the ghetto has to endure constantly. The author saw to that as he planned for his children to have the optimal in security. What the author did not anticipate was how having a famous father can, in some cases, be just as devastating as being poor, living in an inner city. John Wideman was his high school's valedictorian, captain of the basketball team, and destined to have an equally astonishing career at UPenn. Then he goes on to become a great writer. What will be the expectations of such a father for his child? What pressures will be brought to bear?

Wideman's latest novel, *Philadelphia Fire* (1990), has many autobiographical elements. It is about a father so engrossed in his flourishing career that he becomes estranged from his own son and realizes "I've always known next to nothing about him." However, Wideman does not stop there. He raises the question of how society in general regards children. Taking on the persona of Cudjoe who "copped the education and ran" to a distant island, he returns to the mainland in search of the boy who escaped the city-authorized bombing of MOVE's (The Movement) headquarters in Philadelphia in 1985. Jacob and the boy become one and the same as the author uses them to symbolize a wide variety of abuses, "atrocities that prove adults don't give a fuck about kids. The lousy school system, abortion, lack of legal rights…kiddie porn, kids' bodies used to sell shit on TV, kids on death row, high infant mortality." Susan Sontag, in her book *Against Interpretation* (1966), offers this definition of a writer: "As a man he suffers; as a writer, he transforms his suffering into art." *Fire* is certainly a commendable work of art, a tool the author uses to exorcize his own pain. But it also must serve as a warning for society either to wage war against its various formidable demons or concede that they will consume all of us.

James Robert Saunders
December, 1992

UPDATE

Novelist and short-story writer John Edgar Wideman has since published *Fatheralong* (1994), *The Cattle Killing* (1996), *Two Cities* (1998), and *Hoop Roots* (2001). The volume *Conversations with John Edgar Wideman* (written with Bonnie Tusmith) was published in 1998.

In a review of *Two Cities*, which the *Review of Contemporary Fiction* called "narrative and contemplative," Wideman's latest novel was described as one that "maintains the thematic intensity of Wideman's earlier fiction and essays, yet adopts a softer, more haunting tone. . . . The novel ponders the disparities between perception and memory. Everywhere there is slippage; nothing is as it was. As the character Robert Jones says in one of his never-to-be-sent letters to the sculptor Alberto Giacometti, 'When you turn from the model to shape a portrait or clay figure, it's memory and habit, not sight, that guide your hand.'"

Wideman's newest book may gain him a whole new reading audience. In *Hoop Roots*, a memoir about basketball, Wideman—a former player once called the best rebounder one coach had ever seen—examines the impact of the game on his life. *Publishers Weekly* wrote: "Darkened by uncharacteristic spurts of melancholy and regret, this occasionally brilliant tribute to basketball, survival and families linked by blood, joy and tragedy is . . . Exhilarating." And *Booklist* called it "poignant, thought-provoking reading": "[B]asketball has meant far more to him than a stepping-stone to a better life. As he describes his complex relationship with the game, and uses it to conjure memories of his family, especially his grandmother, he recognizes

■ BOOKS BY JOHN EDGAR WIDEMAN

A Glance Away. New York: Harcourt, 1967.

Hurry Home. New York: Harcourt, 1970.

The Lynchers. New York: Harcourt, 1973.

Damballah. New York: Avon, 1981.

Hiding Place. New York: Avon, 1981.

Sent for You Yesterday. New York: Avon, 1983.

Brothers and Keepers (memoir). New York: Henry Holt, 1984.

The Homewood Trilogy (includes *Damballah*, *Hiding Place*, and *Sent for You Yesterday*). New York: Avon, 1985.

Reuben. New York: Henry Holt, 1987.

Fever. New York: Henry Holt, 1989.

Philadelphia Fire. New York: Henry Holt, 1990.

All Stories Are True. New York: Vintage Books, 1992.

The Stories of John Edgar Wideman. New York: Random House, 1992.

Fatheralong. New York: Pantheon, 1994.

The Cattle Killing. Boston: Houghton Mifflin, 1996.

Conversations with John Edgar Wideman (with Bonnie Tusmith). Oxford: University of Mississippi, 1998.

Two Cities. Boston: Houghton Mifflin, 1998.

Hoop Roots. Boston: Houghton Mifflin, 2001.

that basketball still helps him define himself and provides a connection to all that he has been, might have been, or will be. . . . Hoops and writing are vehicles with which Wideman can set his own standards in a white world that often imposes definitions of success on black people."

Greatly admired by readers and critics alike, Wideman, whose literary style and gritty subjects make for profound reading, has been praised by the *Los Angeles Times Book Review* as "the black Faulkner, the softcover Shakespeare."

"By the Light of the Baseball Moon": The Sublunary Magic of Nancy Willard

Once upon a time, when I was twenty, an alchemist with crinkled eyes handed me a stone. But I shrugged, and tossed it back into the river. I still remember how the muddy water sheered to platinum when it splashed.

Or: long long ago, a kind-hearted poet told his young apprentice to read the work of Nancy Willard. But—ensorcelled as the apprentice was by that twisted wizard, Late Adolescence—a blinder lay across her eyes. "What's this about stuffing green peppers?" she murmured as she read a page at random. "How dreadfully ordinary! How…How domestic!" Shuddering, she donned her black turtleneck. "Why not write of leaf-lorn branches in November sleet, of the barbarous heart's-goad that is love?" And yet, before the foolish apprentice set the book aside, she read that poem again.

Or something like that. But as Willard points out in "How to Stuff a Pepper," "Cooking takes time." When I next read that poem—or perhaps it was the time after that, or maybe only just last week—it came to me that something I'd written shortly afterward (an up-to-the-next-level student poem, it was, about slicing into cantaloupes) grew directly from that green pepper's magical seeds.

The moral? Never mind, please, the obvious one about a young writer's high-headed cluelessness and proclivity for unwitting theft. Rather, learn from this tale three things: that Nancy Willard's words cast spells that change mud-brown to a silver-toned flash, that her images linger in the mind, resisting the downhill flow of time, and so, that at its best, her work is a philosopher's stone for preserving human lives and transmuting the dross of this sublunary world. "Surely it is no accident," Willard tells us in one of her essays on the writer's craft, "that in ancient Egypt the god of alchemy was also the god of writing." This, then, is what she's up to: a mage's artful transformation of human experience—from murkiness and loss into something illumined by wonder and meaning—through the supernatural agency of tale and song.

In fact, words like "magical" or "enchanting" show up all the time in reviews and cover blurbs for Willard's long and varied list of books. The danger here is the chance of being dismissed as merely childlike, merely charming—that is, of having the un-self-important mistaken for the unimportant. This response, of course, is one with which the work of anyone making art in the mode of the fantastic, or anyone who writes books that children read, has been too often met. And some of her work (a few of the stories for kids, at any rate) may strike you as suffering from a tad too much unassimilated whimsy. But read on, and even the sourest puss will sweeten; the childlike quality, the naivete, is not faux, but chosen—and becoming more childlike, as Jesus of Nazareth pointed out, might do us all some good. The processes and the results of Willard's alchemy well deserve, and well reward, a closer look, for they demonstrate the lifesaving value of the verbal conjuror's art.

Nancy Willard

Nancy Willard was born June 26, 1936, in Ann Arbor, Michigan. She began creating little books as a child and as a teenager she discovered crow-quill pens and India ink and begin to draw. Her first poem was published in a Unitarian church magazine at the age of seven and her first miniature book was published when she was a high school senior. She received her B.A. from the University of Michigan in 1958, an M.A. in medieval literature from Stanford in 1960, and returned to the University of Michigan to earn her Ph.D. in modern literature in 1963. She has studied art in Oslo and Paris. In 1964 she married the photographer Eric Lindbloom and they have one son, James Anatole. Willard has been a lecturer at Vassar College, an instructor at the Bread-loaf Writers Conference, and a visiting poet at Oberlin College. She is a playwright and illustrator, as well as author of poetry, adult fiction, children's literature, short stories, and literary criticism.

Willard has received numerous honors and awards. For *Skin of Grace*, she received the Dennis Memorial Award in 1967. In 1970 she won the O. Henry Award for best short story. *Sailing to Cythera, and Other Anatole Stories* was selected as one of the fifty books of the year by the American Institute of Graphic Arts in 1974. Since childhood she has admired the poet-painter William Blake, which inspired her to write *A Visit to William Blake's Inn: Poems for Innocent and Experienced Travelers*, for which she received a National Endowment for the

Arts grant in 1976. A filmstrip was based on the book and it also won the first John Newbery Medal for a collection of poetry, the Caldecott Honor Book Award from the American Library Association, and the American Book Award nomination, all in 1982. She also received the Creative Artist Service Award in 1987–88, and *Water Walker* was a National Book Critics Circle Award nomination in 1990. Her work has been featured in many periodicals, including the *Massachusetts Review, Redbook, Esquire, The New Yorker*, and *New Directions*. She and her family reside in Poughkeepsie, New York. ■

Magical, how? Certainly, the stuff of Nancy Willard's scenes and narratives (whether verse or prose) is the stuff of the extra-ordinary. The worlds we see in her crystal balls—her alephs—are inhabited by persuasive hens and mysterious humanoid toads, by ancestors who turn into birds and a baseball team managed by smooth-talking Death himself, by ghosts and angels and saints and everyday eccentrics who see what no dull rationalist apprehends. Even in Willard's kitchen there's a cook who can somehow shrink till she slips inside one of those green peppers and sits "under the great globe / of seeds on the roof of that chamber."

"[A] lot of people can't tell who's real and who isn't," says Kate's mother in the 1978 children's novel *The Highest Hit,* a pleasantly realistic exception to this rule of extra-ordinariness—until you acknowledge with it the annual miracle of "Bushels of tomatoes" from small green plants, or the quietly life-altering one wrought by old Mr. Goldberg's lesson to Kate about "the triumph of right over wrong, joy over grief, weak over strong." In the end, after all, what is more extraordinary than the everyday, what more astounding than the "fever of pearls" inside a green pepper? It's in getting us to see this truth that Willard's magic finally lies.

In order to lead us to that realization, however, many of Willard's poems and stories carry the titles and the archetypal plots of fairy tales or folk-talk of the marvelous: "The Boy Who Ran with the Dogs", "The Tailor Who Told the Truth," "The Wisdom of the Geese," "The Child. The Ring. The Road," "When There Were Trees," "How the Magic Bottle Gave Biddy Its Blessing". One effect of such titles and such story lines is to give the marvels credence, for how could something apparently told so long and so often, something so plain and simply and unhesitatingly said, something so familiar despite its strangeness, be a lie? As Willard writes in an essay called "The Well-Tempered Falsehood: The Art of Storytelling," "Stories that develop archetypal situations have the truth and the authority of proverbs, no matter how fantastic the particular events they describe."

Here, for instance, is one thing that happens to a boy who becomes, through all-too-ordinary parental neglect, that archetypal orphan, the wild child, in a realm of groomed lawns and barbecue grills: "He had stepped too close, he was in the light. The man whirled and lunged but the boy was not there, he was running with the dogs behind and ahead of him, leaving the man to grope in the wilderness at the edge of his land." Again, it is the bringing-together, in content and expression, of what's commonplace (running boy or time-polished linguistic structures) and what's not (the nearness of evil perceived) that leads us to understanding. Our trust in the commonplace reality of any "Boy Who Ran" makes the deathly darkness in the suburbs real.

The fabulous furnishings, the age-old patterns, the samplings from what J.R.R. Tolkien called the "Cauldron of Story" (that long-simmering stew of motifs from which the writer of fantasy may draw) are the most obvious aspect of Willard's magic, but they're also the least of it. Truly, her wizardry lies as much in the telling as in the matter of the tale. Often the voice of Willard's writing articulates the confident Wisewoman voice of oral traditions, the voice of *Starlight-starbright* and *Once there were three brothers*. This is the voice that makes the incredible appear before us, genuine! almost touchable! *alakazam!* It's the voice that told us truths before we aged into the self-absorbed dithering of doubt.

She also uses the voice of ultimate authority in the Judeo-Christian tradition that forms the foundation of Willard's art. Check out the joyful eschatology at the end of the eerily beautiful title story in *The Lively Anatomy of God*. Or take for example this description of a typhoon in her first adult novel, *Things Invisible to See*: "And on the fifth night of the fifth moon a great wind arose, and the sun withdrew and the moon turned away, and darkness settled upon the parched face of Hewitt Island.... And the wind carried away four cubits of the roof to the west and great was the noise thereof..." Who would dare to question the terrible testimony of this storm, or doubt the strange events ("'I can arrange furloughs,' said Death.") that follow it?

In fact, *Things Invisible* begins its loving examination of daily life in the midwestern U.S. of the early 1940's with all the scope and mastery of a seer's report of things unseen—or a mother's comforting explanation of the looming night-time sky: "In Paradise, on the banks of the River of Time, the Lord of the Universe is playing ball with his archangels. Hundreds of spheres rest like white stones on the bottom of the river, and hundreds rise like bubbles from the water and fly to His hand that alone brings things to pass and gives them their true colors." Then, a couple sentences later, "...in a small town in southern Michigan Wanda Harkissian goes into labor with twins. She will name them Ben and Willie, but it's Esau and Jacob all over again." *The stars and planets, my dear,* (that is to say) *are like the baseballs you have fun with, are like the rocks you skip across the river. These two boys I'll be telling you about are like the ones you learned about in Sunday School last week. So you know the universe is not a cruel place, and that my story's true.*

This claiming of authority is a necessary thing: necessary not only to get us to suspend our world-weary disbelief and gasp at the magician's show, but—for this must be her purpose—to get us to exorcise entirely that stolid, sulky unbelieving in anything beyond the senses' paltry range. The Universe plays not only fair but mercifully, *Things Invisible to See* assures us, and being alive is well worth "All the pain, all the trouble." And most assuringly of all: sometimes love and unreasonable hope can overcome even the awful dream team of mortality and human sin and the limitations of faith and flesh.

Similarly, Willard's poems lay claim to the occult power of the most enduring castings-forth of language. They assume not just the titles but the grammar of fables, proverbs, riddles, of passed-down voicings of archaic wisdom. A few examples written over four decades, all taken from the richly various 1996 *Swimming Lessons: New and Selected Poems*:

"So it must be," says my grandfather...
"If they are to make the gold, they must be caught

and made to live in the dark hive."
"Bees Swarming"

In the beginning were the letters,
wooden, awkward, and everywhere.
Before the Word was the slow scrabble of fire and water.
"In Praise of ABC"

Only a man thinks he can live
forever....
"The Animals Welcome Persephone"

Who invented water?
The hands of the air, that wanted to wash each other
"Questions My Son Asked Me, Answers I Never Gave Him"

Mercy is whiter than laundry
"Angels in Winter"

Other poems are hymns, or psalms, language asserting by the bald fact of its utterance that things deserving of praise exist. Language, then, with the miraculous ability to make faith possible:

Let a saint cry your praises, O delicate
desert companion, the flea.
"The Flea Circus at Tivoli"

I praise the brightness of hammer pointing east
"A Hardware Store as Proof of the Existence of God"

More powerfully still, some of the poems are prayers. In this mode, language bespeaks yearning, and so—with luck and skill—captures the uncertain or despairing reader's allegiance, even as it affirms that praying's worth the expenditure of time and breath:

And if a white bear steps from the morning's throat

may I be still enough to hear him,
may I be warm enough to invite him in.
"Fairy Tale"

St. Zita, bless the fire
that boils the water, the air

that dries clothes, and keys
that have lost their doors:
may angels keep them
from the deep river.
"Angels Among the Servants"

Certain poems even assume the form of spells and oracular commands:

I pick up Sad,
I burn it, I scatter the ashes....
Life of the earth,
protect this one
who is going to meet you.
"Blessing for Letting Go"

This is performative language, language that (like a promise or a decree) makes something so by the saying of it:

May those who follow you
find gold but not glowworms
                    ...and not me.
"Charm of the Gold Road, the Silver Road, and the Hidden Road"

Go deep. Save, sift, pack, lose, find again.
Come back as snow, rain, tears, crest and foam.
Come back to baptise, heal, drown.
Come back as Water. Come back as Poem.
"Poem Made of Water"

This uttering of charms is magic indeed.

Of course, magic has its rules. This is also true for baseball or any other art, even literature. And what prodigies may be accomplished with the aid of those shaping principles! Late in *Things Invisible*, in the midst of World War II, the South Avenue Rovers (most of them now weary GIs) reunite on their old diamond: "Today they are playing to be healed, to let the eyes and mouths of the dead fall away from them, to step back into the eternal presence of summer the way they lived as kids, playing till darkness came." The just patterning, the familiar order, of baseball stands against the dark privations and racism and murderous insanity the Rovers have met with off the ballfield. It promises that they may yet "find the timeless space that turns ordinary men into heroes, where the only real world is the game itself, as old and reliable as the stars." What more marvelous transformation could we ask for?

In another essay, citing May Sarton's characterization of writing as a holy game, Willard points out that "a game needs rules that free the players to move about the board." Learn them, and then you can work wonders. Ignore them, and the whole show falls apart. Yet such power does not come without risks.

One danger lies in blind obedience. In one memorable short story, Willard presents a parable of rules run amok. The protagonist of "The Hucklebone of a Saint"—the first in a sequence of portraits of the artist as a young woman—must negotiate between the implacable natural laws studied by her rationalist father and the capricious but powerful precepts of the unseen world her mother teaches her about. The taboos and regulations of childhood superstition begin to bind too tightly, squeezing the girl into compulsion; just then, mortality arrives in the form of her aging grandmother. Words lose their palpable appeal, taking on "the opacity of a magic formula," so that saying *tree* releases "forces beyond your control." Death threatens the joy that language grants: a warning for any writer, any reader, against inflexible theories, or dour, proscriptive formulae.

As Willard writes in her most formal work of criticism, a study of Williams, Ponge, Rilke, and Neruda, "All four poets agree that the death you should fear is the death of your heart, imprisoned in a world wholly measurable, usable, and falling away under your grasp." This is magic gone wrong—the reduction of the gift of tongues to a lust for control. It is murderous dissection upon the altar of the demon Rationality, with no eye for his elusive but far less mean-spirited sisters Clowning Around and sweet Surprise.

Eventually, the girl in "Hucklebone" is rescued from the dark powers of moribund ritual: a droll glimpse of human folly and a quirky, poem-writing uncle's loving-kindness bring her into the light that breaks, in one form or another, at the end of many of Willard's short stories. But first and crucially, she is freed by the orderly, yet beautifully various, sentences of a prayer of exorcism—poem-like words whose efficaciousness can't be quantified, or denied.

It's worth noting that this grand performance of the incantatory power of language ends with a scene of good-natured buffoonery, as "the devil in the mirror" turns out to be a neighborhood silly-billy whose hair has just been turned green by a bad perm. Humor, that wellspring of subversive energy, is one of Willard's mainstays against the forces of stultification: she does not rail, but smiles at the foibles of her characters, the way a hip nightclub illusionist, or one of the jollier bodhisattvas, might. We need the rules, need to declare a difference between strikes and balls, between good grooming and vanity, but we needn't get uptight about it—sometimes humankind's lurching flubs are well worth a laugh.

Such humor heals us. The holy, restorative "hucklebone" of the story's title, in fact, is mistaken by the protagonist for "the place on your elbow that tingled when you accidentally bumped it"—that is to say (*get it?*), the funny bone. And even if you've never read that Yorkshire fellow's books, even if your German's pretty sketchy, ya gotta lighten up and acknowledge the prankish puissance of words when Willard drops into her irresistible second adult novel, *Sister Water*, mention of a veterinarian of "miraculous" curative skill named Dr. Herrgott. Such is the saving grace of jokes, that celebrate the meaning-making force of our lingo's rules—by bending them until (*boi-oing!*) they zing.

In other tales, Willard demonstrates the value of rules-without-rigidity in other ways. An old magician tells Sylvia, heroine of Willard's picture-book retelling of *The Sorcerer's Apprentice*:

We, who are masters of these arts,
learn by our failures, fits, and starts.
If you would learn to cast a spell,
practice till you do it well.

Sylvia, naturally, tries to play the game before she knows how. But like the creations of writers and artists who've transmuted this very tale over the centuries, from Lucian through Goethe to the Disney animators, she brings on a comic debacle of inept spell-casting run amok. In the end, however, Sylvia heeds the magician's lesson, learns the rules, and becomes a teacher of word-magic; her spells (like those of the creative artists, not their creatures, who are now her true predecessors) turn "pencils into pails / and failures into fairy tales." Eat your heart out, Mickey Mouse.

In the four lines quoted above, Willard's versification demonstrates just how a good word-magician finds freedom within the rules she's chosen to play by. The emphatic initial trochees in lines one and two, the arresting headless fourth line, the varied caesuras (some giving the second line its halting, jumpy, fits-and-starts rhythm): these ring changes on a meter that would otherwise risk the ritualistic rigor mortis of singsong—even as the flawless regularity of the third line's insistent iambic tetrameter makes its point.

These are only a sample of the deft metrical variations running through this poem/book. Moreover, internal rhyme, slant rhyme, occasional triplets, frequent yieldings of the couplet form to diverse interlocking rhyme schemes: all these create subtler, multiform sound patterns, and so evoke a multiform, subtly-patterned world. The alchemies of Willard's poetry follow canons more sensitively tuned than a metronome's, more complex than *aa bb cc*.

Another poem collection—or if you will, another picture book—*A Visit to William Blake's Inn*, recounts in its introduction the author's childhood discovery of how Blake's poetry can astonish, and can cure. If poems are mighty medicine, some of that curative art surely lies in the victory of variety over dullness. In various ways, the various poems reveal how the imagination and its journeys can protect and reveal, can nurture and can mend. Sometimes they do this in couplets, or with *abcb* rhyme. But most of the poems carry more complex designs: *abccb*, or *aab ccb*, or *abbcdcd effe*, or others less obvious, but indisputably there.

Further instances of the poet's sound-magic abound. "Wedding Song" (from the 1966 book *In His Country*), offers its evocation of Orpheus calling, Eurydike running, the vegetative world responding, in intertwining subtle rhymes that shift their pattern, stanza to stanza, until it almost begins to seem that all words rhyme—a fine expression of the poem's calling-forth of organic harmonies in nature and in song. We find there redundant rhyme (seas / sees), perfect rhyme (day / lay), assonance rhyme (cress / bed), consonance rhyme (stone / again), and augmented perfect rhyme (falling / calling), as well as such undeniable near misses as hymn / stone.

In the same early volume, evocations of Norse visionary angst contain themselves within more nearly conventional, yet still flexible, rules of rhyming, as in "Ashes," which pushes beyond the Petrarchan sonnet as it runs *abba cddc'ded fefghgh*. (The ' indicates near rhyme: in this case the assonance of "trees" and "me.") A sequence on the tortuous sculptures of Gustav Vigeland employs slippery, inconstant rhymings that manifest phonically Vigeland's profoundly disturbing images of an interconnectedness without redemptive order or grace.

Don't misunderstand—most of Willard's poetry is unrhymed, though not unmusical. But the recent collection's title poem, "Swimming Lessons," testifies to the continuance of a poetic craft refined well before anyone thought to claim an angel's status for rebelling against the straw figure that is contemporary American free verse. It plays out its elegiac sorrow and acceptance on a court bounded by full rhyme and repetition, along with both assonant and consonant rhyme, and echoings as inescapable as "pawns" and "down" or "vest" and "stretch," The result is a moving farewell of daughter to mother, heightened even as it is controlled by such line-end links as "carry," "keep me," "body," "hospital sheets," and "this story." It forms an incantation as obsessive as a sestina's (without that form's potential for ham-handedness), and as intense as grief itself.

Willard's newest book, an anthology of poems being marketed for "young people," reveals the wide reading that must have shaped her sensibility and tuned her ear. It brings phonically rich (and, the marketeers whisper, accessible) free verse from poets like Levertov and Stevens and Clifton together with Mother Goose, the Shakespeare of "Full Fathom Five," Blake's "Tyger," Yeats' "Wandering Aengus," and—but of course!—that childlike queen of sly rhymers, Dickinson. In an essay from the early 80's on "Becoming a Writer," the poet notes the effect upon her of a grad-school year spent compiling an annotated bibliography of Middle English lyrics. "Twenty years later," she tells us, "I have gone back to the forms of those lyrics in some of the poems I want to write now." If you have read *The Ballad of Biddy Early* (1989), you might have guessed as much.

What's more, if you go and read that essay now, you'll have the pleasure of encountering Willard's description of judging that curious contemporary phenomenon, a poetry-book competition: "The more manuscripts I read, the more it seemed to me that all the poems had a single author.... Everypoet—as I named the single voice in these manuscripts—had read his contemporaries. He had taken from them what they had in common, a language close to speech, sometimes indistinguishable from prose. But the variety of experiences and influences that resonates in the work of the best writers was absent." Everypoet's career is going strong. But reading Willard's verse is a fine antidote to the aural ennui he can engender.

She does further homage to the potency of words (in her own distinctive voice, the one that cannot be mistaken for Everypoet's relentlessly nattering prose a la mode) with a series of poems rising from the muck of outrageous puns. In one section of *Water Walker* (1989), sports headlines are transmogrified into titles: "Nets Halt Suns," "Foxes Fall to St. Francis," "Angels' Singer Stops Orioles." What's meant by these sentences transmogrifies as well, from (sorry, sports fans) the mundane to the amazing. Even as one releases the ritual groan, one sees the liveliness, the alive-ness, of words—and of the wit that can spin a golden pun-poem from newsprint's straw.

Clowning, too, requires the skill and diligence and perceptiveness of the alchemist. And paronomasia is, after all, a rhetorical figure that's only out of fashion in the local here-and-now. Ask Donne or Milton, for example, or Dickinson (again!), or any number of poets who wrote in traditional China or Japan. Willard's tomfoolery, her abracadabra, enables her readers to hear, and so to envision, more than the straight-men ever will.

"How can we see an imaginary world except by the light of this one?" asks an essay of Willard's on fairy tales. The artful, playful, illuminating magic she makes is like the baseball invented by the Magician of the Mountains of Detroit in *The Mountains of Quilt*, "that turned into a full moon when the sun went down. Very useful...on nights when the moon turns off her lamp." It glows with the theurgic ability of the language game to overcome, in its way, the dark force of natural law.

By this I certainly mean the death blows dealt by rigid, legalistic common-sense to the consolations of vision, fancy, hope. And certainly, too, I mean the near-brain-death of word-music when literary fashion (or ineptness) tries to kill it off. But Willard also gives us writing as a kind of victory over plain ol' mortality itself.

Again and again, her work memorializes the passing and the past, reconstructing personal and family history in fictive guise. Anatole, Eric(a), Ann Arbor: naming the names of places and persons loved has the fabulous power to give them eternal—or at least, extended—life. "All flesh is grass, cry the birds," at the end of a story in which a woman with the feminine version of Willard's husband's name has just given difficult birth to a fragile boy who will bear the middle name of the writer's son (which is also one name for her fantasy trilogy for children, the Anatole stories), "and all flesh is beautiful." The story's next, and last, sentence offers a deft and paradoxical ambiguity as it tells us how this world's children break "free from the flesh of their parents"—born from the womb into life on earth as if (*as if!*) born into transcendence of it.

Of course, many another writer has hit upon these truths, the one about immortalizing your inamorati, the one about beauty's mom. Many another has clutched at the thought that (as the serpent hisses to Willard's Eve in one parable) loss is the source of song, or that our lives can only be stories because they have endings. And many another has asked (as Willard does in a journal entry turned essay), "For artists, for writers, what body is there but the body of work we leave behind?" Scholars too have figured out that (as Willard puts it) "Fairy tales are a wish unrolled into a story, a wish that when we disappear under the great extinguisher of death, we may not go out forever."

But there's more here than literature as graven tombstone or mortal whiner's fantasy. The magic Willard draws on is the ability of shapely chunks of language to enhance, well, our quality of life: "The stories that the dead tell and that we tell of the dead make life more glamorous, more intense, and more joyful," she tells an audience of writers in "High Talk in the Starlit Wood." The lives of the dead are saved (preserved)—and ours are saved (made worth living)— by the fabulist's, the incantator's, implication that the polished palaver's worth the trouble, that it all makes sense.

Indeed, Willard's stories don't just animate, zombie-like, the dead: they have the salvational power of re-creation, and that of creation, too. Like her nocturnal Tortilla Cat, who sings to and feeds and cures five newly motherless kids when their scientific doctor-daddy can't, our dreamtime yowlings heal us. As the angelic Sam says in *Sister Water*, after advising a young widow to talk to her recently dead husband, "We aren't made of atoms, Ellen. We're made of stories." Tell him a riddle, Sam urges, tell him a joke. Which is to say: pass on a little snappy verbal art. Half a novel later, the riddle-joke Sam has offered her in that crucial moment—a two-liner silly as an elephant joke, profound as a mystic's prayer—saves them both.

But wait. Two issues have been lurking between these lines: genre, and recycling. Each tells us something more about Willard and the rules of litrachure, about how she plays out her thaumaturgic arts.

I snuck in a little punctuational sleight of hand some paragraphs ago. Is that "poem/book," *The Sorcerer's Apprentice*, a poem or a book? Truth is, it's both. Its physical form, like its listing in the card catalogue, marks it as a children's picture book. Willard has published more than thirty books for children, some in prose, some verse, some marketed for one age-group, some for another. (Their labelings by publishers or in lists of her work in the front matter of later works can vary: some are "Children's Books" one time and "Poetry" another, and the "Anatole stories" may be separated from "Children's Books" as a "Fantasy Trilogy.") Also (you may file the following under "adult"—although *Things Invisible* has also been claimed for that especially nebulous category "young adult" in at least one respectable reference work): two novels, nine more volumes of poetry, two books of short fiction, a critical book and three collections labeled "short stories and essays" in the front pages of *Swimming Lessons*—even though one of them contains some fifty pages of poetry, and another includes an interview she conducted as well as the transcript of a speech.

And if *The Ballad of Biddy Early* is "Juvenile," is it altogether proper to include selections from it in a volume of "new and selected" poems for adults? The boundaries of our quotidian categories begin to melt away. Where are the rules now?

And what, really, are we to do not only with *A Visit to William Blake's Inn* (which the Newbery folks counted as "children's literature" when they gave it their highly regarded award— though the book proclaims itself quite clearly in its subtitle to be *Poems for Innocent and Experienced Travelers*), but with a genre-buster like *An Alphabet of Angels*? The simple, mystery-filled language and imagery of this slim volume surely satisfy readers of all ages. ("The angel of alphabets opens the door. / The book angel whispers, 'Go out and explore.'") Its shape and heft assign it to the kids in Generation ABC—but I'll bet that this abcdarium is read as often by adults alone as by or to children.

For this not-your-usual-picture-book, Willard herself took the photographs of her 26 + 2 tableaux, creating artworks—not "illustrations" —integral to her text: an angel probably sold to sit atop a Christmas tree emerges from a pearlescent seashell, another made of sheet copper flies above shadows of apparitional rooftops on a ground of swept snow. The notion of spiritual presence that these three-dimensional collages imply is set up by the Talmudic epigraph. Pub-

■ BOOKS BY NANCY WILLARD

poetry

In His Country: Poems. Ann Arbor, Mich.: Generation, 1966.

Skin of Grace. Columbia, Mo.: University of Missouri Press, 1967.

A New Herball. Baltimore, Md.: Ferdinand-Roten Gallerias, 1968.

Nineteen Masks for the Naked Poet. Santa Cruz, Calif.: Kayak, 1971, Brownsville, Ore.: Story Line Press, 1971, New York: Harcourt Brace, 1984.

The Carpenter of the Sun. New York: Liveright Publishing Corp., 1974.

Household Tales of Moon and Water. New York: Harcourt Brace, 1982.

Water Walker. New York: Alfred A. Knopf, 1989.

Poem Made of Water. San Diego: Brighton Press, 1992.

Among Angels. (With Jane Yolen) New York: Harcourt Brace, 1995.

Swimming Lessons: New and Selected Poems. New York: Alfred A. Knopf, 1996.

Step Lightly: Poems for the Journey, ed. New York: Harcourt Brace, 1998.

novels

Things Invisible to See. New York: Alfred A. Knopf, 1984, New York: Bantam Books, 1986.

Sister Water. New York: Alfred A. Knopf, 1993, New York: Ivy Books, 1994.

short stories and essays

The Lively Anatomy of God. New York: Eakins Press Foundation, 1968.

Testimony of the Invisible Man: William Carlos Williams, Francis Ponge, Rainer Maria Rilke, Pablo Neruda. Columbia, Mo.: University of Missouri Press, 1970.

Childhood of the Magician. New York: Liveright Publishing Corp., 1973.

Angel in the Parlor: Five Stories and Eight Essays. New York: Harcourt Brace, 1983.

A Nancy Willard Reader: Selected Poetry & Prose. Hanover, N.H.: University Press of New England, 1991.

Telling Time: Angels, Ancestors, and Stories. New York: Harcourt Brace, 1993.

children's books

Sailing to Cythera, and Other Anatole Stories. New York: Harcourt Brace, 1974.

The Merry History of a Christmas Pie: With a Delicious Description of a Christmas Soup. New York: Putnam, 1974.

All on a May Morning. New York: Putnam, 1975.

The Snow Rabbit. New York: Putnam, 1975.

Shoes Without Leather. New York: Putnam, 1976.

---

lished two years later, *The Good-Night Blessing Book* plays a similar game; the angels in its assemblages reveal realms of multivalent meaning when they bless, for example, a Milky Way which is both the realm to which our beloved dead ascend and the moo-juice in the icebox. (And by the way, if you're put off by fads, remember Willard was writing about angels long before they showed up on TV and in the greeting-card shops. In fact, you might want to consider what felt needs are being met by the pop culture craze—and what that says about the value of Willard's work.)

In the same way, genre labels assigned to Willard's writings shift over time. Perusal of acknowledgments pages reveals that something called in one table of contents an "essay on writing" was earlier published in an anthology of short stories. ("How Poetry Came into the World, and Why God Doesn't Write It" works either way; the next conference panel on "creative non-fiction" may wish to discuss this.) A chapter in *Sister Water* had an earlier life as a short story—nothing especially unusual, yet it's nice to see the piece presented not as yet-another chapter by the same omniscient narrator, but as a story one character has written for another, and so as one of several little subversions of a novel's tendency to claim monologic truth. Again we see that verbal power is one thing, but simplistic, hide-bound dicta or classifications are an-(undesirable)-other.

But that's not the half of the shape-shifting to be encountered in a study of Willard's works. In the "other books by" lists in various volumes, some early titles vanish, while others reappear.

The Well-Mannered Balloon. New York: Harcourt Brace, 1976.

Simple Pictures Are Best. New York: Harcourt Brace, 1977, London: Collins, 1978, Sydney: Ashton Scholastic, 1993.

Strangers' Bread. New York: Harcourt Brace, 1977.

The Highest Hit. New York: Harcourt Brace, 1978.

The Island of the Grass King: The Further Adventures of Anatole. New York: Harcourt Brace, 1979.

Papa's Panda. New York: Harcourt Brace, 1979.

The Marzipan Moon. New York: Harcourt Brace, 1981.

A Visit to William Blake's Inn: Poems for Innocent and Experienced Travelers. New York: Harcourt Brace, 1981, London: Methuen, 1982.

Uncle Terrible: More Adventures of Anatole. New York: Harcourt Brace, 1982.

The Nightgown of the Sullen Moon. New York: Harcourt Brace, 1983.

Night Story. New York: Harcourt Brace, 1986, London: Methuen, 1986.

The Voyage of Ludgate Hill: A Journey with Robert Louis Stevenson. New York: Harcourt Brace, 1987.

The Mountains of Quilt. New York: Harcourt Brace, 1987.

The Ballad of Biddy Early. New York: Alfred A. Knopf, 1989.

The High Rise Glorious Skittle Skat Roarious Sky Pie Angel Food Cake. New York: Harcourt Brace, 1990.

Pish Posh, Said Hieronymus Bosch. New York: Harcourt Brace, 1991.

Beauty and the Beast. New York: Harcourt Brace, 1992.

Firebrat. New York: Alfred A. Knopf, 1988, New York: Bantam Books, 1992.

The Sorcerer's Apprentice. New York: Scholastic, 1993.

A Starlit Somersault Downhill. New York: Little, Brown, 1993.

An Alphabet of Angels. New York: Scholastic, 1994.

Gutenberg's Gift. New York: Harcourt Brace, 1995.

The Good-Night Blessing Book. New York: Scholastic, 1996.

Cracked Corn and Snow Ice Cream: A Family Almanac. New York: Harcourt Brace, 1996.

The Tortilla Cat. New York: Harcourt Brace, 1997.

The Magic Cornfield. New York: Harcourt Brace, 1997.

Raggedy Ann and The Christmas Thief. New York: Simon & Schuster, 1999.

Shadow Story. San Diego, Calif.: Harcourt Brace, 1999.

The Tale I Told Sasha. Boston: Little, Brown, 1999.

The Moon and Riddles Diner and The Sunnyside Cafe. San Diego, Calif.: Harcourt Brace, 2001.

play

East of the Sun and West of the Moon. New York: Harcourt Brace, 1989.

Poems from out-of-print small-run collections find new lives reprinted in new contexts. The protagonist of "The Hucklebone of a Saint" is "Anne-Marie" when she first shows up in book form in 1968; she's transmuted into "Erica" when the piece reappears twenty-three years later in the sequence of five Erica stories—a stand-alone tale turned into something like a novella-chapter.

There's more at work here than realities of late-twentieth-century publishing: juxtapositions of the 70's and the 90's strike sparks; new themes emerge and voices return transposed into different keys. Go look at those assemblages in *An Alphabet of Angels* and *The Good-Night Blessing Book*, where two or three objects brought together by the artist create—this is their magic—an organic whole that's greater than their inanimate sum. Variations on a single family constellation (the senile grandmother, the scientist father) link the fictions, as do certain resonant acts (an elopement, an undertaker's fatuous remark). And of course, within the corpus of the work, vibrant images like water, cats, trains, the moon, donkey heads, all sorts of fruits and vegetables, cycle round and round again—as if within a single poem, yet in each new con-text, made new again.

Even the writerly tendency to take single-minded hold over a book gets a nudge from that gentle insurrectionary, the elbow bone. Willard uses epigraphs throughout her work, but it's more than that: there's a decorous hint of a postmodern pastiche about some of the books. Both adult novels occasionally evade their omniscient narrators in favor of texts within texts—a chapter of letters or a journal entry. These novels also acknowledge sources ranging from Jerry Garcia to a piece in a 1942 issue of *Life*; my favorite of these is the fictional passages, based on a West African folktale, ostensibly from *Prevention* magazine. It's no surprise that the essays on writing further this sense of low-key intertextuality, packed as they are with quotations from other writers. More distinctively, there's a 1995 book co-authored with Jane Yolen via a sequence of poem exchanges, and a poem ("song lyric," really) by Peter S. Beagle that shows up in a two-poem exchange within *Water Walker*.

In that wonderfully mixed bag, *A Nancy Willard Reader: Selected Poetry and Prose* (1991), we find, recycled to serve as an introduction, her letter to an inquiring reader: "[E]ach work chooses its own form, and I try to follow its lead—story, poem, novel, or essay. I hope the connections between them are clear. They all come from the same well, a metaphor I don't take lightly." And one of Willard's newest children's books, *Cracked Corn and Snow Ice Cream: A Family Almanac*, stitches together oral histories, recipes, old photos, poems, and country lore, celebrating as no monolithic memoir could the rich diversity of lives in the American heartland. Here's what all this points to: fluidity of textual form, status, ownership, sequencing, boundaries—Willard's oeuvre revealed itself as hyper-text well before that word entered common parlance, before technology took the next step in its apprentice's imitations of art.

In all this hyper-linking, shifting, and renaming, all this blurring of categories and bringing-together of disparate parts, we see again the writer's refusal to accept logically-chopped pigeon-holes and straight-and-narrow linearity. Rather, this celebration of the flexible and the associative enacts the imagination's cat's-cradle, which in turn enacts Willard's mythopoeic cosmos:

It's not to warm anything that
you gather and fold the string
but to hold the Protean act
together

the stick figures that your mind
makes between stars
"String Games"

Hidden and a-rational connections, like those that transcend genre labels, like those of words' sounds—what's sauce for the writer-magician is sauce for the reader, too. Often in Willard's fiction, our delight and our instruction lie in discerning the secret working-out of things. We are pleased and astounded as we read, for example, *Sister Water*: by the slowly revealed identity of the here-again/gone-again one-armed toad; by the inexplicably mapped network of underground waterways linking homey Ann Arbor, Michigan, to the mythic town of Drowning Bear, Wisconsin; by the recurring manifestation (prophetic, accusatory) of a woman in water—on a hallucinatory video, on plans for a shopping mall, in the form of a comical fish-shaped party hat; and by the granting after decades, generations, of one wish by the duty-bound Angel of Death.

This is a key to Willard's method, this diviner's revelation of order beyond our knowing, of laws beyond the merely natural ones. It's the philosopher's careful unraveling and re-knitting of reality, with a little flash-and-dazzle erupting—*ta-dum!*—at the finale. It's the alchemist's (not the chemist's) value-laden and inexplicable rearrangement of the elements, the contemplative's rapturous report on the secret structure of the cosmos—revealed albeit not analyzable, and if not always lucid, surely luminous.

But credit where it's due—this method, Willard's spell-casting, her writerly hoodoo, is rooted in something peculiar to all us chattering *Homo saps,* if only we will give ourselves over to it, the way good apprentices should. As Willard's Eve says of poems, "some things only humans can make." Such sublunary magic is a triumph of the meaning-making animal over the info-kipple, the data-debris, of our own techno-culture's nest-fouling ways. The magic of art's patternings, like any intimation of the supra-mundane, helps us differentiate among all (theories, e- & junk- & voice-mail, history and histories, cable channels, dueling web browsers and rival search engines, interlocking economies, shiny new paradigms, software upgrades, Dilbertesque management strategies and assessments of outcomes assessments, lies, opinions, faxes, facts) that bombards us now. Like the philosopher's stone, when this linguistic wonder-working selects and connects, it extends the merely mortal and alters the sadly base. Nancy Willard's writing, then, offers us this transforming magic: the triumph over undifferentiated, deadening chaos of the word.

Jeanne Larsen
October, 1998

The Novels of
John Williams

■ I

John Williams' *Augustus* appeared in 1972, almost unnoticed, but the following spring it and John Barth's *Chimera* won the National Book Award for fiction. Unfortunately, winning this award did not lead to the wide recognition that *Augustus* and two of Williams' other novels, *Butcher's Crossing* (1960) and *Stoner* (1965), deserve (he also has published *Nothing But the Night* and several books of poetry). As his career has progressed he has developed several important themes more incisively while using more sophisticated literary techniques, until he created *Augustus,* his major work so far and a novel that deserves a permanent place in American fiction's pantheon.

■ II

Butcher's Crossing is the story of a clergyman's son who leaves Harvard for the Western frontier, but it is not a recapitulation of *Roughing It,* not a comic tale of a tenderfoot among those who have learned that it is good to be shifty in new territory. William Andrews comes to Butcher's Crossing to meet McDonald, a dealer in buffalo hides who long ago knew Andrews' father. Andrews, uninterested in business enterprise, rejects McDonald's offer of a job, but he falls victim to Miller's oft-failing scheme to convince someone to finance a search for an isolated plateau that once teemed with buffalo. Andrews, Miller, Hoge and Schneider start off, find the plateau, annihilate thousands of buffalo there and begin carting back as many hides as possible. But they lose the hides in a river swollen by the spring melting, and when they return to Butcher's Crossing they learn that the market for buffalo hides has collapsed.

Like many American books set in the West, *Butcher's Crossing* is a meditation on the West as a symbol of a quality latent in Americans and in American society, a quality that perhaps became extinct before it became manifest. About to speak for the first time to McDonald, who he thinks can put him in touch with persons able to explain the West, Andrews tries to identify the quality he seeks: "Whatever he spoke he knew would be but another name for the wildness that he sought. It was a freedom and a goodness, a hope and a vigor that he perceived to underlie all the familiar things of his life, which were not free or good or hopeful or vigorous. What he sought was the source and preserver of his world, a world which seemed to turn ever in fear away from its source, rather than search it out, as the prairie grass around him sent down its fibered roots into the rich dark dampness, the Wildness, and thereby renewed itself." This sounds like the voice of a Platonist seeking to shuck off the impediments to the Spirit or the American accents of Thoreau and Emerson or the voice that would have been heard had others who sought a kind of salvation by traveling west been able to explain their motivation.

To experience wildness Andrews endures physical suffering that is minutely portrayed. First, the four men nearly die of thirst because they travel across arid country on a shortcut

John Williams

John Williams was born August 29, 1922, in Clarksville, Texas. He took his B.A. in 1949 and his M.A. in 1950, both from the University of Denver in Colorado. In 1954 he took his Ph.D. from the University of Missouri, in Columbia. He taught at the University of Missouri and at the University of Denver, where he was director of the creative writing program and later Laurence Phipps Professor of Humanities. In 1963 he was awarded the English Speaking Union Fellowship for travel and study at Oxford University and in 1973 he won the National Book Award for *Augustus*. In 1986 Williams moved with his wife, Nora, to Fayetteville, Arkansas, where he lived until his death in 1994. ■

rather than follow a river. In his laconic, emotionally charged prose Williams describes their plight just before they find water: "Andrew's hands clung to the saddle horn; they were so weak that again and again they slipped from it, and he hardly had the strength to pull them back. Breathing was an effort of agony; slumped inertly in his saddle, he learned to snuffle a little air through his nostrils and to exhale it quickly, and to wait several seconds before he repeated the process. Sometime during the night he discovered that his mouth was open and that he could not close it. His tongue pushed between his teeth, and when he tried to bring them together a dull dry pain spread in his mouth." Later Williams exactly and copiously describes the men clambering up the steep slope to the plateau, skinning the buffalo and loading the hides on the wagon. One of the chief tortures is winter's onset, which catches them before they can leave the plateau. After all these torments it is no wonder that Schneider, immediately before he is killed by a blow from a horse's hoof, "was frowning a little, as if vaguely puzzled, and his lips were twisted in a slight grimace of annoyance and contempt."

These experiences of wildness effect two changes in Andrews. First, passion awakes. Before leaving for the hunt he refuses the sexual favors of a kindly prostitute, but she correctly predicts that he will return changed, and they spend a sensuous interlude together before he again leaves Butcher's Crossing. Second, while certain of their lesser mental functions are sharpened, Andrews and the others nearly lose higher functions, becoming virtually mindless. That is, they, especially Miller, become expert at hunting and at performing the attendant logistical operations. In fact, *Butcher's Crossing* is to buffalo hunting as Hesiod's *Works and Days* is to farming: a compendium of information. To hunt successfully, however, the men must avoid thinking too much; Miller recognizes that "'I thought about what would happen if I didn't get a clean shot. I broke a leg. If I hadn't thought about it, I could have got the whole herd.'" The irrationality of the buffalo and the necessity of blotting out the slaughter's meaning in order to continue it also encourages mindlessness. Of the buffalo Miller says, "'You think about what they're going to do, and you get yourself in trouble; all a man can do is not think about them, kill them when he can, and not to try to figure anything out.'"

During the night when Andrews realizes that to kill a buffalo is to snuff out its noble self and fears that the hunt is having the same effect on him, he keeps his hand on his face as he sleeps, seeking reassurance that he has a self. This is not what he had in mind when he came to the West. At the book's end, contemplating the prostitute and his own coming of age, "he could hardly recall, now, the passion that had drawn him to this room and this flesh, as if by a subtle magnetism; nor could he recall the force of that other passion which had impelled him halfway across a continent into a wilderness where he had dreamed he could find, as in a vision, his unalterable self. Almost without regret, he could admit now the vanity from which those passions had sprung." He had tracked wildness through labyrinthine ways but had taken the wrong route and had found instead the monster within himself.

This novel, as its title suggests, is also about a Western town, and the scene there after the men return is significant. The energy of frontier existence has dissipated, and as the town has lost its economic base, the trade in buffalo hides, it has dwindled into lethargy. The only energy left is violence, and it explodes when Miller, enraged by the hunt's futility, sets fire to McDonald's warehouse. *Butcher's Crossing* is thus a parable of the frontier experience, a tale of frontier vigor and heroism, albeit of a mindless variety, being transformed into boredom, economic inutility and violence.

■ III

Stoner is the story of a farm boy who goes to the University of Missouri to study agriculture, switches to English and stays on to earn a Ph.D. and to become a professor. As Williams narrates that life he develops some of the themes that are prominent in *Butcher's Crossing*: the primal passion that motivates various kinds of quests, its manifestations in love and other forms, and the adversity that those driven by it must endure. Stoner, although ignored by others, is heroic because he maintains his integrity throughout his quest and understands and articulates the primal passion's meaning.

Stoner's introduction to adversity occurs much earlier than does Andrews'. Rather than leaving a comfortable existence and a university to search for a wilder life, he leaves the grinding, life-sapping poverty of a farm for a university. His West has been formed by many years of the decline evident in *Butcher's Crossing*, but that experience stands him in good stead: "William Stoner knew of the world in a way that few of his younger colleagues could understand. Deep in him, beneath his memory, was the knowledge of hardship and hunger and endurance and pain. Though he seldom thought of his early years on the Booneville farm, there was always near his consciousness the blood knowledge of his inheritance, given him by forefathers whose lives were obscure and hard and stoical and whose common ethic was to present to an oppressive world faces that were expressionless and hard and bleak." Even Stoner's family is an affliction. He marries a young woman, one of the first he has known, and she never grows up; the only meaning of her life is the agony she causes for him. She breaks the bond of affection between him and his daughter, who then begins her descent into loneliness and alcoholism. Finally, Stoner, heavily sedated and full of cancer, fades away into death.

One of his solaces is the academic world. Inexplicably, in a British Literature course taught by an irascible and sarcastic professor he finds his vocation as an English professor. One of his friends claims that Stoner stays at the university because he is a dreamer unfit for life elsewhere. This friend is a cynic who dies in World War I but, as Stoner realizes, is in a sense reborn in Lomax, Stoner's chairman, and in Walker, a student who is Lomax's protégé and caricature. After Stoner votes to fail the fraudulent Walker on his Ph.D. exam, Lomax stops speaking to him and begins to retaliate in every way he can conceive and carry out: denying him advanced courses (until Stoner begins to teach medieval literature in Freshman Composition), denying him promotions and driving away his lover. Stoner comes to think that Lomax and Walker are the world that the university must keep out.

Despite these hardships, Stoner keeps alive his passion and eventually realizes that it is composed of learning and love, not mindlessness and sexuality, which is all that Andrews in *Butcher's Crossing* could see in it. His marriage is loveless; after publishing a book early in his career he stops writing and except for a brief timespan he cannot communicate his love of learning to his students, but he always has potential for and reverence for love and learning, and during an affair with a graduate student he realizes that potential. His relationship with Katherine Driscoll, meaningful both intellectually and physically, is the zenith of his life, the one experience that makes all the adversity endurable and, along with his steadfast adherence to his dream, makes him heroic. With her he learns that "love is not an end but a process through which one person attempts to know another." They achieve an epiphany: "'lust and learning,' Katherine once said. 'That's all there is, isn't it?' And it seemed to Stoner that that was exactly true, that that was one of the things he had learned." Years later, after he has lost her, he reads the book that she wrote with his help and dedicated to him and he thinks of the primal passion: "He had, in odd ways, given it to every moment of his life, and had perhaps given it most fully when he was unaware of his giving. It was a passion neither of the mind nor of the flesh; rather, it was a force that comprehended them both, as if they were but the matter of love, its specific substance. To a woman or to a poem, it said simply: Look! I am alive."

■ IV

By means of letters and documents *Augustus* tells the story of Augustus Caesar's adult life, beginning shortly before he learns of Julius Caesar's death and ending with his own death. Williams uses documents more effectively to develop characters, a setting and themes than does Thornton Wilder in *The Ides of March*. Williams' characters reveal themselves as they describe other characters and narrate events. For example, some of them are differentiated and developed because they write in the three prose styles that Cicero explains in the *Orator*: Cicero himself in the middle style, Maecenas in the plain style, and Julia and Augustus in the vigorous style. The documents also lend to this novel an aura of historical authenticity, but none of the major purported sources exist. Williams does mention and once in a while paraphrases or quotes from one real source, *Res Gestae Divi Augustus,* an autobiographical work. Our knowledge about Augustus derives not from the sources Williams pretends to cite but from such works as Suetonius' *The Twelve Caesars,* Tacitus' *The Annals of Imperial Rome,* Plutarch's lives of Antony and Cicero and such minor historians as Velleius Paterculus, Appian and Cassius Dio.

Augustus is multi-faceted and positive, a character who, like Robert Graves' Claudius, is morally superior to the society he rules. In the first document Julius Caesar explains the course of study that Augustus pursued, and later Strabo quotes the opinion of Augustus' tutor that he could have been a scholar. Frequent references to his delicate health and his slight body make his accomplishments seem more admirable. Other attractive traits are his clemency after he has obtained power, his love for his daughter, Julia, and his unpretentiousness, which his austere house makes especially evident. His modesty is obvious in his long letter to Nicolaus, this novel's climax, because in it he contemplates his life: "I am a man, and as foolish and weak as most men; if I have an advantage over my fellows, it is that I have known this of myself." His supporters in this novel deny that he is authoritarian, and Augustus of course agrees, claiming that he transferred power to the Senate and the Roman people and asserting that "of power I possessed no more than those who were my colleagues in any magistracy." He seems almost totally lacking in cruelty, particularly in the scene when the triumvirs negotiate their proscription list. Maecenas asserts that Augustus took little interest in the negotiations, acted as though they were distasteful but unavoidable, refused to add any names to the list, and tried to dissuade Antony from having Cicero killed.

Early in this novel Augustus' allies are quickly and deftly characterized when they discuss his obligations after Julius Caesar's death. Agrippa, revealing the careful, orderly mind of the military commander and administrator, recommends doing nothing until they receive more information. Rufus advises immediate attack, exhibiting the same impetuosity that later makes him turn against Augustus. Maecenas, although mocked by many as a fop, offers the best advice because he thinks like the poets he later supports financially, is oblivious to power, and understands human motives. He advises Augustus to "return quietly, with his friends and his grief—but without the soldiers." Augustus' youth and inexperience make waiting in Rome the best tactic, and Antony's recklessness and the Senate's desperation assure the success of this tactic.

Although Cicero dies early in this novel, he is portrayed extensively. At first he vastly underestimates Augustus and his three colleagues, writing of the former, for example, "The boy is nothing, and we need have no fear." After a while, however, in a letter to Brutus he writes more respectfully of Augustus' capabilities and indicates his plan to manipulate him so that he will destroy Antony, restore power to the Senate and re-institute the Republic. Decimus Brutus mentions Cicero's witty statement that Augustus must be complimented, honored and *"tollendum"* (raised, got rid of). Cicero's support of Julius Caesar's assassins gives Antony one reason to have him killed, but Augustus has the same motive for revenge and does not seek it. Williams barely mentions the Phillipics that Cicero delivered in the Senate against Antony, which were the main cause of Antony's desire for revenge. In short, by making Antony's motives less clear than they really were, Williams makes them seem irrational and thereby makes Cicero's death seem more lamentable.

Julia is sensitive, even in regard to her affairs, which cause problems for her father. For example, she writes in her journal, "Before that afternoon, I had not known the pleasures of love…And in the months that came that pleasure fed upon itself, and multiplied." Her journal demonstrates her intelligence and poetic sensibility: she often analyzes events more incisively than do the other characters. However, she has an affair with Julius, Antony's son, who plots against both Tiberius and Augustus. (She writes in her journal that she may have expressed a desire for the death of Tiberius, her husband, so she can marry Julius.) Augustus invokes a law against adultery to banish her in order to save her from a treason charge.

Augustus' enemies differ considerably. Antony's irrational contempt for the young Augustus is clear during their meeting to discuss Julius Caesar's will soon after Augustus' return to Rome. Antony himself reports on their meeting in a letter that describes Augustus in offensive terms: "that whey-faced little bastard, Octavius, came around to see me yesterday morning." Brutus, however, is genuinely noble. In a letter to Augustus he shows his regard for Rome and his relative disregard for his own interests, writing, for example, "let us forget proscriptions and assassinations; if you can forgive me the death of Caesar, perhaps I can forgive you the death of Cicero. We cannot be friends to each other; neither of us needs that. But perhaps we can be friends to Rome."

Even more extensively than he does in *Butcher's Crossing*, in *Augustus* Williams describes the society in which his characters live. Julius Caesar expresses a negative view of Rome: "We have seen murder, theft, and pillage in the name of the Republic—and call it the necessary price we pay for freedom. Cicero deplores the depraved Roman morality that worships wealth—and, himself a millionaire many times over, travels with a hundred slaves from one of his villas to another." Similarly, in the penultimate document in this novel Augustus writes, "There is now upon the Roman face a look which I fear augurs badly for the future. Dissatisfied with honest comfort, he strains back toward the old corruption which nearly robbed the state of its existence." He also warns against the barbarian waiting to conquer the empire. This novel's last words are, "Let us pray to the gods that, under Nero, Rome will at last fulfill the dream of Octavius Caesar." In one sense these words are vitriolically ironic; Nero certainly did not fulfill Augustus' dream of a world secure, ordered and reasonably free. In another sense, he did fulfill the dream of his own death that Augustus had just recounted. Nero will help that dream become true for the empire, and the barbarian will complete the project.

Other characters echo Julius Caesar's original charge that hypocrisy is rampant in Rome. Maecenas points out that the Senate thanked the killers of Julius Caesar and then passed laws Caesar had supported and that Antony fraternized with the assassins both shortly before and shortly after the murder. Beneath the surface of political alliances and marriages lies the primary motive of political advantage, as the dizzying pace of new alliances and new marriages indicates. As Nicolaus, the credible outsider, notes, during this era noise and danger dominate everyday existence. This does not mean that Rome is totally repulsive; Nicolaus also says that living there makes him feel that he is at the world's center. During Augustus' administration the outward condition of Rome changed vastly for the better, but he himself mentions the dangers lying behind the attractive facade, and Nicolaus also senses a disturbing uneasiness. Similarly, Ovid attacks as mere pretense the virtues that most Romans claimed to possess: "those 'virtues' of rank, prestige, honor, duty, and piety have simply denuded man of his humanity."

From the portraits of the characters and of Rome several themes emerge. Learning and love, which in *Stoner* are the two components of the primal passion, are metamorphosed into halves of two dichotomies; action-contemplation and power-love. Maecenas is crucial to the development of the former dichotomy. Very early in this novel Rufus quotes him: "'I have been projecting a poem that examines the active versus the contemplative life. The wisdom of the one I know; I have been observing the foolishness of the other'." As Augustus' second most influential advisor he lives in the world of power, and as the patron of Horace, Virgil, Propertius and probably Ovid he lives in the world of poetry. Horace writes to another poet, Tibullus, that he and Virgil are among Augustus' closest friends. Horace also revises the myth of Orpheus by saying that his Eurydice is knowledge and his underground is his enemy at Philippi, an allusion to the fact that Horace fought there for Brutus and against Augustus. Maecenas tells Livy about Horace's belief, contrary to "Ars Poetica," that in writing a poem he begins with a feeling and then conceives of "'an end, as simple as I can make it, toward which that feeling might progress'." Maecenas, again showing that he understands both the world of poetry and the world of power, tells Livy that a politician reacts similarly. Ovid illustrates the dangers that poets face when they consort with power; Augustus banishes him, partly because of *The Art of Love*. A poet need not always lose, however. Lucius Varius Rufus, a minor poet, in a letter to Virgil assumes a moral position superior to that of the powerful:

> What games they must play, those who have power in the world! And how ludicrous must they seem to the muses! It must be that those who are nearest to the gods are most at their mercy. We are most fortunate, my dear Vergil, that we need not marry to ensure our posterity, but can make the children of our souls march beautifully into the future, where they will not change or die.

This dichotomy of power and poetry closely relates to the dichotomy of love and power, which Antony and Cleopatra dramatically illustrate, as they do in Shakespeare's play. When

■ **BOOKS BY JOHN WILLIAMS**

novels

Nothing But the Night. Chicago: Alan Swallow, 1948.

Butcher's Crossing. New York: Macmillan, 1960.

Stoner. New York: Viking Press, 1965.

Augustus. New York: Viking Press, 1972.

poetry

The Broken Landscape. Chicago: Alan Swallow, 1949.

The Necessary Lie. Denver: Verb Publications, 1965.

their affair begins, it seems merely to be an excess of love dissipating power and causing outrage in Rome. Some of the female characters show poignantly what happens when love meets power. Hirtia does so inadvertently when she describes her meeting with Augustus. Her account follows the account of Augustus' victory at Actium, but when he meets her he is on his way to denounce his beloved daughter. Hirtia's uncomplicated love sharply contrasts with the machinations and values of the powerful. Augustus realizes later that had she been in his place she would have chosen love over power, would have saved Julia and lost the empire. Julia and Octavia, Augustus' wife, know that love and power often are mutually exclusive. The world of power draws them, as it draws the poets, out of the world in which they are comfortable. Even at the age of nine, Julia senses at one of her father's triumphs that matters of state are pulling him away from her. Later she resists so vigorously her own drift into the world of power that her love becomes obsessive. The tragic Octavia also knows that power threatens her world of love. After many years as a pawn in the games of power politics, she resists Augustus' plans to have her daughter, Marcella, divorce Agrippa so that Augustus can arrange an even more politically advantageous marriage: "I do not persuade myself that the possession of fame and power is worth the price of it." Julia sums up the degradation of love by power: "One even loved for power; and the end of love became not its own joy, but the myriad joys of power."

Finally, Williams integrates his two main themes. Poetry and love interact when Virgil reads to Augustus, Octavia and others the passage in the *Aeneid* about Octavia's dead son, Marcellus:

Fate shall allow the earth one glimpse of this young man —
One glimpse, no more. Too puissant had been Rome's stock, ye gods,
In your sight, had such gifts been granted it to keep.
What lamentations of men shall Campus Martius echo
To Mars' great city! O Tiber, what obsequies you shall see
One day as you glide past the new-built mausoleum!

Although it disturbs Octavia, poetry harms her less that power does. The world of power has killed her son; poetry merely reports the killing. Late in this novel these two themes come together in a different way. Even though love in its common forms cannot defeat power, in other forms it can. By redefining it Augustus proclaims its ultimate victory: "There is a variety of love more powerful and lasting than that union with the other...it is the love of the scholar for his text, the philosopher for his idea, the poet for his word." In this sense love and poetry triumph, as they did for Williams when he wrote *Augustus.*

■ **V**

John Williams has written a western novel, an academic novel and a historical novel, but in each he has developed the same important themes. His moral vision has allowed him to create in these three sub-genres works that are more than entertainments. His techniques are interesting and appropriate but have not dominated his work to the exclusion of meaningful content.

That is, like Stoner, he has maintained his integrity and has kept alive his dream. Like Stoner, too, he deserves more attention.

John Stark
October, 1980

Miller Williams

Miller Williams, born in Hoxie, Arkansas, in 1930, came out of a peculiar educational background for an academic poet, for he took a B.S. in biology from Arkansas State College, Conway, in 1951 and an M.S. in zoology from the University of Arkansas, Fayetteville, in 1952. In 1961 Williams applied for and was awarded a poetry fellowship at the Bread Loaf Writers' Conference at Middlebury College. Subsequently the director, the late John Ciardi, appointed Williams a member of the staff, and in 1963 he was awarded the Amy Lowell Traveling Scholarship. Williams began his career teaching biology at McNeese State College, went to Loyola University in 1966, and after some wandering about returned to Fayetteville in 1971, where he taught in the Fayetteville English department and writing program until eventually he became a University Professor of English and, at last, director of the University of Arkansas Press, a position he has used to build the Press into one of the foremost publishers of poetry and poetry criticism among the smaller university presses. Williams has also contributed to the literature of his time two important anthologies which have been widely used as textbooks, *Contemporary Poetry in America* (1973) and *Patterns of Poetry: An Encyclopedia of Forms* (1986).

In the early 1960s Williams participated in a writers' conference held at the Cleveland Poetry Center of Fenn College, now Cleveland State University, where he made a number of cogent comments, but in the course of a panel discussion on "The Poet's Masks" he said one thing in particular that is relevant to a discussion of his work: "The poet lies to tell the truth." As an illustration of this thesis the poet used an incident that involved his son. One day the boy ran into the house and said, "A lion's chasing me!" Of course, there was no lion in the yard, but out of courtesy to childhood Williams looked—and there *was* a lion in the yard...in the form of a fair-sized dog. The point Williams made was that to an adult the animal was a dog, but the quality of the boy's experience was that he had been threatened by something as large and menacing to him as a lion would be to an adult, so the child had "lied" in order to convey the magnitude of the experience to an older person. Williams' poems in his first book *A Circle of Stone* (1964) were, in these terms, a pack of lies. Each of them was an exaggeration, an attempt to get a mode of seeing and thinking down on paper in such a way as to help the reader to achieve the poet's original experience, or at least its essence.

Williams was and continues to be equipped to find the right words with which to lie well, for he knows how to compose his work, not merely invent images or murk about for the sake of darkening, although he is, perhaps, a "Southern Gothic" poet in the sense that he has a real feeling for the strange in mankind. He puts words down in an order that gets them into the reader's mind and makes them stay there.

Williams' second book published in the United States (*Recital*, in a bilingual edition, appeared in Chile, also in 1964) was *So Long at the Fair* (1968). *The Only World There Is* followed

Miller Williams

A poet, professor, and editor, Miller Williams was born in Hoxie, Arkansas, in 1930. He received a B.S. in biology from Arkansas State College and an M.S. in zoology from the University of Arkansas. He has taught at McNeece State College, Millsaps College, Louisiana State University, and Loyola University, as well as the University of Arkansas at Fayetteville. His poetry has appeared in *Poetry, Saturday Review, American Scholar, Shenandoah,* the *Oberlin Quarterly,* and *Prairie Schooner.* In 1961 he was honored with a Breadloaf fellowship and in 1963 received the Amy Lowell Traveling Scholarship in Poetry. He won the John Williams Carrington Award for excellence in literature, 1994, and the National Arts Award in 1997. Williams chairs the comparative literature program at the University of Arkansas at Fayetteville and directs the University of Arkansas Press. ■

(1971), and then *Halfway from Hoxie* in 1973. *Why God Permits Evil* appeared four years later, in 1977, and another four years passed before *Distractions* was published in 1981. *The Boys on Their Bony Mules* was published in 1983, and *Imperfect Love* in 1986. Reading through his *Living on the Surface: New and Selected Poems* (1989) is not merely a pleasurable tour through the best work of these volumes, it is a fascinating introduction to a strong personality, an interesting revelation of the development of a fine and individual literary style, and an educational experience.

One of the features of Williams' style is the tone of the Baptist preacher, a down-home diction combined with a pulpit rhetoric harnessed to serve an elevated purpose, as in the elegy which is also a prayer, "For Clement Long, Dead," subtitled *"lines written in the dark,"* a poem which the poet unfortunately did not include in his most recent volume:

Lord listen, or heaven is undone.
He will not spell your name or take your hand,
will hee-haw at the gate with a held breath,
will run away to the end where death is real.

Lord if you chase him like a wheatfield fire
till hallelujahs and a choir of angels
sing him coming and the grand gates open,
still he will stand against your house
where no sin ever is and no flesh fails,

If even he has treasures, let the mouse
discover the grain, take the worm to the tree.

Give his potential pleasures to the poor,
or watch him. And watch him well. And watching see
how he subverts the angels, whispering this:

ninety and nine returned and deserve attending;
surely the faithful one, the unoffending
son should have the calf; God, it's a small grace
to be a counter of coins in the first place.

The images are organic to the poem; although they would be unusual in the mouth of a real preacher, in the lines of Williams they are unobtrusive. The contexts of his poems allow the overtones one associates with the pulpit, but literary associations are not blocked out either, and the poems can be read on two levels—the literal and the allegorical. Williams walks this fine line between rhetoric and symbolism as well as anyone has done during the past quarter century.

If we examine the first poem in *Living on the Surface*, "The Associate Professor Delivers an Exhortation to His Failing Students," we can isolate many of these elements and subsequently follow their development in the body of Williams' work. This piece combines something of the poet's characteristic oratorical quality with what is the major concern of the book, survival. At a glance, the poem appears to be "free verse"—that is, line-phrased prose: each line a phrase or a clause of some kind. The typographical level also tells us that the poem is strophic rather than stanzaic: there are twenty-nine irregular sections, some as small as a line in length. Here are the first two strophes—clearly, the professor is a biologist:

Now when the frogs
that gave their lives for nothing
are washed from the brains and pans
we laid them in
I leave to you
who most excusably misunderstand
the margins of my talks
which because I am wise
and am a coward
were not appended to the syllabus

but I will fail to tell you
what I tell you
even before you fail to understand
so we might in a manner of speaking
go down together.

An examination of the poem on the sonic level, however, quickly discovers that this is no kind of prose but variable accentual-syllabic prosody. The meter is variable iambics, each line ranging in length from monometer to hexameter:

I should have told you something of importance
to give at least a meaning
to the letter:

how, after hope, it sometimes happens
a girl, anonymous as beer,
telling forgotten things in a cheap bar

how she could have taught here as well as I.

Better

The first line of strophe three is iambic pentameter verse (see the scansion above), though it has some variations: a promotion of the central unstressed syllable, in a series of three, in the fourth foot and the substitution of an amphibrach in the fifth foot. The next line seems to consist of two iambs and an amphibrach, in that order, and the third line of strophe three would then look like two trochees. However, if one were to put lines two and three together, it would look and scan like this:

to give at least a meaning to the letter:

In other words, lines two and three of strophe three, taken together, are metrically a duplicate of line one. What we have here, really, is two lines of iambic pentameter verse with falling endings—or, to be descriptively more accurate, iambic hendecasyllabic (eleven-syllable) verse.

Taking a hint from this discovery, we may look back at the beginning of the poem and see that "lines" 1–2 are also equal to one line of iambic pentameter verse, as are "lines" 3–4. The next two combined "lines," however, equal one hexameter, so not everything is going to boil down to pentameter, but it becomes fairly clear that the line-phrasing of the poem is not a strong component of the prosody; rather, it is a disguise of the fact that Williams is writing verse. Perhaps this practice was itself a poetic survival mechanism during "The Great Hiatus" of twenty years and more in American formalist poetry—during the 1960s, 1970s and early 1980s—when versewriting was proscribed and only "free verse composition" was allowed.

Taken at face value, however, we may call Williams' prosody in this poem line-phrased, variable accentual-syllabics, and the meter is variable iambics, the range for the lines being from monometer to hexameter. There are great numbers of other sorts of variations in the meters; we can see some of them if we look at strophe 7. Williams substitutes other sorts of verse feet, including anapests,

The day I talked about *the conduction of currents*
I meant to say

an occasional double iamb,

be careful *about getting* hung up in the brain's things

(This line may very well be the thesis of the poem, but more about that a bit later.)

that send you screaming like madmen through the town
or make you like the man in front of the Safeway store
that preaches on Saturday afternoons
a clown.

In the beginning of the poem Williams did not do much with outright rhyme, but there are some line-ending repetitions linking strophes one and two: *you/you/you* and *misunderstand/understand*; consonances between strophes two, three, and six: *together/letter/Better*, and within strophe (couplet) five: *beer/bar*. True rhyme shows up in strophe seven: *town/clown*. This rhyme continues in strophe eight:

The day I lectured on adrenalin
I meant to tell you
as you were coming *down*
slowly out of the hills of certainty
empty your mind of the hopes that held you there.
Make a catechism of all your fears

512

and say it over:

this is the most of you…who knows…the best
I where God was born
and heaven and confession
and half of love

from the fear of falling
and being flushed away
to the gulp of the suckhole and that rusting gut
from which no Jonah comes

that there is no Jesus and no hell

This passage is the thesis of the poem stated overtly. The lecturer is delivering a sermon on the subject of religion or the lack thereof in the existential modern world—the associate professor, like Williams, is a biologist and, also like Williams, one of the lapsed and disillusioned faithful. The "failure" here is the failure of both students and teacher, each in the same and different ways. The ideational level of the poem is as important as the sonic.

Returning to a consideration of the latter, we note that from this point in the poem rhyme becomes an important consideration, and it grows as close as couplet rhyme, though more often it is still random (as usual, the emphases are mine):

that God
square root of something equal to *all*
will not feel the imbalance when you *fall*

that rotting you will lie unbelievably *alone*
to be sucked up by some insignificant oak
as a child draws milk through straws
to be his *bone*.

These are the gravity that holds us together
toward our common *sun*

every hope getting out of hand
slings us hopelessly outward one by *one*
till all that kept us common is *undone*.

Rhyme (*sun/one/undone*) links strophes fifteen and sixteen; the latter ends, in fact, in a heroic couplet. As the poem progresses it is pulling together, becoming more and more formal, although Williams has maintained his disguises.

The sensory level of the poem is not complex. The basic tropes are descriptions rather than similes and metaphors. There are more rhetorical tropes than images—allusion in particular:

The day you took the test
I would have told you this:
that you had no time to listen for questions
hunting out the answers in your files
is surely the kind of irony
poems are made of

that all the answers at best are less than half

and you would have remembered
Lazarus
who hung around with God or the devil for days
and nobody asked him

anything

The primary schemas are constructional—grammatic parallels mostly, but Williams also avoids punctuation throughout the poem: there are few marks of terminal punctuation, not many internally, either. Williams generally indicates a new sentence or paragraph, as he does in the next strophe, twenty-one, simply with an initial capital letter:

But if they do
if one Sunday morning they should ask you
the only thing that matters after all
tell them the only thing you know is true

tell them failing is an act of love
because
like sin
it is the commonality within

Now rhyming has progressed to such an extent that the next strophe, number twenty-three, becomes a heroic quatrain consisting of two couplets; Williams says to tell them—that is, the students,

how failing together we shall finally pass
how to pomp and circumstance all of a class
noble of eye, blind mares between our knees,
lances ready, we ride to Hercules.

With the puns on "pass" and "class" Williams works his way into the subdued metaphor that has lain dormant throughout the poem till now. This strophe also contains the only overt metaphor of the poem—we are all knights, Don Quixotes de la Mancha, riding out to do battle with Death; we will simultaneously fail and pass on.

Another heroic couplet begins the penultimate strophe twenty-four which then returns to a semblance of prose—

The day I said this had I meant to hope
some impossible punk on a cold slope
stupidly alone
would build himself a fire
to make of me an idiot

and a liar

But the last two lines are now obviously yet another disguised heroic couplet; indeed, if the word *himself* were not present, the last two "strophes" would be another heroic quatrain and might be written out like this:

The day I said this had I meant to hope
some impossible punk on a cold slope
stupidly alone would build…a fire
to make of me an idiot and a liar

The poem ends without punctuation, but Williams has asked a question, not made a statement. The mood of the poem is one of disillusion; there is a touch of bitterness in it—gall brought on by a loss of faith, and perhaps of despair staved off at a great cost of will. The viewpoint is dramatic, for, though Williams clearly draws on his own background, he has created a persona who speaks a monologue to an assumed audience of his students. The level of diction is intelligent but not overly intellectual, and the style is mean, not high. If the subject itself is the human intellect, then Williams' thesis is that, though the mind may be an untrustworthy guide through life, intellect is the only guide that mankind has.

The major genre of the poem, then, is dramatic; the specific form is the monologue, though if this were written subjectively it would be a sermon with a strong didactic element. The levels emphasized are the sonic and the ideational, though the typographical is important to Williams' disguise of his prosody, and toward the end of the poem there is heavier emphasis on the sensory.

The poem balances the conflict of intellect with mystery extremely well, especially, it seems to me, for an early poem. All, or nearly all of the elements of Williams' mature style are here, and the poem is a good one for that reason as well as for intrinsic considerations.

"Voice of America," from *The Only World There Is,* finally gives up all technical disguises and announces itself typographically as a verse-mode poem written in quatrain stanzas. Sonically, it is written in normative accentual-syllabics—the running foot is iambic and the line length is tetrameter, but as in the earlier poem there are many variations. The rhyme scheme is *abcb*; thus, the specific form is long measure, from the family of common measure stanzas. It is a cautionary speech in the form of a lyric utilizing the devices we have already noted including repetition and parallelism ("Do not imagine…" begins many stanzas and lines), alliteration, consonance, echo, and assonance.

The sensory level contains, again, primarily descriptions, but there is irony too, and the main image is a simile, "like a bullet hitting a head" the sperm "crashes in" upon the egg to begin the process of reproduction. It appears to be a garish image until, reading closely, we understand that the real comparison is with a rifle bullet entering the head of its victim to finish a life in the same way that life began. The mood of the poem is tense and ominous.

Eventually it will occur to the reader that the subject of the poem is not reproduction but assassination. The schemas Williams uses here are repetitional primarily, the repetitions conjuring up an obsession. The viewpoint is narrative and the syntax is objective—a cautionary tale is being told with illustrations. The level of diction is that of a parent or a teacher (or even a preacher) warning an older child by means of illustrations. The poem, then, is a didactic lyric with a strong narrative element. The levels are in balance—there is even a typographical hiatus in the penultimate line of the eleventh and last stanza to suggest the hole the bullet is making in the head of its victim. This is a poem about the death of John F. Kennedy, or Martin Luther King, or Robert Kennedy…or anyone in this world who meets a violent end.

Williams' most ambitious and longest poem, "Notes from the Agent on Earth: How to be Human," appeared in *Why God Permits Evil*. It appears at first glance to be a verse mode poem built in both long sections and short—cantos and strophes; none of the cantos are titled. Scansion shows that, indeed, it is verse, normative accentual-syllabic prosody, in fact: the meters are iambic pentameter, but it is not quite blank verse—as in many of his other poems, there is random end-rhyme which at times becomes couplet rhyme, and there are other sorts of sonic devices often taking the place of rhyme, such as consonance and repetition. Williams' jazzy variations haven't changed, either. The general form of the poem is that of the elegy, and the Southern preacher inhabits the voice of this poem, as it does in other Williams works, so that at times it partakes of the sermon.

There are seven cantos here and, though there are no titles, each of the middle five begins with a parallel: "This is about…"; the first canto is an introduction—the scene is Rome, St. Peter's Basilica. The speaker is looking at statuary: St. Gregory sits on a slab under which "the devil, winged and dog-faced, cat-pawed and crooked / turns in his agony and bares his teeth, / bares his broken claws, turns his nostrils / almost inside out."

The last canto is the summation, a coda. It begins, "There is much that matters. What matters most is survival." Williams' lifelong theme is thus stated in so many words. In between the prologue and the epilogue the cantos announce themselves: "This is about Love and how to tell it." "This is about Faith and how to tell it." "This is about the Will to Power, Envy, Covetousness, Ambition.… " "This is about Death and how to tell it." "This is also something about Ambition. Also Love. And Faith also. And Death."

The sensory level contains, like the earlier poems, primarily descriptions that sometimes ascend to metaphor, but far outnumbering these are the rhetorical tropes; in particular, Williams here displays a real talent for coining aphorisms: "Love is Fear and Loneliness fed and sleeping: / Faith is Fear and Loneliness explained, / denied and dealt in; Ambition which is envy / is Fear and Loneliness coming up to get you; / Death is Fear and Loneliness fading out." The emotional thrust of the poem is thoughtful tranquillity shot through with neurotic disillusion.

The ideation of the poem revolves around the subject of existence. As we can see, the schemas used are repetitional and constructional, in particular the long parallels of the cantos. The voice here is only partly narrative, for Williams steps out from behind all his masks in this poem to assume the subjective viewpoint and the egopoetic stance. The syntax follows the form of his thought and only now and again the form of an action. The level of diction is slightly elevated, but the style is mean, not at all florid, though there are some gothic scenes, especially in the prologue. One might be tempted to call the form of the poem georgics, for it is a handbook on how to get through life.

Fusionally, the poem is lyrical and didactic and the levels are balanced, though clearly the ideational is most heavily weighted. For all its preacherly qualities, the poem is most readable, for Williams is ever the musician of language.

In *The Boys on Their Bony Mules* Williams wrote with a greater sense of story. His rhythms and tropes were so well grounded in meter and in the particular that the reader hardly noticed the large issue, the thought rising from its base. Williams, despite his scientific background, is one of those poets who were trained, or who trained themselves, in the basics of verse composition and built from that foundation a style of writing and an angle of vision that enabled them to range widely and plunge deeply into the world and the self.

As always in his work, the poems in *Imperfect Love*—formal lyrics and short narratives— considered the human condition in its myriad formations and transformations in such a way as to provide the reader with both insight and delight, as in "A Little Poem":

for Jack Marr

We say that some are mad. In fact
if we have all the words and we
make madness mean the way they act
then they as all of us can see

are surely mad. And then again
if they have all the words and call
madness something else, well then —

■ BOOKS BY MILLER WILLIAMS

A Circle of Stone. Baton Rouge: Louisiana State University Press, 1964.

Recital. Valparaiso, Chile: Ediciones Oceano, 1964.

So Long the Fair. New York: Dutton, 1968.

The Only World There Is. New York: Dutton, 1971.

Halfway from Hoxie: New and Selected Poems. New York: Dutton, 1973.

Why God Permits Evil; New Poems. Baton Rouge: Louisiana State University Press, 1977.

Distractions. Baton Rouge: Louisiana State University Press, 1981.

The Boys on Their Bony Mules. Baton Rouge: Louisiana State University Press, 1983.

Imperfect Love. Baton Rouge: Louisiana State University Press, 1986.

Patterns of Poetry: An Enclyclopedia of Forms. Baton Rouge: Louisiana State University Press, 1986.

Living on the Surface: New and Selected Poems. Baton Rouge: Louisiana State University Press, 1989.

Adjusting to the Light. Columbia: University of Missouri Press, 1992.

Points of Departure. Urbana: University of Illinois Press, 1995.

The Ways We Touch. Urbana: University of Illinois Press, 1997.

Some Jazz a While: Collected Poems. Urbana: University of Illinois Press, 1999.

well then, they are not mad at all.

Also in 1986 Williams took a role to the forefront of the blossoming Neoformalist movement with the publication of his text/anthology, *Patterns of Poetry: An Encyclopedia of Forms,* of which the late John Ciardi said, "Miller Williams has performed a brilliant service in this book.... I recommend it to everyone who dares to think he can teach anyone to be a poet." Through this volume's pages the new generation of poets is beginning again to understand that when a poet writes formally the burden of tradition need not inhibit him in the treatment of the particular subject in hand. This is the true reason that many of the poets of the past two decades have shuddered at the thought of traditional forms: they feel smothered, and indeed they are, but when someone comes along, like Williams, who can understand and release the power of the old constructs in an individual and imaginative manner, the form helps the poet to say the necessary thing.

Miller Williams, then, has done contemporary poetry a singular service in that, during the indulgent decades, he maintained a level of artistry committed both to tradition and to a personal vision. This poetry of balance, of intelligence as well as feeling, will serve as a benchmark to the new generation of poets who are feeling their way back to a sense of writing as literature, not merely self-expression. But his commitment to the craft of poetry takes more forms than just the maintenance of high personal standards. Williams remains the teacher or, if you will, the preacher who exhorts his audience by precept and example. He uses his pulpit to spread the word and the book.

Lewis Turco
April, 1989

UPDATE

Williams has since published five volumes of poetry: *Living on the Surface: New and Selected Poems* (1989), *Adjusting to the Light* (1992), *Points of Departure* (1995), *The Ways We Touch* (1997), and *Some Jazz a While: Collected Poems* (1999).

"Best known for narrative, dramatic poems about ordinary people in ordinary speech," according to *Publishers Weekly,* Williams became better known after President Clinton asked him to write and deliver a poem at the 1997 inaugural ceremony. Even before the event, readers were looking for his earlier work.

The Dictionary of Literary Biography describes Miller Williams as the most gifted poet of the American South of his generation, one who has grown with each new book. "Williams's poetry exhibits a remarkable consistency of vision and voice throughout his career. . . . The result of this long and steady artistic development is a mature and informed art that is being written by a major poet only now reaching the height of his powers."

The Mississippi Quarterly once wrote, "Gradually you get drawn into Williams' world of bafflement and awe, of humility and profoundness. No other poet I can think of has achieved the combination of intellectual sophistication and modesty we find in individual poems and the work as a whole."

Contributor Notes

JOHN ALEXANDER ALLEN was a longtime professor of English at Hollins College (now Hollins University). Among his books are a collection of poems, *The Lean Divider,* and the anthology *Hero's Way: Contemporary Poems in the Mythic Tradition.*

DON BELTON has taught literature and writing at the University of Michigan, University of Massachusetts in Boston, and Bennington College. He is the author of the novel *Almost Midnight* and the editor of *Speak My Name: Black Men on Masculinity and the American Dream,* winner of the 1996 Gustavus Myers Humanitarian Award.

NICHOLAS BIRNS teaches at New School University in New York and was a research visiting fellow at the University of Newcastle, Australia. He is editor of *Antipodes* and of *Powys Notes* and has published articles and reviews widely.

TERRI BROWN-DAVIDSON is a lecturer at the University of Nebraska at Lincoln. After receiving her Ph.D. in English in 1995, she is currently pursuing a second Ph.D. in philosophy. Her poetry, fiction, essays, and reviews have appeared widely in journals.

EMILY MILLER BUDICK is professor of American studies and chair of the department at the Hebrew University of Jerusalem, Israel. She is the author of *Emily Dickinson and the Life of Language: A Study in Symbolic Poetics, Fiction and Historical Consciousness: The American Romance Tradition, 1850-1990,* and *Nineteenth Century American Romance: Genre and the Democratic Construction of Culture.*

DAN CASEY is the president of Burlington College in Vermont. He wrote a prize-winning study of Benedict Kiely for the Bucknell Series. He also co-edited *Irish American Fiction: Essays in Criticism* and a companion anthology of short fiction, *Friends and Relations,* both with Robert Rhodes.

KELLY CHERRY is professor emerita at the University of Wisconsin, Madison, where she was Eudora Welty professor of English and Evjue-Bascom professor in the humanities. She is a contributing editor of *The Hollins Critic* and the author of six books of poetry (most recently, *Rising Venus*), five novels, one collection of short fiction, a collection of essays, a memoir, and verse translations of plays by Seneca and Sophocles.

AMANDA COCKRELL is the managing editor of *The Hollins Critic* and director of the graduate program in children's literature at Hollins University. She is the author of several novels, most recently *Pomegranate Seed.*

PHILIP COOPER taught at Hollins College and the University of Maryland, Baltimore County. He is the author of *The Autobiographical Myth of Robert Lowell.*

GEORGE CORE is the editor of *The Sewanee Review* and *Southern Fiction Today.* He is co-editor of several books, the latest of which is *Selected Letters of John Crowe Ransom.*

HERBERT R. COURSEN, JR. is professor emeritus of English at Bowdoin College. A prolific writer, he is the author of over two dozen books of poems and eight novels, as well as many books of Shakespearean criticism and scholarship, among them *Christian Ritual and the World of Shakespeare's Tragedies,* *Shakespeare on Television,* and *Shakespearean Performance and Interpretation.*

JOSEPH DEWEY is associate professor of American literature at the University of Pittsburgh. He is the author of *In a Dark Time: The Apocalyptic Temper of the American Novel in the Nuclear Age* and *Understanding Richard Powers,* as well numerous articles and reviews.

R. H. W. DILLARD is the editor of *The Hollins Critic* and professor of English at Hollins University, where he has been chair of the creative writing program since 1971. He is the author of six volumes of poetry (most recently, *Sallies*), two novels, a collection of short fiction, verse translations of plays by Aristophanes and Plautus, and two critical monographs, *Horror Films* and *Understanding George Garrett.*

JOHN DITSKY is a professor of English at the University of Windsor, Ontario. He has published poems, reviews, and essays in numerous journals.

GARRETT EPPS is associate professor of law at the University of Oregon. He is the author of two novels, *The Shad Treatment* and *The Floating Island,* as well as *To an Unknown God: Religious Freedom on Trial.*

SHARON FELTON has taught at a number of American and Canadian universities and is the director of Teaching Technology of Nashville, Tennessee.

CHARLES FISHMAN served as director of the SUNY Farmingdale visiting writers program for eighteen years. His books include *Mortal Companions, The Firewalkers, Blood to Remember: American Poets on the Holocaust,* and *The Death Mazurka.* He is poetry editor for

Cistercian Studies Quarterly and is a poetry consultant for the U.S. Holocaust Museum.

WILLIAM L. FRANK is professor emeritus at Longwood College. In addition to his ongoing work on William Hoffman, he has written and edited books and articles on Sherwood Bonner, Robert Penn Warren, and Allen Wier.

PHILIP FRIED is the founding editor of the *Manhattan Review.* His poems, essays, and interviews have appeared in numerous publications.

MIRIAM FUCHS is associate professor of English at the University of Hawai'i at Manoa. She is the co-editor of *Breaking the Sequence: Women's Experimental Fiction* and has published essays on William Gaddis, Marguerite Young, Hart Crane, T. S. Eliot, and the Maori writer Patricia Grace, as well as Djuna Barnes.

THOMAS GARDNER is professor of English at Virginia Tech. He recently received a Guggenheim fellowship to complete a book on Emily Dickinson and contemporary writers.

EDWARD HIRSCH is professor of English at the University of Houston. He is the author of five books of poems, most recently *On Love,* and two critical books, the latest of which is *Responsive Reading.* He was awarded a MacArthur fellowship in 1998.

DAVID HUDDLE is a poet, novelist, short story writer, and essayist who teaches literature and writing at the University of Vermont and the Bread Loaf School of English. His most recent books are *Summer Lake: New and Selected Poems* and the novels *The Story of a Million Years* and *La Tour Dreams of the Wolf Girl.* He is a contributing editor of *The Hollins Critic.*

JOSEPHINE JACOBSEN is a poet, short story writer, and critic. She is the author of numerous books, most recently *In the Crevice of Time: New and Collected Poems.* She was inducted into the American Academy of Arts and Letters in 1994. See the essay on her work in this collection.

ANNE GOODWYN JONES is associate professor of English at the University of Florida. She is the author of *Tomorrow*

Is Another Day: The Woman Writer in the South, 1859-1936 and the editor of *Haunted Bodies: Gender and Southern Texts.*

STEVEN G. KELLMAN is Ashbel Smith professor of comparative literature at the University of Texas at San Antonio. He is the author of *The Self-Begetting Novel* and *Translingualism and the Literary Imagination* and co-editor of *Into the Tunnel: Essays on William Gass's Novel* and *Leslie Fiedler and American Culture.*

THOMAS E. KENNEDY is a fiction writer, literary critic, translator, and editor. He is the author of *The Short Fiction of Andre Dubus* and *Robert Coover: A Study of the Short Fiction,* as well as three novels and two collections of short fiction. He is an American who has lived in Europe for the past two decades, most recently in Copenhagen, Denmark.

BENEDICT KIELY is the author of ten novels, five volumes of short fiction, and seven other books, including *Drink to the Bird: A Memoir.* See the essay on his work in this collection.

MARY KINZIE is director of the English major in writing and professor of English at Northwestern University. She is the author of five books of poetry, including *Summers of Vietnam, Autumn Eros,* and *Ghost Ship,* two volumes of critical essays, *The Cure of Poetry in an Age of Prose* and *The Judge Is Fury,* and *A Poet's Guide to Poetry.*

TODD KLIMAN is a freelance writer in Washington, D.C. He has taught at Prince George's Community College in Maryland and acted as the director of development for the Writer's Center in Bethesda, Maryland.

JEANNE LARSEN is professor of English at Hollins University and a contributing editor of *The Hollins Critic.* She is the author of a collection of poems, *James Cook in Search of Terra Incognita* (winner of the AWP Poetry Prize in 1980), a trilogy of Chinese metahistorical novels (*Silk Road, Bronze Mirror,* and *Manchu Palaces*), and *Brocade River Poems: Selected Works of the Tang Dynasty Courtesan Xue Tao.*

STEVEN LEHMAN teaches English composition and literature at John Abbott College in Montreal. He has

written for *Science Fiction Studies, Paradoxa,* and *The Montreal Gazette,* among other publications.

JEB LIVINGOOD is a part-time lecturer at the University of Virginia, where he is faculty advisor for *Meridian.* He has published fiction and creative nonfiction widely and is the editor of George Garrett's *Going to See the Elephant: Pieces of a Writing Life.*

KAREN MACEIRA is a widely published poet who lives in Louisiana.

ROBERT MCGOVERN is editor of the Ashland Poetry Press and is professor emeritus at Ashland University. He has published his poetry and criticism extensively, and among his books are the recent anthologies *Scarecrow Poetry—The Muse in Post-Middle Age* and *And What Rough Beast—Poems at the End of the Century,* both co-edited with Stephen Haven.

FRANK MCSHANE was professor in the writing division of the School of the Arts, Columbia University. He edited *Selected Letters of Raymond Chandler* and was the author of literary biographies of Chandler, Ford Madox Ford, James Jones, and John O'Hara.

ROBERT MIKLITSCH is associate professor of English at Ohio University. He is the author of *From Hegel to Madonna: Towards a General Economy of "Commodity Fetishism"* and *Roll Over Adorno: Critical Theory and Popular Culture in the Post-Marxist Period.*

CHARLES MOLESWORTH is professor of English at SUNY Buffalo. He is the author of three books of poetry and *Donald Barthelme's Fiction, Gary Snyder's Vision: Poetry and the Real Work,* and *Marianne Moore: A Literary Life.*

JANET C. MOORE directs the Saint Leo College Center at MacDill Air Force Base in Tampa, Florida, where she teaches communications and literature. A poet, she has also published articles on literary and film theory.

HOWARD NELSON is a contributing editor of *The Hollins Critic.* He is the author of five books of poetry as well as *Robert Bly: An Introduction to the Poetry* and the editor of *On the Poetry of Galway Kinnell* and a recent collection of Walt Whitman's nature poems. He lives in the Finger Lakes district of New York.

MICHAEL PEARSON is professor of English at Old Dominion University. He is the author of *Imagined Places: Journeys into Literary America, A Place That's Known: Essays,* and *John McPhee.*

JULIA RANDALL, a former associate professor of English at Hollins College, is the author of seven books of poetry, most recently *The Path to Fairview: New and Selected Poems.* See the essay on her work in this collection.

ELLEN CRONAN ROSE is professor of women's studies and chair of the department at the University of Nevada, Las Vegas. She is the author of *The Tree outside the Window: A Study of Doris Lessing's* Children of Violence, *The Novels of Margaret Drabble,* and *Meeting the Challenge: Innovative Feminist Pedagogies in Action,* as well as numerous articles and edited volumes.

EARL ROVIT is professor emeritus of English at the City College of New York. He is the author of books on Elizabeth Madox Roberts, Ernest Hemingway, and Saul Bellow, as well as numerous essays on literary topics and three novels.

JAMES ROBERT SAUNDERS is professor of English at Purdue University. A widely published author and editor, he is most recently the author of *Tightrope Walk: Identity, Survival, and the Corporate World in African American Literature.*

KATHLEEN WESTFALL SHUTE, a fiction writer and critic, taught at Hollins College and Oklahoma State University. Prior to her untimely death in 1992, she was working on a critical study of the short fiction of Vladimir Nabokov.

DAVID R. SLAVITT is the author of over seventy books, among them novels, collections of poetry and short fiction, translations, and a critical study of Virgil. He also co-edited with Palmer Bovie both the *Complete Roman Drama in Translation,* published by the Johns Hopkins University Press, and the *Penn Greek Drama Series,* published by the University of Pennsylvania Press.

JOHN STARK, an attorney, has published two books of literary criticism, a reference work, and numerous articles.

MICHAEL STEPHENS lives and works in New York City. Among his books are *Green Dreams: Essays under the Influence of the Irish,* winner of the 1993 AWP Prize for Creative Nonfiction, two novels, a collection of poems, and the memoir *Lost in Seoul.*

ROBERT B. STEPTO is professor of African-American studies, American studies, and English at Yale University. He is the author of *From Behind the Veil: A Study of Afro-American Narrative* and the memoir *Blue as the Lake: A Personal Geography,* as well as editor of four other books on American and African-American literature.

ROBERT STOCK is professor of English at the University of Nebraska at Lincoln. He is the author of *Samuel Johnson and Neoclassical Dramatic Theory, Johnson's Literary Criticism, The Holy and the Daemonic from Sir Thomas Browne to William Blake,* and *The Flutes of Dionysus: Daemonic Enthrallment in Literature.*

KAREN ADAMS SULKIN teaches in the graduate program in children's literature at Hollins University. She is the author of *The Mystery of Roanoke* and four other serialized adventure stories for children, which have been syndicated in more than thirty newspapers around the country.

NANCY SULLIVAN is professor emerita at Rhode Island College. She is the author of *Perspective and the Poetic Process* and two books of poems, one of which, *The History of the World as Pictures,* was the first winner of the Devins Award in 1965.

HENRY TAYLOR is professor of literature at the American University. He is the author of five books of poetry, among them *The Flying Change,* which was awarded the Pulitzer Prize in 1987, and *Brief Candles,* a collection of clerihews which earned him the Michael Braude Award for Light Verse from the American Academy of Arts and Letters in 2002. He is also the

author of *Compulsory Figures: Essays on Recent American Poets* and is a contributing editor of *The Hollins Critic.*

TONY TREMBLAY teaches world literature and cultural studies at St. Thomas University in Fredericton, New Brunswick. He is the editor of a new collection of essays on the work of David Adams Richards.

LEWIS TURCO is professor emeritus of English at SUNY College at Oswego and was founding director of both the Cleveland State Poetry Center and the program in writing arts at Oswego. Among his many books of poetry and scholarship are *The Book of Forms: A Handbook of Poetics, Visions and Revisions of American Poetry* (winner of the 1986 Melville Cane Award for literary criticism), *The Shifting Web: New and Selected Poems,* and, most recently, *The Green Maces of Autumn: Voices in an Old Maine House.* See the essay on his work in this collection.

ANNE BRADFORD WARNER is associate professor of English at Spelman College. Her poems and critical essays have appeared in journals and anthologies.

GERALD WEALES is professor emeritus of the University of Pennsylvania. He is the author of numerous books, among them *American Drama Since World War II, Odets the Playwright, Religion in Modern English Drama,* and a study of film comedies of the 1930's, *Canned Goods as Caviar.*

ED WEYHING has published fiction and essays in numerous journals.

HARRIET ZINNES is professor emerita of English at Queens College of the CUNY. She is the author of seven books of poetry, most recently *My Haven't the Flowers Been?,* as well as a collection of short fiction and a book of translations of the poems of Jacques Prévert. She is a contributing editor of *The Hollins Critic.*

DANIEL ZINS is associate professor of liberal arts at the Atlanta College of Art. He has published articles on the Vietnam War and arms control as well as on literature.

"Observation Tower, The" (Turco), 2: 422–423

Occupant Please Forward (Summers), 2: 371, 2: 377–379, 2: 380

O'Connor, Flannery
Gaitskill, and writings compared to writings by, 1: 323, 1: 325, 1: 327, 1: 331, 1: 334
Munro, and influences of, 2: 110, 2: 111, 2: 113
"Good Man Is Hard to Find, A," 1: 263, 1: 327
"Parker's Back," 1: 325

O'Connor, Frank, 2: 407

Odd Woman, The (Godwin), 1: 361–362, 1: 365

"Ode: Intimations of Immortality" (Wordsworth), 1: 479, 1: 530

"Ode to a Nightingale" (Keats), 1: 446, 1: 479

"Ode to Joy" (Beethoven), 1: 466

"Ode to Tenochtitlan" (Harper), 1: 430–431

"Odyssey of Big Boy" (Harper), 1: 432

"Of Geoffrey, My Cat" (Smart), 1: 31, 1: 396

"Of Islands" (Smith), 2: 325

Of Memory and Desire (Swan), 2: 383, 2: 390

"Of Memory and Desire" (Swan), 2: 385–386, 2: 387

O'Faolain, Sean, 1: 559

"Old Apple Trees" (Snodgrass), 2: 341

Old Boys, The (Trevor), 2: 407, 2: 408, 2: 409, 2: 410

"Old Bull" (Trevor), 2: 416

"Old Dominion" (Hass), 1: 447, 1: 449

"Old Fascist in Retirement, The" (Baxter), 1: 100

"Old Man Feeding Hens" (Francis), 1: 321

Old Scores, The Latin Lover and Other Stories (Raphael), 2: 257

"Old Woman, An" (Richard), 2: 281

Old Yeller (Gipson), 1: 70–71

"Oldest, and the Longest Married, The" (Summers), 2: 378

Oliver Twist (Dickens), 1: 529

Olivier, Laurence, 2: 322

Olsen, Tillie, 2: **163–170**
biography of, 2: 163, 2: 164
books by, 2: 169
picture of, 2: *164*
on Davis, Rebecca Harding, 2: 166

"From the Thirties," 2: 168
"I Stand Here Ironing," 2: 164, 2: 167
Tell Me a Riddle, 2: 167–168
"Tell Me a Riddle," 2: 164
"Women Who Are Writers in Our Century: One Out of Twelve," 2: 167
Yonnondio, 2: 163

Olson, Charles
Maximus Poems, The, 1: 81, 2: 202
"Projective Verse," 1: 83

Olson's Push (Paul), 1: 82

"Ommateum" (Ammons), 1: 2

"On a Painting by Patient B" (Justice), 1: 541

"On Accepting the Gold Watch" (Summers), 2: 374

"On Looking at Television's Late Movies" (Summers), 2: 372

"On Seeing Films of the War" (Coxe), 1: 203

"On the Birth of a Black/Baby/Boy" (Knight), 1: 605

"On the Death of Friends in Childhood" (Justice), 1: 539

On the Edge of the Desert (Swan), 2: 383, 2: 390

"On the Edge of the Desert" (Swan), 2: 389, 2: 392

"On the Eve of the Next Revolution" (Swan), 2: 385–386, 2: 387, 2: 388–389, 2: 390

On the Island: New and Selected Stories (Jacobsen), 1: 519

"On the Island" (Spires), 2: 354–355

"On the Islands which Are Solomons" (Smith), 2: 324

On the Poetry of Galway Kinnell: The Wages of Dying (Nelson), 1: 577

"On the Pulse of Morning" (Angelou), 1: 20

"On Water" (Tomlinson), 2: 401

"Once opened..." (Turco), 2: 420

"Once Upon a Time" (Summers), 2: 372–373

Ondaatje, Michael, 2: **171–183**
awards/prizes, 2: 172, 2: 182
biography of, 2: 171, 2: 172, 2: 173, 2: 178–179
books by, 2: 183
picture of, 2: *172*
reviews of writings, 2: 183
Anil's Ghost, 2: 172, 2: 183
"Burning Hills," 2: 175–176

Cinnamon Peeler, The, 2: 171
Collected Works of Billy the Kid, 2: 173–175
Coming through Slaughter, 2: 171, 2: 176–178
English Patient, The, 2: 171
"Heron Rex," 2: 172–173
In the Skin of a Lion, 2: 171, 2: 181–182
"King Kong Meets Wallace Stevens," 2: 175
"Plot," 2: 181
Rat Jelly, 2: 171
Running in the Family, 2: 172

One Hundred Years of Solitude (Garcia Marquez), 1: 456

"One is a quiet person..." (Dickinson), 2: 43–44

"One More Thing" (Carver), 1: 184–185

"One Out of Twelve" (Olsen), 2: 167

O'Neill, Eugene, *Iceman,* 1: 267

O'Neill, Moira, 1: 547
Grace for Light, The, 1: 547
"Grace for Light, The," 1: 551

Only Children (Lurie), 1: 615

Only World There Is, The (Williams), 2: 509, 2: 515

Open Secrets: Stories (Munro), 2: 118

Operation Wandering Soul (Powers), 2: 214, 2: 216–217, 2: 219, 2: 221, 2: 223, 2: 225

Oppen, George, 1: 72, 2: 395

Orator (Cicero), 2: 504

Orb Weaver, The (Francis), 1: 313

"Orb Weaver, The" (Francis), 1: 318–319

Orchard Keeper, The (McCarthy), 2: 23, 2: 24

"Orchid" (Gaitskill), 1: 331

"Origins of the Negative Dialectic, The" (Buck-Morss), 2: 209

O'Rourke, David, *Essays in Canadian Writing (Winter 1980-81),* 2: 57

Orpheus Hesitated Beside the Black River; Poems, 1952-1997 (Justice), 1: 545

Orrie's Story (Berger), 1: 126

Orwell, George, "Politics and the English Language," 2: 453

Other Concerns & Brother Clark (Summers), 2: 381

Other People's Worlds (Trevor), 2: 413

"Ottawa Valley, The" (Munro), 2: 115

"Ounce of Cure, An" (Munro), 2: 112